PAPER WORKS

GINGKO PRESS

PAPER WORKS

ISBN 978-1-58423-432-6

First Published in the United States of America by Gingko Press
by arrangement with Sandu Publishing Co., Limited

Gingko Press, Inc.
1321 Fifth Street
Berkeley, CA 94710 USA
Tel: (510) 898 1195
Fax: (510) 898 1196
Email: books@gingkopress.com
www.gingkopress.com

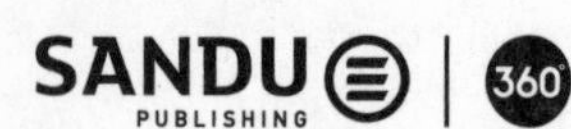

Sponsored by: Design 360° – Concept and Design Magazine
Chief Editor: Wang Shaoqiang
Executive Editor: Feng Huimin
Chief Designer: Wang Shaoqiang
Book Designers: Leo Cheung, Zhu Yingqi
Sales Managers:
Niu Guanghui (China), Daniela Huang (International)
Address:
3rd Floor, West Tower,
No.10 Ligang Road, Haizhu District,
510280, Guangzhou, China
Tel: (86)-20-84316758
Fax: (86)-20-84344460
sandu.sales@gmail.com
www.sandu360.com

Printed and bound in China

Jum Nakao

Paper-Designer
São Paulo – Brazil

In front of the immensity of a blank sheet of paper, I'm still frozen for a moment before writing a dedication or preface, or before drawing initial sketches for a project. It is not the fear of the word, trace, line, brushstroke, cut mark, or fold, but the fascination with the infinite possibilities of that moment. I still remember my first drawing class, when the sweet murmur of my teacher's words brought my hands to overlap two pastel colors, red and yellow. Like magic, an apple appeared on a sheet of paper. In my first origami classes, I discovered that a single square sheet of colored paper can hold an entire universe of possibilities. A wrinkled map of innumerous pathways and crossroads appeared on the glossy paper surface - the correct fold choices brought to the surface a three-dimensional world of birds, animals, fishes, vehicles, airplanes, houses, and flowers. Many children's first gifts on Mother's Day or Father's Day were, like mine, built out of a single sheet of paper. Combined with drawings and words, these crudely folded pieces of paper became gifts of affection and devotion.

The versatility and ease of paper handling allowed me to accomplish my first projects as a child: cars, castles, rockets, spaceships, buildings, and cities. These were the prototypes for my dreams.

My first nightmares were also born on paper: school report cards with disciplinary notes. Not that I was a bad student - quite the contrary. My competitive mind circled around in patterns of restlessness that fueled my sleepless nights. I have learned to relieve these pieces of paper of their marks, numbers, and grades over the years - thus revealing unseen creative possibilities.

I remember the professional gift packers of a previous era; these people were hired by stores to enhance gifts through their precise paper folds that would enclose our memories of Christmas day, birthdays, Valentine's day, weddings... A skilled haute couture gift wrapper could create unique patterns through the rhythm of each geometric fold. Were they packaging designers, surface designers, or clothing designers for the gifts?

When my first important school paper was bound, I felt like a book publisher! I realized the significance of graphic design - the importance of precise paths creating a map through a forest of pages. I learned that words and images need a soul, or they are incapable of creating a universe.

None of the most important pieces of writing, formulas, or theories could exist without a piece of paper as the base. My first formulas and equations, school essays, letters, diaries, testimonies, and thoughts consumed pages and pages which were later balled up or saved as a record of my early existence. Years later, I decided to work in fashion. My first discovery was the perception of a body moving through space and the endless possibilities to dress this form sculpturally. Around the body, lines and strokes created a garment, arising from a paper pattern. Pattern making is more than a birth certificate - it certifies the garment's continued existence and renewal.

In TV, film, theater, and opera scene design, we still use paper models as a raw material for prototyping furniture, sculpture, and characters. The paper supports many performances and works of art. Each application requires specific techniques, but all of them count on the friendly support of the paper.

Paper is the place of our life designs - sketches of our childhood dreams, our first diary notes, our notes on the outlandish, messages exchanged as youths, letters which used to be sent within an envelope also made of paper, packages that wrapped gifts, our semester grades, diplomas, certificates, professional and personal contracts, our first paychecks, our first payable accounts, the results of our diagnostic tests, the wedding invitations of friends, birth and death announcements. Paper holds memories for eternity.

It is also where we plan out projects before they become a reality - where skyscrapers are planned, where constitutions are written, where formulas and theories develop and extend the frontiers of human knowledge, and where poems, novels, and stories are written to move our minds to other worlds. In this book a new dimension of paper is brought to the surface - a dimension which adds to the poetic nature of the medium. The artists featured on these paper pages show us how the lightness, fragility, and transience of a single sheet of paper can, through these artists' visions, reveal another world that is full of possibilities.

Ingrid Siliakus

Paper-Architect / Artist
Amsterdam – The Netherlands

Although we live in a computer-dominated world, computers have never replaced paper entirely and they never will do so, in my opinion. Paper is still being used in so many ways. In our modern world, not a day goes by without the use of paper in one way or another. If you look around carefully, you will find you are surrounded by paper: newspapers, posters, money, name cards, tickets, and so on. A world without it is unthinkable.

Fibers, plants, cotton, linen and even old cloths are a few materials being used to make paper. Magazines, newspapers, and letters are being dropped in our mailboxes daily. Often these types of paper are recycled and end up in the hands of artists as beautiful basics for their new pieces of art. There are many materials and ways to make paper - too many to describe here - and still people that love to make their own paper are experimenting every day to see what kind of materials and techniques will create the most extraordinary papers.

The number of artists working with paper grows; they continually create amazing artworks, whether from homemade or recycled paper, whether small or large scale, whether white or multi-colored. Paper art and artists are becoming more and more well-known all over the world and are being featured in internationally renowned museums and galleries. This gorgeous book you have in your hands is a showcase of the best work by these amazing internationally recognized artists. When you flip through the book, you will see the many ways paper has inspired artists to create new artworks - from life-size functional furniture to very delicate clothing - from paper castles to fancy eyelashes - from unique headwear to handbags.. You'll be surprised what has been created out of paper.

Although working with paper isn't new – it has been used in art for ages – why this revived trend of artists choosing paper as a material for their artworks? I think the advantages of paper are being rediscovered because of its unique qualities. What are these unique qualities one might ask? I only can speak of my own experiences working with paper of course, although it would not surprise me if it is similar to that of my fellow paperartists.

The main advantage of paper to me is that it is sturdy (as mentioned before) and yet flexible at the same time. For instance it can be creased (think of Origami), cut, folded, bent, engraved, painted, written on, printed and manipulated in a number of other ways. Therefore it is the ideal material for many type of art - such as the paper architecture I create.

Let me explain a little bit about the technique I create my artworks with: the technique paper-architecture is the art of creating objects out of a single piece of paper only by means of cutting and folding. This technique has its origins in Japan (founded in the eighties of the previous century by the Japanese professor Masahiro Chatani). Some of my works (including books) are created by attaching several of these objects – made out of a single piece of paper – together, mainly with integrated slits and tabs. All of the pieces can be folded inwards and outward over and over again. Before I can begin cutting and folding, a design has to be made. Since my artworks are created out of a single piece of paper only by means of cutting and folding, it is necessary to calculate the design very accurately to a 100th of a millimeter. The design stage takes a long time, sometimes months, depending on the difficulty of the design.

I like to challenge myself to make more complicated works and to get as many cuts and folds as possible out of a single piece of paper. It also is a challenge to try to get very tiny objects out of a piece of paper. In recent years I have designed skylines of Amsterdam and New York. Skylines seem to be very graceful subjects for my work, which involves a lot of time making the designs - each is truly a great new challenge. What I also like about the technique paper-architecture is that the sky seems to be the limit when it comes to the topic for a piece.

When I first started working with paper-architecture – about 15 years ago – I fell in love with the technique. But it is impossible not to fall in love with paper as soon as one starts working with this material and gaining respect for it. I am sure my fellow artists have experienced the same thing. I have said it before and I keep saying it: working with paper forces me to be humble because paper has a character of its own that asks for cooperation rather than manipulation. It is a challenge to find this cooperation with each different piece of paper I work with. I experience an ultimate satisfaction at the critical moment when the paper, with a silenced sigh, surrenders and becomes a blade-sharp crease. The sound of the paper, which guides this surrendering, to me is incomparable.

Enjoy this book-I hope it inspires you to experiment with paper in one way or another.

"airvase"

This is a paper bowl that enfolds air. You can freely change its shape by molding it into a dish, a small bowl or a vase according to the intended usage. The thin and lightweight paper gives strength and resistance to the bowl and allows it to be folded compactly when not in use. This intriguing bowl will catch your eye as the colors on each side of the paper create a different impression every time you look at the object.

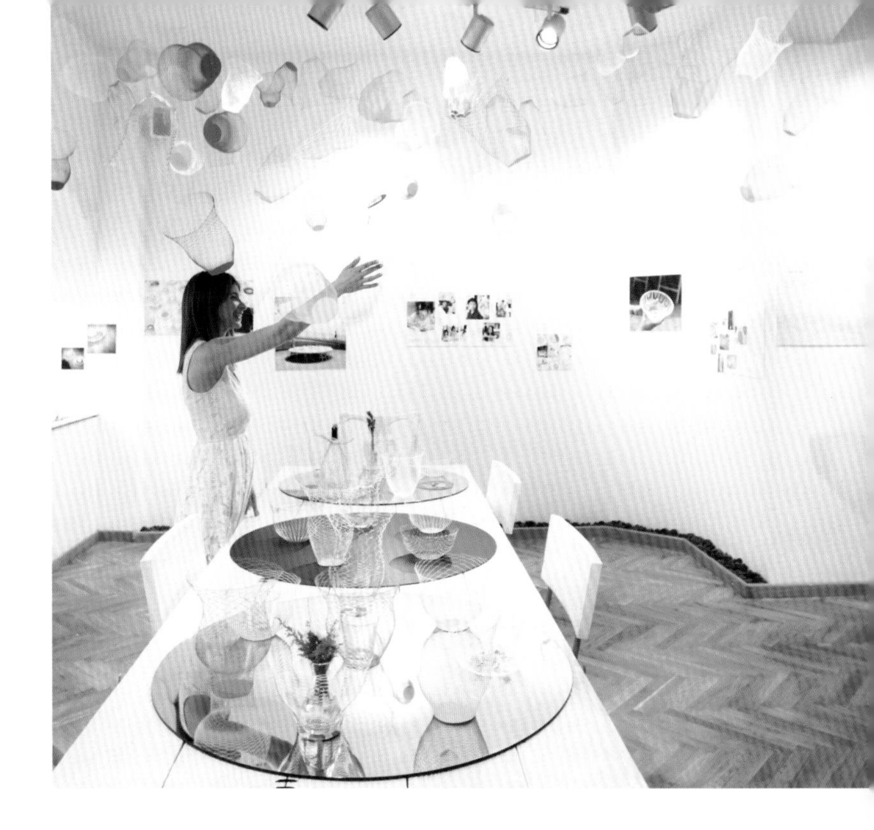

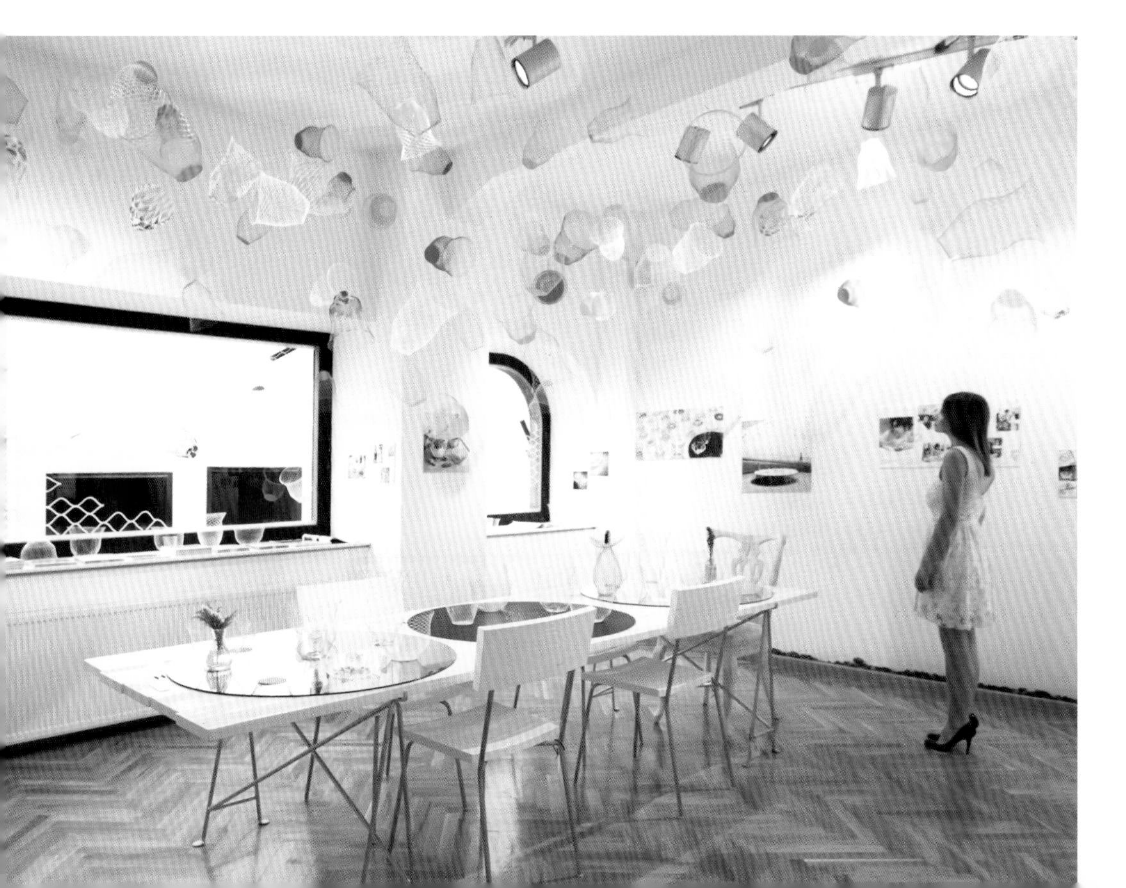

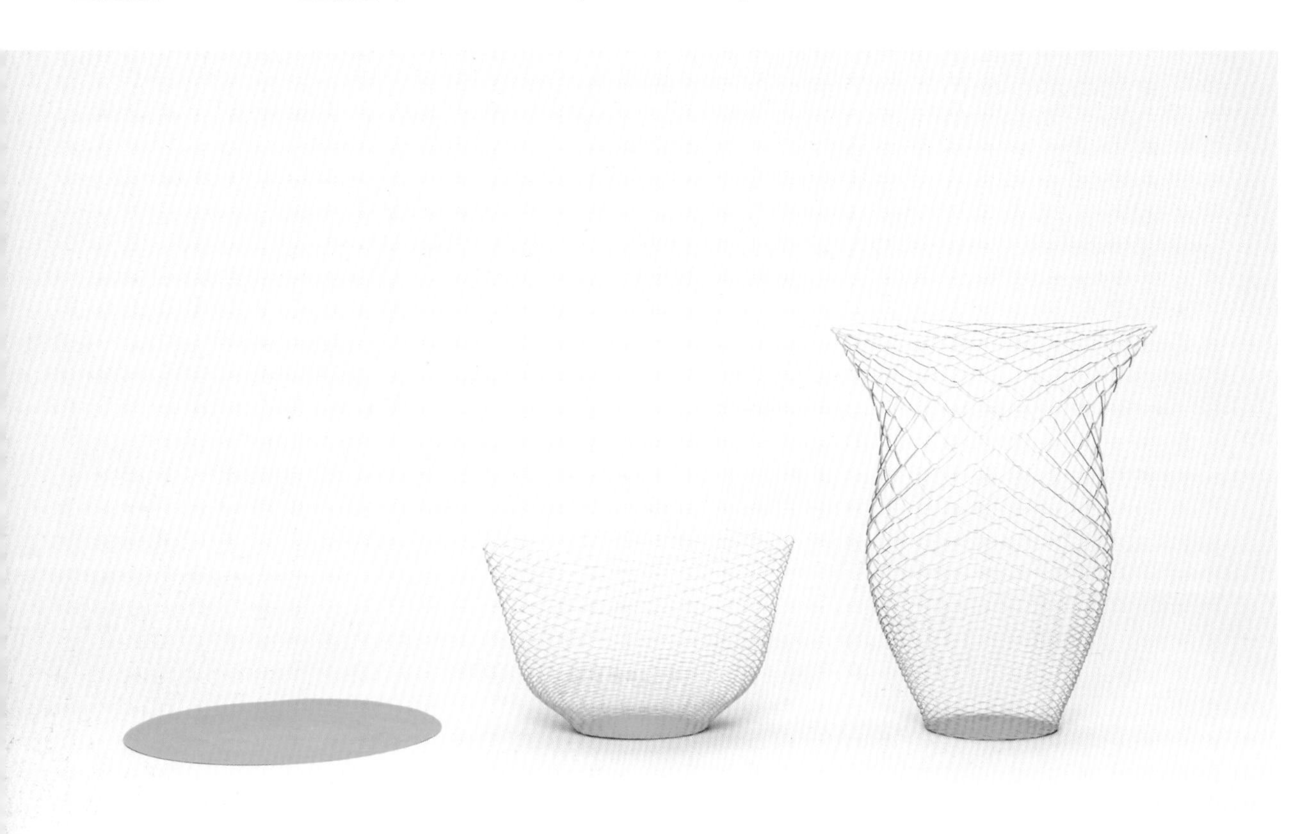

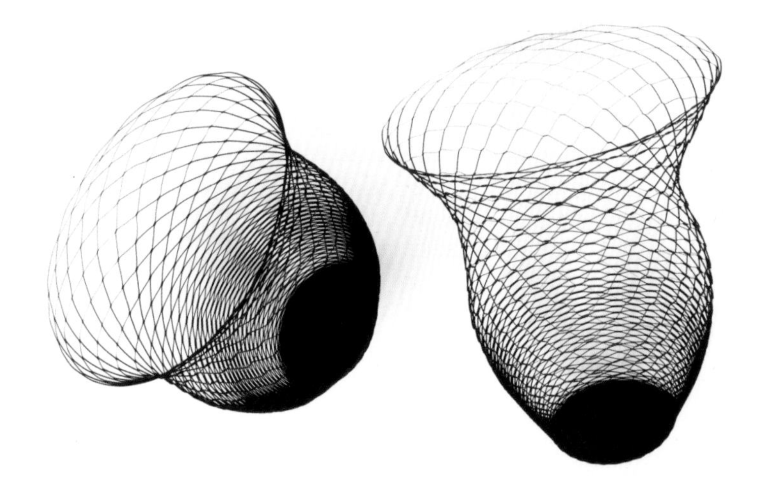

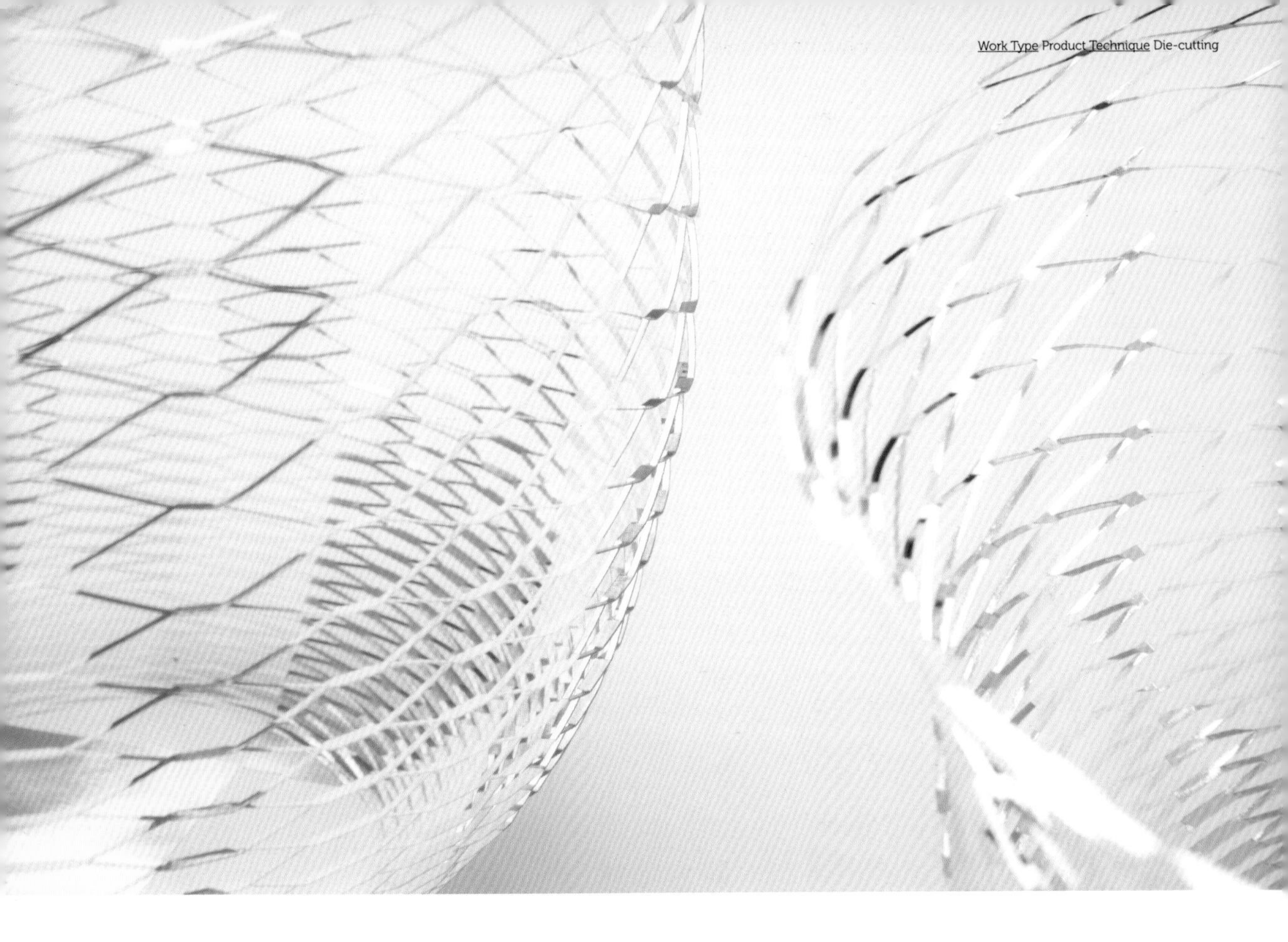

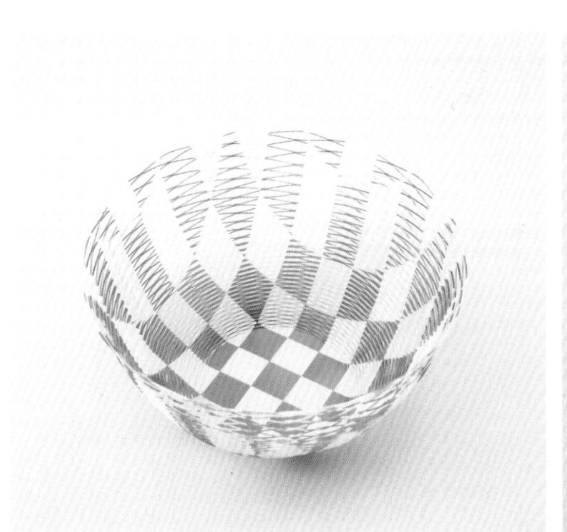

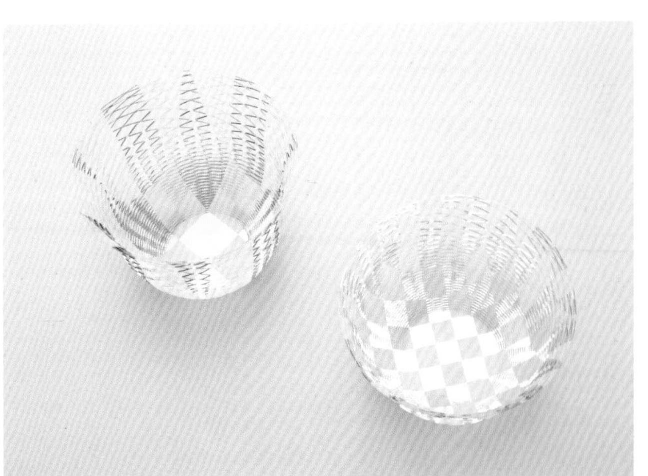

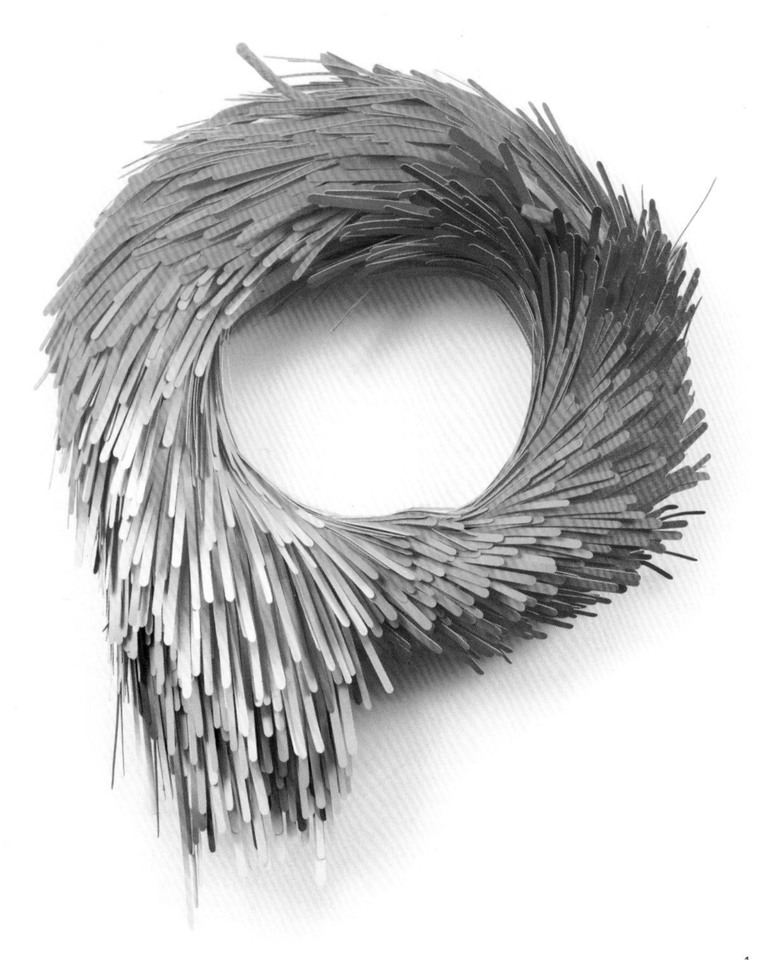

Wreaths and Garlands

1 / The Unending Amends We've Made (Imperishable Wreath)
2 / Schism Chasm Cataclysm
3 / Emptying Marco Polo's Knapsack
4 / Inverted Continuum
5 / Both Sides in Equal Parts

This work explores the fragmented nature of contemporary culture and spiritual identity, employing the tropes and formal devices of various cultures' metaphysical dialogues with the infinite, as well as the talisman-like forms of Modernism such as the monochrome painting, the plinth, and the grid. Constructed primarily from papier-mâché and painted paper, the sculptures are as temporal as the subjects they address. Collectively the work points to confusing, uncertain, but inevitable relationships with the infinite.

1

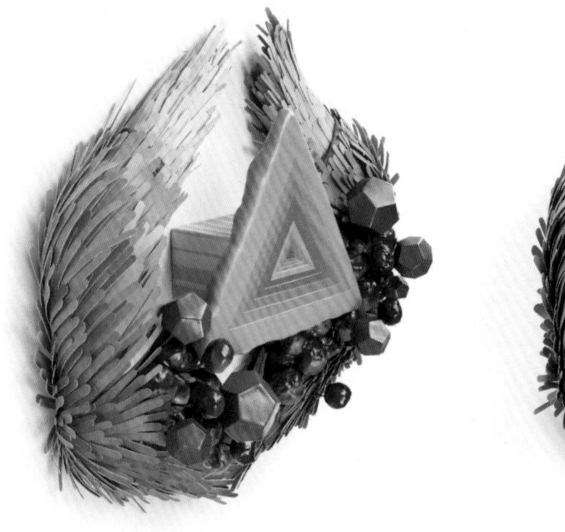

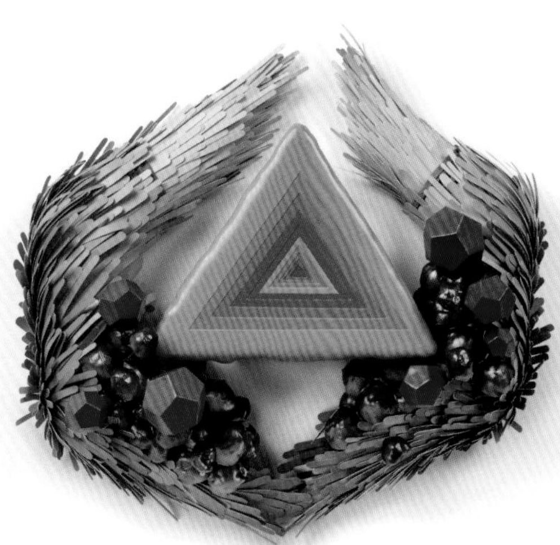

2

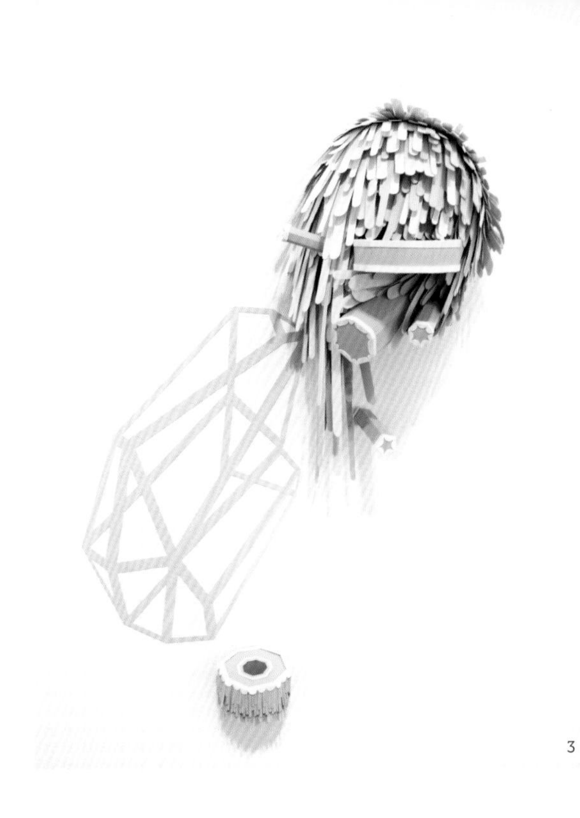

3

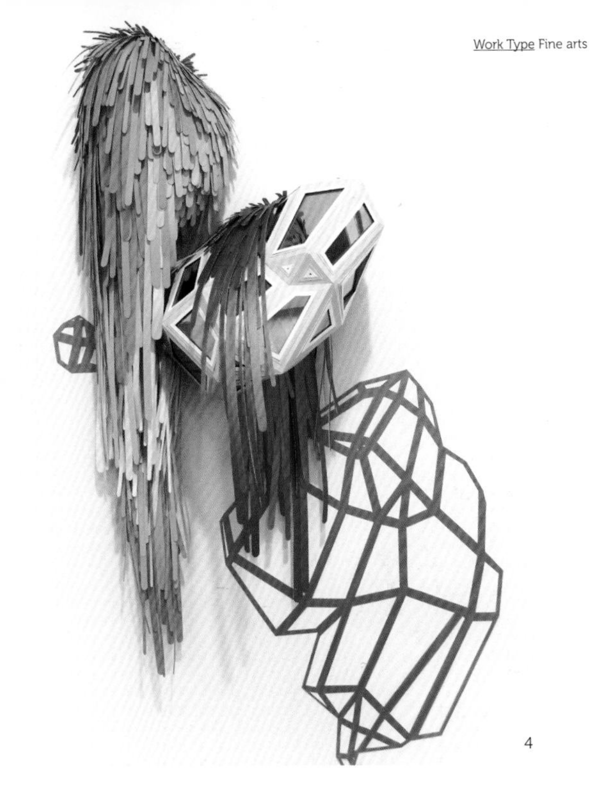

4

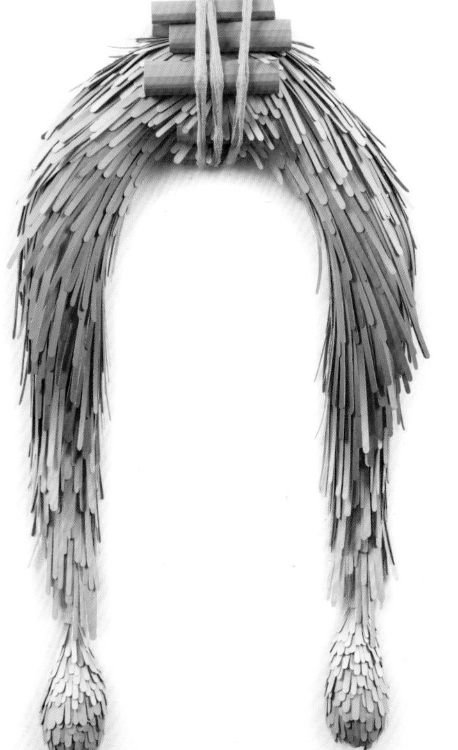

5

Artist Stuart McLachlan Photographer 1, 2, 3, 4 Ian McPherson/ 5 Wendell Teodoro/ 6, 9, 10 Simon Cardwell/ 7, 8 Jordan Graham/ 11, 12, 13 Amelia Soegijono Technique Hand cut and constructed paper

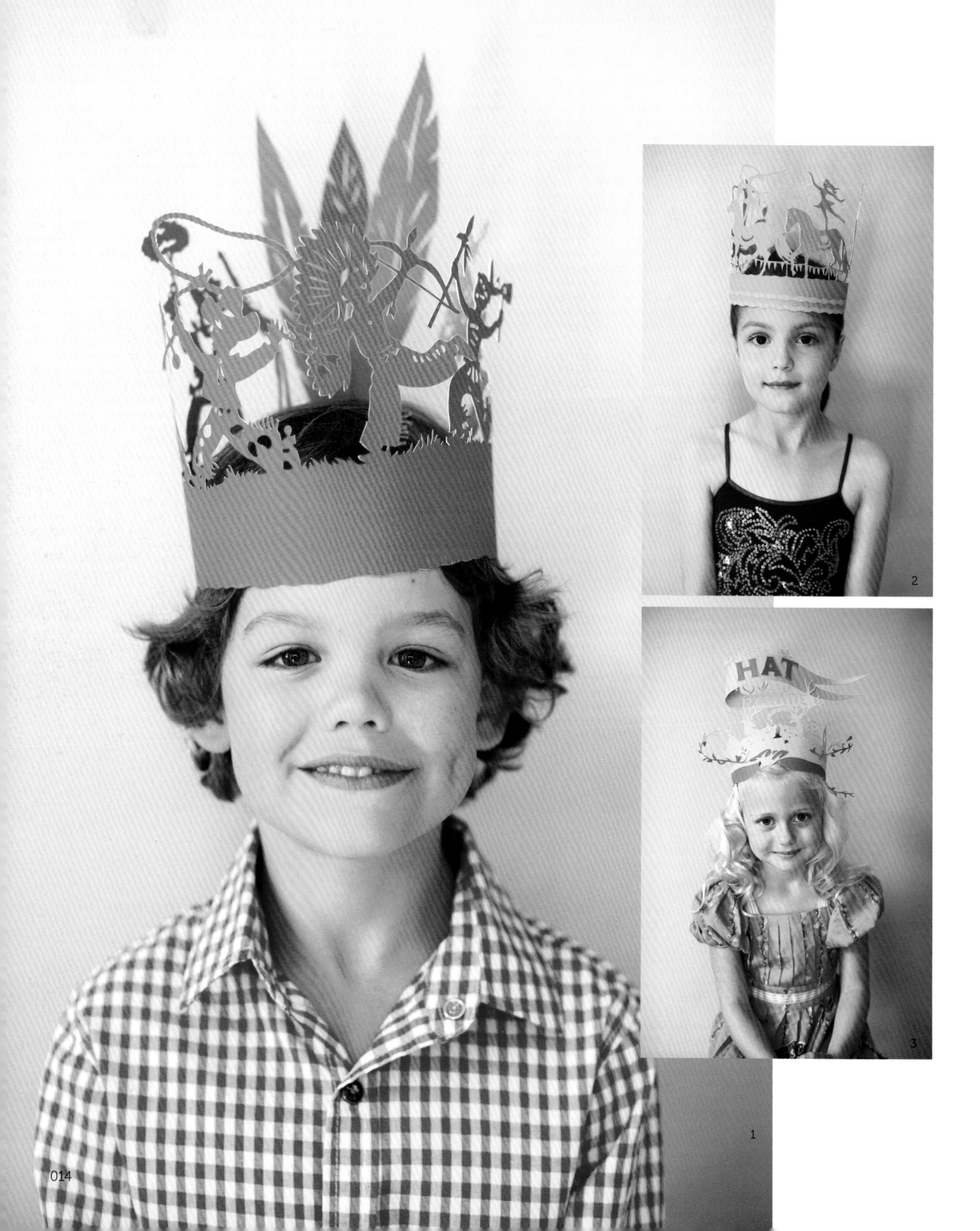

2

3

1

Model 6 Ana Calle/ 7 Milla De Wit/ 8 Jess Hart/ 9 Monique Wright/ 10 Leanne Proctor/ 11, 12, 13 Stacey Lobb Client 1, 2, 3, 4 Lmnop.com.au/ 5 Fred Bare/ 7, 8 Karen Magazine Work Type Fashion

Wearable Paper

1 / Hat Parade & Cowboy / Indian hat
2 / Pony Ring Hat
3 / Hat Parade
4 / Circus
5 / Bunny Hop
6 / Cathedral
7 / Pond Dress
8 / Black Stairway
9 / Lady of the Lake
10 / Bird Girl
11 / Soaring Veil
12 / The Call
13 / Metamorphosis

Although diverse in application, the paper works that McLachlan makes follow a classical graphic silhouetted structure. Whether creating hats for children or imagery for art or fashion, the intention is to create a story or at the very least, a mood, which the viewer can connect to. All pieces are hand cut and the tactile nature of working with paper is the greatest appeal for the artist. The aspect of McLachlan's work that he finds most intriguing is experimenting with live forms and how they interact with the two dimensionality of paper to create a story or image. "Paper is a medium without boundaries, one which can be cut or molded, large or small into almost anything. This is what I endeavour to explore in as many ways as possible through my art. While most things are mass produced these days, the need to explore what we as artists can 'hand make' is an aspect that is very integral to what I do."

4

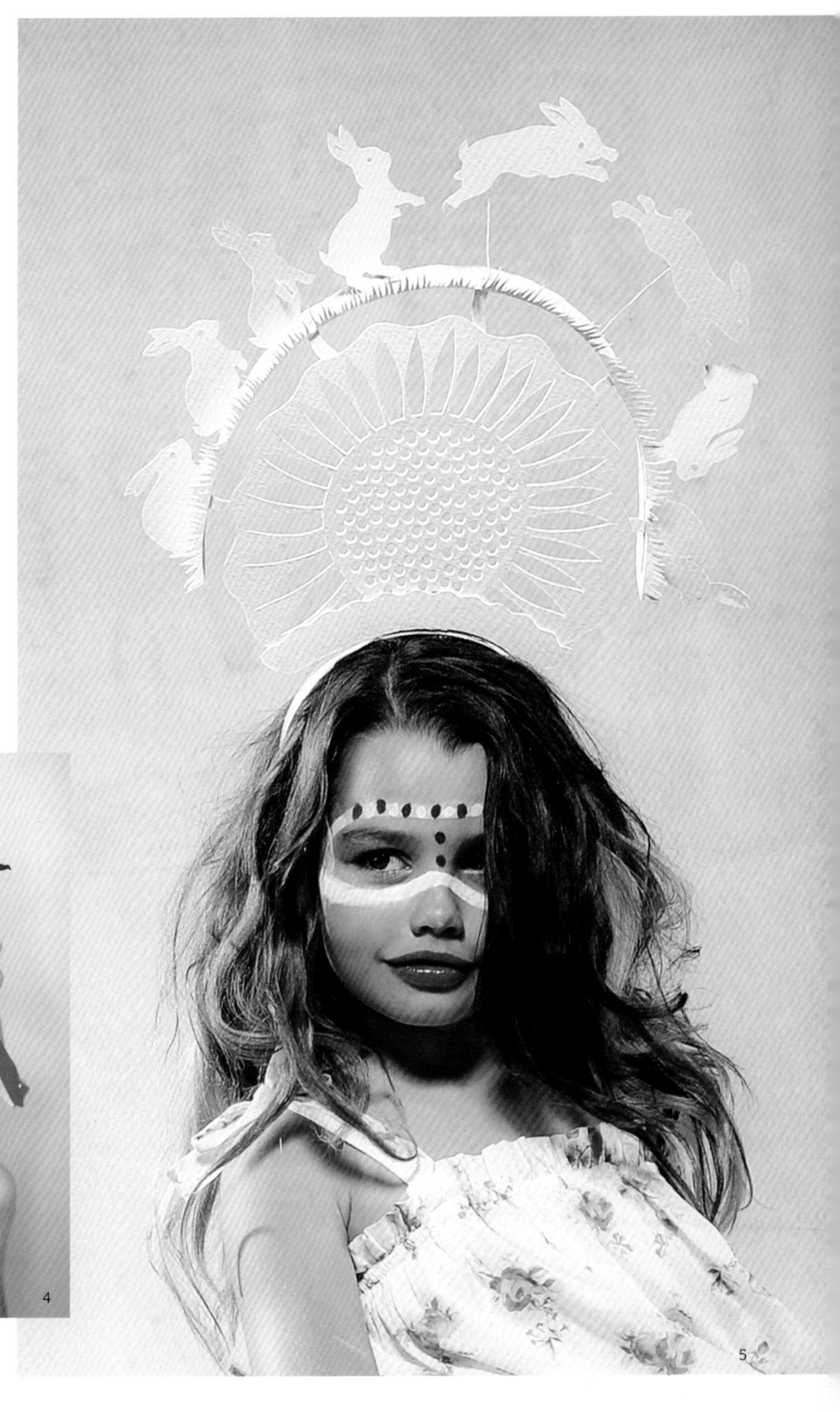

5

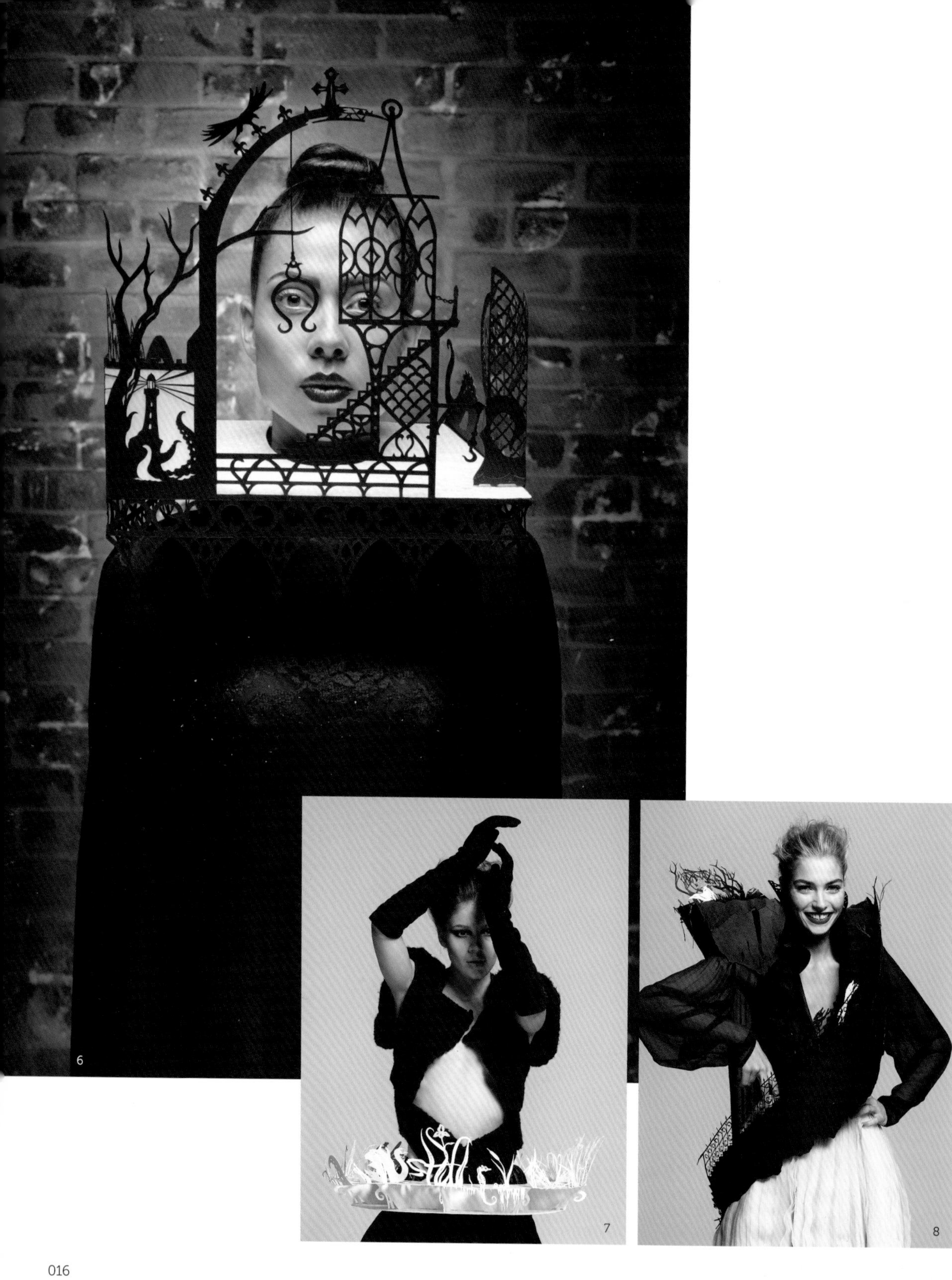
6
7
8

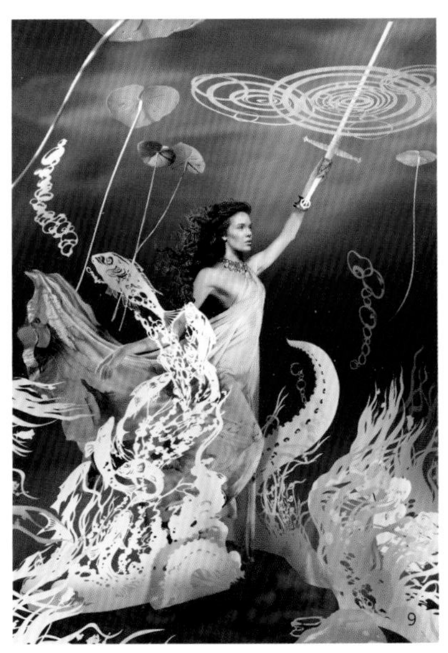

9

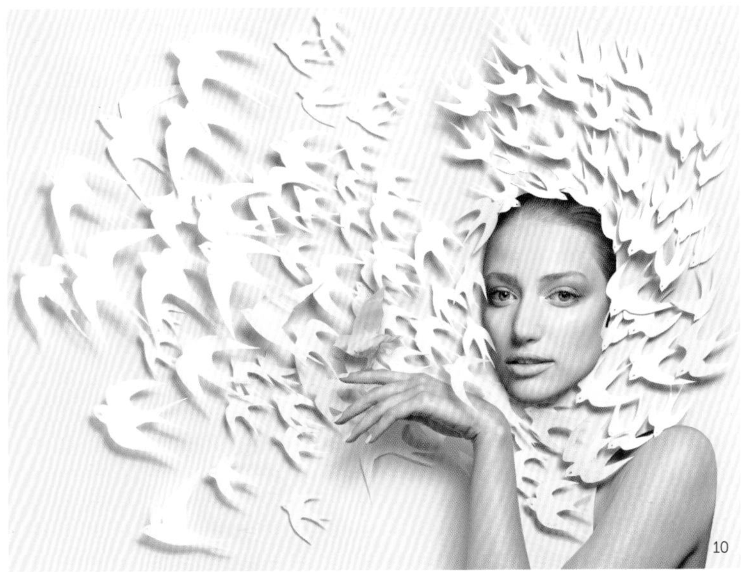

10

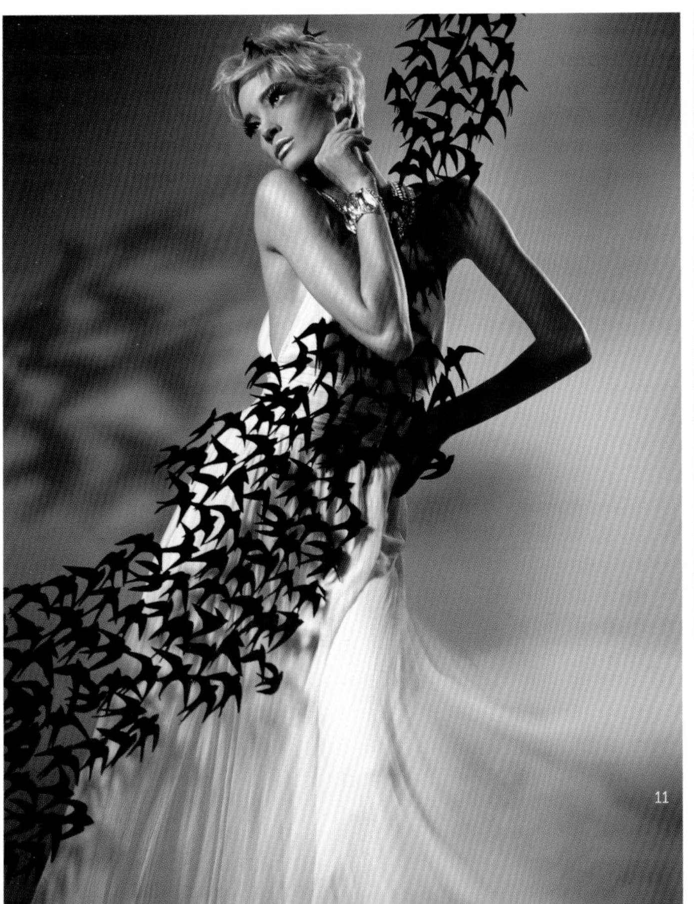

11

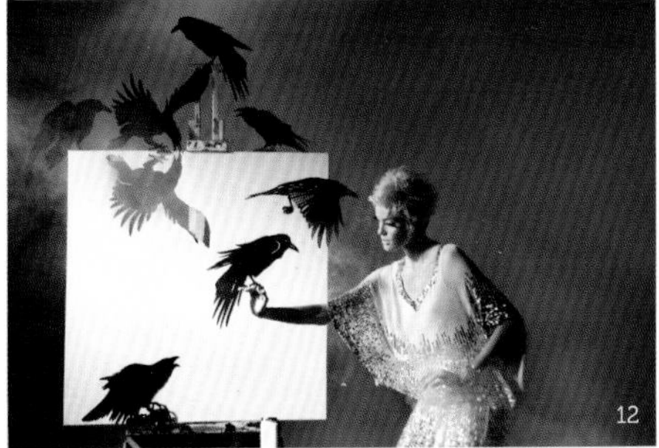

12

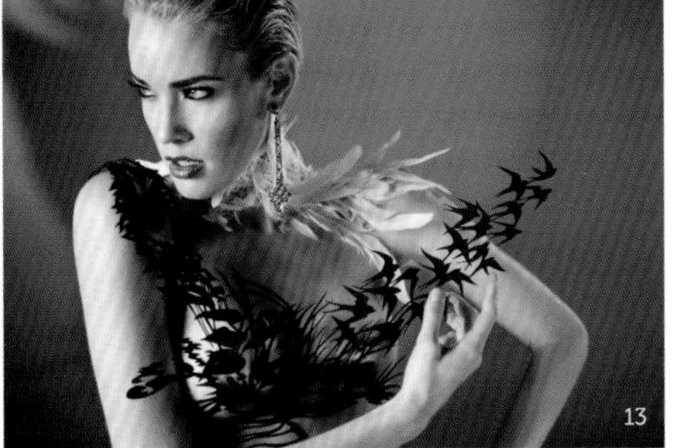

13

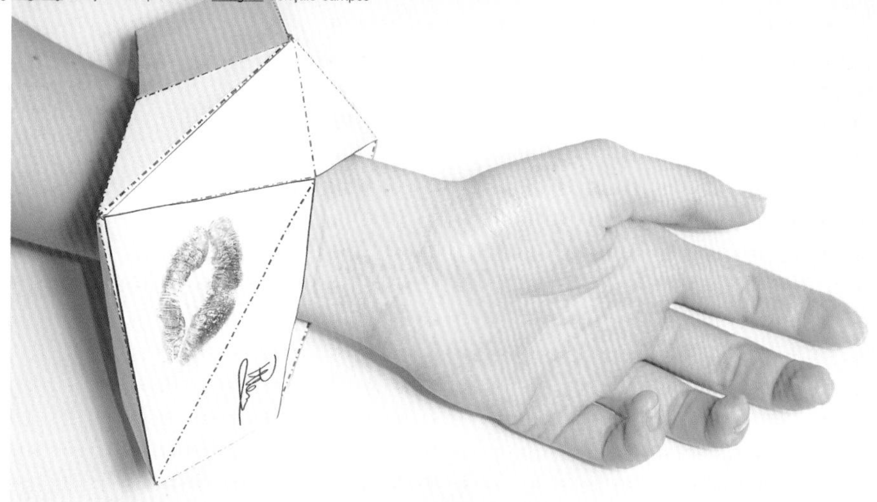

OLY Bracelet

OLY Bracelet is a paper bracelet that anyone can download and build, like a children's game, using glue and scissors. It's a really special and distinct accessory. You can use it at any time that you like, without being afraid of losing or breaking it, because it's just made of paper and can always be rebuilt. It comes in two versions, a patterned one and a blank one, so you can print the guide lines over scrap paper, your own drawings, patterns, pictures, coloured paper, recycled paper, etc...

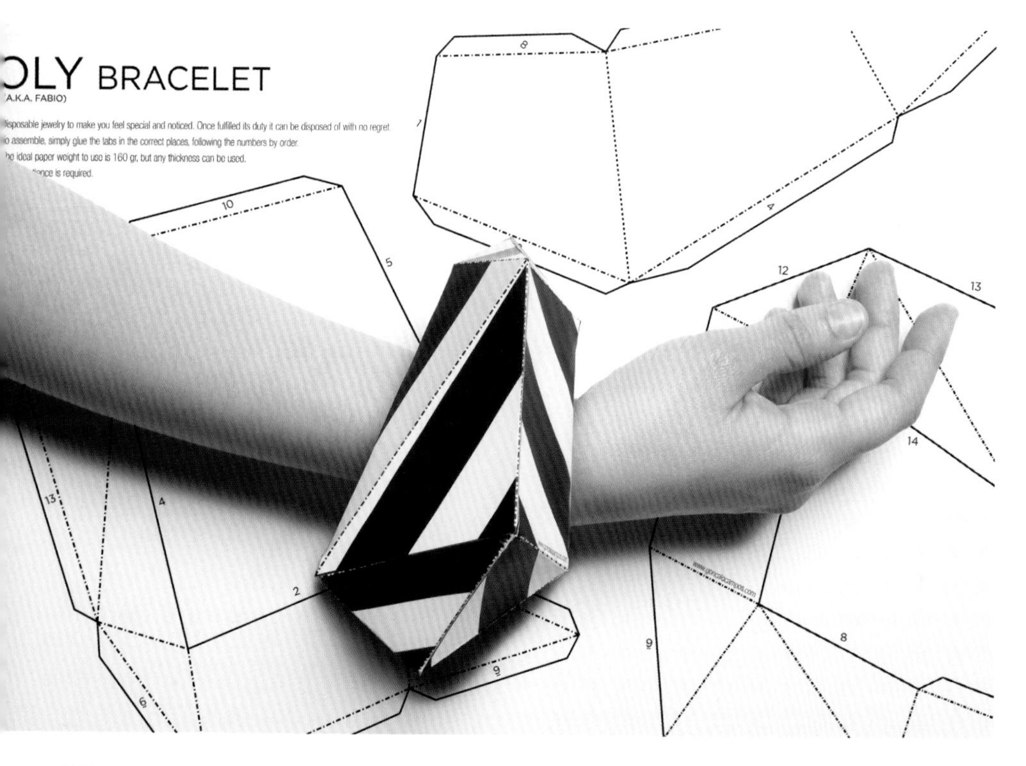

Work Type Fashion Technique Printing, gluing, pasting

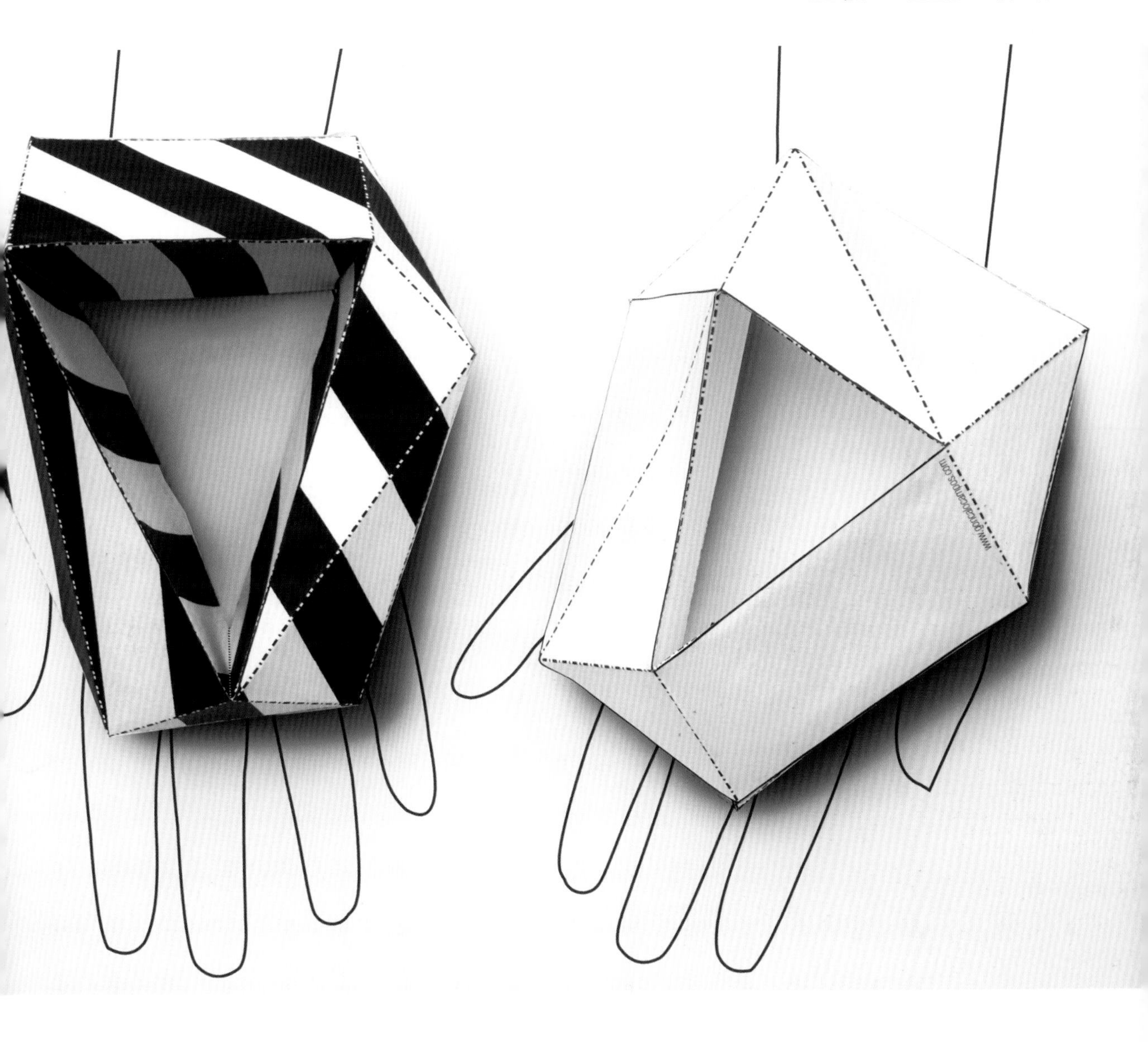

Design Agency Oaddx Ltd Designer Ting-Yu Wang Photographer Iki Chen Producer PAPERSELF

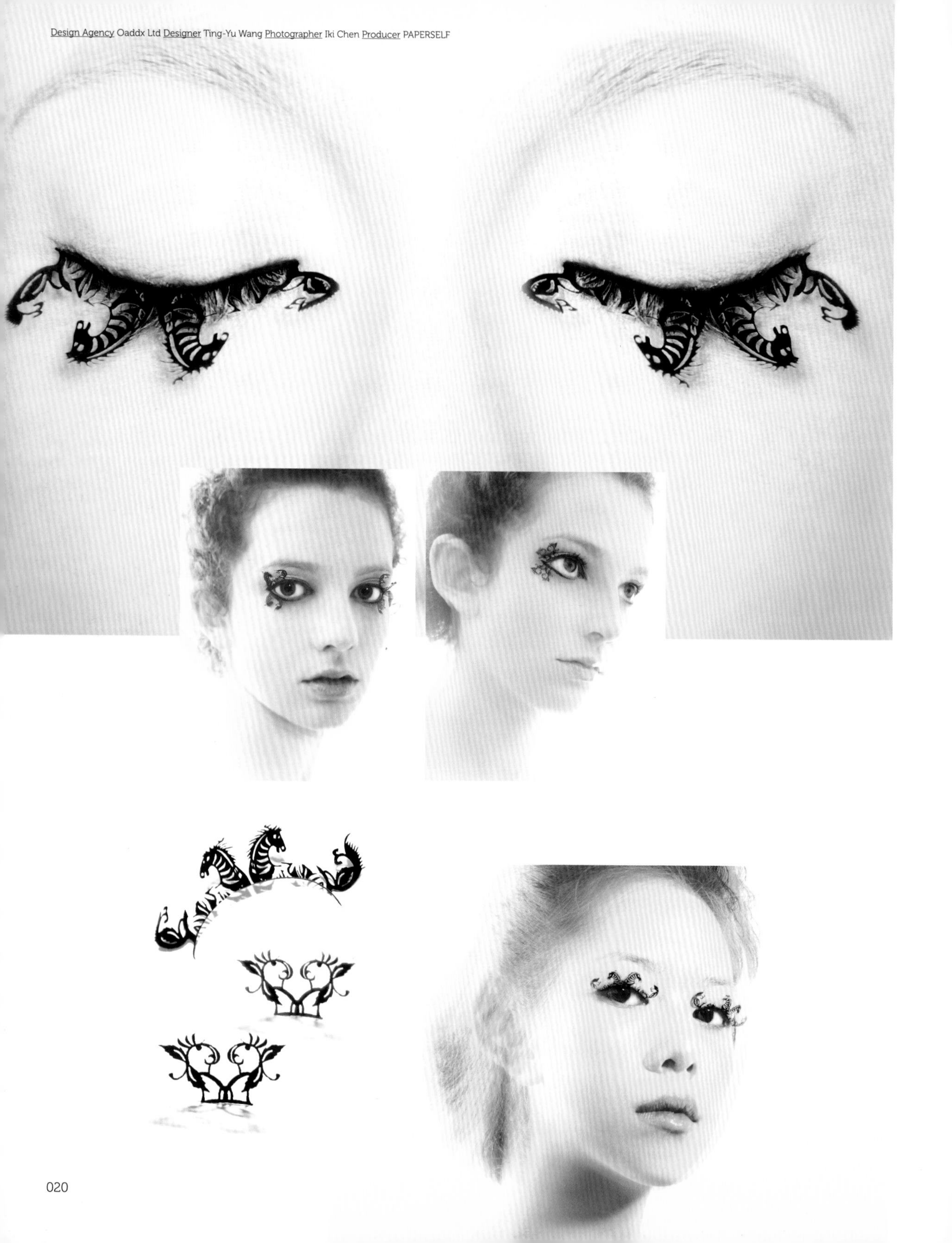

PAPERSELF Paper eyelashes

Paper eyelashes are the newest addition to PAPERSELF. The paper cut eyelashes concept is designed by Ting yu Wang, and developed and produced by the PAPERSELF team. Inspired by the art of Chinese paper-cutting, these eyelashes blend an element of traditional culture with contemporary design. Unique and expressive, the paper eyelashes come in two sizes: wearers can choose to accentuate the corners of their eyes for a subtler daytime look, or make a statement with the full lashes for a special occasion. Intricately cut and delicately pretty, the paper eyelashes are available in three styles, each infused with symbolic meaning rooted in Chinese culture:
Horses: symbolic of success
Peony: for happiness and good fortune
Peach blossom: a symbol of love and romance

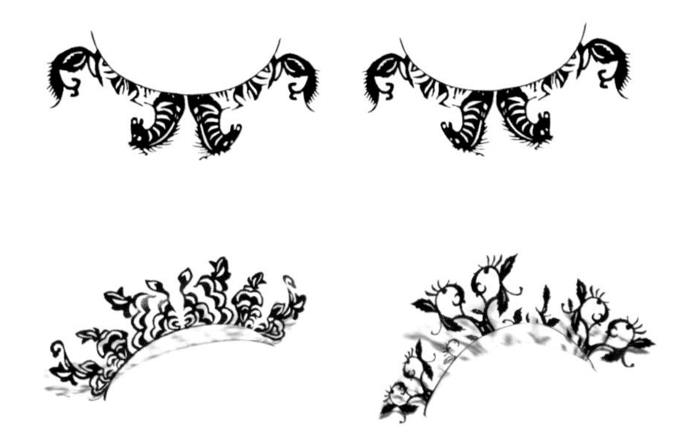

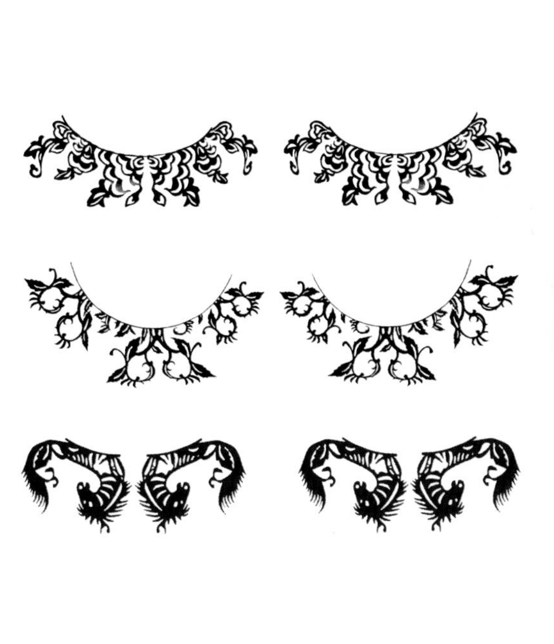

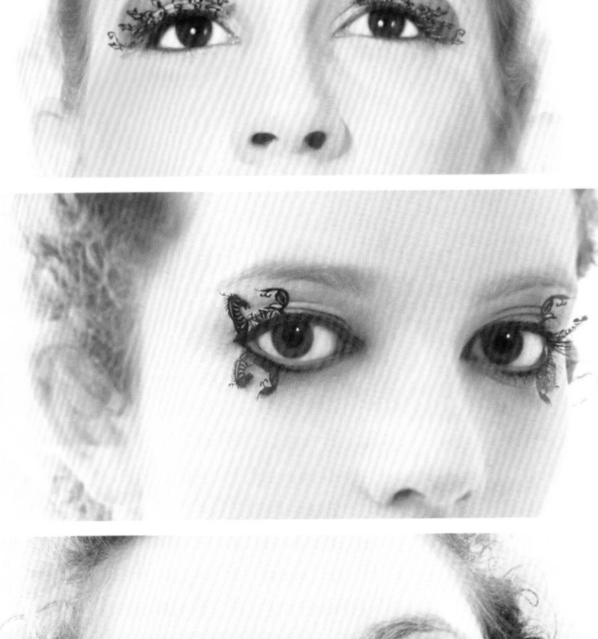

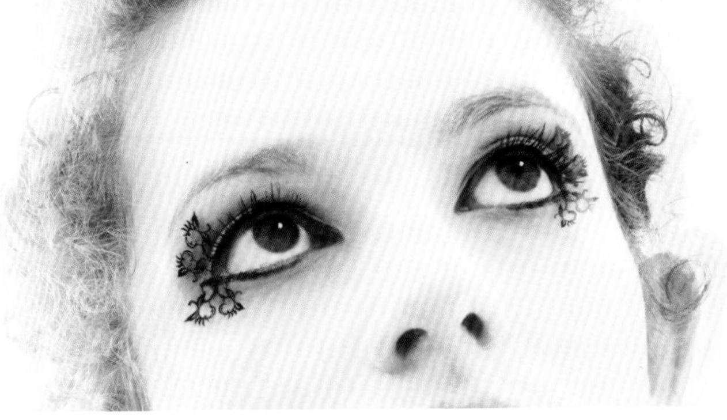

Design Agency Kapsule Kollektive Designer DORA KELEMEN Photographer Tamás Réthey-Prikkel

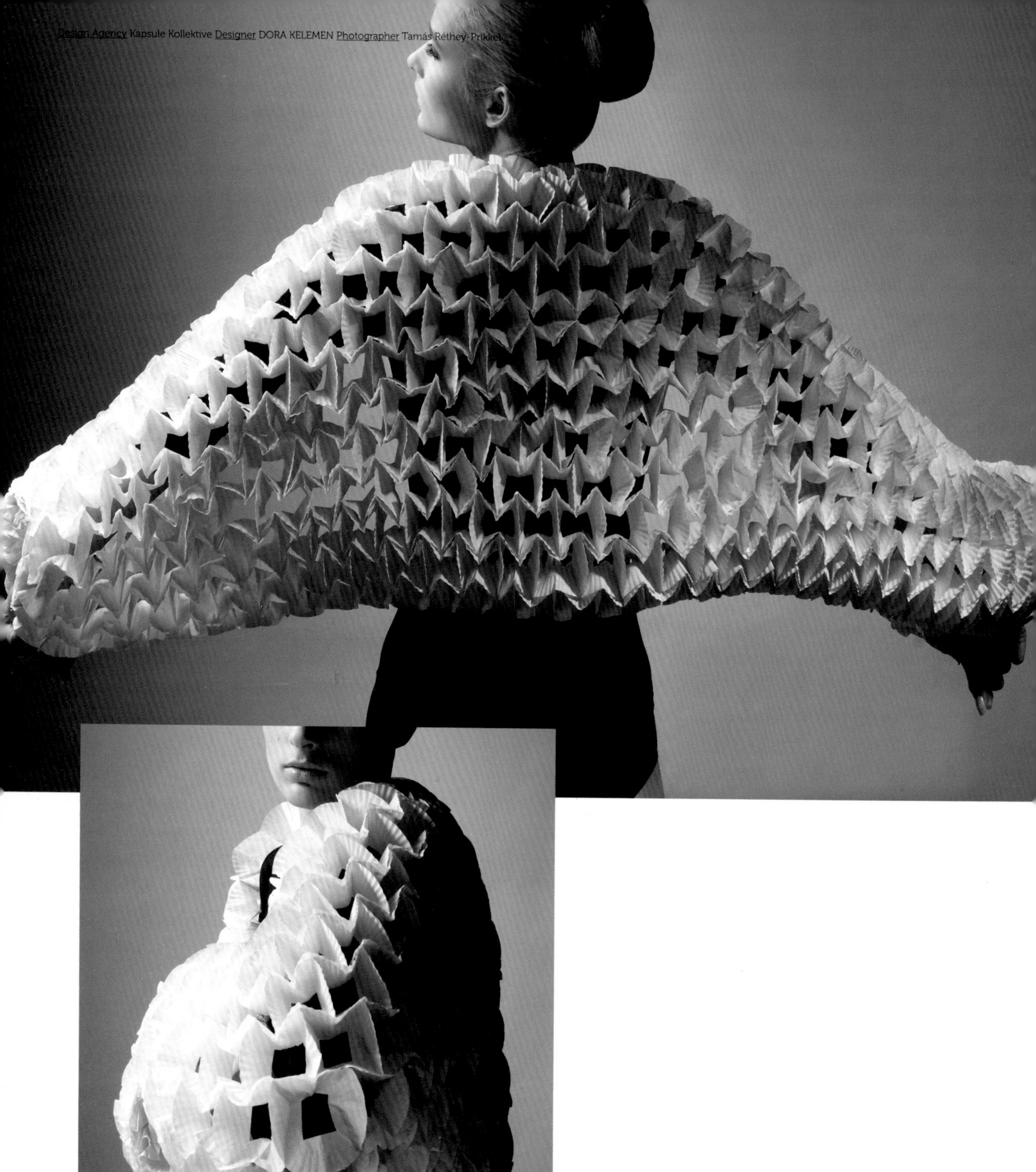

Angel

The "Angel" is a folded paper object which moves with the body and has a constantly changing shape.

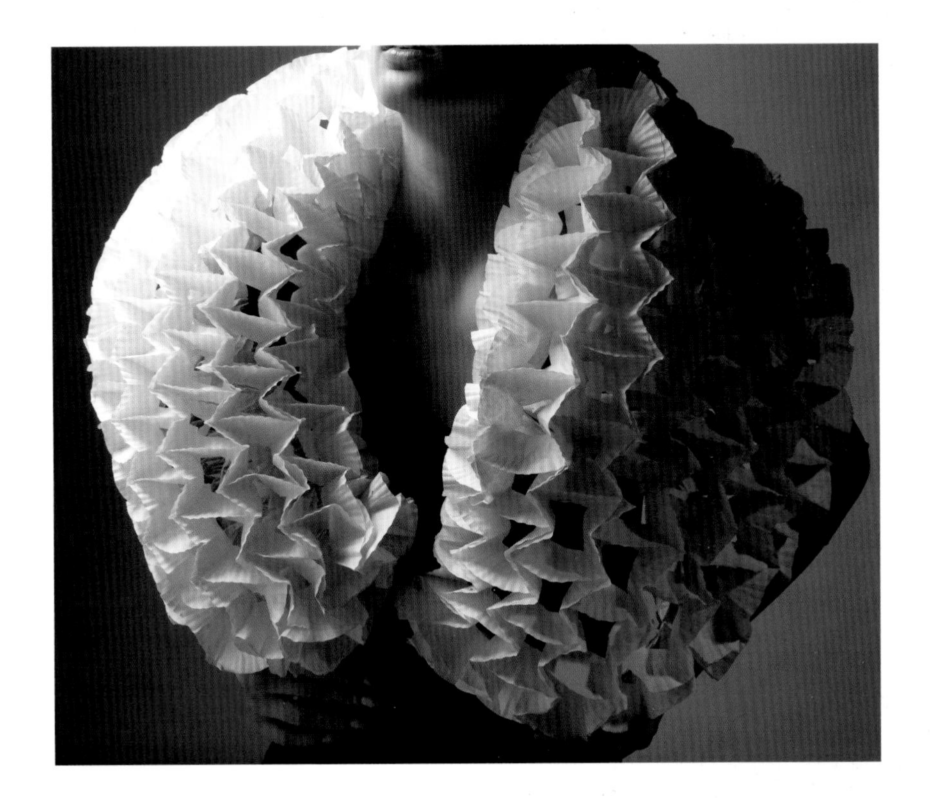

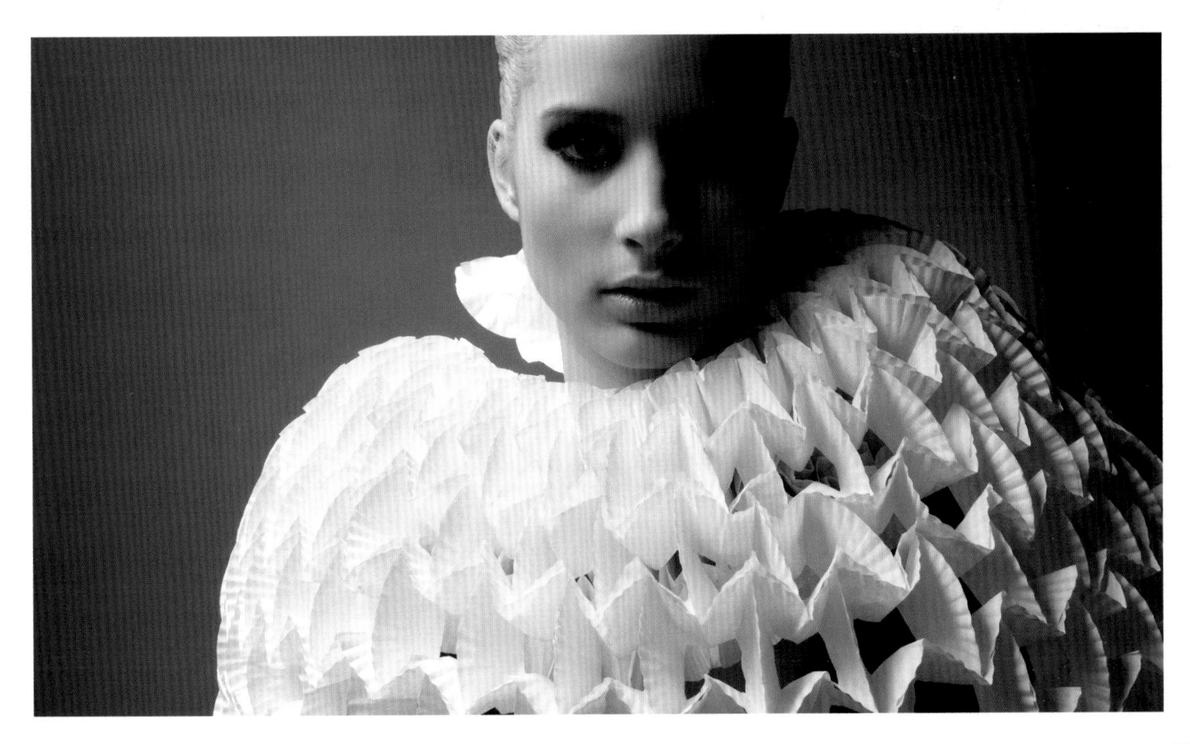

Design Agency GAIAdesign Designer Gloria Pizzilli, Arianna Petrakis, Ilaria Pacini, Adele Bacci Photographer Alessandra Cinquemani, Luca Nelli & PhotoFlo

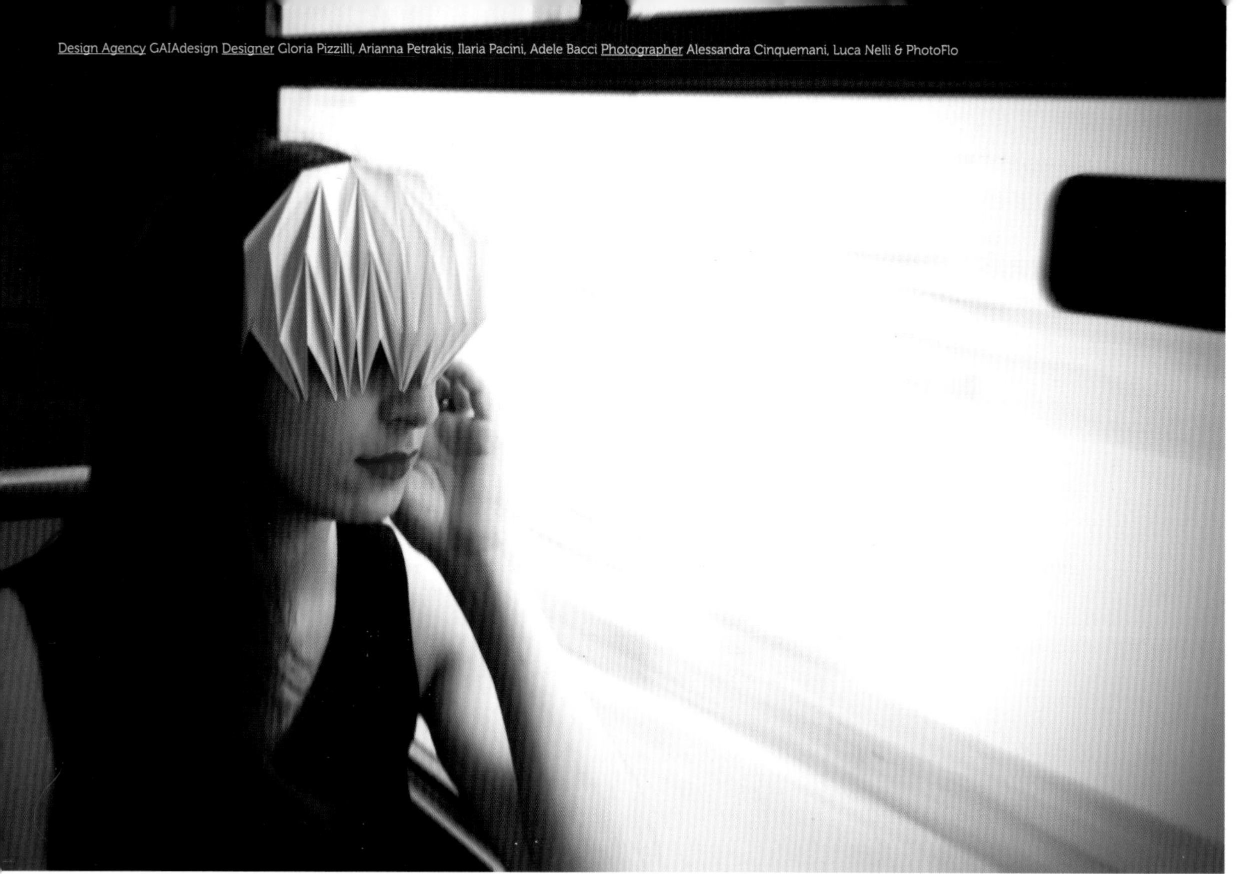

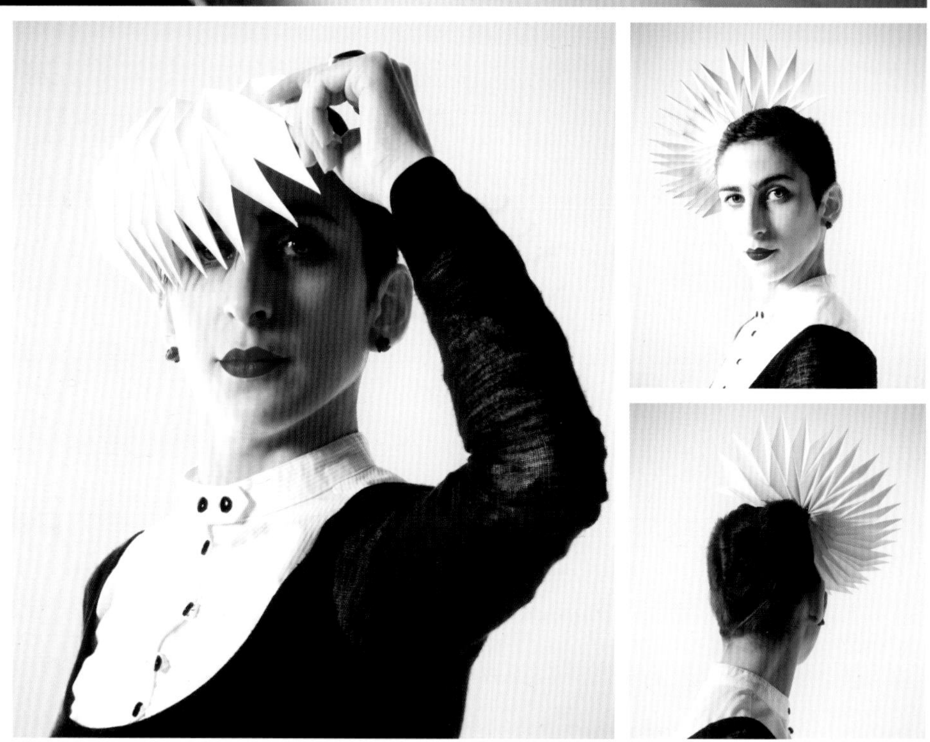

Veasyble – unfold a beautiful intimacy

VEASYBLE is a 4-piece collection of wearable design accessories for unfolding your contextual presence into a state of beautiful intimacy – wherever, whenever. VEASYBLE is made of paper bonded to polyethylene and fabric. A common folded pattern shapes each VEASYBLE piece, which varies in scale and proportion according to your demand of intimacy. VEASYBLE is based on three keywords: isolation, intimacy and ornament.

The idea comes from a reflection on the change in our bodily relationships within the public environment: due to the effects of our increased intersubjectivity and interpersonal life, GAIA has wondered how our sense of intimacy is creating new demands. In March 2009 the project resulted in the design of 4 pieces that work as screens for 4 different parts of the body – eyes, ears, face and upper body. Through shape and colour, VEASYBLE expresses our desire for different levels of intimacy at any time, any place.

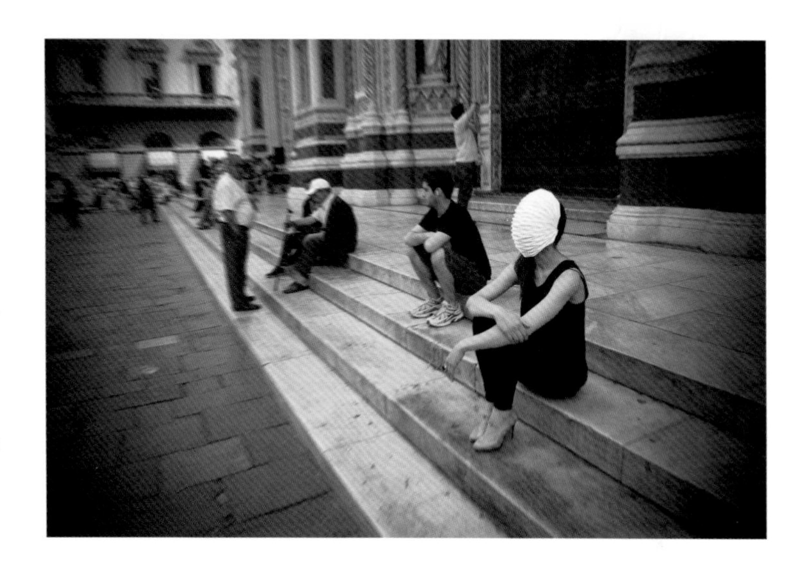

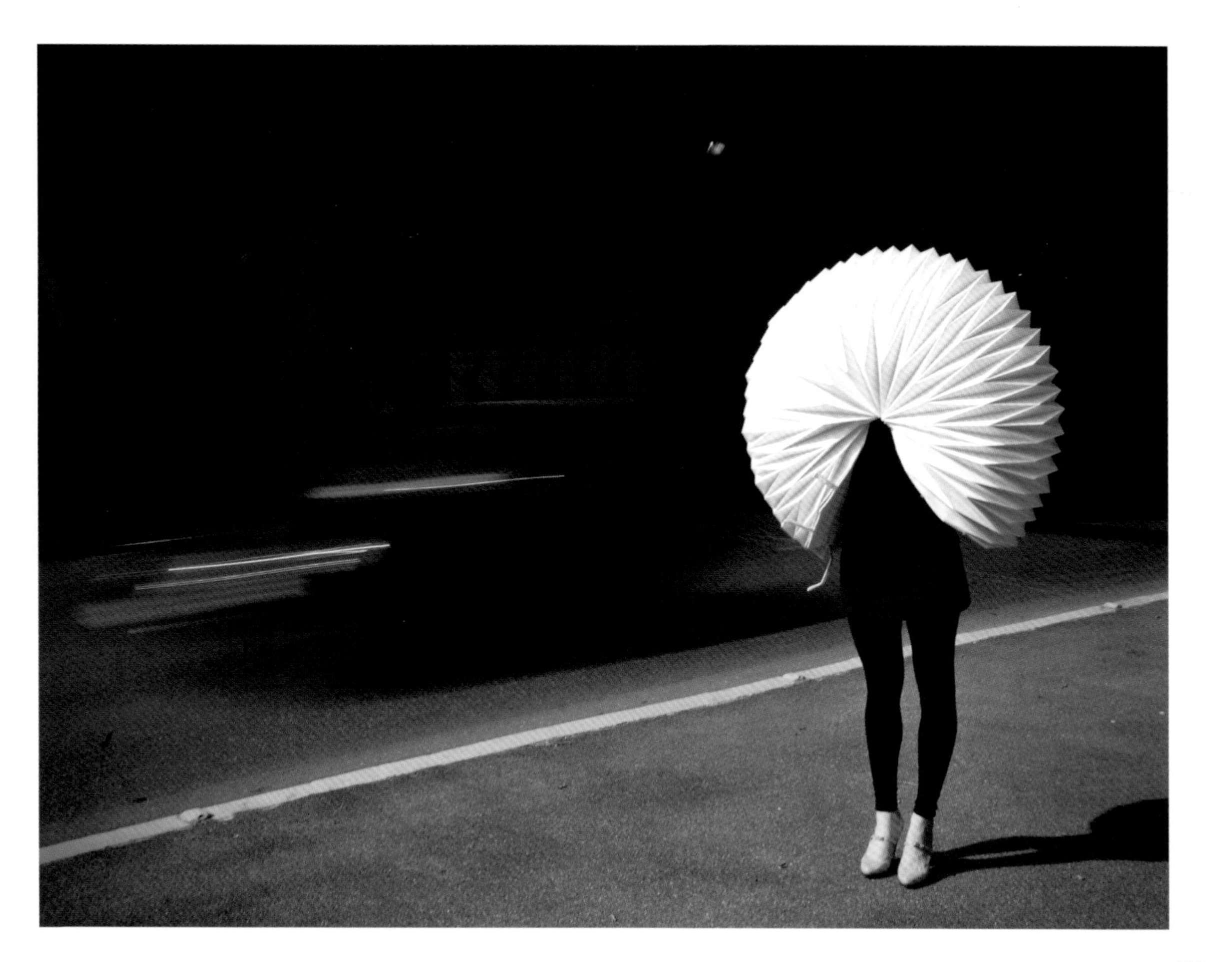

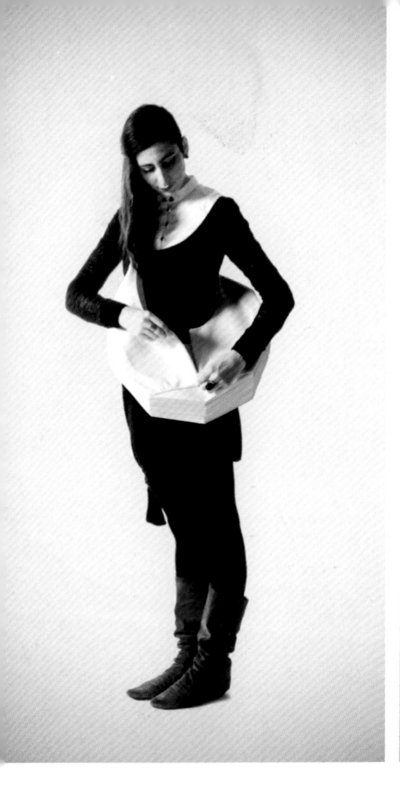

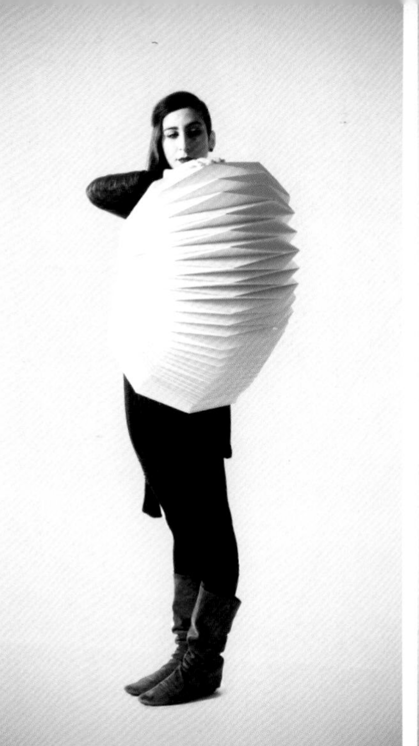

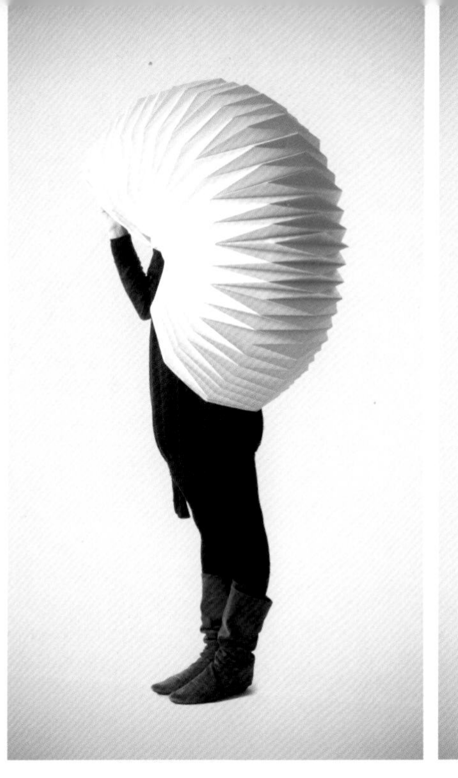

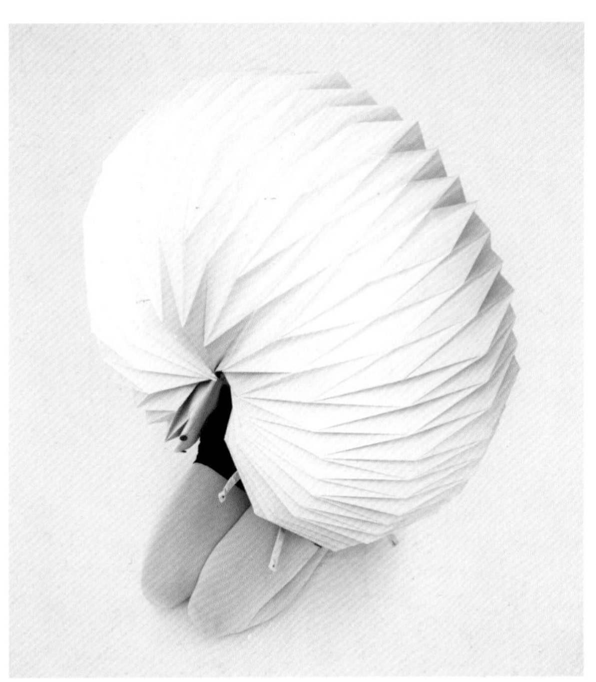

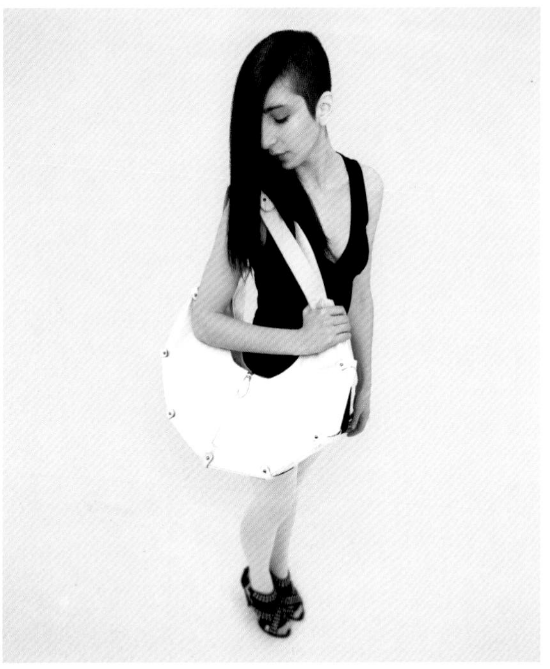

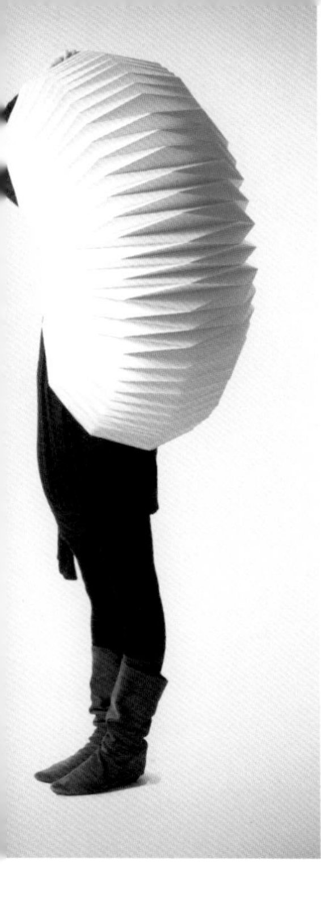

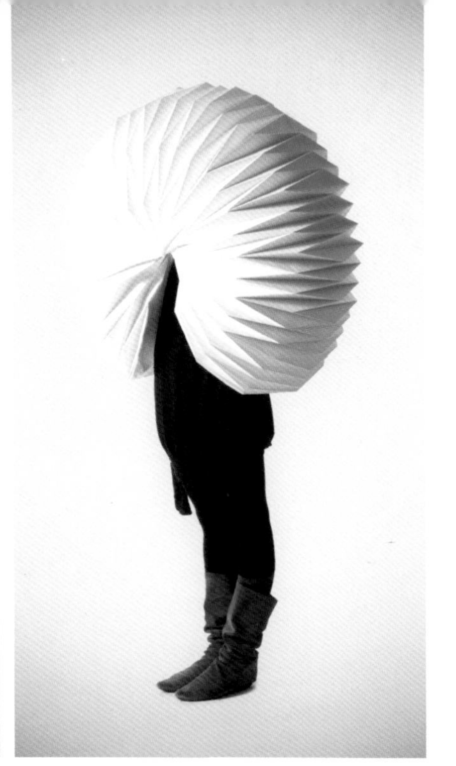

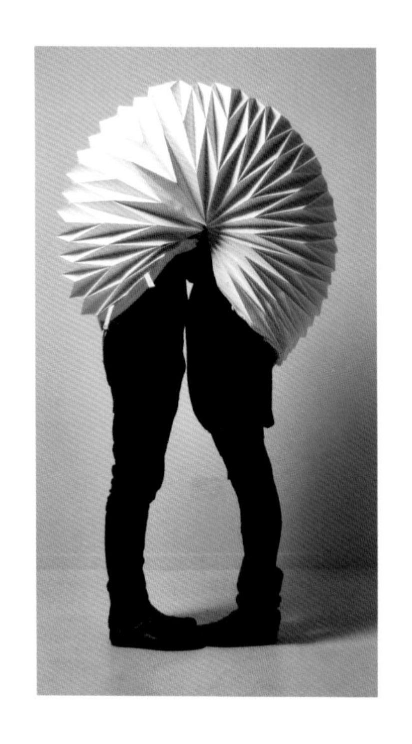

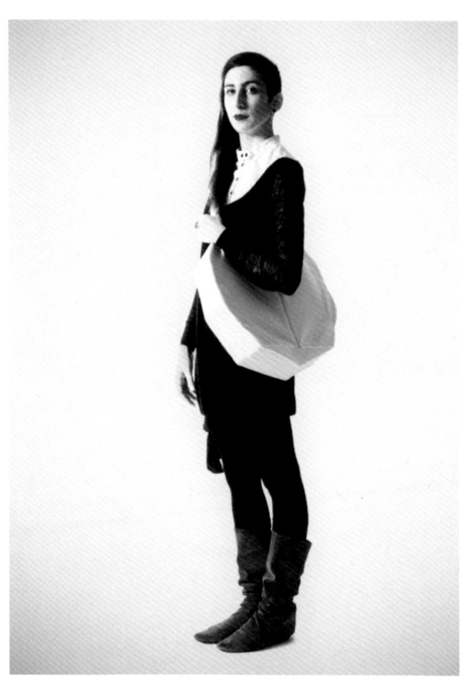

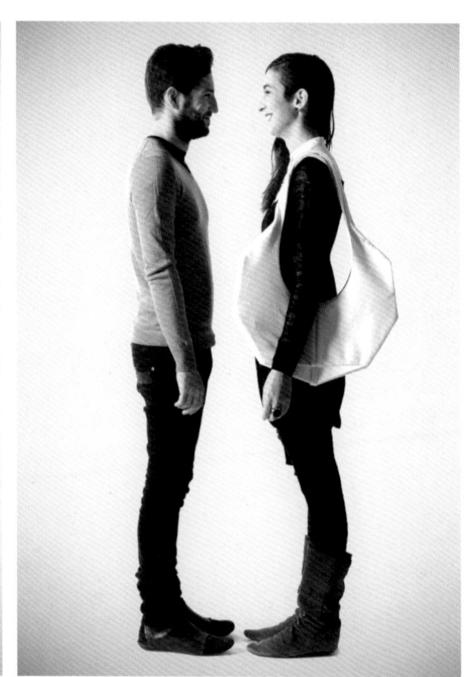

softwall + softblock modular system

softwall + softblock are a modular space shaping system at the core of molo's soft collection. Utilizing flexible honeycomb structures that expand, contract and flex to form sculptural spaces and seating topographies, soft is a research driven exploration of materials, structures and space making. The elements of the soft collection have been designed to be uniquely shaped for a specific occasion or space, folded away for storage and reshaped again in variable and dynamic ways; replacing inflexible alternatives for partitioning and arranging space. The tactile, experiential qualities of the textile softwall + softblock system are suited to shaping more intimate ephemeral areas within larger open spaces. softwall + softblock further provide a medium for shaping the acoustics and light of a space. The cellular structure and vertical pleats that run the course of an expanded wall serve to dampen sound while translucent or opaque versions of softwall + softblock can sculpt the light of a space.

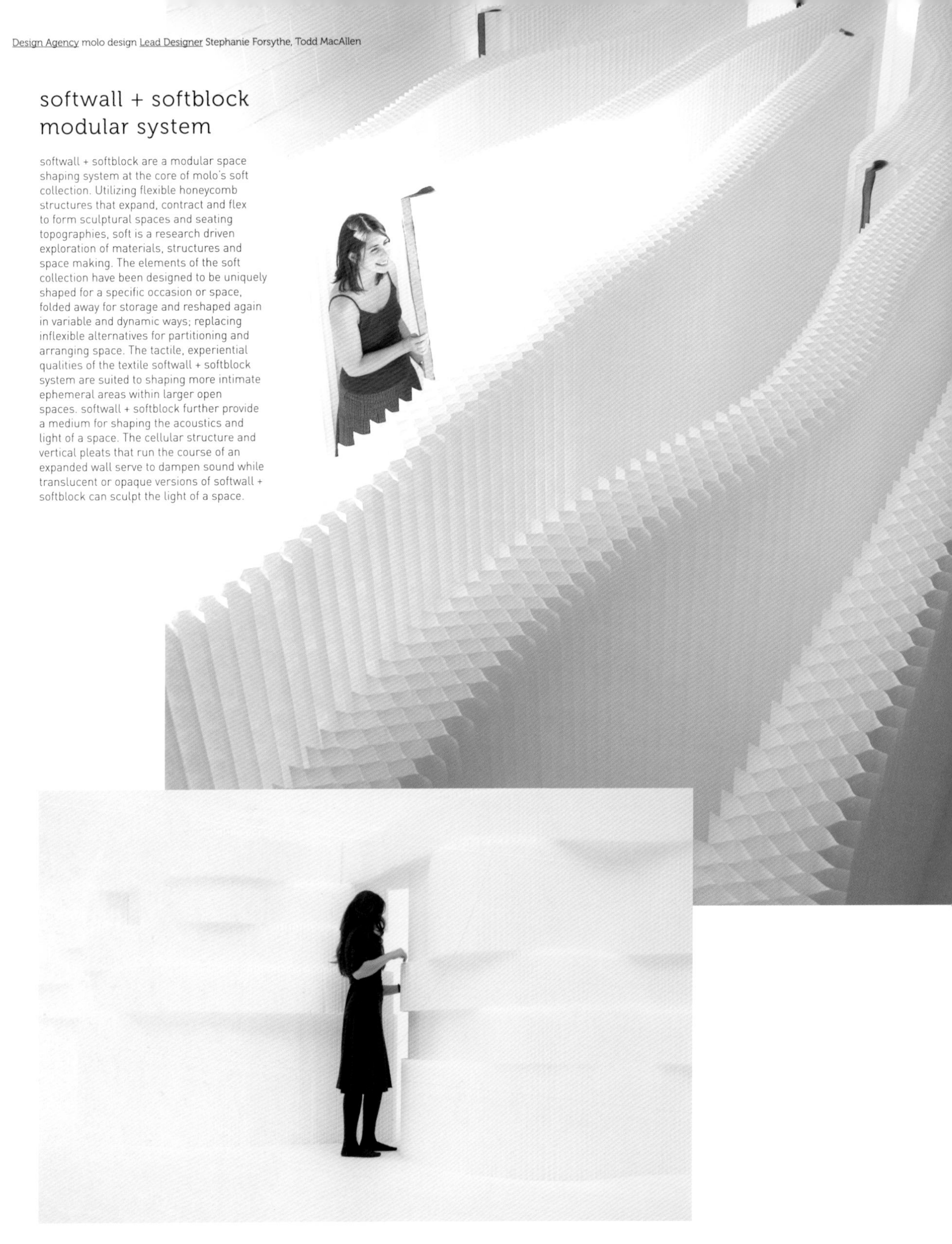

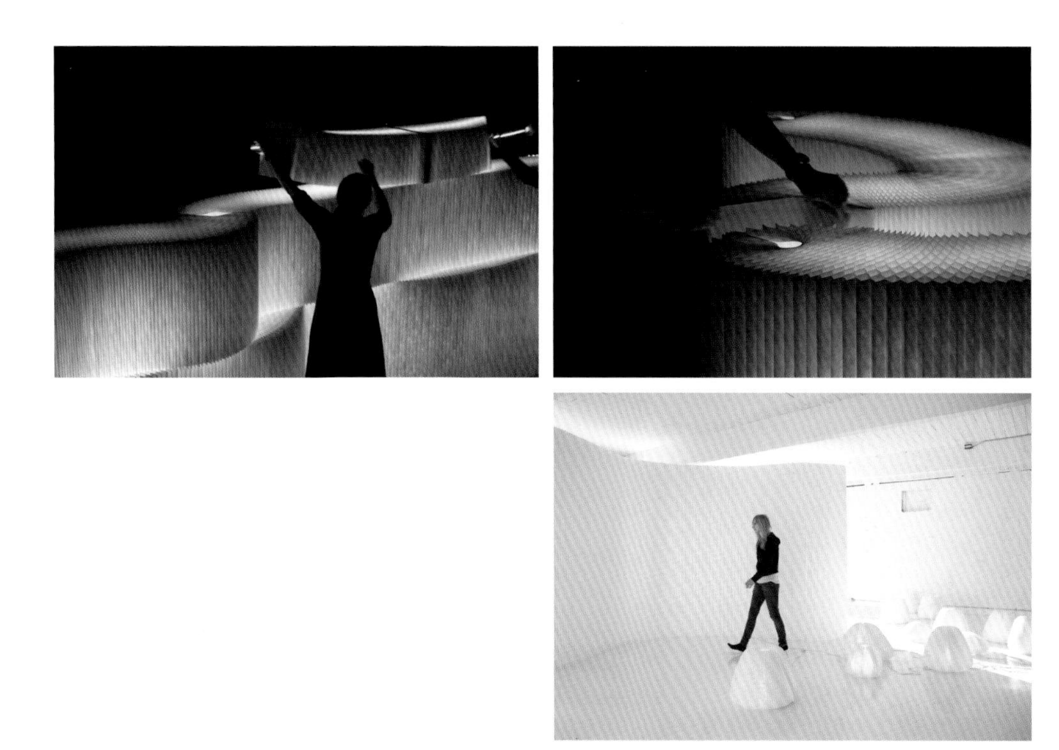

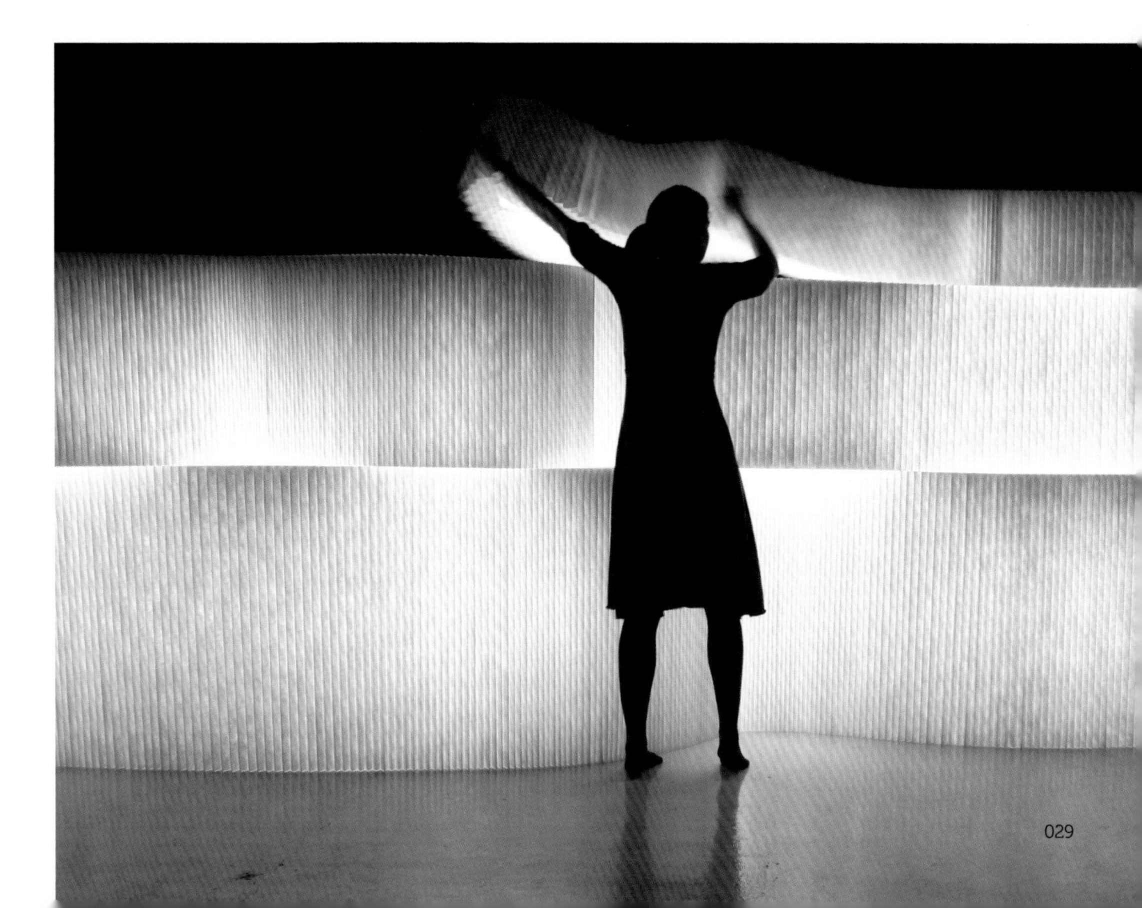

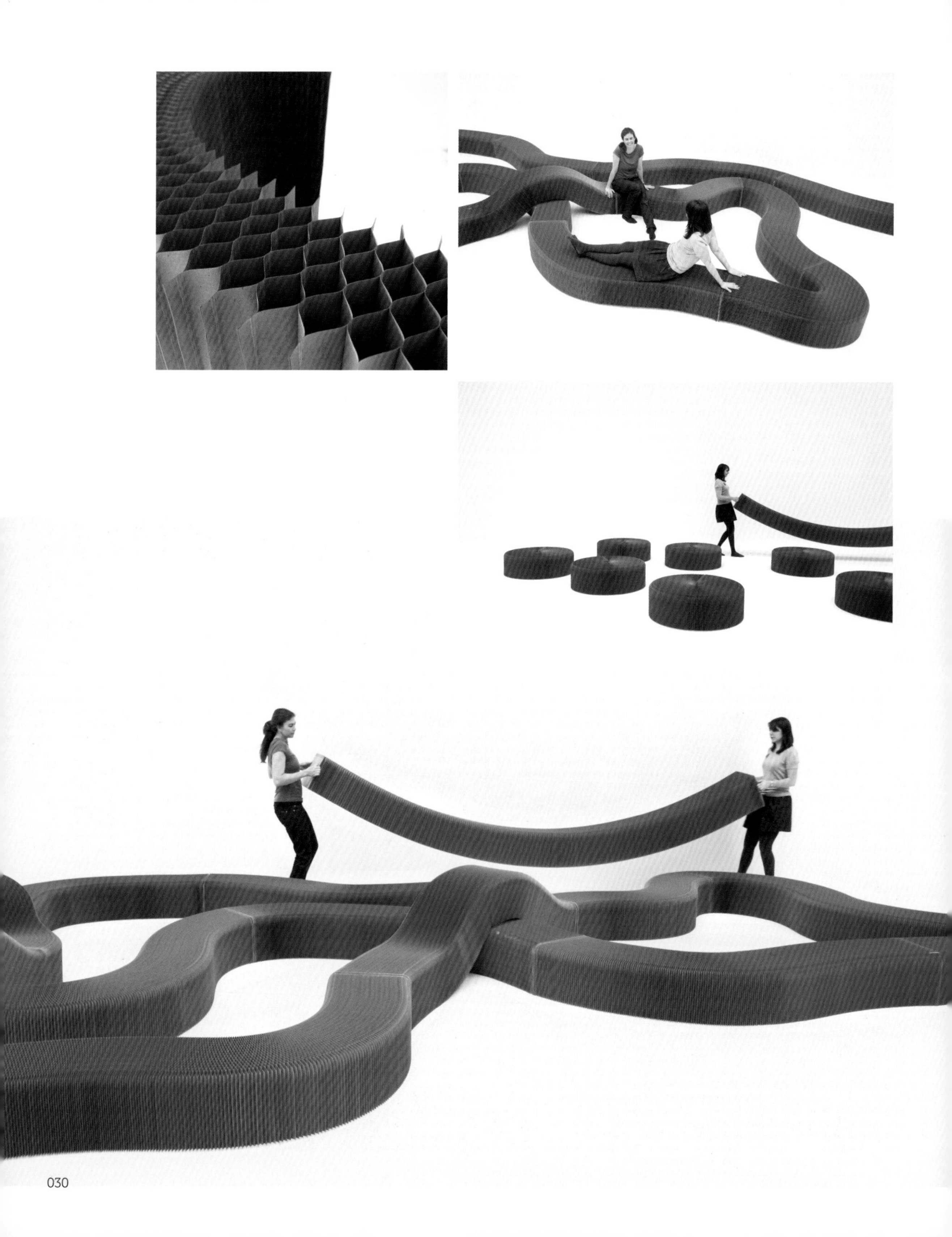

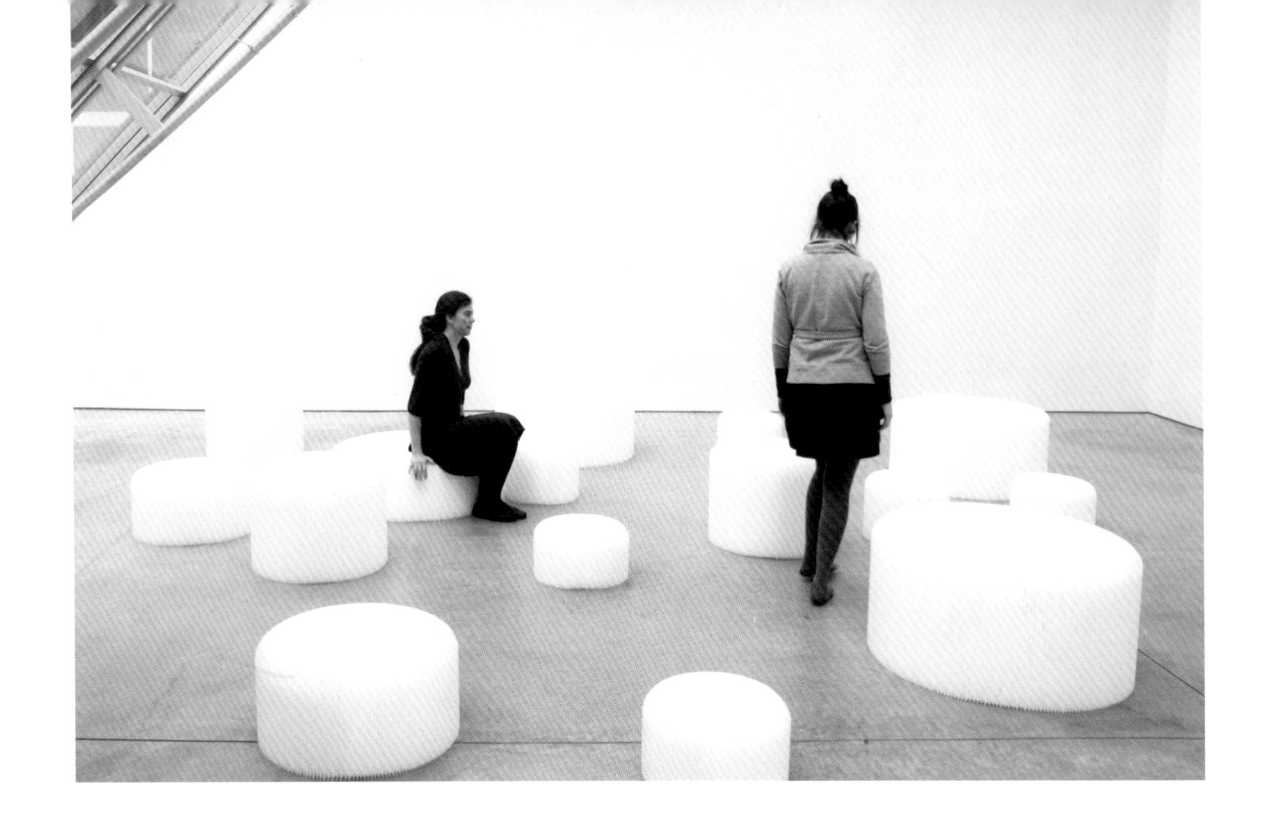

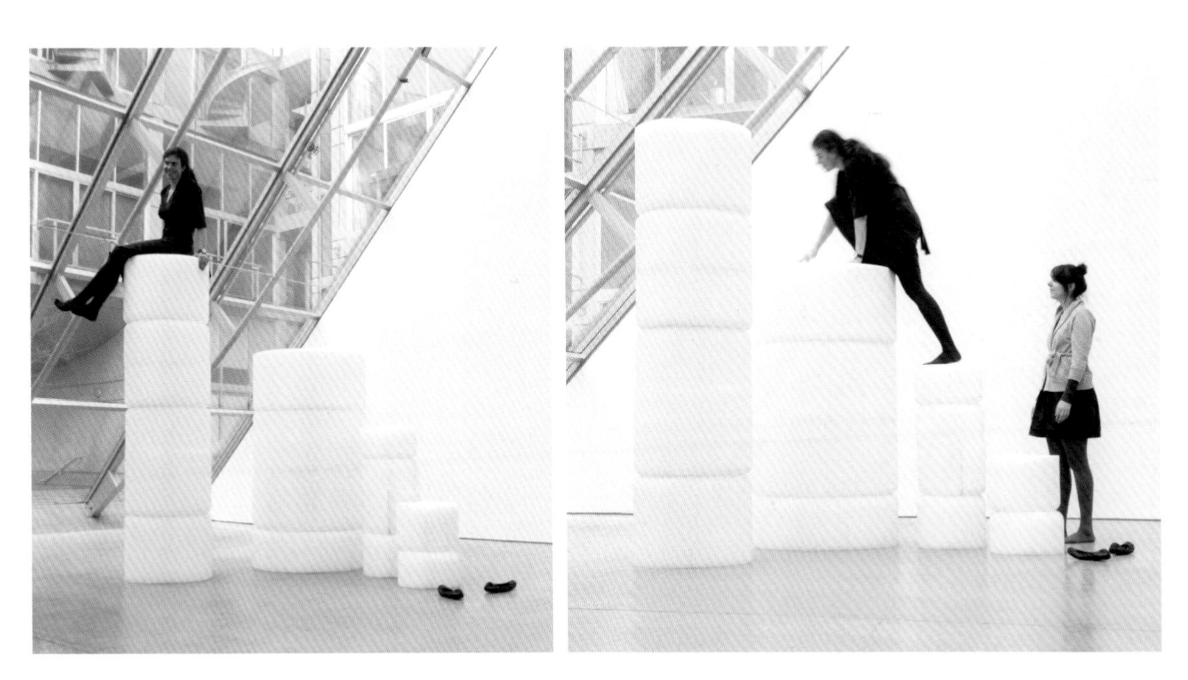

Honey-pop (2000-2001)

Light and strong, the naturally created honeycomb is ultimately an architectural structure. This chair is made with sheets of glassine paper that were piled together and cut along specific lines so that the paper magically opens up into a honeycomb structure. The final form of the chair is set when in use, as it responds to the shape of the sitter's bottom. This is now a part of the permanent collection at the Museum of Modern Art (MoMA), Vitra Design Museum, the Pompidou Center, and Victoria and Albert Museum.

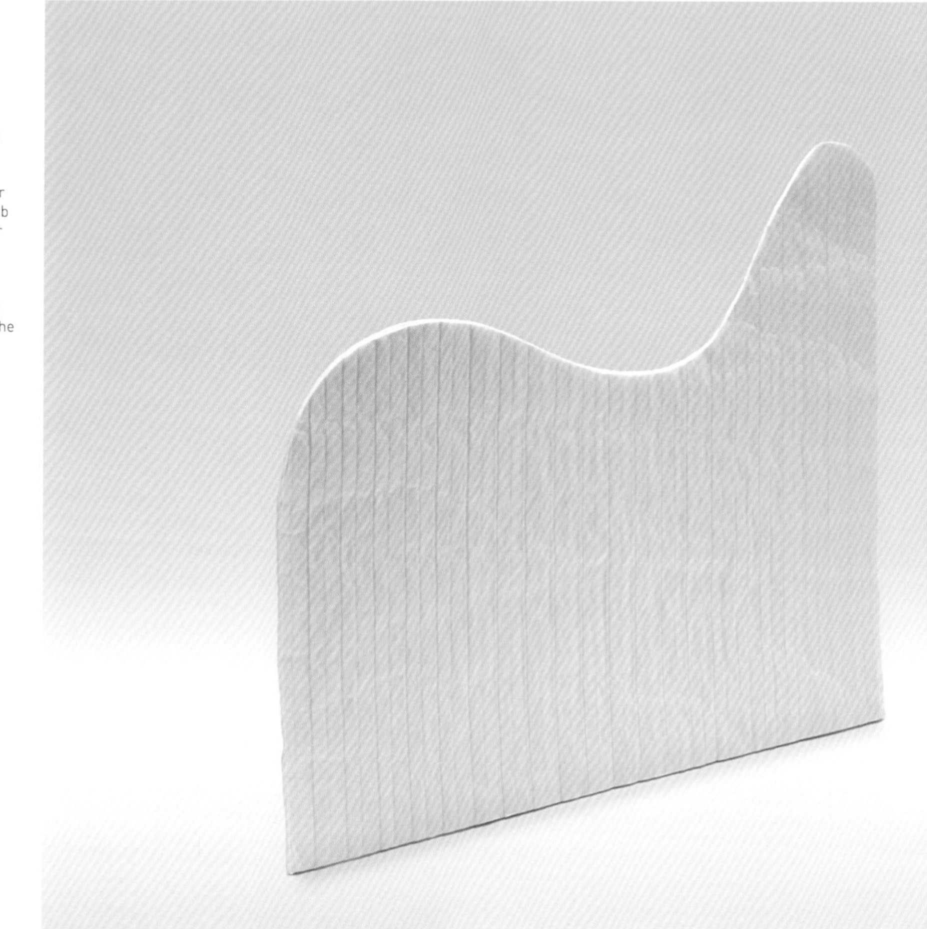

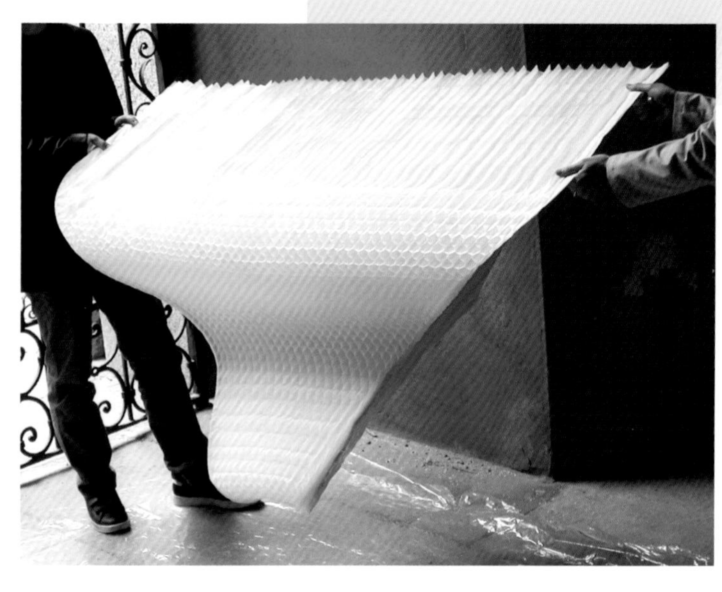

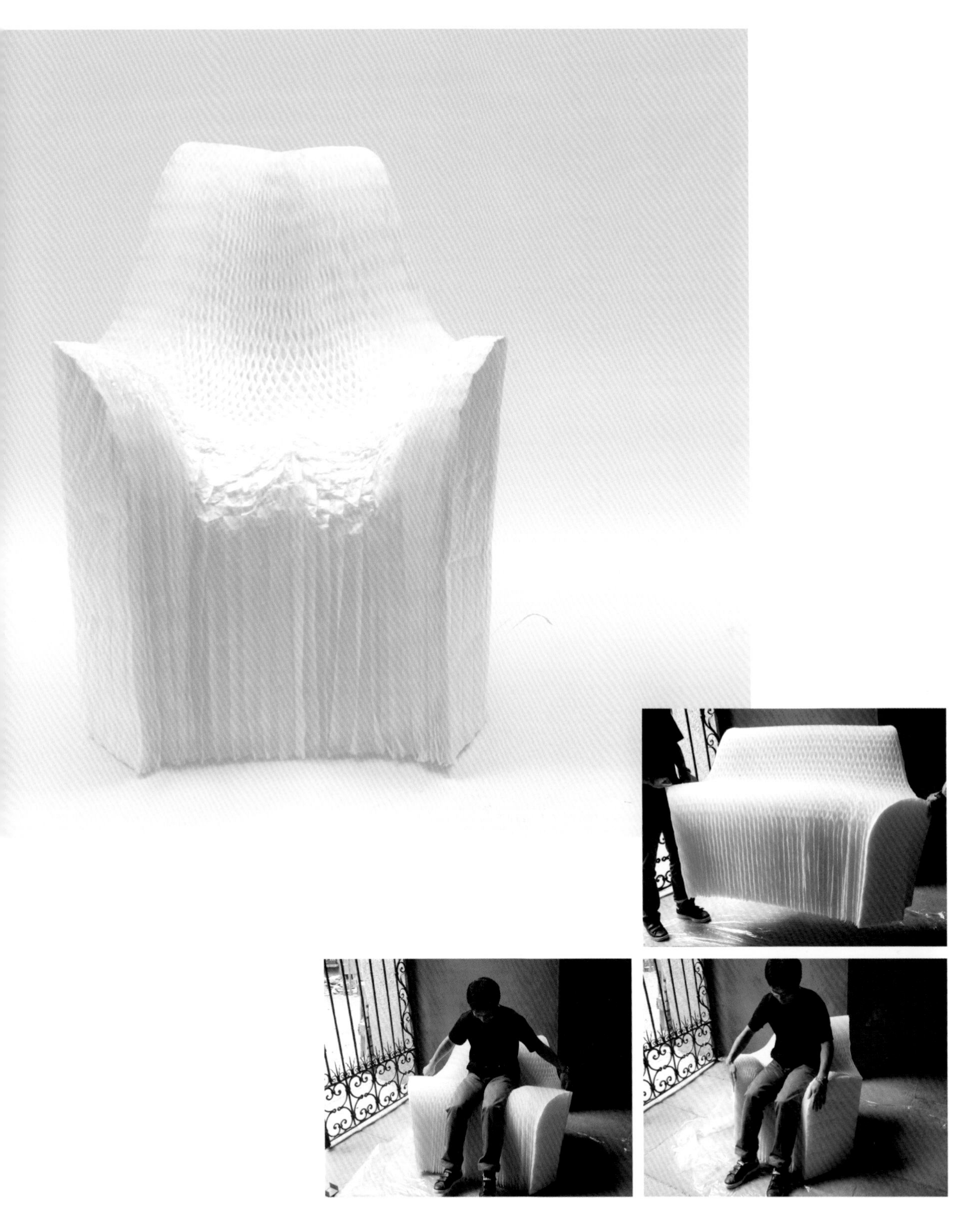

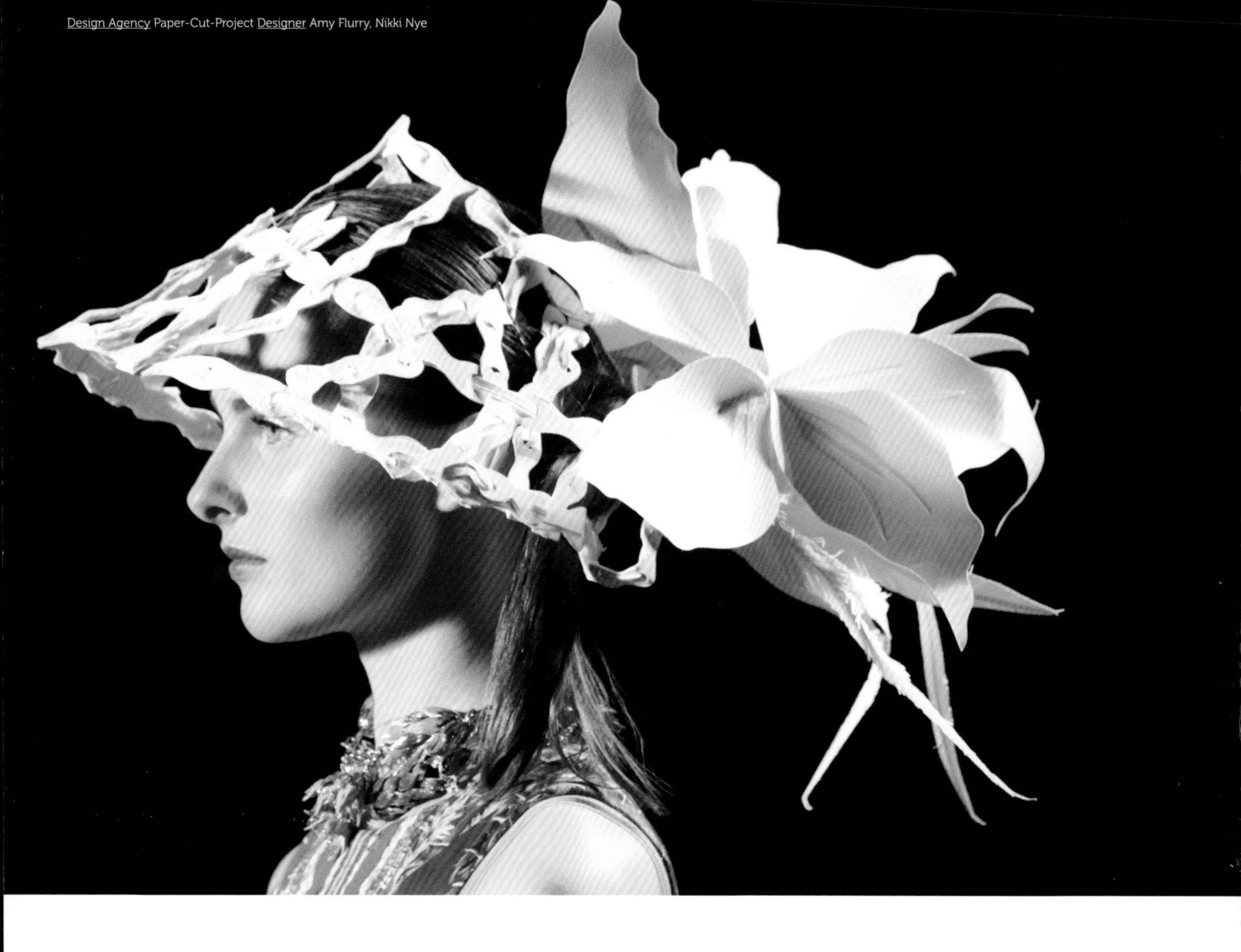

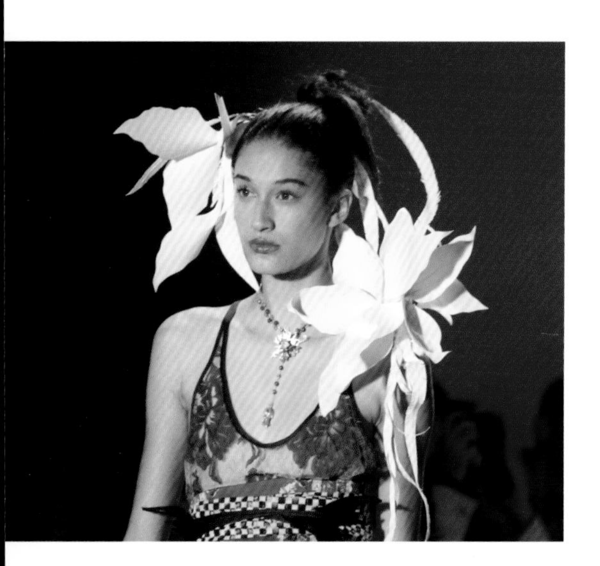

Jen Kao 2012

Paper-Cut-Project collaborated with American designer Jen Kao for her spring/summer 2012 collection at Lincoln Center during Fashion Week. Our ten-piece accessories collection included paper cuffs, a shoulder cage, a floor length cape, belts and multiple headpieces, all inspired by poisonous flora in an urban streetscape.

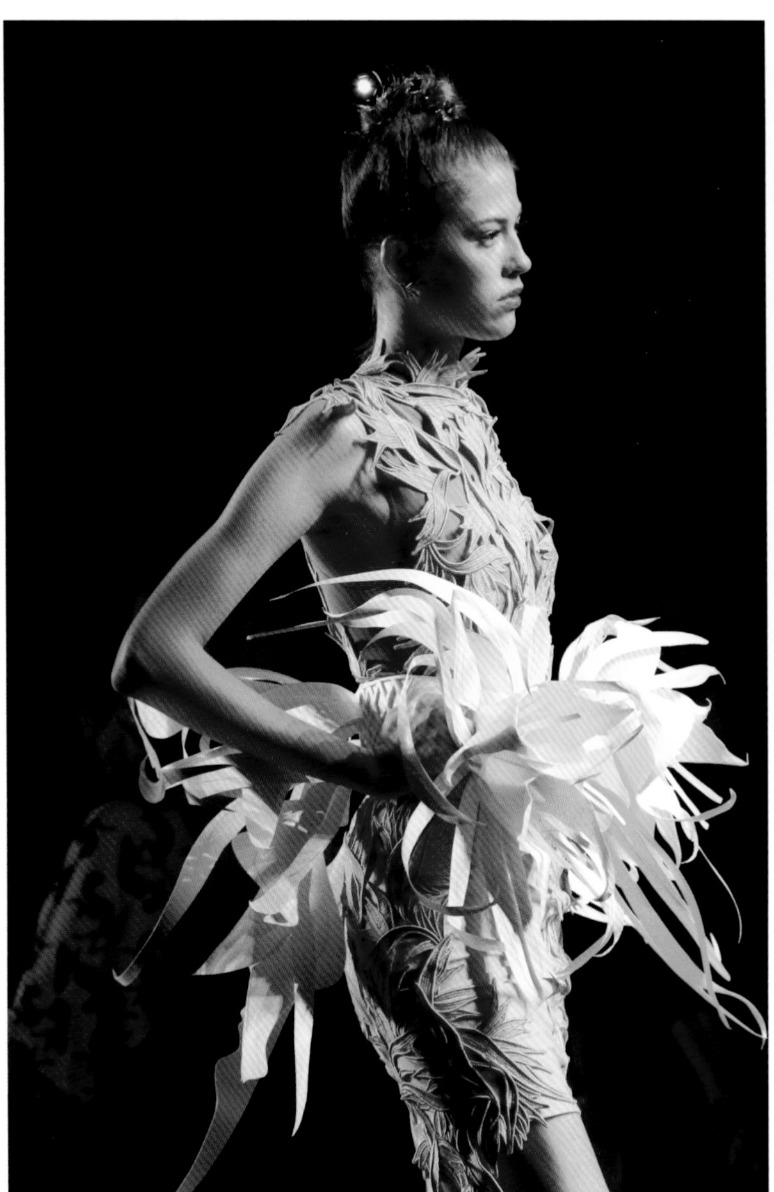

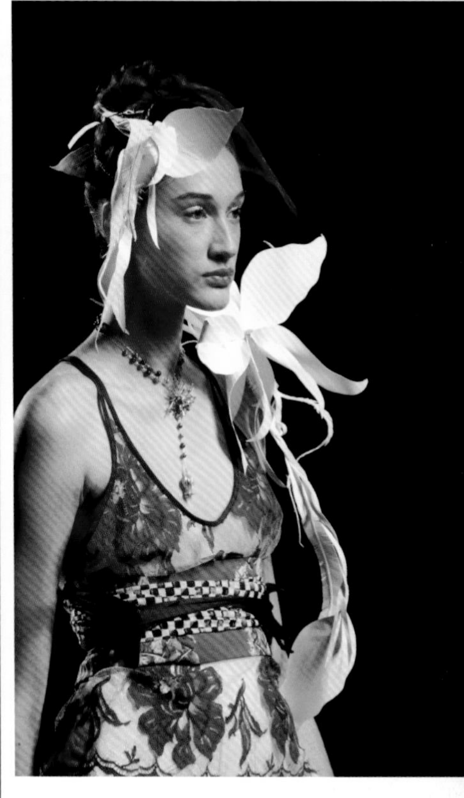

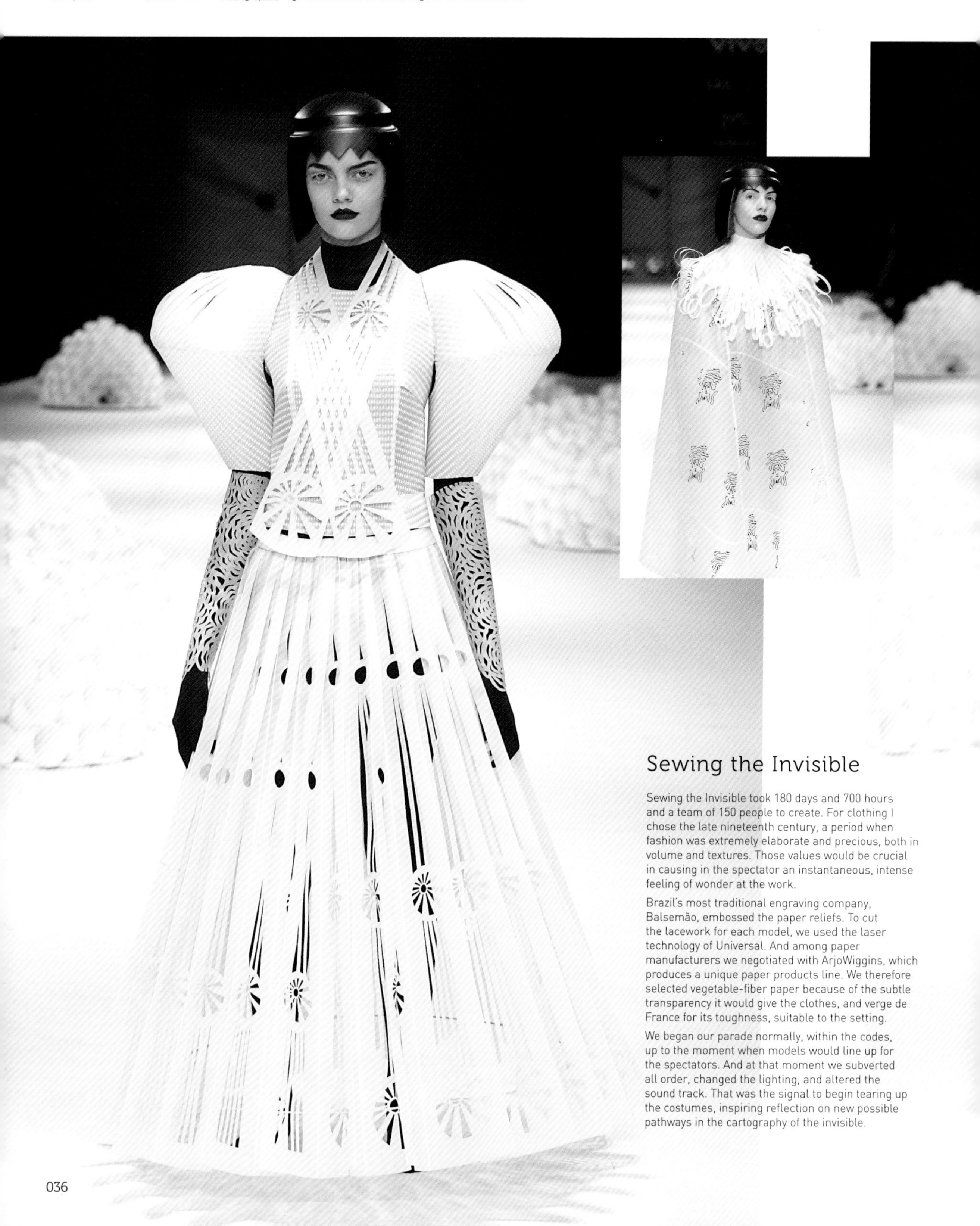

Sewing the Invisible

Sewing the Invisible took 180 days and 700 hours and a team of 150 people to create. For clothing I chose the late nineteenth century, a period when fashion was extremely elaborate and precious, both in volume and textures. Those values would be crucial in causing in the spectator an instantaneous, intense feeling of wonder at the work.

Brazil's most traditional engraving company, Balsemão, embossed the paper reliefs. To cut the lacework for each model, we used the laser technology of Universal. And among paper manufacturers we negotiated with ArjoWiggins, which produces a unique paper products line. We therefore selected vegetable-fiber paper because of the subtle transparency it would give the clothes, and verge de France for its toughness, suitable to the setting.

We began our parade normally, within the codes, up to the moment when models would line up for the spectators. And at that moment we subverted all order, changed the lighting, and altered the sound track. That was the signal to begin tearing up the costumes, inspiring reflection on new possible pathways in the cartography of the invisible.

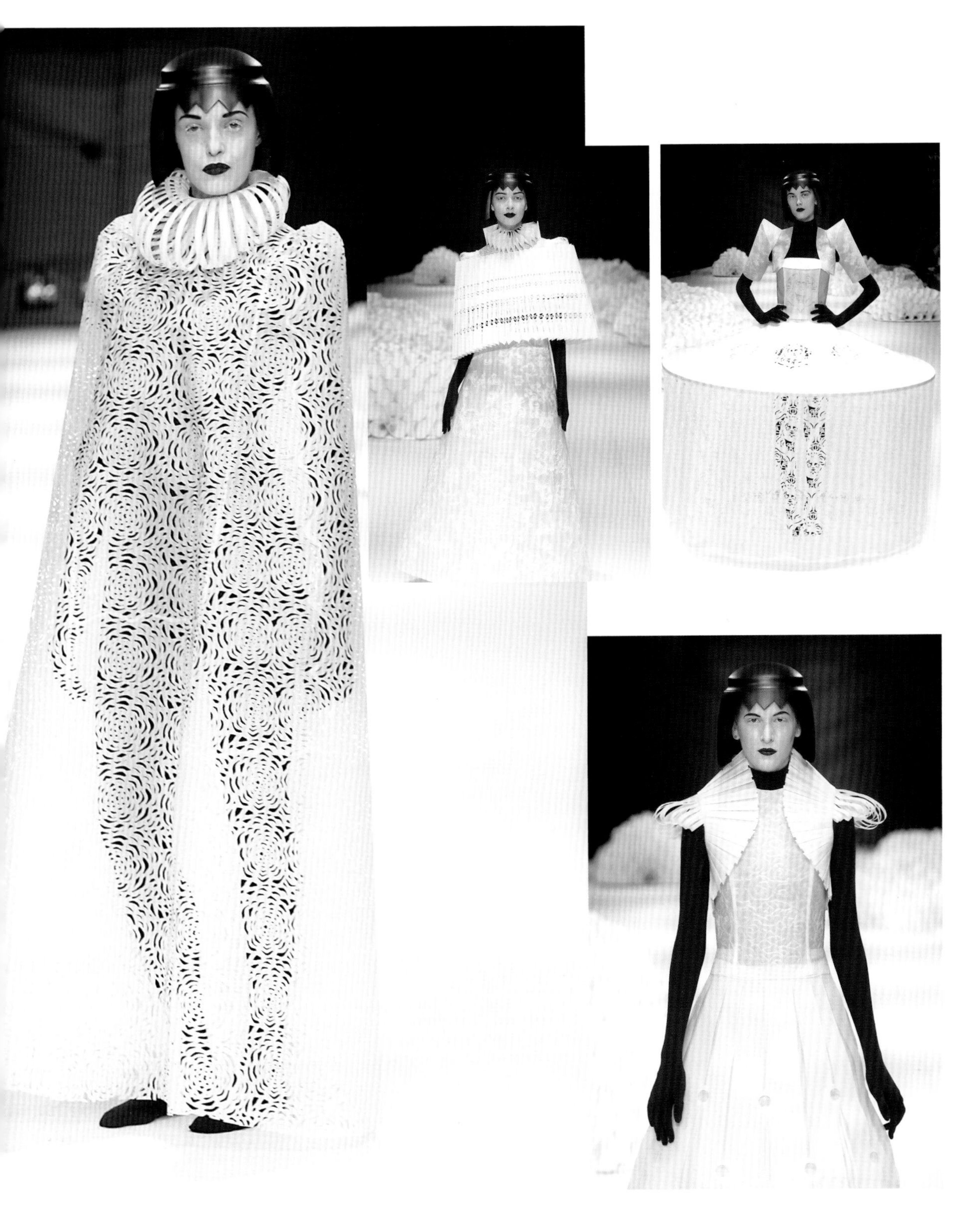

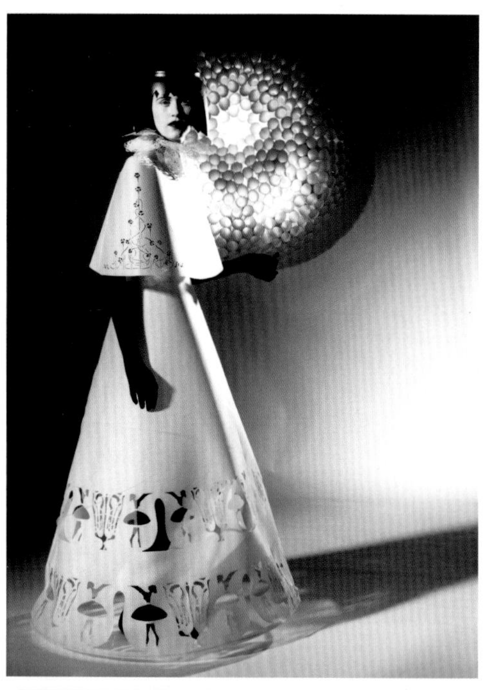

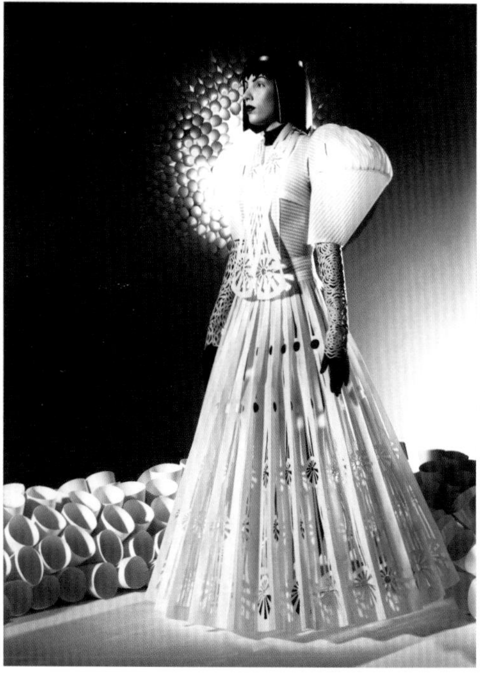

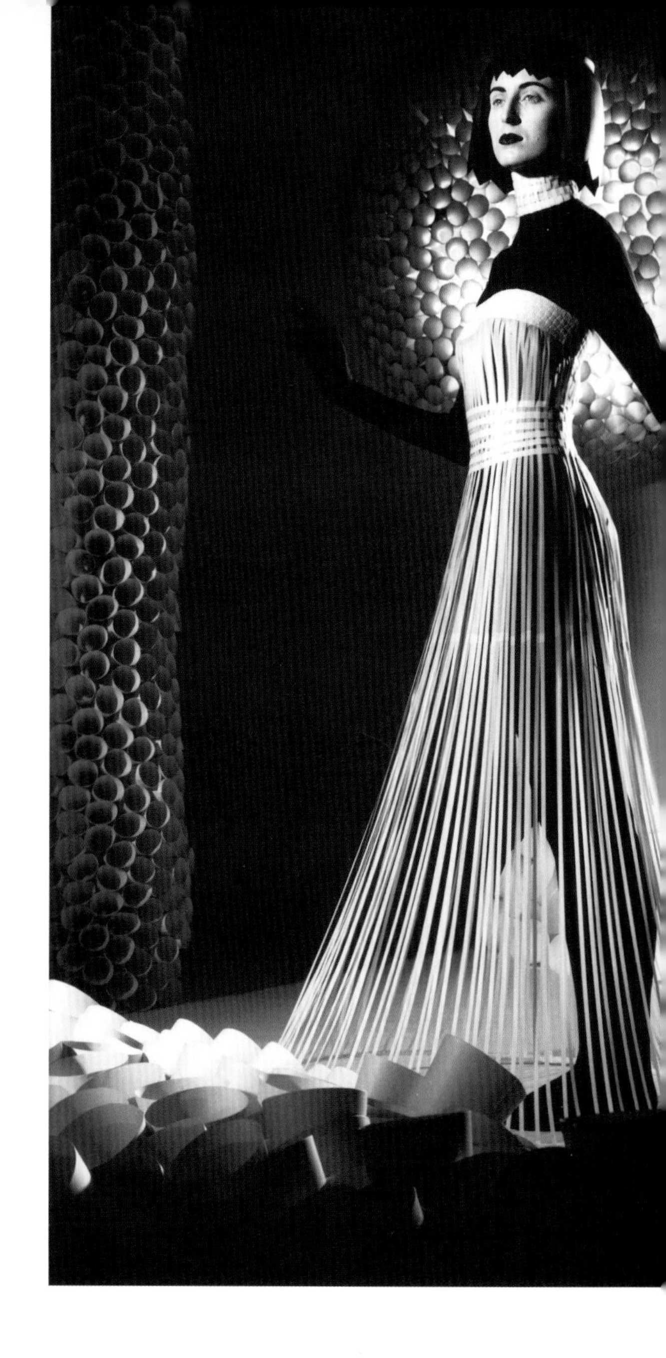

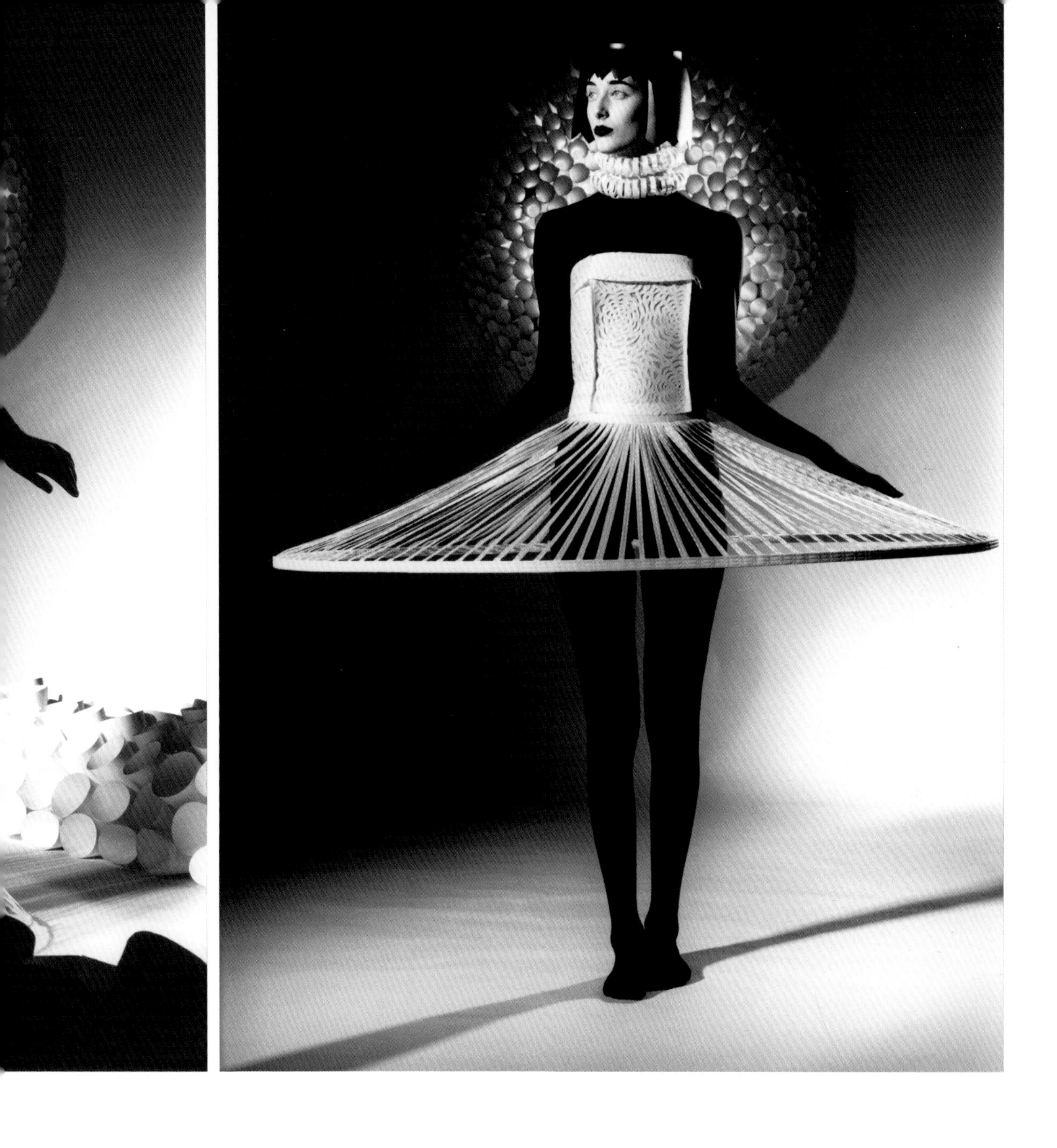

Design Agency Test Shoot Gallery Creative Director/ Designer Ashburn Eng Photographer Soon Tong Hair and Make-up Chris Ruth

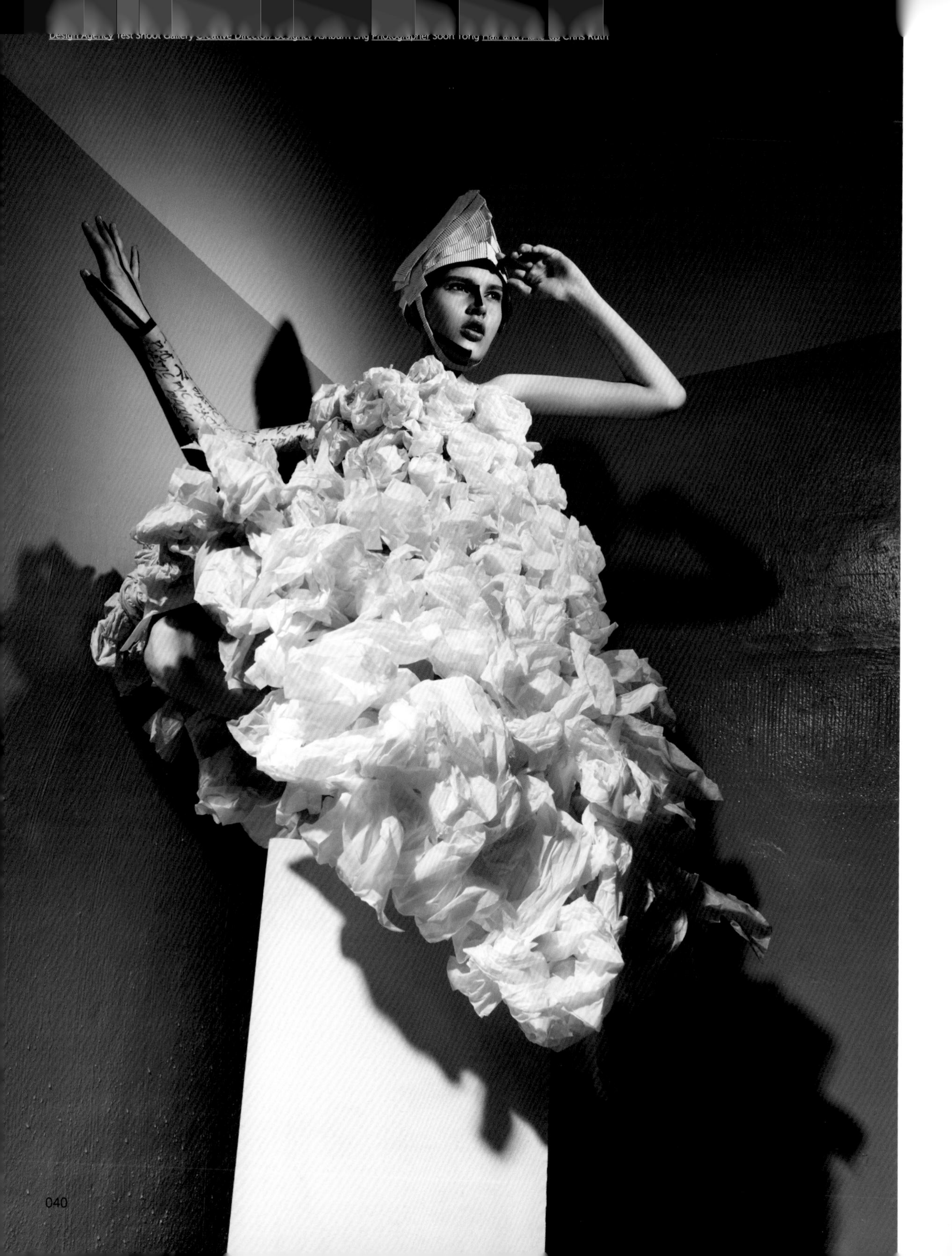

Copywriter Joyceline Tully Assistant Designer Shanna Matthew Model Weronika H (Ave. Management) Work Type Fashion

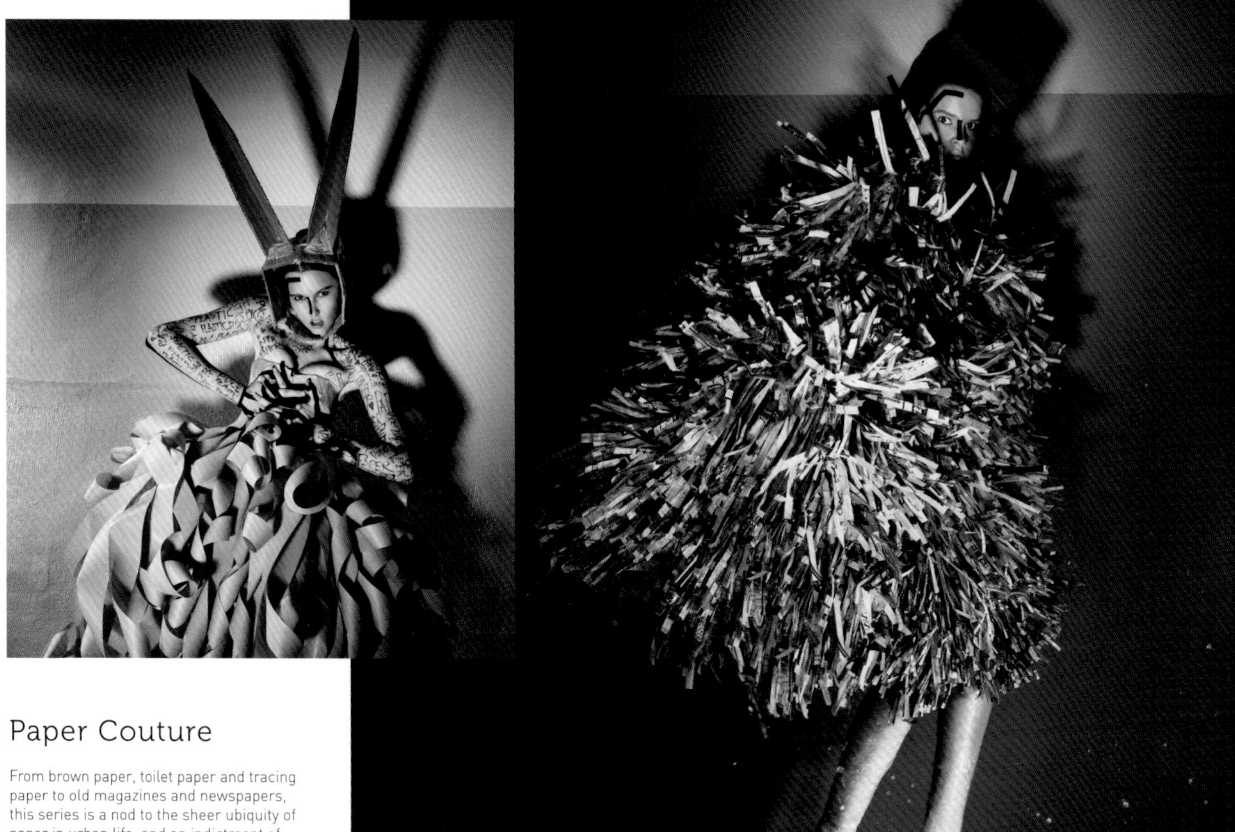

Paper Couture

From brown paper, toilet paper and tracing paper to old magazines and newspapers, this series is a nod to the sheer ubiquity of paper in urban life, and an indictment of its wanton waste. But a little imagination and some assistance—in the form of gum tapes, raffia string, aluminum foil, cling wrap, egg trays, bubble wrap and last but not least, trash bags—go a long way in transforming rubbish into wearable art, a truly modern artefact, or what we like to call, paper couture. With paper, you can scrunch it up to create crinkle effects, as well as twist, braid, weave, pleat and fold to achieve astonishing and remarkable shapes, details and texture. Ashburn Eng and his design assistant spent much time on the outfits. Each of the outfits were painstakingly put together through multiple fittings of pieces of recycled paper, with the level of detail required by fashion's best.

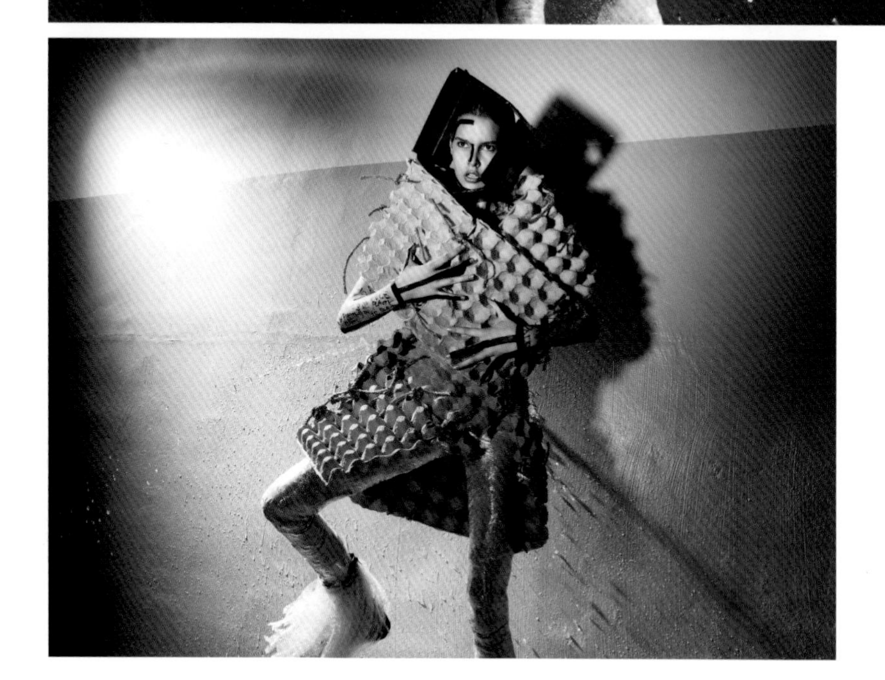

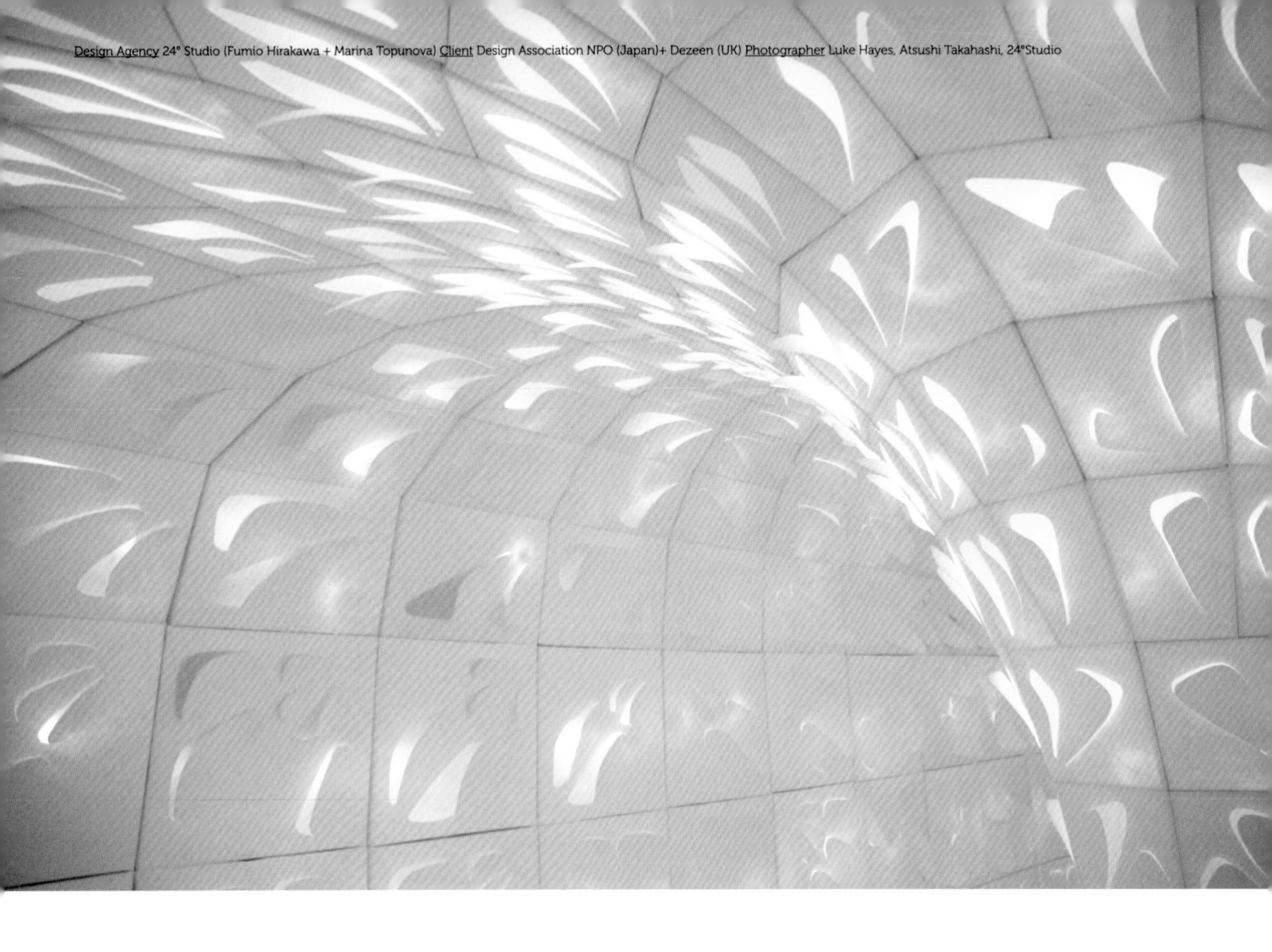

Design Agency 24° Studio (Fumio Hirakawa + Marina Topunova) Client Design Association NPO (Japan)+ Dezeen (UK) Photographer Luke Hayes, Atsushi Takahashi, 24°Studio

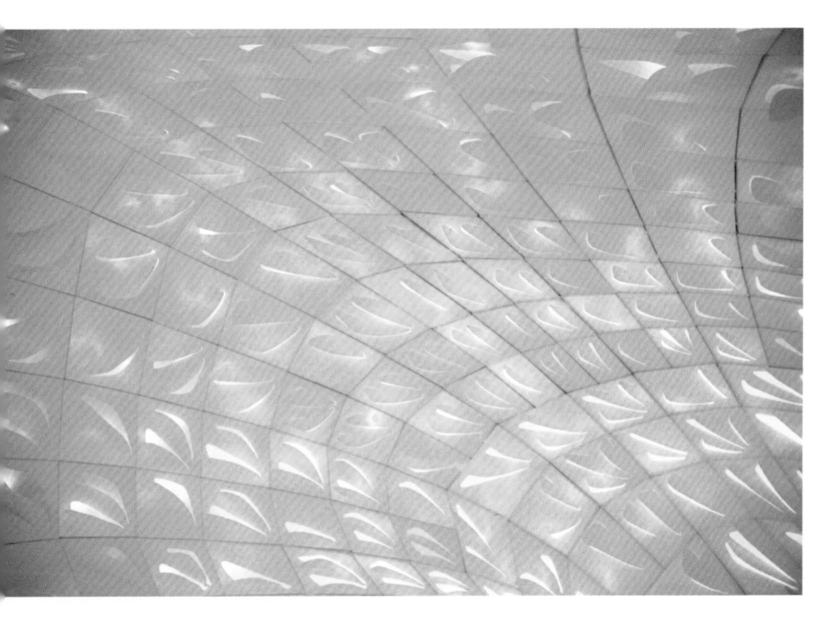

Hope Tree

The symbol of a tree was chosen as a departing point that we universally can identify with. Throughout the ages, trees have been the most primitive form of shelter, abundance, and companionship. With human innovation and intervention, trees have advanced our lives, from a simple paper sheet to a complex house. Every fruit, flower and leaf from a tree symbolizes change and hope for tomorrow. But, even a mighty tree can be frail - if we don't take the proper care, we can cause species to become endangered. Hope Tree installation invites viewers to experience their surrounding environment anew through a single tree and the space that unfolds around its grace.

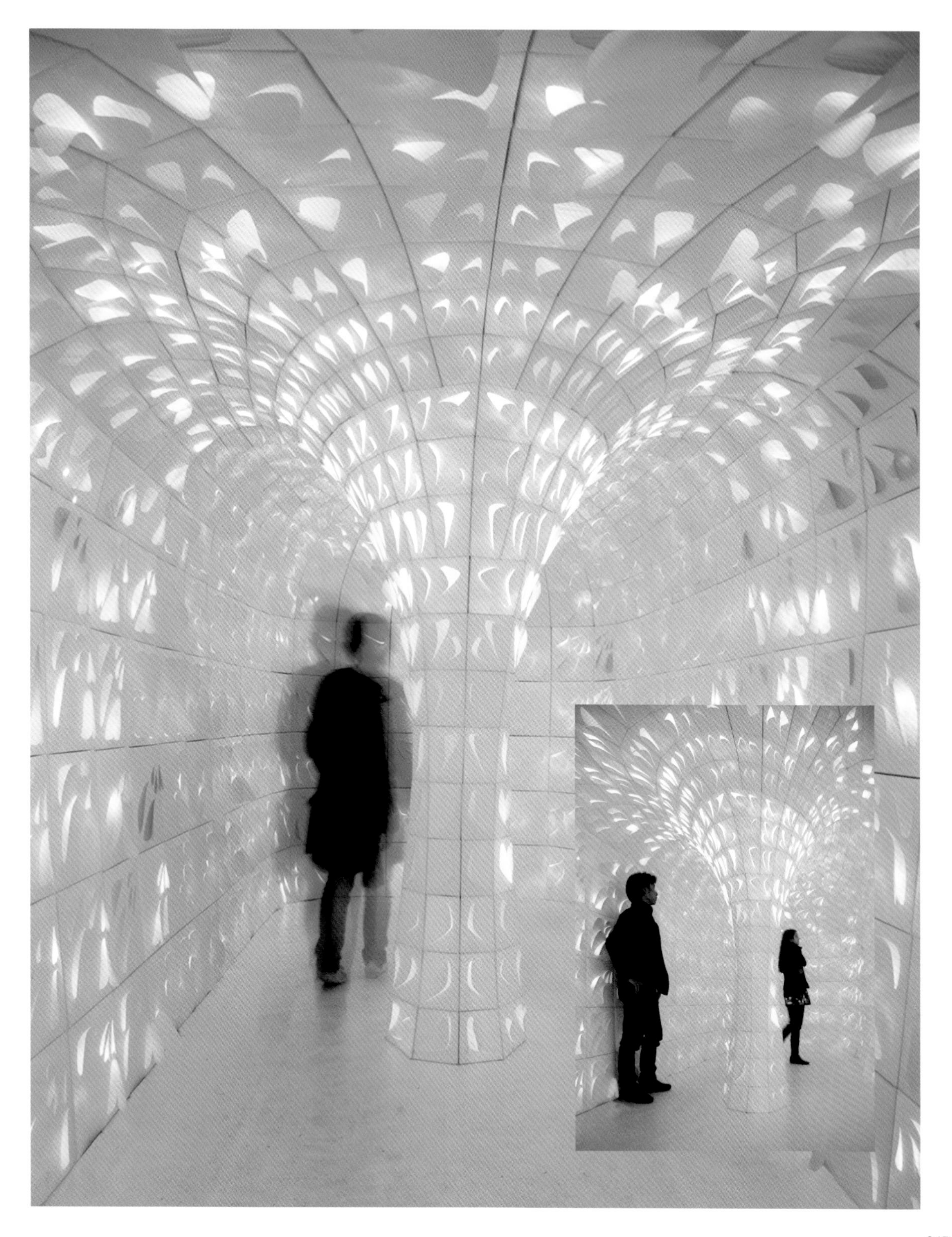

Artist Jolynn Krystosek Photographer Cary Whittier

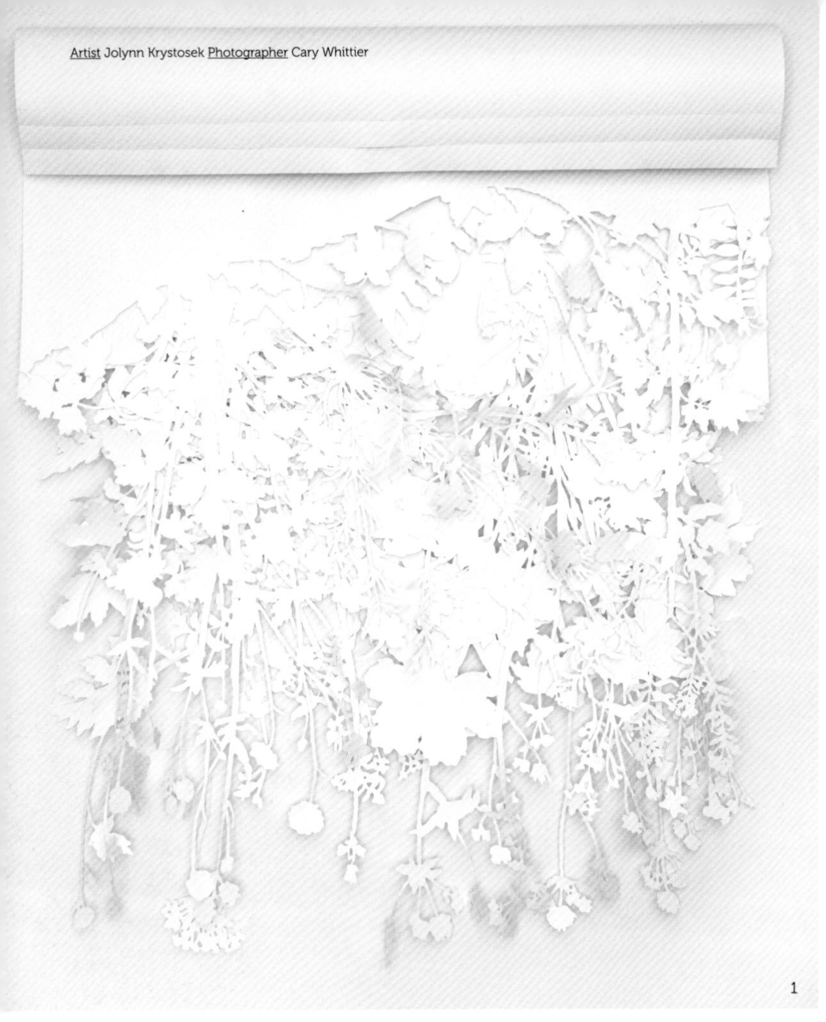

1

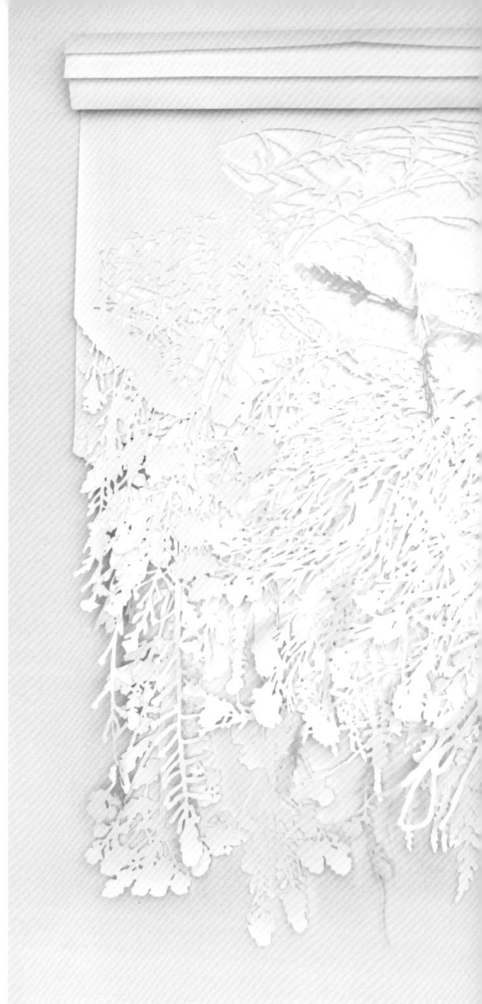

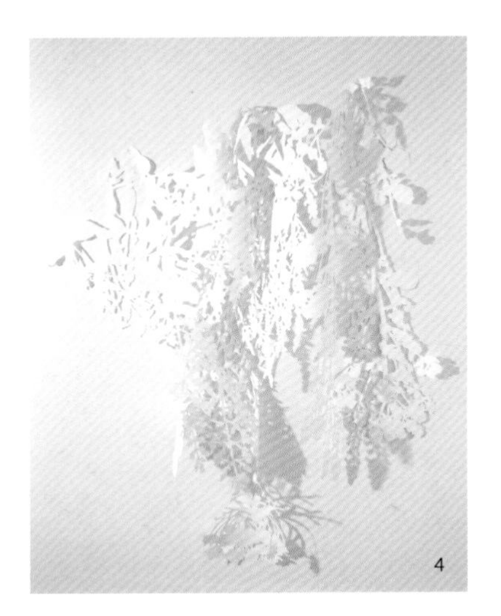

4

Hemlock and lace

1 / Wildflower2
2 / Tumbleweed
3 / Thistle and Poppies
4 / Hemlock and lace
5 / Rockrose
6 / Trumpet
7 / Meadowsweet

Jolynn Krystosek's large scale floral paper cut-outs blend harshness with malleable beauty, pushing the material to its limits of sustainability. The paper cut-out's overgrown and entangled density is achieved through a process of layering intricate botanical silhouettes. Using a hand cut process, the artist creates images of great opulence that present the subject at its most glorious and lush - yet through the rich expansive design, a fragility can be glimpsed that suggests impending demise.

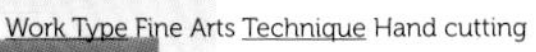

2

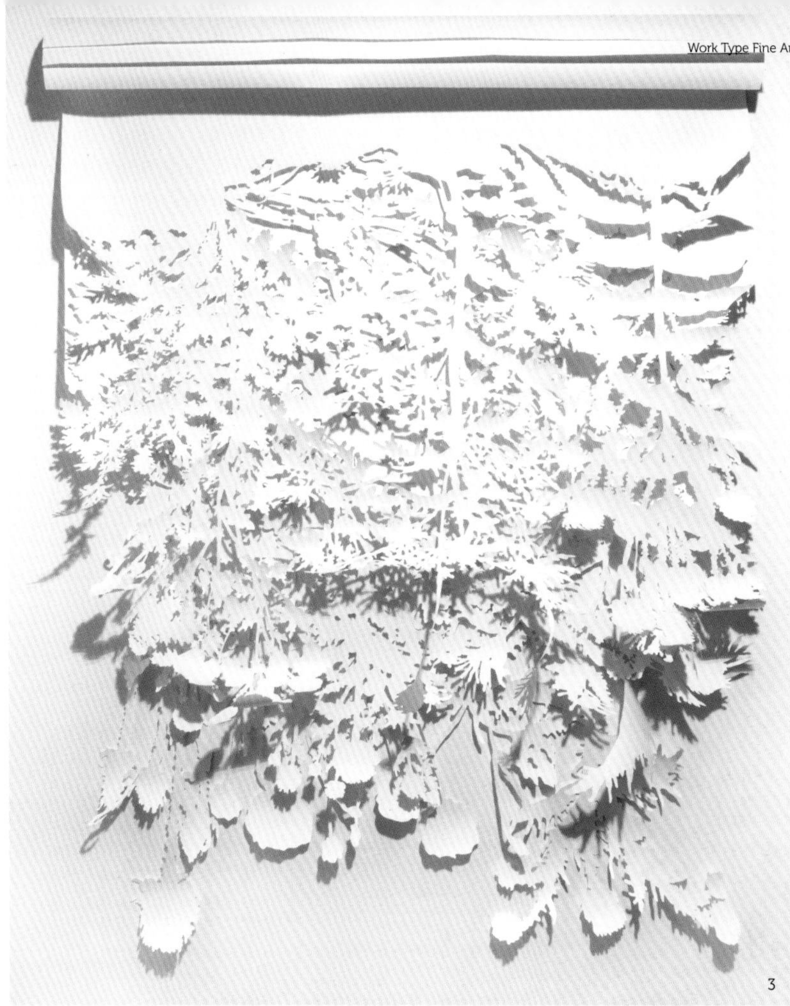

3

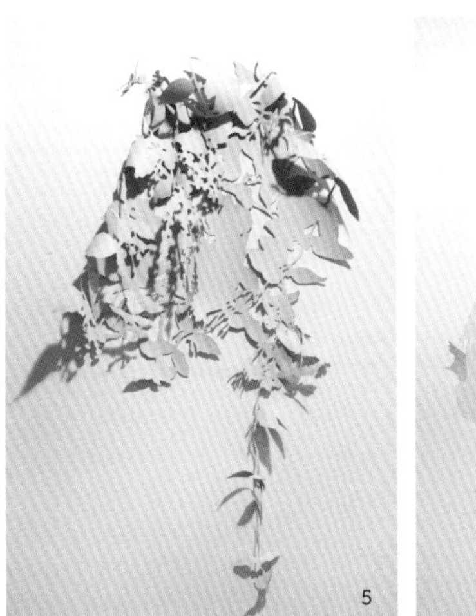

5

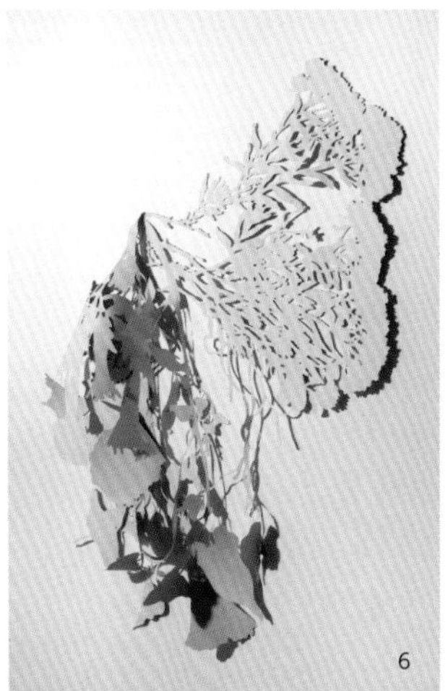

6

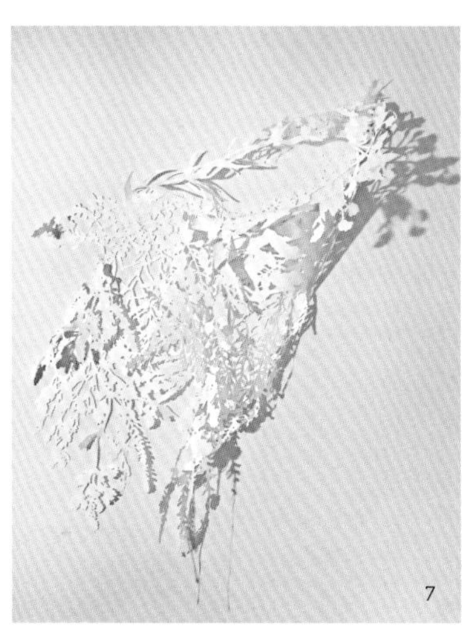

7

Artist Lee Huey Ming Photographer Ivan Liang

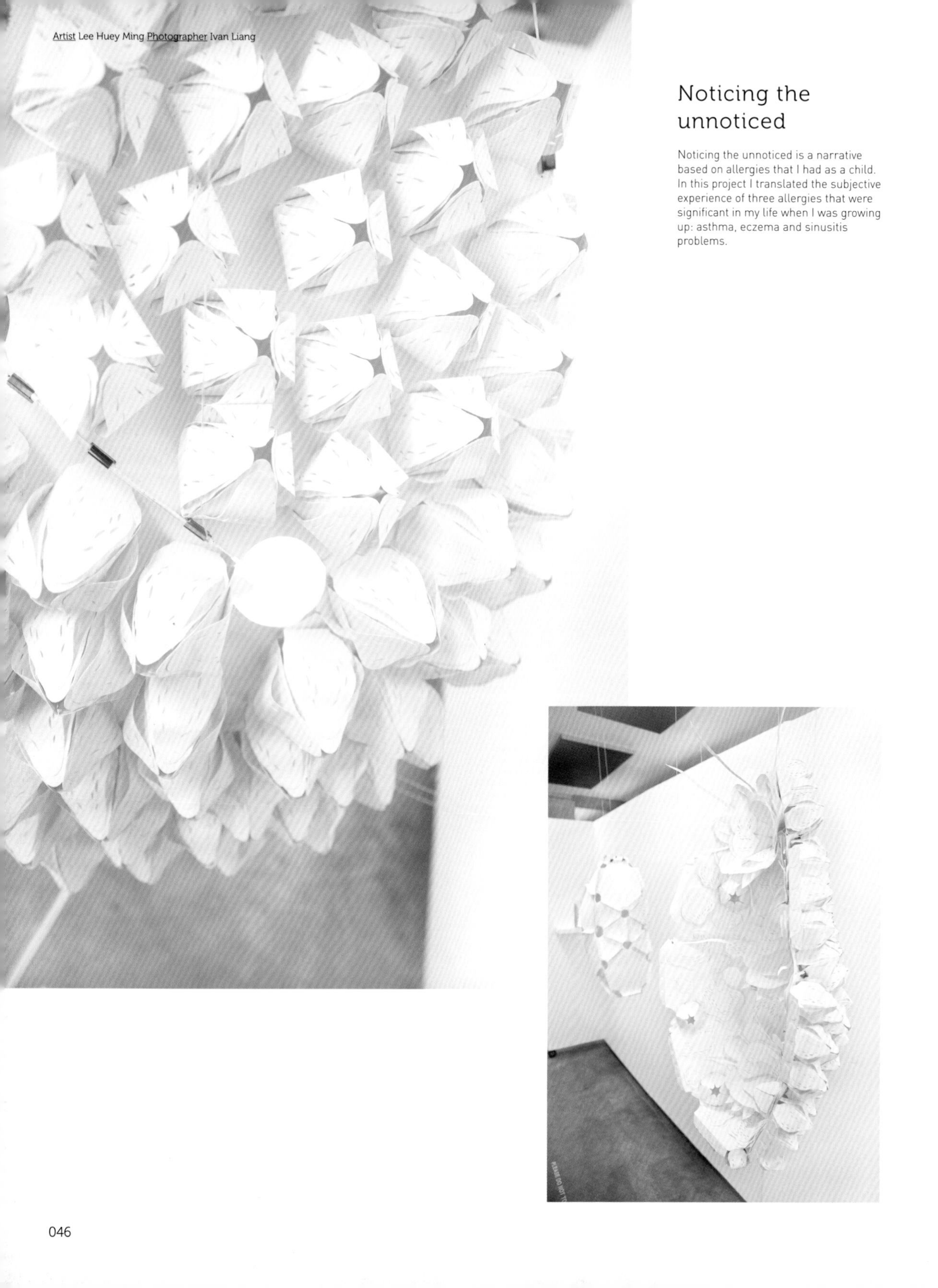

Noticing the unnoticed

Noticing the unnoticed is a narrative based on allergies that I had as a child. In this project I translated the subjective experience of three allergies that were significant in my life when I was growing up: asthma, eczema and sinusitis problems.

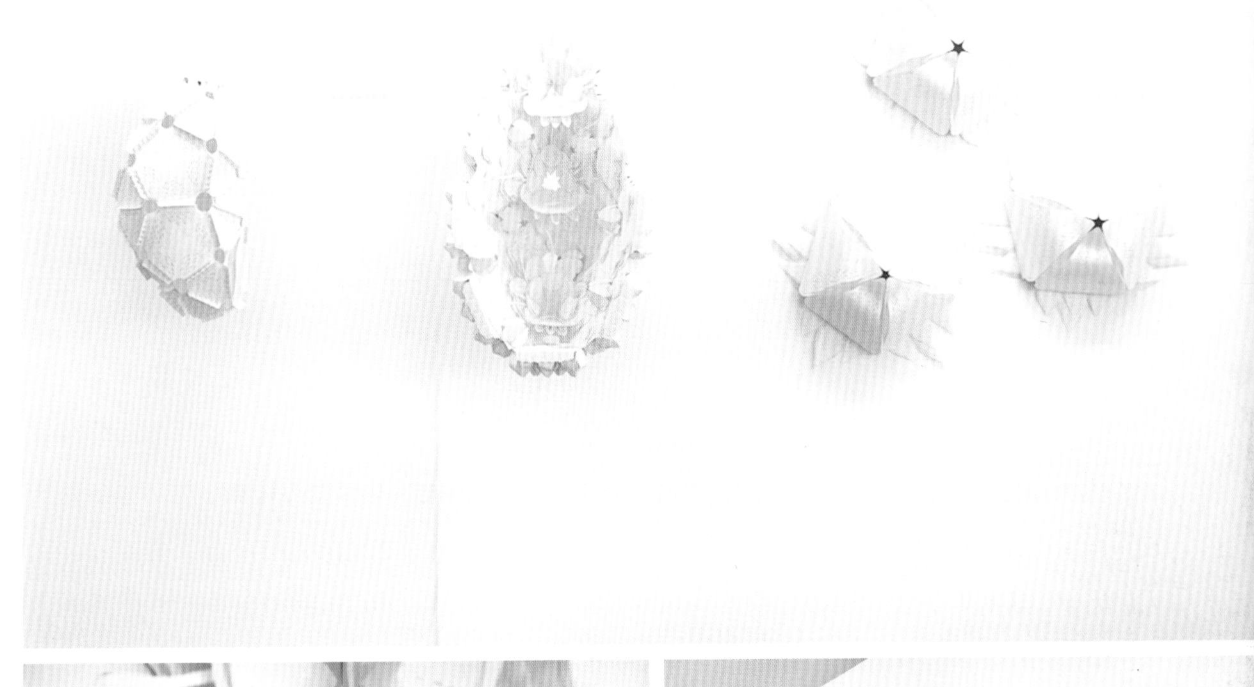

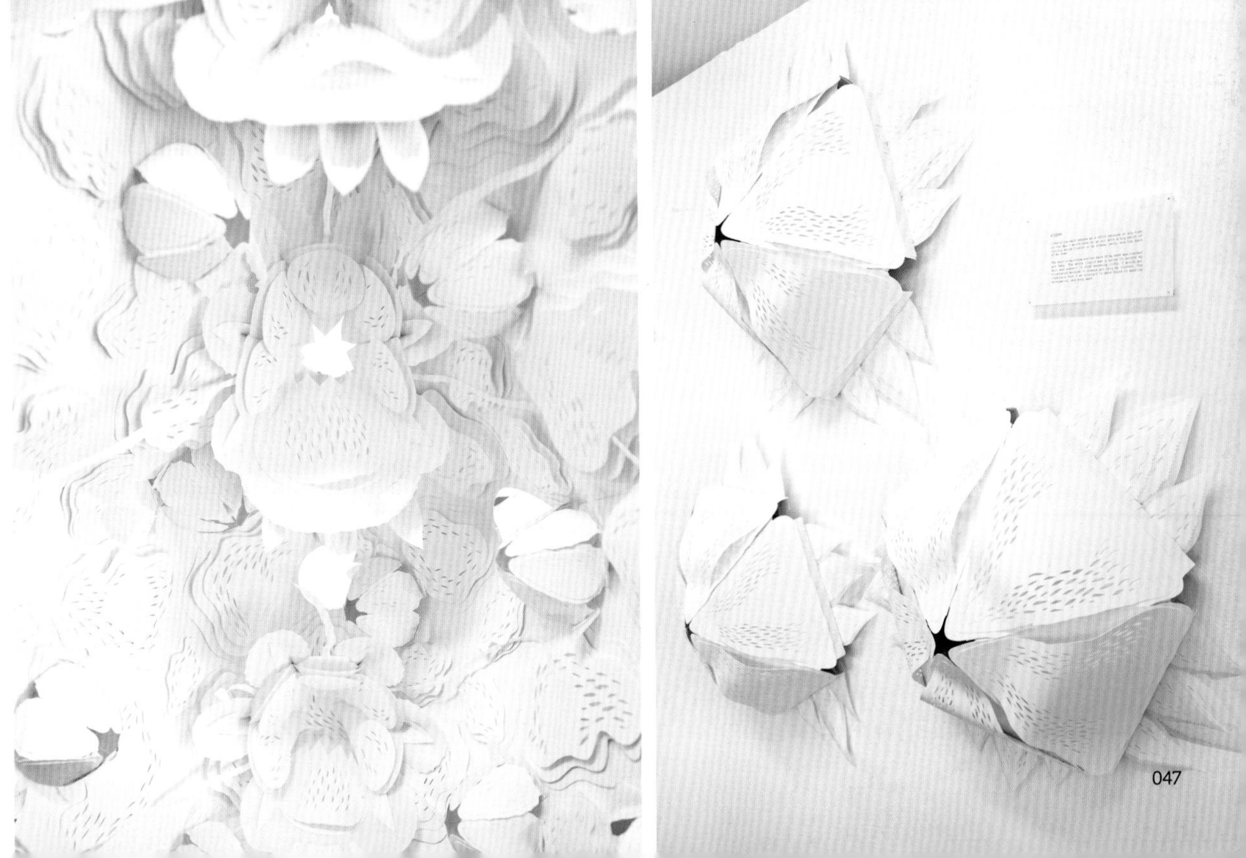

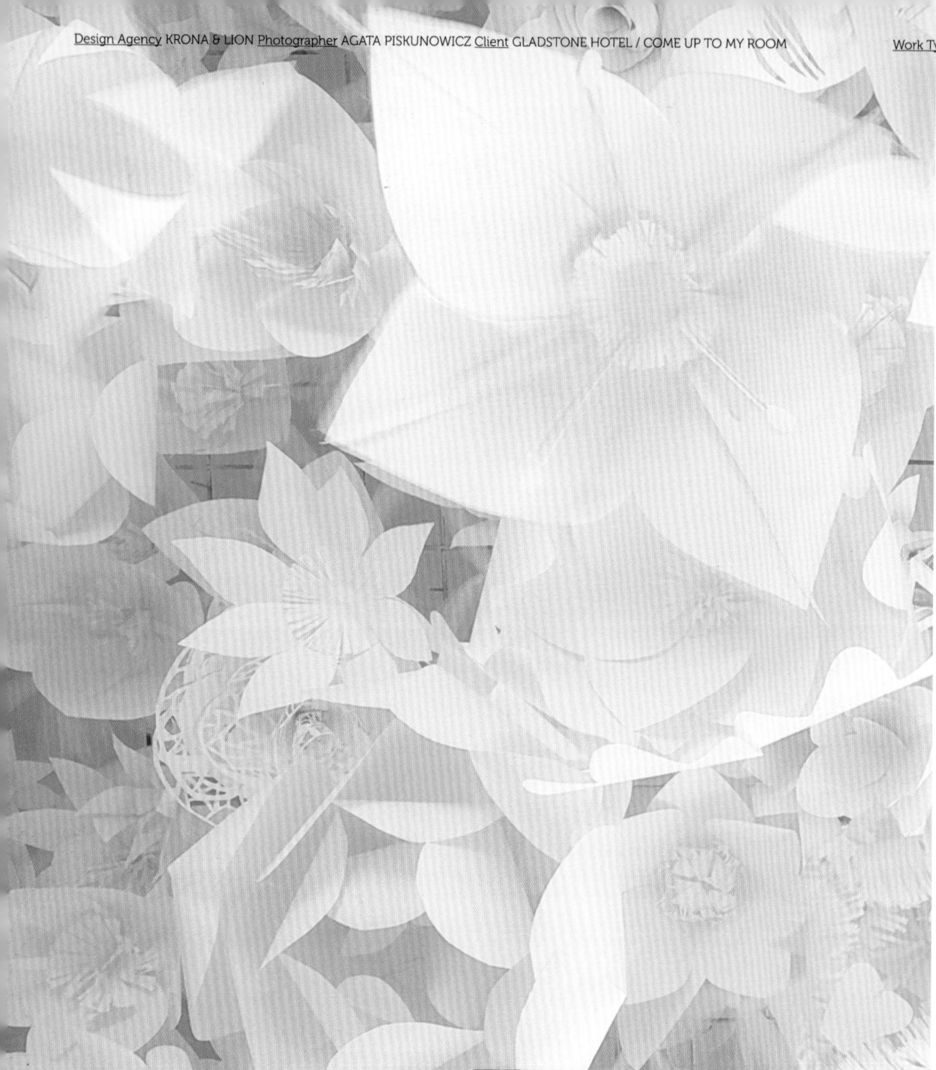

ROOM 211

Room 211 by KRONA & LION celebrates paper, using the seemingly ordinary material to transform an empty hotel room into an awe-inspiring place of discovery. This project began by challenging the conventional strategies involved in hotel room design, resulting in a subversion of traditional decor. The installation expands the definition of conventional light fixtures, taking advantage of the translucency of the paper to soften light and cast shadows. During waking hours, the installation helps to create ephemeral wallpaper. The white colour palette was used to magnify the quality of light in the room, create instant visual impact, and retain the visual association to paper. The typical hotel guest spends a large part of their stay in bed. To address this fact, the physical "wallpaper," normally hung on walls, was hung from the ceiling so that the ideal vantage point became the bed. Great care was also taken to finely detail and craft an extensive variety of flowers. This allowed the slow discovery of new objects and spatial moments that were not visible upon first glance.

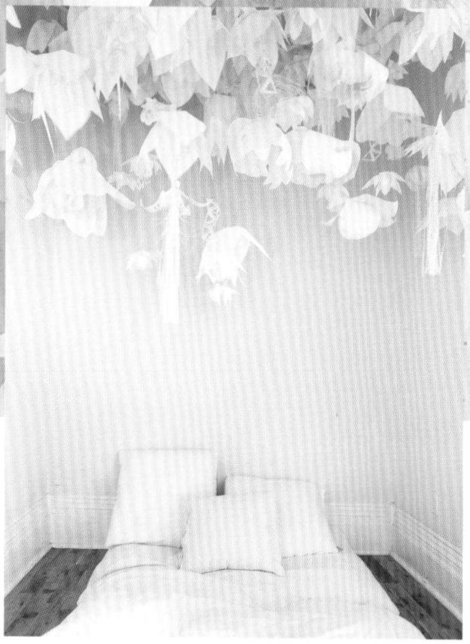

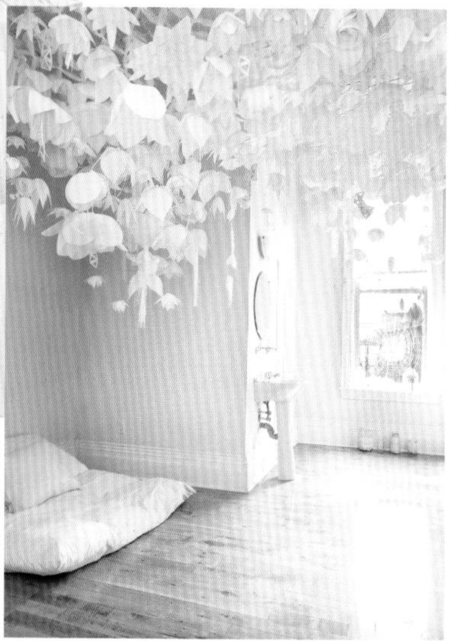

Cloud Softlight

Cloud Softlight creates a luminous, undulating overhead canopy, tailored to the individual space they are shaping. Taking inspiration from the wondrous mobile constructions of Alexander Calder, a mobile of luminous clouds is suspended, moving with a gentle buoyancy in the air currents overhead. The mobile structure allows for a broad canopy of cloud forms, hung from a single point, to provide light and a sense of intimate enclosure. The hollow cloud forms are internally lit by LED light, making the sculptural three dimensional forms mysteriously radiant when viewed from any direction. Alternately, individual pendants in four different sizes can be suspended. You decide the topography of your own cloudscape, positioning how it rises and falls through and over a space. Discover the possibilities of an intimate, gentle space beneath the clouds.

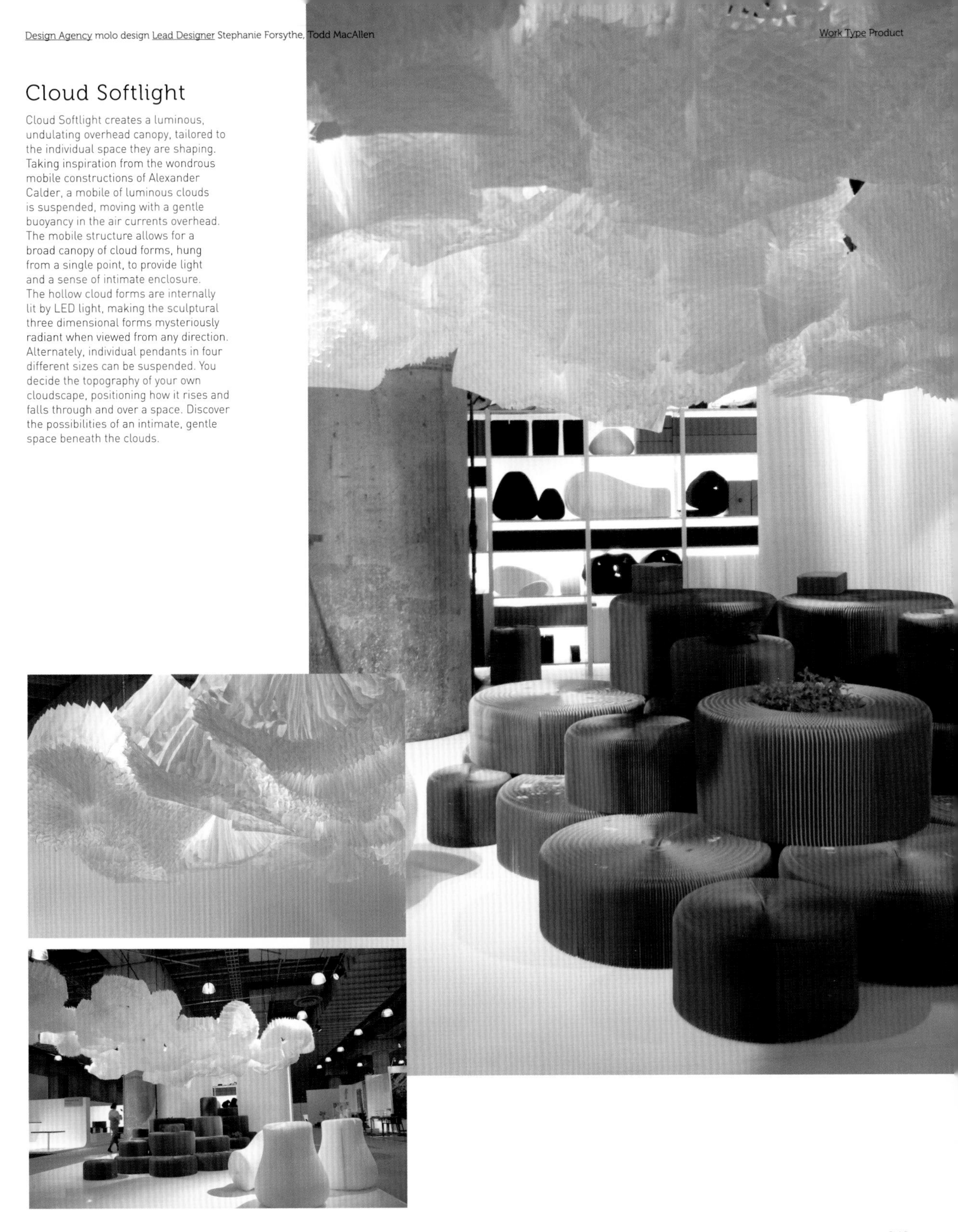

Designer Yuriko Kaneko Photographer Takayasu Hattori

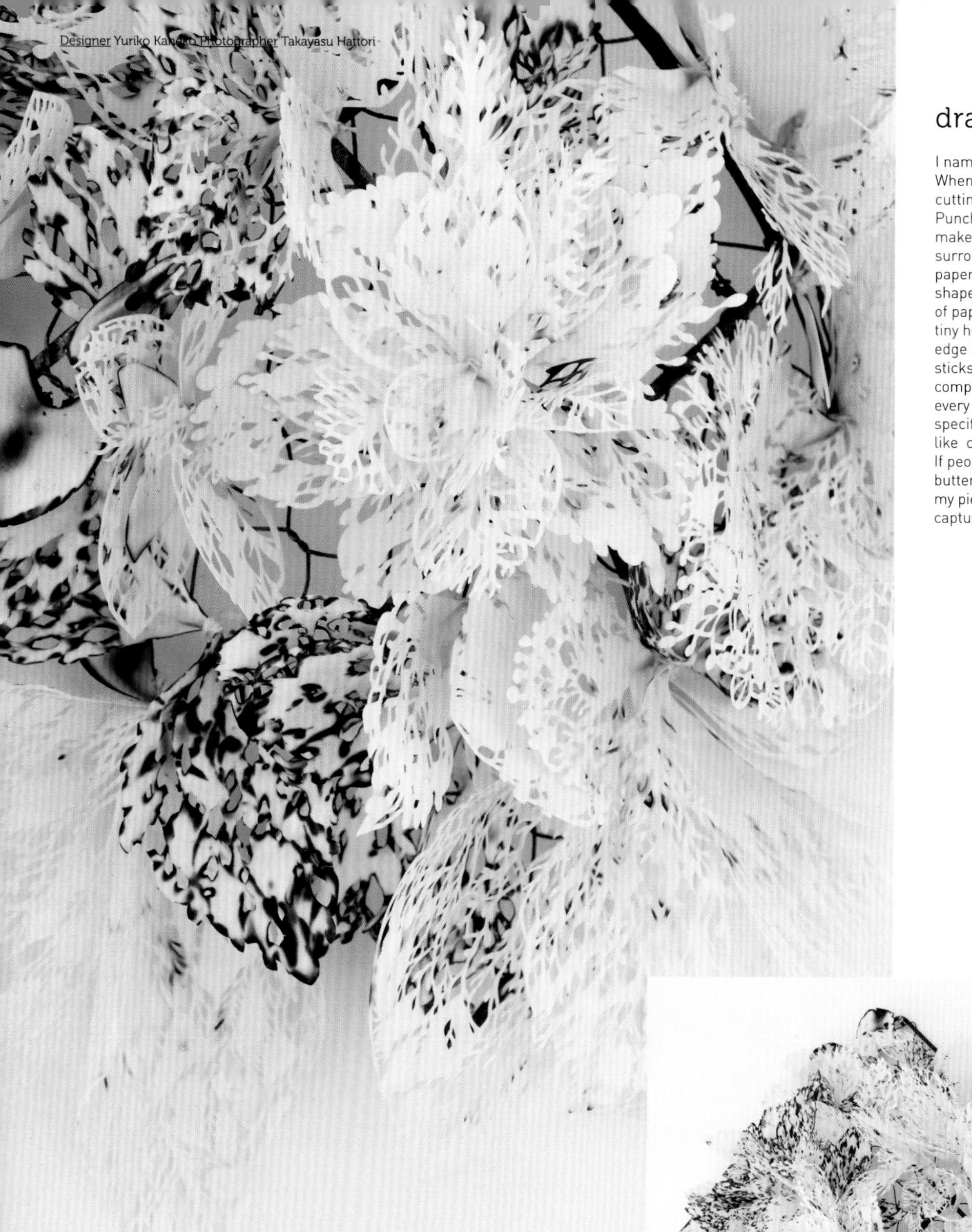

drawing-lace

I name all of my works "drawing-lace." When I touch a piece of paper, I start cutting it, following how it moves. Punching small holes in the paper makes me feel that the air and light surrounding it are swallowed up in the paper. I use a paper cutter to make shapes and holes. To make a piece of paper looked weathered, I make tiny holes, scorch the paper and its edge by flame of candles and incense sticks. It takes almost one month to complete one "drawing-lace." However, every shape I make does not have specific models. I often make things like creatures or plants unconsciously. If people see flower petals, flocking butterflies, mushrooms, or crystals in my pieces, they feel the energy of life I've captured.

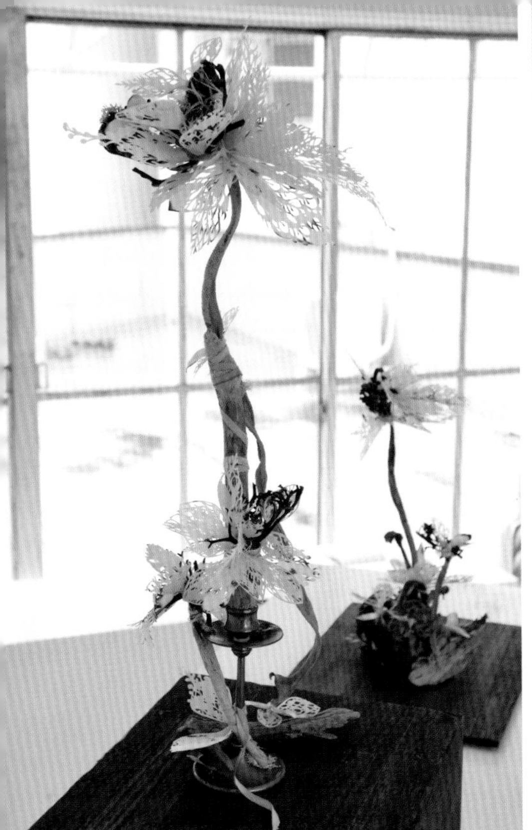

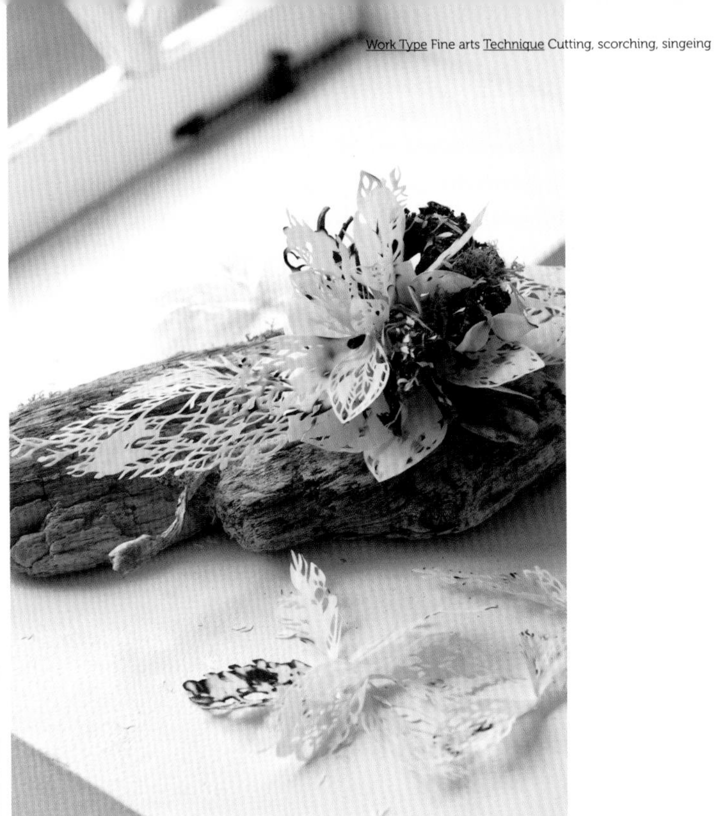

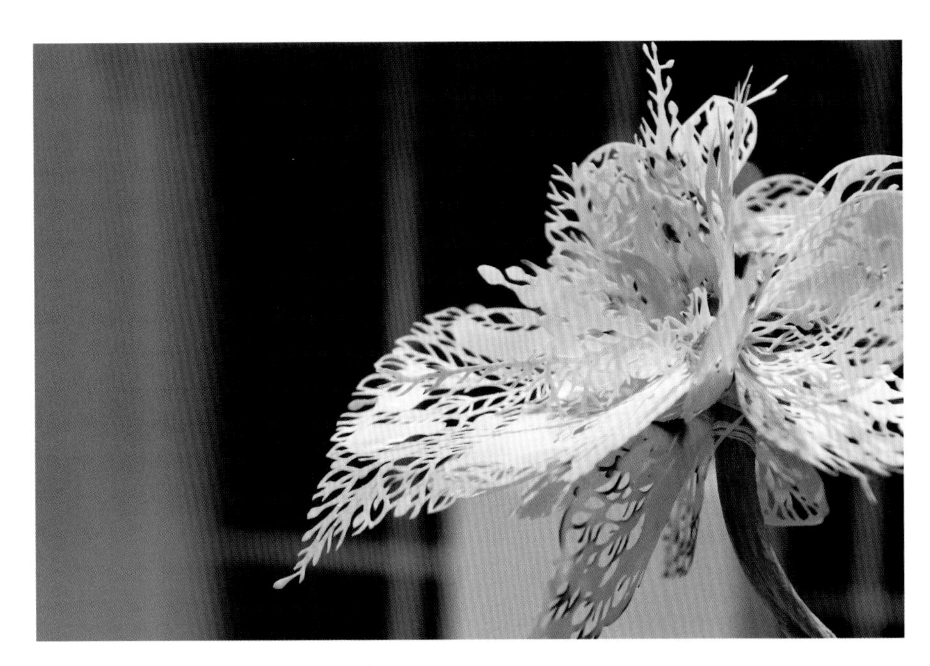

Fashion Statement

Fashion Statement is an artist book to be worn as a dress or displayed as a sculpture. On the dress are hand-cut different statements about fashion, making it a "Word-Robe".

On the dress you can read expressions such as "up my sleeve" and the following quotes:
"We are shaped and fashioned by what we love." Goethe
"Personality begins where comparison ends" karl lagerfeld
"The only way to atone for being occasionally a little over-dressed is by being always absolutely over-educated." Oscar Wilde
"Clothes make the man. Naked people have little or no influence on society." Mark Twain
"What a strange power there is in clothing." Isaac Bashevis Singer
"Change of fashion is the tax levied by the industry of the poor on the vanity of the rich." Nicolas de Chamfort
"A woman's dress should be like a barbed- wire fence: serving its purpose without obstructing the view." Sophia Loren

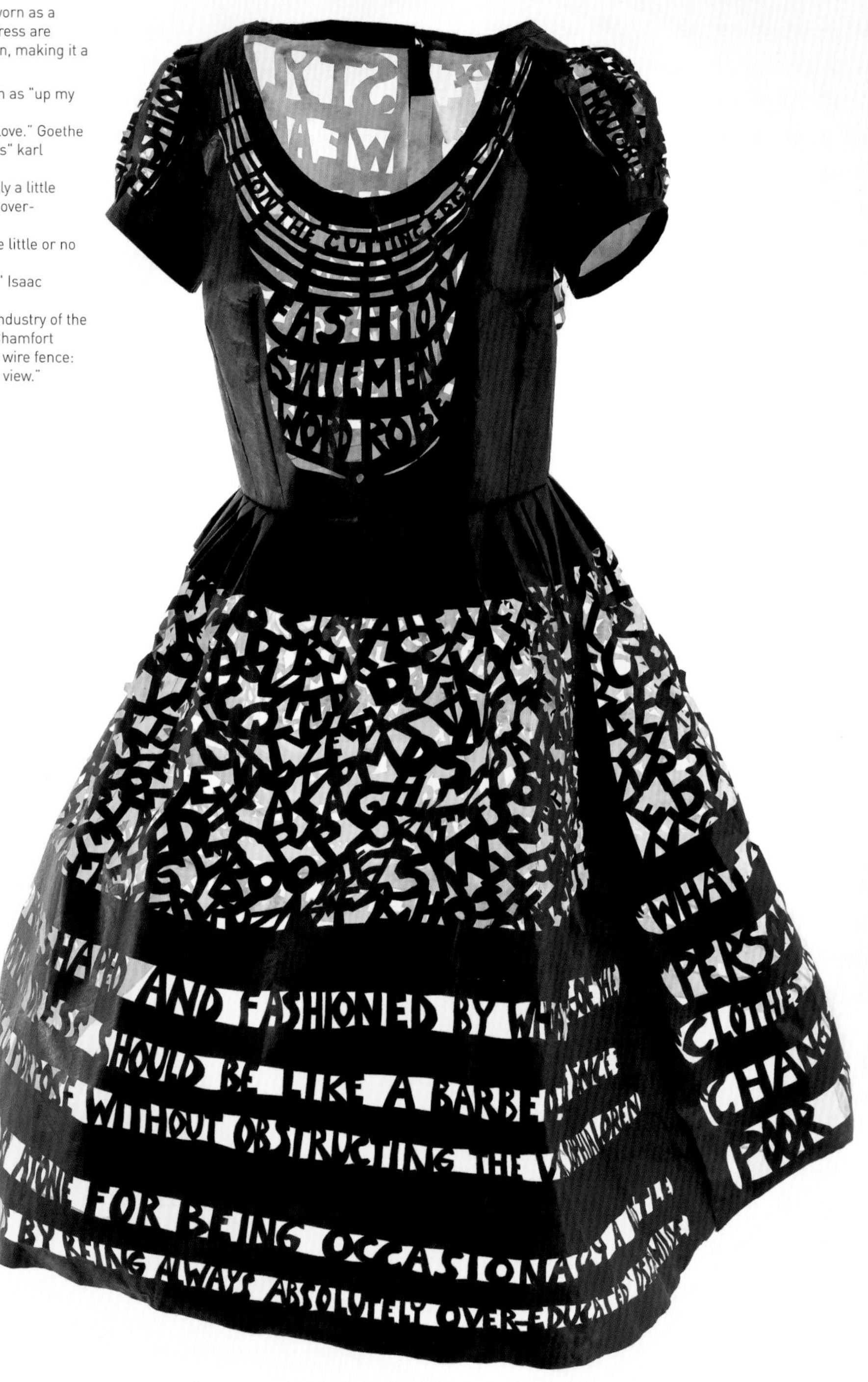

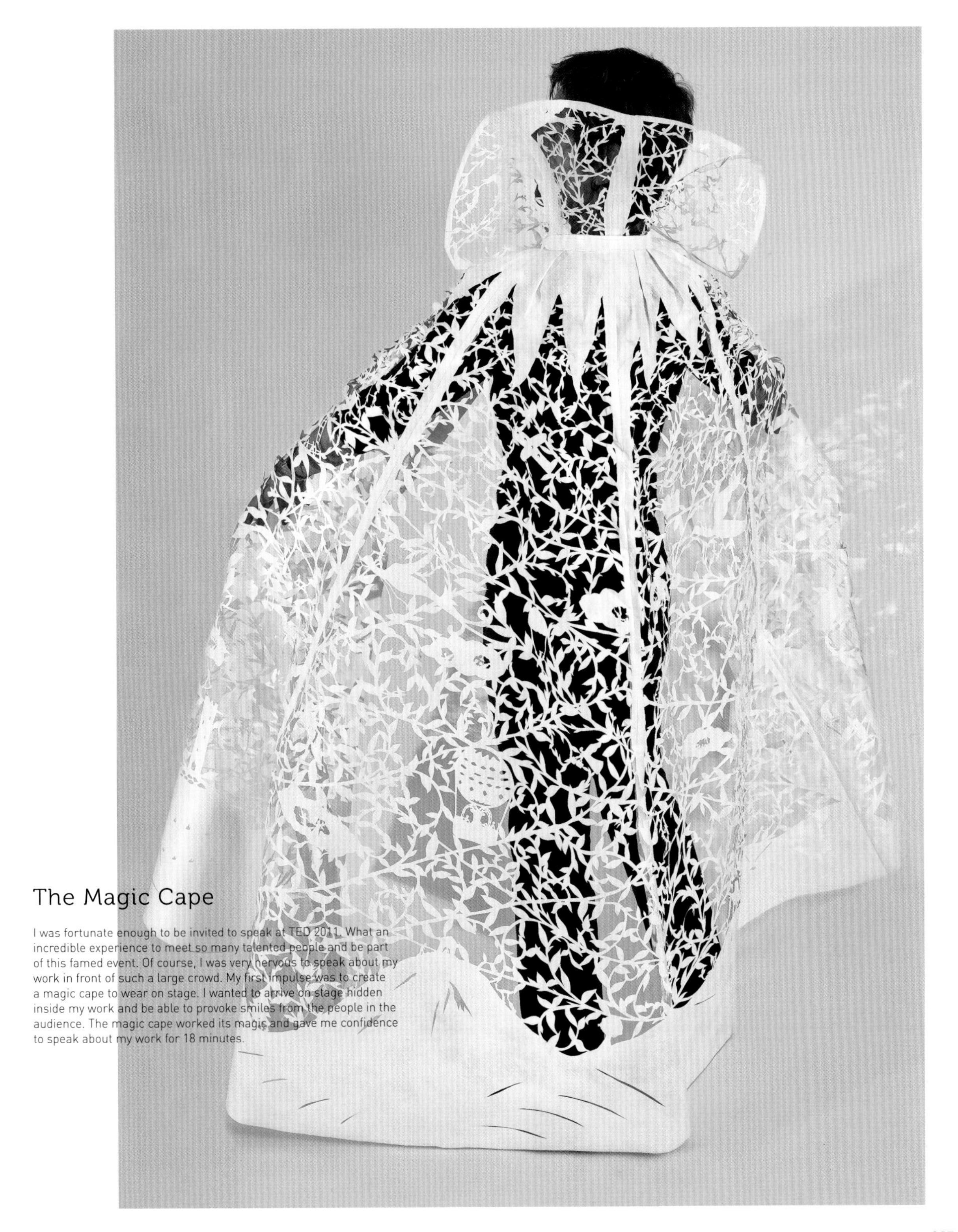

The Magic Cape

I was fortunate enough to be invited to speak at TED 2011. What an incredible experience to meet so many talented people and be part of this famed event. Of course, I was very nervous to speak about my work in front of such a large crowd. My first impulse was to create a magic cape to wear on stage. I wanted to arrive on stage hidden inside my work and be able to provoke smiles from the people in the audience. The magic cape worked its magic and gave me confidence to speak about my work for 18 minutes.

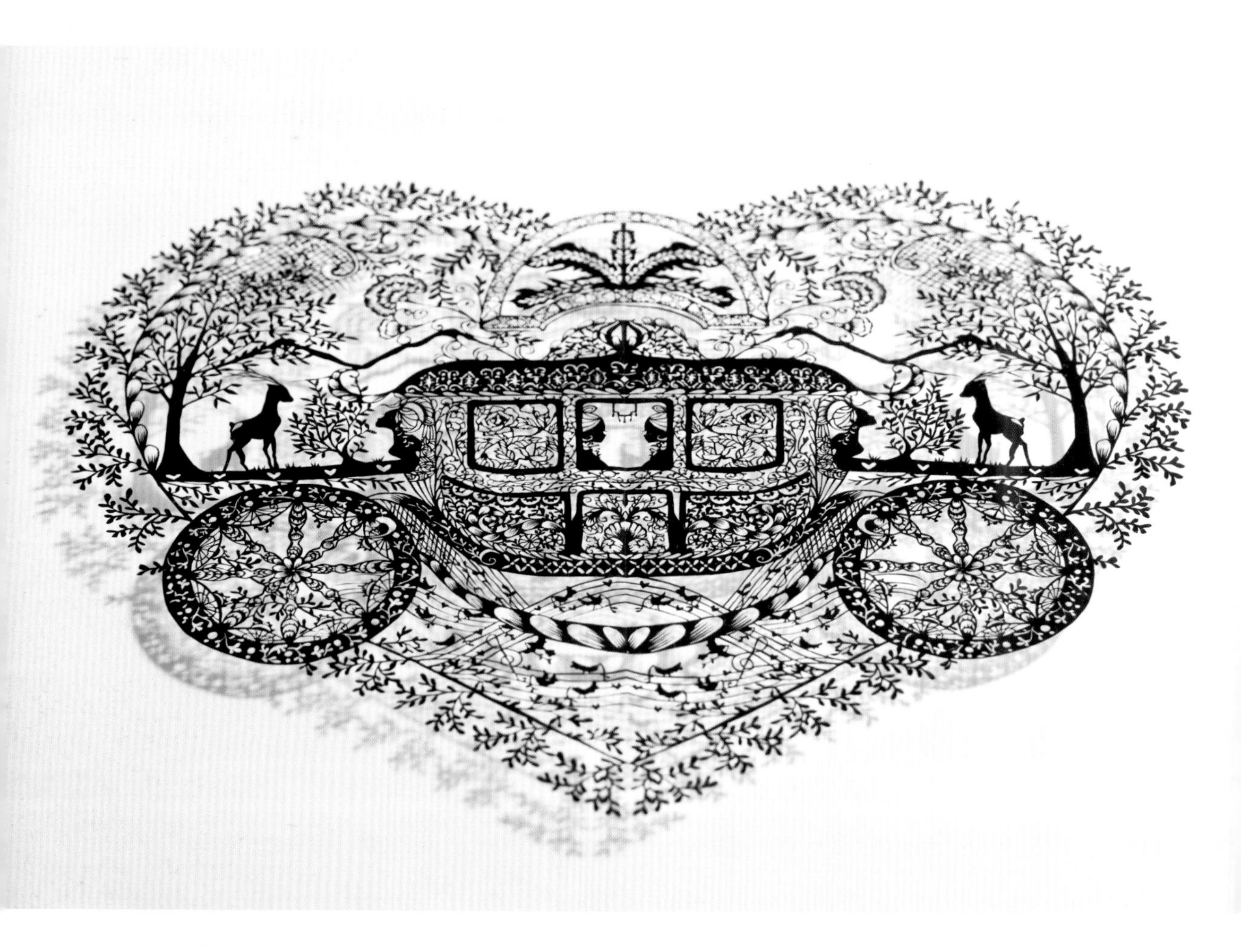

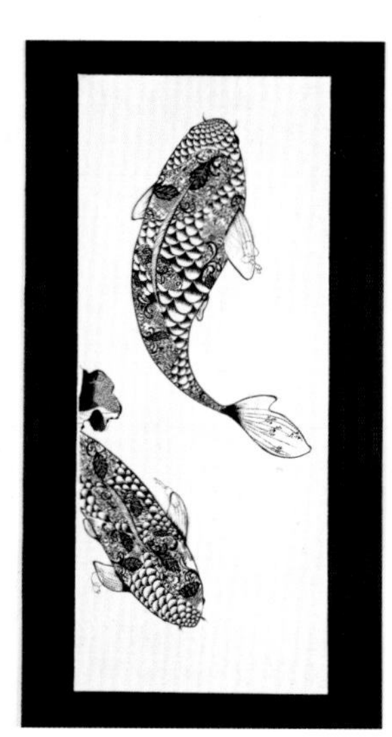

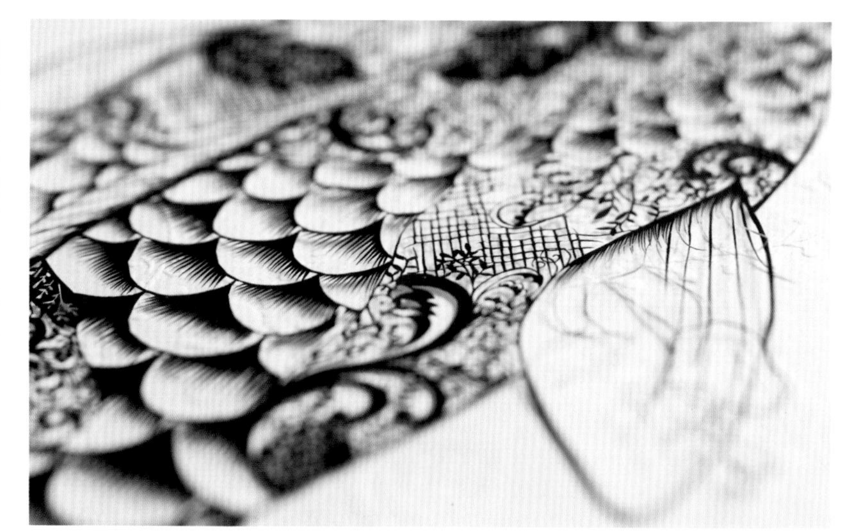

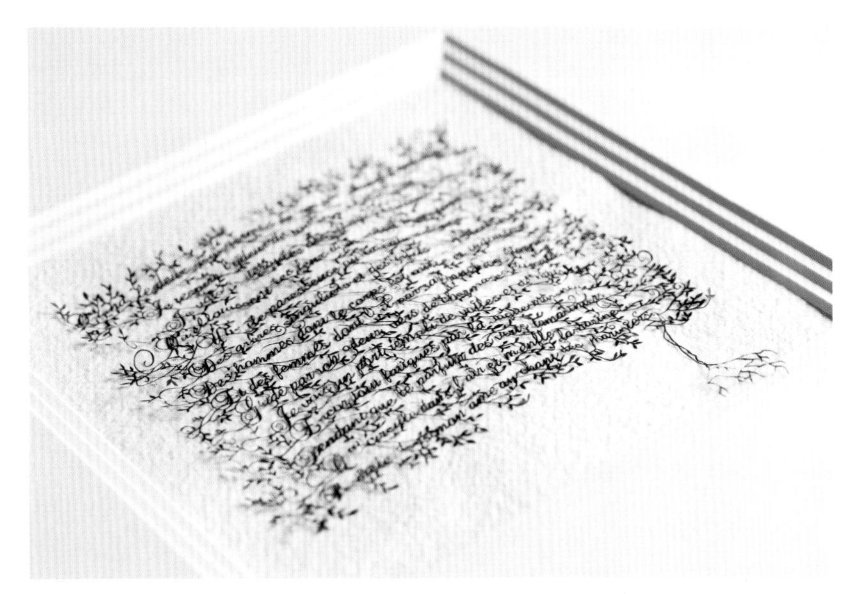

Lacy-paper-cuttings

The pieces are super fine lacy-paper-cuttings done by a simple pair of scissors. My passion is to create intricate works that go beyond the most time-consuming lace needlework. I don't follow tradition but instead try to create a mixture of traditional and modern styles in order to produce my own world through this very precise paper cutting technique.

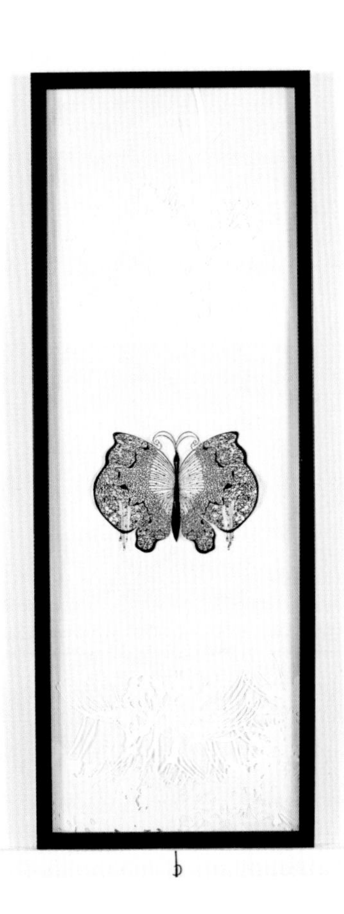

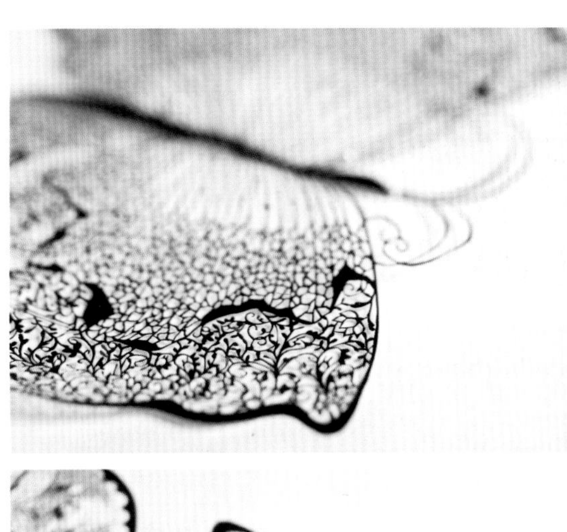

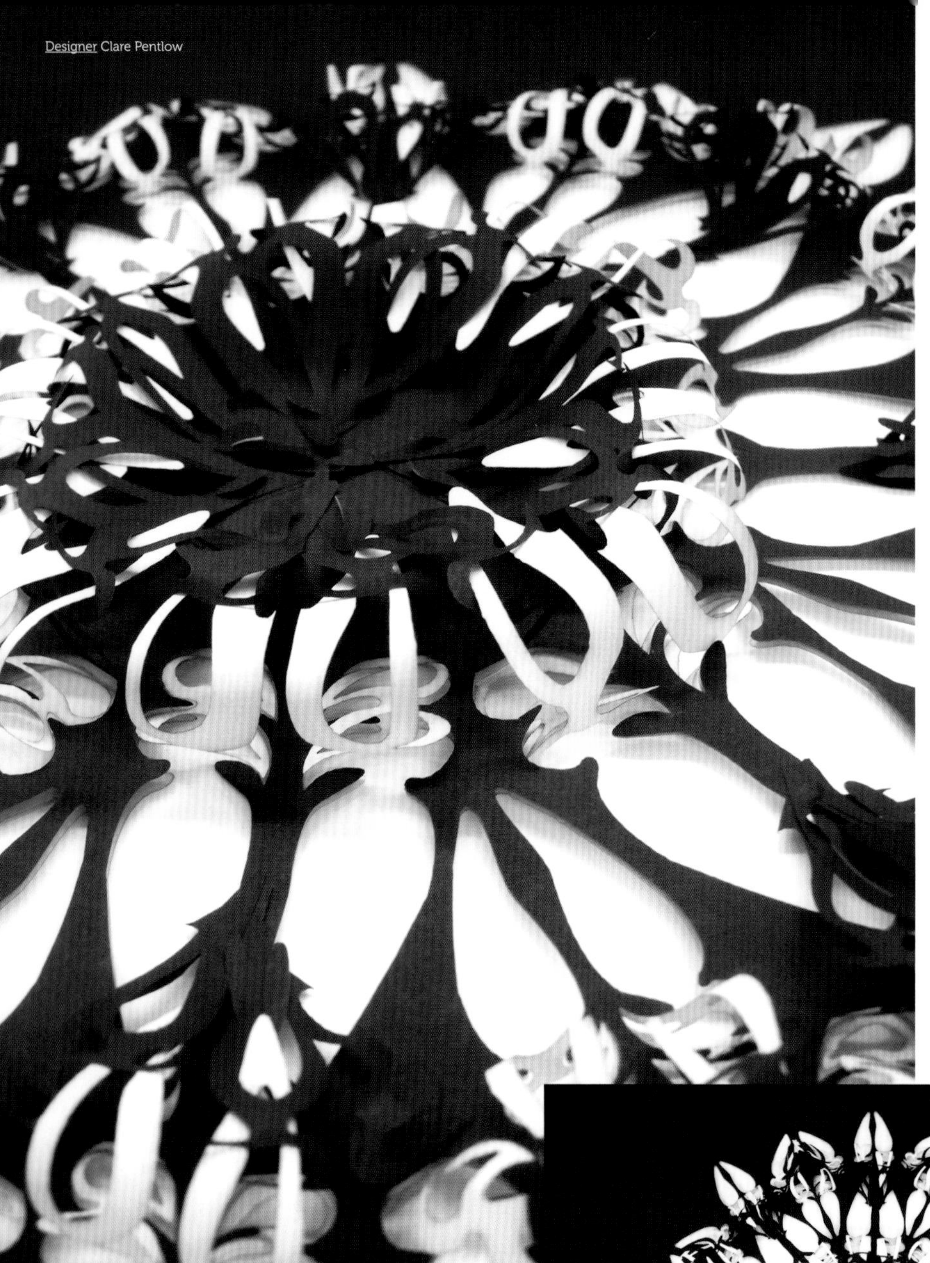

Water Inspiration

My inspiration for the pieces came from the fluid movement of water, the uniformity yet randomness of waves. The paper represents the strength and power of the waves, in contrast to the fragility and smoothness of the water. When light and shadow play on the paper sculptural pieces, they highlight and accent different parts and cast unusual and playful shadows that represent the sporadic nature of the waves. I decided to use neutral colours in my work so as to give the most importance to the form; however, the subtle differences in paper types and surface shapes are visible and create intrigue.

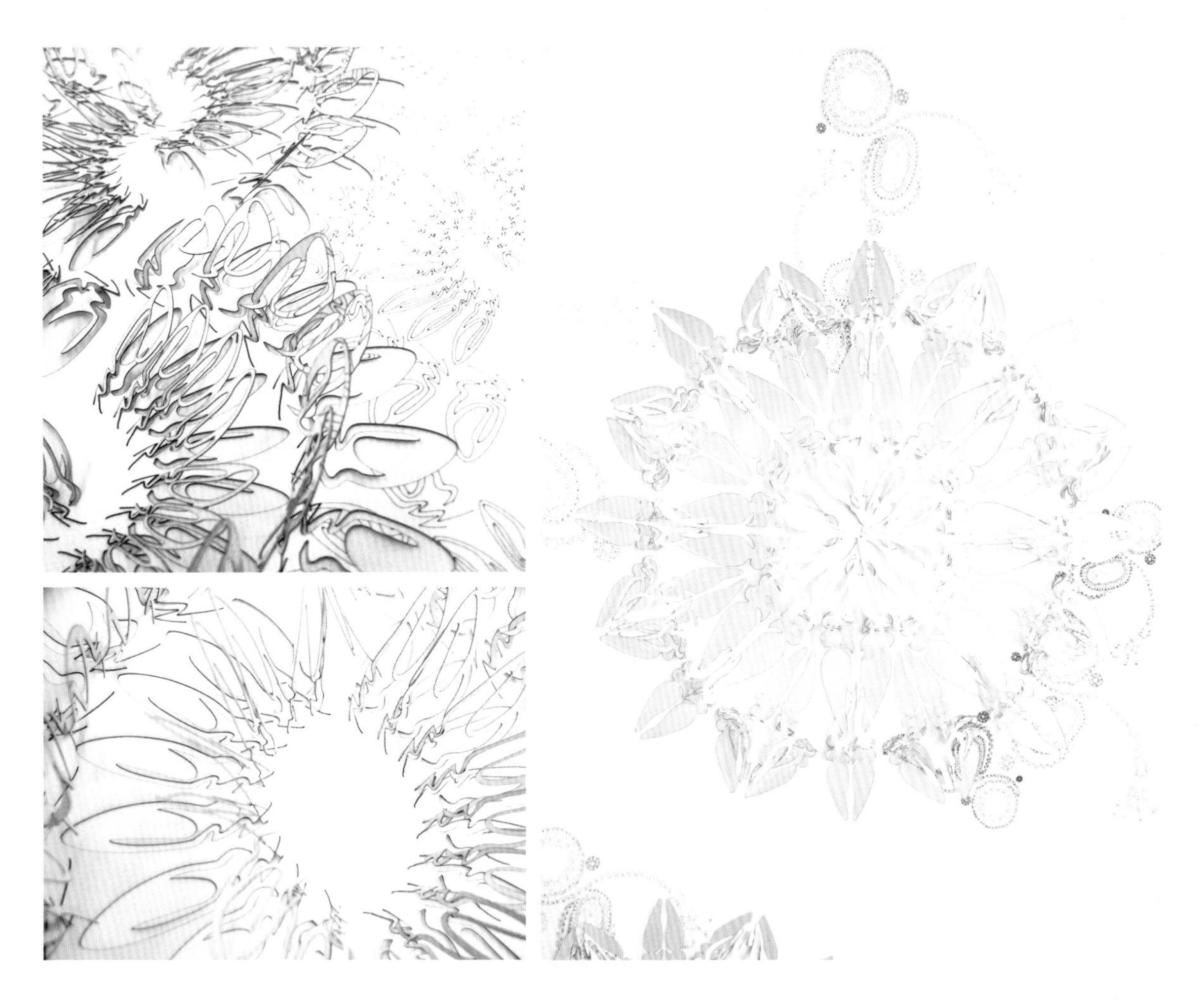

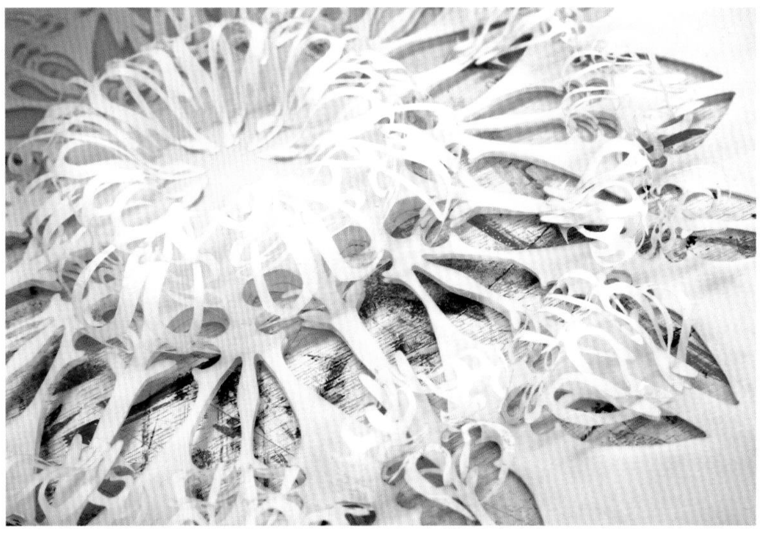

Artist Claire Brewster Photographer Paul Minyo

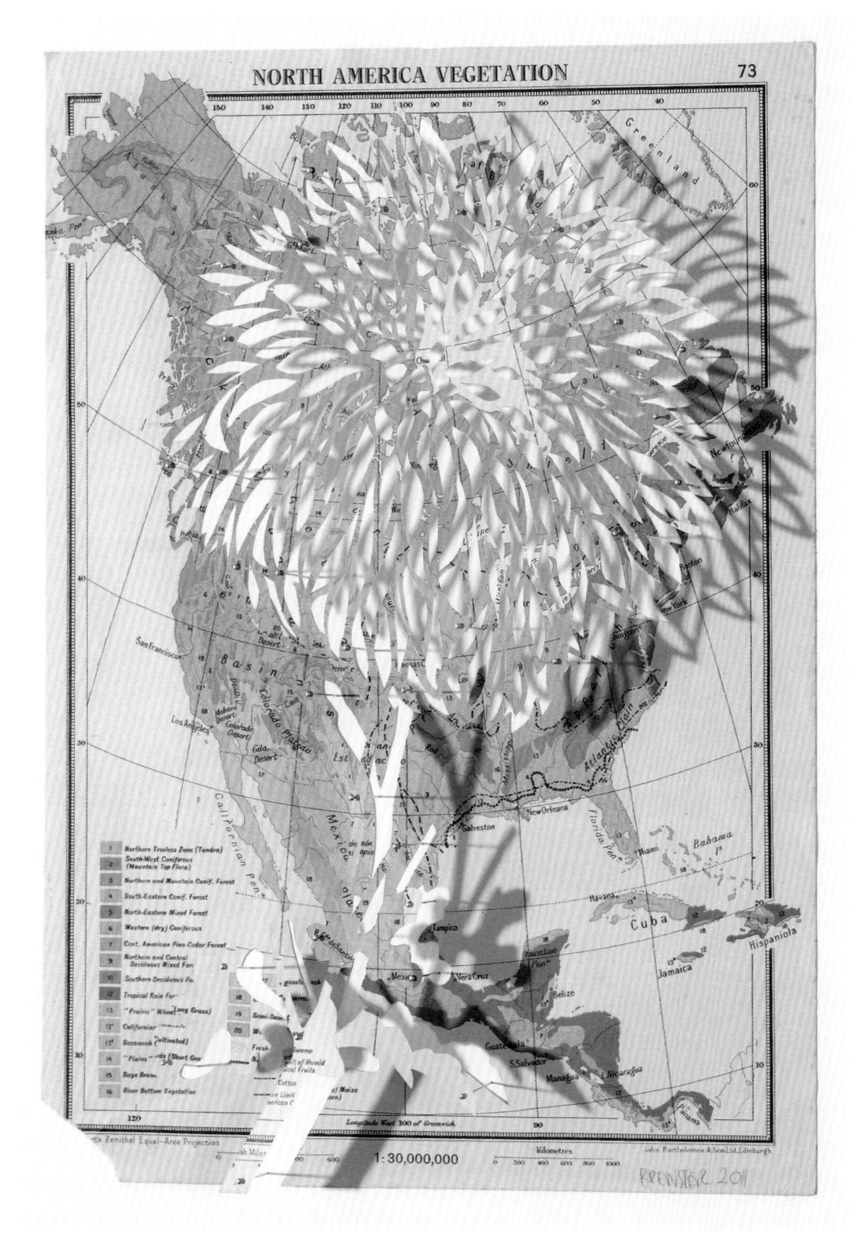

Map Cutting

Claire Brewster's work is about retrieving the discarded, celebrating the unwanted and giving new life to the obsolete. Claire uses old and out-of-date maps and atlases as her fabric, with which she creates her intricate, delicate and detailed paper cuts. Claire takes inspiration from the environment, creating entomological installations of flora and fauna from imagined locations. Her birds, insects and flowers transcend borders and pass freely between countries with scant regard for rules of immigration or the effects of biodiversity. The shadows created when light is shined on them give the structures a three dimensional quality and create a feeling of movement.

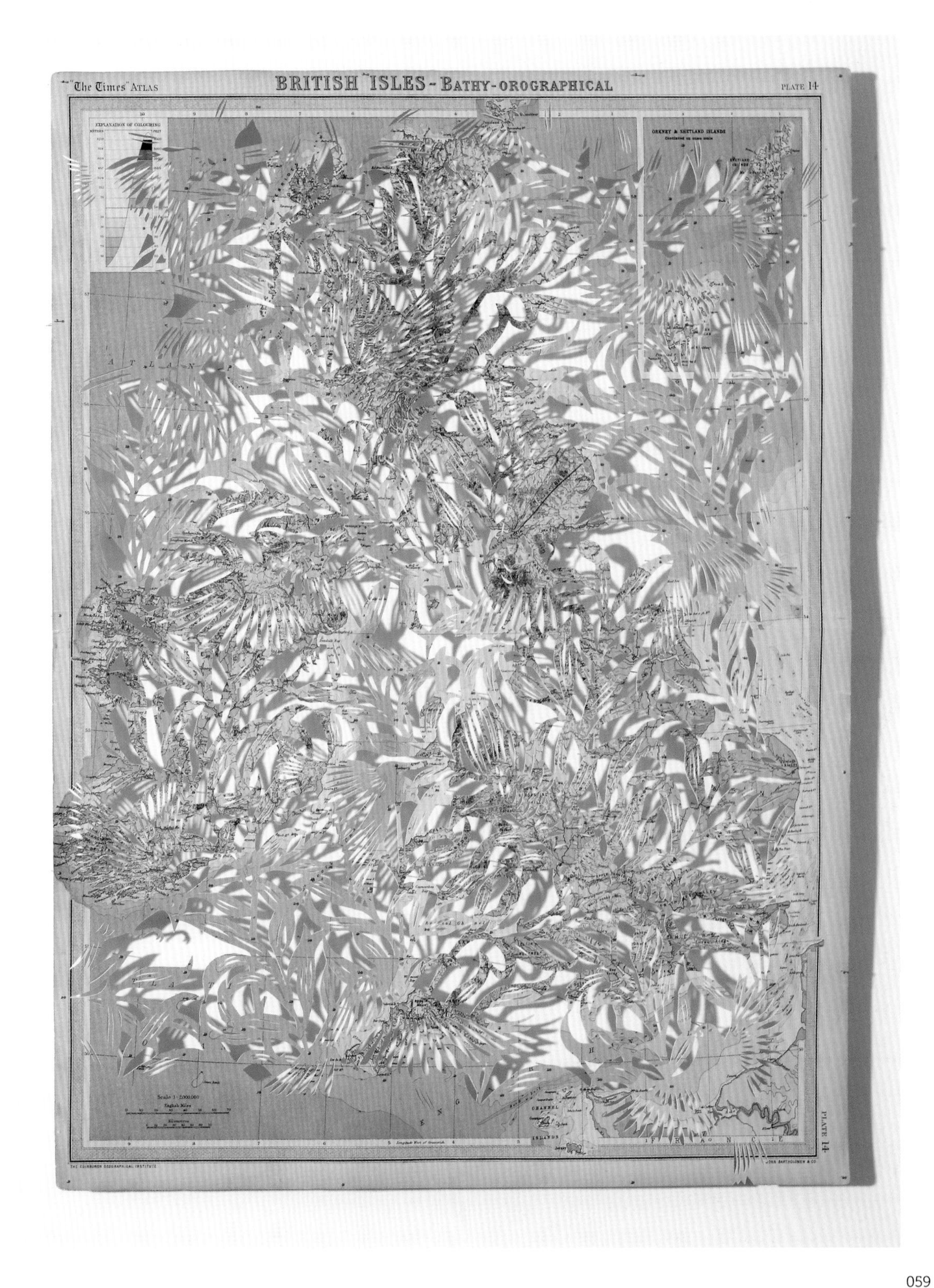
"The Times" ATLAS
BRITISH ISLES - BATHY-OROGRAPHICAL
PLATE 14
EXPLANATION OF COLOURING
ORKNEY & SHETLAND ISLANDS
CHANNEL
ISLANDS
PLATE 14
THE EDINBURGH GEOGRAPHICAL INSTITUTE

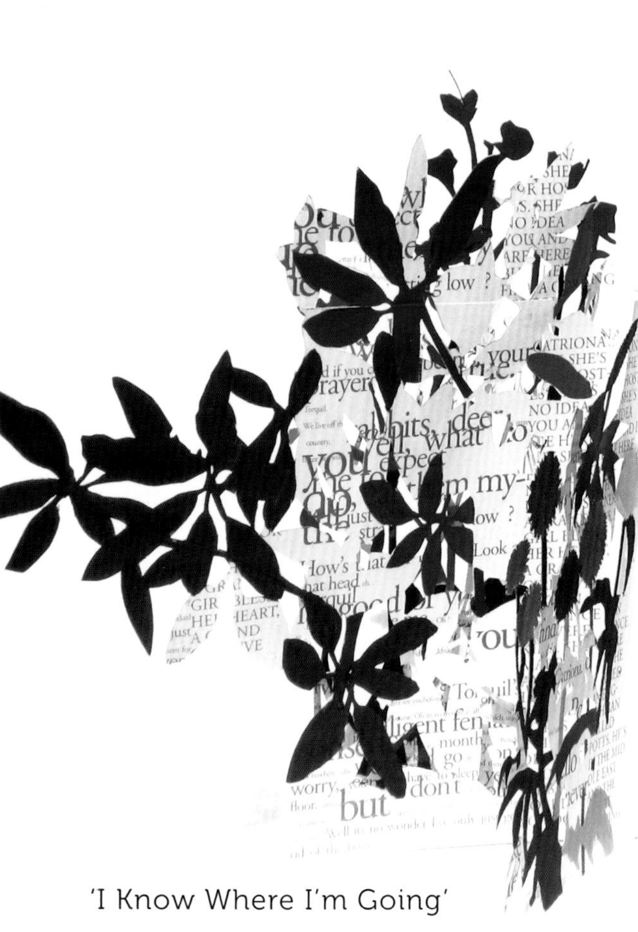

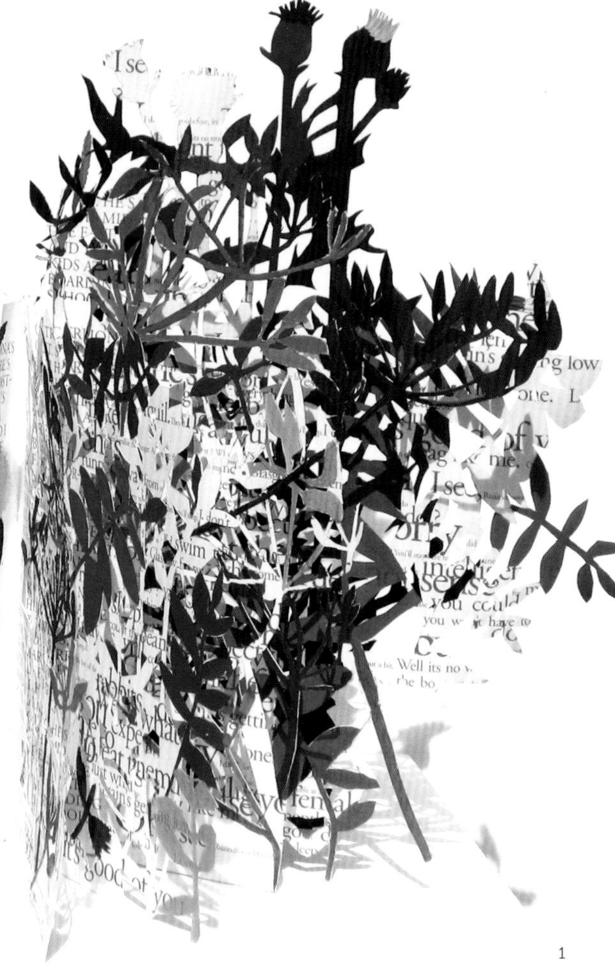

1

'I Know Where I'm Going'

1 / Catriona's Second Book
2 / Torquil's Book
3 / Catriona's Book
4 / Box Book
5 / Now Master Torquil

This series of Artist's Books was inspired by a film made in 1945 called 'I Know Where I'm Going' (Powell & Pressburger). They reflect aspects of the characters in the film, the events and the setting of the film. The structures I used for the books were often driven by parallels I found between film-making and books. The structure of a film is often received unconsciously. We don't step away as we watch and register the editing, for example, as we are caught up by the narrative; just as when we are reading we are not consciously aware of the structure of the book - the placing of words and their visual and physical impact. Instead we are caught up in the story. My books are about that unnoticed physical impact, the importance of the shape of the book itself, as well as the intimate connection between form and content. I try to highlight the presence of a book - the very shape of it conveys something about what is inside. Perhaps too in an age of increasing use of electronic devices for reading, I am driven by the need to highlight a key aspect of the physical book and the reading experience which is missing from the electronic reader.

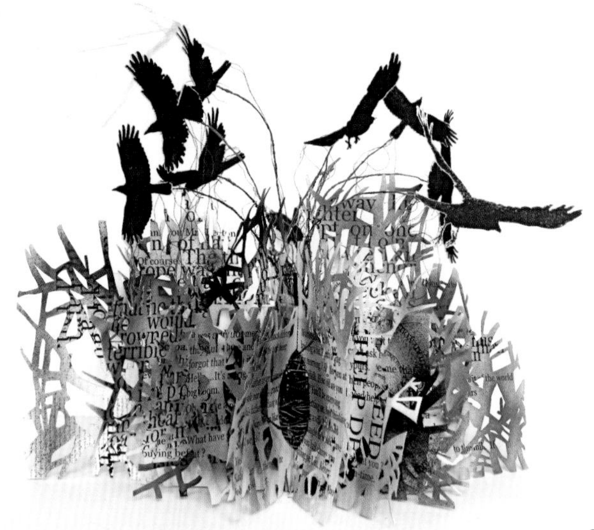

2

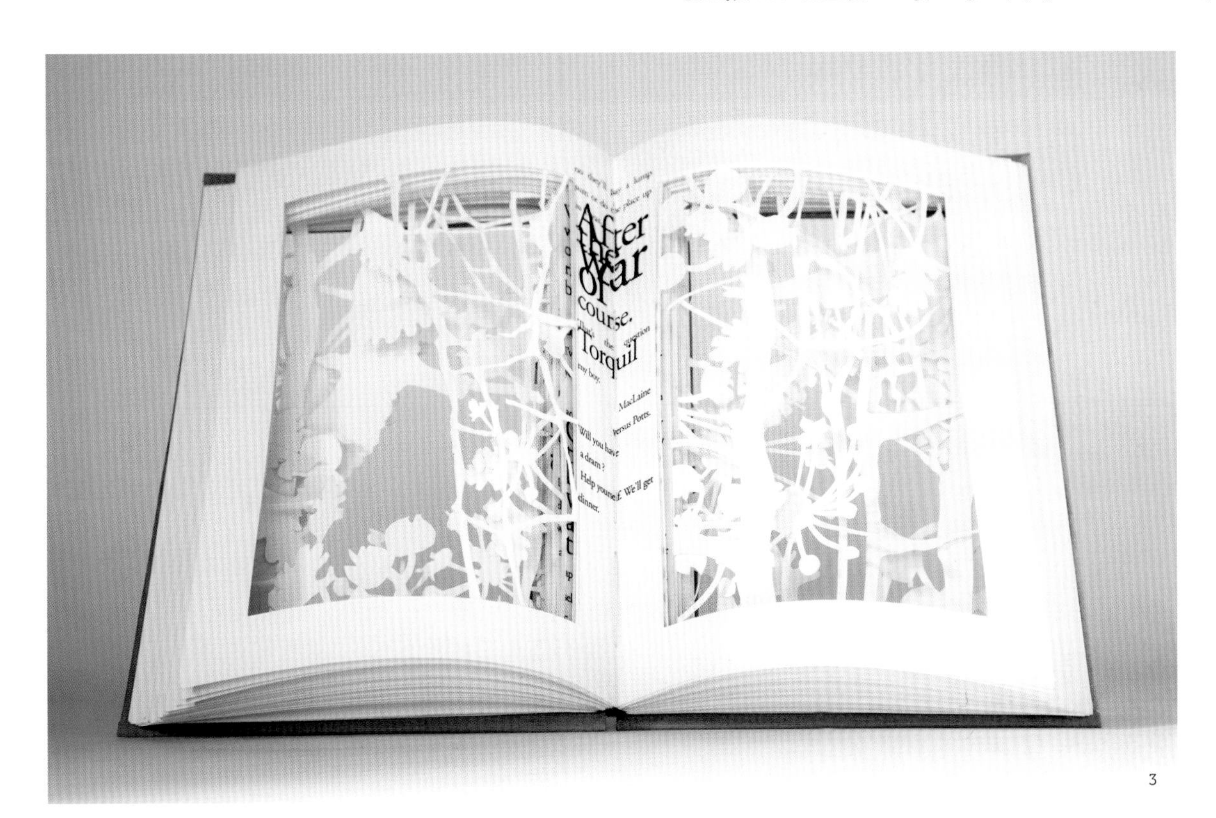
After the War
of course.
Torquil
MacLaine versus Potts.
Will you have a dram?
Help yourself. We'll get dinner.

3

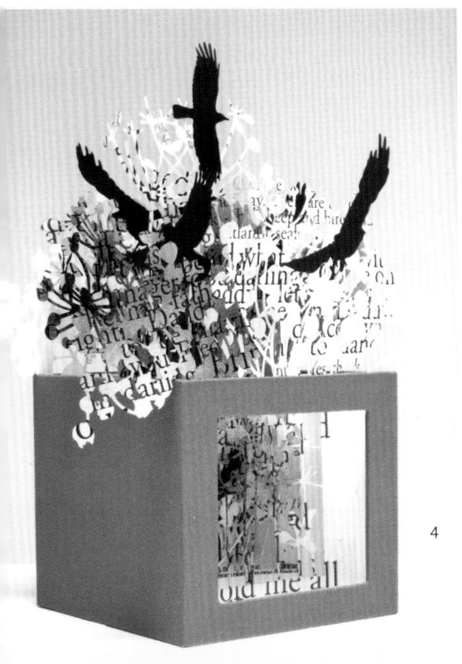

4

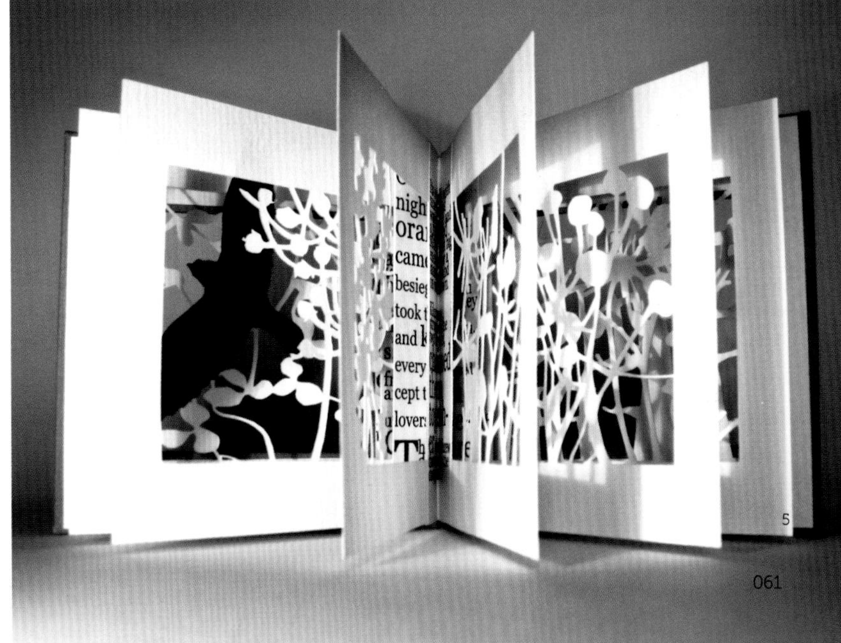

5

Artist Lizzie Thomas Photographer Lizzie Thomas

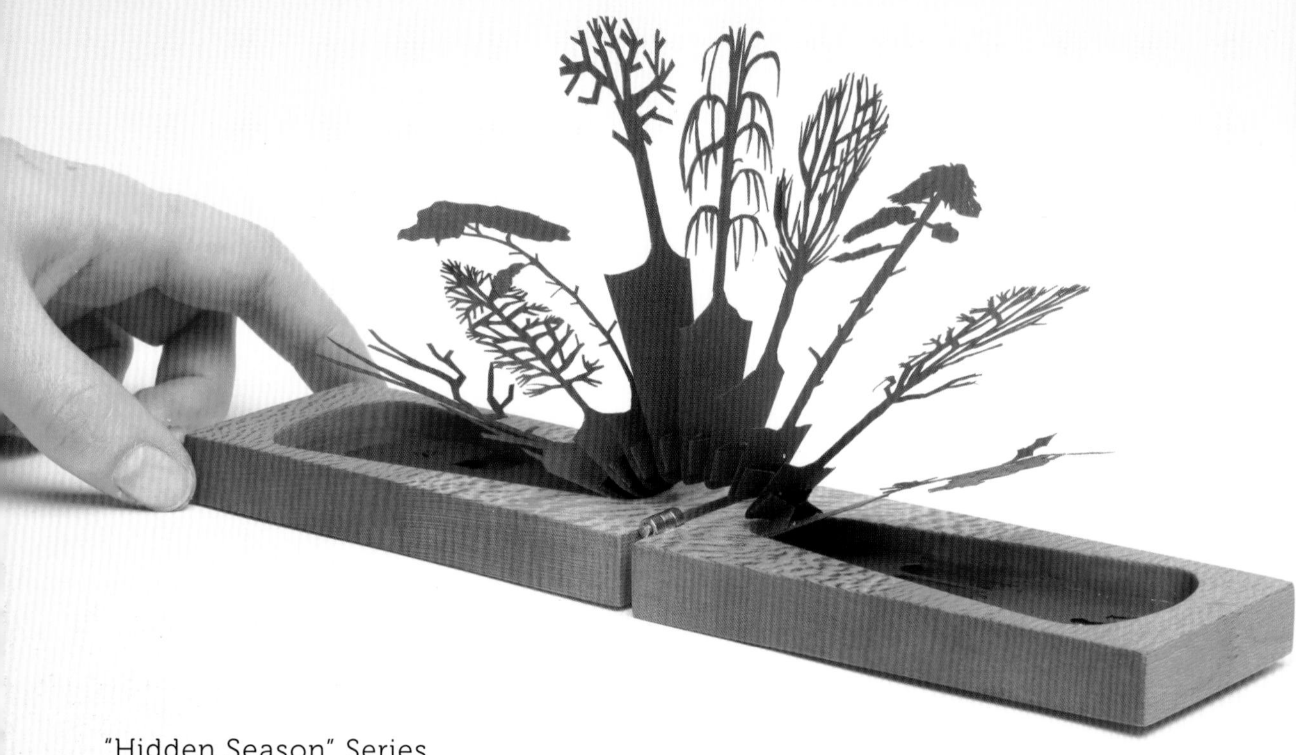

"Hidden Season" Series

The "Hidden Season" Series aims to surprise the viewer; each piece contains an entire season waiting to burst out at any time of the year. Lizzie Thomas was inspired by the transience of both nature and paper and introduced movement into the materials by layering 2D pages in order to create a 3D environment.

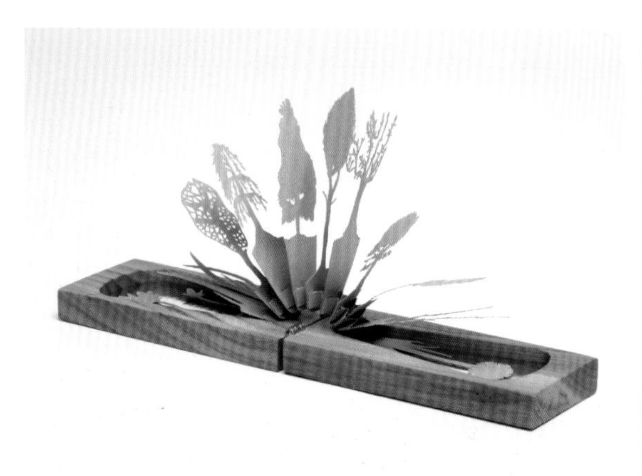

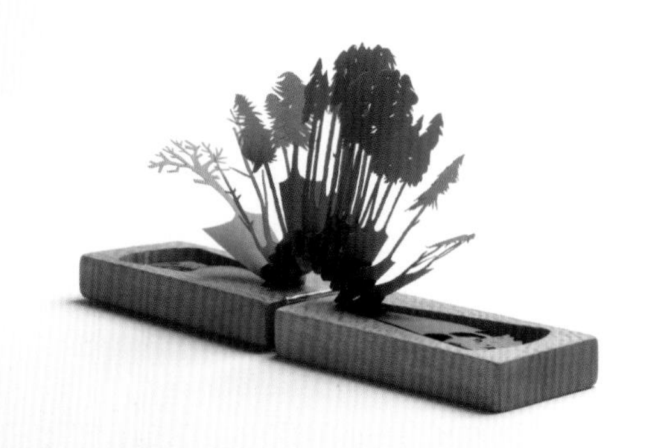

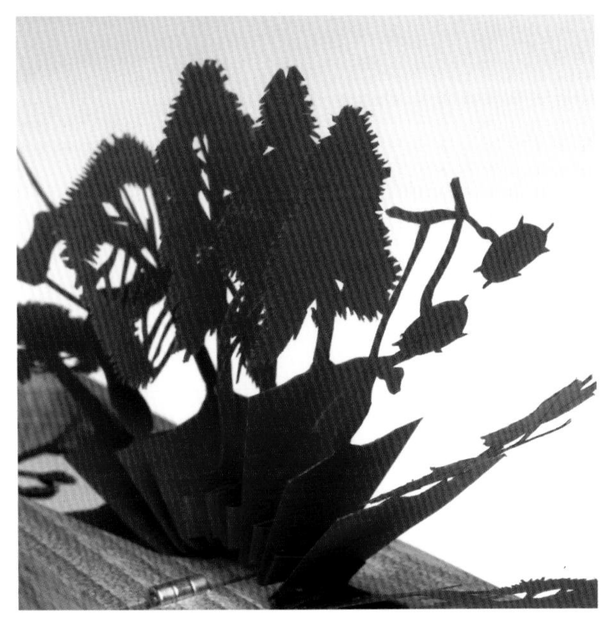

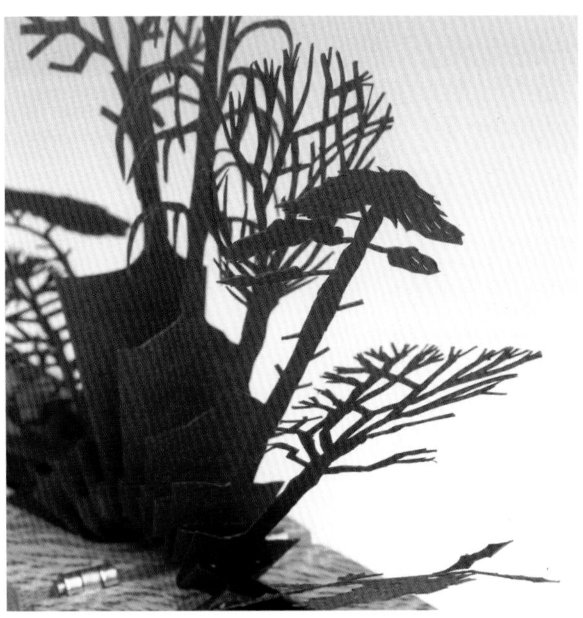

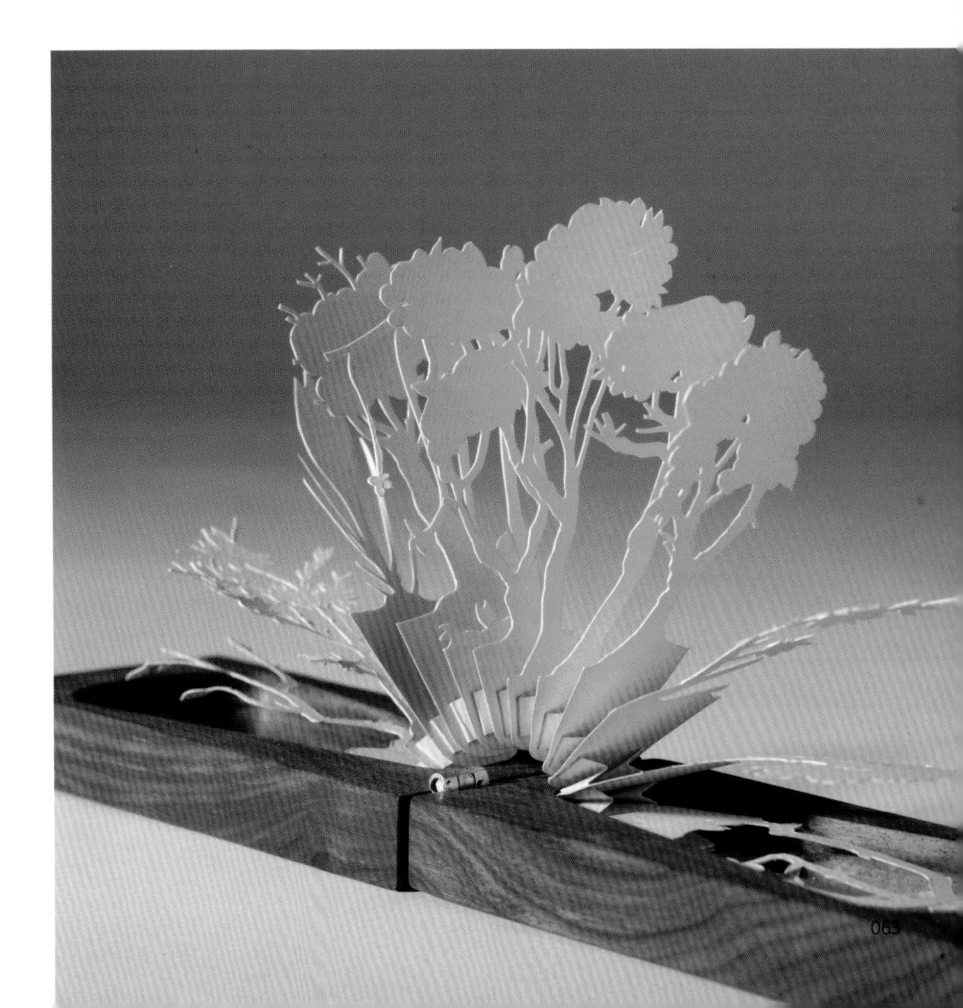

Artist Molly Bosley Photographer Molly Bosley

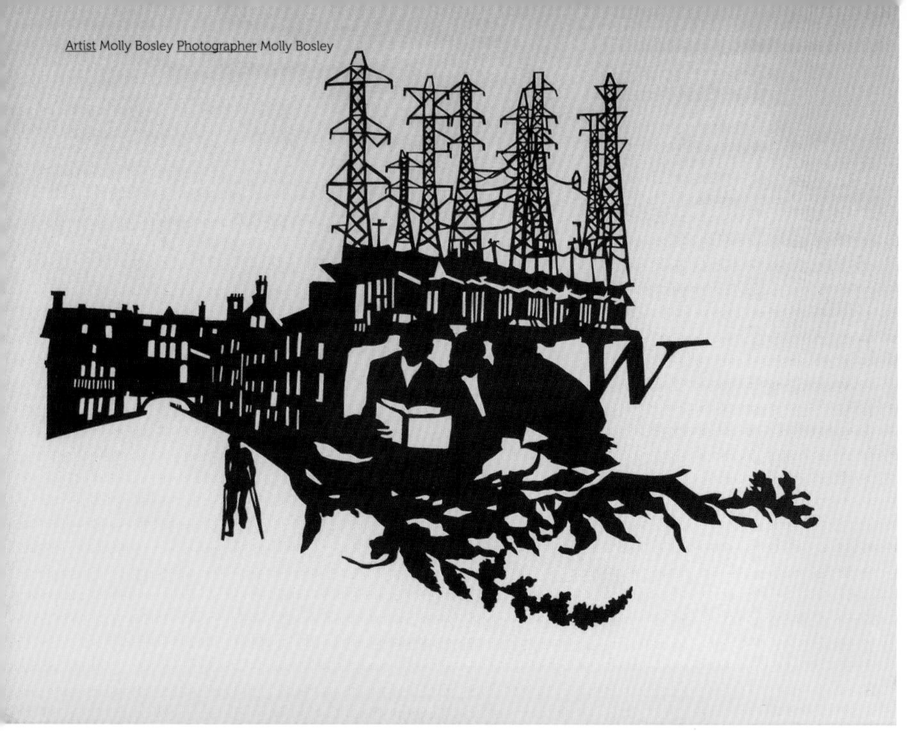

The Nature of Things

The Nature of Things series depicts imaginary landscapes inhabited by figures from discordant imagery. Each scene is sourced from entirely different origins, yet the characters within are gathered as familiars. This collection of artwork explores a fascination with the unfamiliarity, unsophistication, and unworldliness of innocence in contrast with the inevitable impurity ingrained in human nature. The combinations of different techniques and materials emphasize the contrasts which exist in these scenes. Much like reflections of our living world, these things come together and create a chaotic balance.

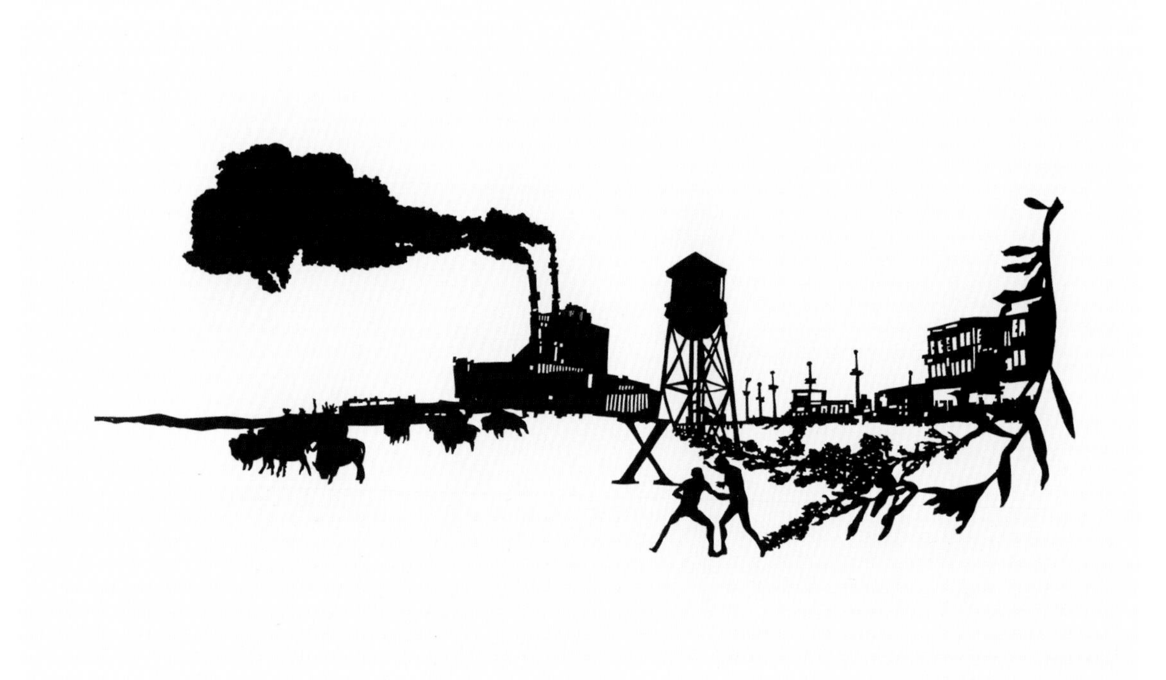

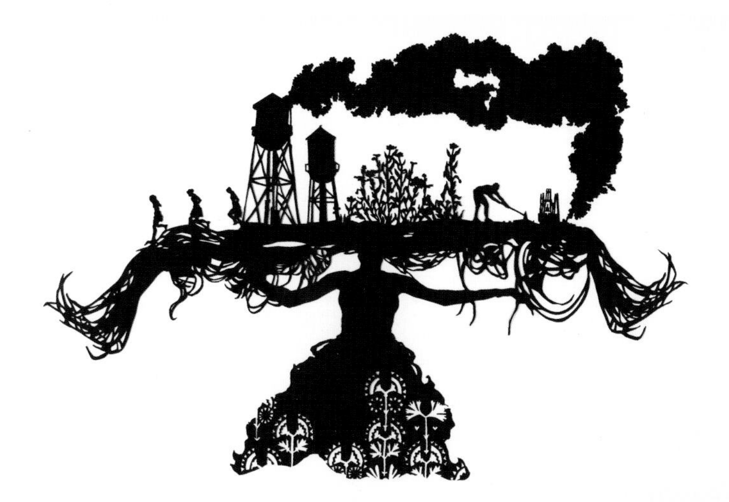

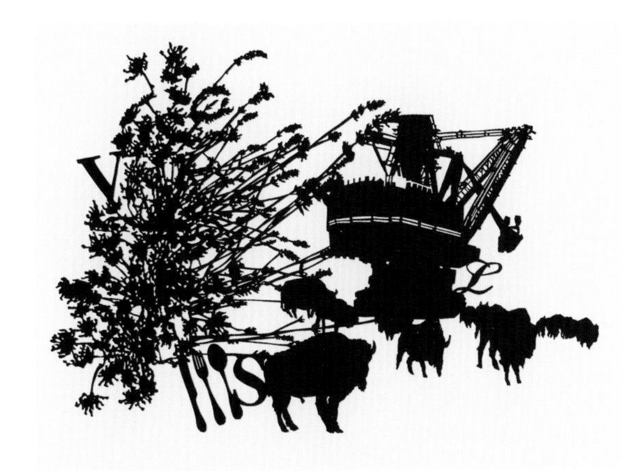

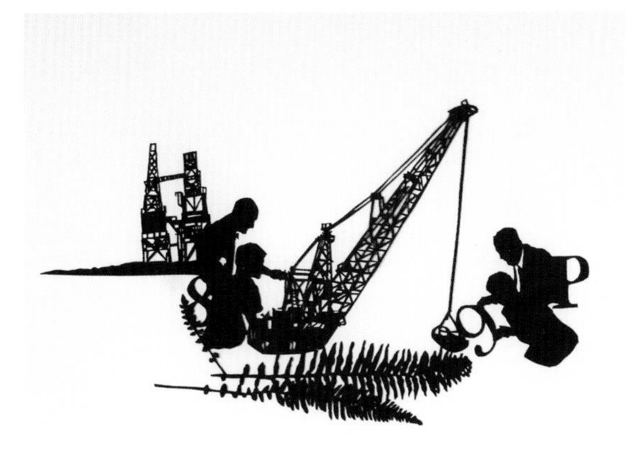

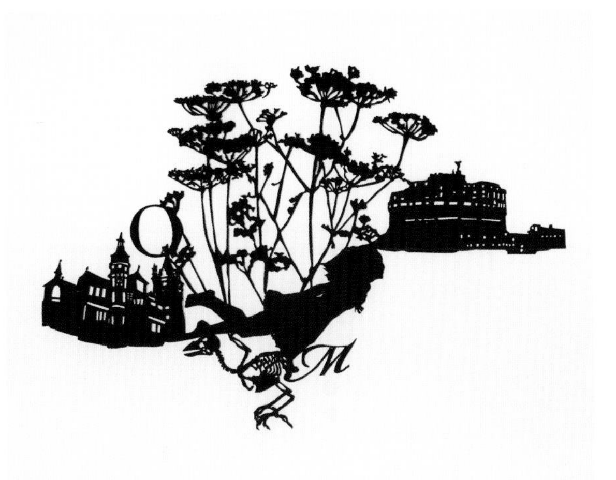

DREAM

1, 3 / Take me to a circus
2, 4 / Dream

Take me to a circus was created for an exhibition called "Designers: dream whisperers", introducing designers and artists who evoke in our memory a time when we used to be living in our dreams and fantasies. I set a theme of a circus that brings us to a time separated from daily life. A circus carriage gave me an image of the black box, which contains something unusual and magical waiting to happen. A thick frame was used like a container so as to keep secrets and dreams within the circus. I illustrated the figures on paper and then cut them out. For the plants coming through the carriage I used different thicknesses of paper in order to get texture. Dream is an experimental work created in a gap year between my foundation course and Masters. I brought a sense of depth to a flat illustration in order to add a more dreamy texture. Paper engineering such as folding, cutting and layering is magical. It creates negative and positive space, beautiful shadows and different tones. I believe that these three-dimensional components enhance visual perception as well as the image of fantasy.

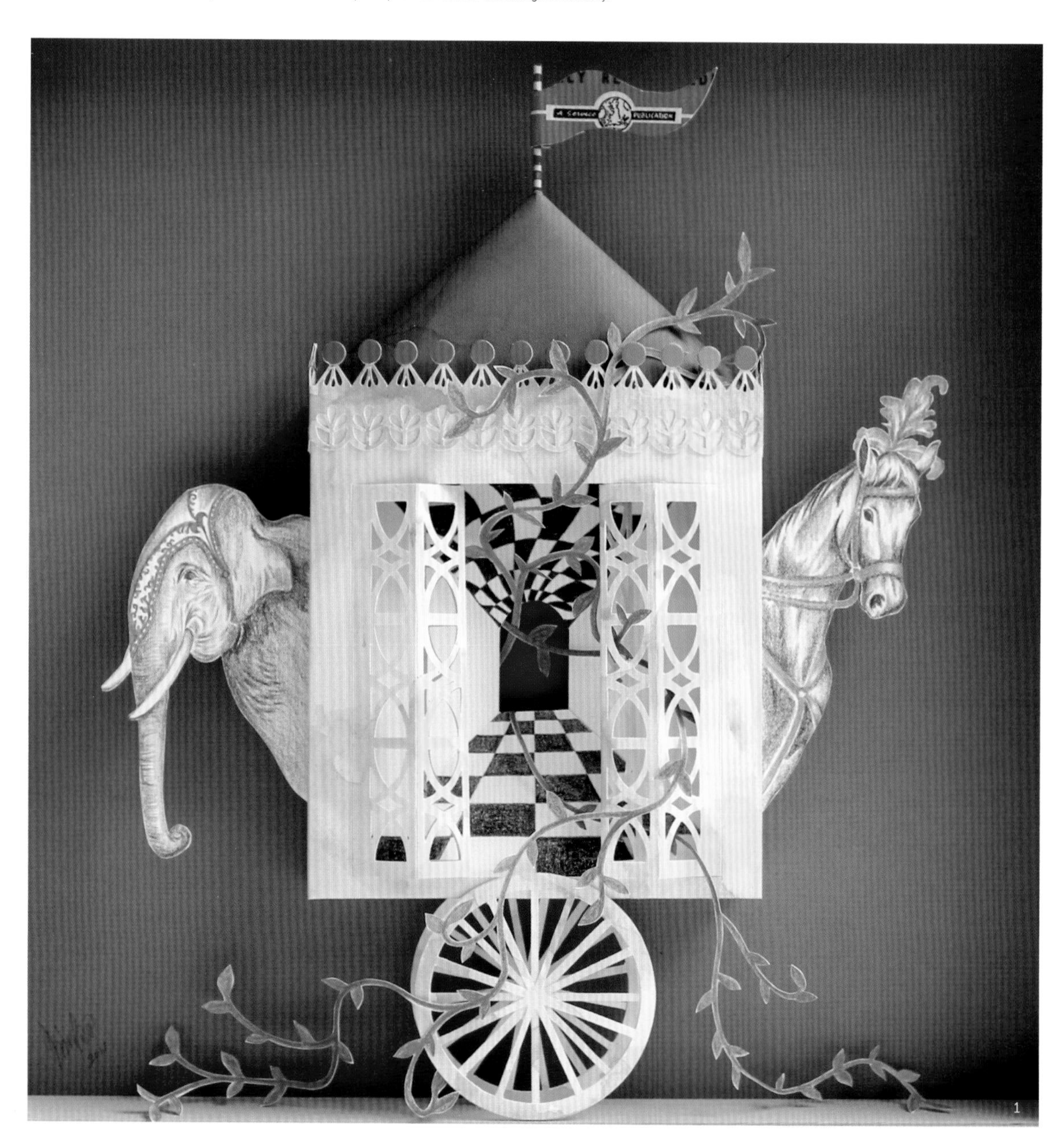

1

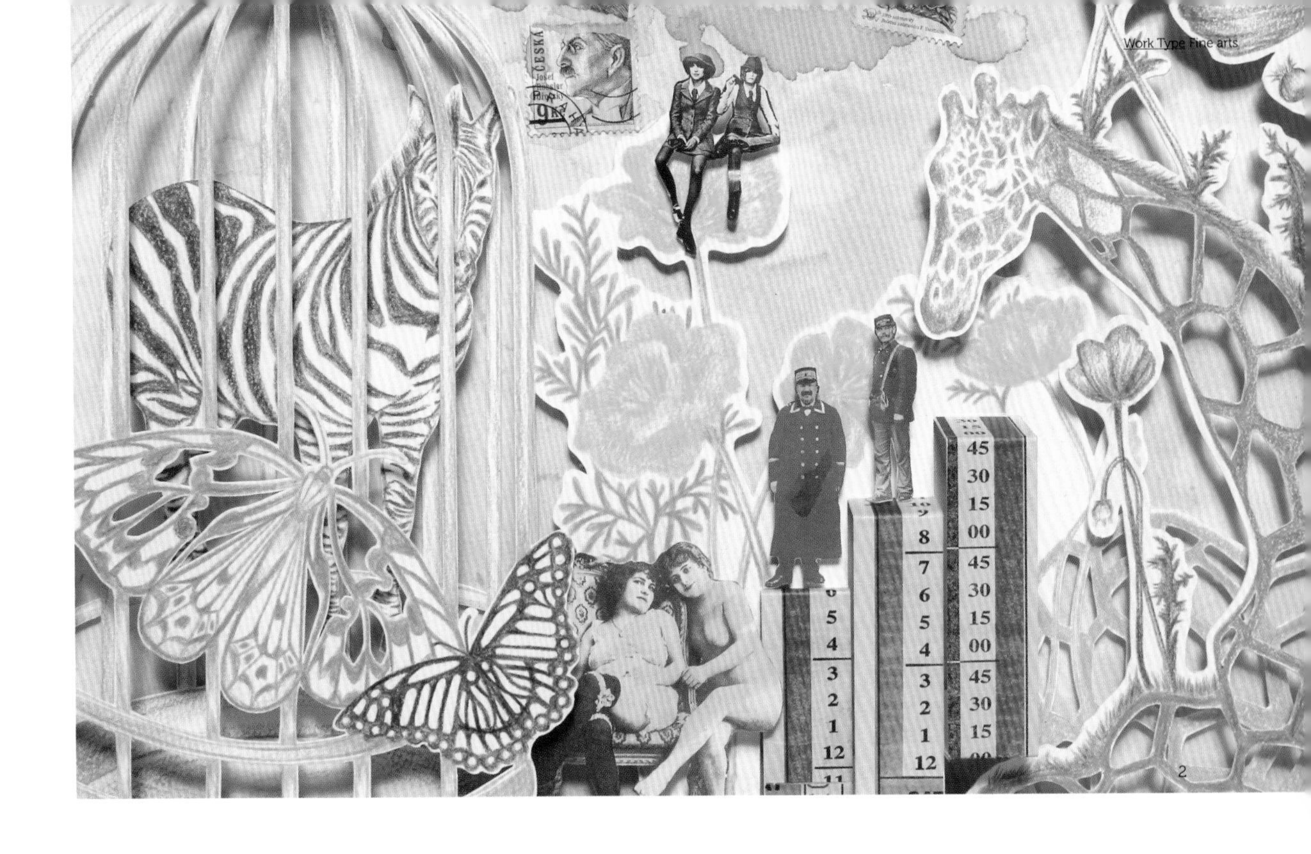

2

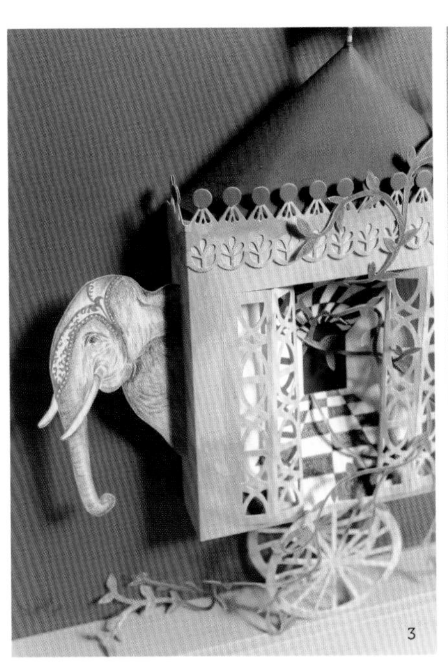

3

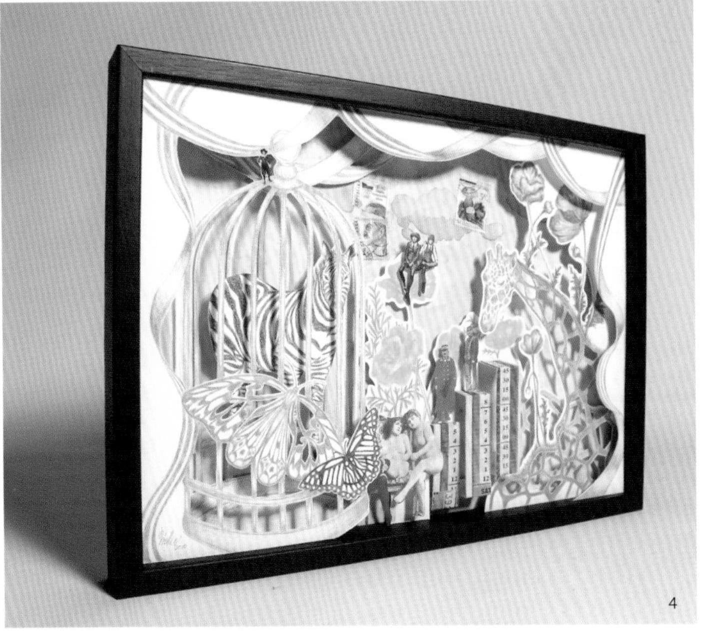

4

Kips Bay Showhouse 2009

For the 2009 Kips Bay Decorator Showhouse, designer Amy Lau used Maya Romanoff's wallpaper in collaboration with artist Jo Lynn Alcorn to create a dynamic and three-dimensional stairwell. Using the magnolia trees outside of the Frick Collection as her inspiration, Lau used Wall Mica as the background paper by Maya Romanoff who also created all the papers for the space including a custom color for the branches and hand painted paper for the leaves. While playing off the gilding and architecture of the house, Lau's design evoked the feeling of springtime and the feeling that you could simply pick the flowers off the wall.

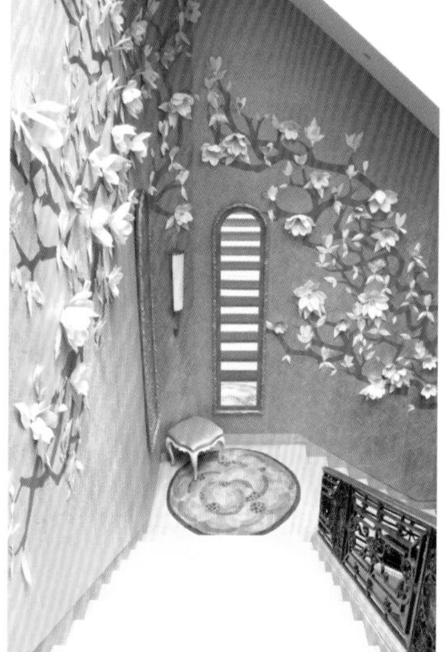

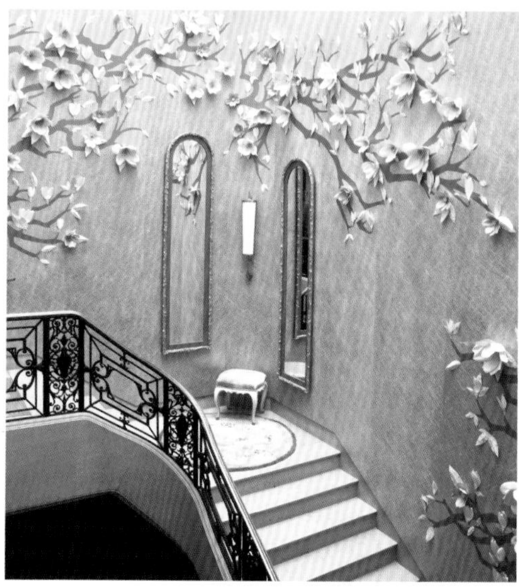

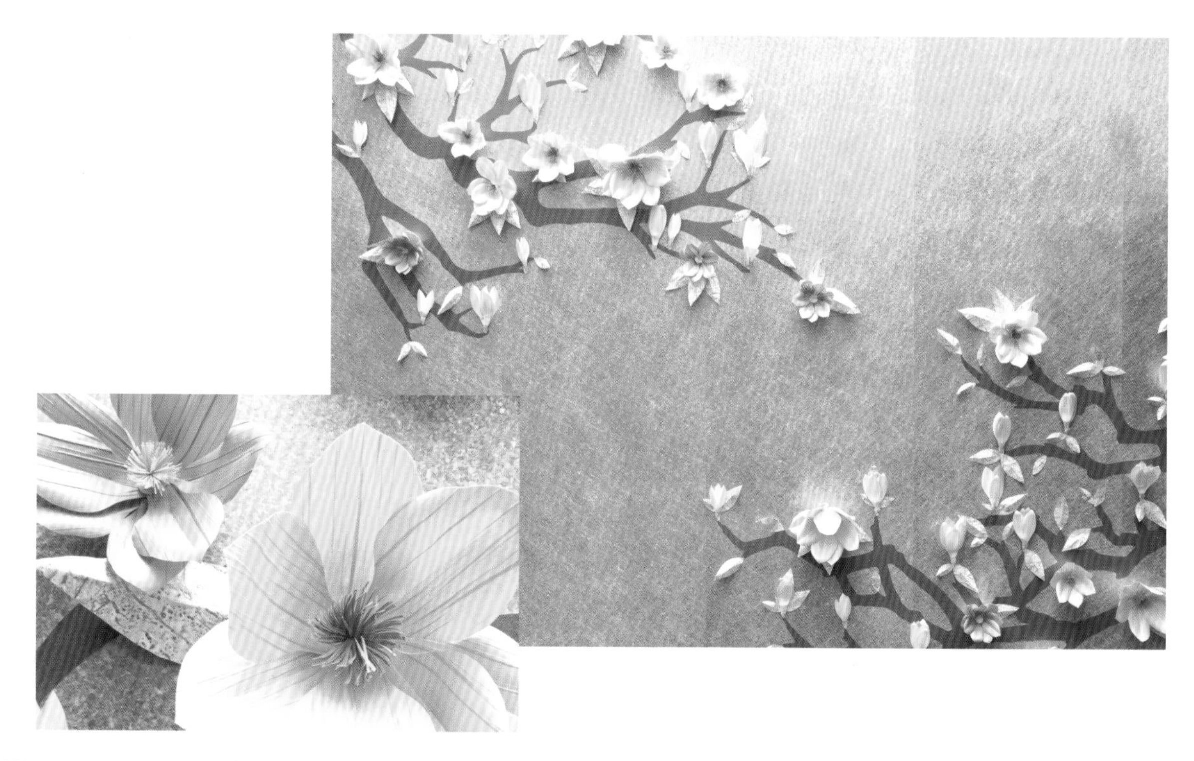

Design Agency Amy Lau Design Designer Amy Lau Photographer Amy Lau Design

Work Type Installation Technique Laser cutting

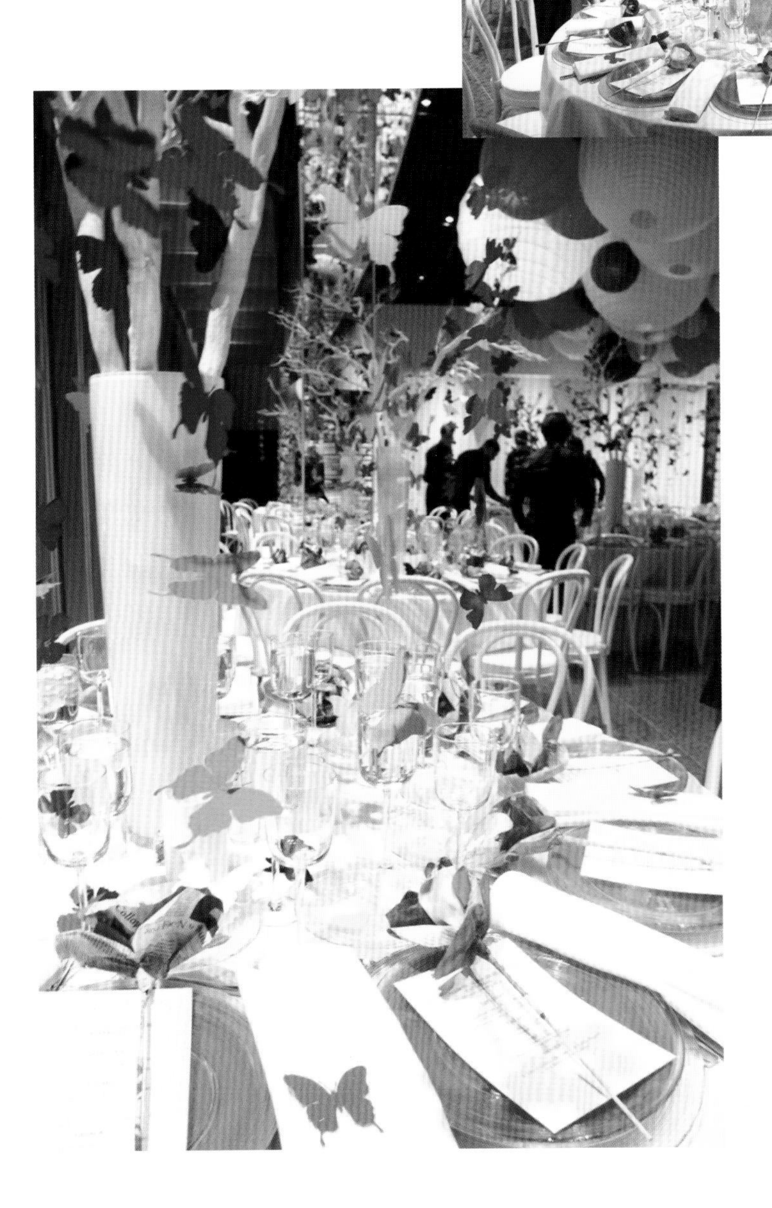

MAD Paperball 2009

In 2009, designer Amy Lau was asked to decorate the dining area for the Museum of Art and Design's first annual MAD Paperball, in celebration of the museum's first anniversary. Inspired by the exhibition featured at MAD entitled, Slash: Paper Under the Knife, Lau's design was made completely out of paper. With an intricate butterfly pattern in hand, created by MAD featured artist Andrea Mastrovito, Lau laser cut 6,000 red, white, and black butterflies to adorn the tablescapes, dangling from white branches that were placed in a vase in the center of each table. To complete the look, paper lanterns covered the ceiling, creating a soft glow.

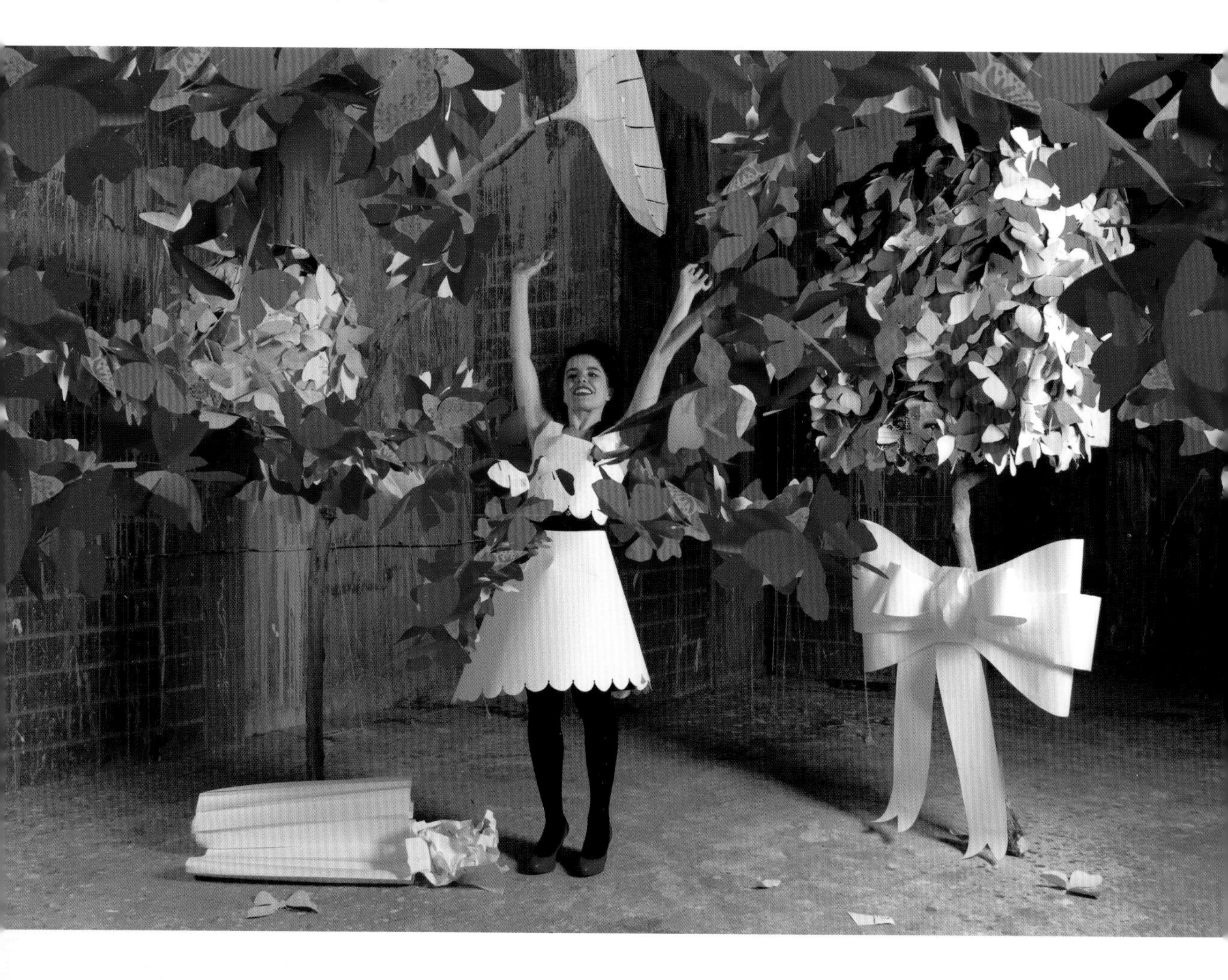

"In All the World I Dream in Paper"

"In all the world I dream in paper" is a short stop frame animation project by artist Petra Storrs, and singer Paloma Faith. The animation is set in an imaginary paper and paint world constructed by Petra Storrs and Sarah Lloyd as an installation for the Designers Block Illustration Festival. The piece stars Paloma Faith dressed in a multilayered paper dress; she slowly peels off and rips its layers until it is gone. This dress was developed as part of her stage show. The photography was done by James Champion, and the music was specially composed by Pierre Forcioli Conti. The set was built over a few days and a tower of scaffolding was constructed in the centre of the space, from which the paint was thrown in every direction and colour. Once this was dry the trees were assembled and hung in the space. The thousands of butterflies were cut by hand over a few days and pinned to the polystyrene tree forms. The paper dress was cut, folded and stapled.

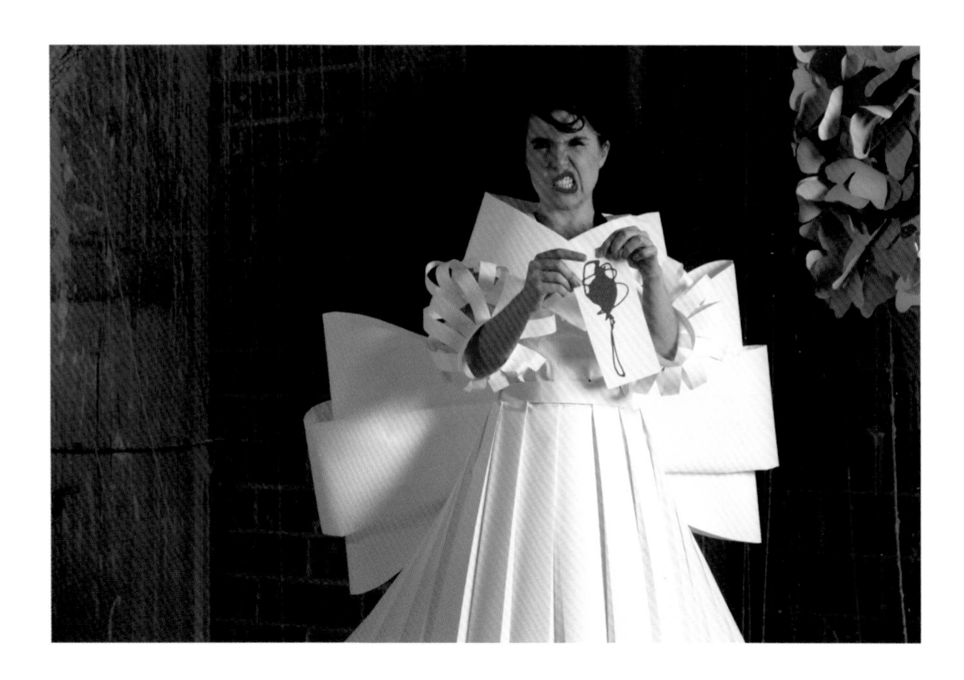

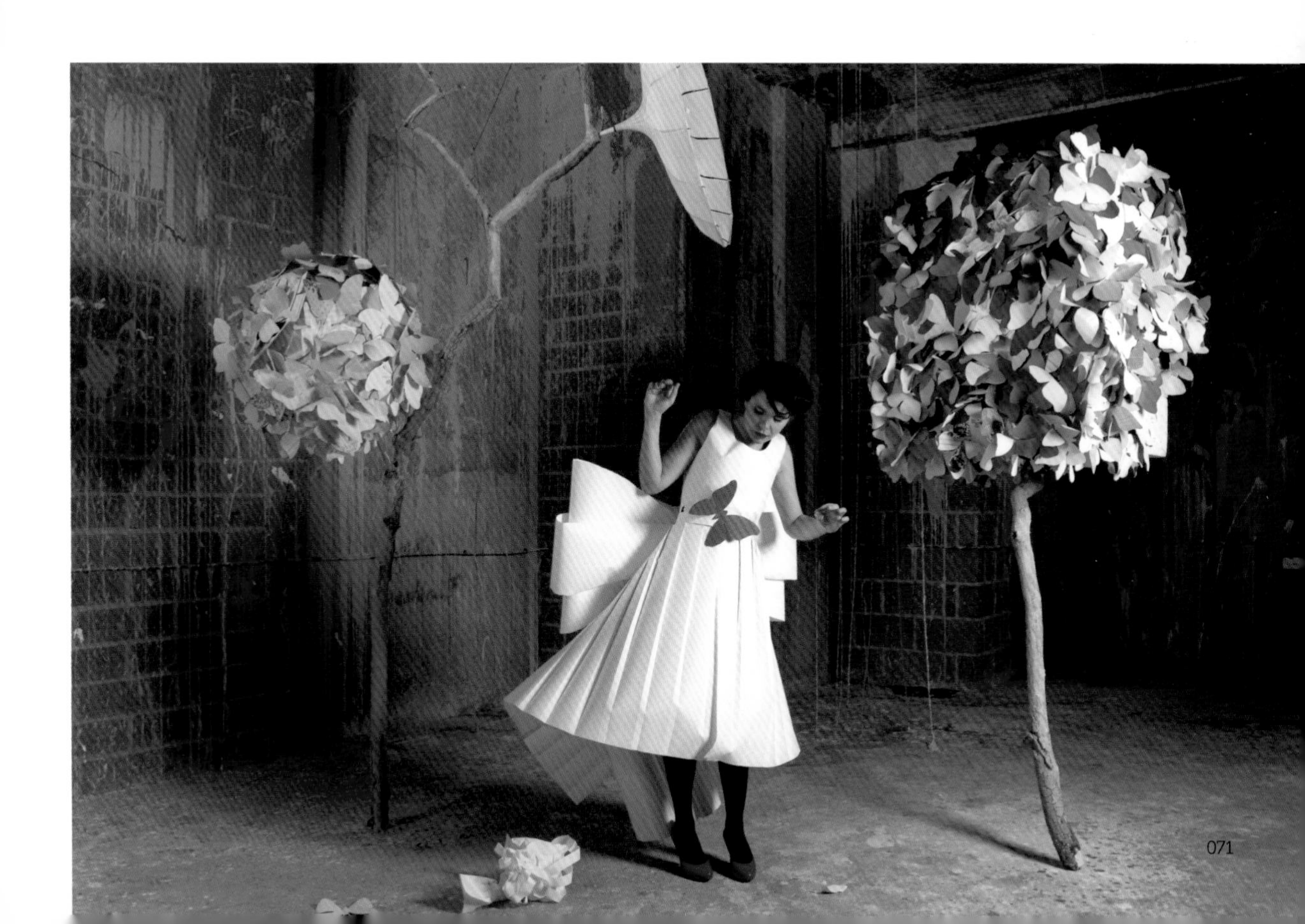

Artist Brian Dettmer Photographer 1, 4, 5 Image Courtesy of the Artist and Kinz + Tillou Fine Art/ 2, 6, 8 Image courtesy of the Artist and Packer Schopf Gallery
3 Image Courtesy of the Artist and Toomey Tourell Fine Art/ 7 Image Courtesy of the Artist and Wexler Gallery

Book Sculpture

1 / Saturation Will Result
2 / New Books of Knowledge
3 / Wagnalls Wheel
4 / Mound 2
5 / The New Century
6 / The Life of Vertebrates
7 / Absolute Authority
8 / Compiled Upon A New Plan

In this work I begin with an existing book and seal its edges, creating an enclosed vessel full of unearthed potential. I cut into the surface of the book and dissect through it from the front. I work with knives, tweezers and surgical tools to carve one page at a time, exposing each layer while cutting around ideas and images of interest. Nothing inside the books is relocated or implanted, only removed. Images and ideas are revealed to expose alternate histories and memories. My work is a collaboration with the existing material and its past creators and the completed pieces expose new relationships of the book's internal elements although they are still exactly where they have been since their original conception.

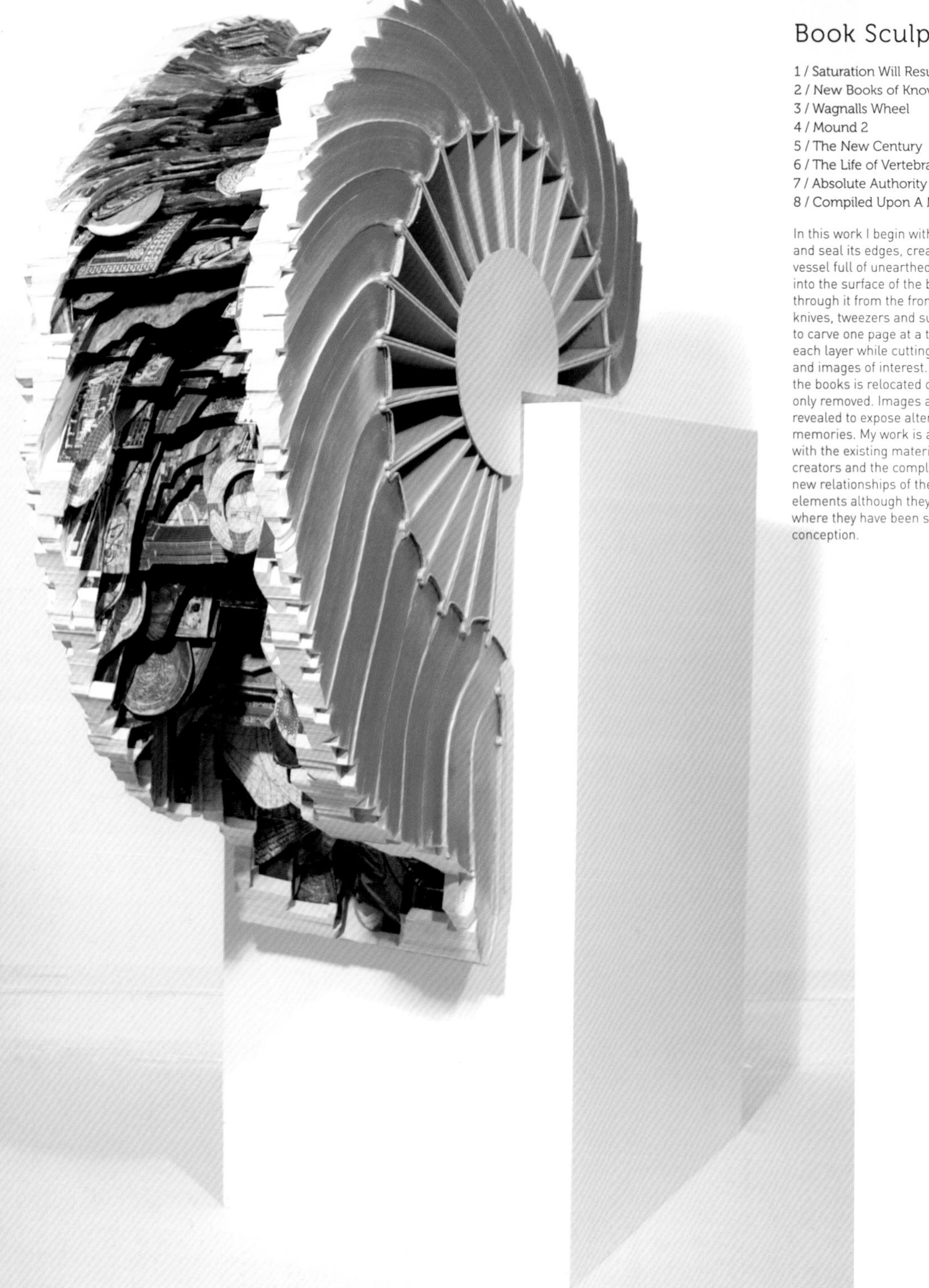

1

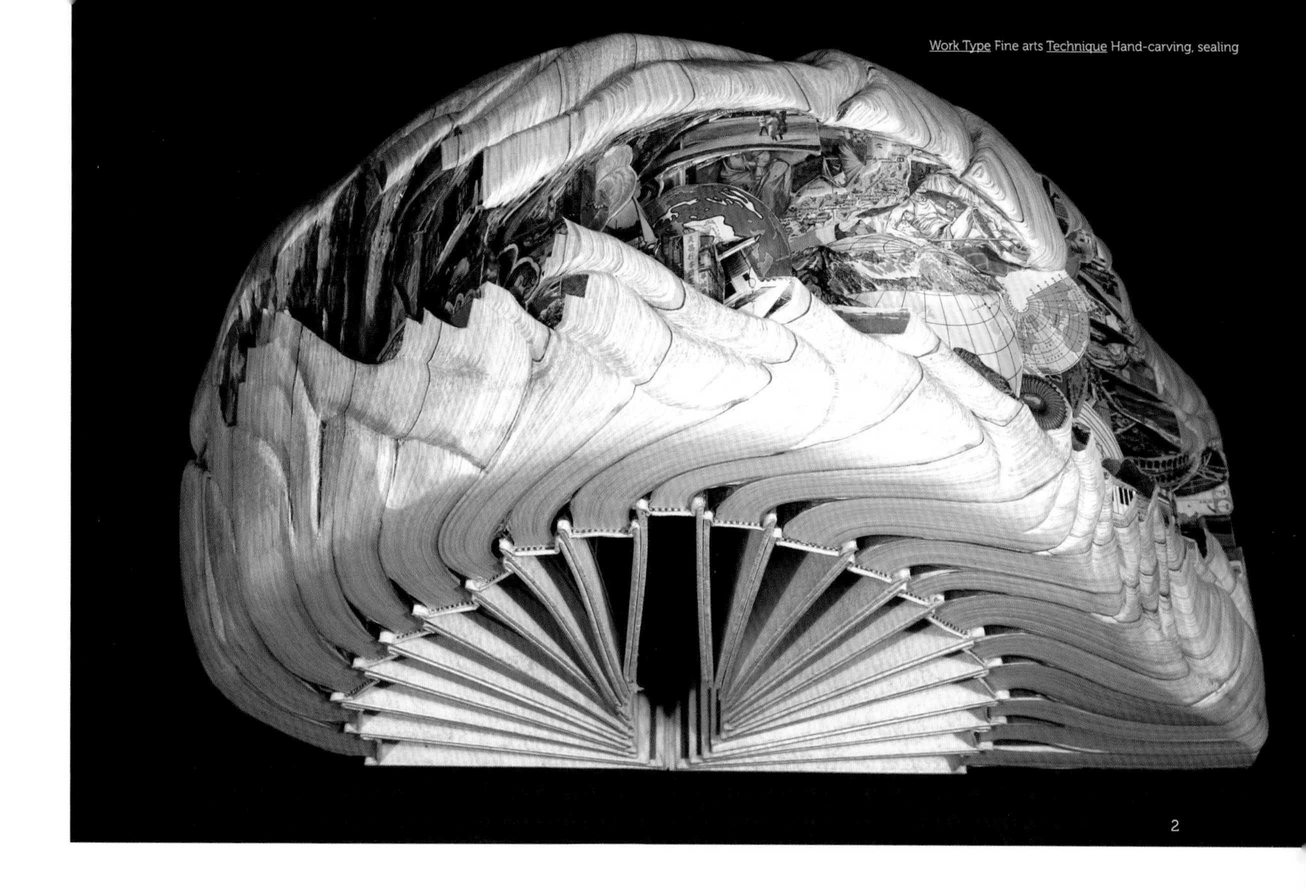
Work Type Fine arts Technique Hand-carving, sealing

2

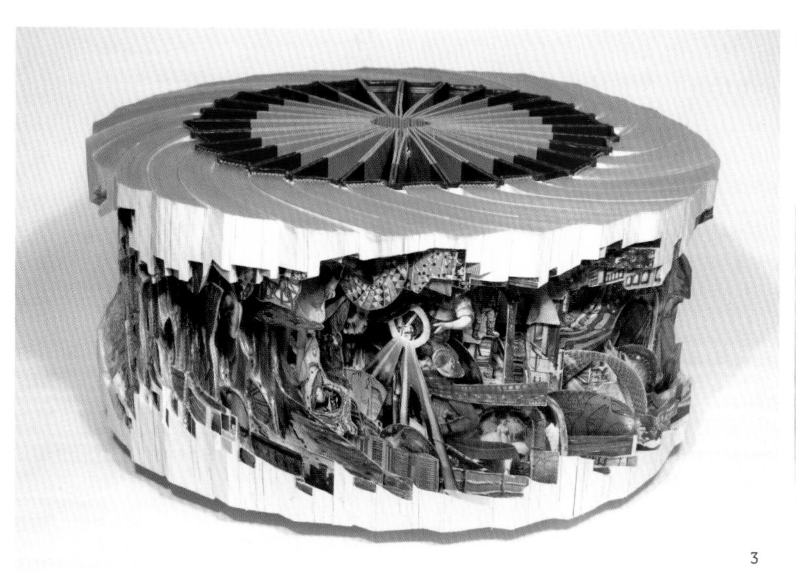
3

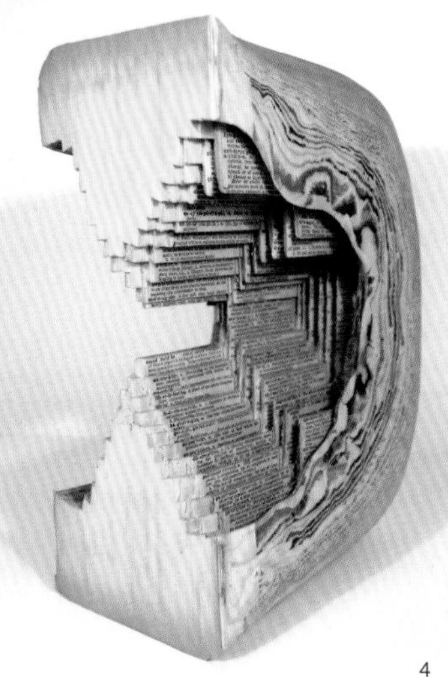
4

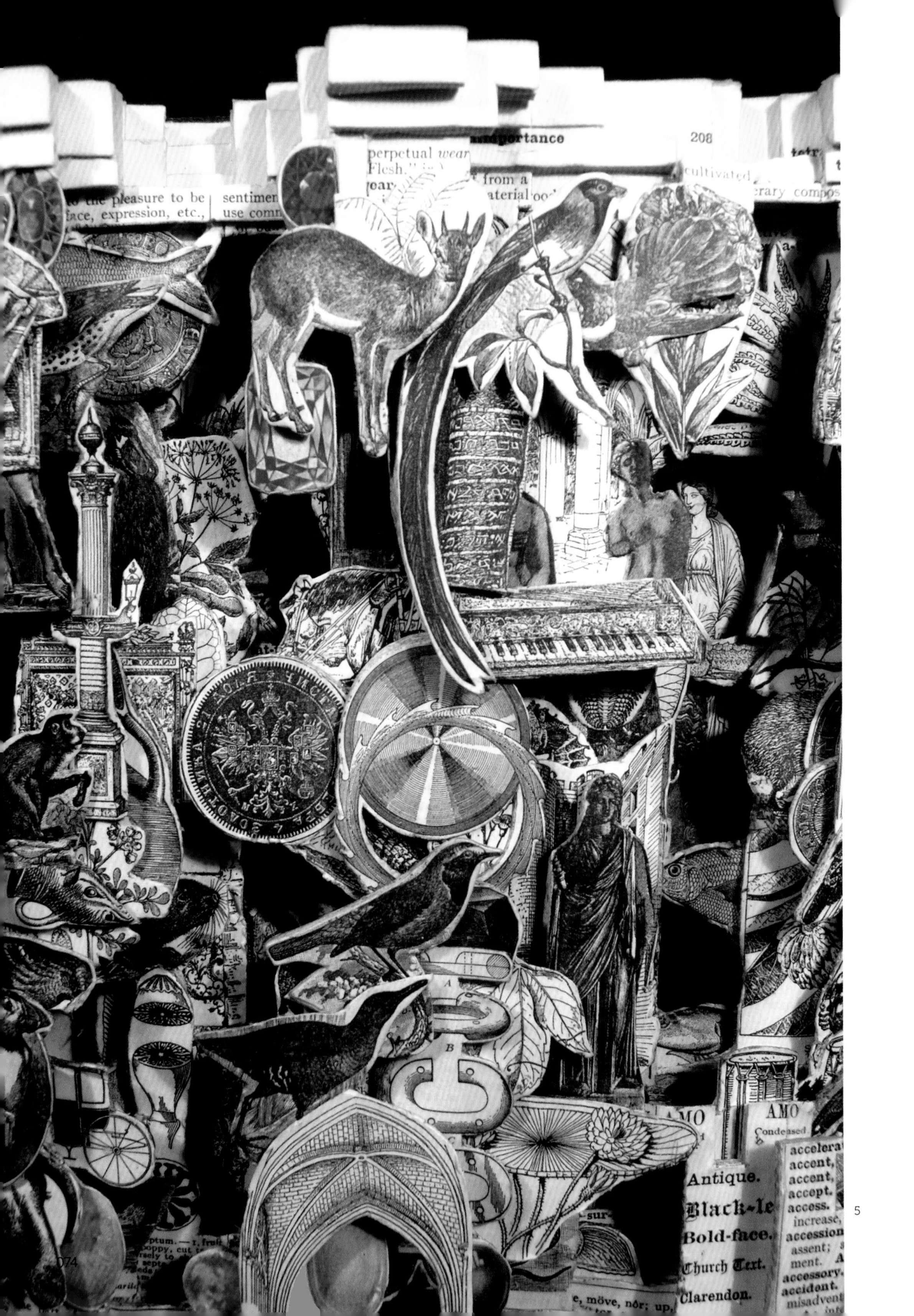

importance
208
perpetual wear
Flesh."
from a
cultivated
the pleasure to be
face, expression, etc.,
AMO
AMO
Condensed
Antique.
Bold-face.
Church Text.
Clarendon.
accent,
accent,
accept.
access.
increase,
assent;
ment.
accessory.
accident.
e, möve, nôr; up,

5

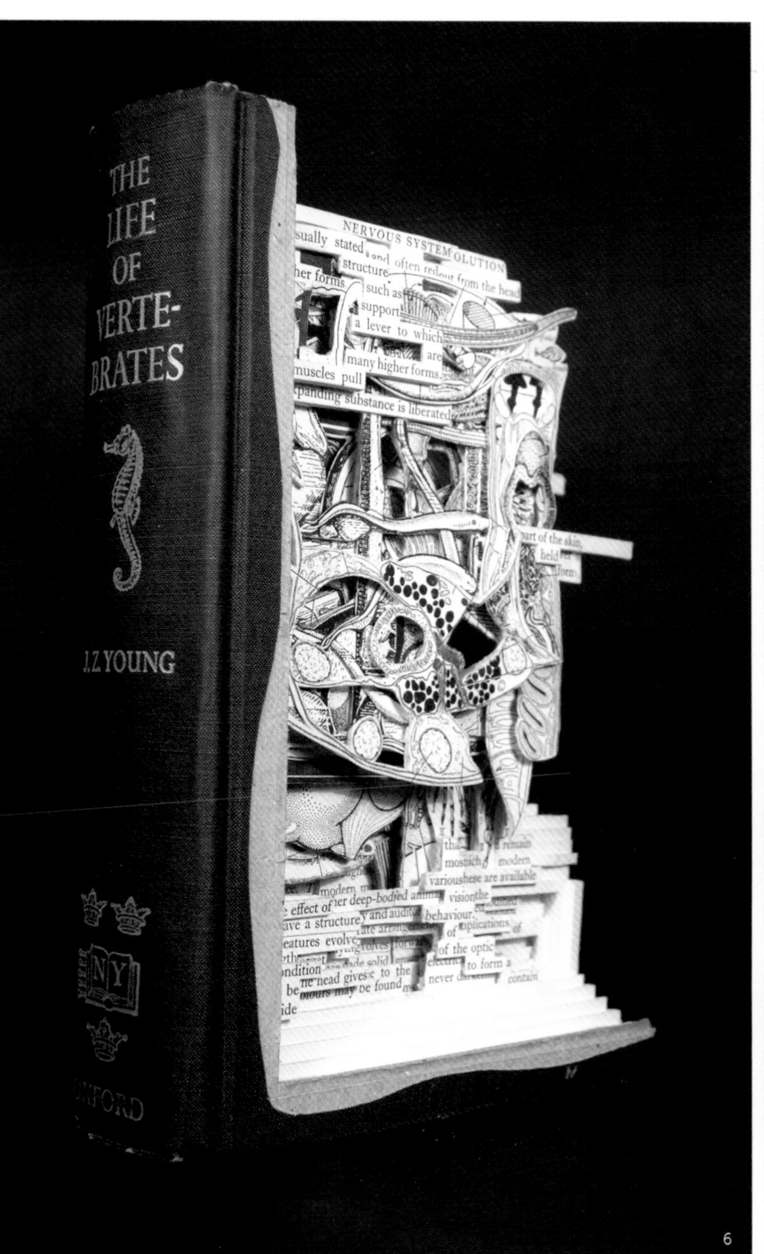

6

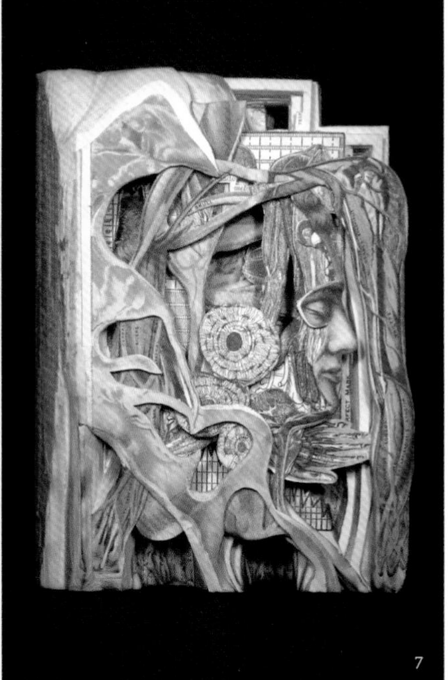
7

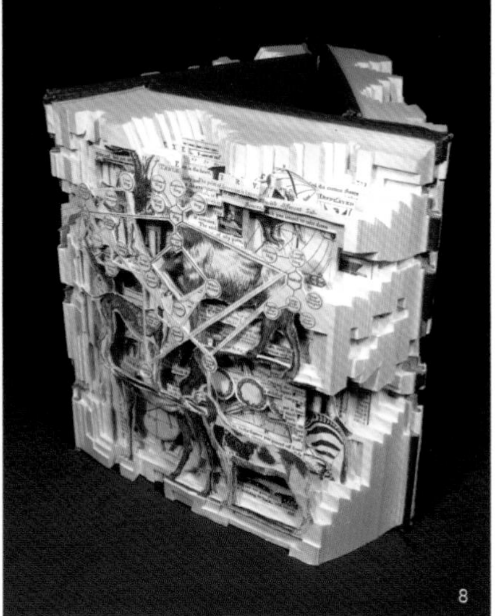
8

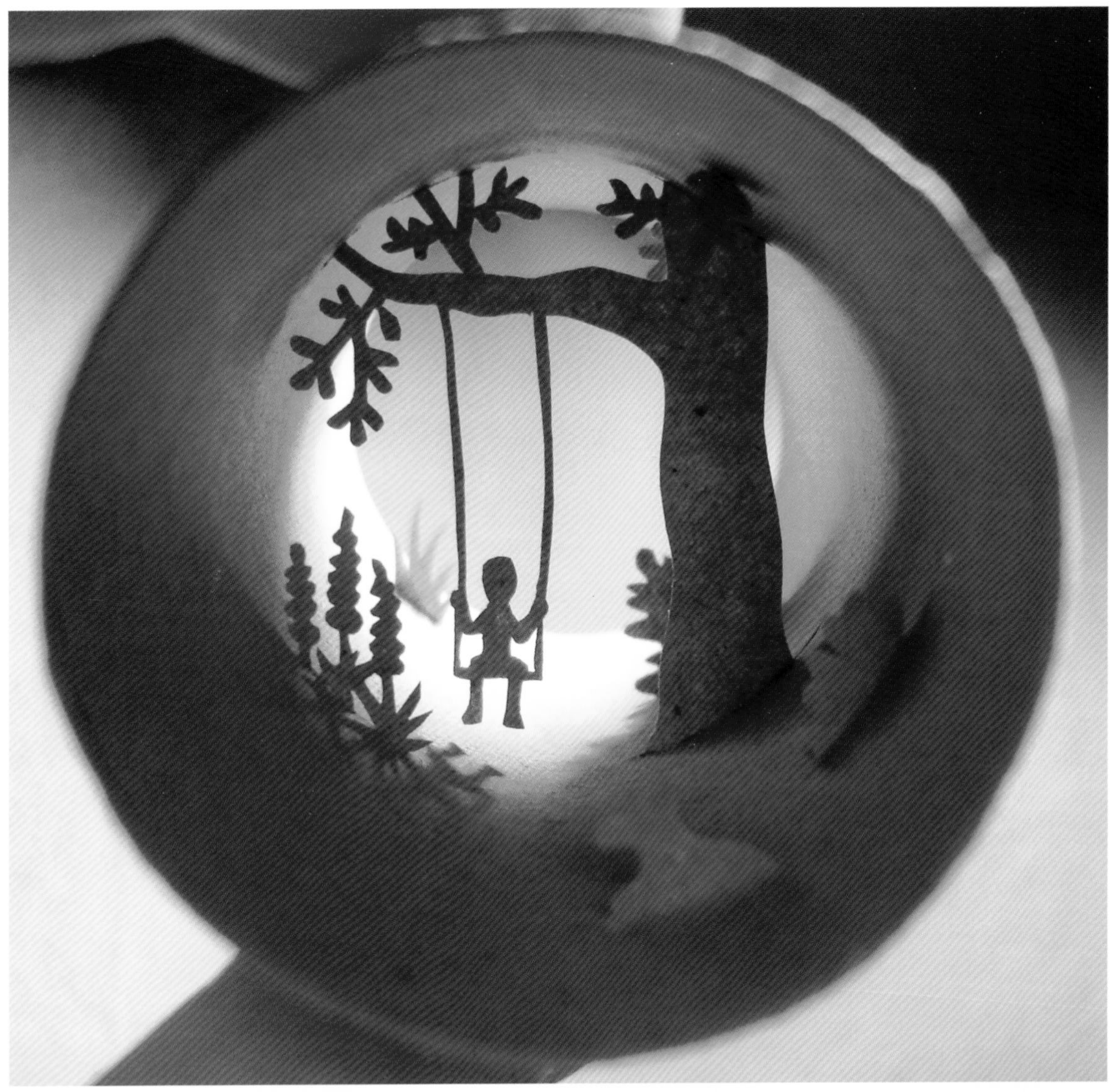

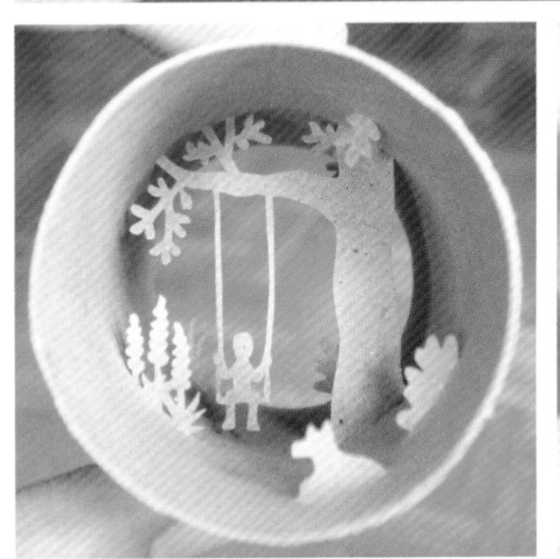

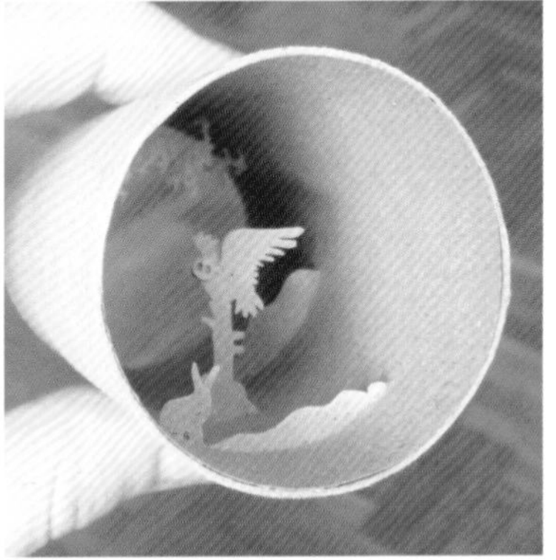

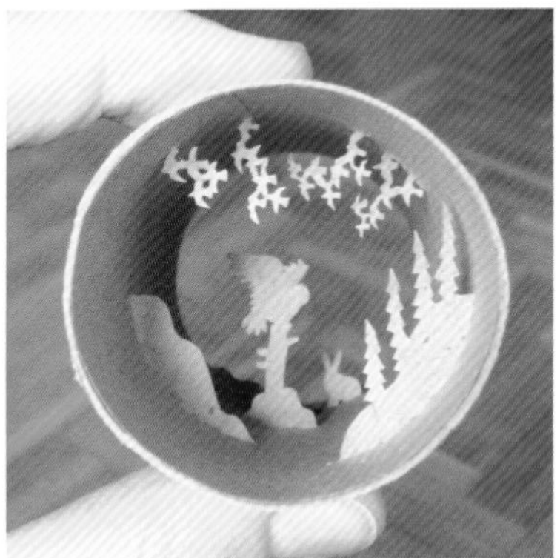

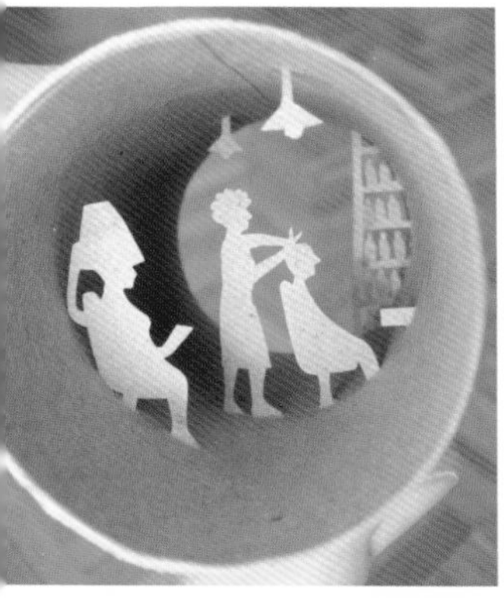

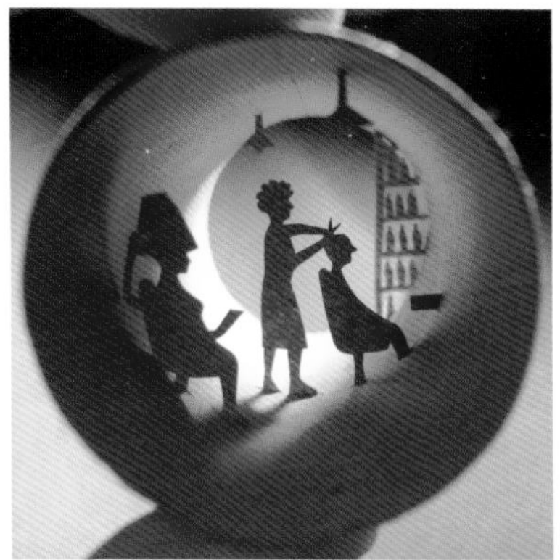

Paper Rolls

I have fun finding out what I can do with recuperated materials. The imagery of this work comes from our common daily trifles: hairdressing salon, pedestrian crossing, queue and swing. All these small events of everyday life often go unnoticed. But it is these details that make up a life. So I wanted to put these neglected events on a pedestal and show that everyday life is not boring. I use manicure scissors and a cutter to cut the small paper shapes. I select paper of the same color as the roll. It gives the illusion that the paper figures make part of the roll. I use tweezers to manipulate the paper shapes. I pay attention to the arrangement of elements to ensure that they best capture the light.

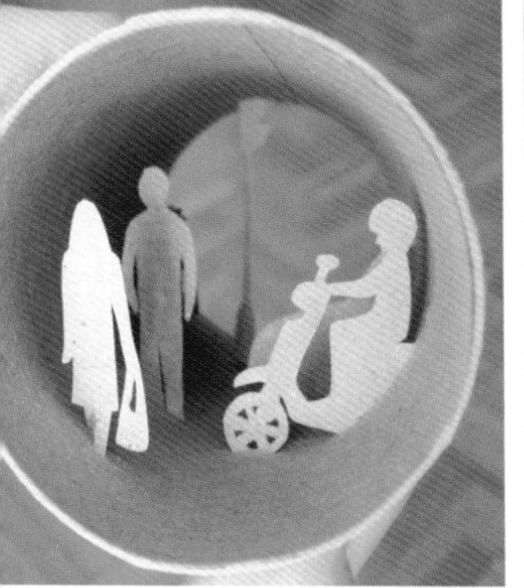

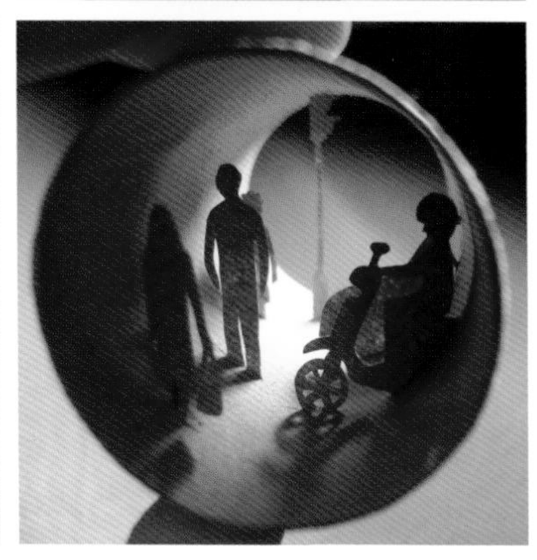

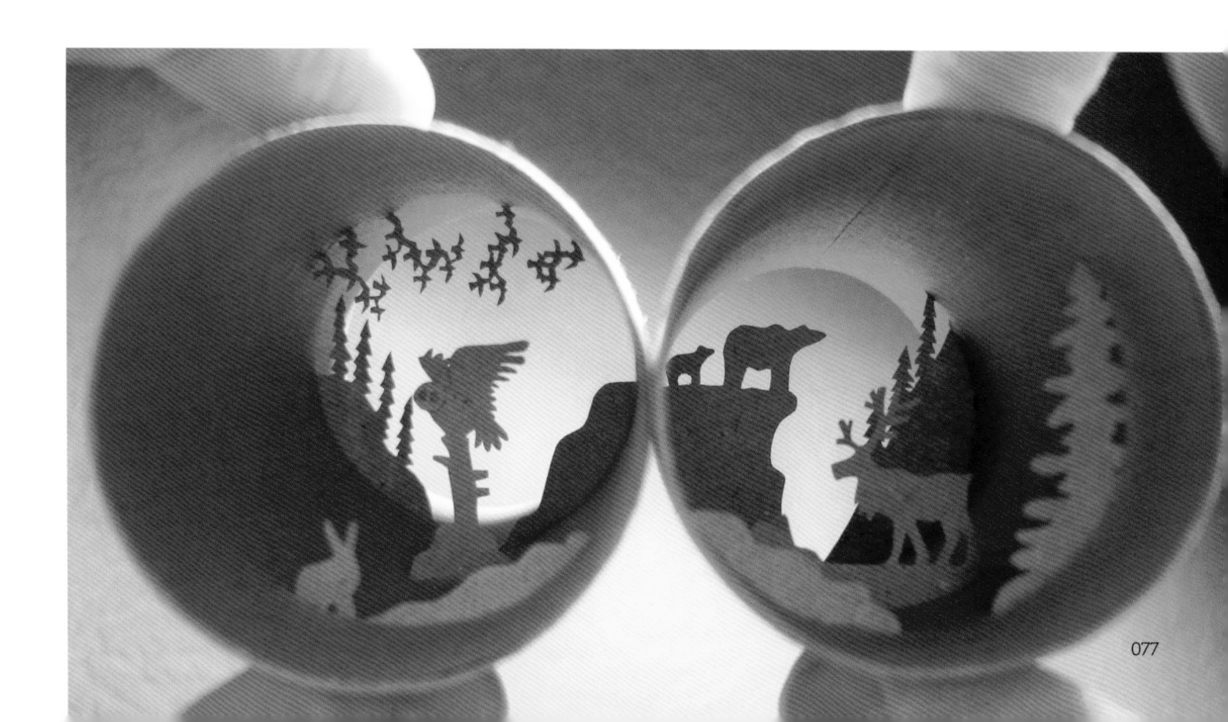

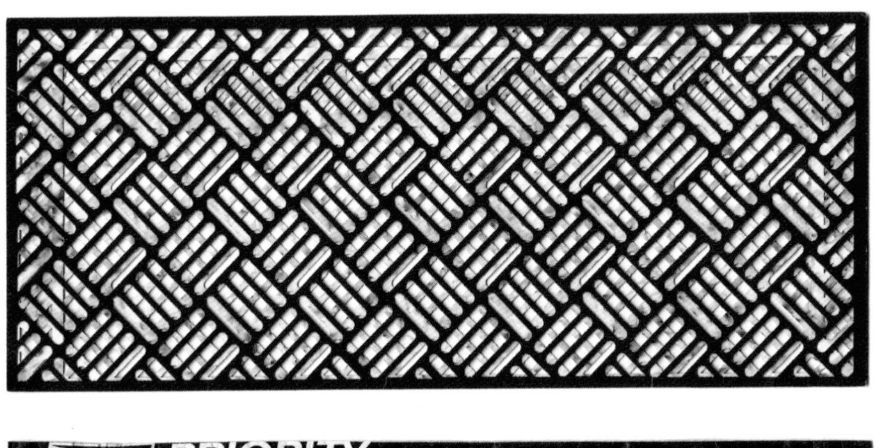

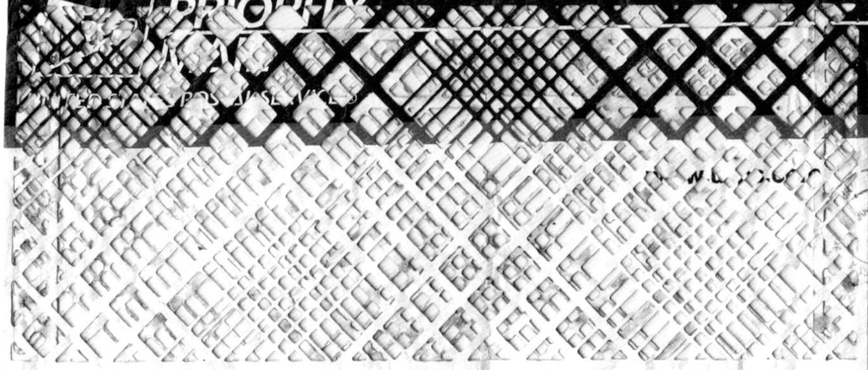

Insecurity Envelopes

Insecurity Envelopes are a series of laser-cut envelopes that are based on the patterns printed inside security envelopes.

JONATHAN KELLER-CAA
39221 WOODWARD AVE
BOX 801
BLOOMFIELD HILLS 48304
37 USA
37 USA
37 USA
KEETRA DIXON
PO BOX 1632
BIRMINGHAM MI 48012-1632

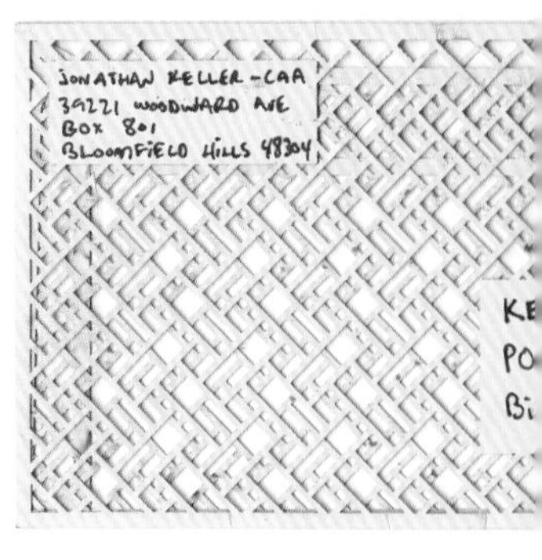
JONATHAN KELLER-CAA
39221 WOODWARD AVE
BOX 801
BLOOMFIELD HILLS 48304

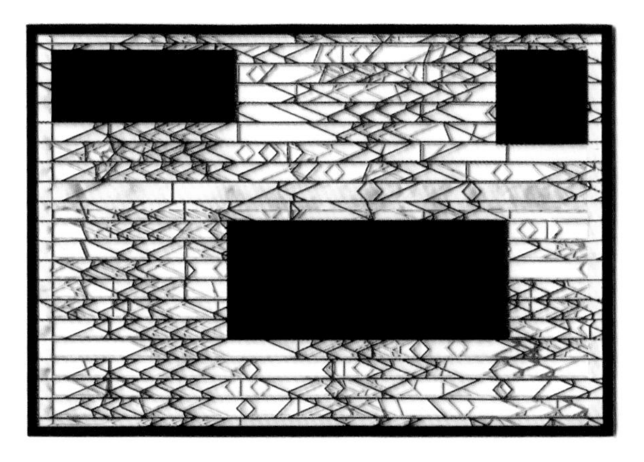

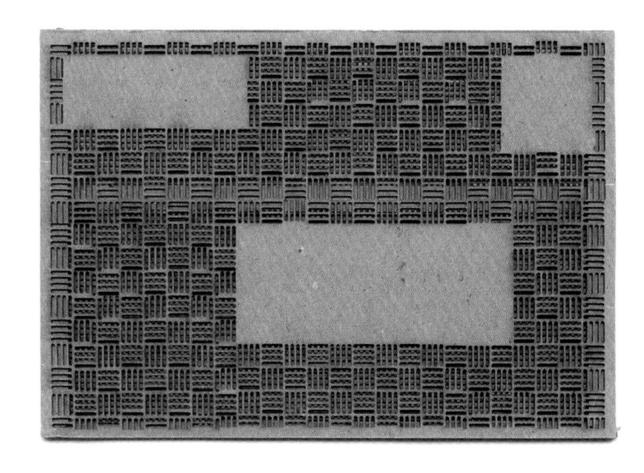

"Les Robes Géographiques"

"Les Robes Géographiques" started as a series of studies and sketches in 2002. As a cartographer, Lecourt depicts maps to understand the world we live in; Lecourt forces the maps to take the shapes of clothing, representing the wearer's habitat and identity, forming an intimate connection with the wearer. Within Les Robes Géographiques Lecourt uses maps forming clothes and garments as a rubbing of the body and soul. It's a continuation of personal thoughts found throughout her work, which she creates using a range of materials to provoke and extract emotions.

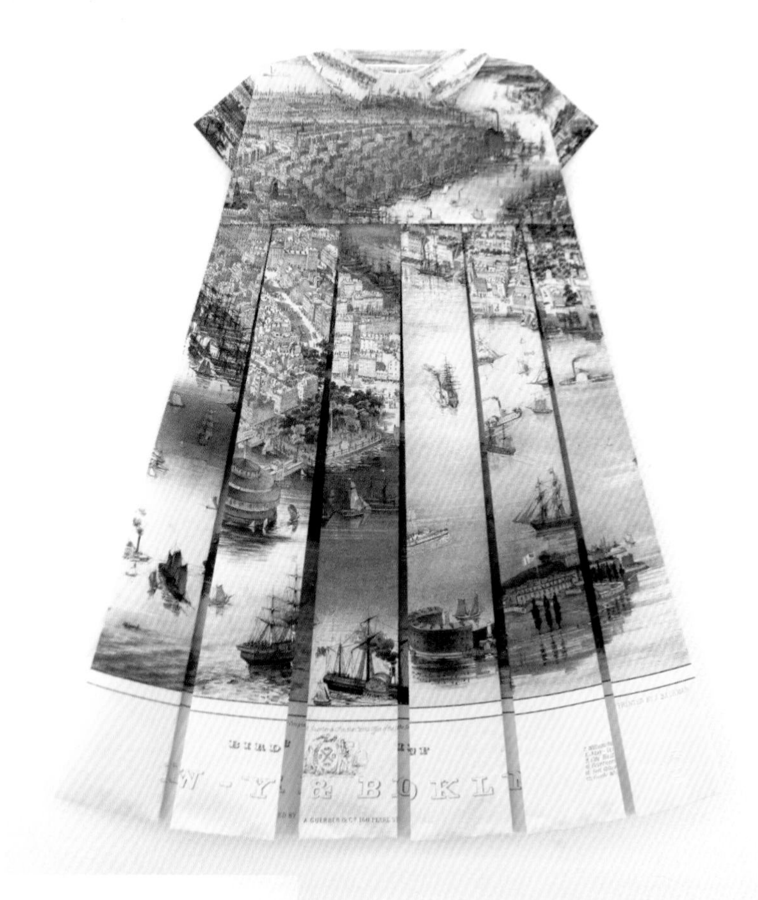

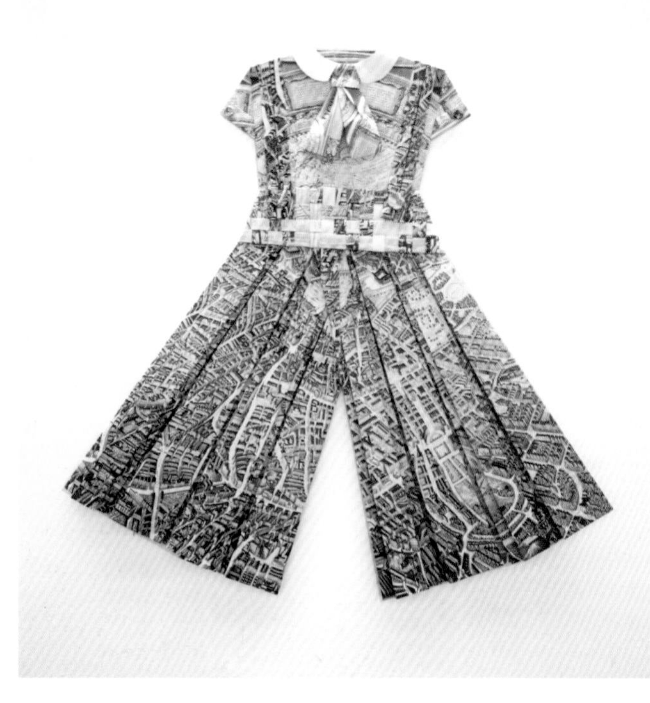

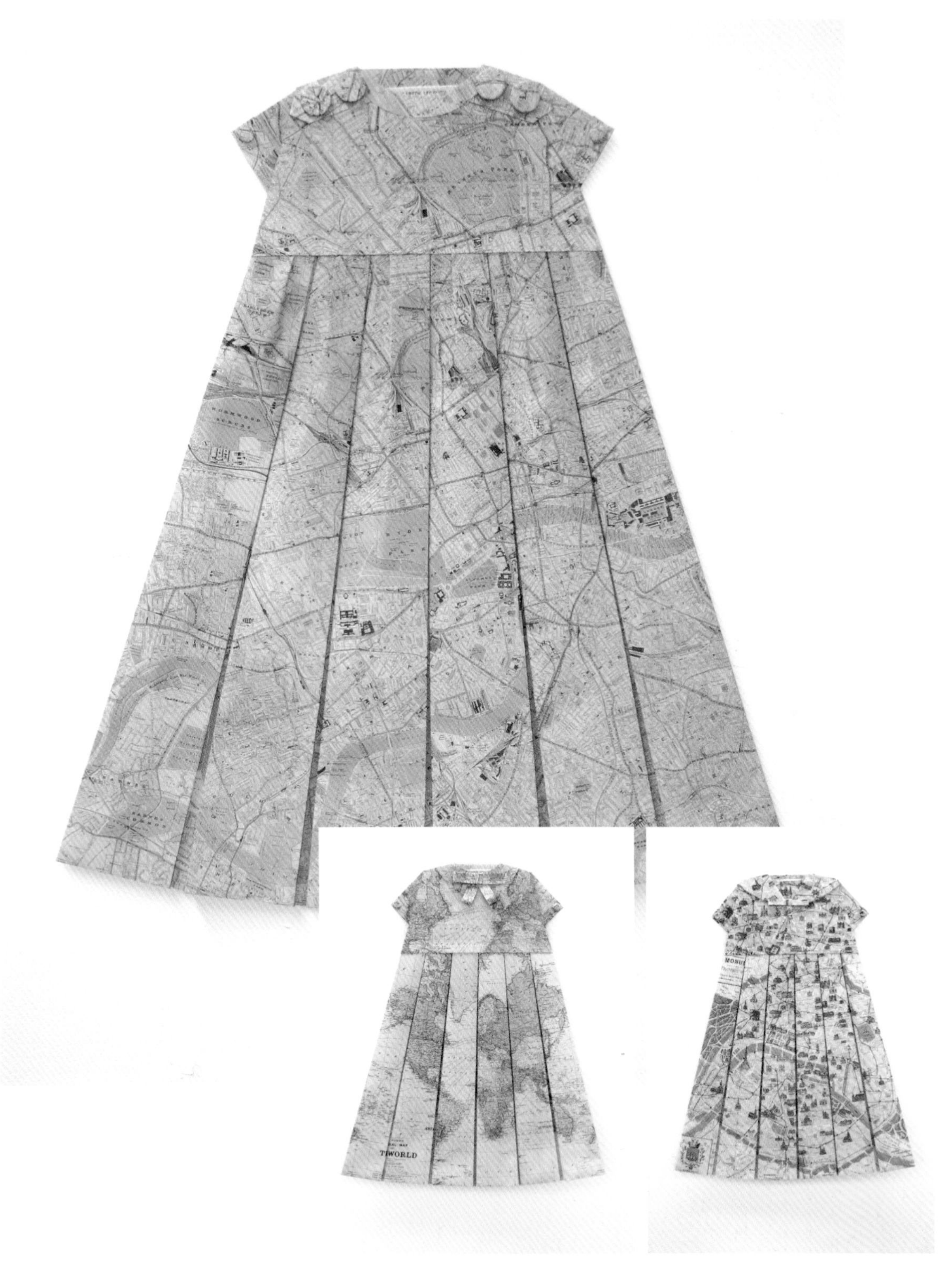

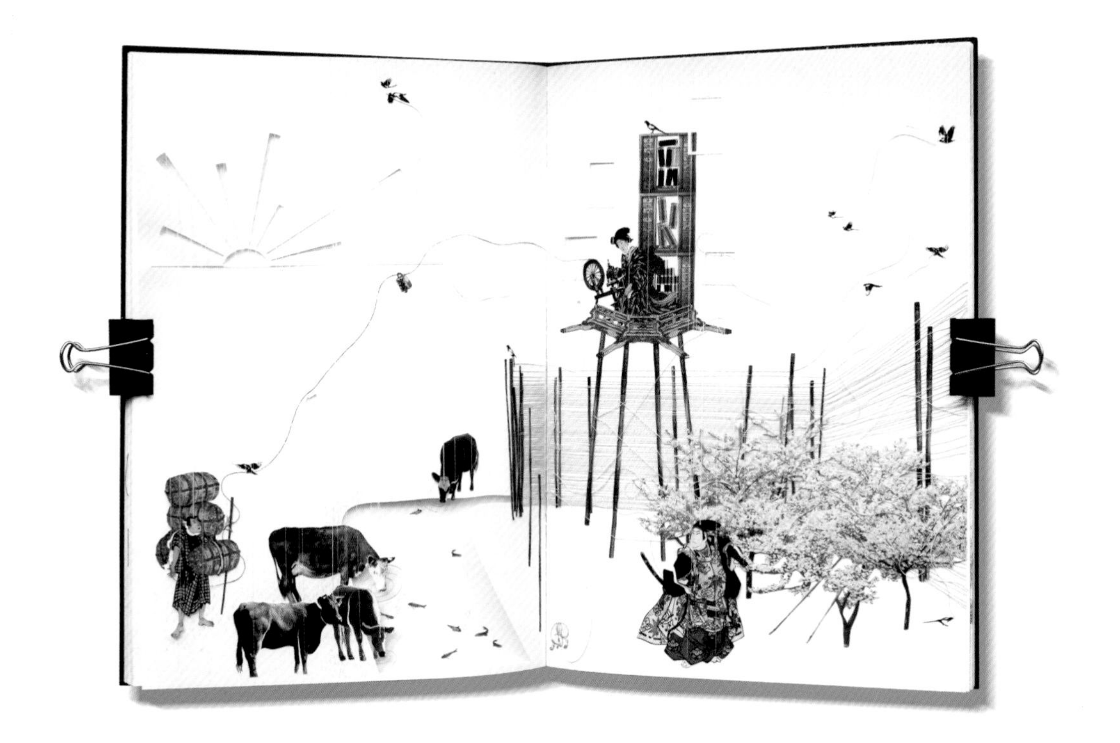

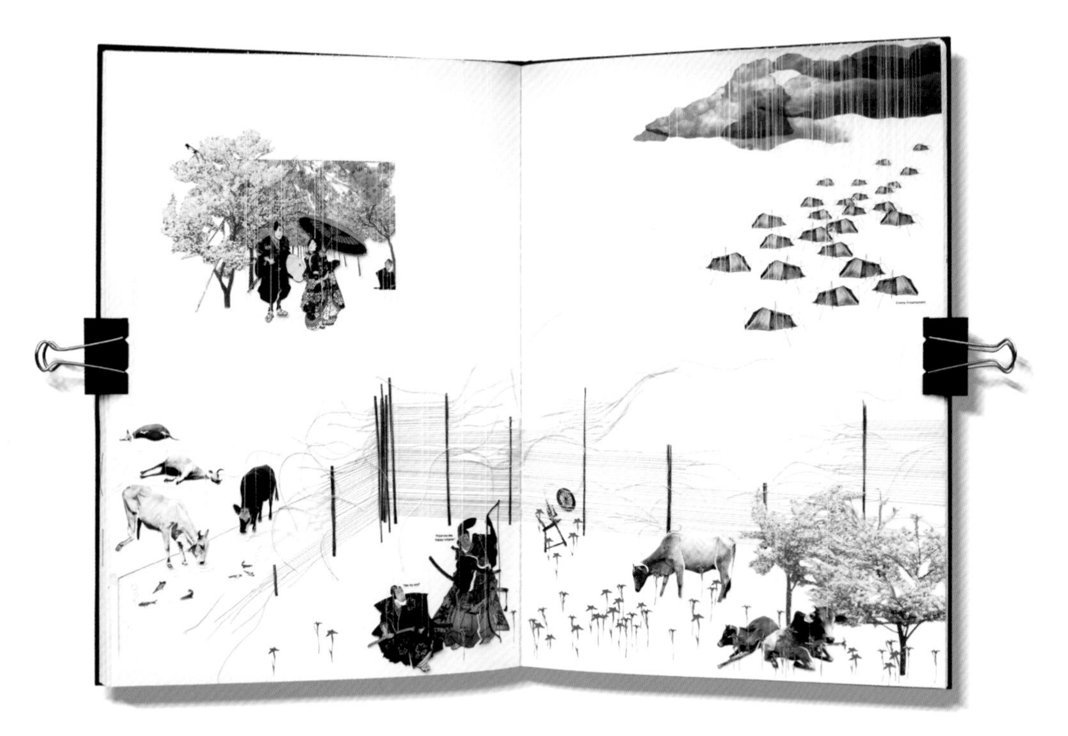

The Emperor's Castle

The Emperor's Castle originates from a mythical and ancient tale hidden within a woodblock landscape scene created by Japanese Ukiyo-e printmaker, Ando Hiroshige. This tale charts the story of two star-crossed lovers, the weaving Princess and the Cowherd, who have been separated by the Princess's father, the Emperor. These characters have been replaced and transformed into architectonic metaphors that create an urban theatre within the grounds of the Imperial Palace in central Tokyo. This piece of narrative architecture was the vehicle to examine current day cultural and social issues in Japan such as unconditional piety, relentless work ethic, and conservative attitudes towards love. The aim of the Emperor's Castle was to provoke thought but never patronise or attempt to solve all the world's problems.

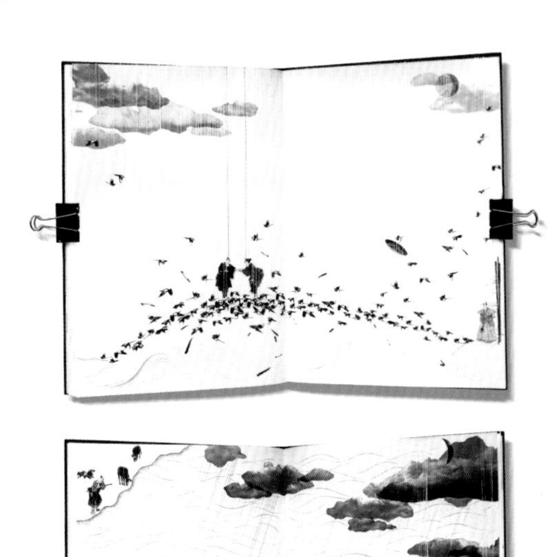

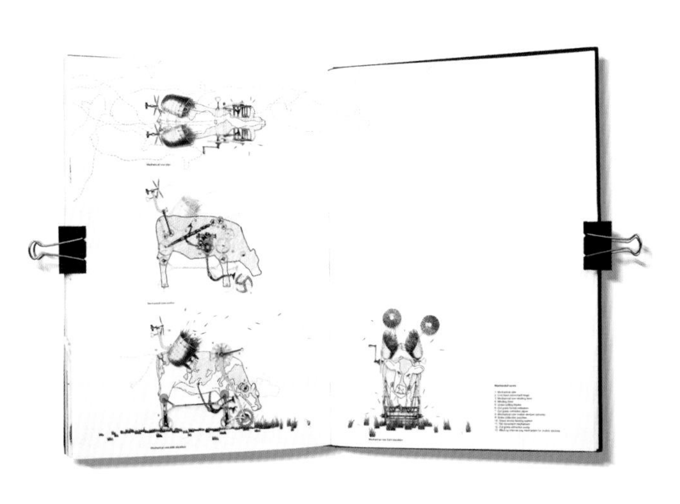

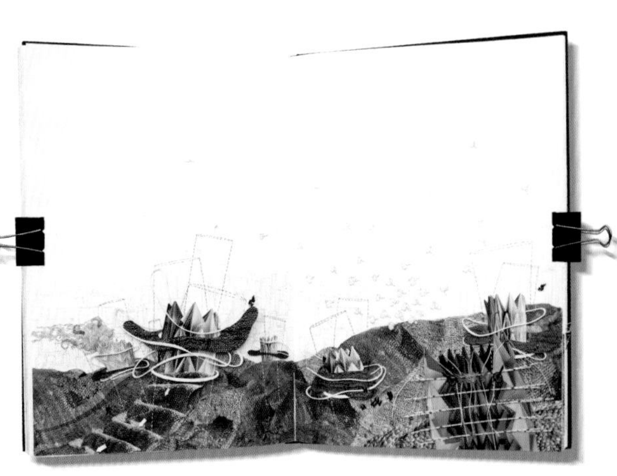

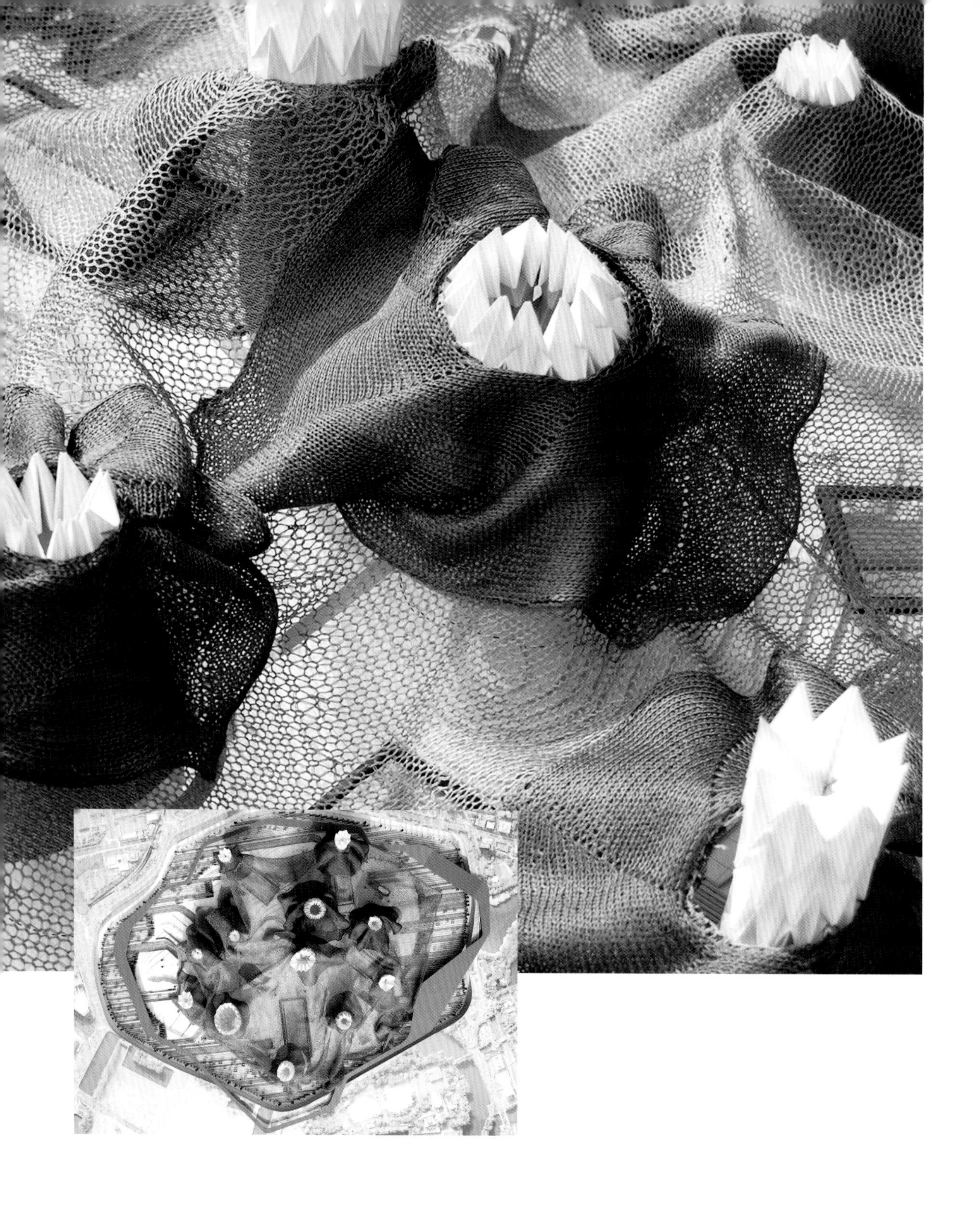

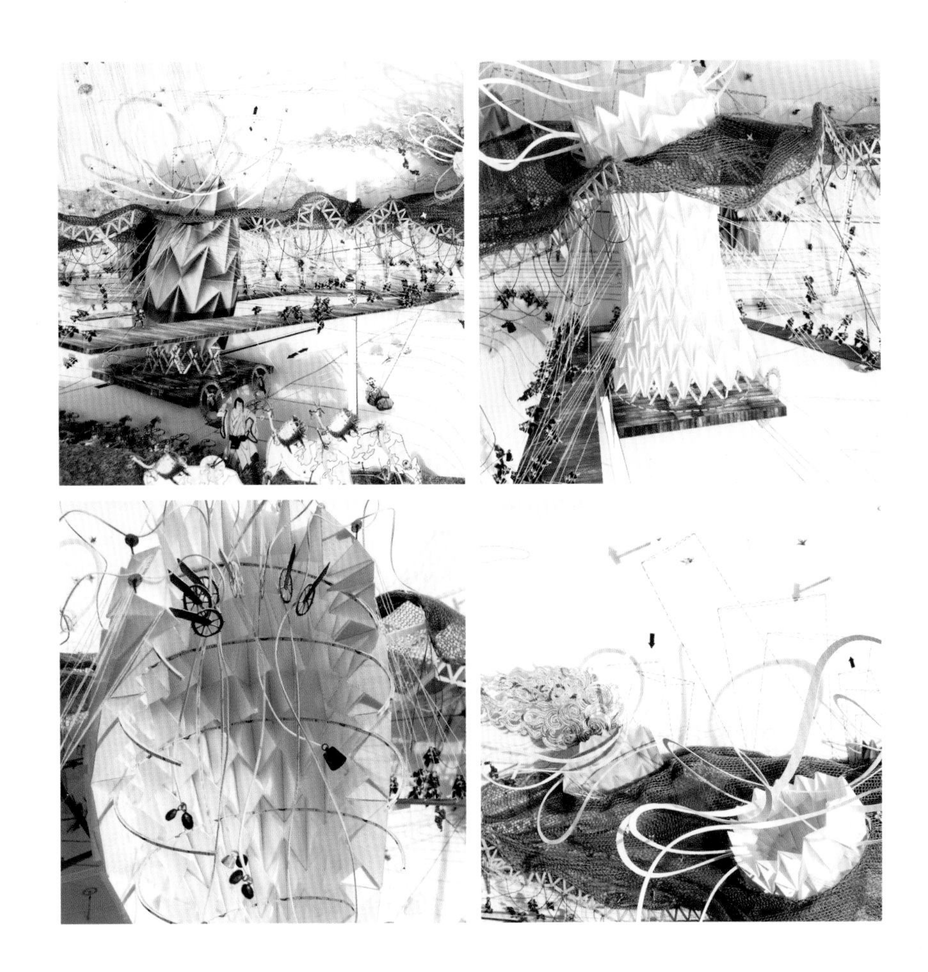

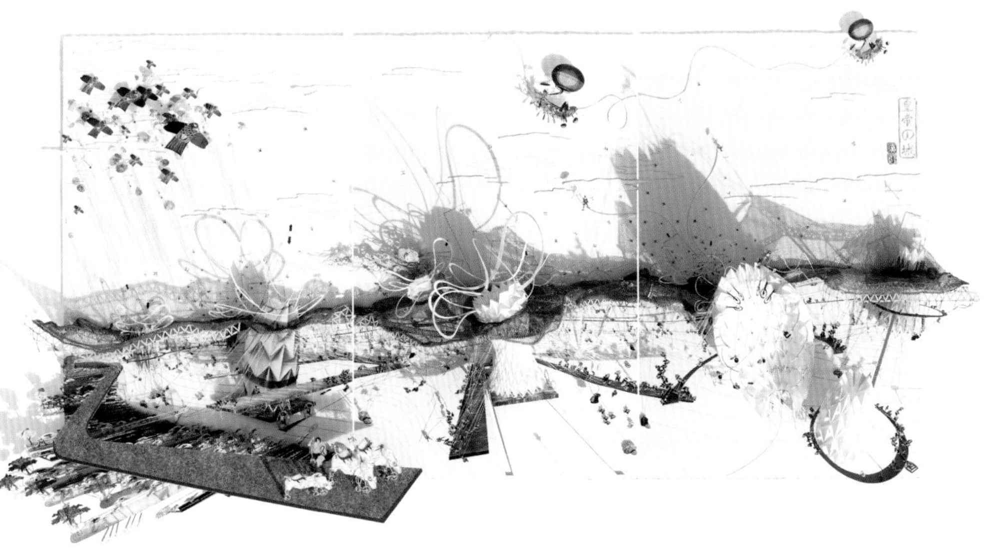

Architect Thomas Hillier Photographer Thomas Hillier

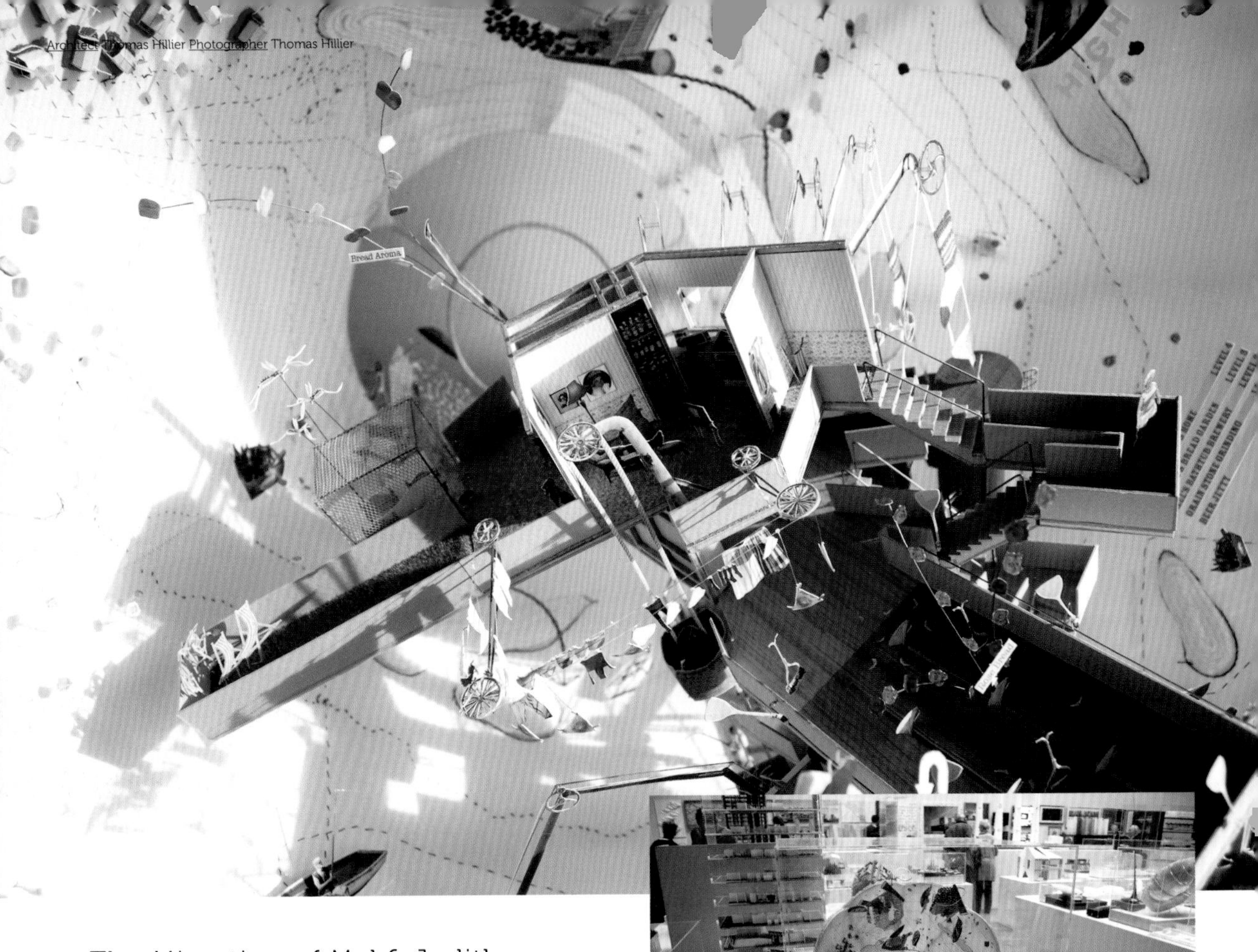

The Migration of Mel & Judith

This architecture tells the story of a couple, Mel & Judith. Becoming bored with Europe, Mel & Judith eventually decide to settle down to a new life in Luxor, Egypt. They now live on a small, uninhabited island situated on the River Nile, where in their weird and wonderful 'Do-It-Yourself' English manor Mel brews beer in his bathtub brewery while Judith bakes rose-bread in the bread-garden. Their island comes alive during the holiday season creating an English retreat in the middle of Luxor, a retreat that lures in English tourists with the opportunity to be surrounded by the sights, sounds and smells of home. The smell of roses and freshly baked bread drifts through the air while the temptation to drink beer (which is illegal in Luxor) is impossible to resist. So if you are ever in Luxor and miss the familiarity of home, take a rowboat over to Mel and Judith's island for a little piece of England. The architecture is created and built for the specific needs and functions of the two users, not for its aesthetic appeal. The scheme aims to be beautiful in its ugliness, a building with a sustainable lifecycle that allows Mel & Judith to 'live off the land'.

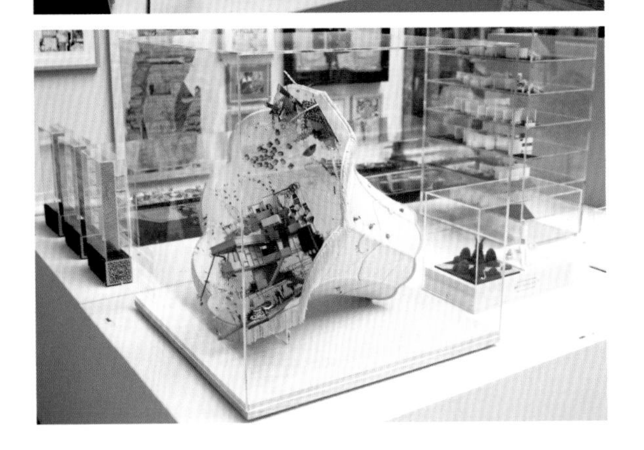

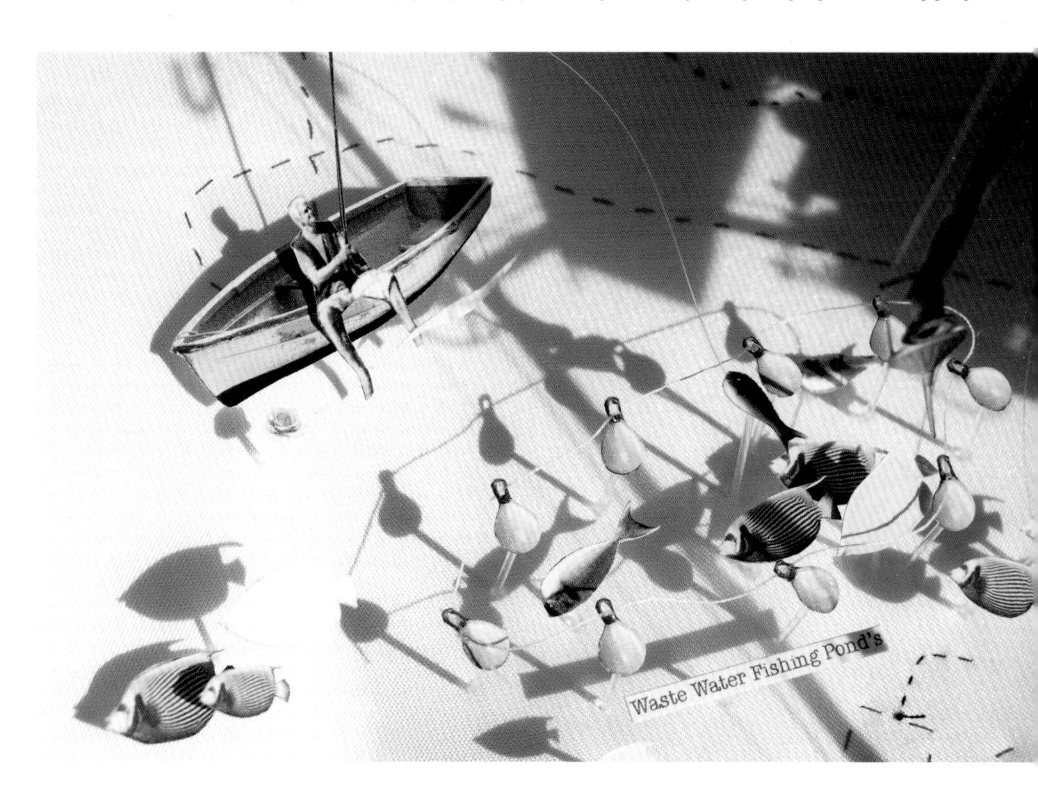
Waste Water Fishing Pond's

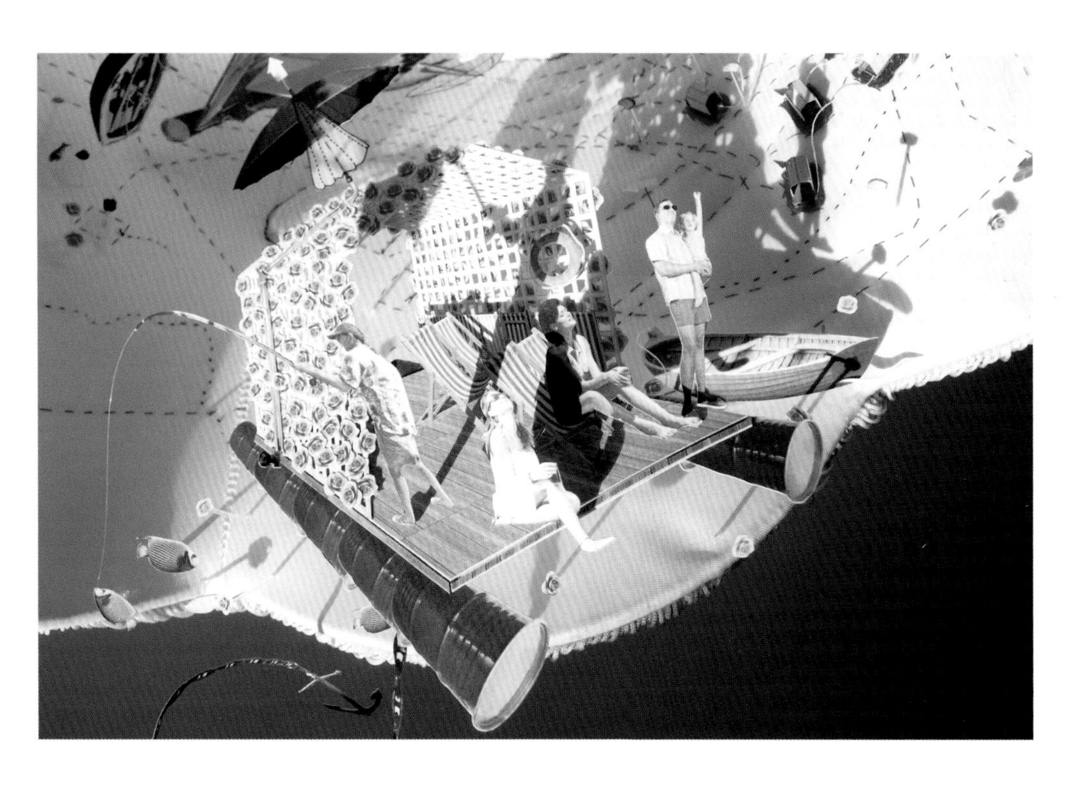

Artist Laura Cooperman

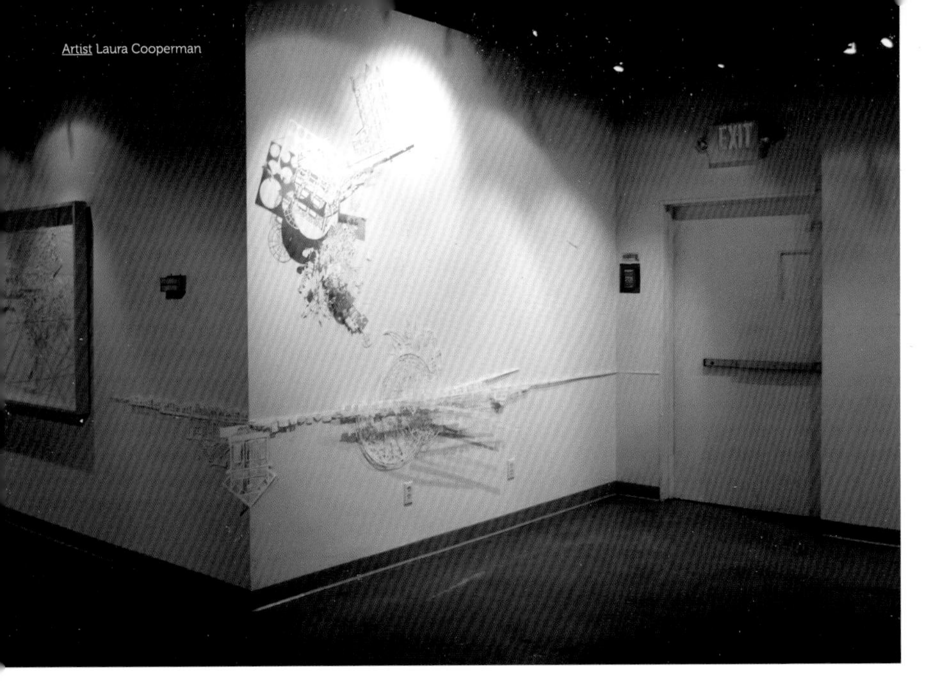

Multiple Art Works

Through the use of intricate layered paper cut outs, I investigate our associations with the built environment. My work refers to a fluid space where personal, geographical, and physical borders fluctuate to challenge one's definition of place, origin, and ownership. My mechanical pieces emerged after a period of time spent in Cedar Key, Florida where after listening to the mechanistic voice on the weather radio describing the timing of the tides, I began to incorporate gears in my work to express motion and thus the passage of time. I further explored the theme of time in Beijing as I watched the tearing down of historic Hutong neighborhoods and the erection of skyscrapers to present the face of progress in time for the 2008 Olympics. At the same time, I continually heard the sound of fireworks celebrating the Chinese New Year. I associated the sounds of demolition and construction with the fireworks and expressed them as explosions amidst symbols of modernity in my work.

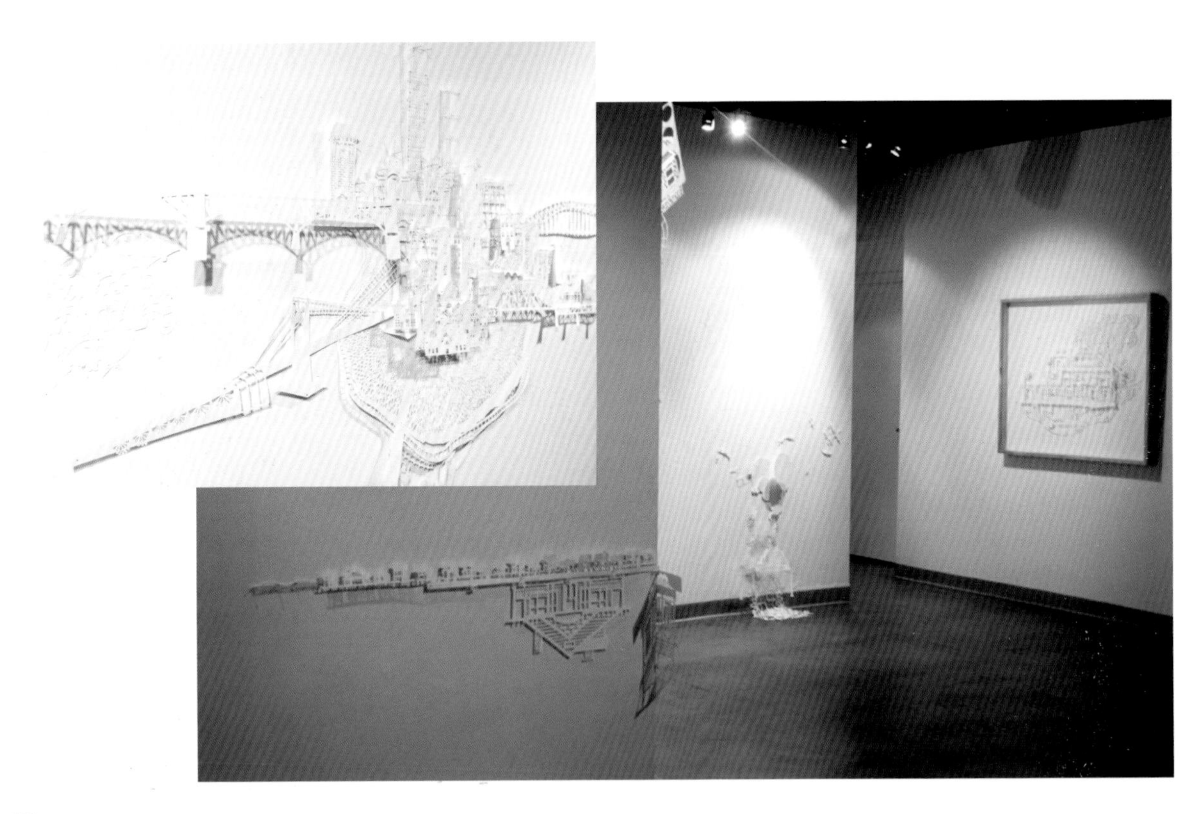

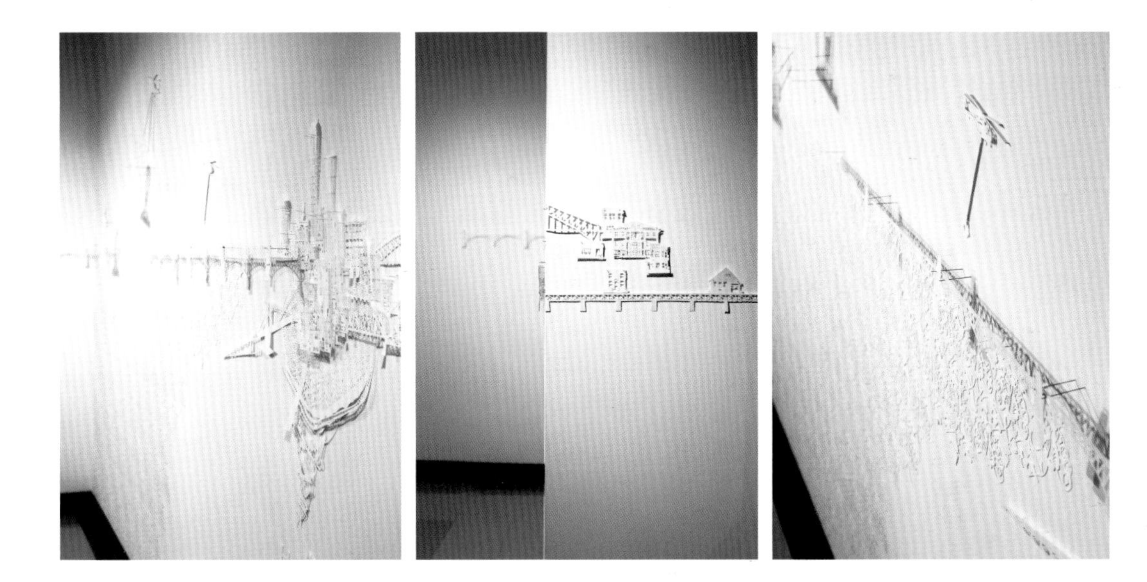

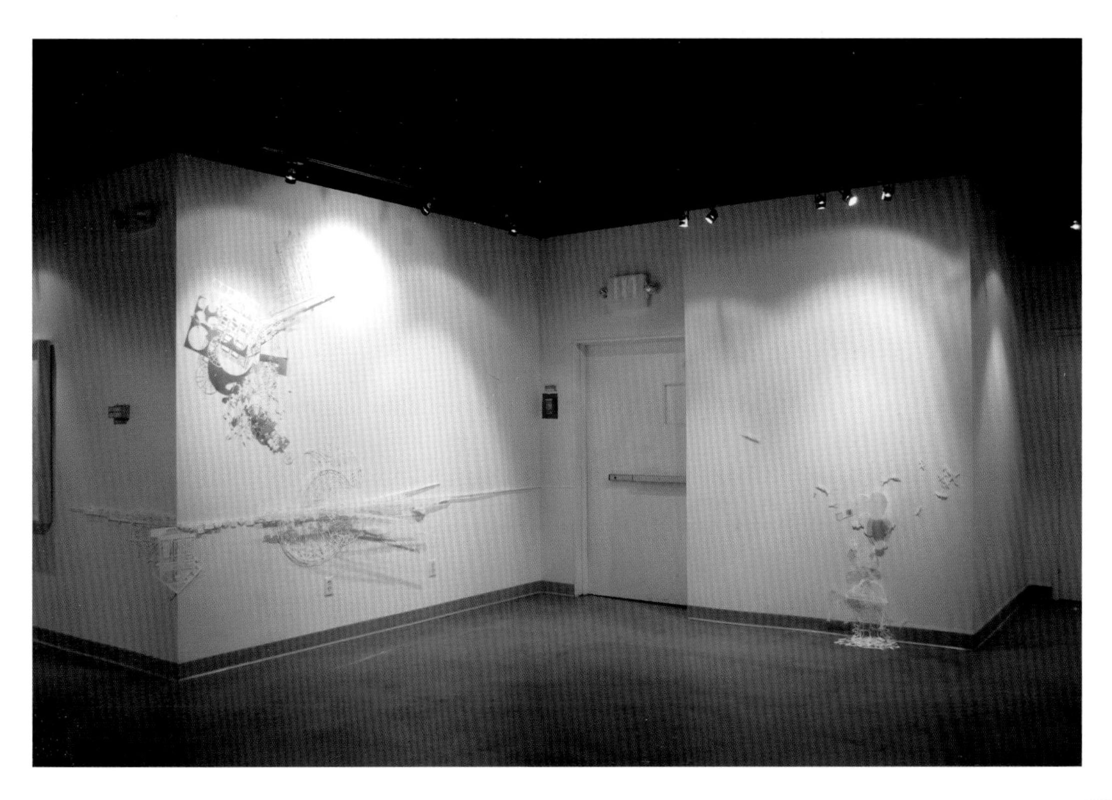

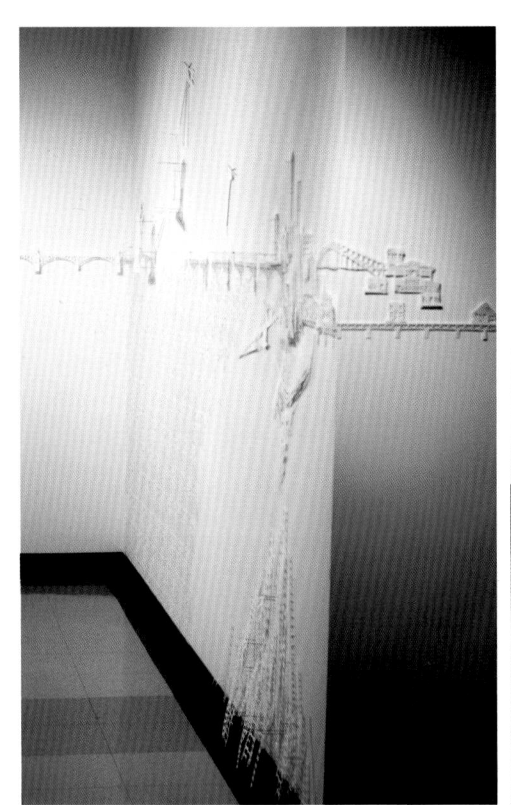

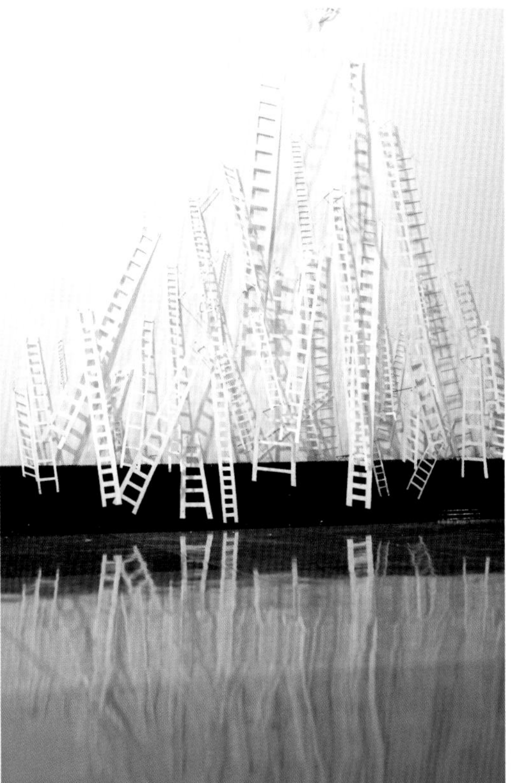

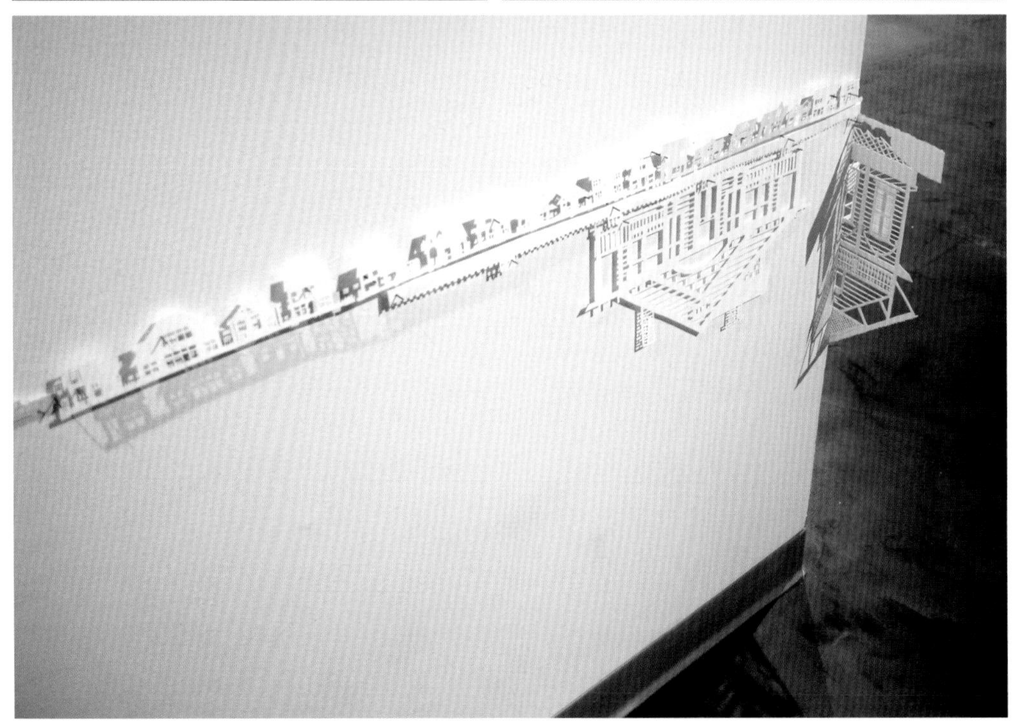

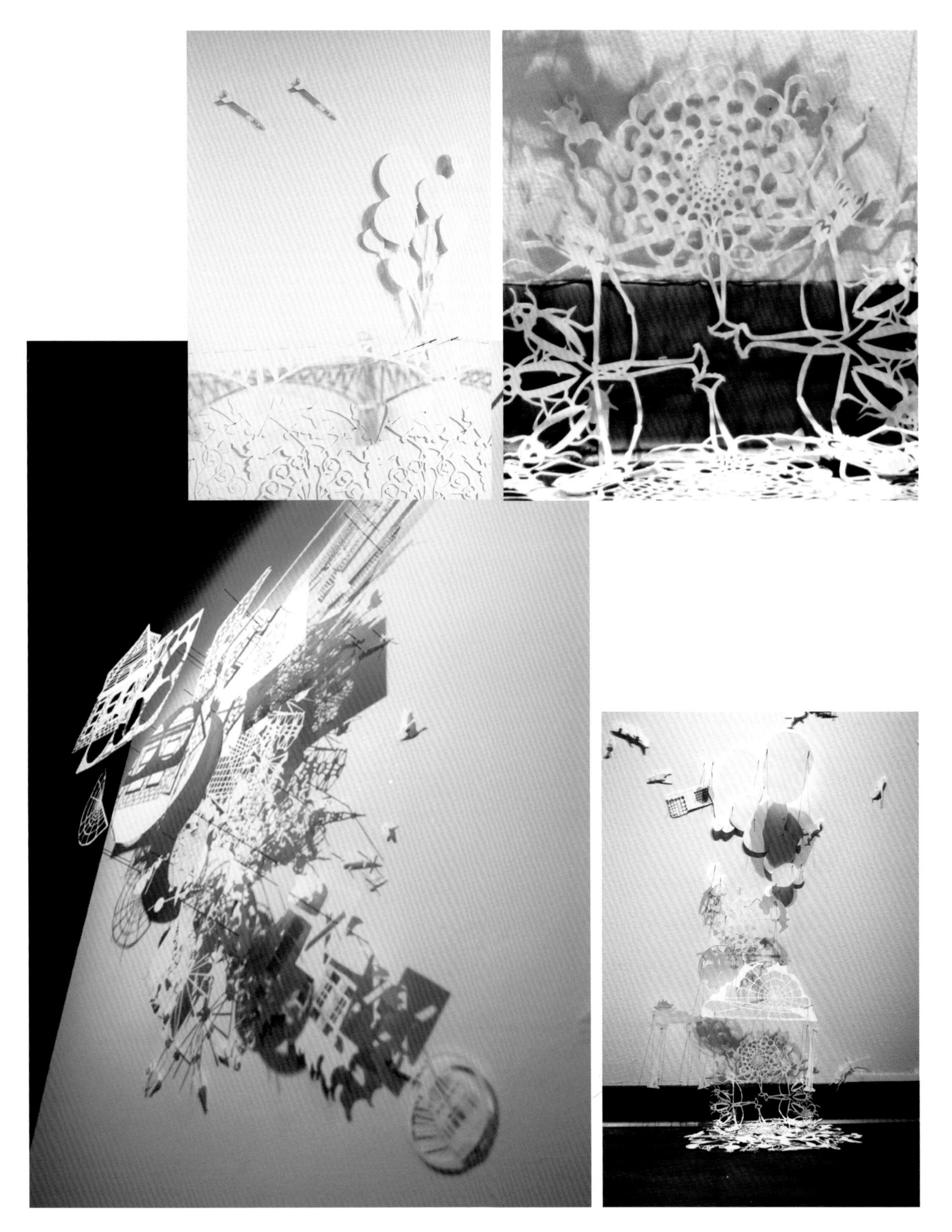

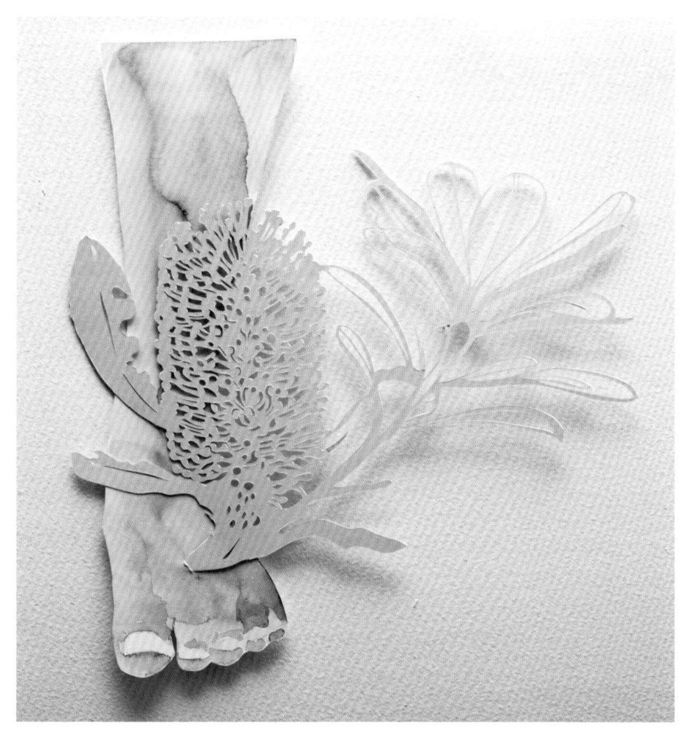

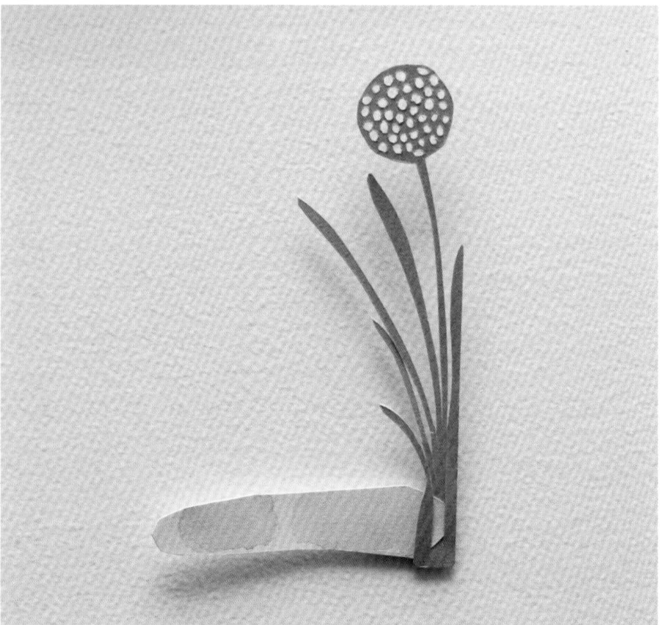

The Bush has ceased to weep, and when she smiles, she is a mistress not to be denied

This self-portrait completes a cycle of semi-self portraits I have made over the past two years. I now realize the piece is a critical self-examination of the theme "homecoming." I finished this piece thinking of the following passage from Roberto Calasso's The Marriage of Cadmus and Harmony:

A Maenad had a fawn tattooed on her soft, bare right arm. She was breast-feeding a fawn, stroking and playing with it. Then she grabbed it, tore it to pieces, and sank her teeth into the still pulsing flesh. Why this sequence? And why must this sequence forever take the form of a sudden raptus, when really it was a ceremony? ... Altarless, she wandered through the trees. Dismembering the fawn, the Maenad dismembered herself, possessed by the god. Hence, in devouring the fawn she devoured the god, mixed in its blood. She who was possessed thus tried herself to possess a part of the god. But what happened afterward? A great silence. The sultry heat of the woods. Strips of bleeding flesh glimpsed through the leaves. The god wasn't there. Life – incomprehensible, opaque.

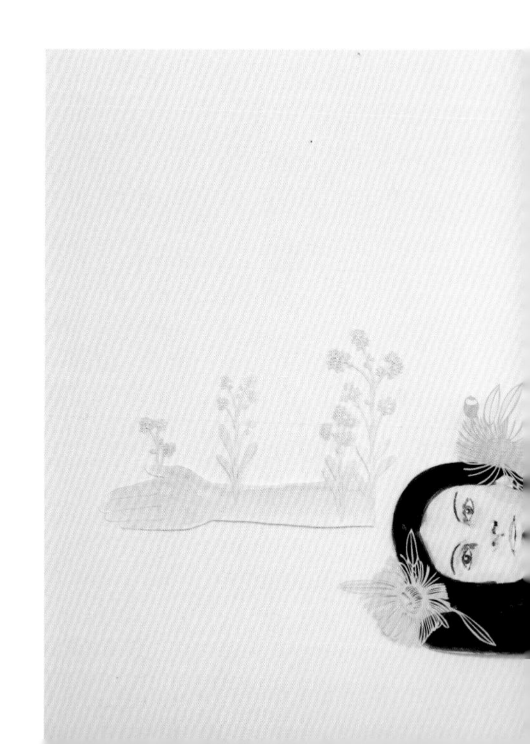

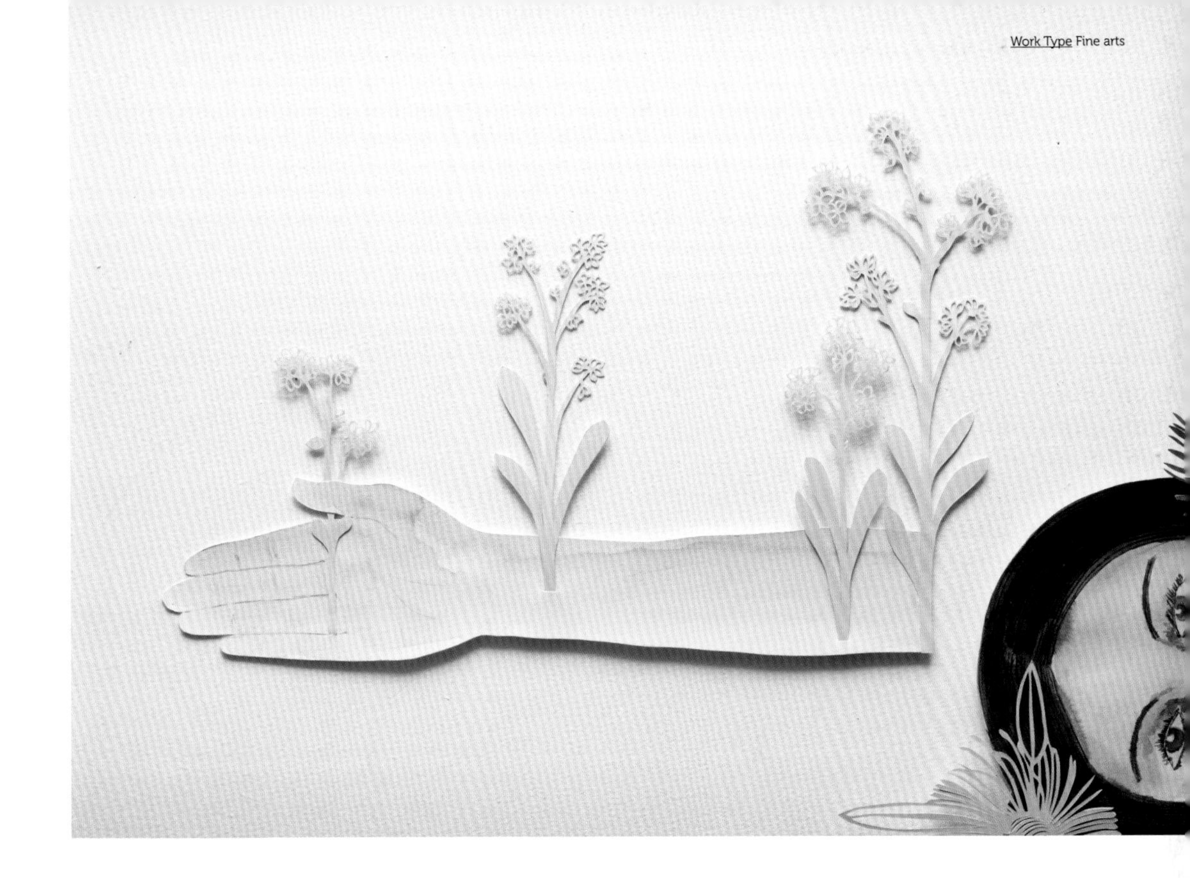

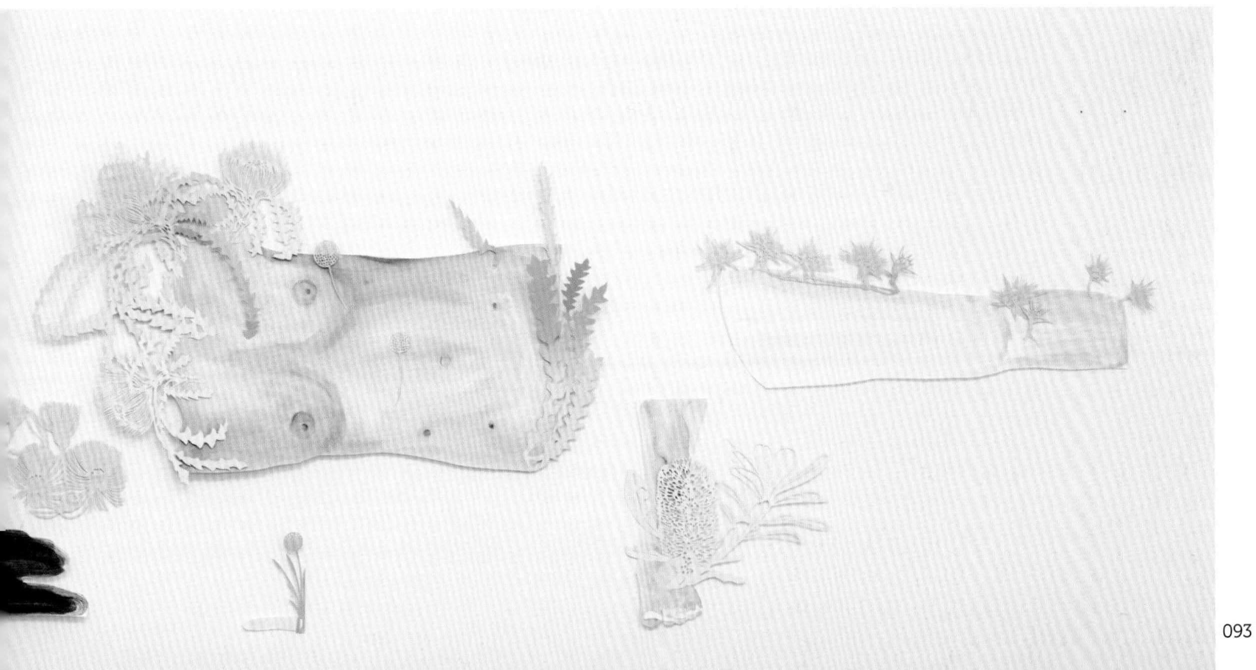

Artist Peter Callesen Photographer 1, 2, 3, 8, 9, 15 Anders Sune Berg/ 6, 7, 13 Adam Reich

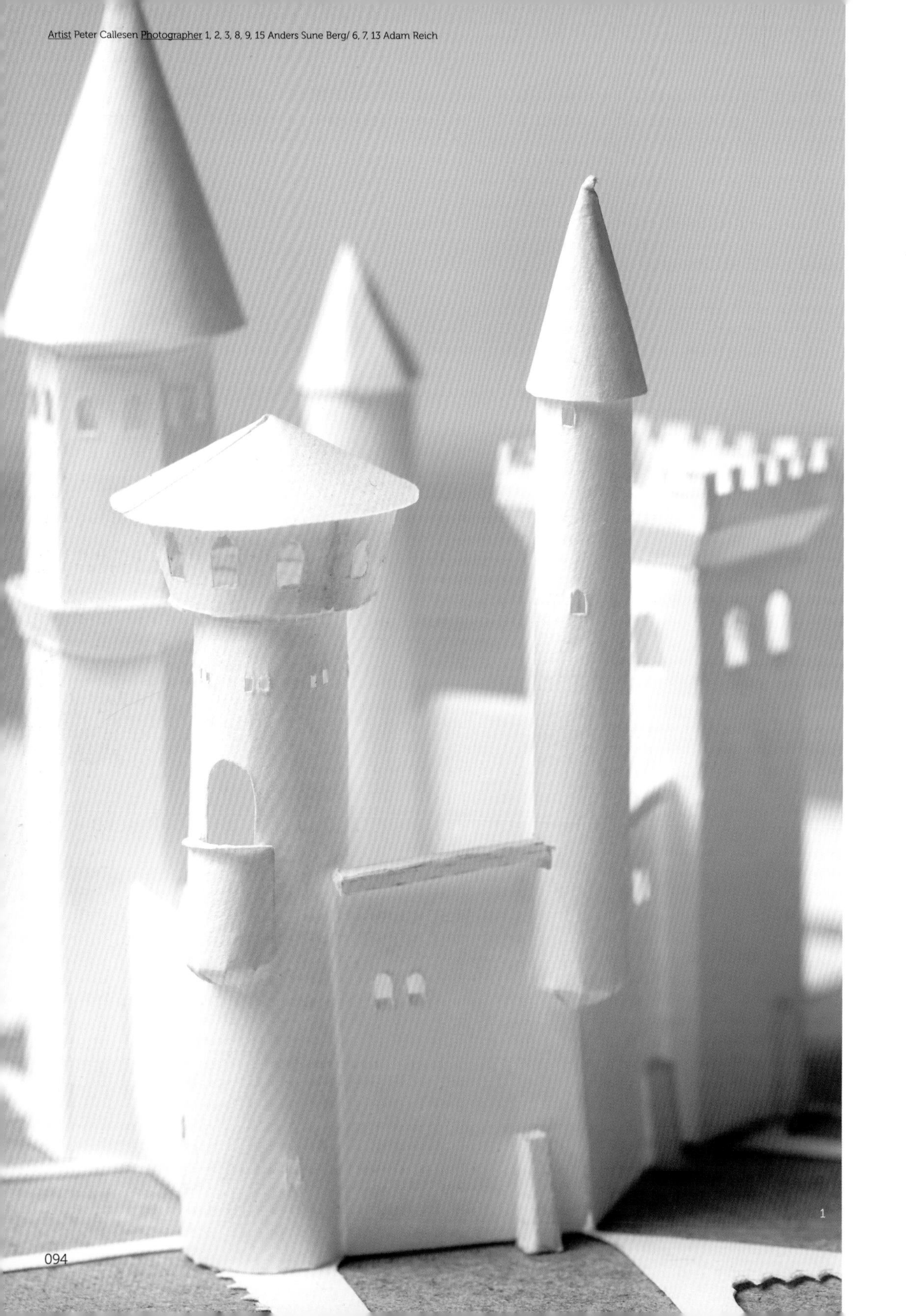

1

A4 Paper Creation

1, 2 / Impenetrable Castle
3 / Single Double Bed
4, 5 / Birds Trying to Escape their Drawing
6 / The Core of Everything
7 / Three Dead Angels
8 / Hanging Image
9 / On the Other Side
10 / Broken Flowers
11 / Cowboy
12 / Holding on to Myself
13 / Fall
14 / Looking Back
15 / Transparent God

A large part of my work is made from A4 sheets of paper. It is probably the most common and consumed media used for carrying information today. By taking away all the information and starting from scratch using the blank white A4 paper sheet for my creations, I feel I have found a material that we are all able to relate to, and at the same time the A4 paper sheet is neutral and open to fill with different meaning. The thin white paper gives the paper sculptures a frailty that underlines the tragic and romantic theme of my works. The paper cut sculptures explore the probable and magical transformation of the flat sheet of paper into figures that expand into the space surrounding them. The negative and absent 2 dimensional space left by the cut, points out the contrast to the 3 dimensional reality it creates, even though the figures still stick to their origin without the possibility of escaping. In that sense there is also an aspect of something tragic in many of the cuts.

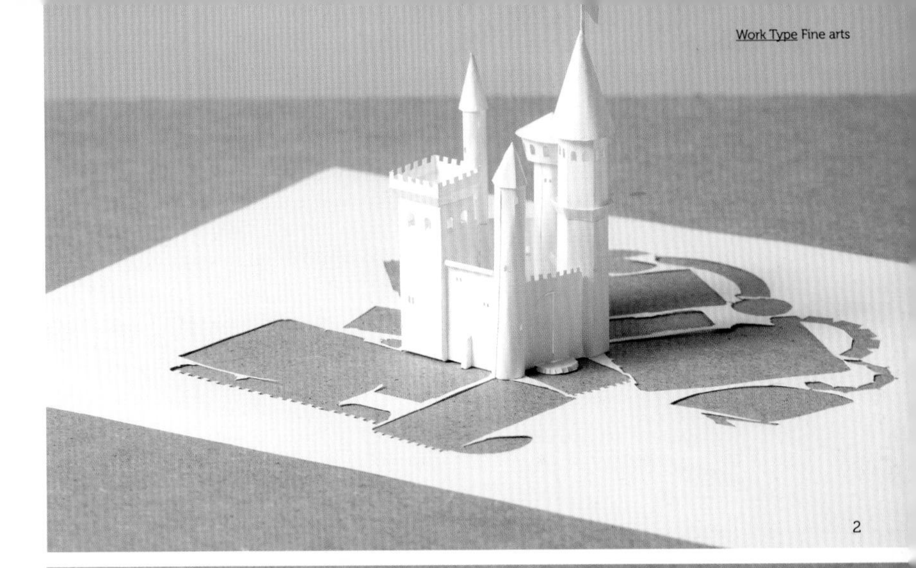

2

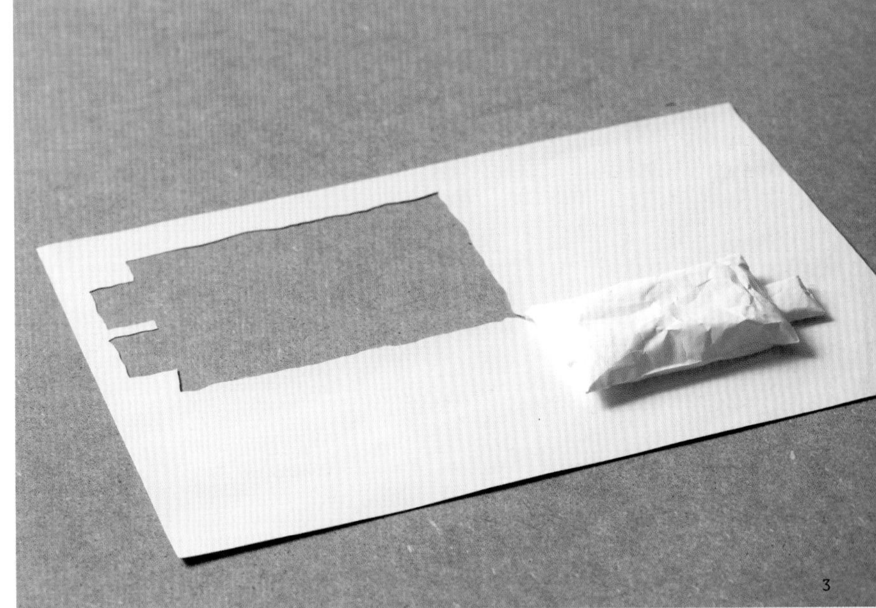

3

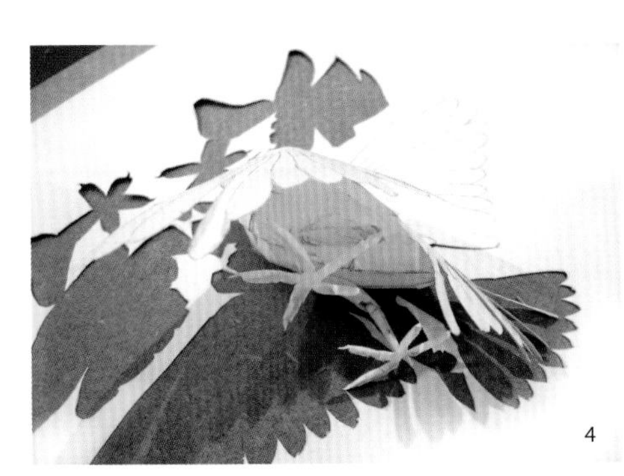

4

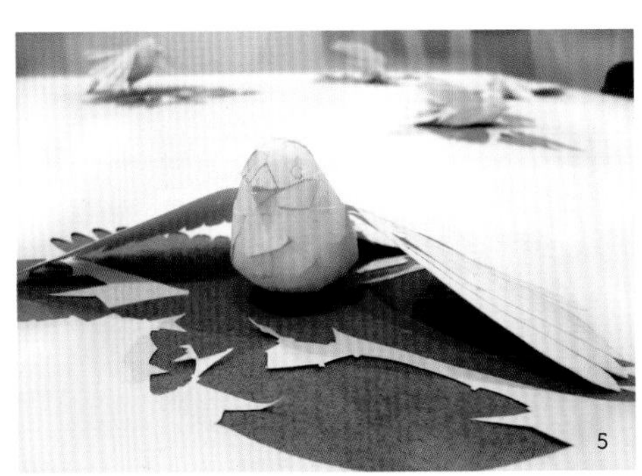

5

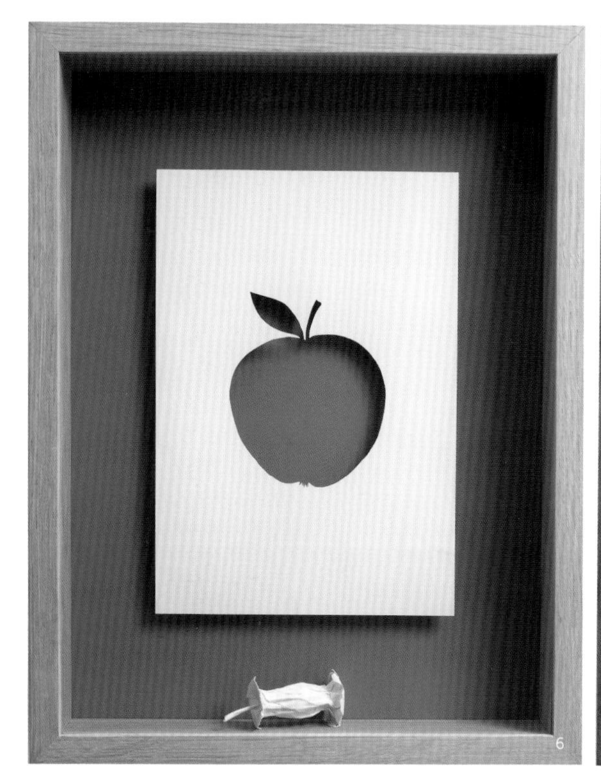

6

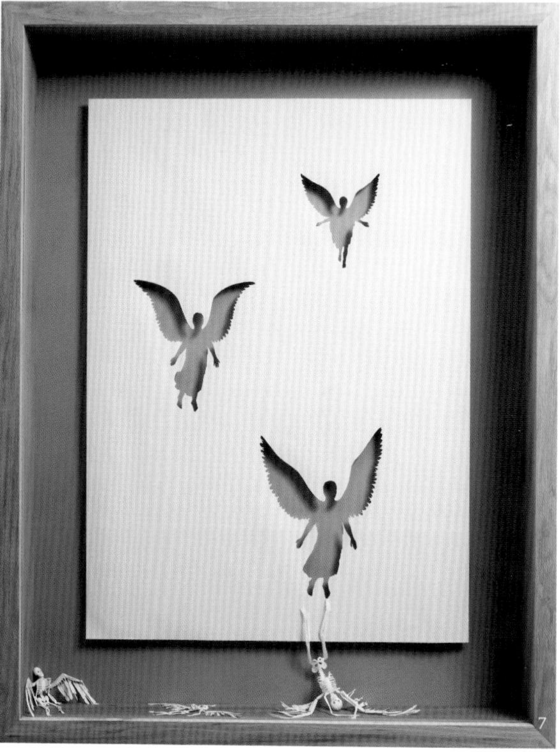

7

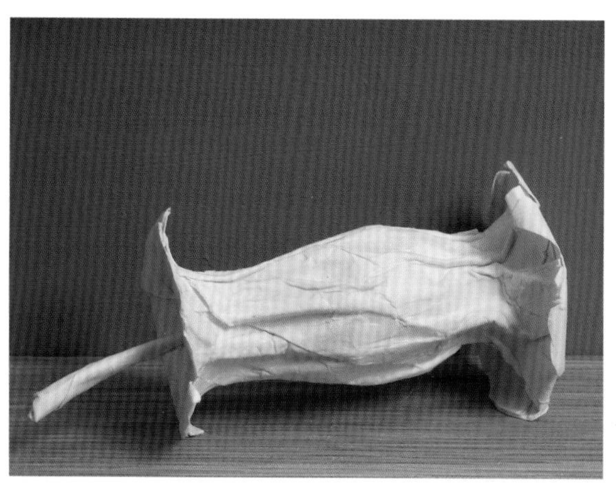

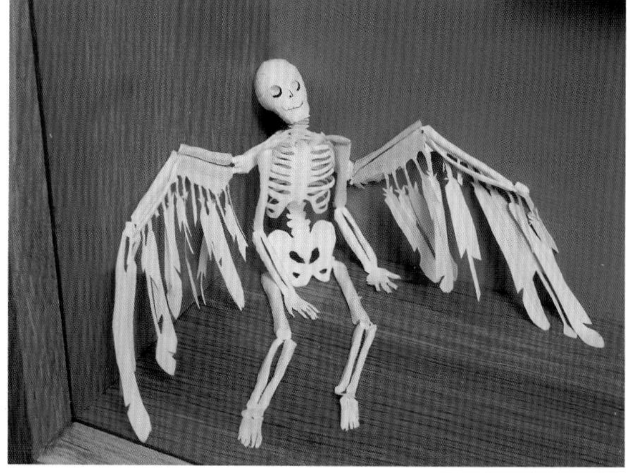

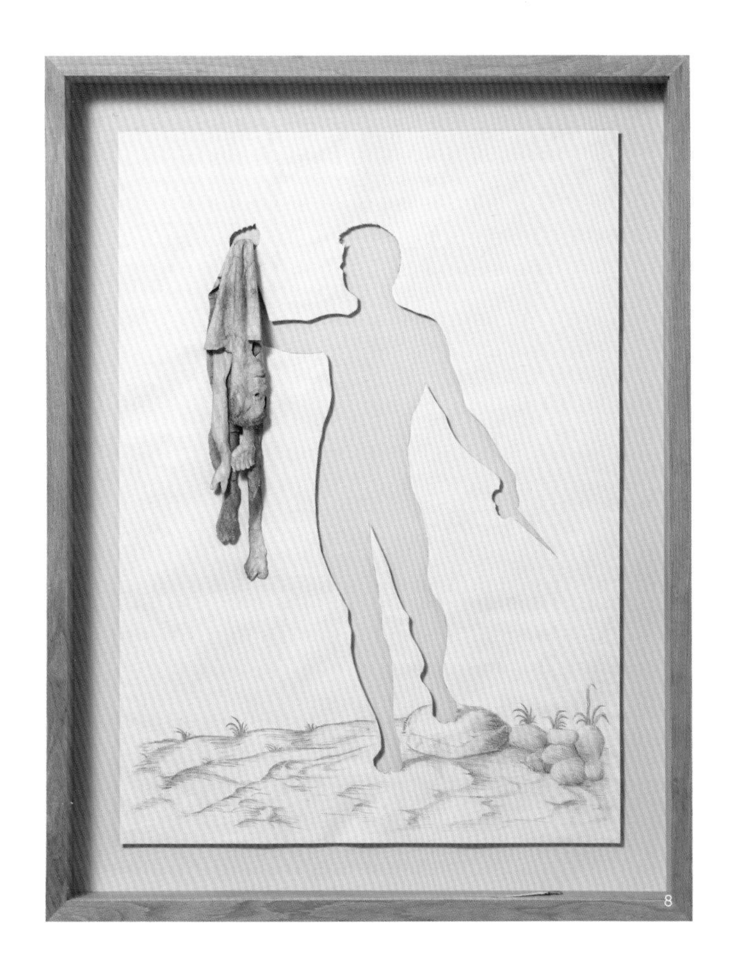

8

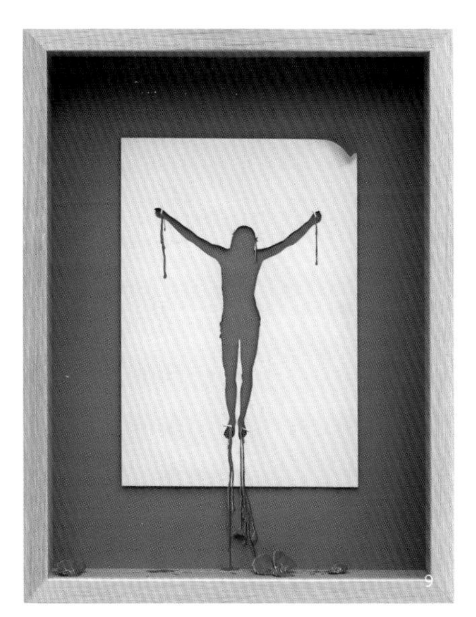

9

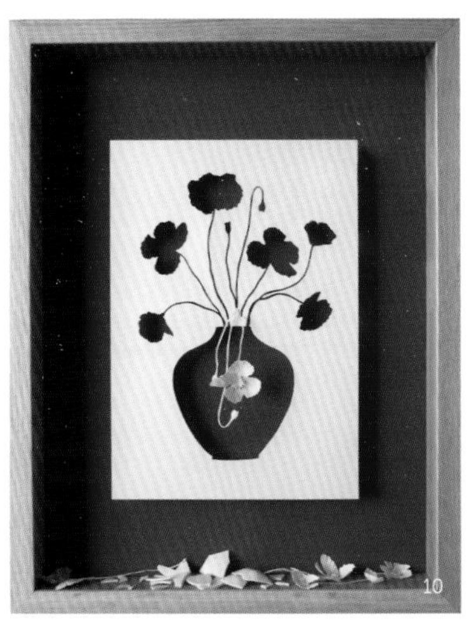

10

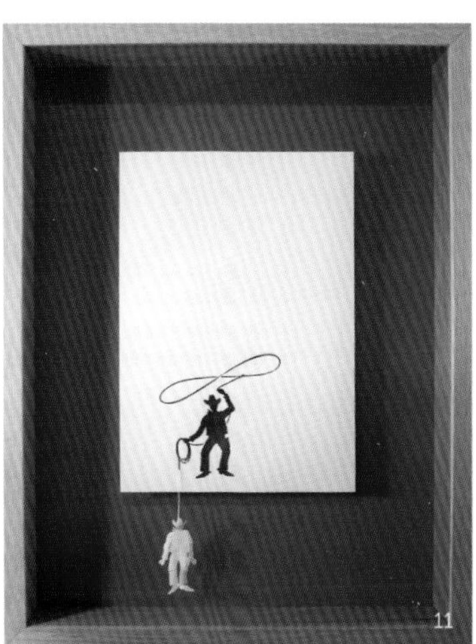

11

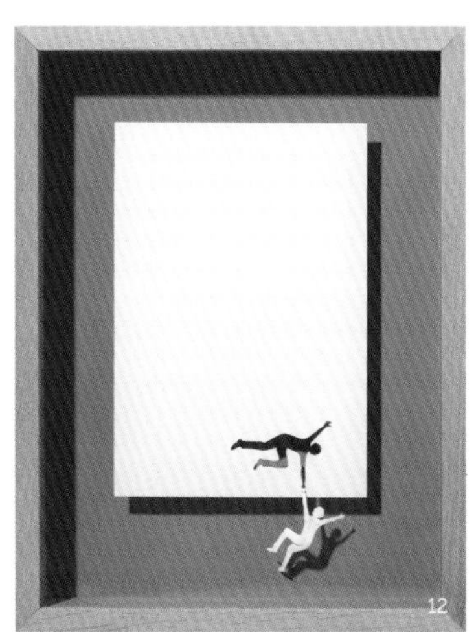

12

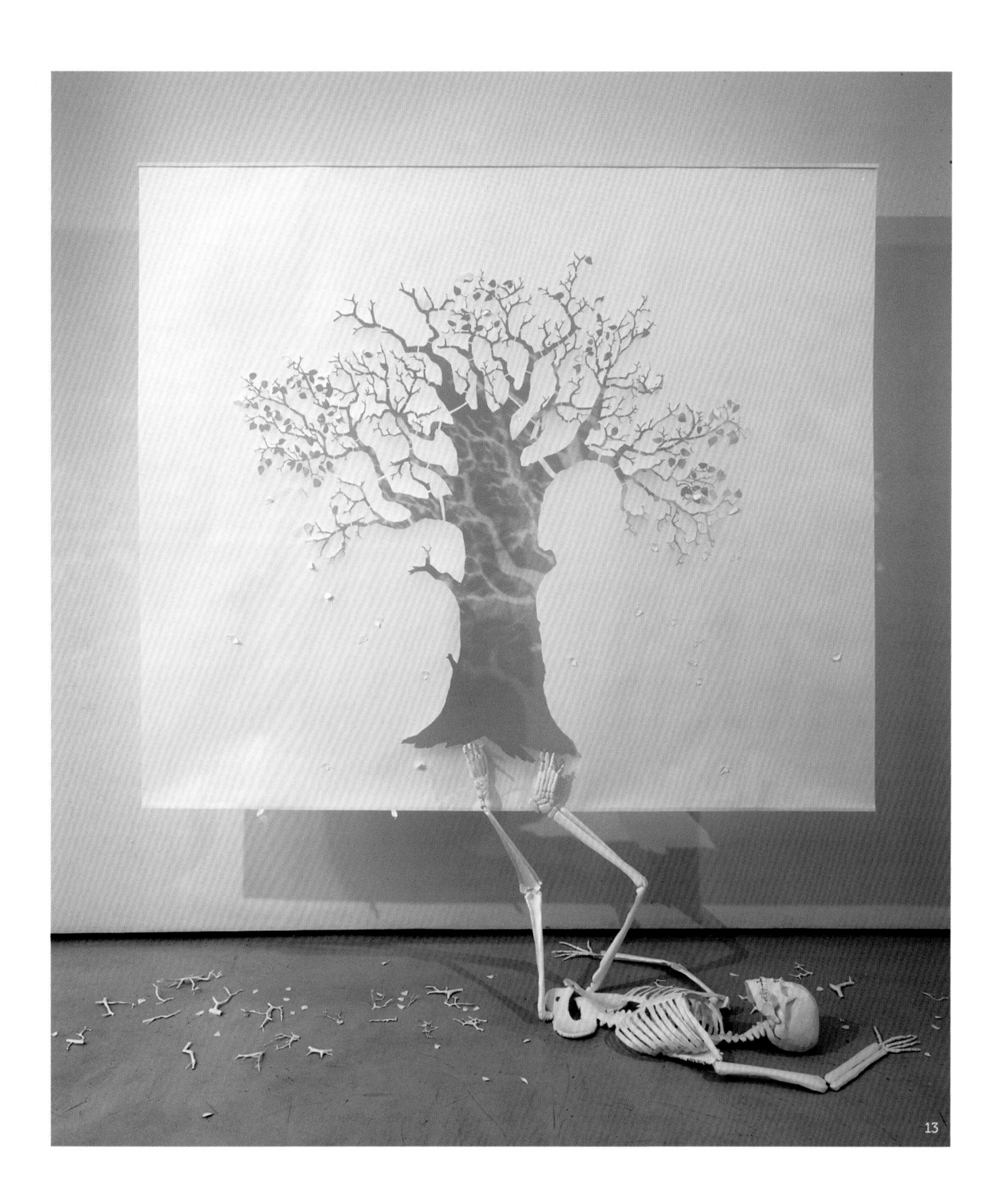
13

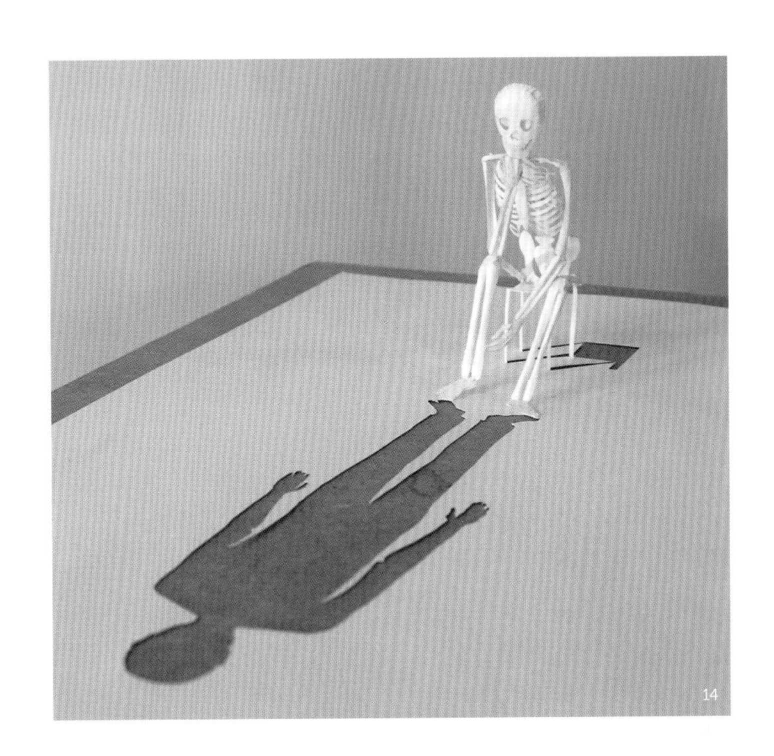
14

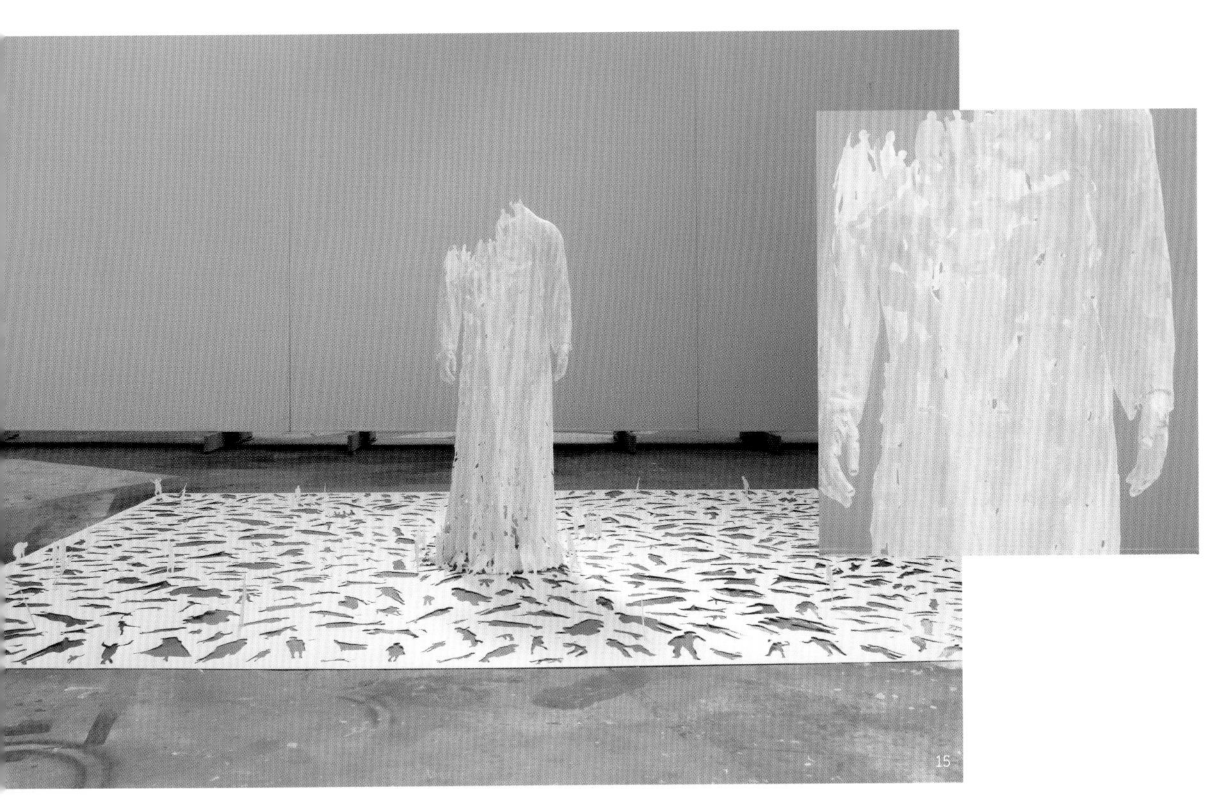
15

Paper-tattoos

1 / Mayflower
2 / Sea serpent
3 / Three sheets to the wind
4 / Panther
5 / Owl
6 / Portraits
7 / Vanitas
8 / Wounds man
9 / Anjuan skull

With the use of a traditional tattoo machine, this young Danish artist creates "Paper-tattoos" that take the craftsmanship and imagery of tattooing into a new context. To create these delicate paper works, the artist works straight on top of a special paper. With the tip of a non-inked tattoo-needle he carefully draws lines into the upper layer of the paper, disrupting the fiber-structure. This rearrangement of the paper fibers causes the soft pulp to rise and cast a drop shadow of which the image is created. The artist merges the material and technique with the chosen subject matter, for which the artist finds inspiration in the maritime history, 16th century woodcuts, and traditional tattooing.

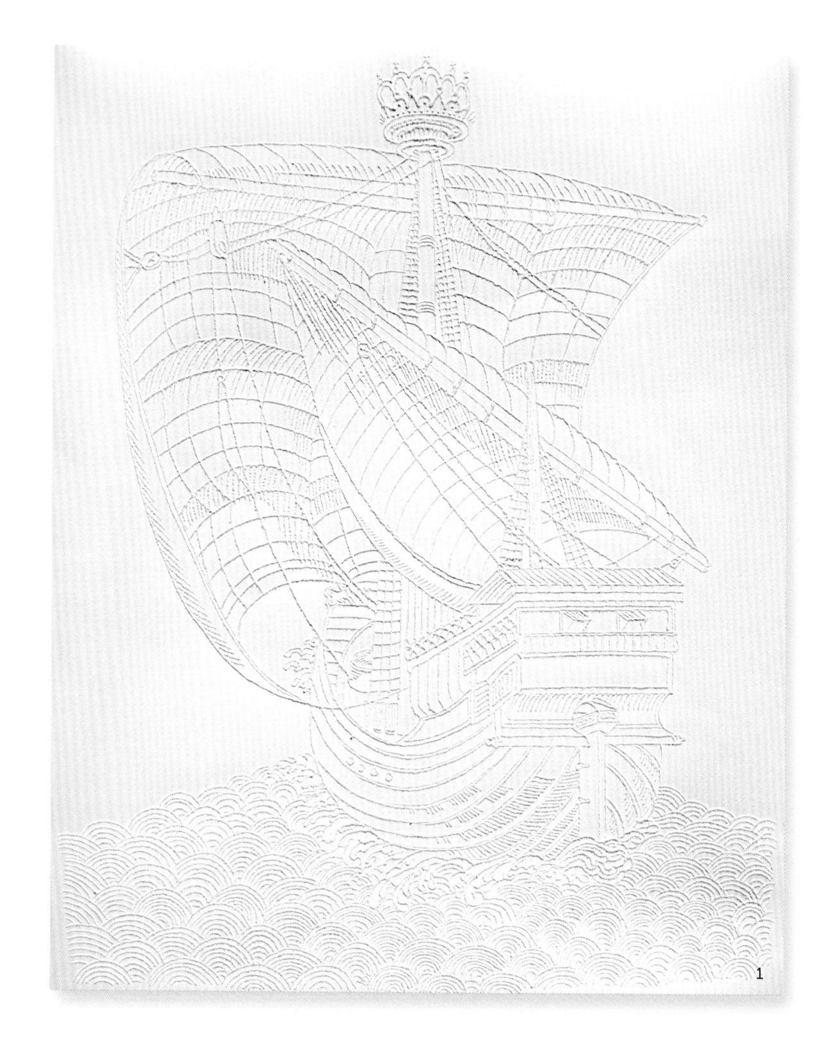
1

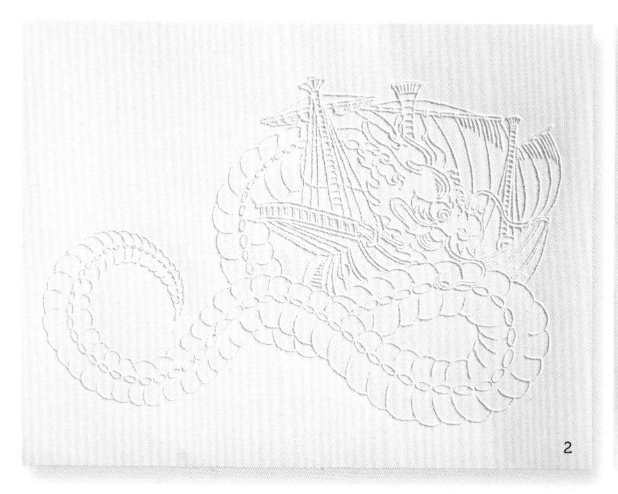
2

3

4

5

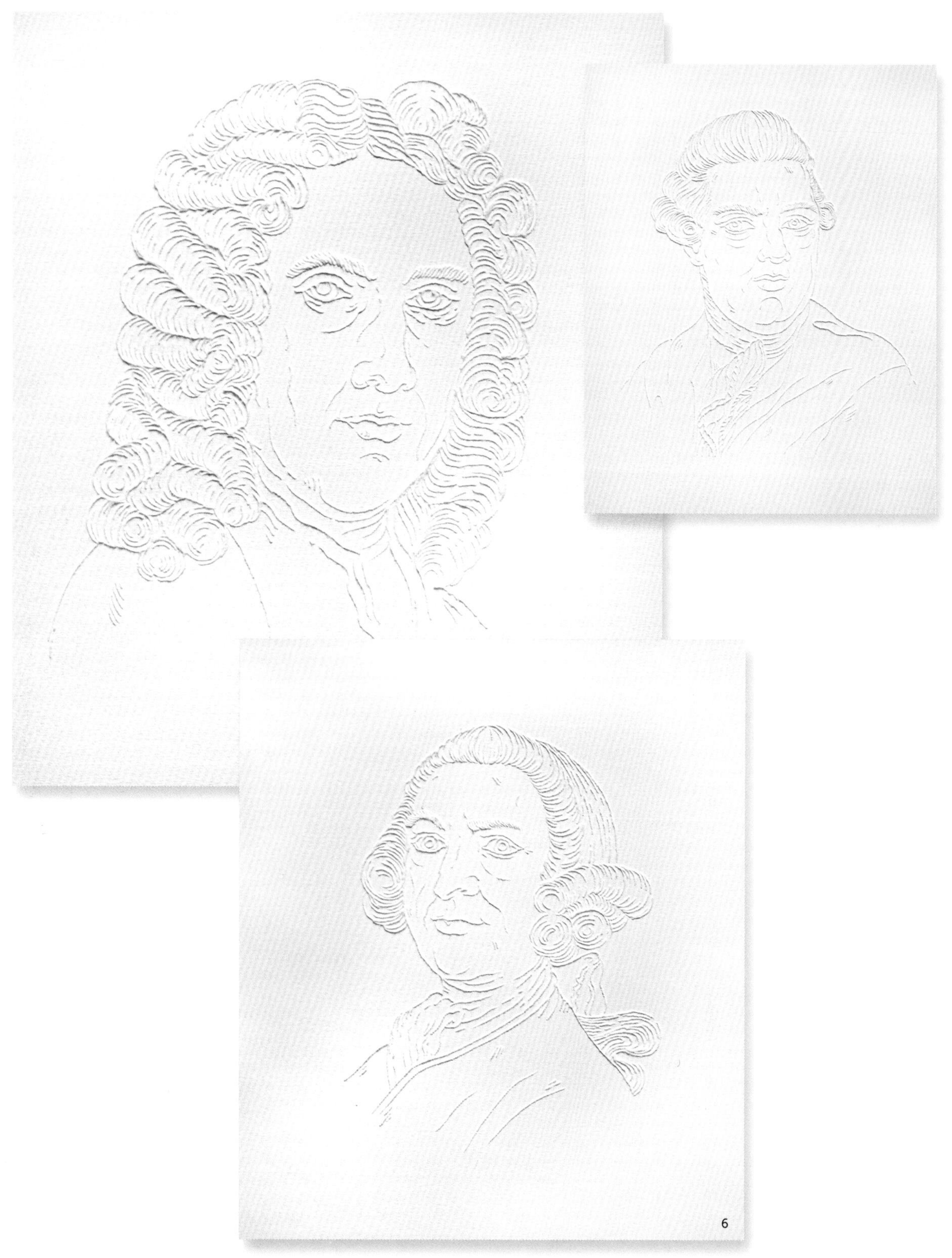
6

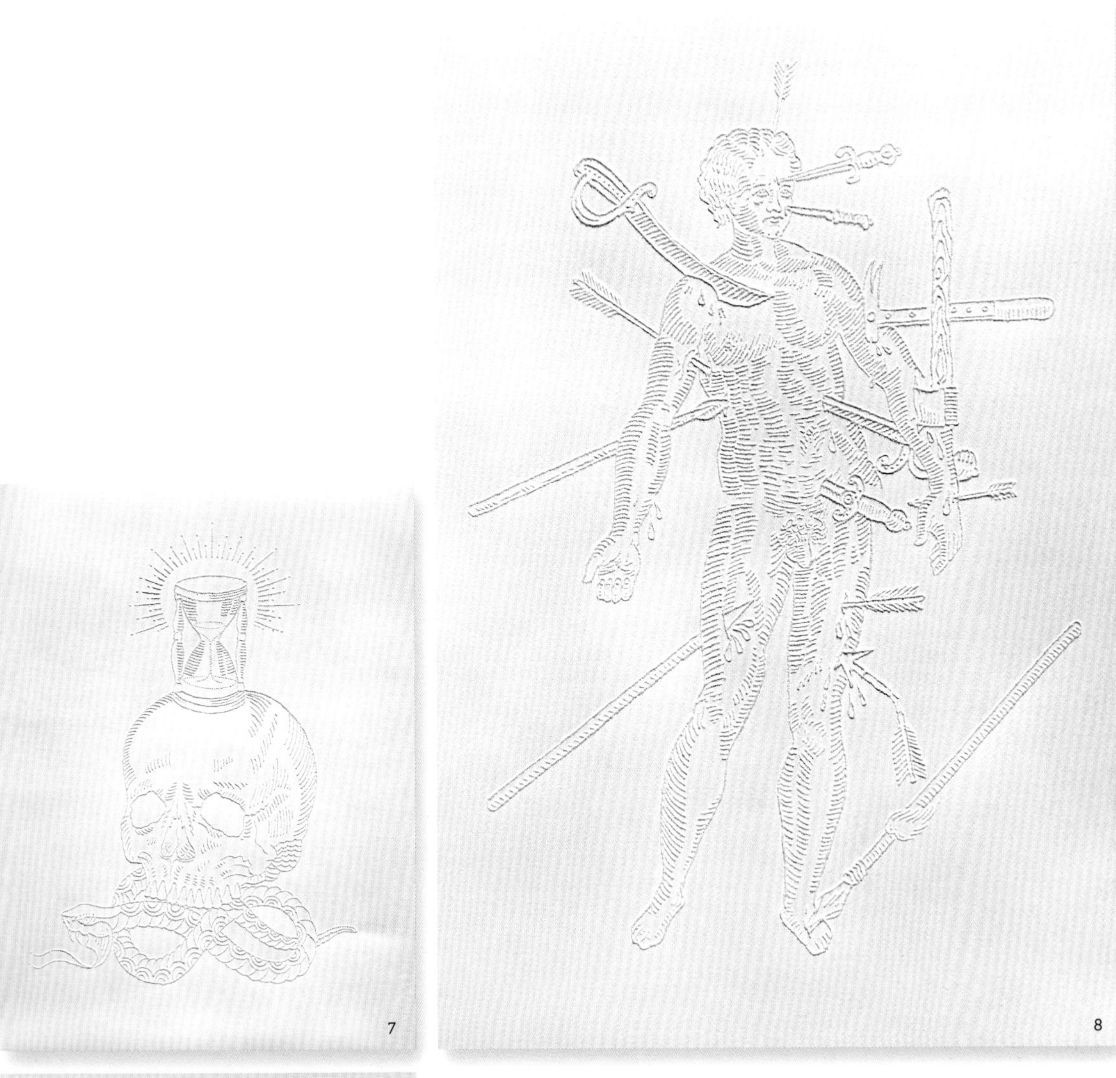
7
8

9

Artist Simon Schubert Photographer All images copyright by Simon Schubert, courtesy of Kudlek van der Grinten gallery

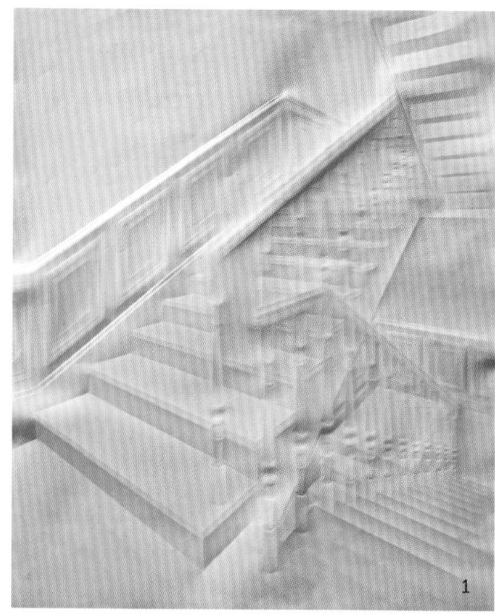

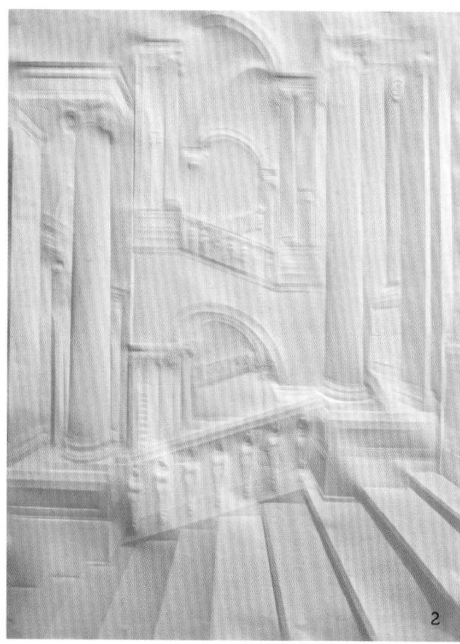

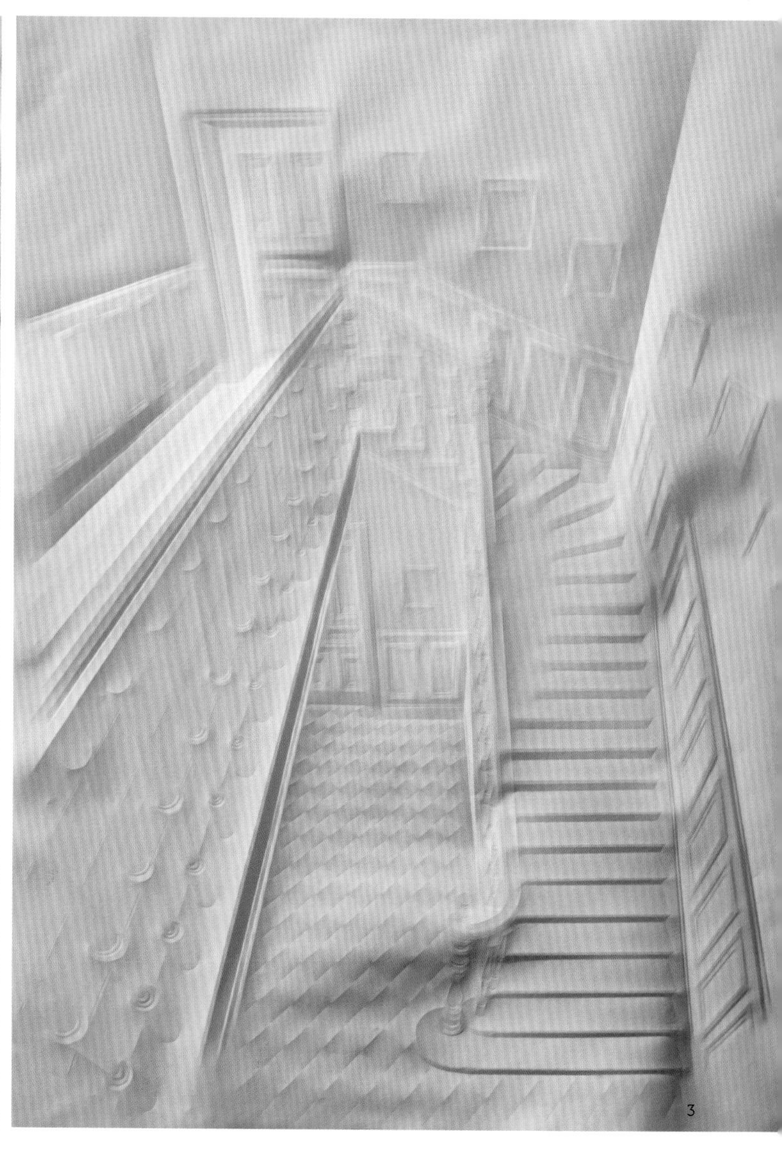

Rich Plain Paper

1 / Staircase with figure, 100 cm x 75 cm
2 / Berlin Stadtschloss (grand staircase), 100 cm x 75 cm
3 / Staircase, 100 cm x 70 cm
4 / Stairwell, 75 cm x 100 cm
5 / Mirrors and mirrors, 75 cm x 100 cm

The paper works are made of plain paper. The papers are entirely folded and uncoloured. No pencil or colour is used. The three-dimensionality of the pictures is a result of a special technique. Simon Schubert invented the technique of the process, which took years to develop. The lines, angles and circles are raised several millimetres as the result of positive and negative folding. Those reliefs change in the interplay of shadow and light and move between two and three dimensionality.

In different lighting, like the changing of daylight, the pictures change from nearly vanishing into a complex illusion of three-dimensionality and space. Through mirrors, windows and different perspectives the pictures become very complex and confusing. Three-dimensionality becomes folded two-dimensionality or the illusion of it.

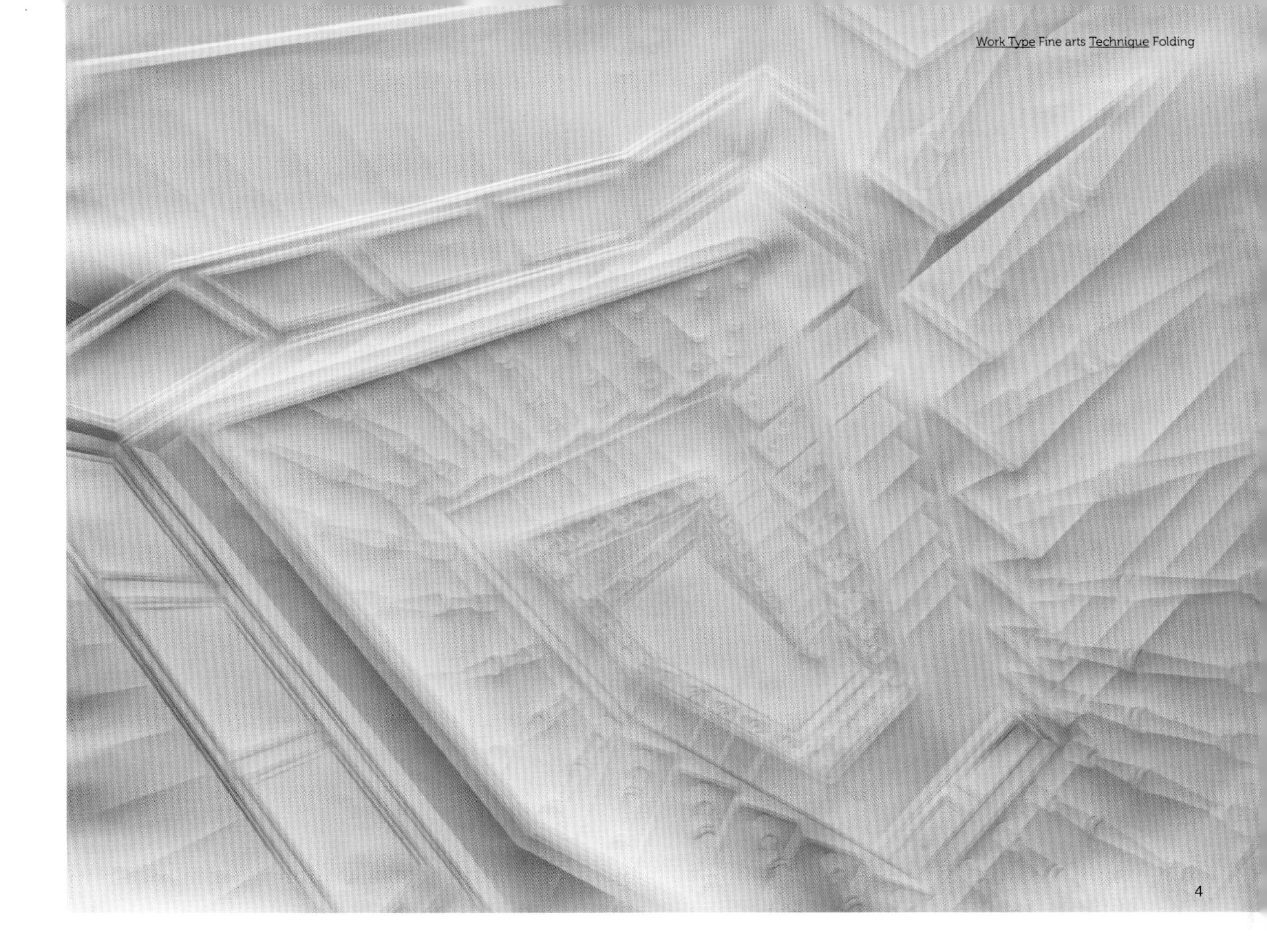

4

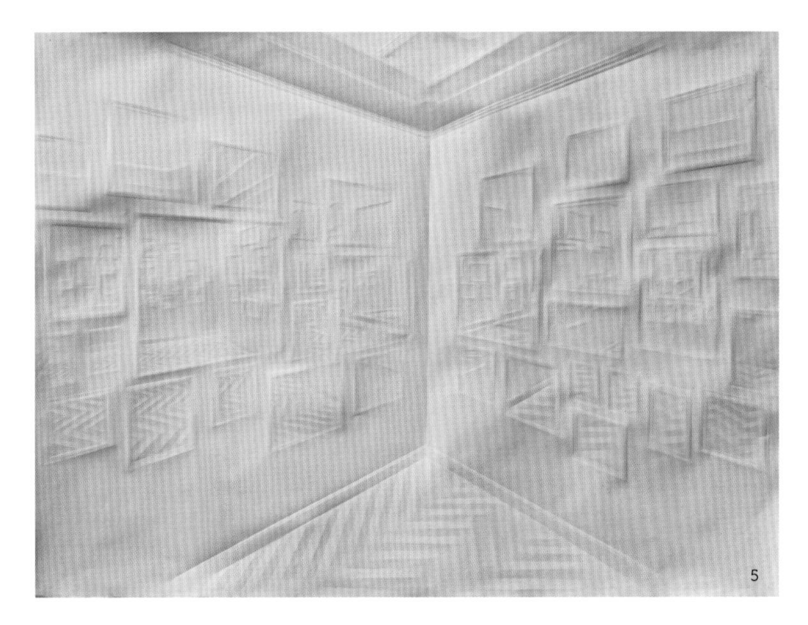

5

Designer Jeff Nishinaka Photographer Ed Ikuta

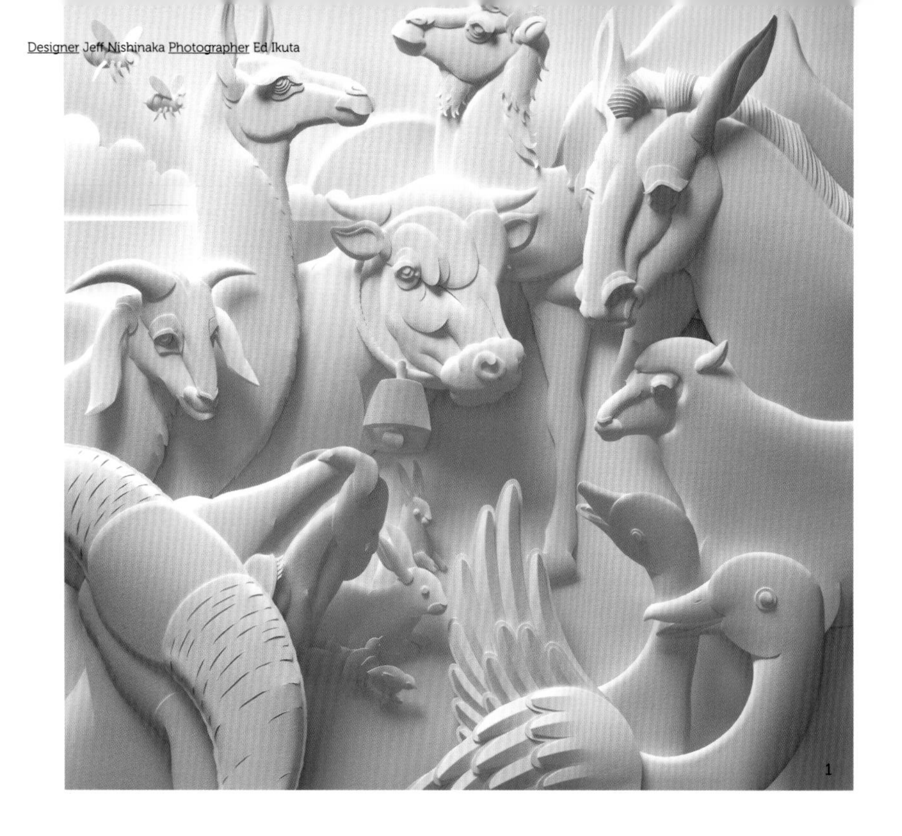

1

Paper Sculpture

1 / Heifer International
2 / Summer Festival
3 / Secret Stone Wine
4 / Landmarks of the World

I began experimenting with paper sculpture as part of a project during my student days at The Art Center College of Design in Pasadena, California. We could choose any type of medium, like matchsticks, nails or clay. I chose paper and made a fish sculpture - it was an 'ah-ha!' moment for me. After that I quickly developed a feel for working with paper. I began experimenting with different types of papers, finding ways to shape, bend, and round edges on it. I knew I was destined to make paper sculptures. I feel that paper is a living thing with energy of its own. All I try to do is redirect that energy. Though they look 3D, they're actually 2D. The illusion is achieved by layering and lighting.

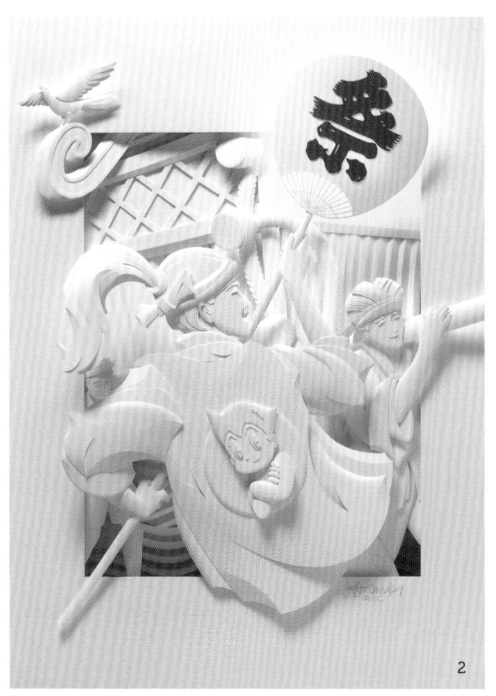

2

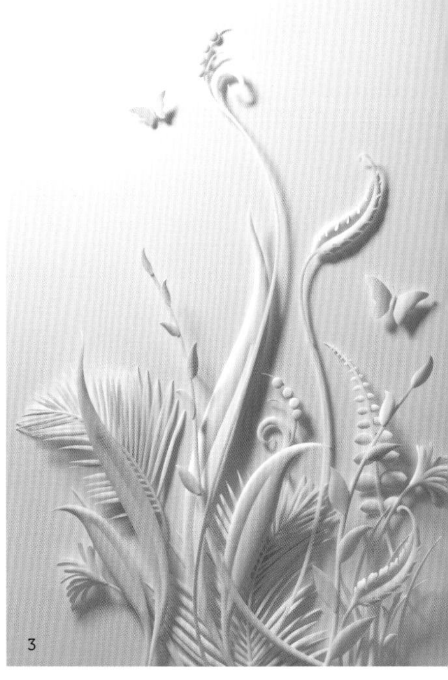

3

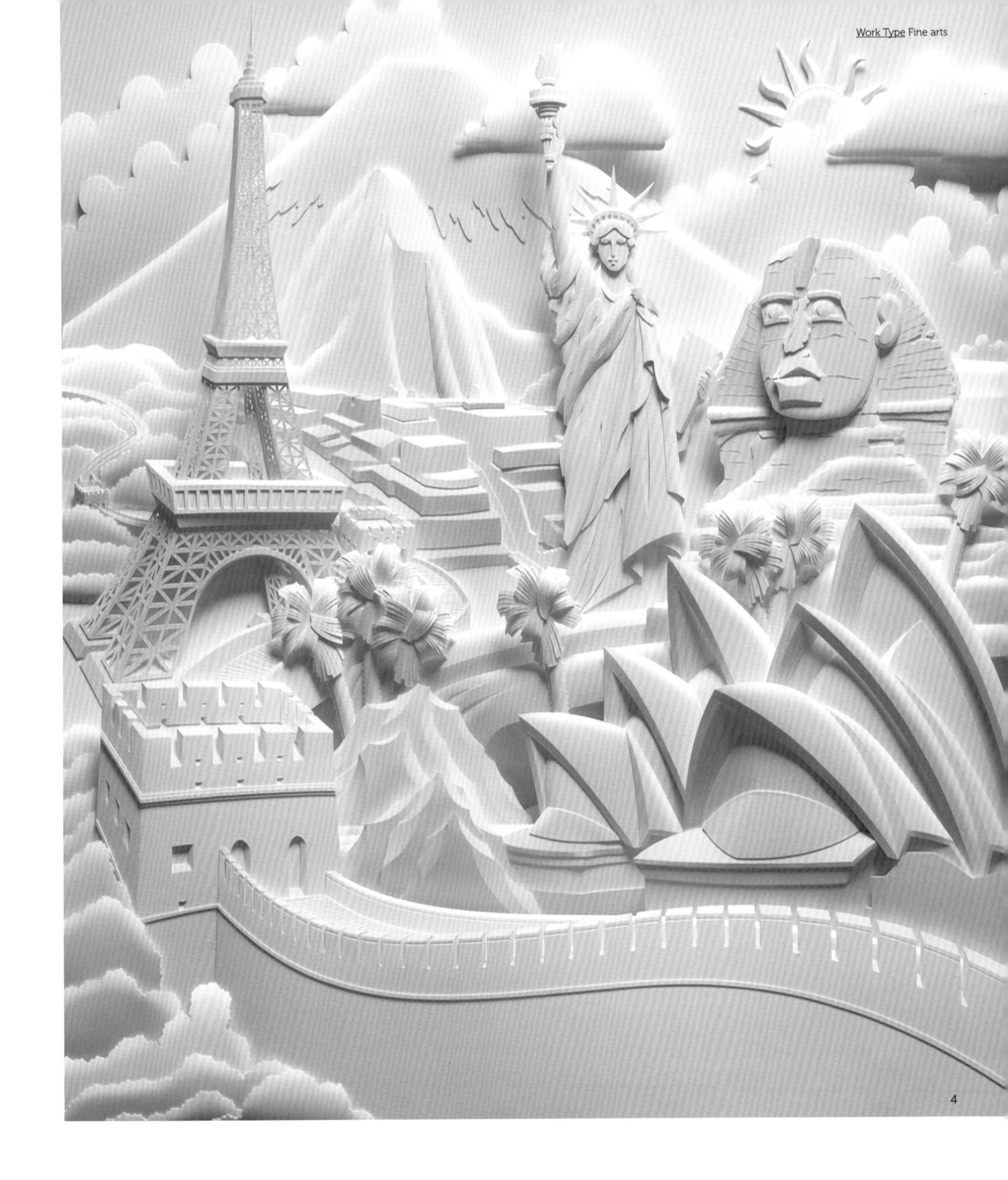

4

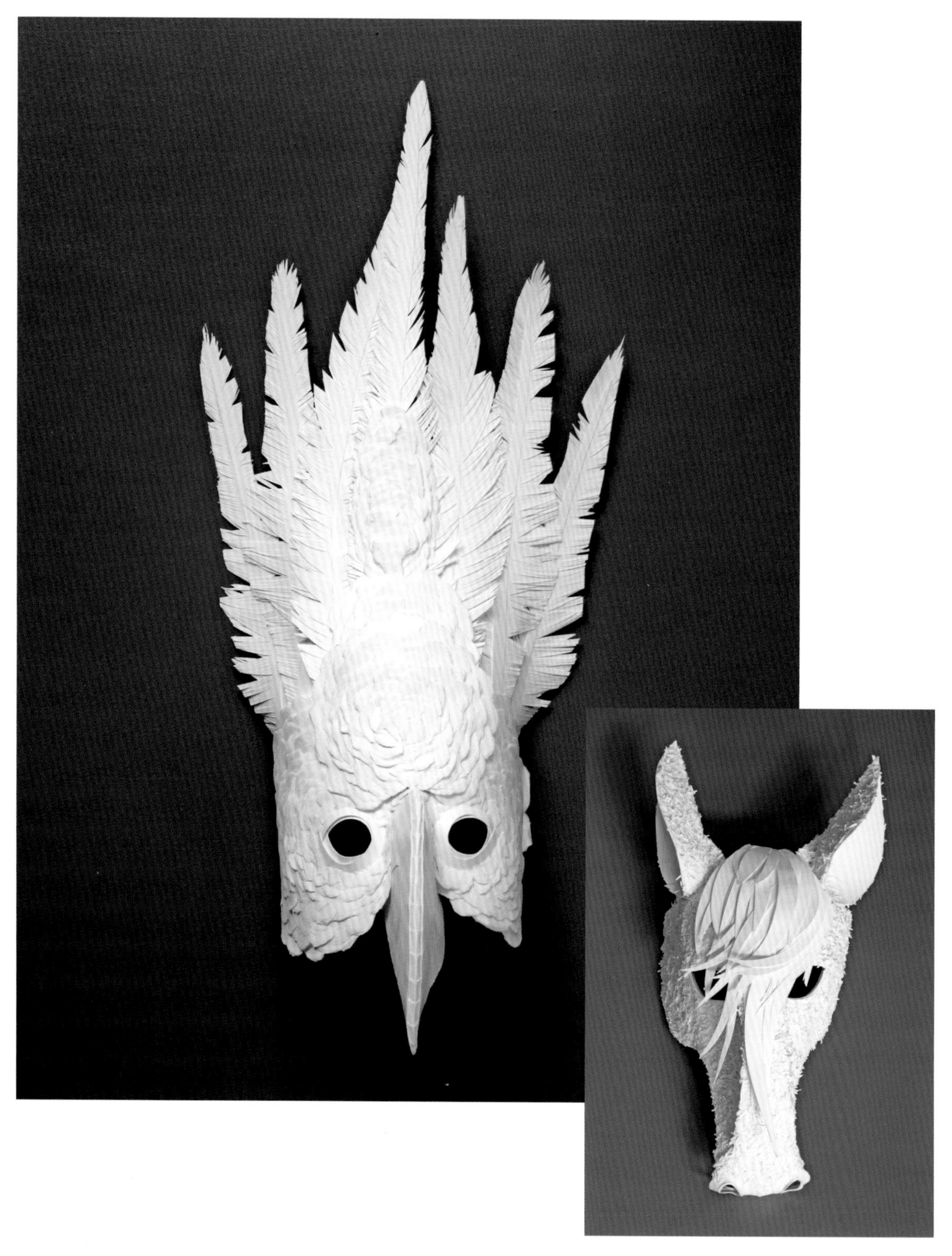

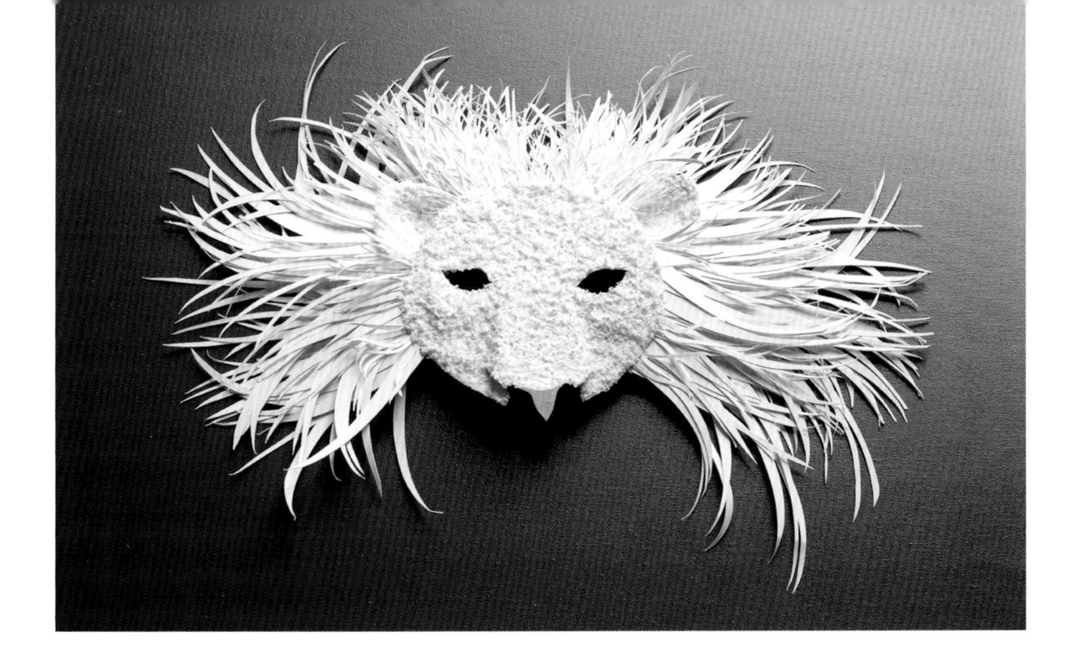

Animalia Series/ Hermes April-October 2010

The Paris-based fashion house commissioned thirty animal masks, each different from the last, to use at the openings of new boutiques in Asia and in Europe in 2010. Models wore the masks and greeted guests who came to the boutique openings.

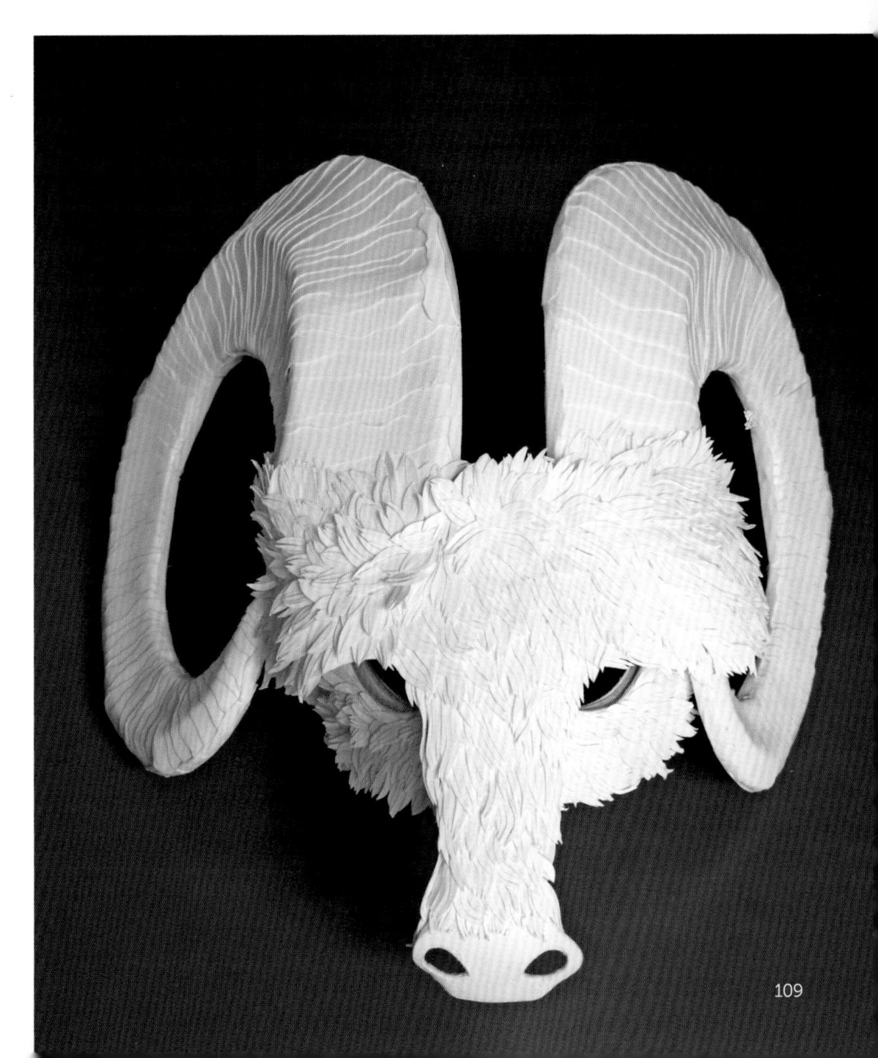

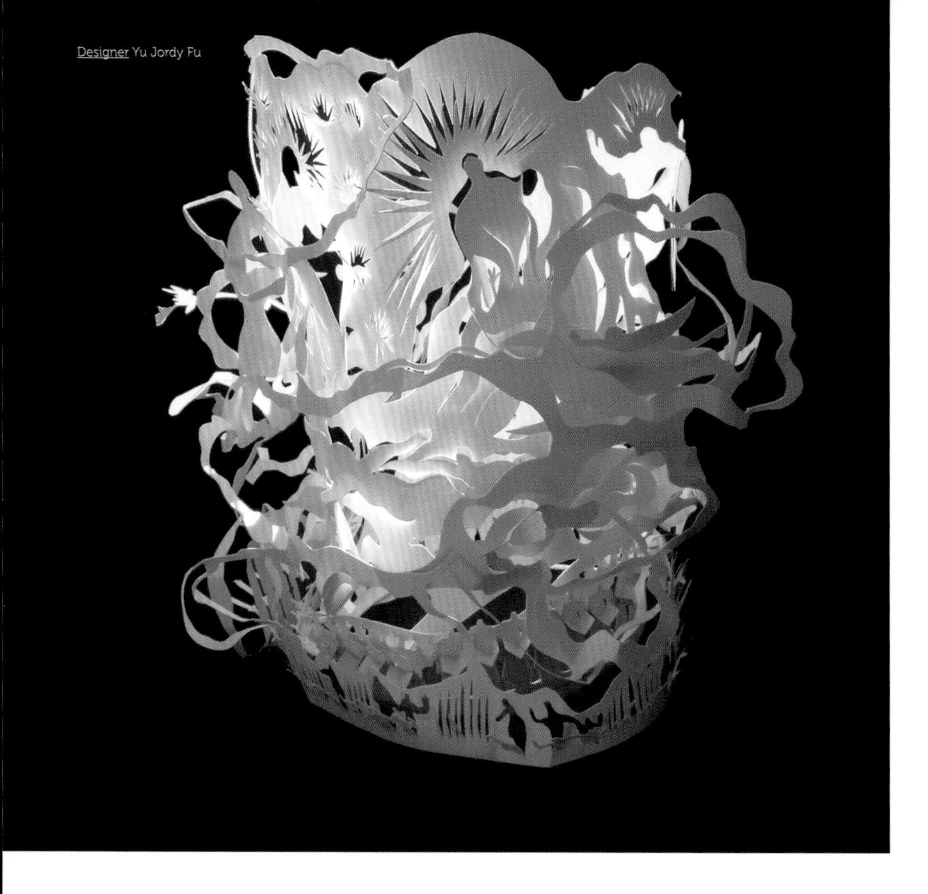
Designer Yu Jordy Fu

Cloud Lamps

These delicate lampshades are inspired by Jordy's architectural design projects and scaled at 1:50, each lamp is a sensational space, and they instantly transform the atmosphere of a home. The Cloud lamps are sustainable: the material is recycled paper, the method of production is handmade, and the product is to be used with energy saving light bulbs. By introducing the Chinese paper-cutting tradition into a contemporary use, the Cloud Lamp is sustaining a culture.

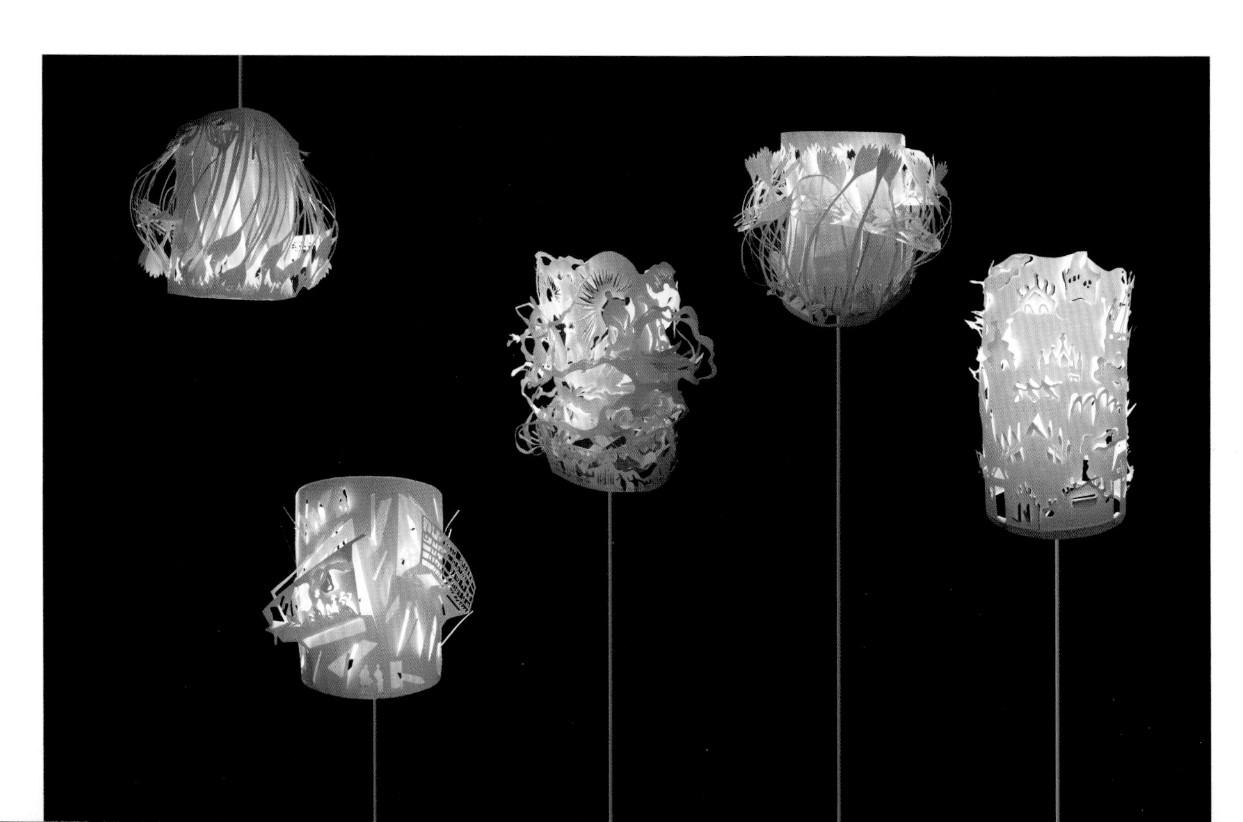

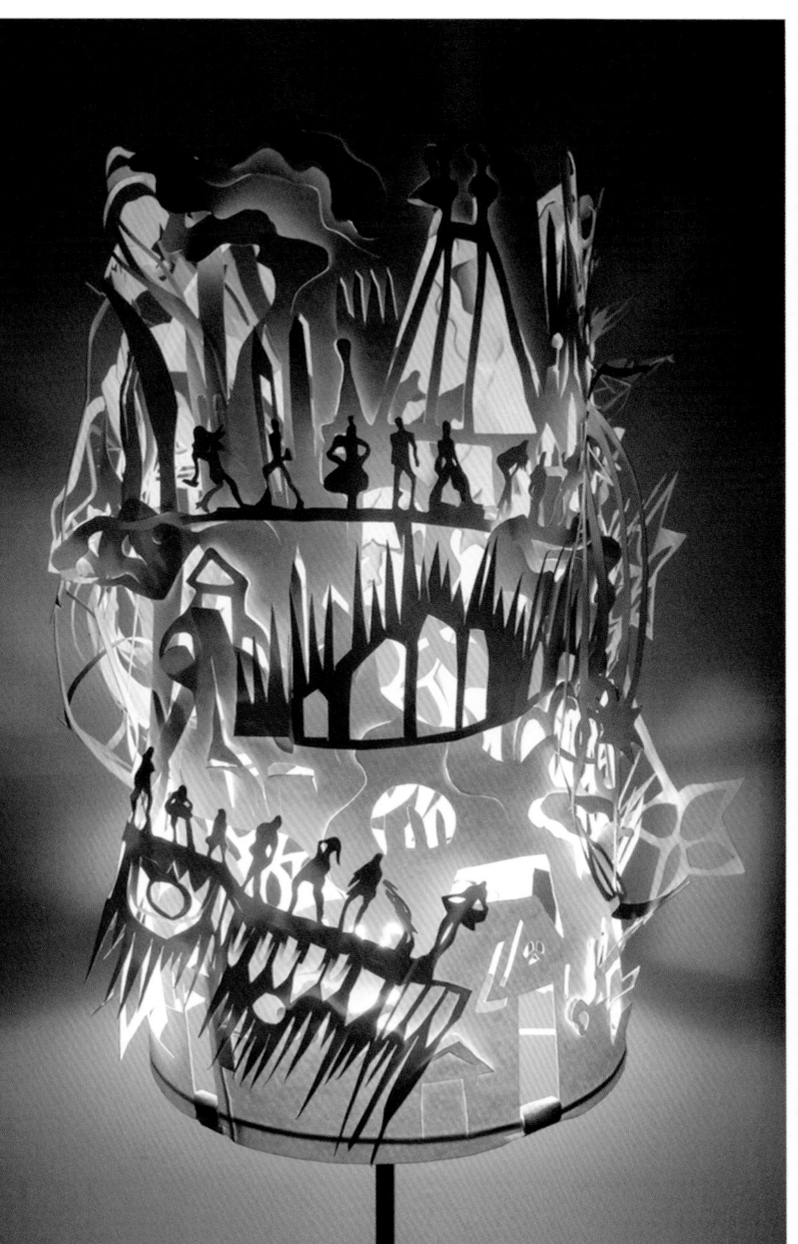

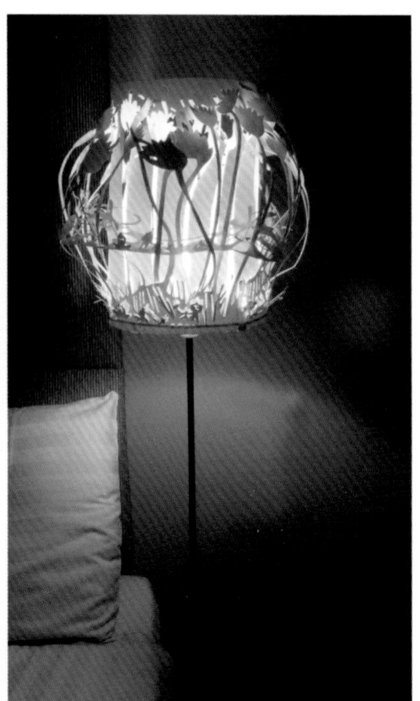

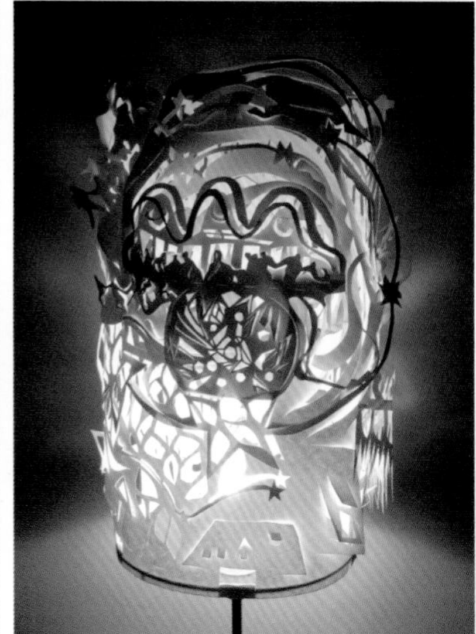

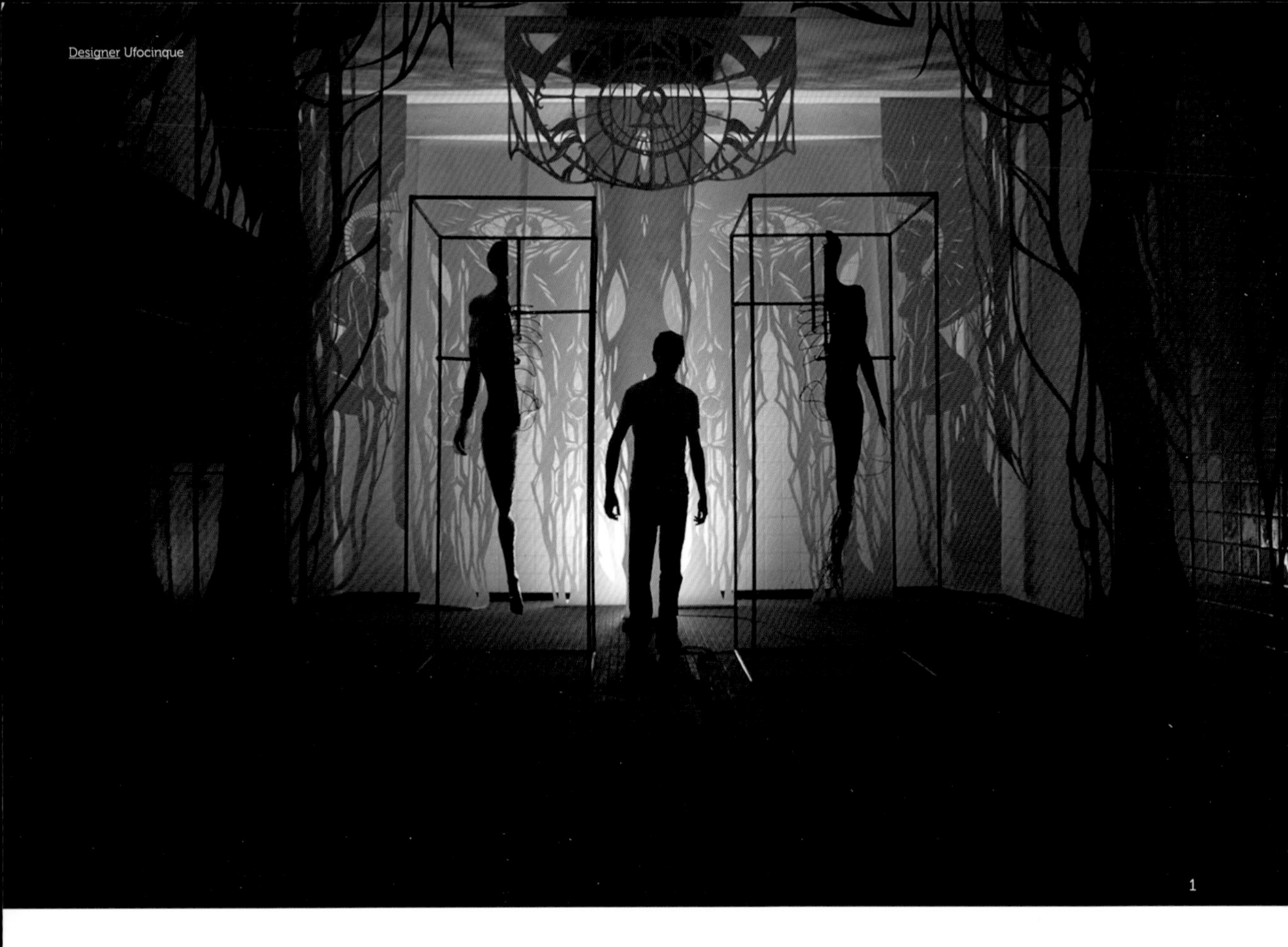

1

Papercut Layers

1 / DICOTOMIA SIMMETRICA 2011
2 / GAEA, 2009
3 / CRACKEN, 2011
4 / KEITH HARING, 2011
5 / THE FOX, 2010

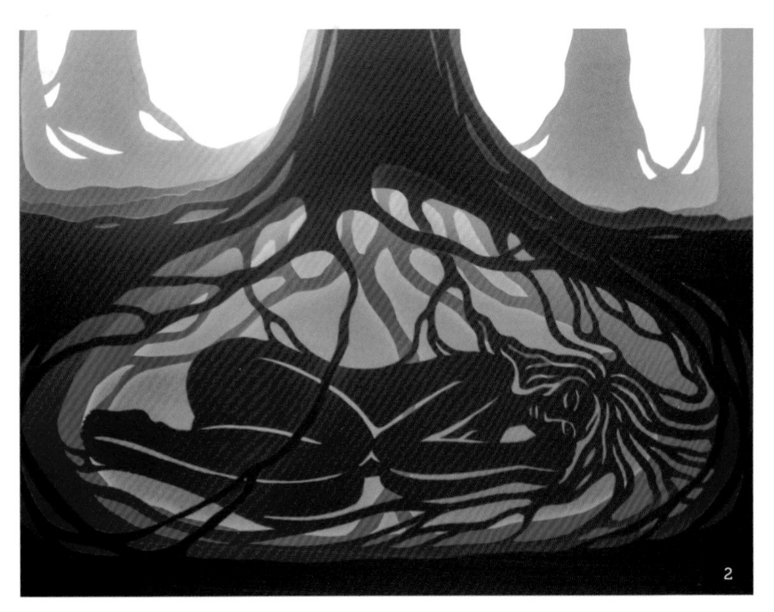

2

Ufocinque's pieces start from the urge to communicate a message. The creative process can be divided in two phases: the planning and the execution phase. The key steps of the planning phase is to evoke suggestive images, to accurately evaluate the boundaries within which the piece has to be executed (especially relevant for installations) and to develop roughs to visualize how each layer will interact in the composition.

The next step is to cut the paper. As opposed to the preliminary studies, this phase is driven by instinct: the disposable knife is used as a pencil and forms come to life out of the blank sheet of paper. Once each layer has been created it's of great importance to produce a frame able to neatly keep the composition in place, like boxes, wooden frames or feather-light metal wires. The only self-imposed limitation is to adopt non-invasive solutions that, in case of installations, once dismounted won't leave a trace of their existence. The final element added to the piece is light. Ufocinque feels that all the different layers of papers are just an instrument to make shadow and light to vibrate within the composition.

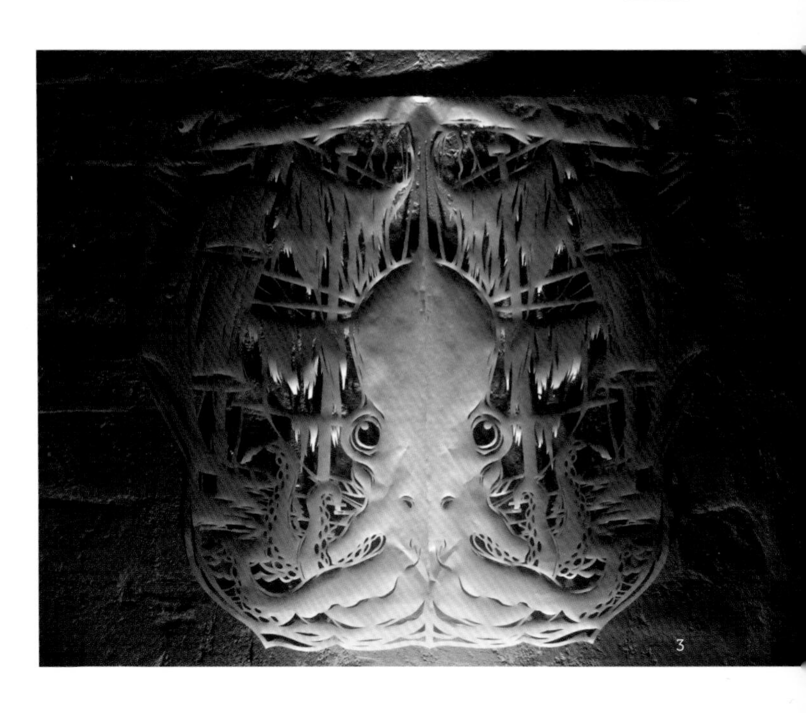
3

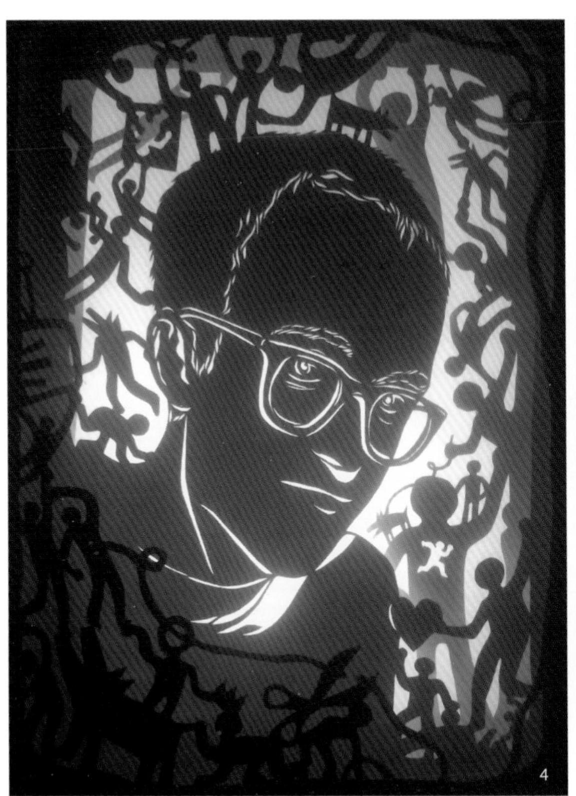
4

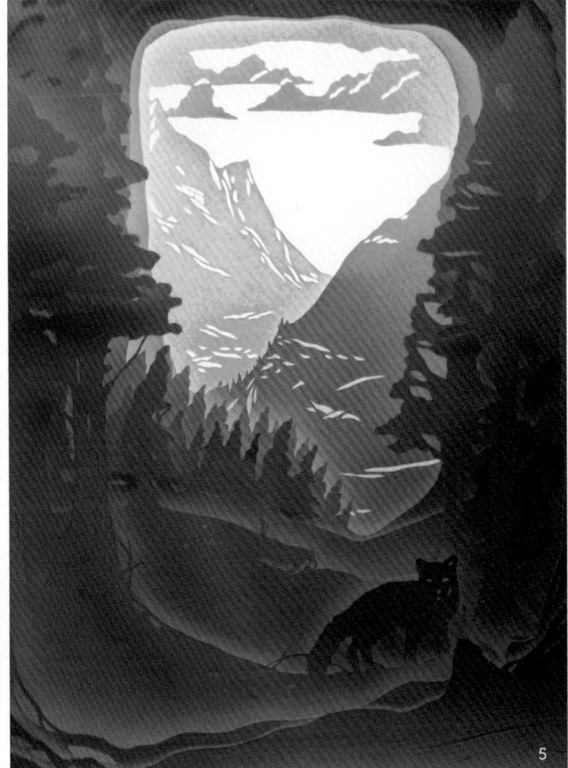
5

Artist Studio Bovey Lee Studio Artist Bovey Lee Photographer Tricia Nicolas, Bovey Lee

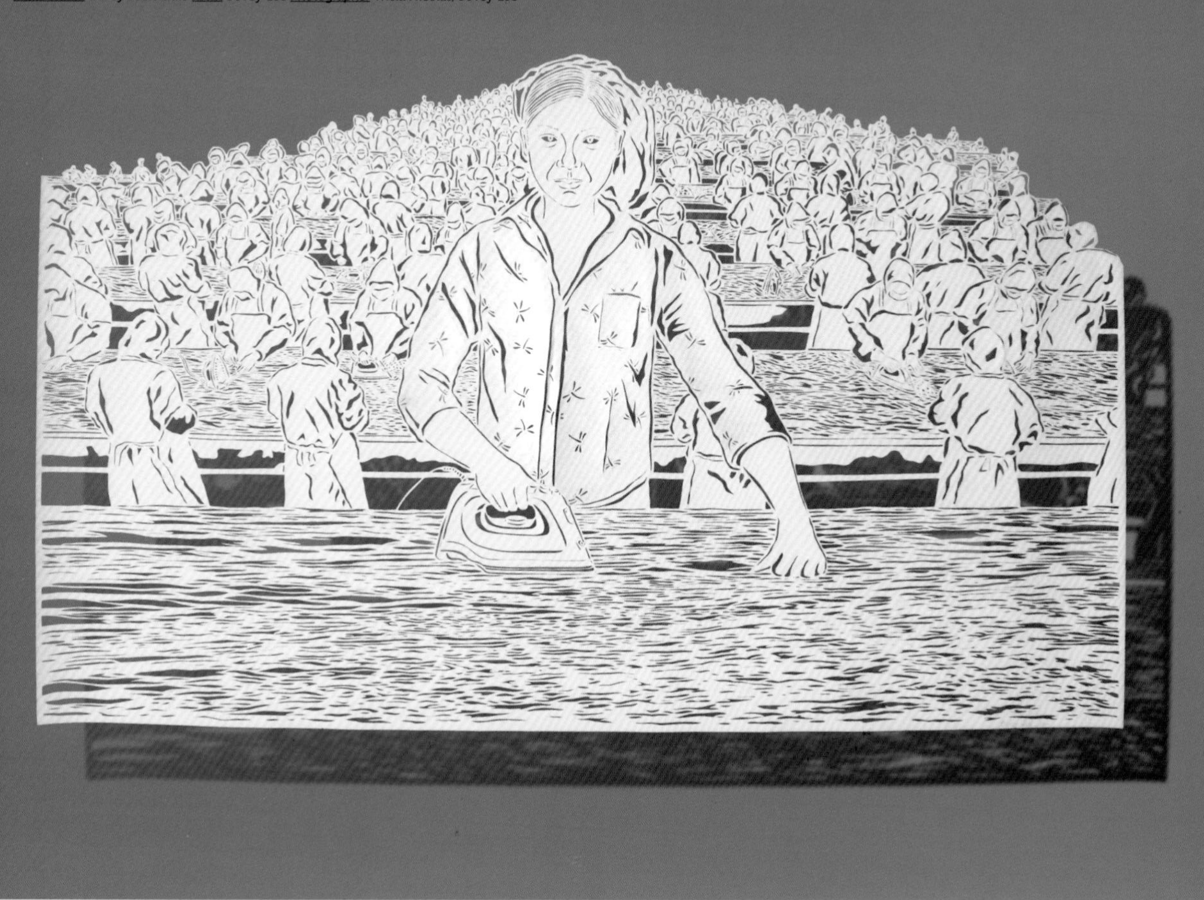

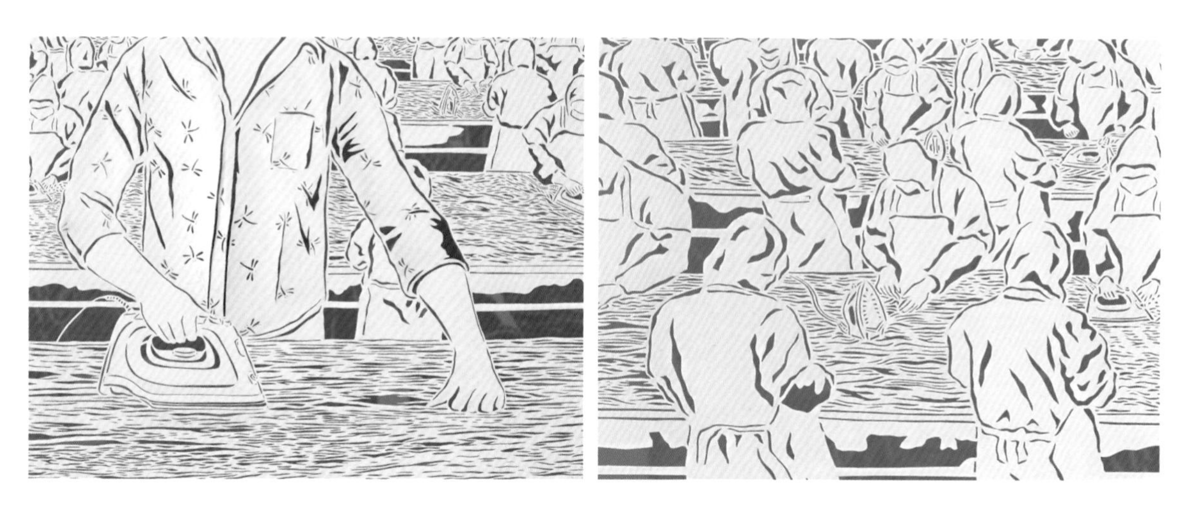

"Sewing Highways" and "Ironing Oceans"

Power, sacrifice, and survival are the underlying narratives in my cut paper works. Within the parameters of these three subjects, I create layered and dramatic stories referencing my life experiences, response to headline news, and concerns for urban and environmental issues. I hand cut each work using Chinese rice (xuan) paper mounted on silk. "Sewing Highways" and "Ironing Oceans" are among the new body of works that tie closely to the theme of survival in the 21st century. Specifically, the economic fiasco created by mega corporations, banks, and Wall street inspired me to think about the work that we do and its ripple effect on not merely a single country or continent but the world. Because my own work is intrinsically physical and laborious, I want to redirect our focus onto the everyday working people who underpin societies and nations.

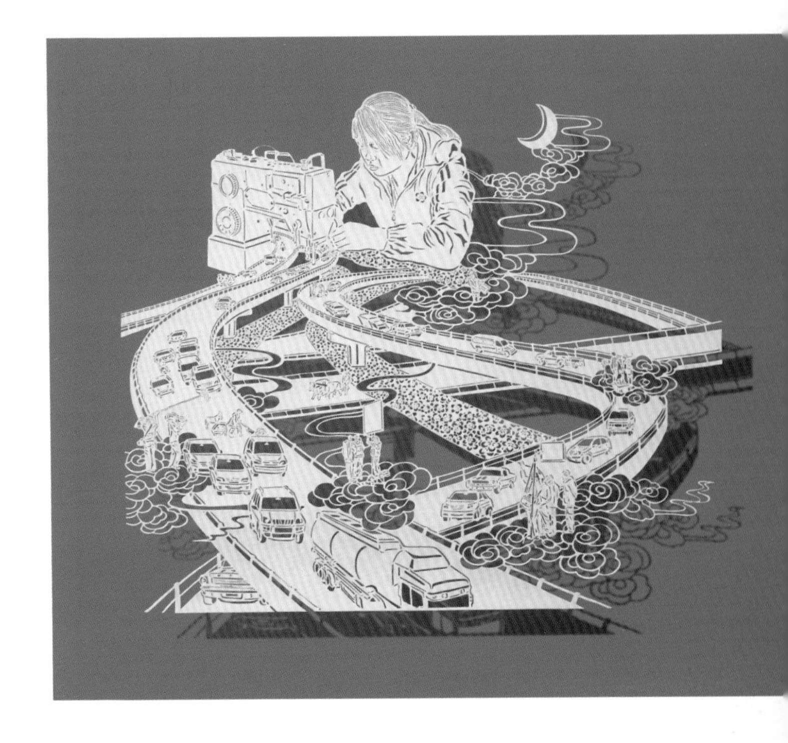

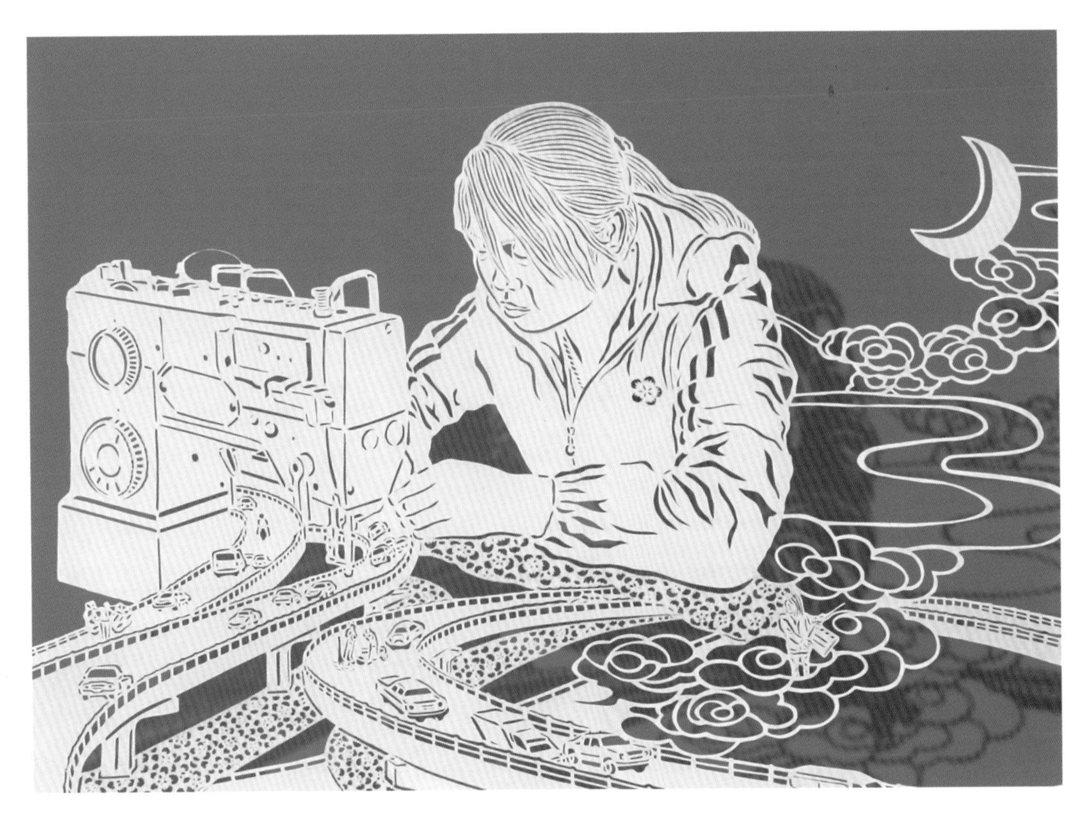

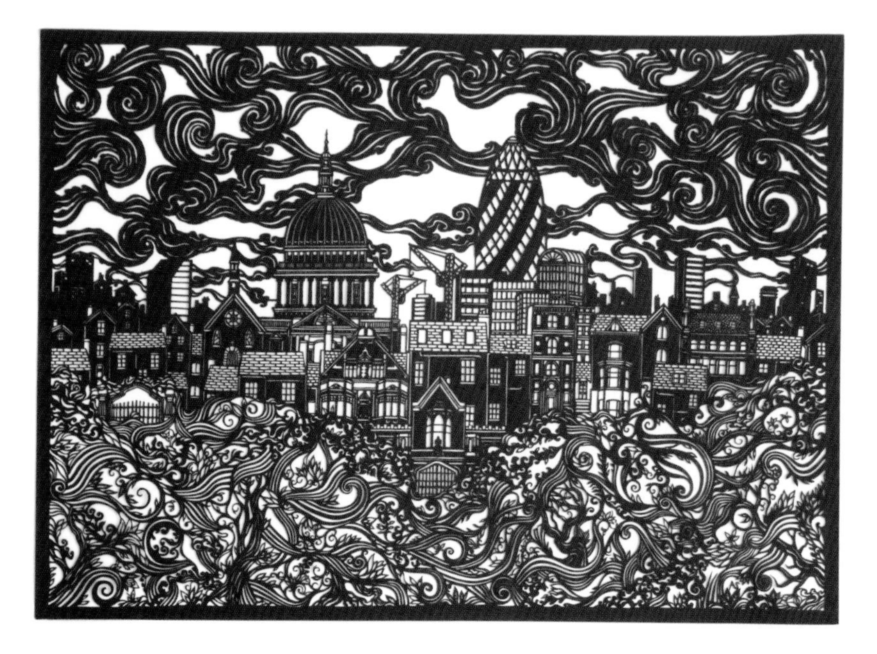

London Cityscape

A privately commissioned paper cut art work based on some of London's famous skyline buildings, including St.Paul's Cathedral and "the Gerkin" skyscraper. The piece took over one hundred and fifty hours to complete and is made up of architectural and organic forms. The work size is 60cm x 45cm.

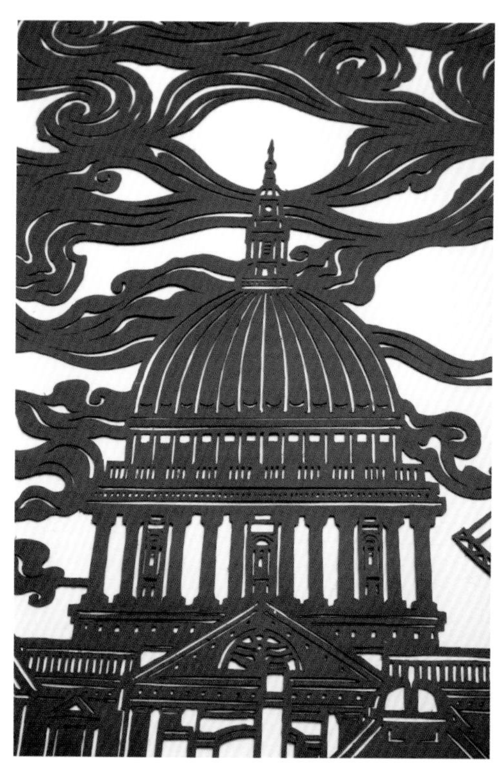

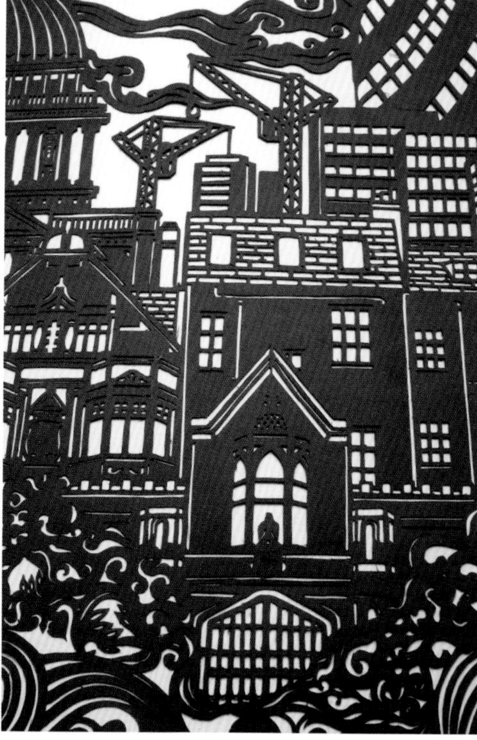

Space of Fantasies

Space of Fantasies is a model based on my imagination about the hybrids of different animals and plants.

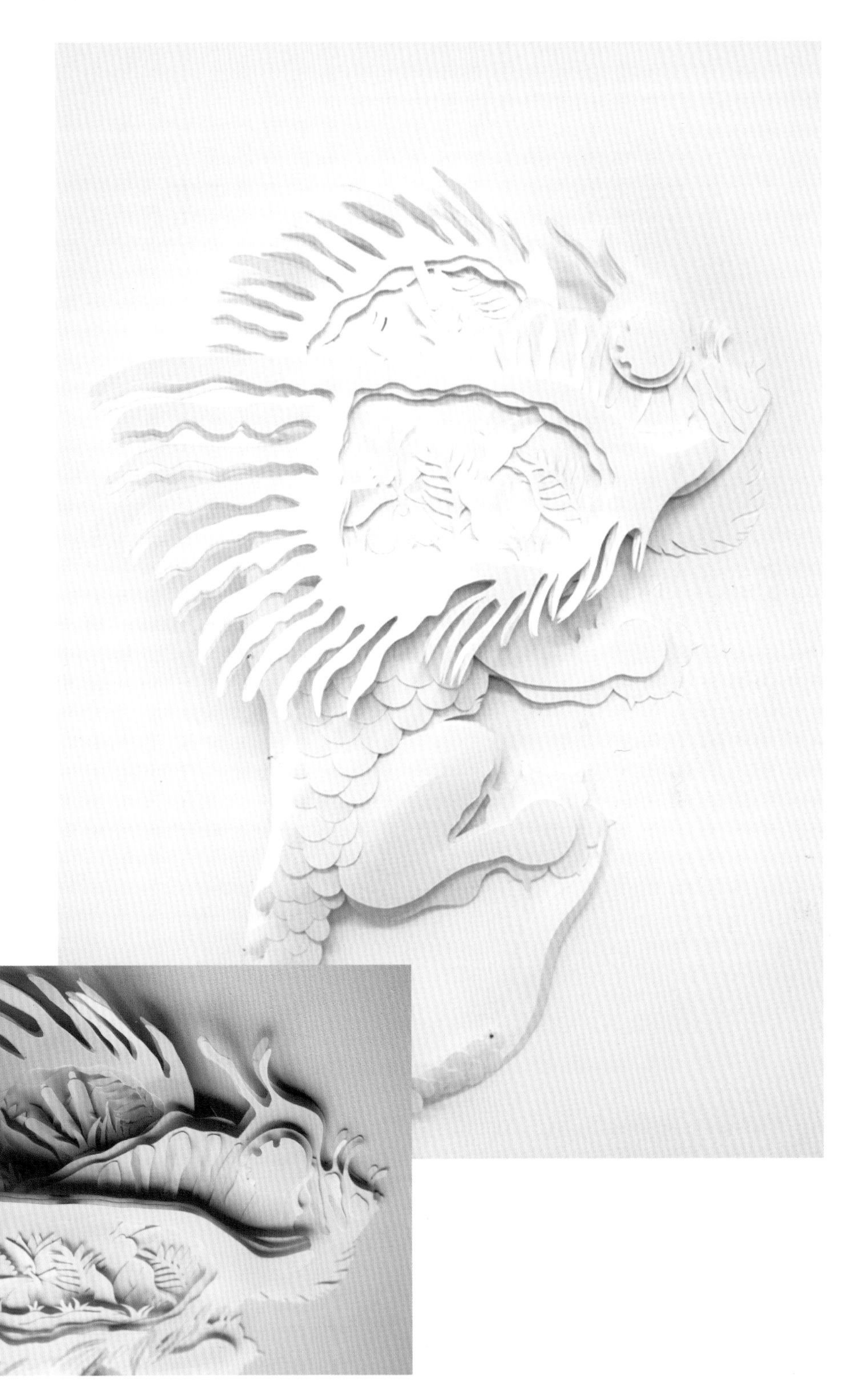

Shadows and reflections

Paper sculptor Kris Trappeniers creates pristinely twisted and complex portrait stencils, then completes each piece on canvas with spray paint or acrylics. The process from drawing to finished work is completely analogue, without the use of software or photo filters.

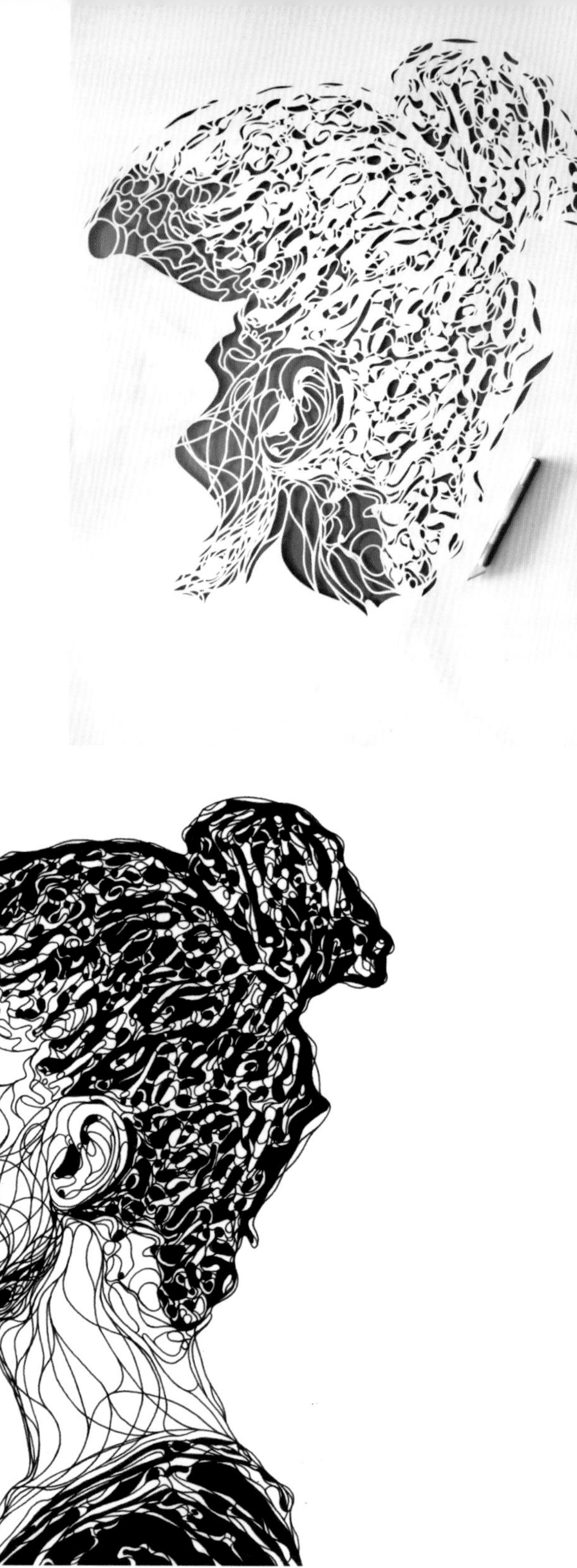

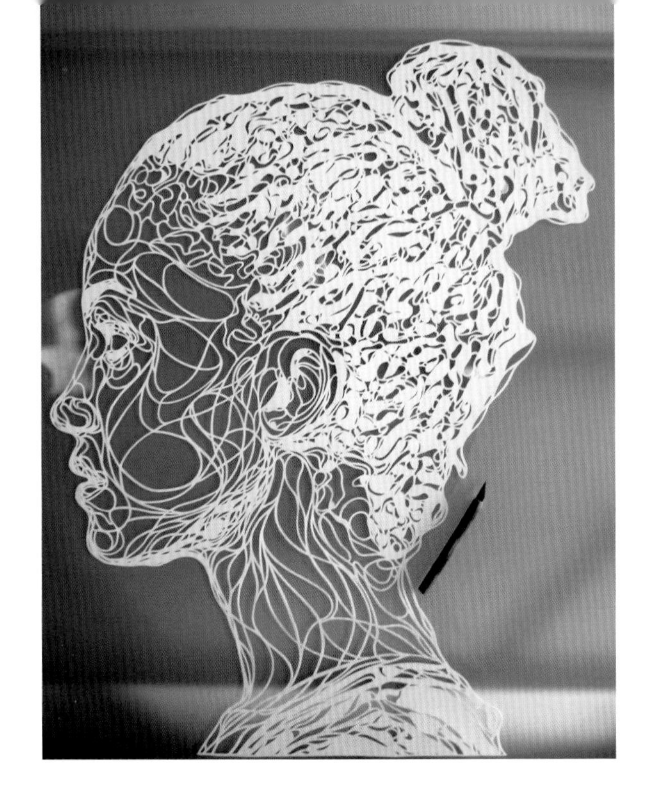

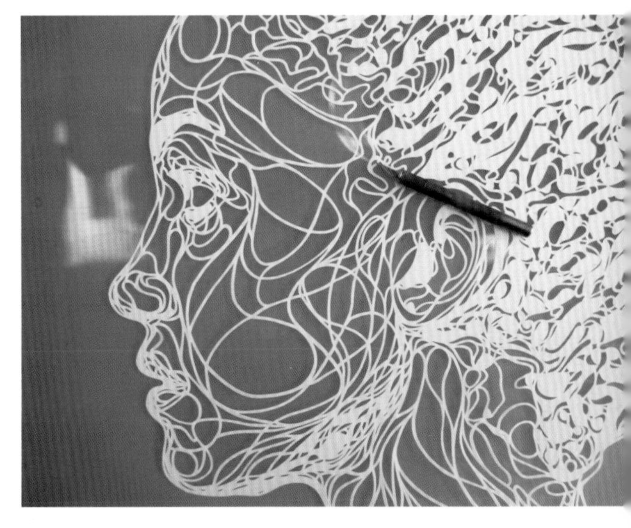

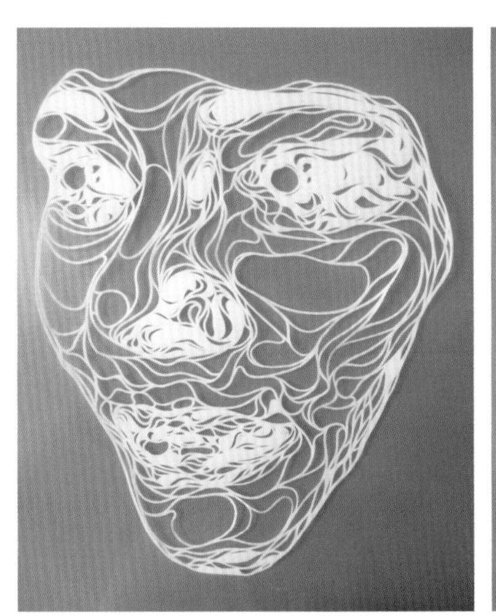

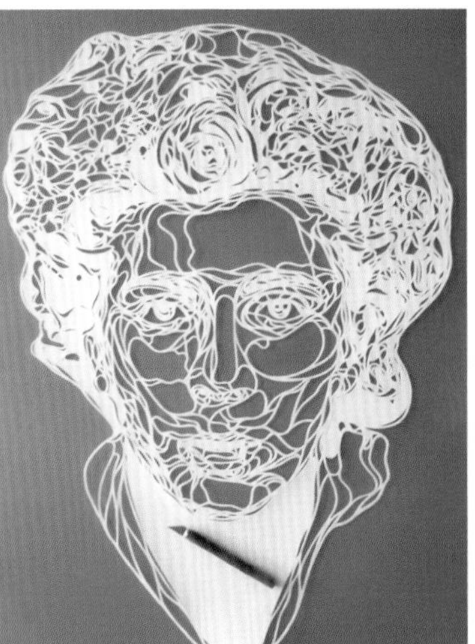

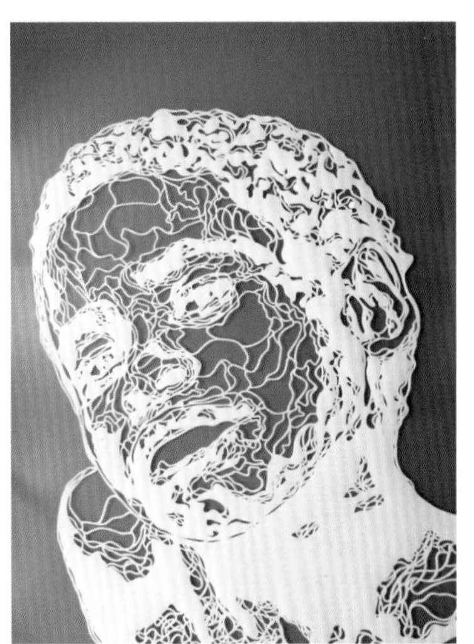

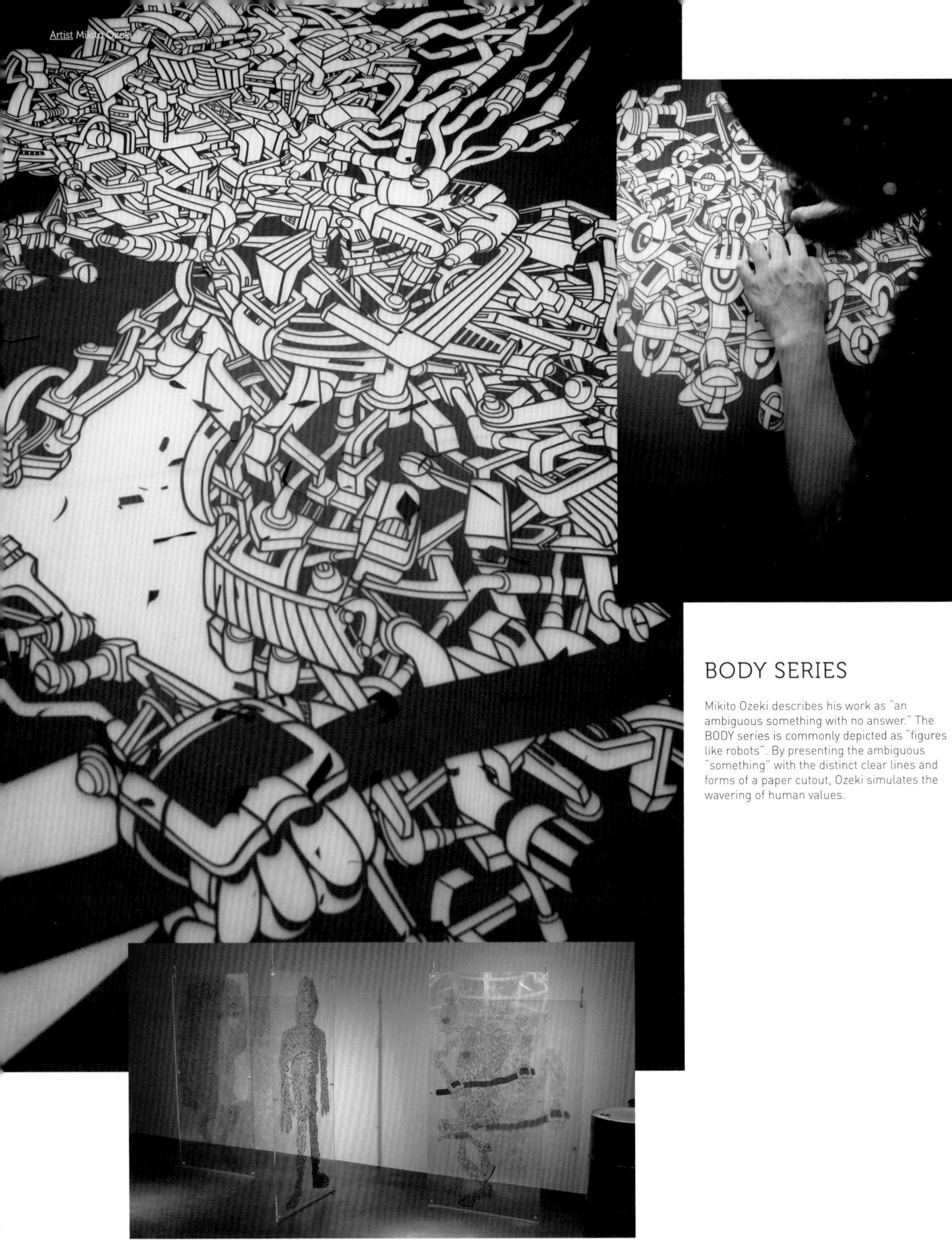

BODY SERIES

Mikito Ozeki describes his work as "an ambiguous something with no answer." The BODY series is commonly depicted as "figures like robots". By presenting the ambiguous "something" with the distinct clear lines and forms of a paper cutout, Ozeki simulates the wavering of human values.

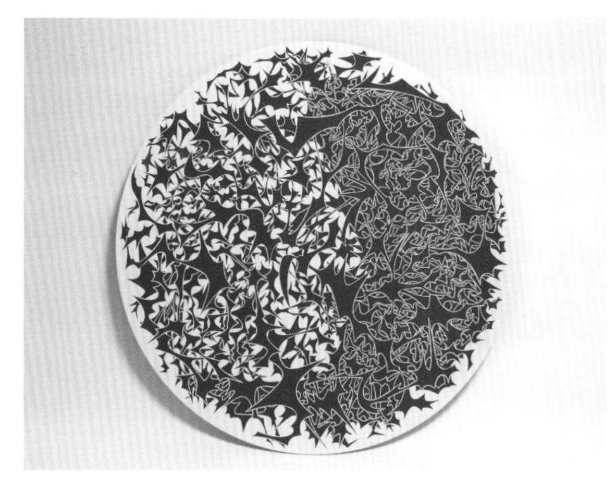

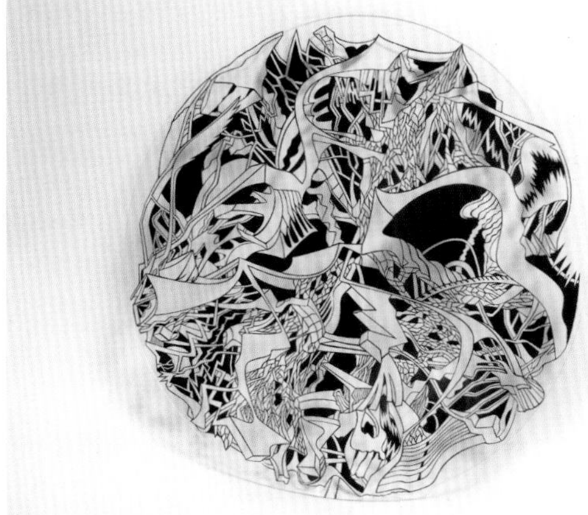

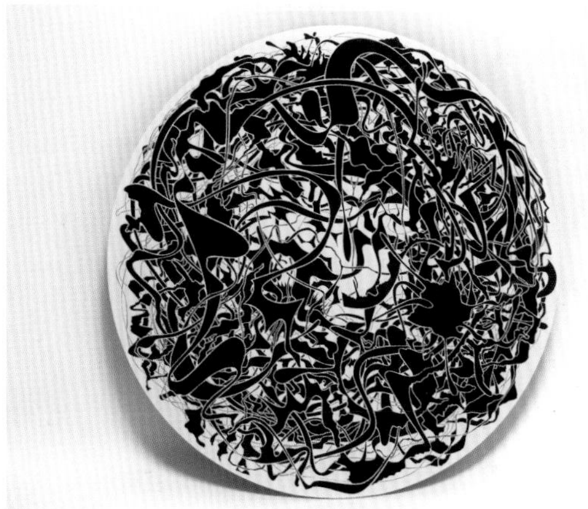

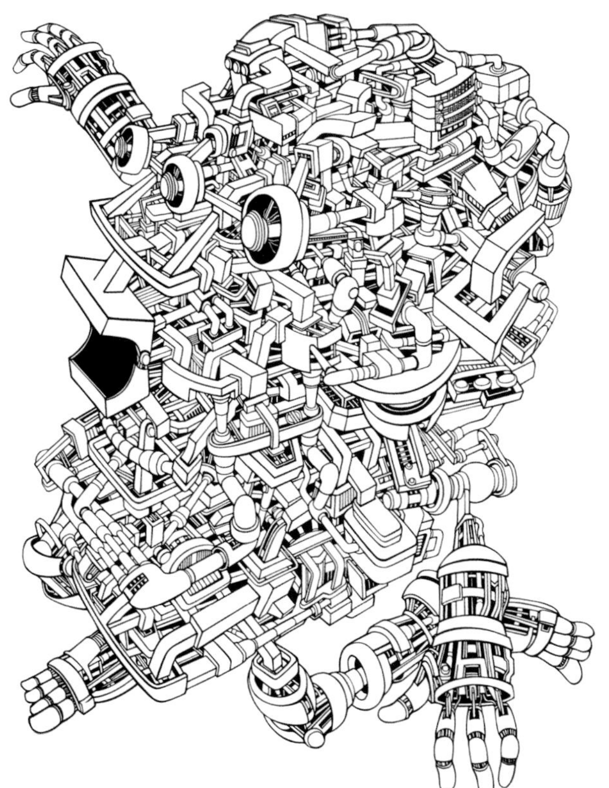

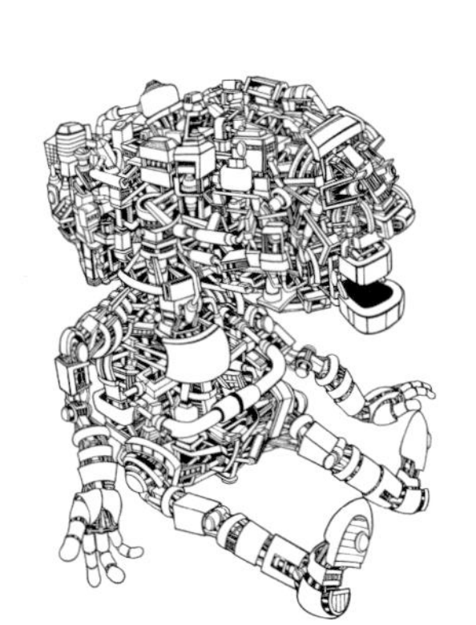

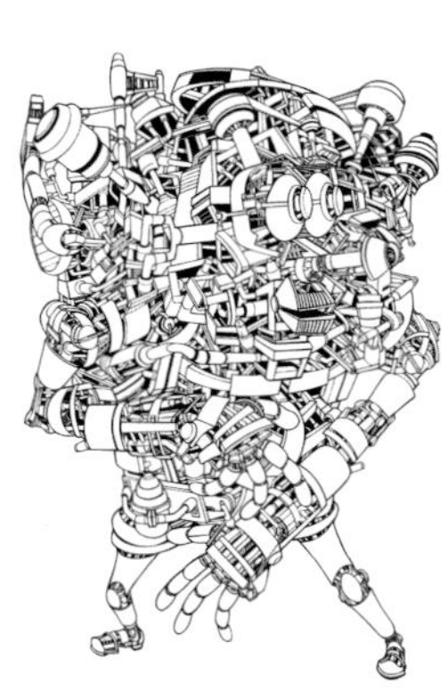

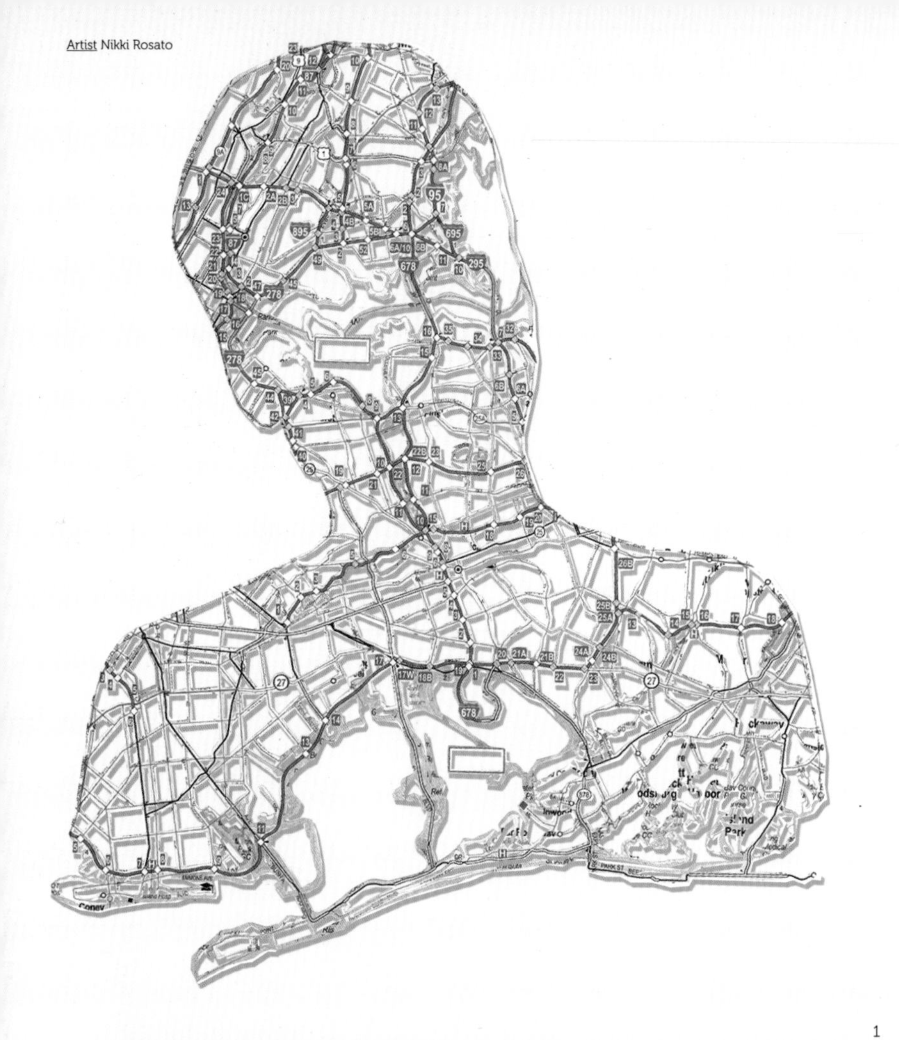

1

Cut Map

1 / Tom: Jamaica, NY
2 / Installation View: Dimensions Variable
3 / Two Bostons
4 / Connections
5 / Untitled (Childhood Portrait)

Our physical bodies are beautiful structures full of detail, and they hold the stories that haunt and mold our lives. The lines on a road map are fascinatingly similar to the lines that cover the surface of the human body. In my work involving maps, as I remove the landmasses from the silhouetted individuals I am further removing the figure's identity, and what remains is a delicate skin-like structure. Through this process, specific individuals become ambiguous and hauntingly ghost-like, similar to the memories they represent. The figures in the Connections series find themselves bound by the roads that both separate them as well as lead them to one another. People are often separated by distance, and these connected lines represent the roads that are either explored to bring these figures together or left untraveled, further symbolizing not only their physical distance but also psychological and emotional space.

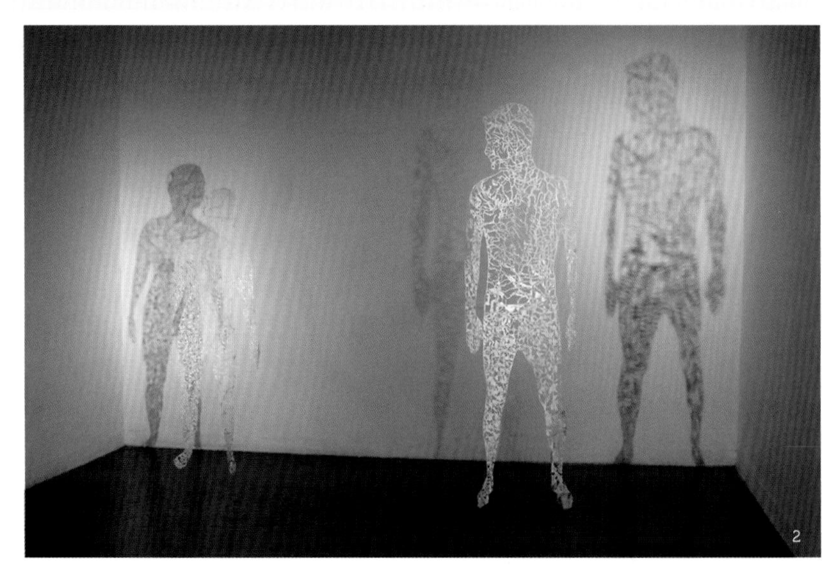

2

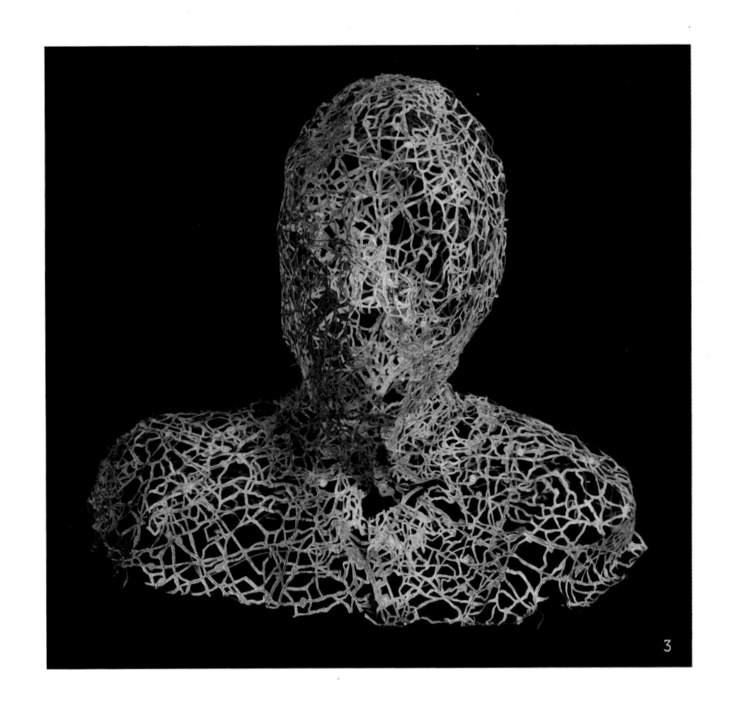

3

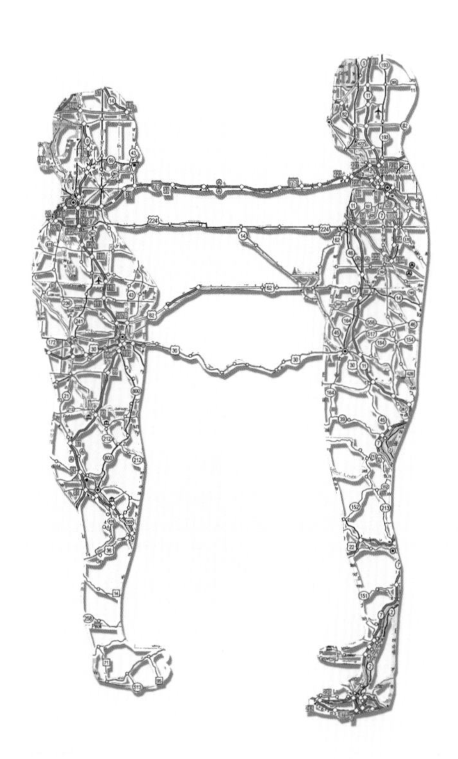

4

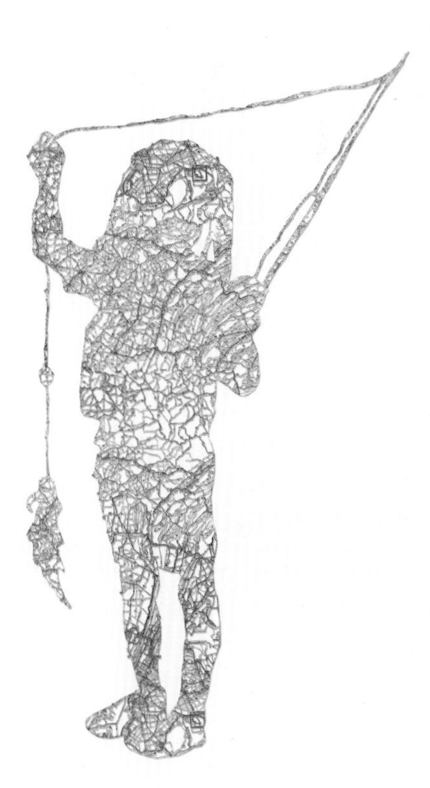

5

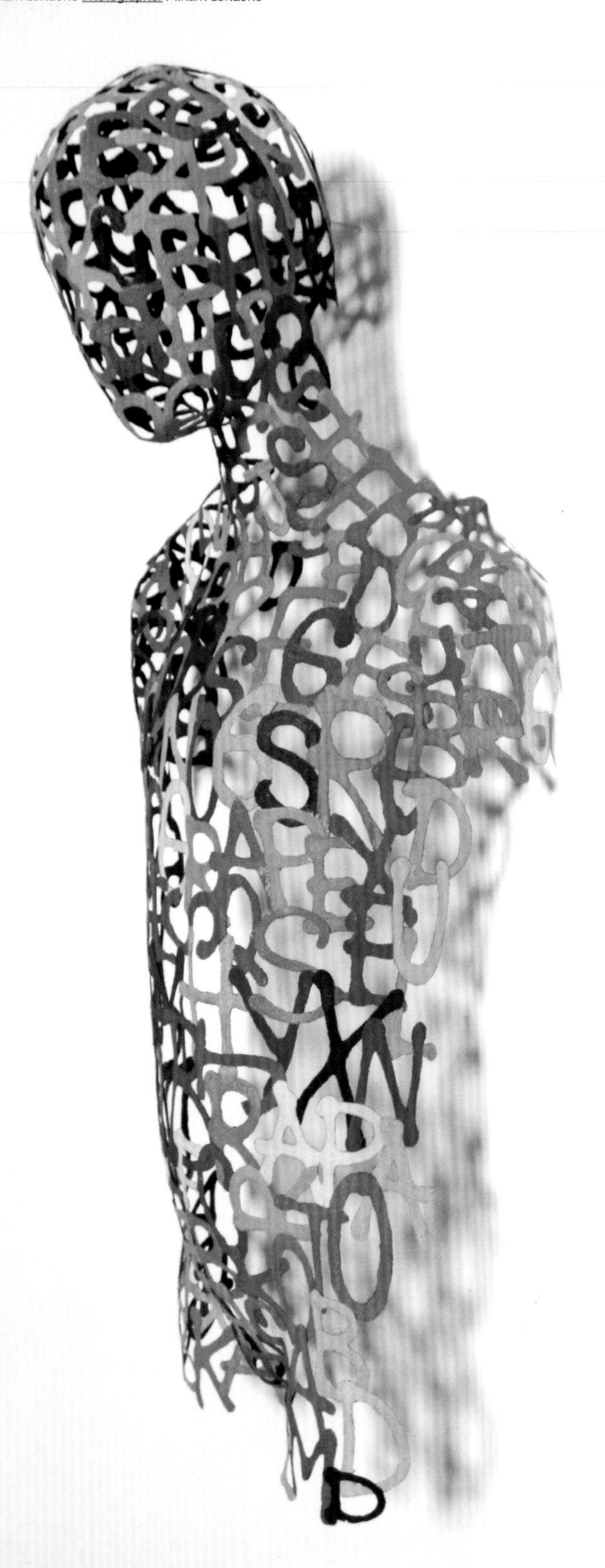

Line drawing

Line drawing is always associated with something slender, very slender. How, then, to make lines consisting of paper, drawings without their traditional support and that can hold themselves up on their own, while at the same time retaining the freshness of lines etched on paper? These are some of the questions Miriam Londoño asked herself during the course of her work, seeking new paths to extend the possibilities of drawing into the third dimension. The technique Londoño uses, drawing with liquid pulp, allows the flow and movement of a line just as if it were set on paper, shifting the expressiveness and narrative qualities of line drawing into space. Her calligraphic project is an attempt to reflect upon the meaning of communication with letters we construct words, sentences and stories. By using our own words and telling our own stories, we create our identity.

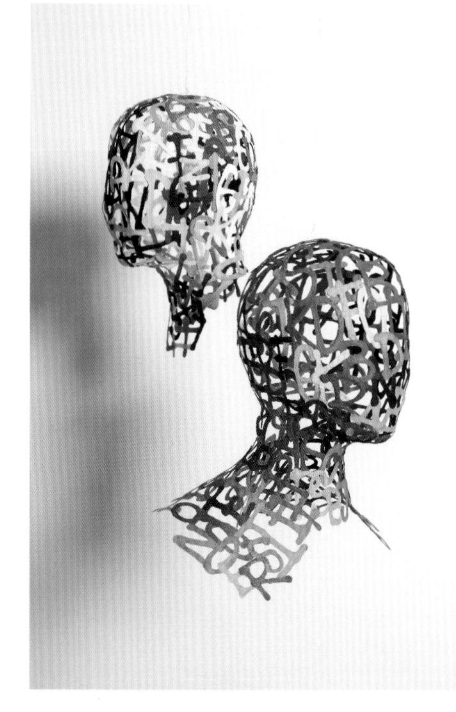

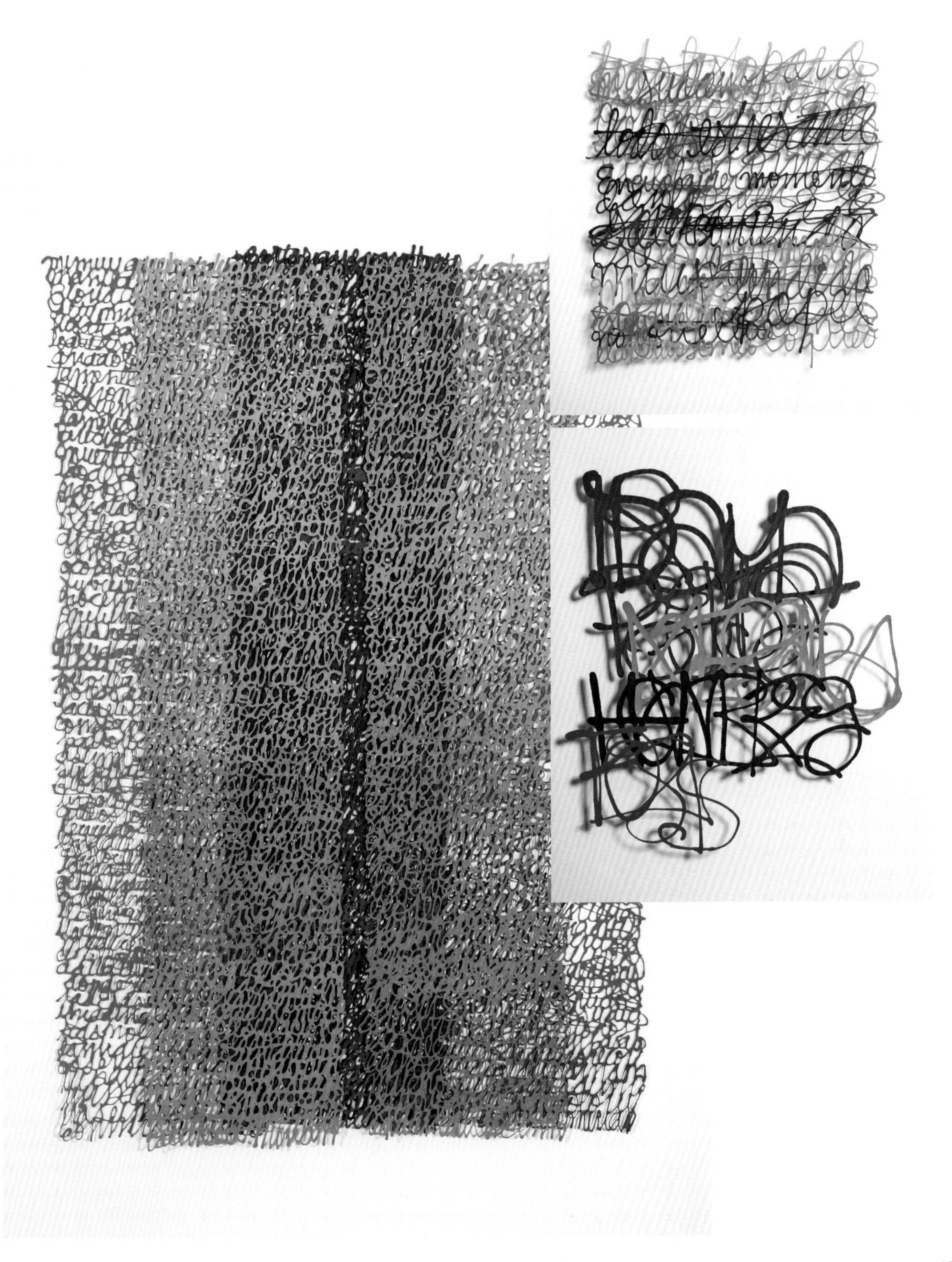

Tangible Handwritten Letter

A letter is physical confirmation of who we were at the moment it was written, or all we have left of a person or a time. I have been working with cut out correspondence for the past four years. I meticulously recreate notes and letters that I have found, written, or received by enlarging the documents onto a new piece of paper and intricately dissecting the negative spaces with an Exact-o knife. The handwriting and the lines support the structure of the cut paper, keeping it strong and sculptural, despite its apparent fragility. In these paper cutouts, I focus on the text, structure, and emotion of the letter in an elaborate investigation into the properties of writing and expression. Penmanship, word choice, and spelling all contribute to possible narratives about who that person is and what they are like. My recreating the letters is an extended concentration on peoples' inner lives and the ways they express their thoughts through writing.

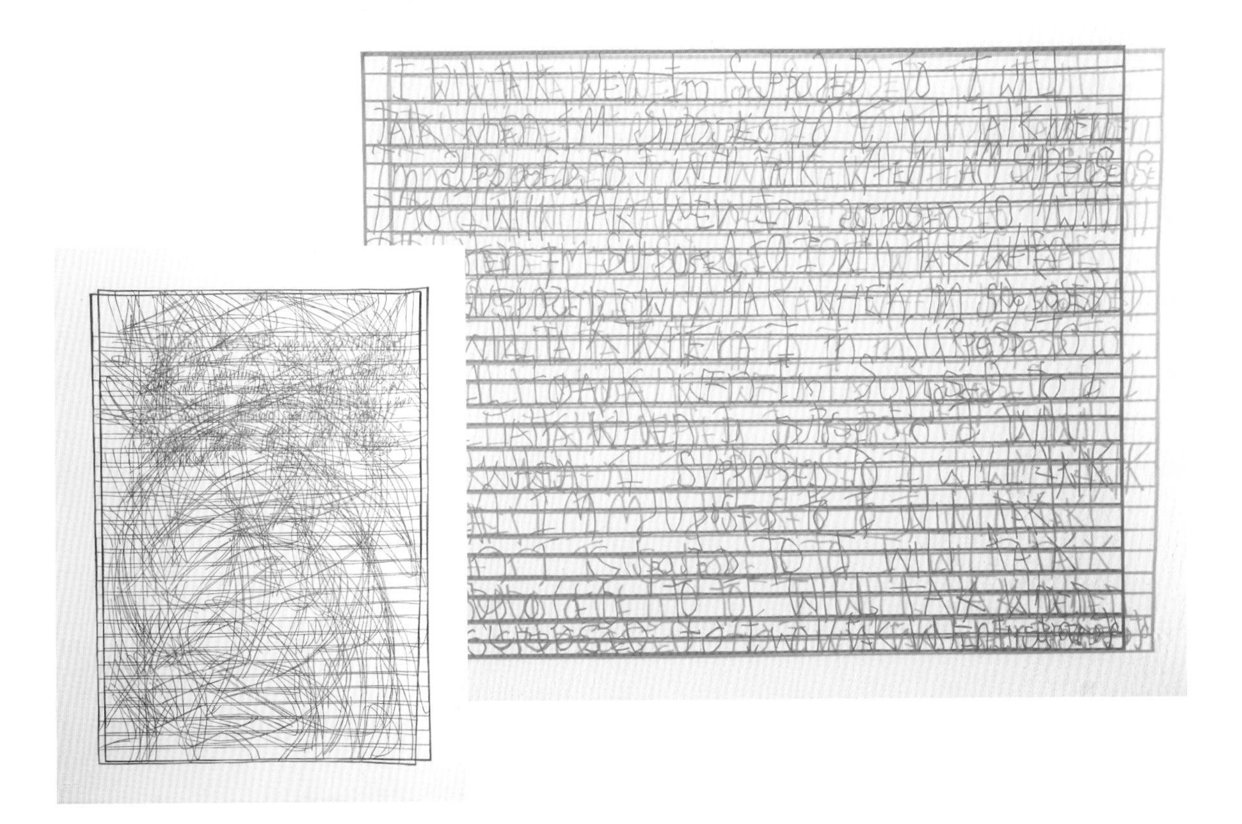

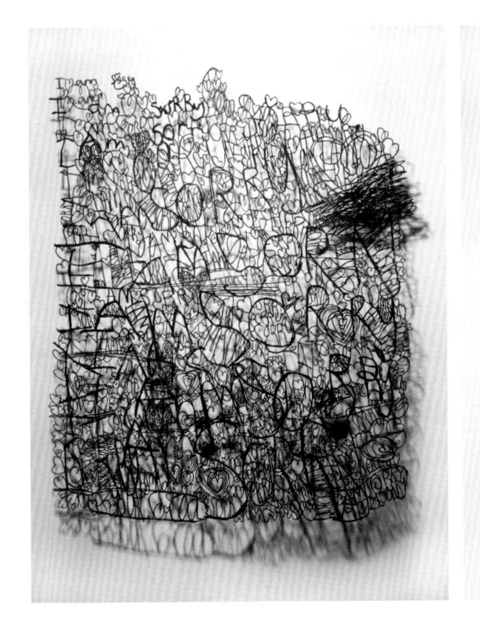

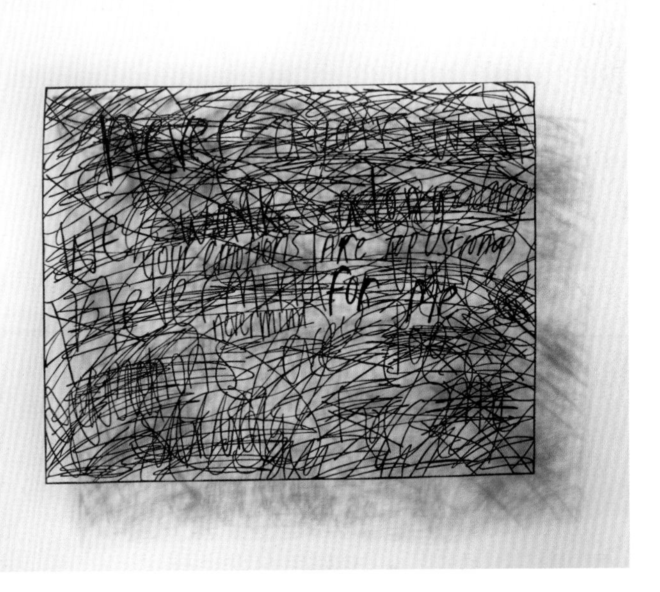

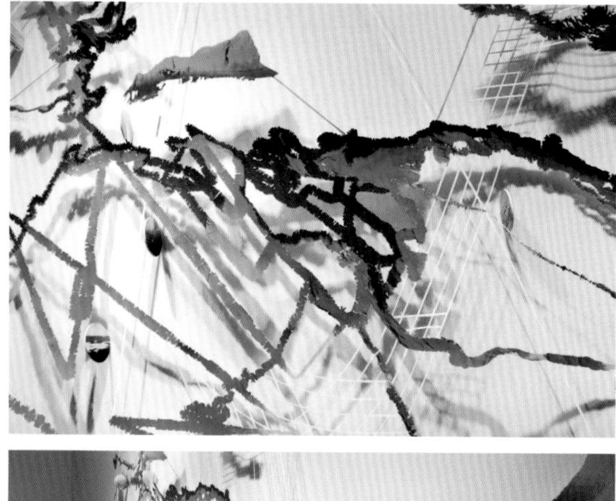

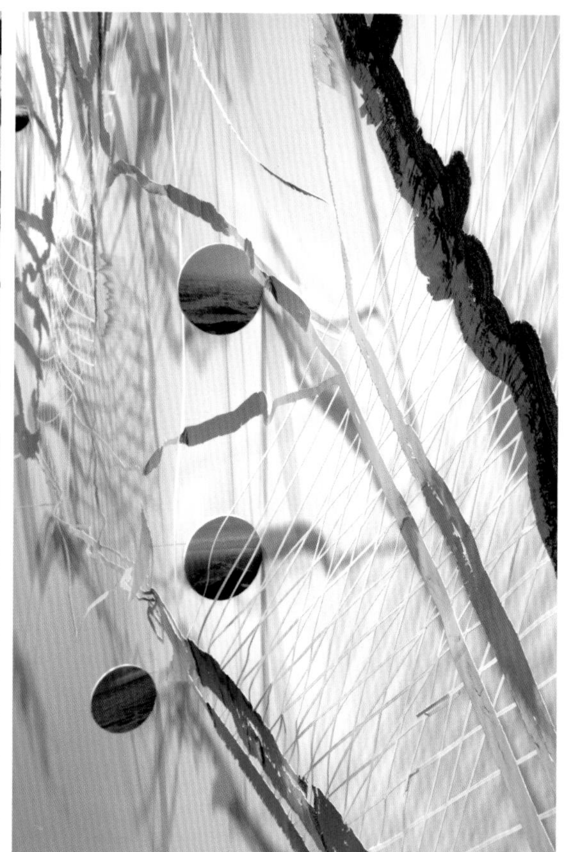

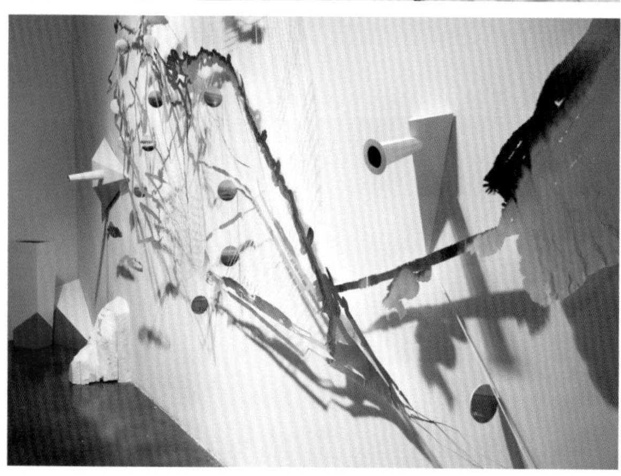

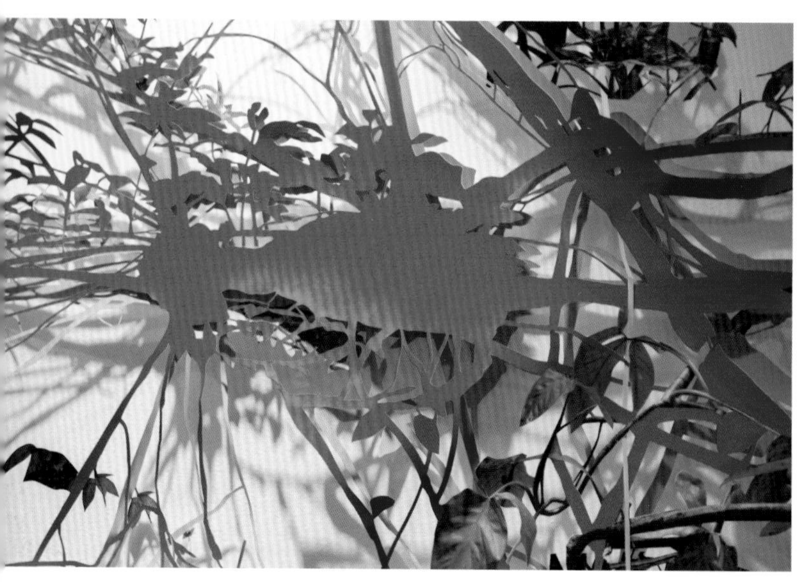

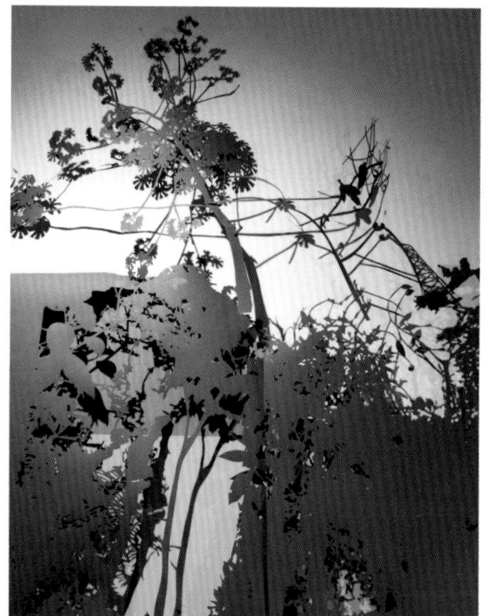

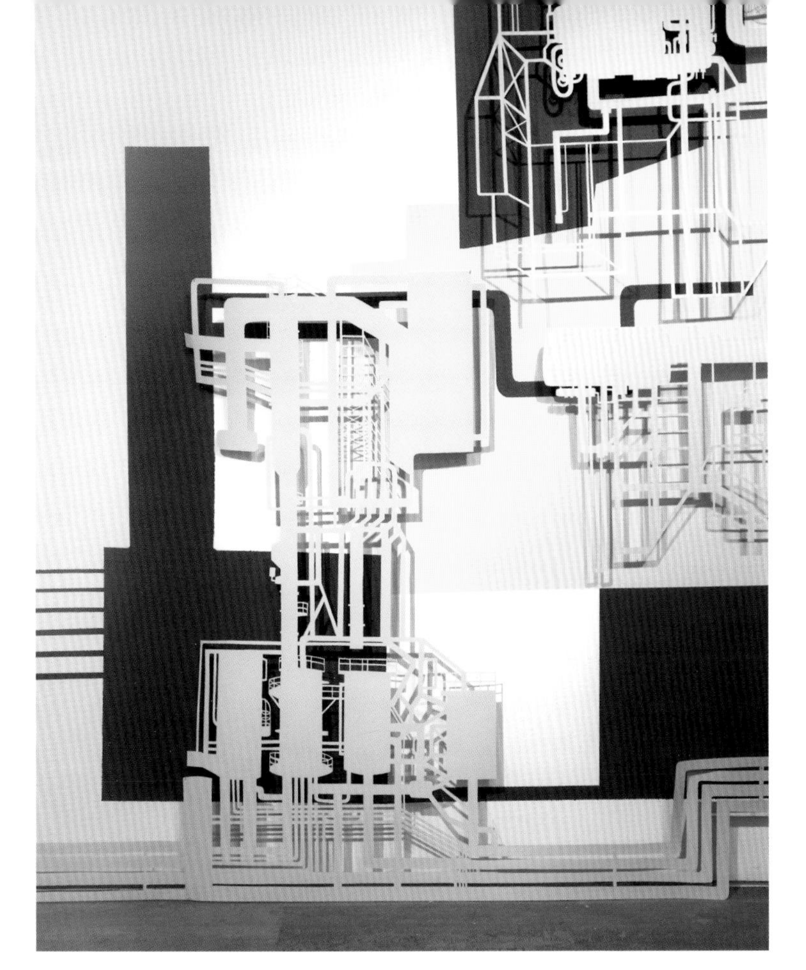

Human and Nature

Adriane Colburn's work consists of large-scale installations, comprised of layers of hand cut paper, digital prints and projected light, that investigate the complex relationships between human infrastructure, earth systems, technology and the natural world. These works, derived from scientific data, images and video collected through research and while participating in scientific expeditions, look at how mapping is used to investigate fragile and inaccessible ecosystems along the edges of the Earth's last vestiges of wilderness. Colburn's installations are created by transforming images through a system of physical removal, cutting out everything except imperative lines, thus creating constructions that are informed by voids as much as by positive marks. Through this process of cutting and display, an intricate array of shadows results.

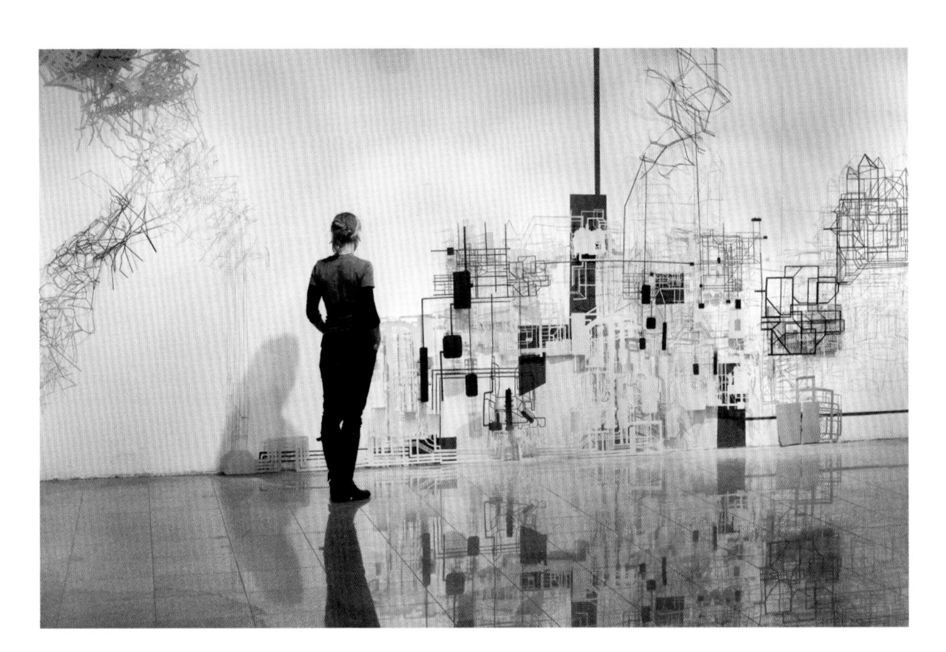

Artist Pat Shannon Photographer 5 D. Hyland

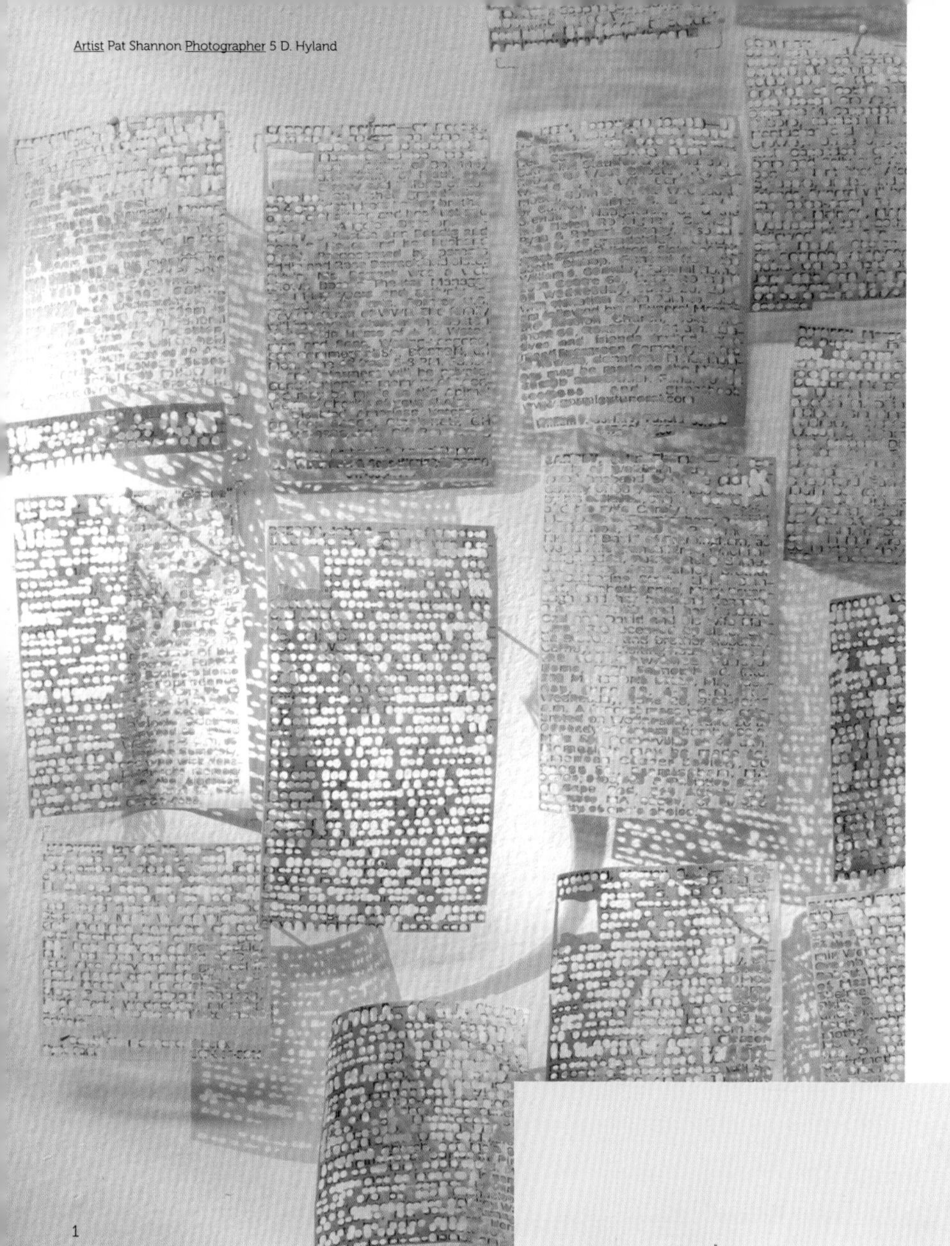

1

2

Newspaper Cutting

1 / Beloved
2 / Open House
3 / Wall Street Journal, Boston Globe, New York Times
4 / Cape Cod Times
5, 6 / Sunday New York Times

My work with newspapers grew from an ongoing curiosity about how we experience the passage of events in time. It was through this concern that I was first drawn to the newspaper's temporary nature and social function as a carrier of world events. In this body of work, I physically manipulated newspapers as a source to address temporal issues. The activity of cutting through the surface of the paper to remove all text and images became a type of extended dialogue, a form of non-verbal communication. There was this disruption of a narrative experience that compelled me both in the process and the results. Each seemed to satisfy a deeply felt personal yearning for momentary stillness.

Work Type Installation Technique Hand cutting

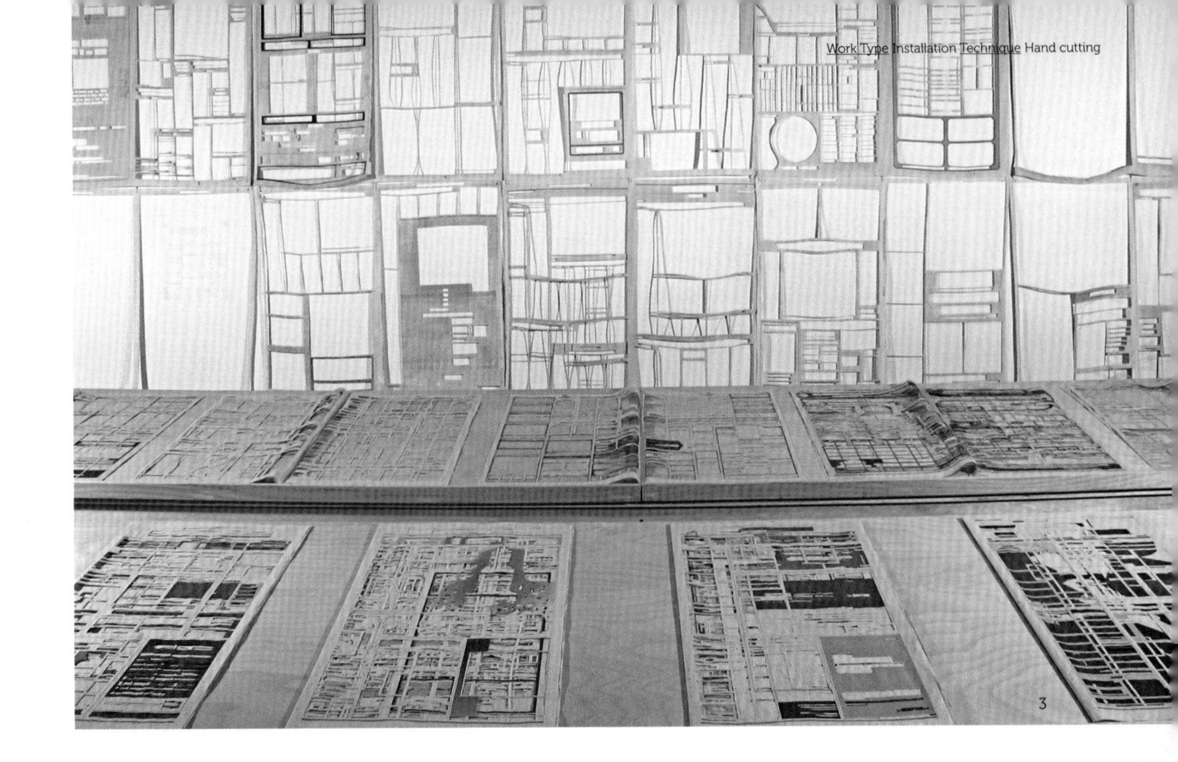
3

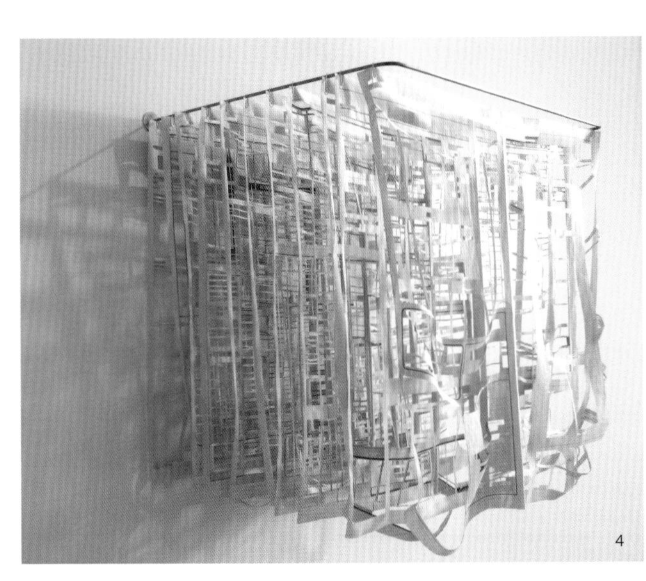
4

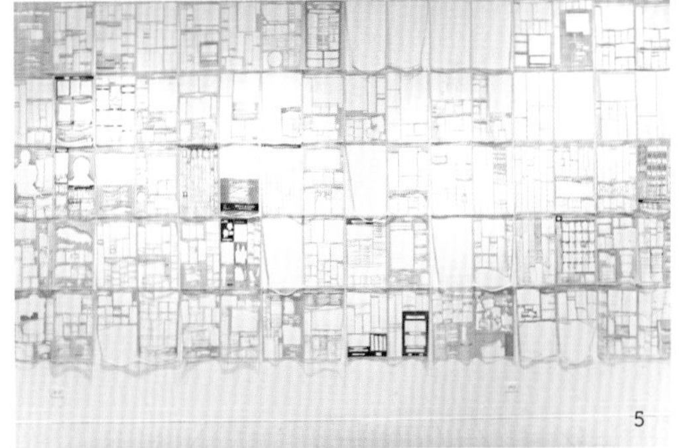
5

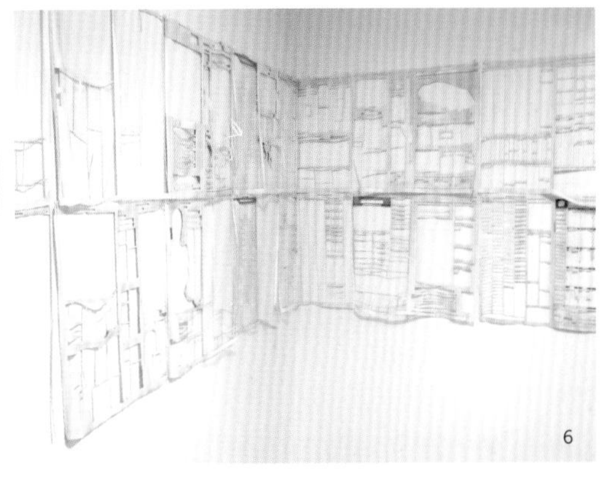
6

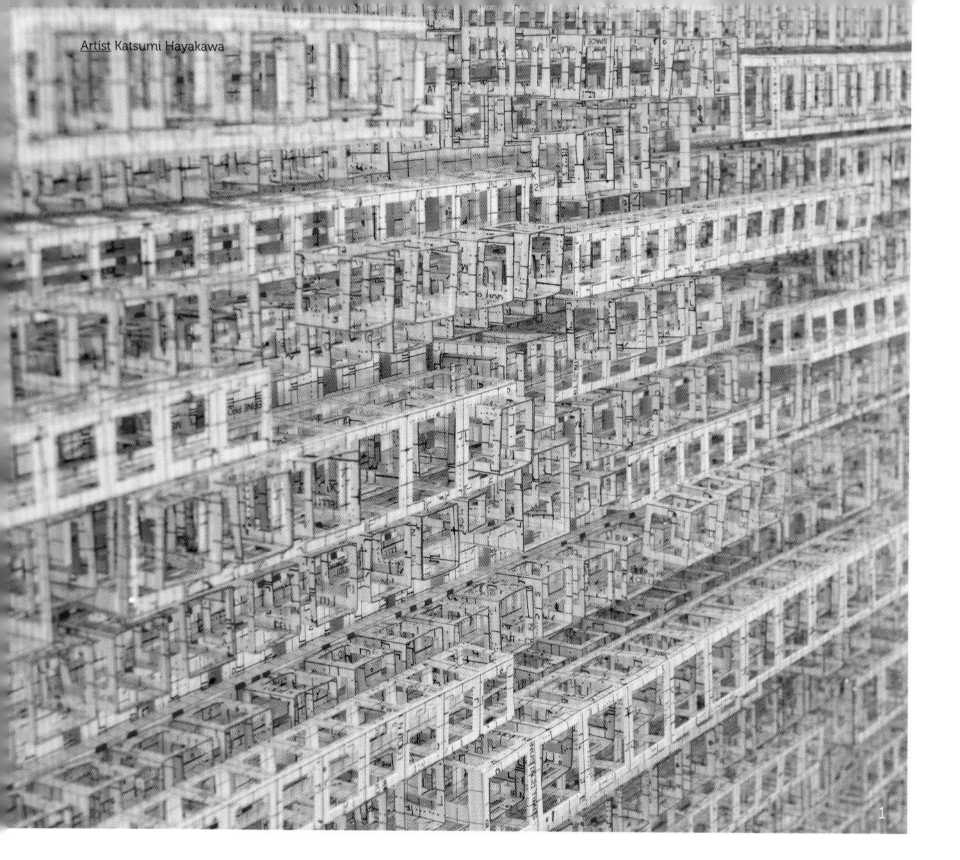

1

Architectural Paper Sculptures

1 / Composition 15
2 / Level 30 (86 x 116 cm)
3 / Hakomono 2 (54 x 69 cm)
4 / Detail of Hakomono 2
5 / Transcolor 3 (60 x 50 cm)
6 / Detail of Blue Lines

The absence of existence, the absence of nothingness, and the absence of absence; this is what I refer to as "space". A familiar example is a doughnut hole. Does it really exist or not? In my last solo exhibition, I explored various thoughts on two-dimensional space by using basic perspective drawing. In this exhibition, several types of rectangular solids and cubes made with paper were composed to make real spaces which are not illusions. By keeping color to a minimum, I am presenting a series of works made by trial-and-error thinking about the picture's composition and structure from different angles. I am pursuing the possibilities of new expression through the study of the relevance of the virtual and the real aspects of the concept of space, and the relationship between the work and the viewers.

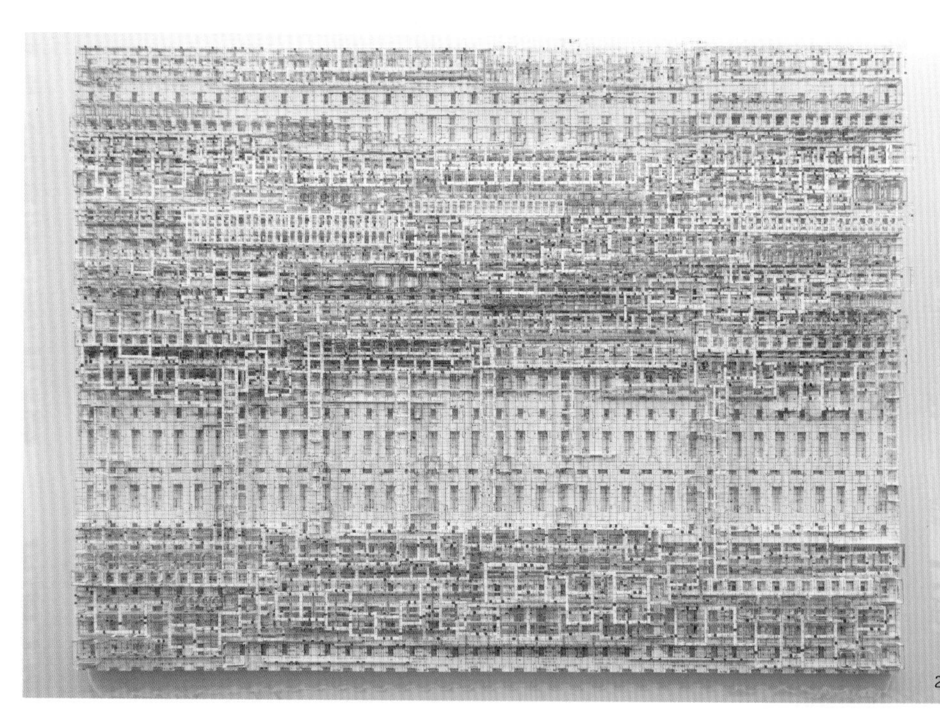

2

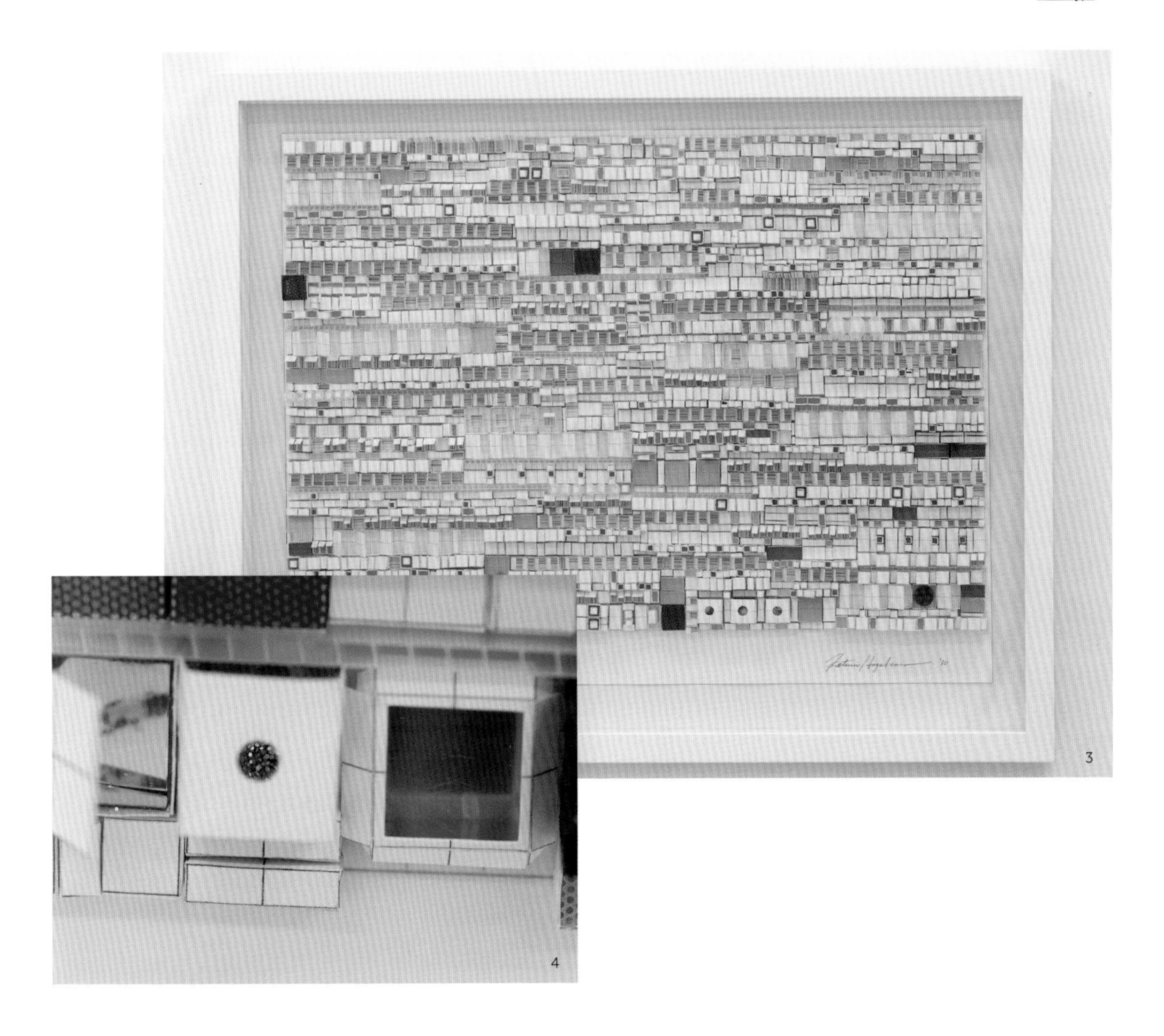

3

4

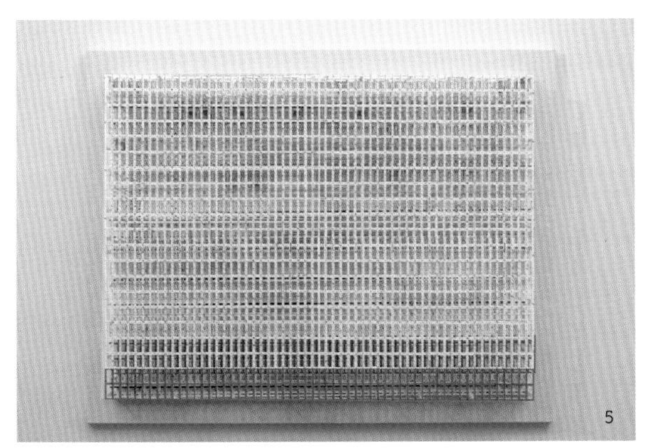

5

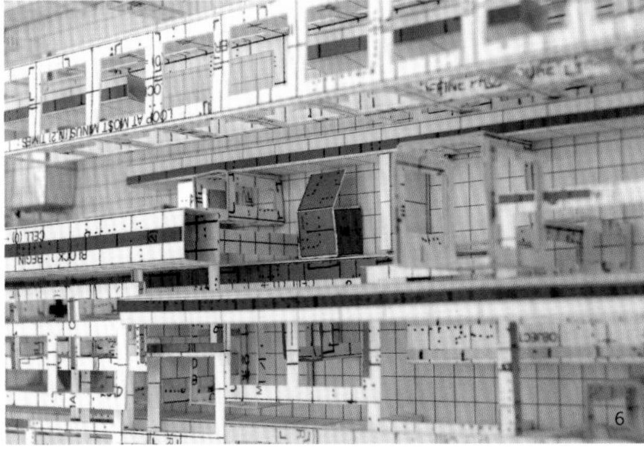

6

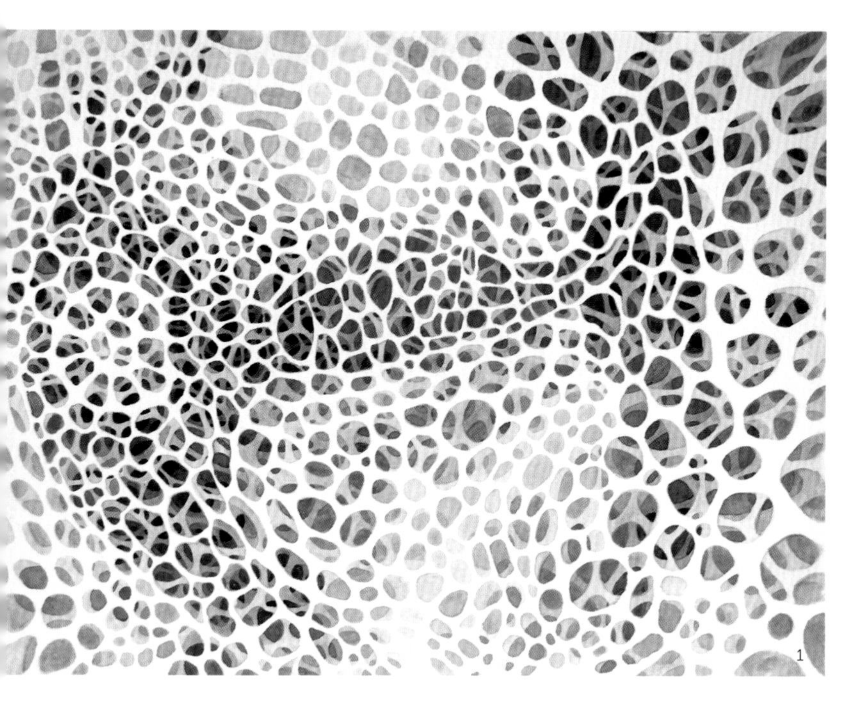

1

Monochromatic Paper Creations

1 / Untitled 15
2 / Untitled 18
3 / Untitled 20
4 / Aircooled 26
5 / Aircooled 25

My work on paper seeks to engage the viewer by adding a 3D dimension to 2D work. I allow the viewer to enter into the work by creating the appearance of space under the surface. My palette is monochromatic and limited to a range of tonality from black to white. Arches, Canson and Fabriano are my preferred paper manufacturers. I choose to work in 300gsm or thicker watercolor paper. My work process is to puncture the 2D space of the sheet of paper either by cutting with a knife to expose the underlying sheet which is lighter or darker in color; or by the following means:

Light work on paper: I start out painting with gouache or acrylic, circular or oval shapes with a slightly darker tonality than the paper color. The part that is not painted becomes the "white" structure or "screen" and will remain "untouchable" for the duration of the painting process. I paint a second or deeper layer with a darker tonality than the first layer within the first layer of cells (lightest tonality), limited by the white screen. And on it goes until there are no less than 3 layers that seem to penetrate deep into the sheet. Often black is the deepest and last layer.

The black works on paper are a reversal of the white process. For these works, I start with a blacked out gessoed sheet and work backward so that the last (deepest) layer is white.

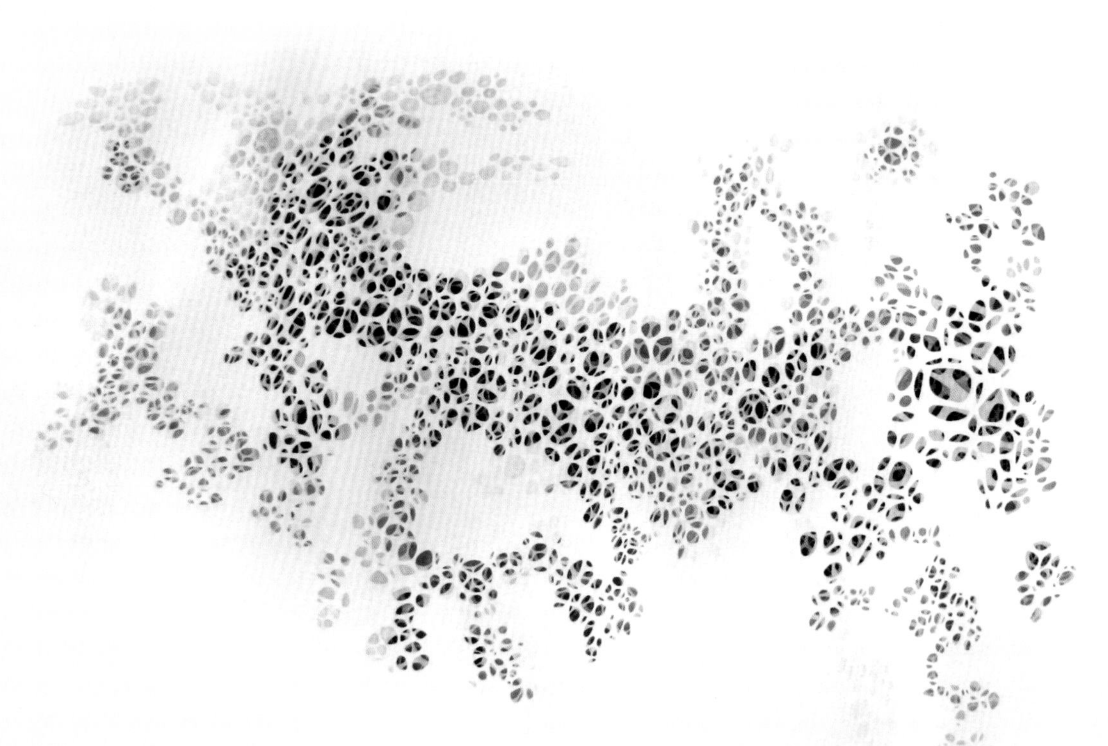

2

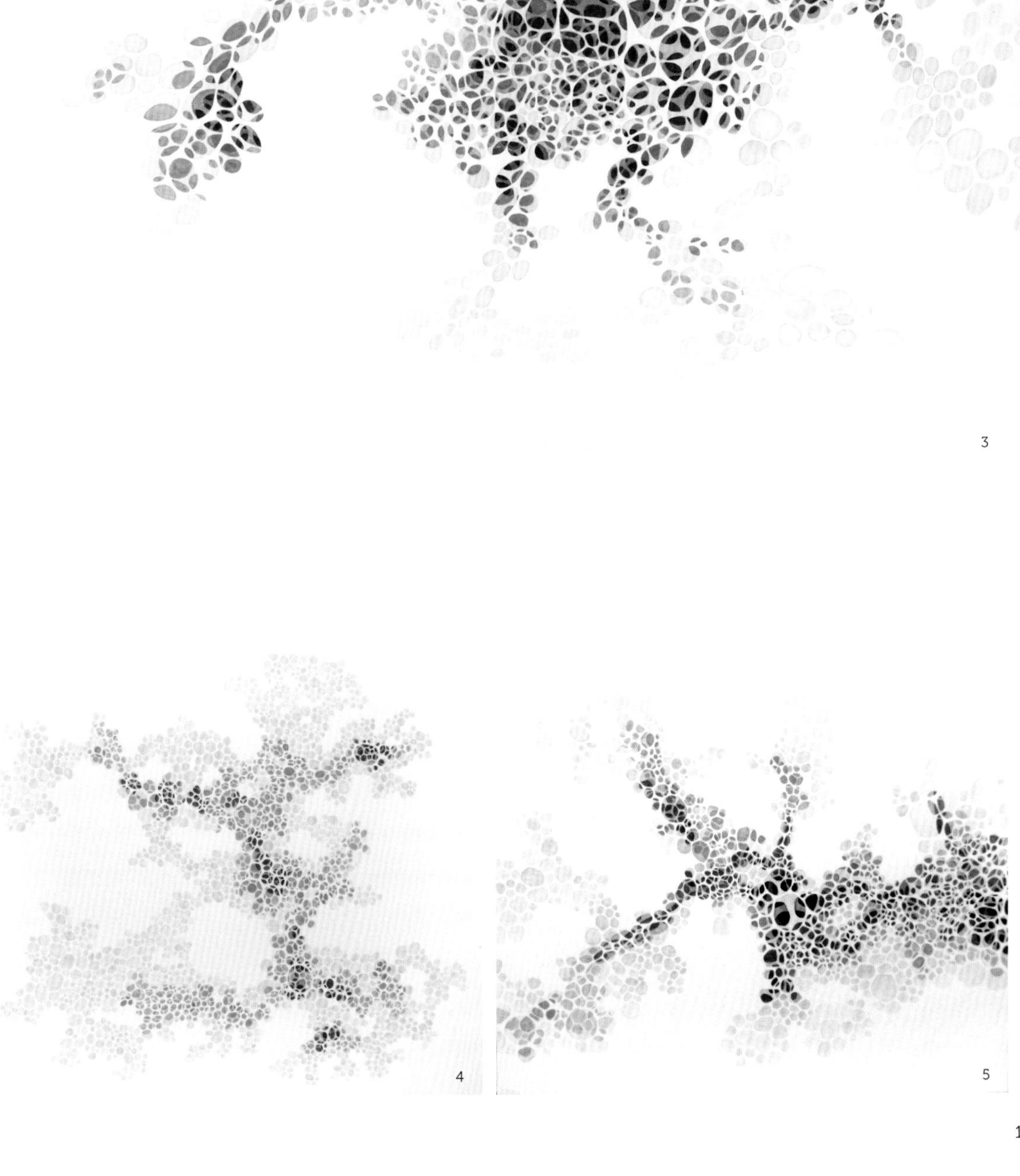

3

4

5

Map Exploration

1 / Lake
2 / Valley
3, 4 / Harbor
5 / Museum Complex

The map pieces explore the flexibility of simple patterns, shapes and textures to evoke ideas of place, information, development and time. I enjoy creating different "societies," which I characterize by their patterns of settlement; some are organic and chaotic, others exaggerate the human tendency towards order and rigidity in pattern. The pieces are not replicas of specific places but are inspired by my memories of places I have been or seen or dreams of places I would like to see. By subverting the idea of a "map" of a specific site, I hope to provide the viewer with an environment in which she can bring her own memories of place and time to the landscape she is viewing.

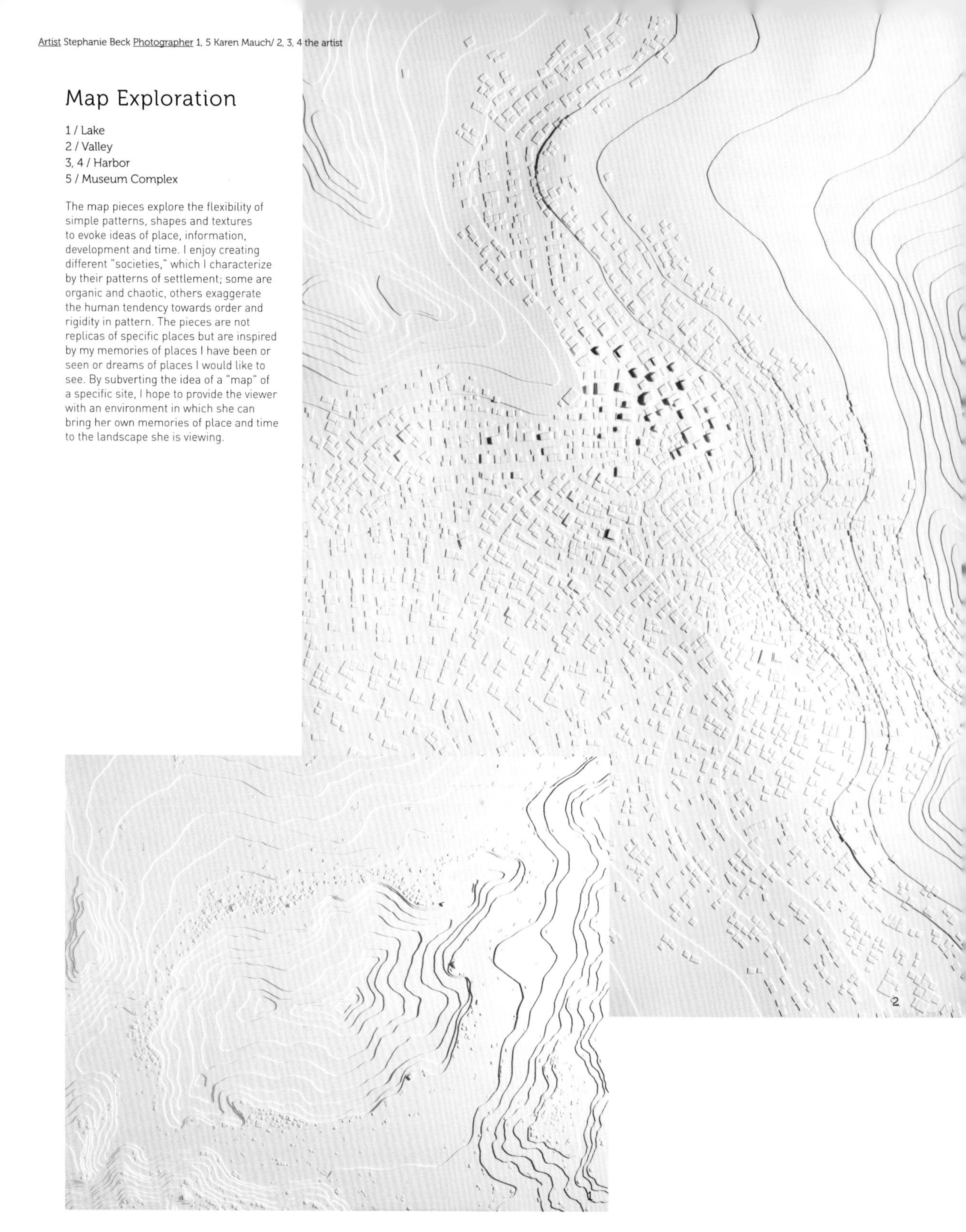

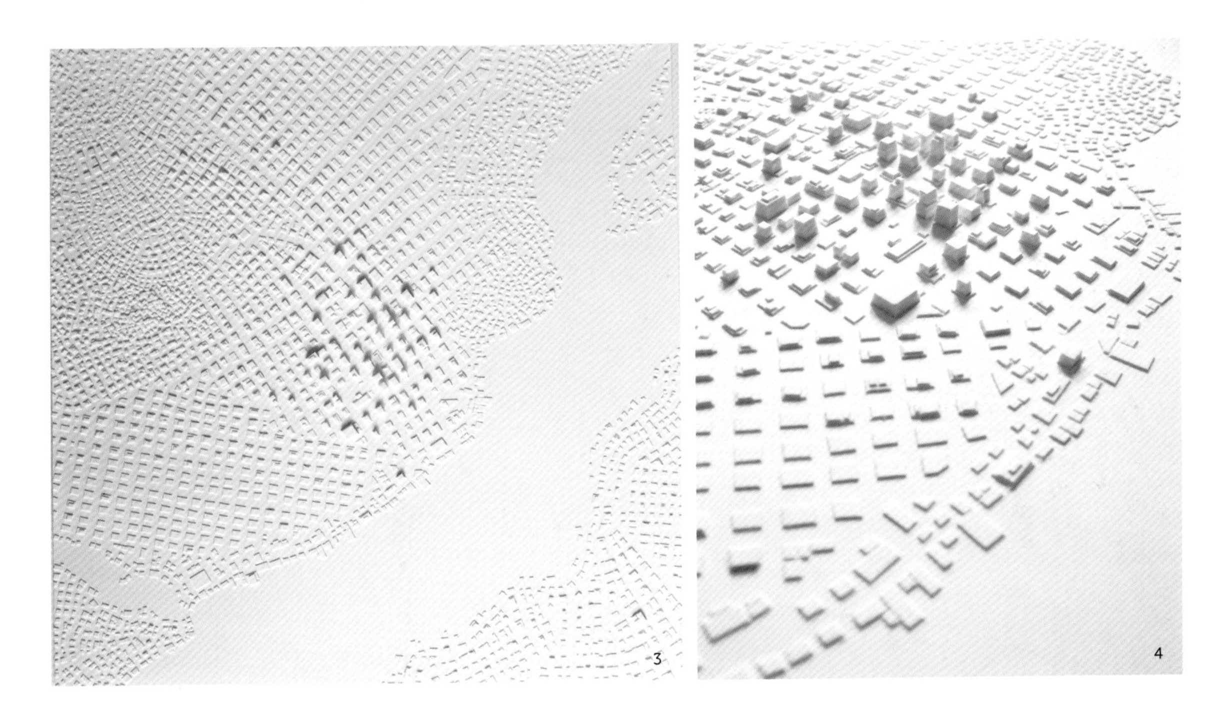

3

4

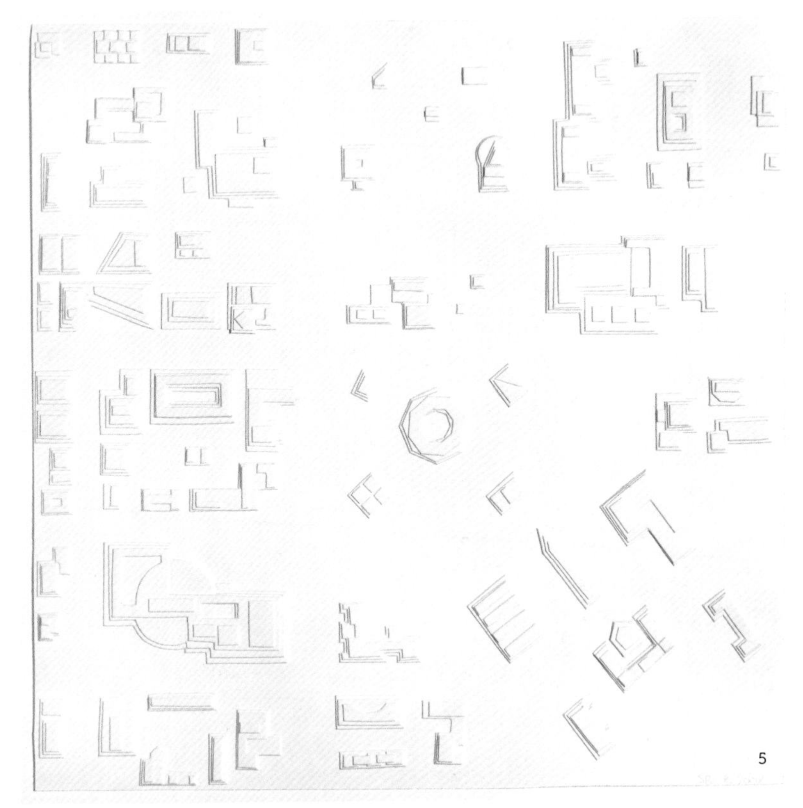

5

Aviary

"Aviary" is inspired by a downtown skyline in flux, with skyscrapers, construction cranes, and a bridge to nowhere. Each building also functions as a cage and shadow-puppet theater for various birds, which live inside, playing out the roles that we play in these spaces.

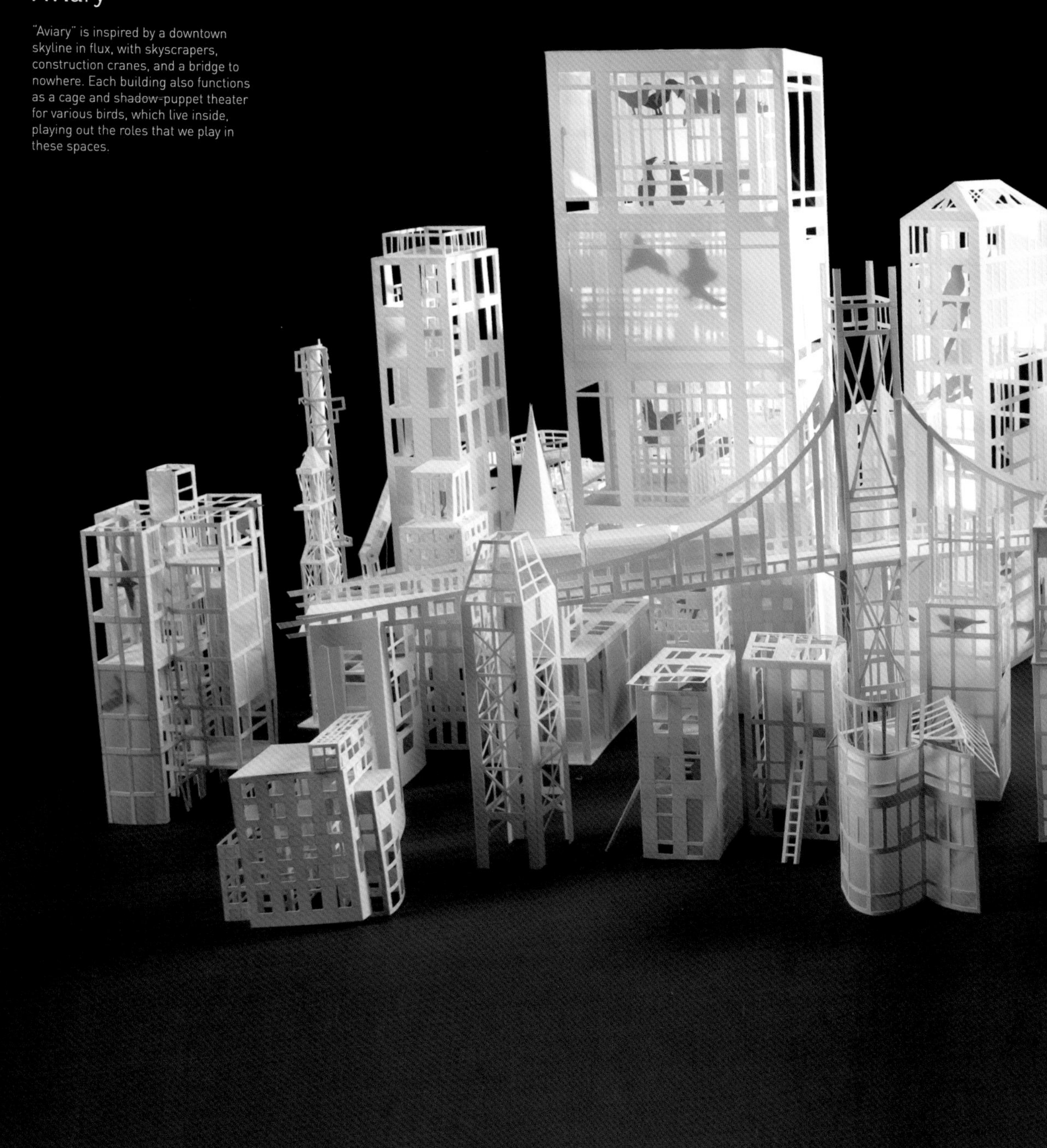

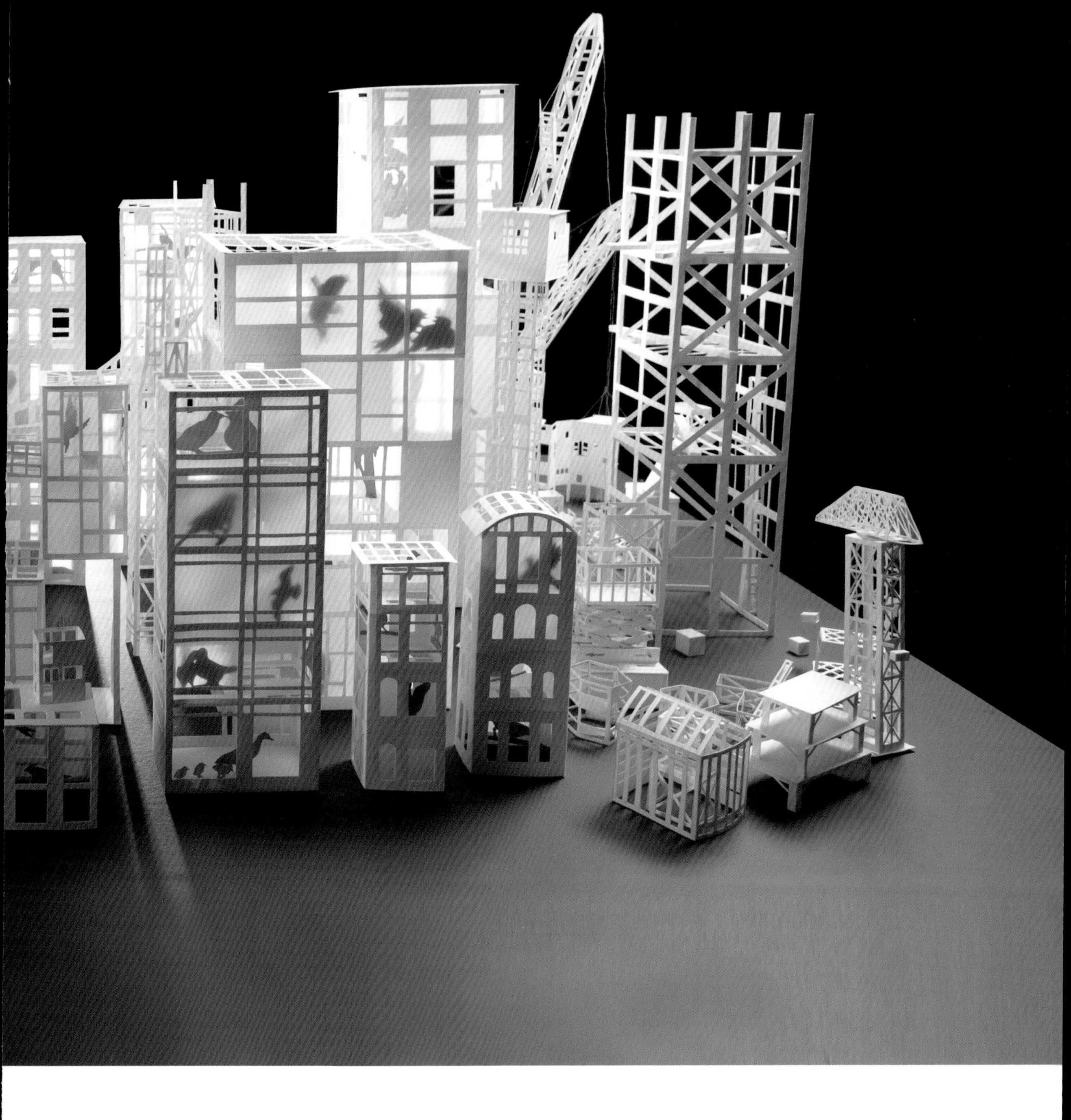

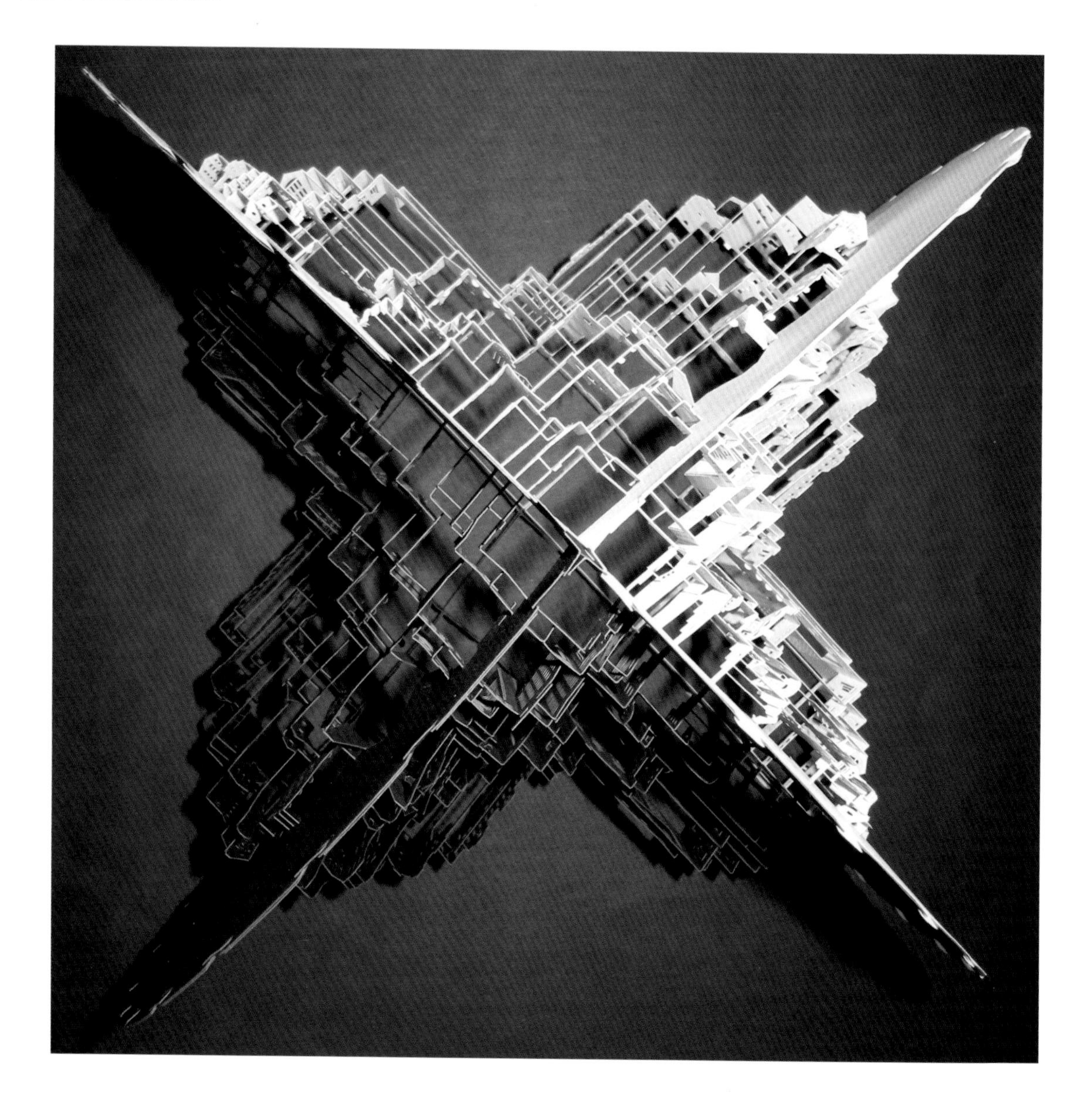

Big City, Amsterdam, 2011

This artwork consists of four sides, each connected to the other by means of integrated tabs/slits. These can be loosened, and after that the artwork can be folded into a two-dimensional surface. Also all four sides can be loosed and individually folded flat to the original piece of paper. The topic of this artwork is the hometown of the artist, namely Amsterdam. Paper-brand: Rives Artist and Envelopprint. This work is 30 x 40 x 40 cm.

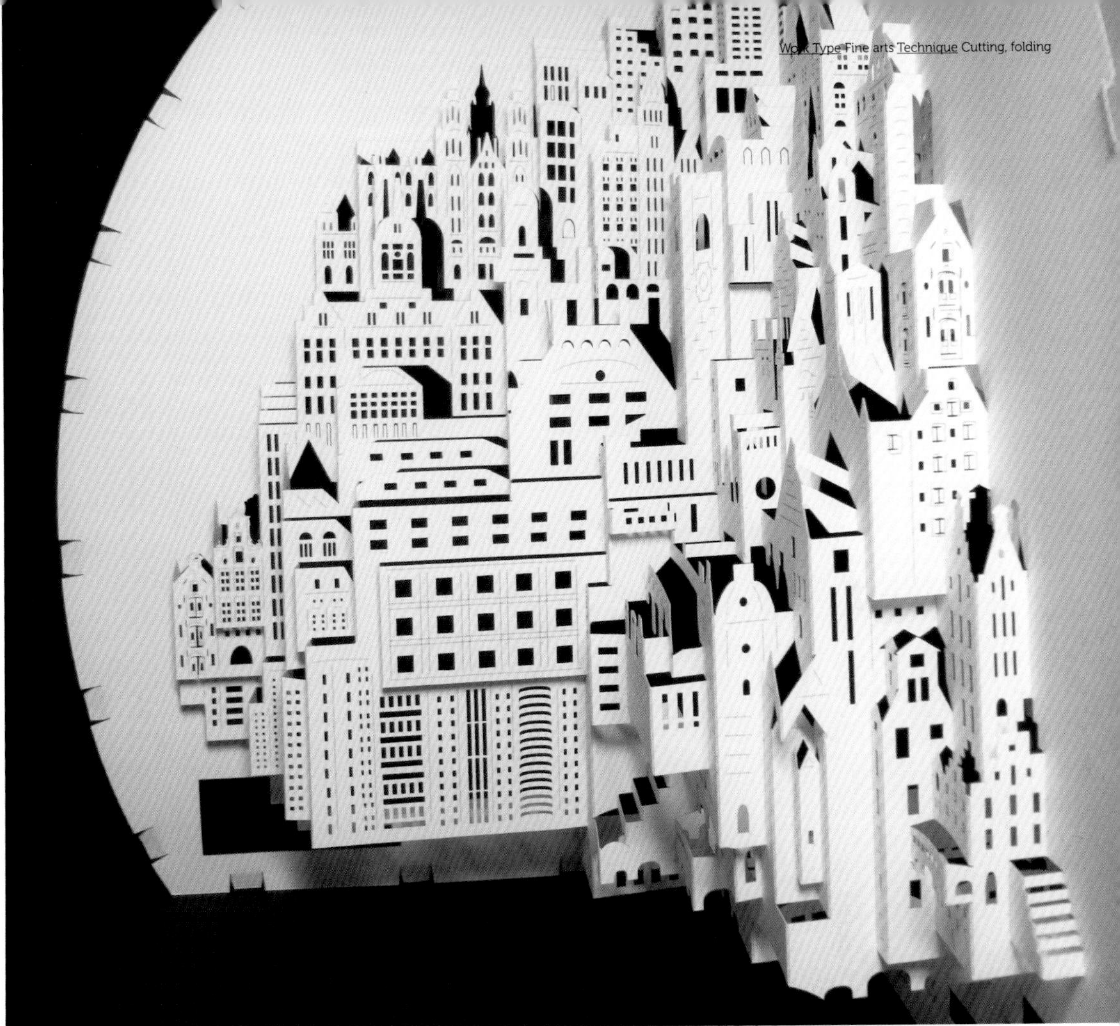

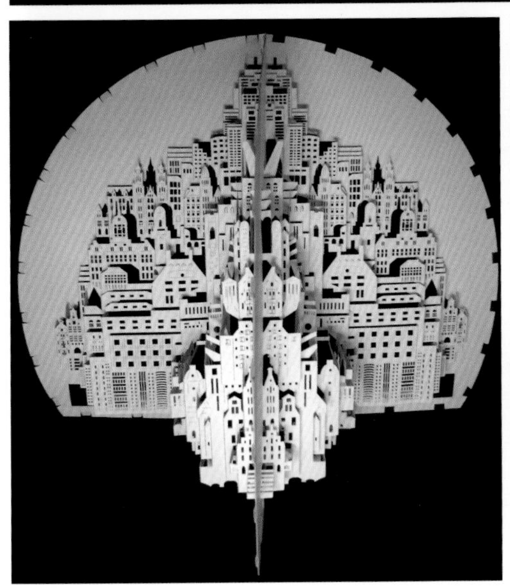

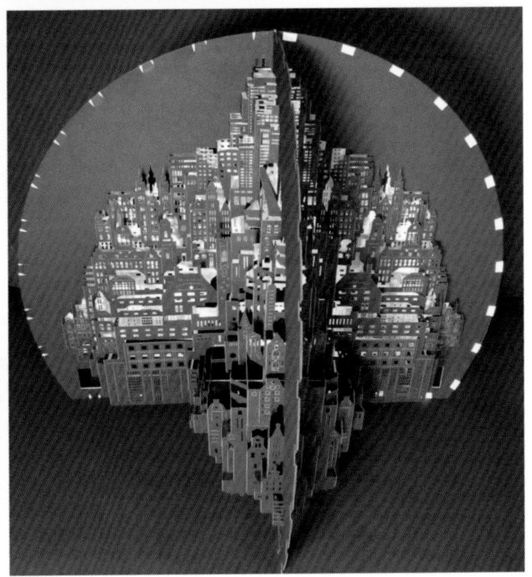

Reflection on Sagrada Familia

This project is based on the Sagrada Familia in Barcelona (Spain). The original basilica in Barcelona was designed by the famous Catalan architect Antoni Gaudi. It is a terracotta paper-brand with a size of 60 x 30 x 30 cm. The artwork consists of four outsides and also has an inside design (which is light-colored). The entire artwork can be folded flat to a two dimensional surface.

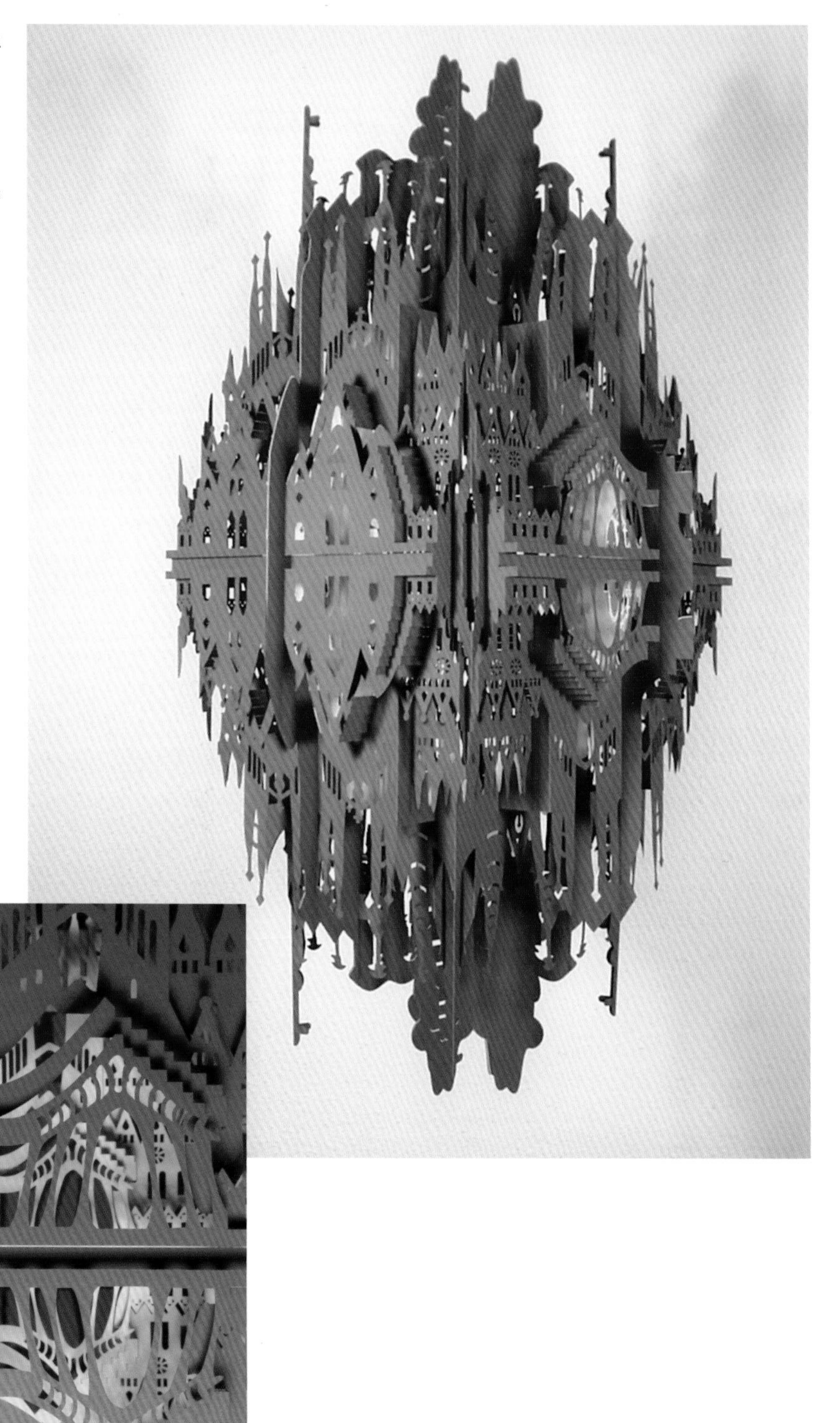

Reflections

Reflections is an abstract artwork with architectural characteristics. This artwork is cut and folded out of one piece. This artwork can be unfolded to a two-dimensional flat surface. The size is 30 x 15 x 15 cm.

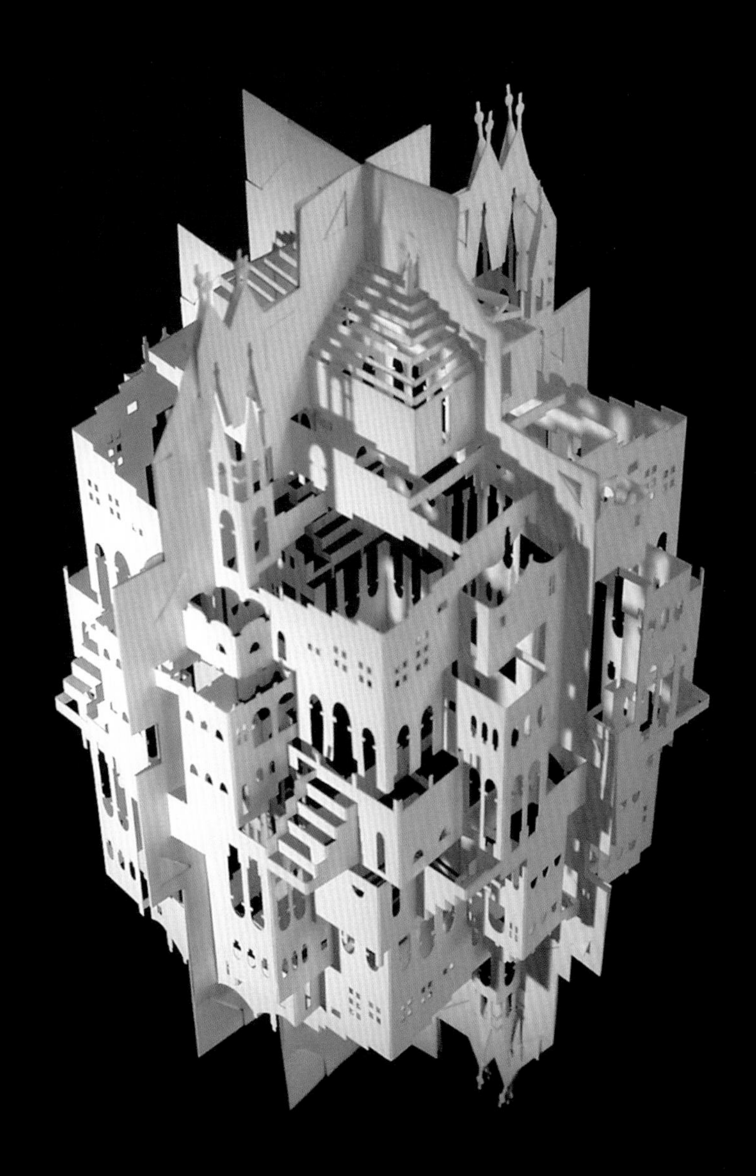

Wunderboxes

Wunderboxes is a temporary installation designed for the V&A Friday late programme "Archive Live" in the grand entrance hall of the V&A museum in London. Postlerferguson was commissioned to visualize parts of their research and the design team responded with an installation of differently formatted cardboard boxes — each one housing a bright orange light box displaying a variety of three dimensional models to create an abstract but strangely familiar collection of "things". Spectators were encouraged to come closer and examine the partly hidden and camouflaged objects being drawn in by the warm and hypnotizing orange glow of the boxes.

From a tiger attack helicopter to Han Solo in Carbonite - from a Lobster to the iconic "Nike Swoosh" the objects represent the designers' diversified interests and fields of research from science to popular culture.

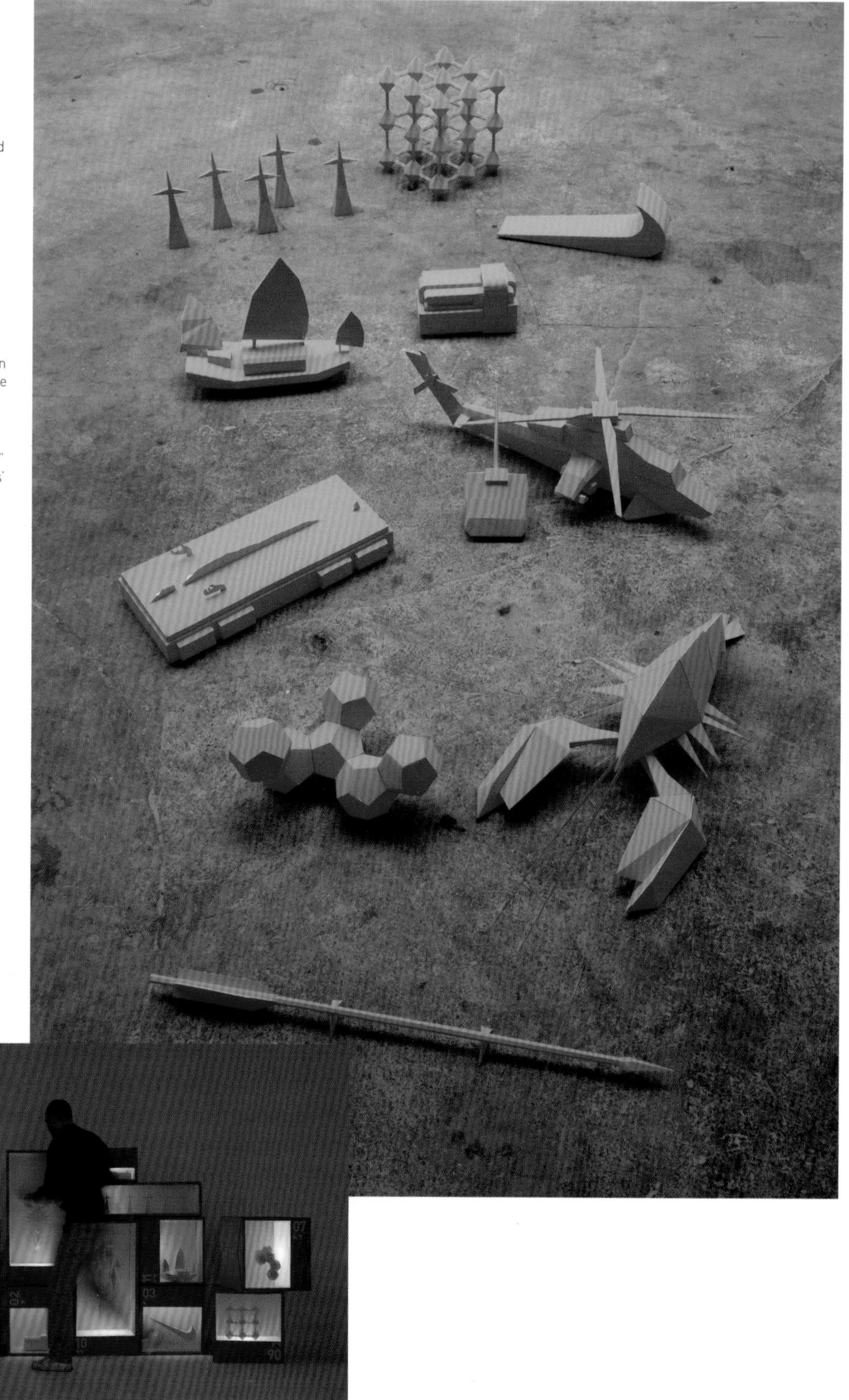

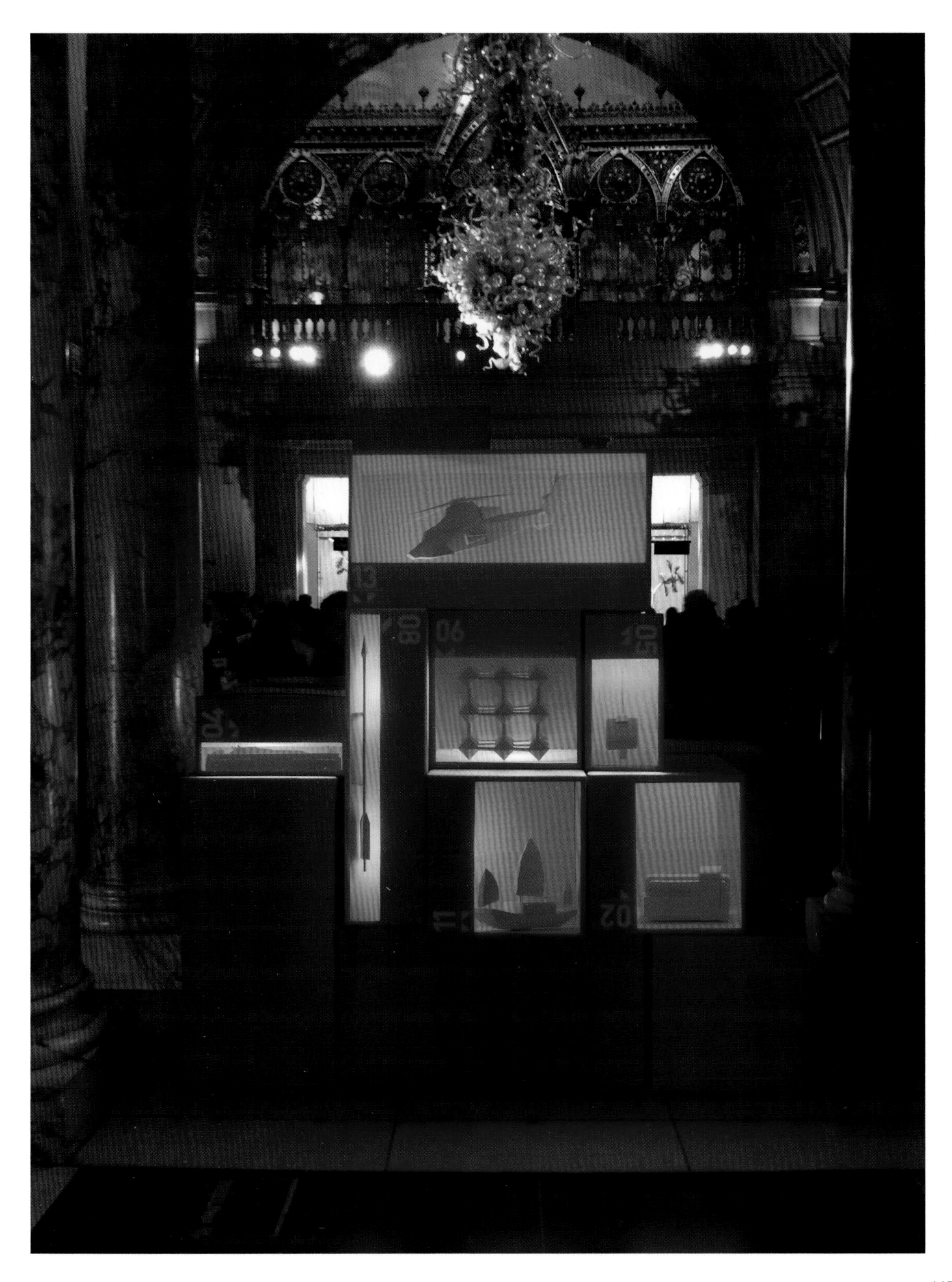

Free Range Birds

As sponsors of Free Range 09, Grafik Magazine commissioned an installation of recycled paper birds made from old copies of the magazine. A cluster of birdhouses also provided a messaging system, inviting people to comment on the work in the show by writing on a paper feather and posting it into a birdhouse.

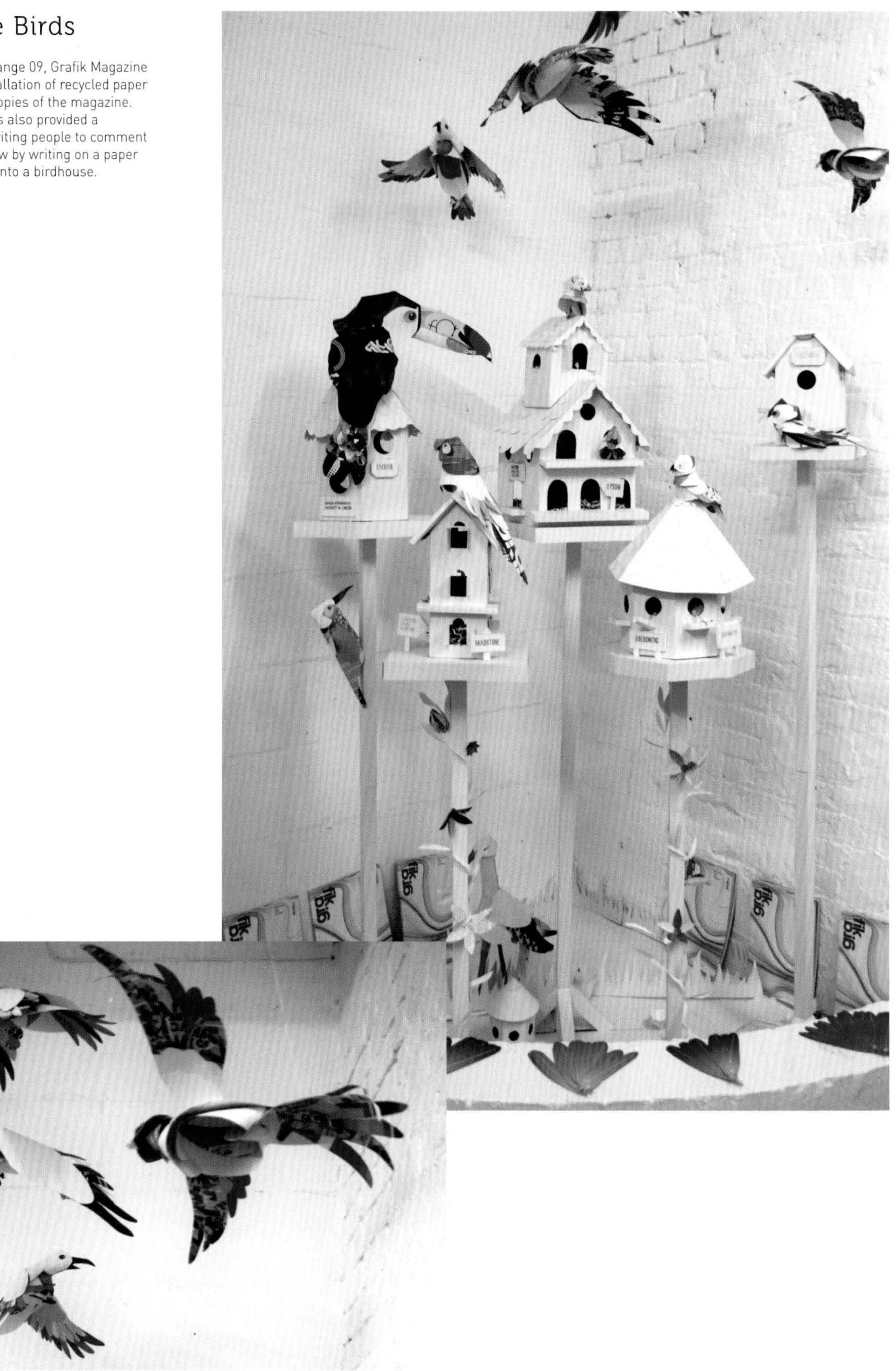

Designer Andy Singleton Photographer Sylvain Deleu Client Crafts Council and Liberty Partnership

Work Type Fine arts Technique Hand cutting, scoring, folding

They Loved What They Found

This project is commissioned by the Crafts Council to celebrate the opening of the Liberty stationery room. The work consisted of a multiple site paper installation situated in a window and the stationery room. Andy Singleton created 26 handmade bird sculptures to go with three handmade paper trees and numerous other objects such as books, pens and ink wells, all constructed from paper.

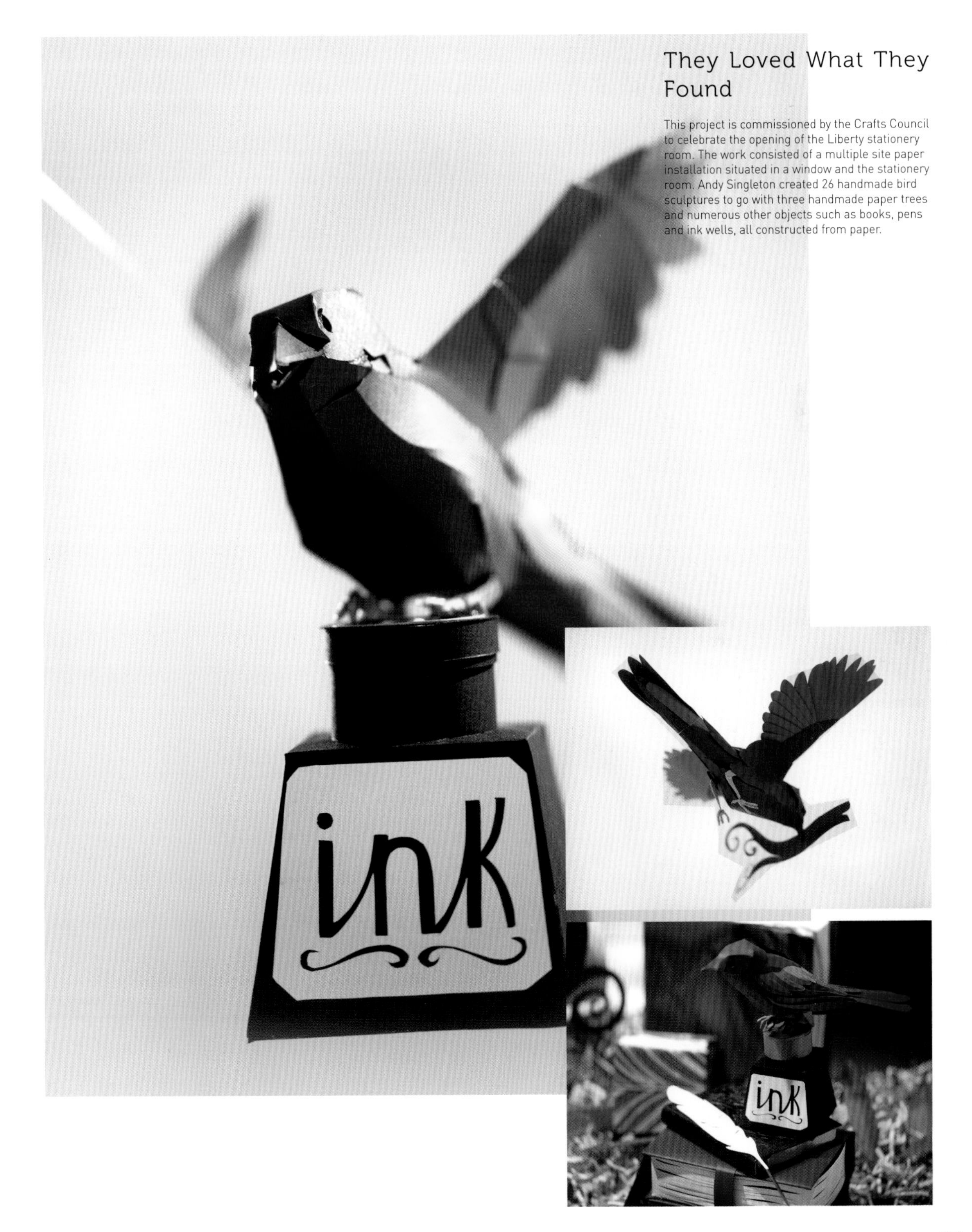

Designer Sloppy James Photographer Michel Dubreuil

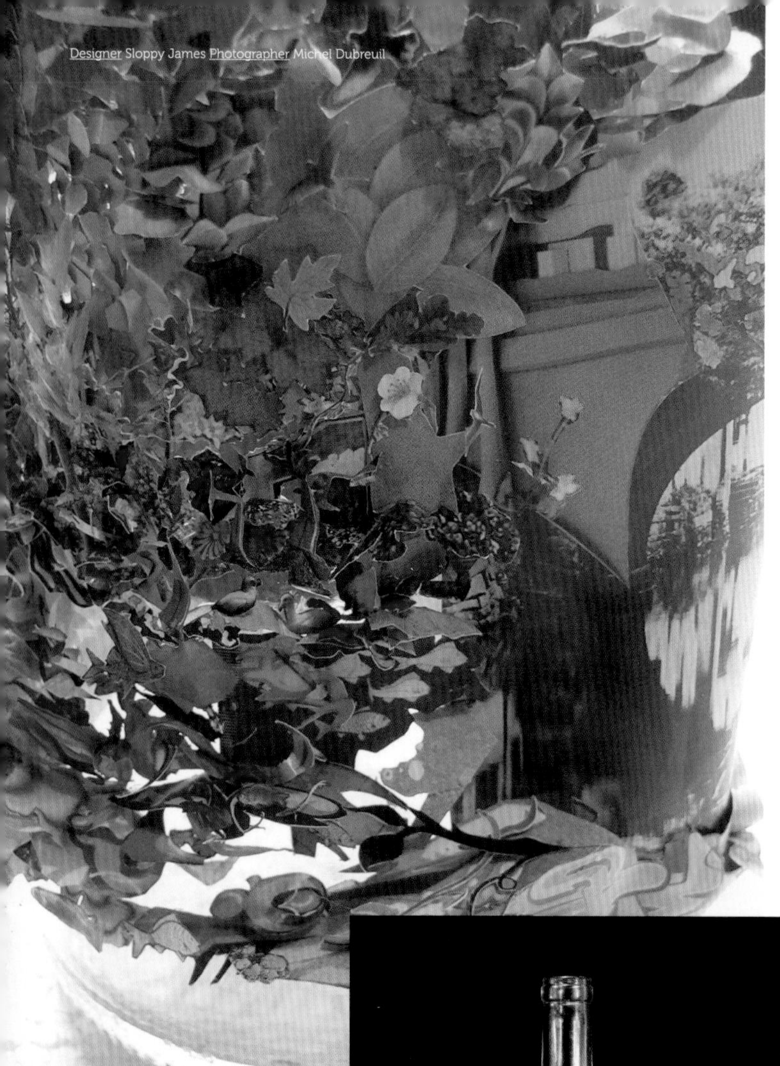

That The Sky is Above Us, Even When We Do Not See It

This particular piece is part of a project that I immersed myself in for a little over two years. Some said that I had fallen off the planet during this time, but I was there (in my studio) day and night working happily on a series of collages that would eventually evolve into collage-sculptures. This project was the beginning of my exploration not only into collage, but more importantly, into paper, color, concept, placement and pattern.

'That The Sky is Above Us, Even When We Do Not See It' is one of four collage-sculptures that I worked on during this period. I created each on a bottle that I used as a glass canvas, and like the Greek vases of red or black figures, each bottle was meant to be rotated to be able to better understand and view the entire narrative gist or story.

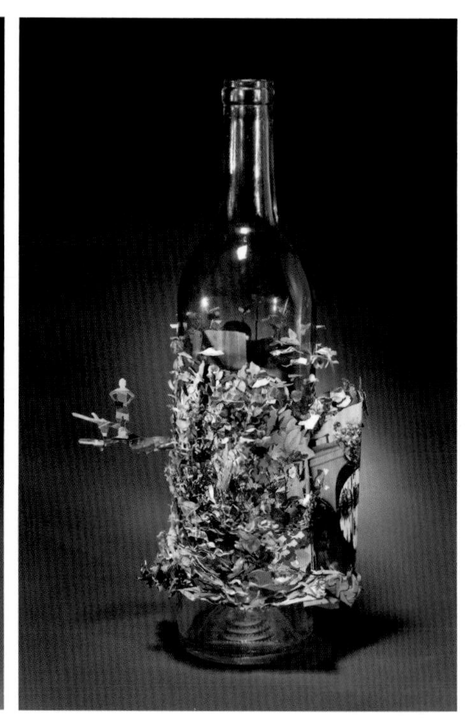

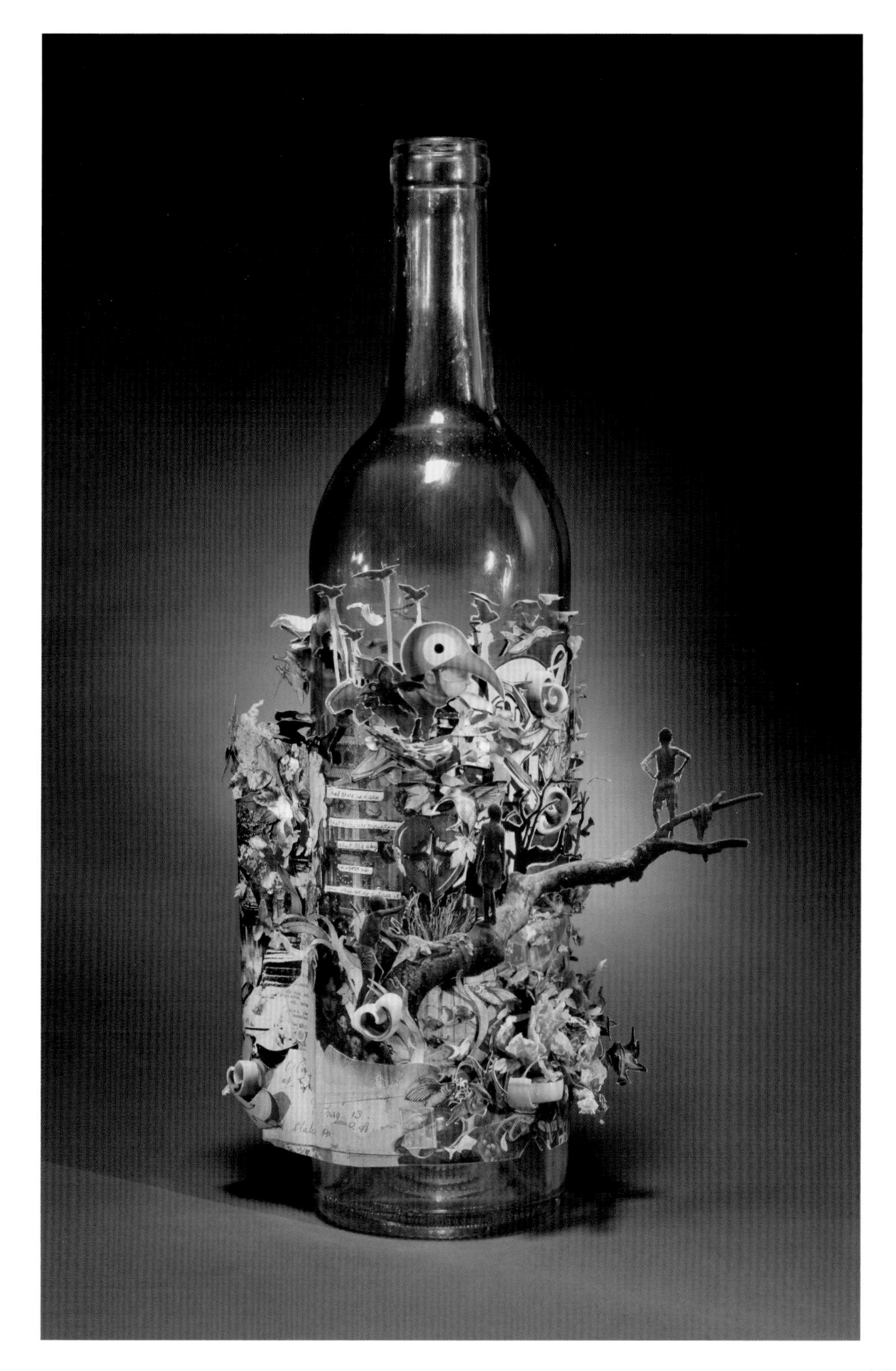

Design Agency Packaging UQAM Designer Justin Lortie, Nadine Sigouin-Cantin, Aleksandra Krakowiak Client Packaging UQAM | Sylvain Allard

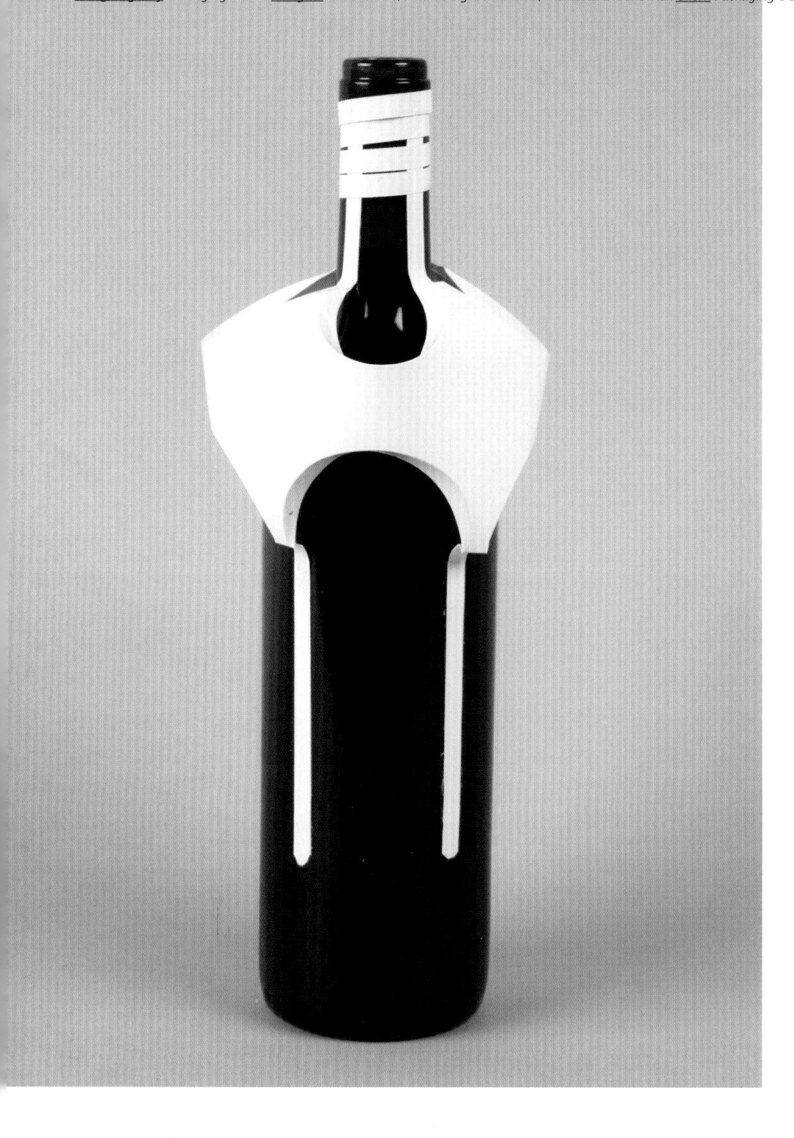

Wine Label

To begin our session and create a complete immersion in the world of packaging, I invited the students to do this exercise during their first course in 2010. The two-dimensional sheet of paper takes shape and becomes a volume. Therefore, shadows and light act on the white surface and create an image. The assignment was to design and create a label for a bottle of wine from a single sheet of paper. Through manipulation, bending, cutouts, and mechanisms or in repeated patterns and structures, the students created an image solely of paper. All of the projects explored the potential of paper; printing was not allowed. Since it was meant to be an exploration to push the limits of paper, transportation constraints, marketing and handling were not an endpoint. In contrast, research, innovation, virtuosity, originality and skill were the criteria for evaluation.

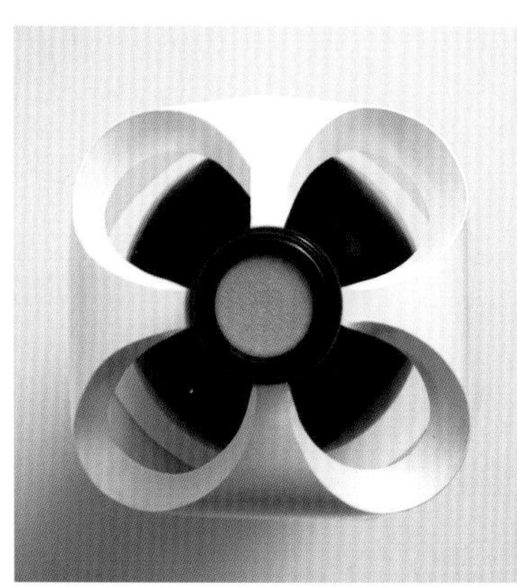

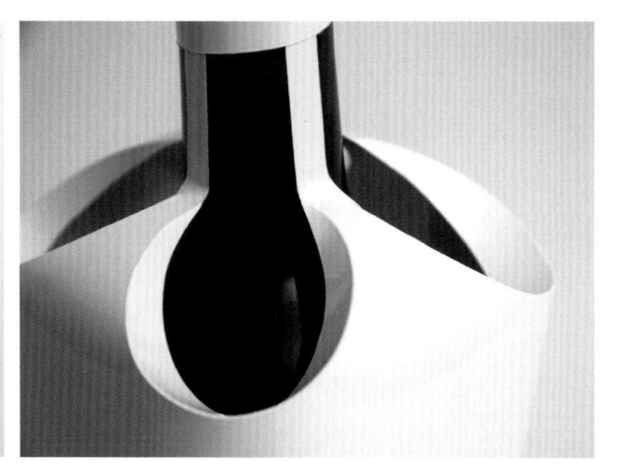

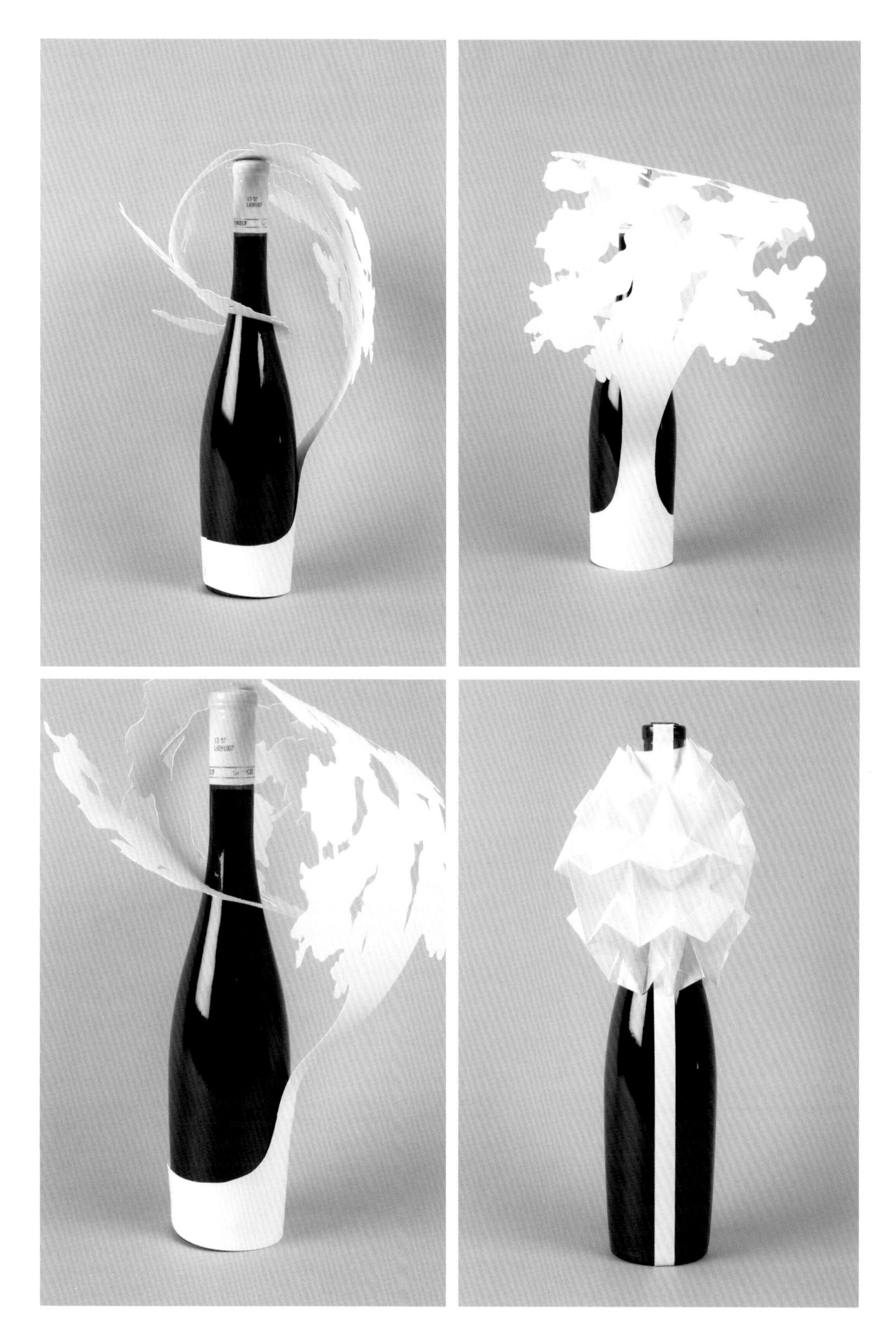

Curious Story

These are images for ArjoWiggins' catalog and website for their "Curious" paper collection.

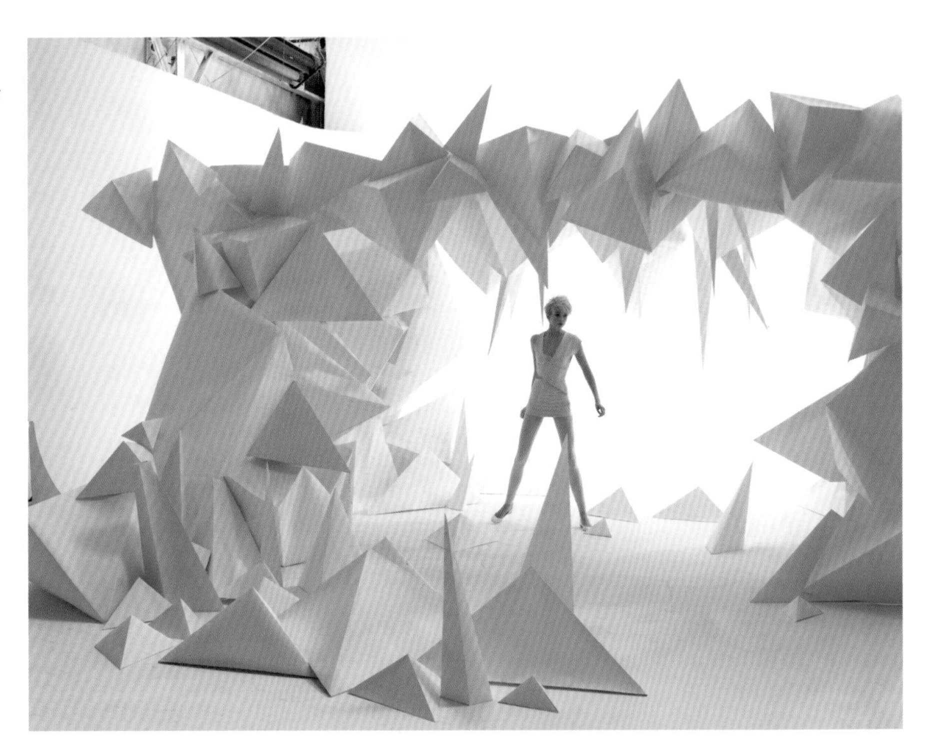

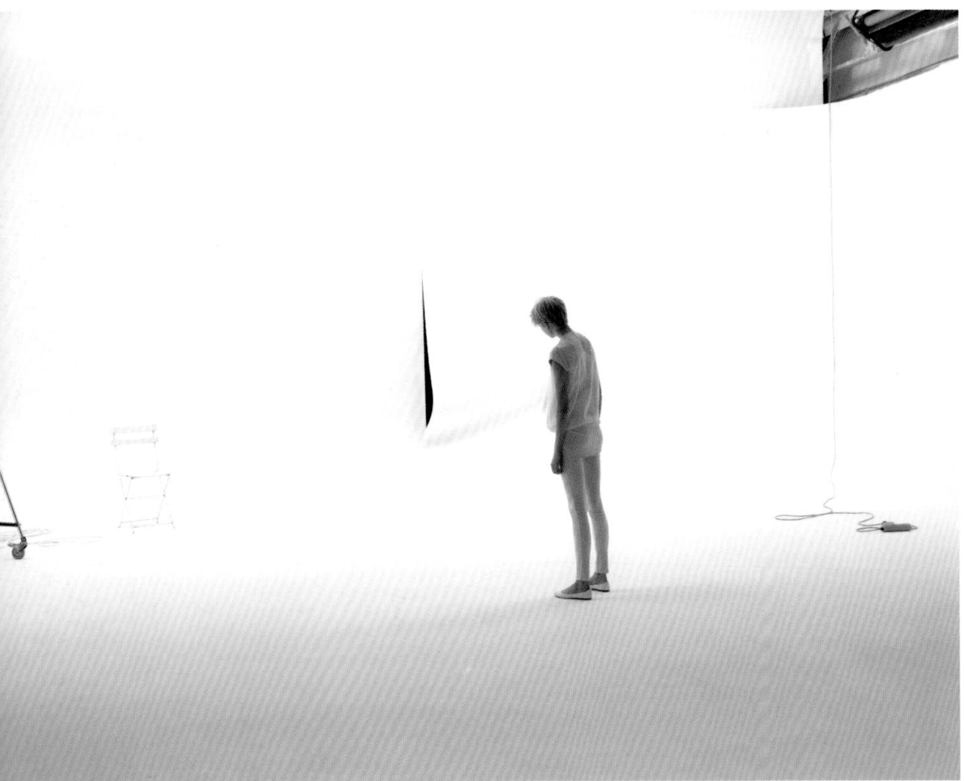

Art Director Frédéric Teyssere Creative Director Nicolas Champion Set Designer Hervé Sauvage Work Type Fashion

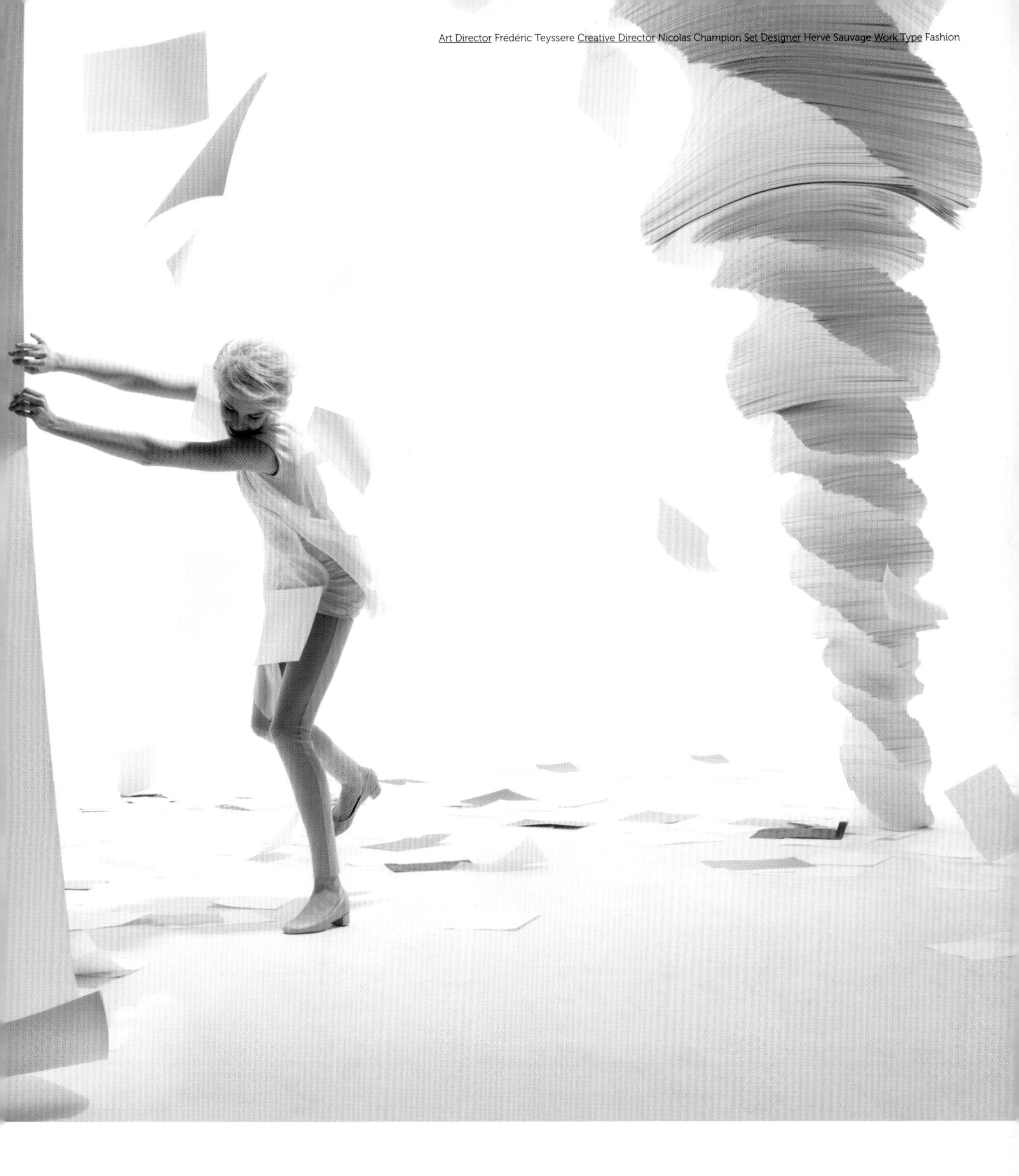

Designer Yuko Takada Keller Photographer 1, 2 Masaki Tada 3, 4 Allan Hansen 5 Yuko Takada Keller

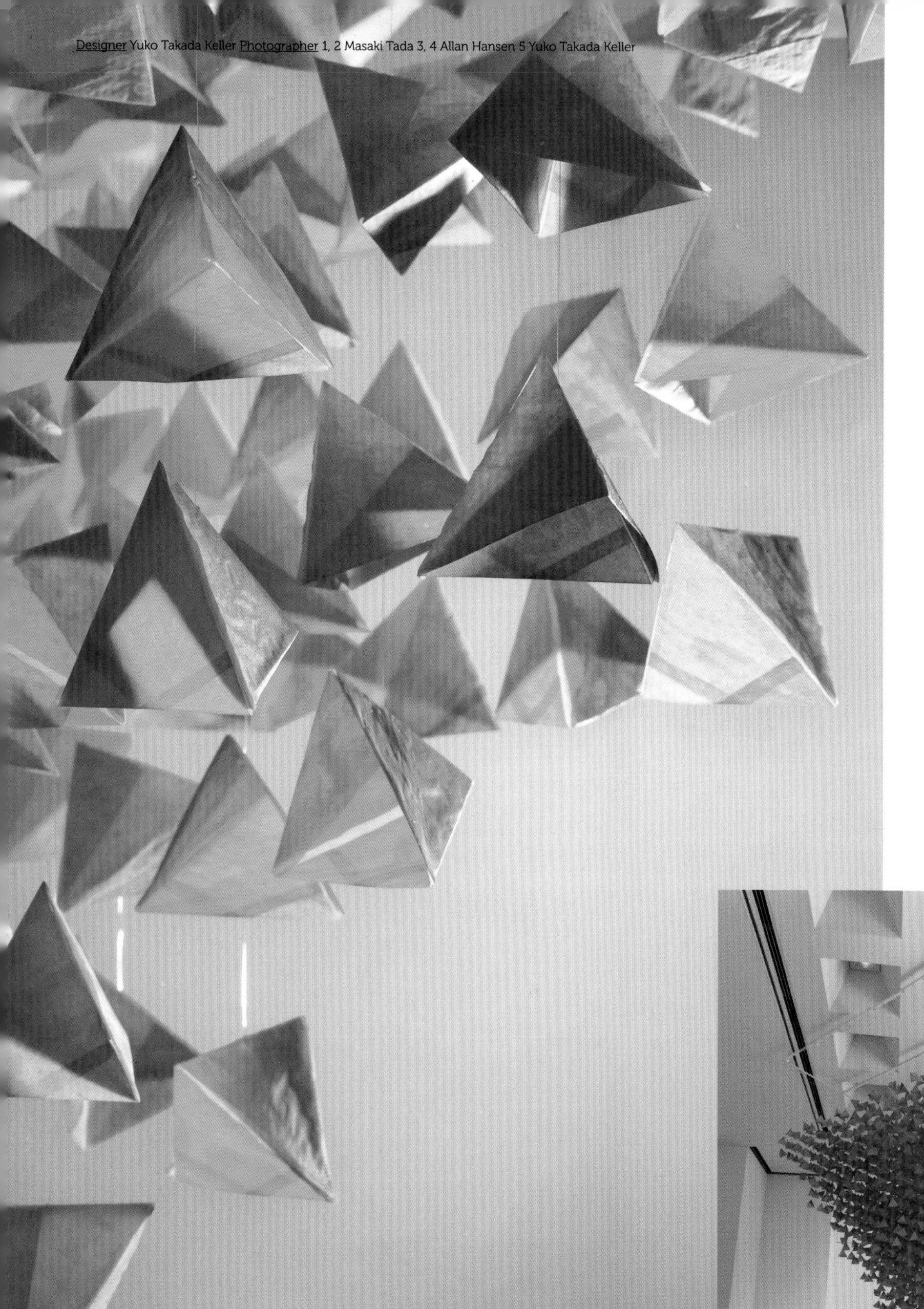

1

Pointillism in the Air

1, 2 / Prismatic 2011
3, 4 / Spring Breeze
5 / Between the Air

Yuko Takada Keller has been using tracing paper for 25 years. At the beginning of her exploration of tracing paper, she hoped her works would remind the viewer of something pure and natural in this world. But she gradually began to be conscious of a skin membrane in between the transparency and untransparency that tracing paper has. So she wanted to represent something more than what is pure and natural in this world. Sometimes we can't see things visually but they exist in our minds.

She uses small triangle pieces in her work. The triangle symbolizes something like a molecule - of water, light, or air. She would like to use the small triangle piece in a way similar to the dots which are building blocks in a pointillist painting. "Between the Air" represents something like this feeling. When she is conscious of a skin membrane in the air, she can feel invisible things, she said. "It's something we have already forgotten or we don't try to see. But we have to remember, and we have to try to see. There is a value in this invisible world. There are always things you can't see."

2

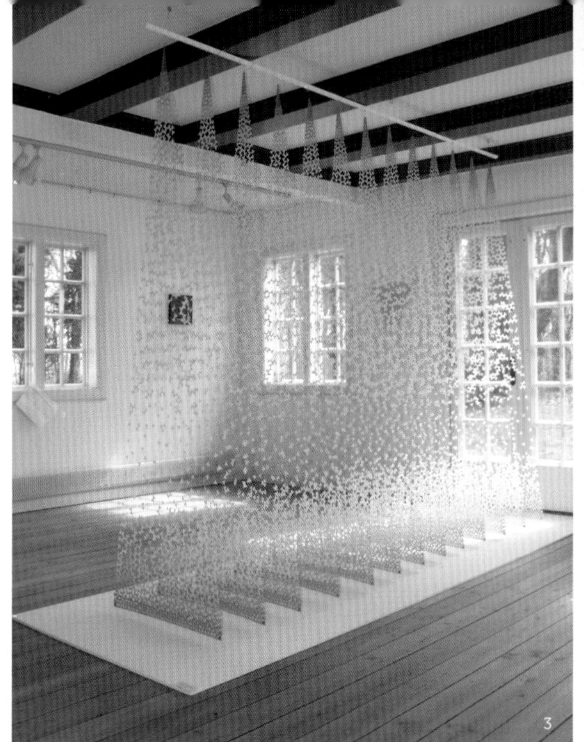

3

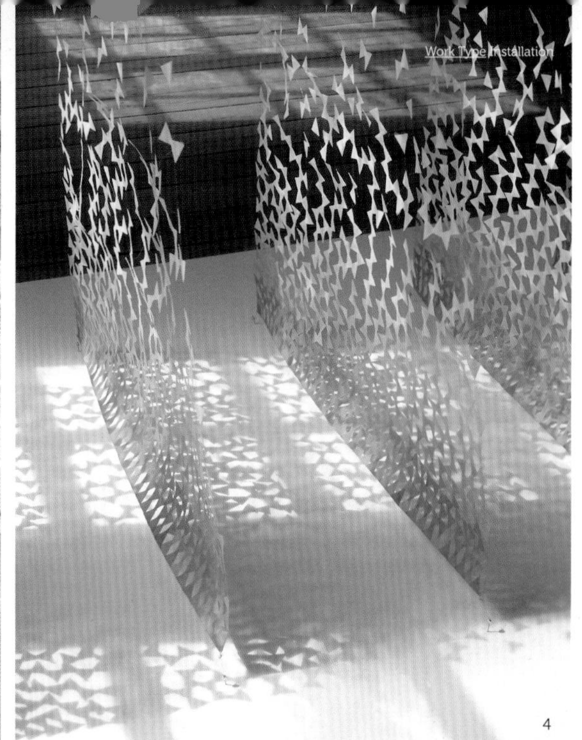

4

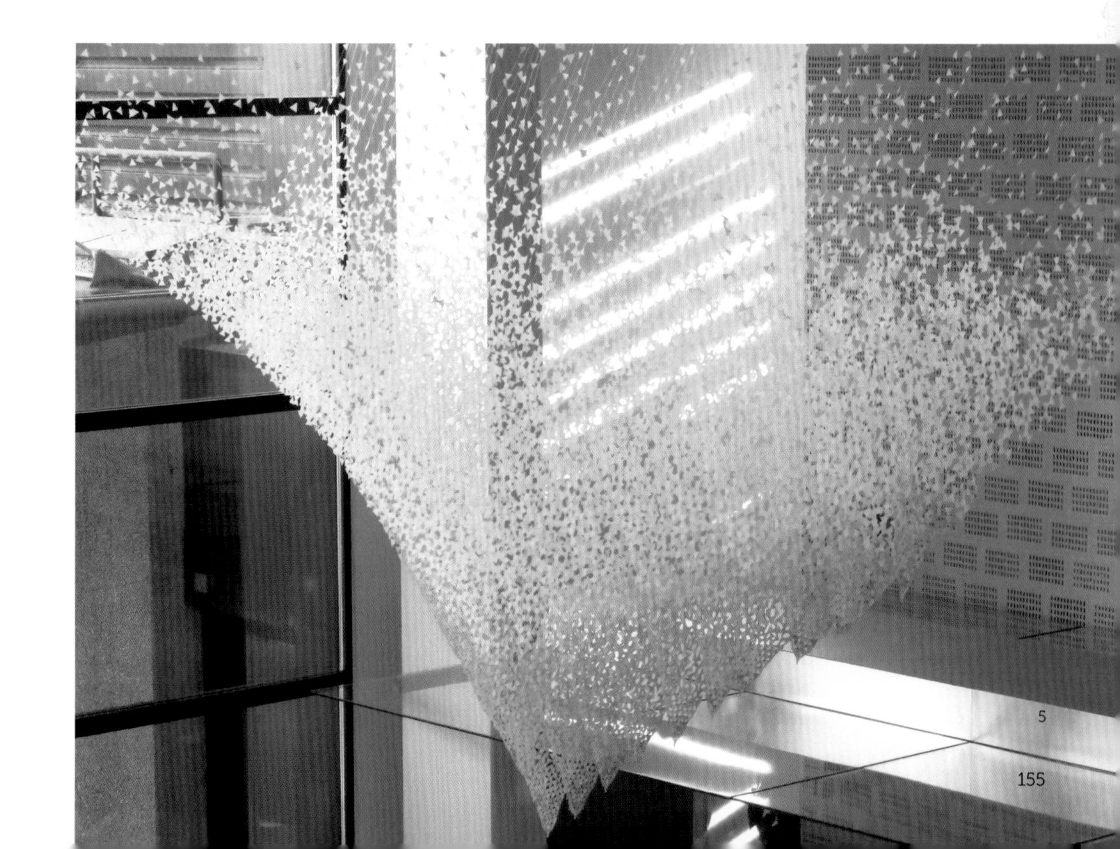

5

Art Director Julien Vallée + DixonBaxi Designer Julien Vallée Photographer Simon Duhamel Client MTV-One

MTV

This project was proposed to MTV-One in collaboration with Dixon-Baxi.

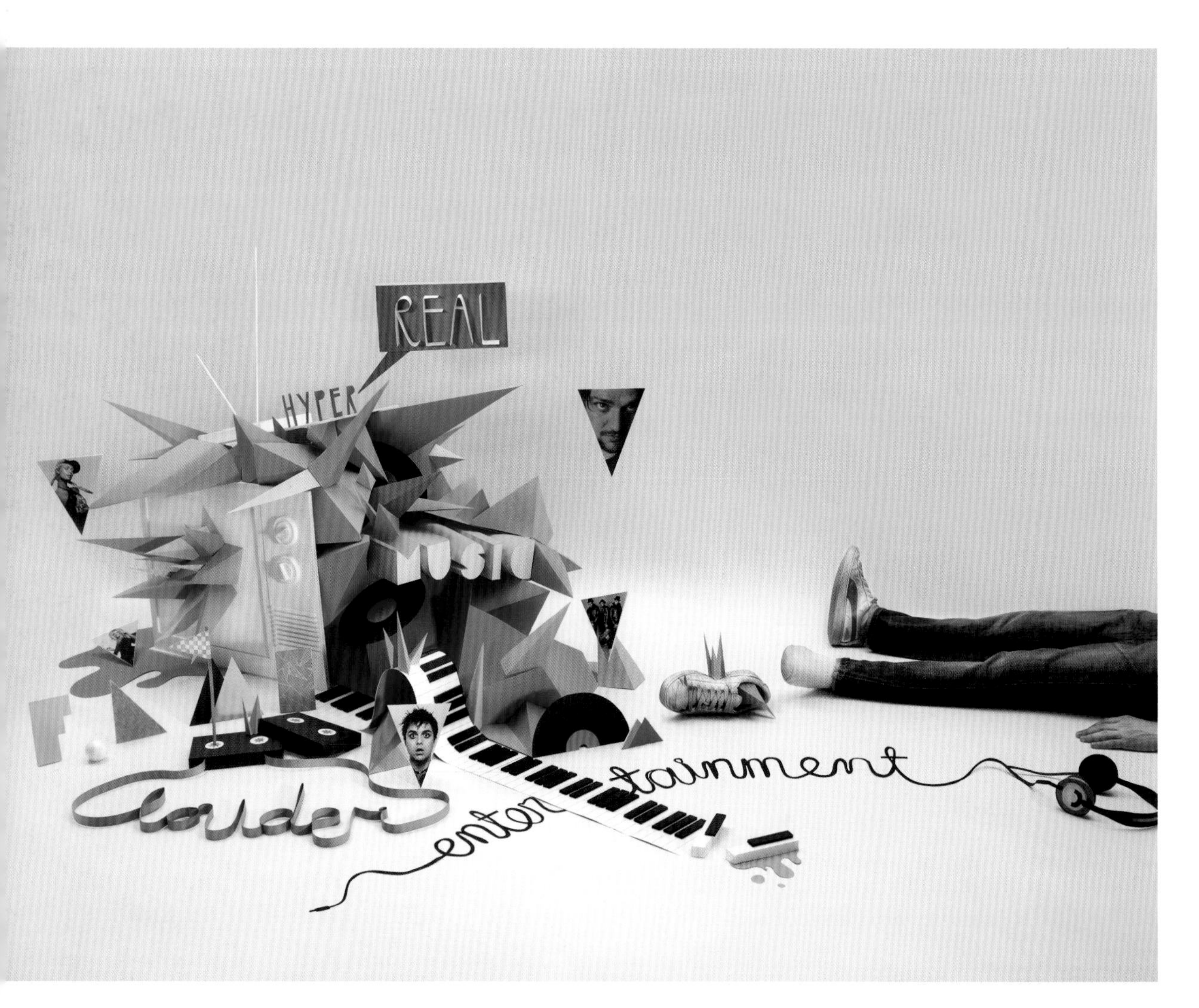

Work Type Installation

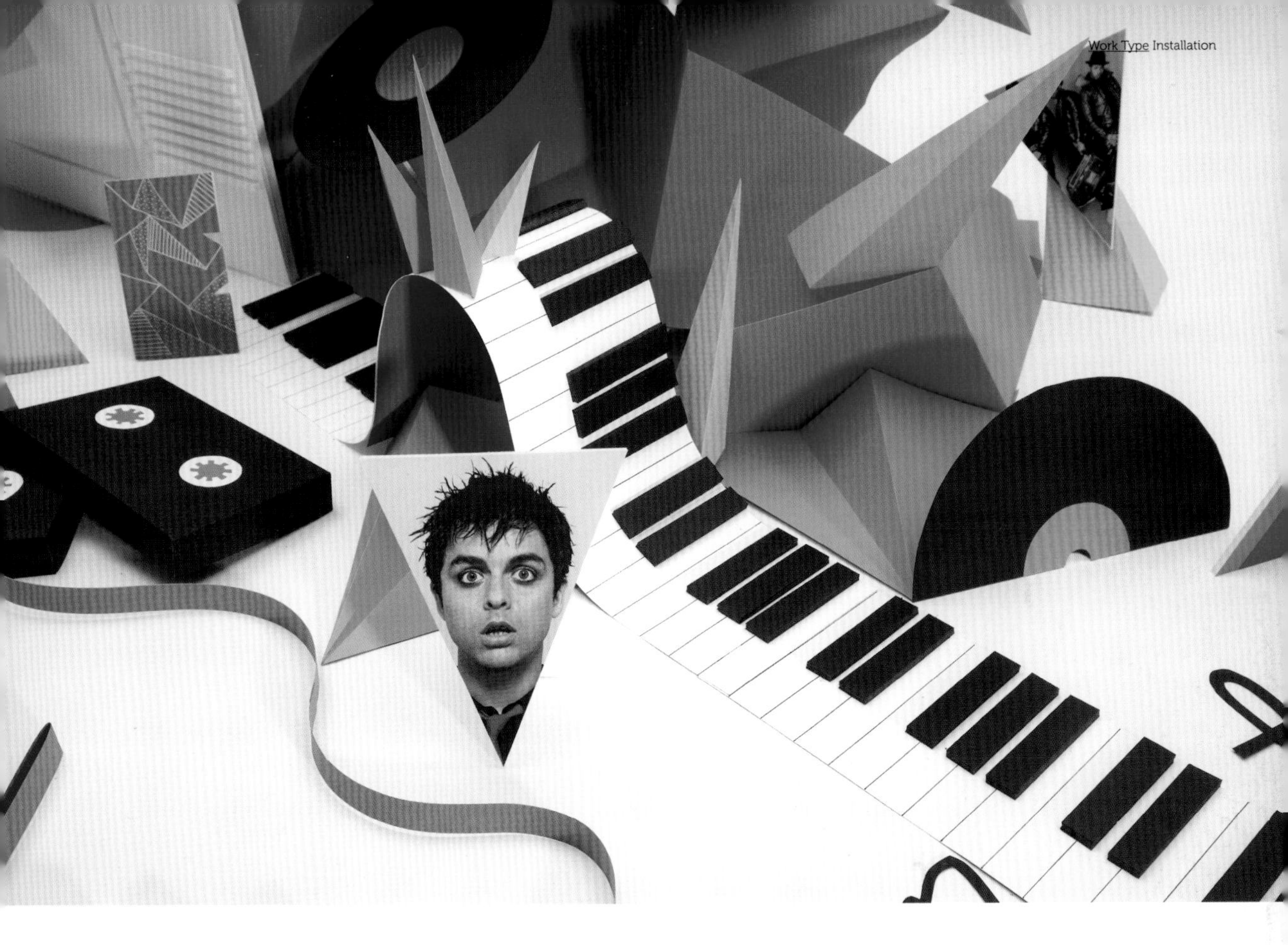

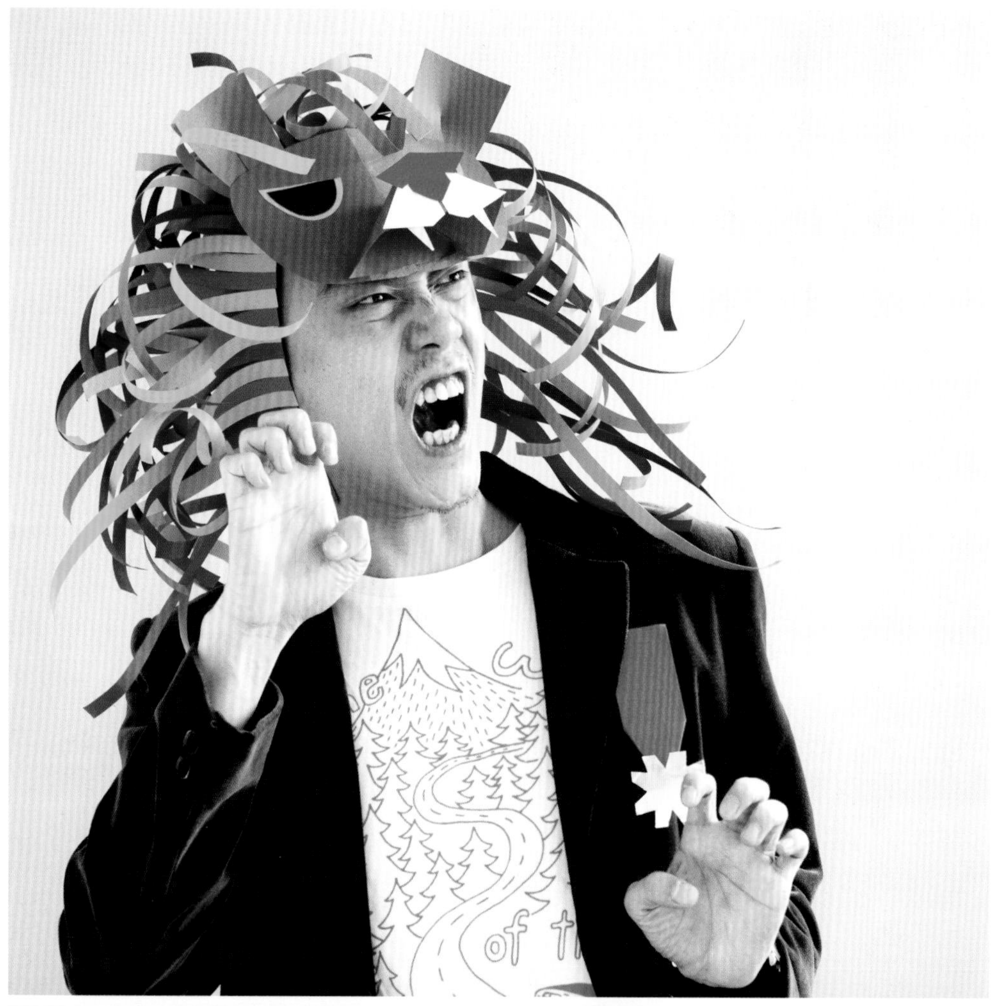

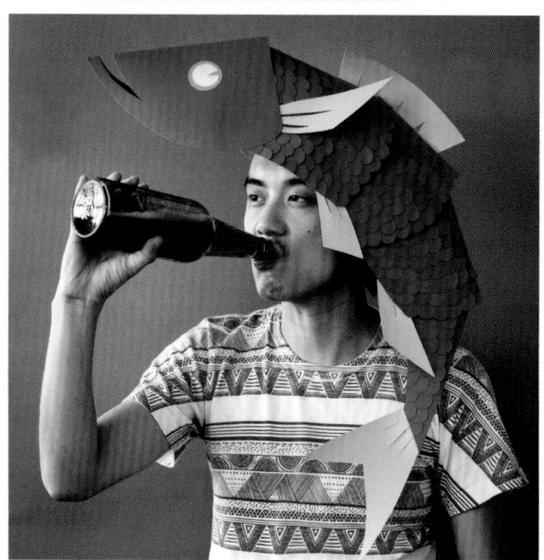

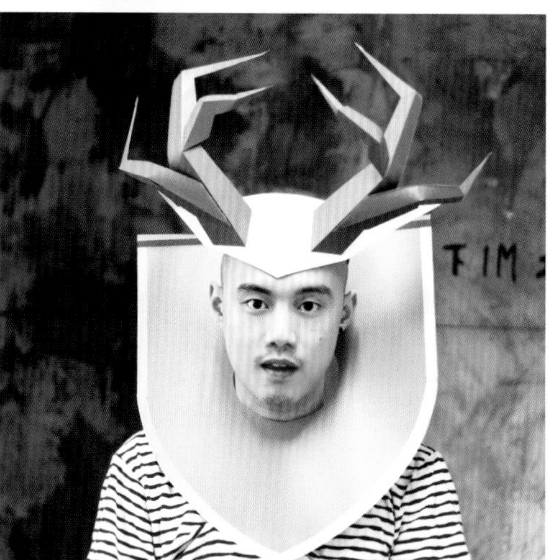

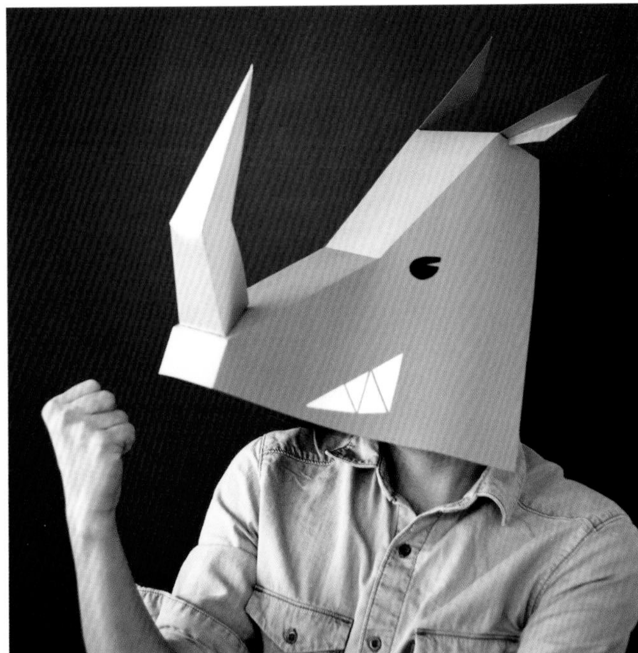

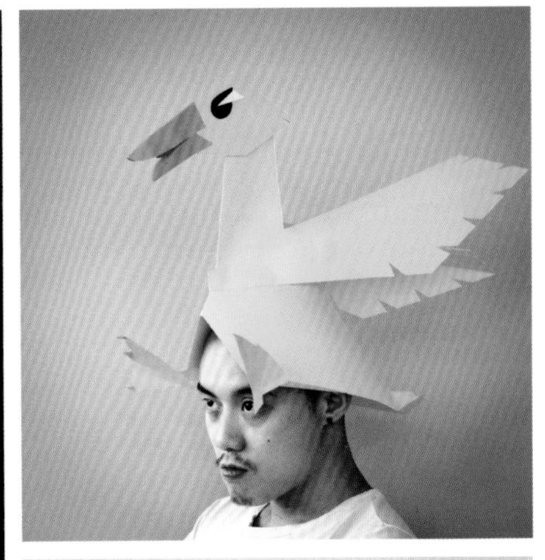

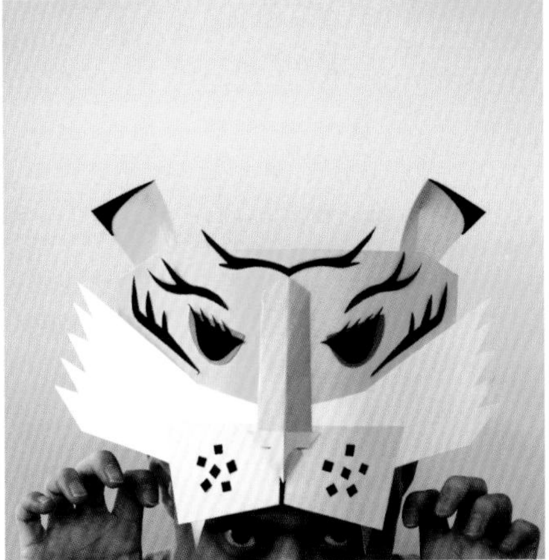

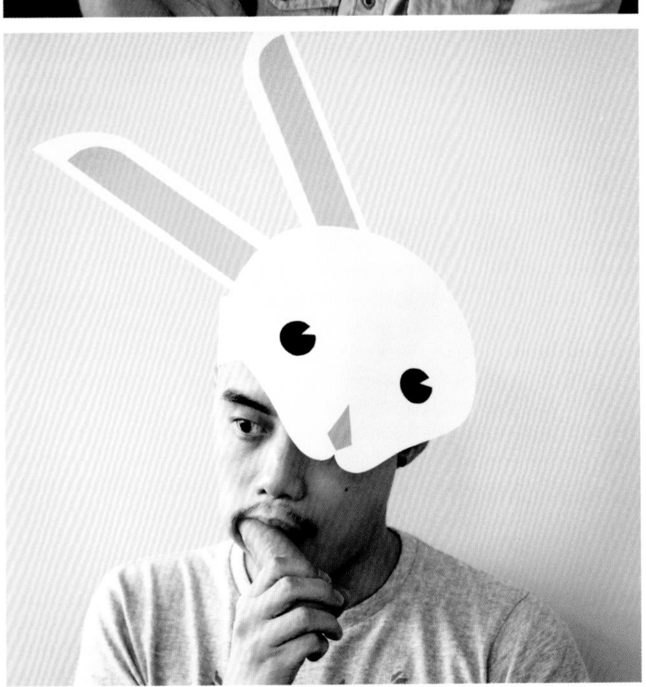

Linus Knows How

In 2011, Linus worked on a daily self-portrait project called "Linus Knows How". It is run almost daily on his Flickr blog. He used paper artworks, along with photography and written articles to discuss mundane problems, and how to brave them in a humorous way. It combines paper costumes and an advice column on how to tackle and handle daily chores, relationships, sex and our own existence in a light-hearted way.

Design Agency Nexus Productions Designer Johnny Kelly Photographer 5 Linda Brownlee/ 6, 7 Johnny Kelly Client 1, 2, 3 Adobe/ 5 Don't Panic

Paper Discovery

1, 2, 3 / The Seed
4 / Pirate
5 / Democracy poster
6, 7 / Mask

Democracy poster is a paper illustration commissioned by Don't Panic. This is distributed as an A2 poster inside their flyer packs. Mask shows a paper mask prototype. Pirate is a character made in 2008. The Seed is a two-minute animated voyage through nature's life cycle, following the trials and tribulations of a humble apple seed.

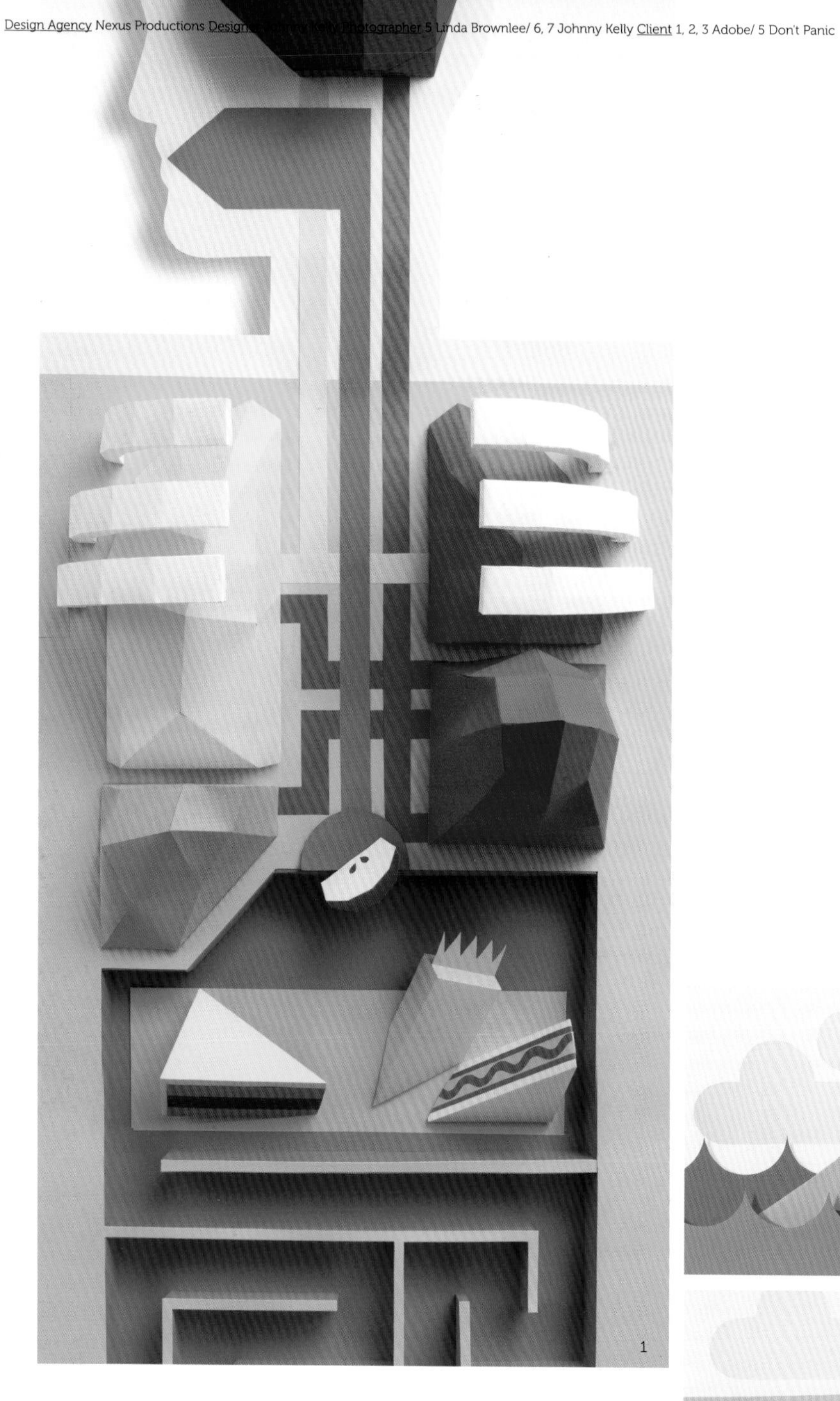

1

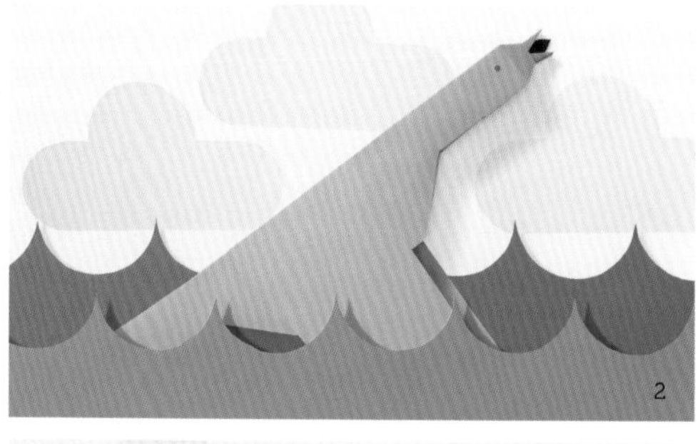

2

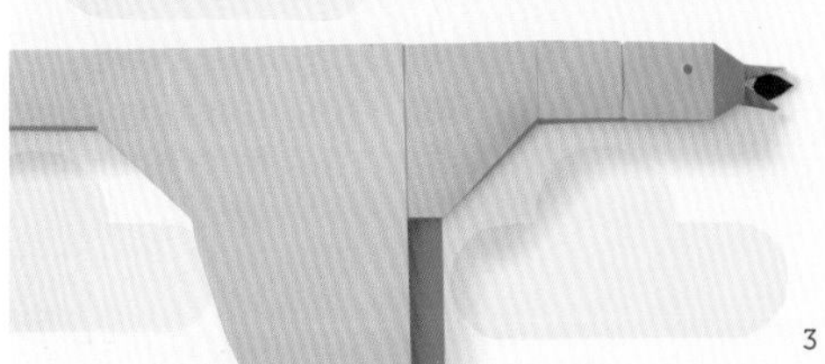

3

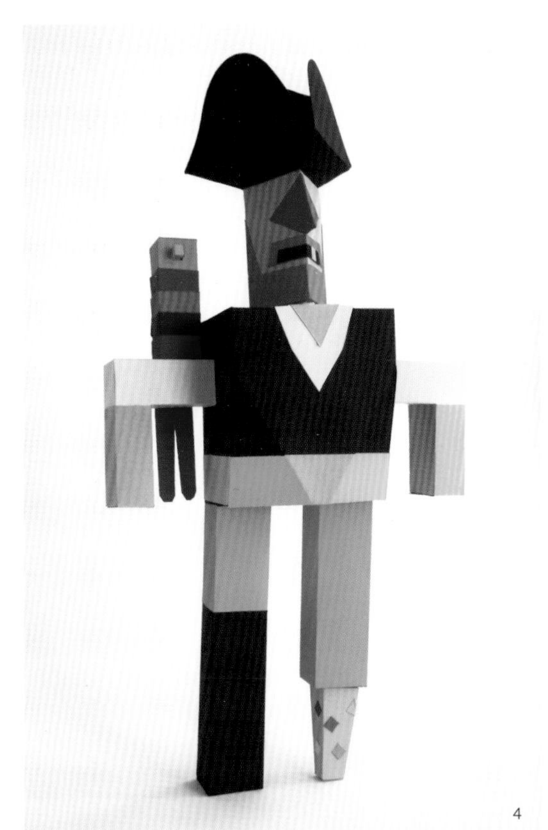
4

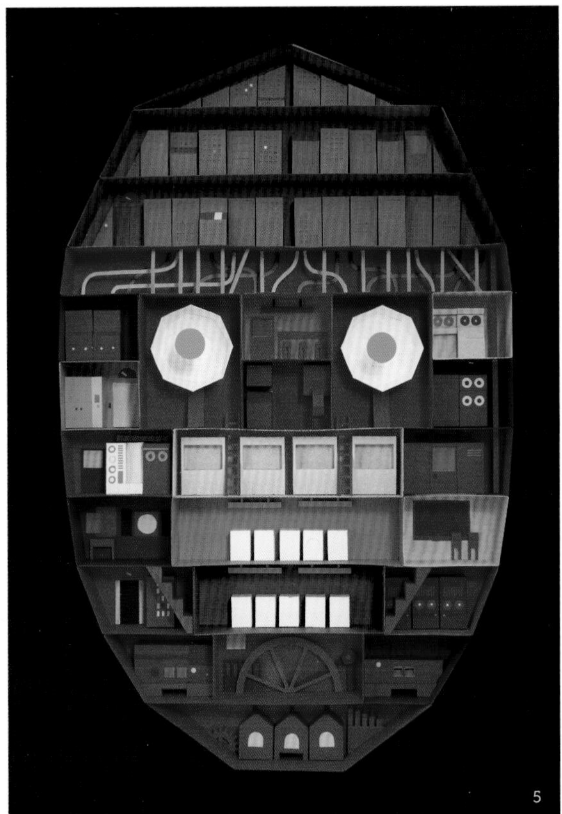
5

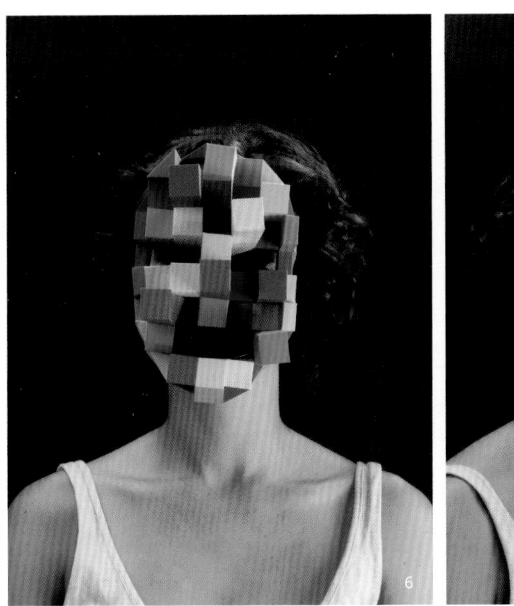
6

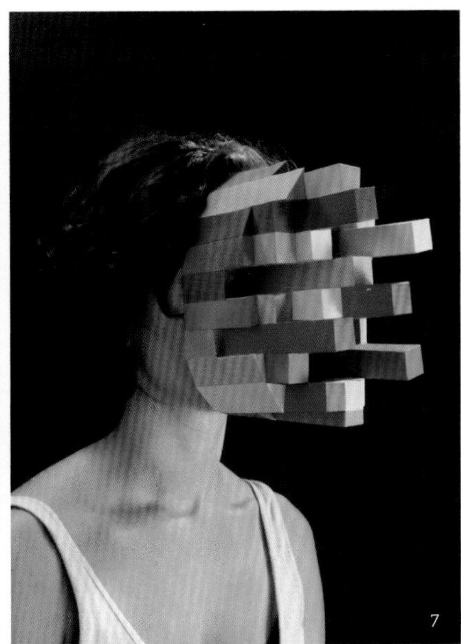
7

Designer Toby Edwards Photographer Toby Edwards Client YCN/Fedrigoni UK

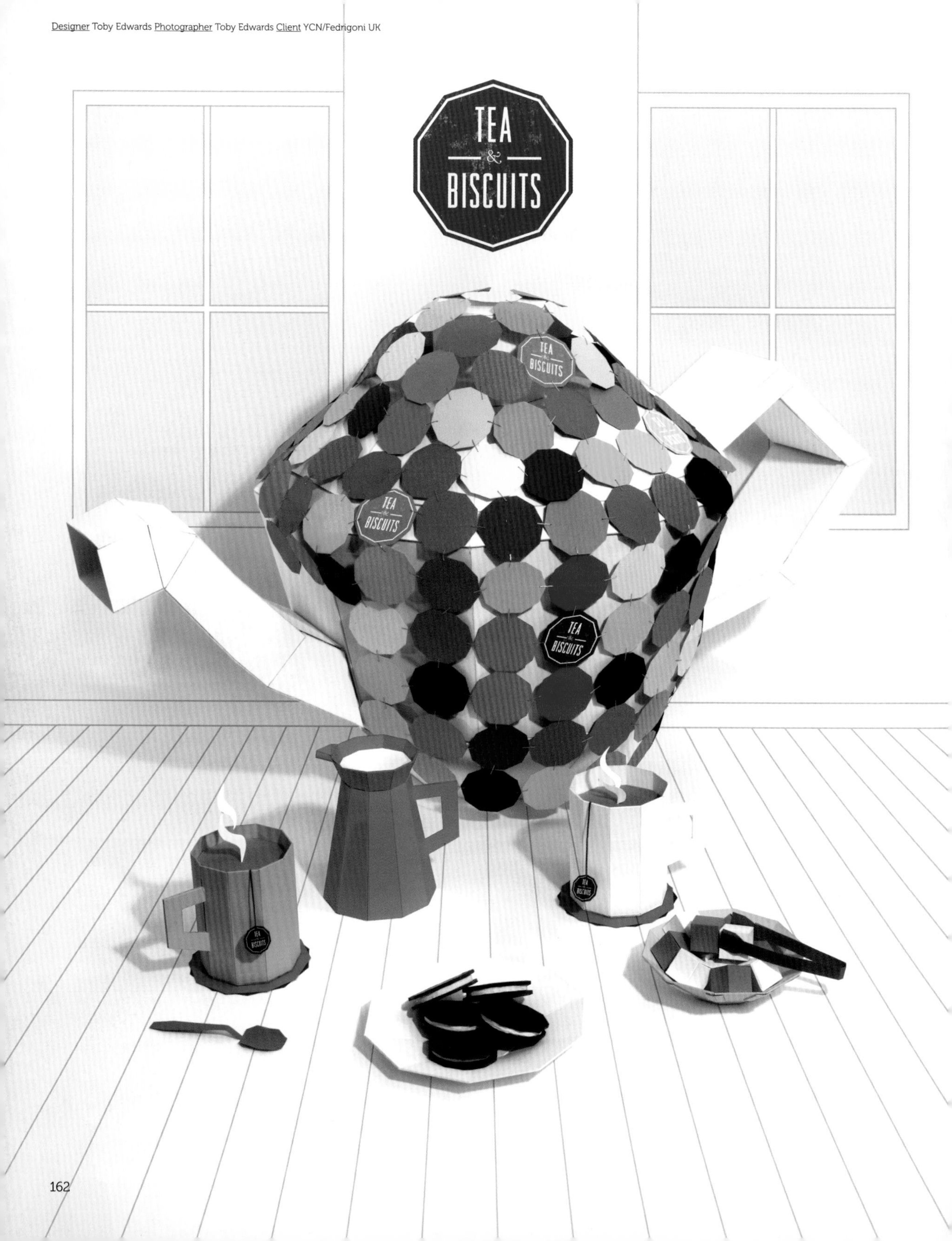

Fedrigoni Showroom Promotion

This project was undertaken while in my final year of university. The brief set by Fedrigoni, through YCN, called upon students to devise a way to promote the Fedrigoni Showroom to fellow designers.

Fedrigoni produces fine Italian paper stocks and uses a their showroom to demonstrate the extensive range of paper manufactured by the company. Clients looking for stocks to use in various different projects can use the space to speak to merchants, collect samples and view an array of documents produced using Fedrigoni paper. To encourage visitors to feel at ease in the space, I created an event themed around a traditional homey welcome, tea and biscuits. I built a giant paper teapot that stood at about 6 feet tall, to stand inside the showroom to showcase all of the available colours, weights and textures offered by Fedrigoni.

The Tea & Biscuits identity was inspired by the shape of old biscuit tins from the 1930s. Typographically, inspiration was taken from vintage Italian poster designs. The decagon shape became the basis on which the installation piece was built. Invitations containing a Fedrigoni branded tea bag were also produced as a teaser for the event. Visitors were encouraged to take a paper mug home with them after filling it with paper swatches of their choice.

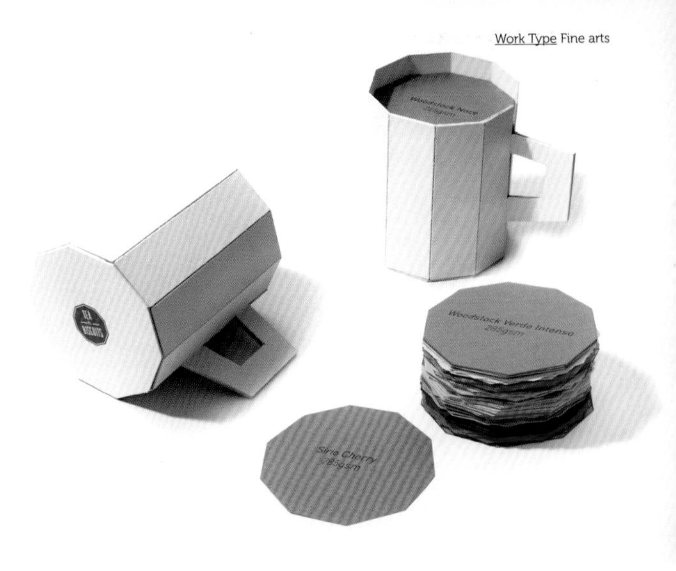

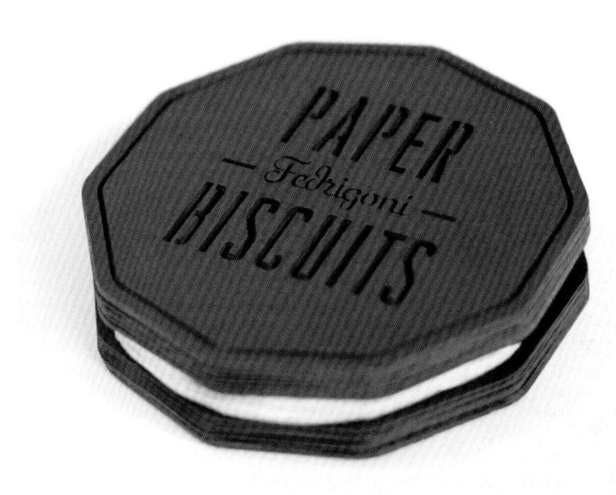

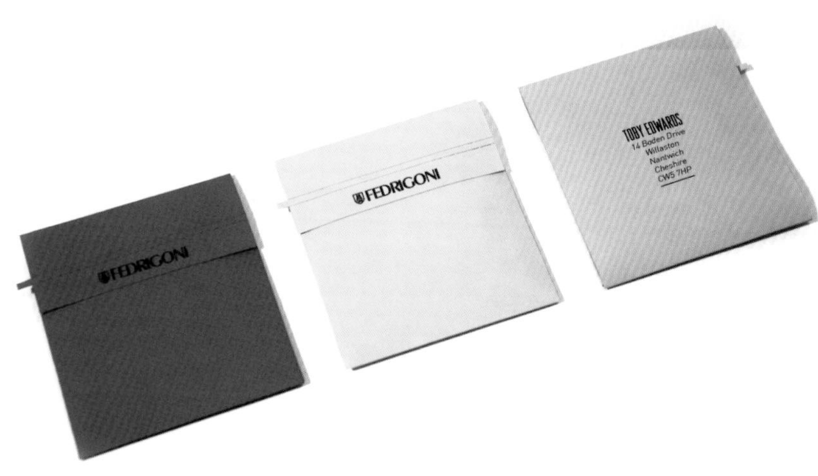

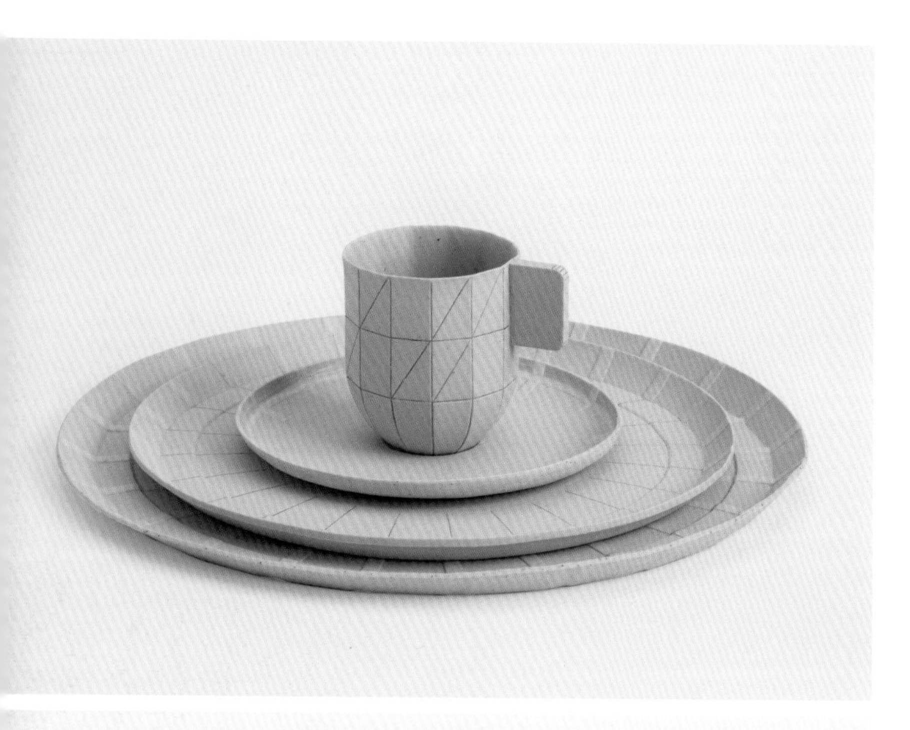

Paper Table

"Paper Table" by Scholten & Baijings combines subtlety with elegance. The folded cardboard models for the crockery are translated into light grey, unglazed porcelain cups and plates, playing with the suggestion of cardboard delicately. For the table linen the duo offers a contemporary solution: they designed two sets containing napkins and table runners which can be used in various combinations. Their design is complemented by a set of sober shaped glassware and cutlery.

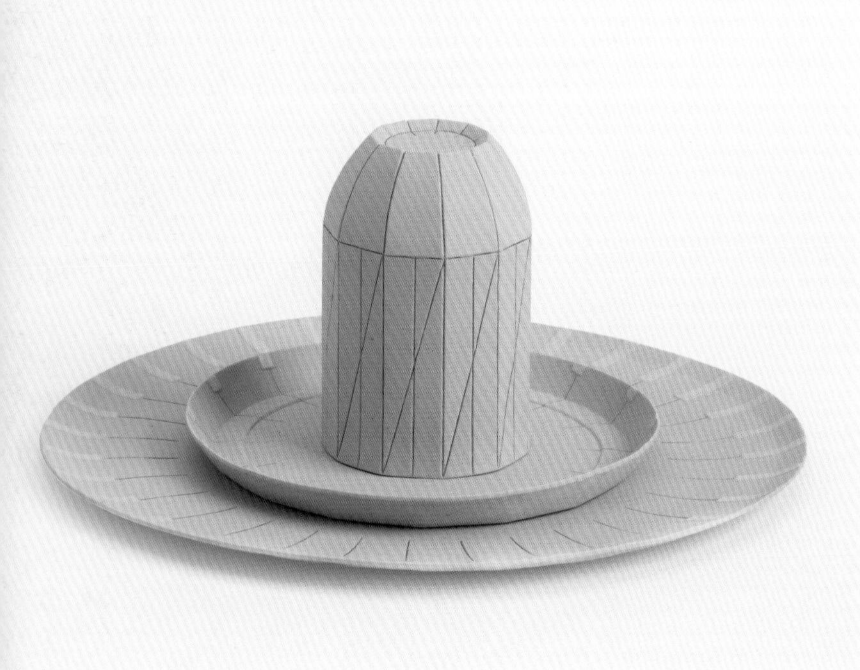

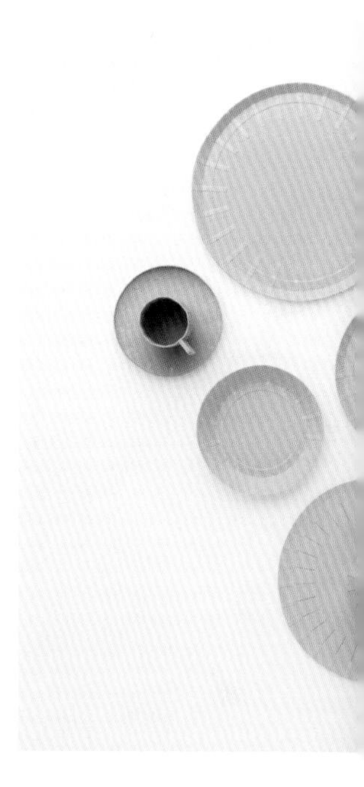

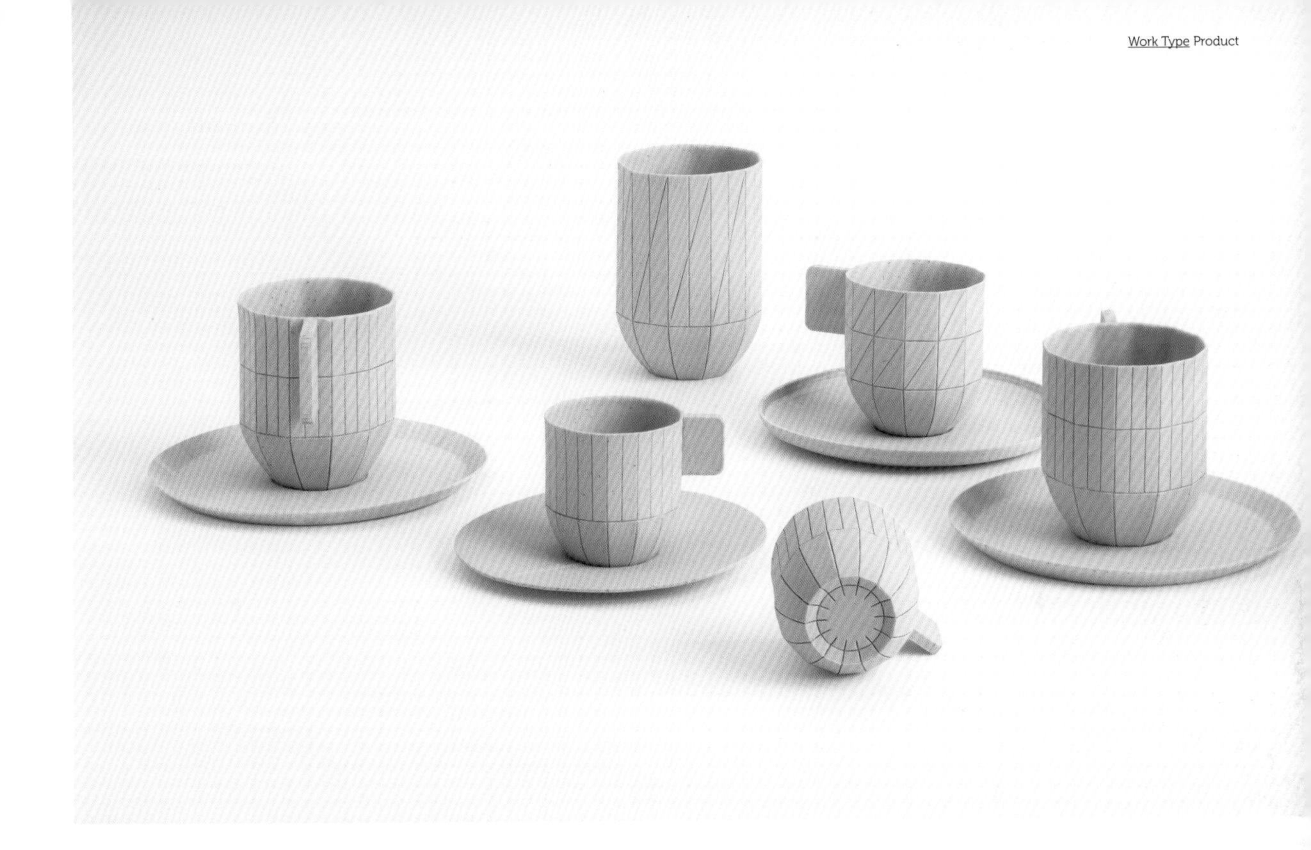

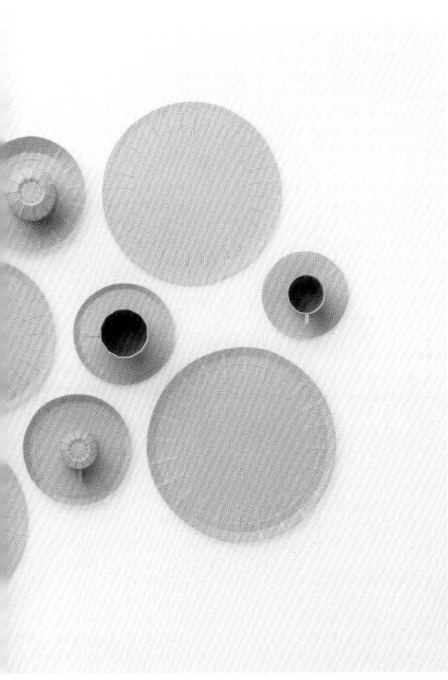

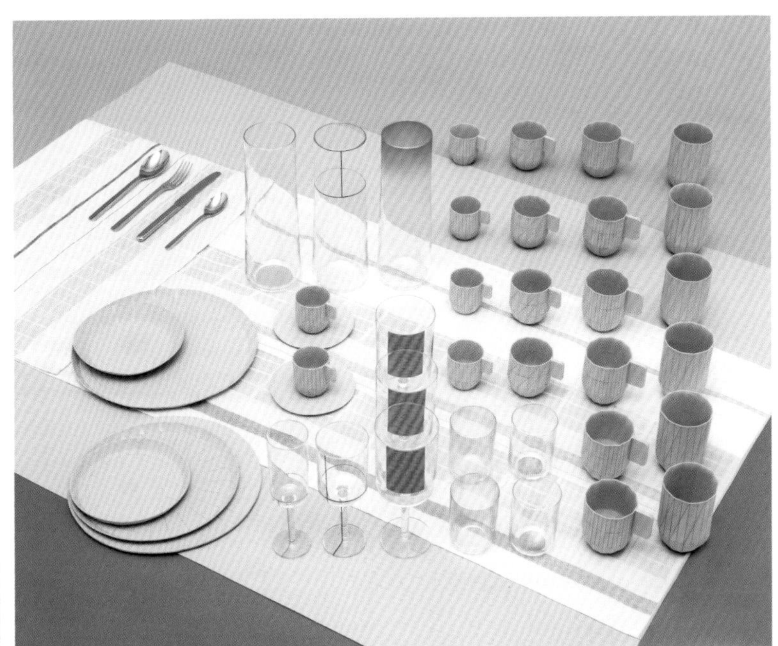

Design Agency Paper Donut Client Arjowiggins Photographer Fanette GUILLOUD

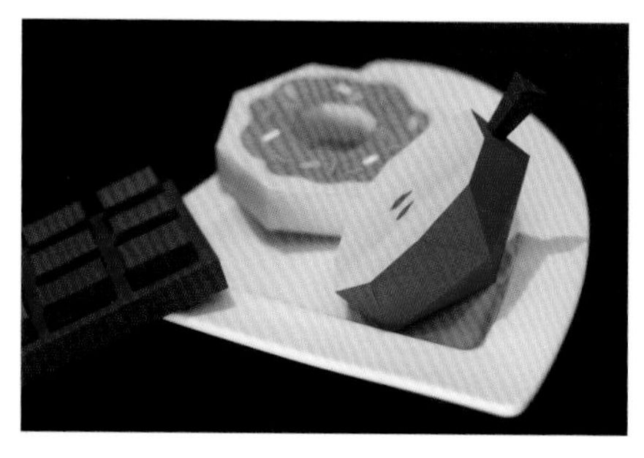

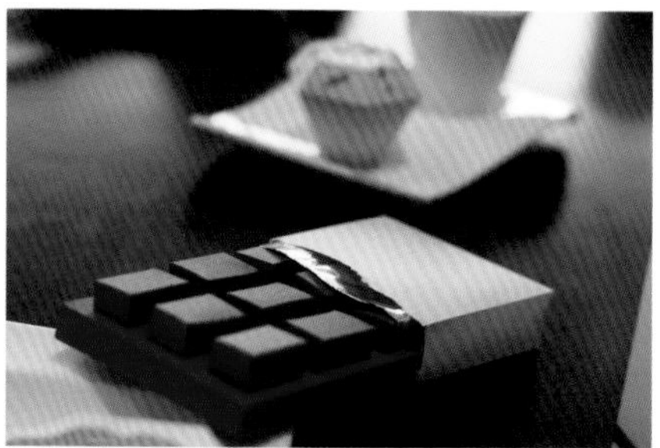

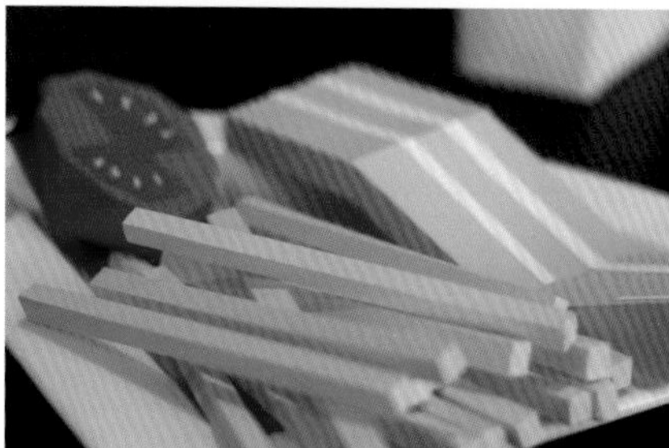

Curious Breakfast

Soul soul! Imagine your own story with our curious paper breakfast. Go on and be creative! We imagined many possible cliche French and American breakfasts for you to choose from. Imagine your very own home breakfast - choose from good butterfat or a cupcake with coffee. Enjoy and bon appetit!

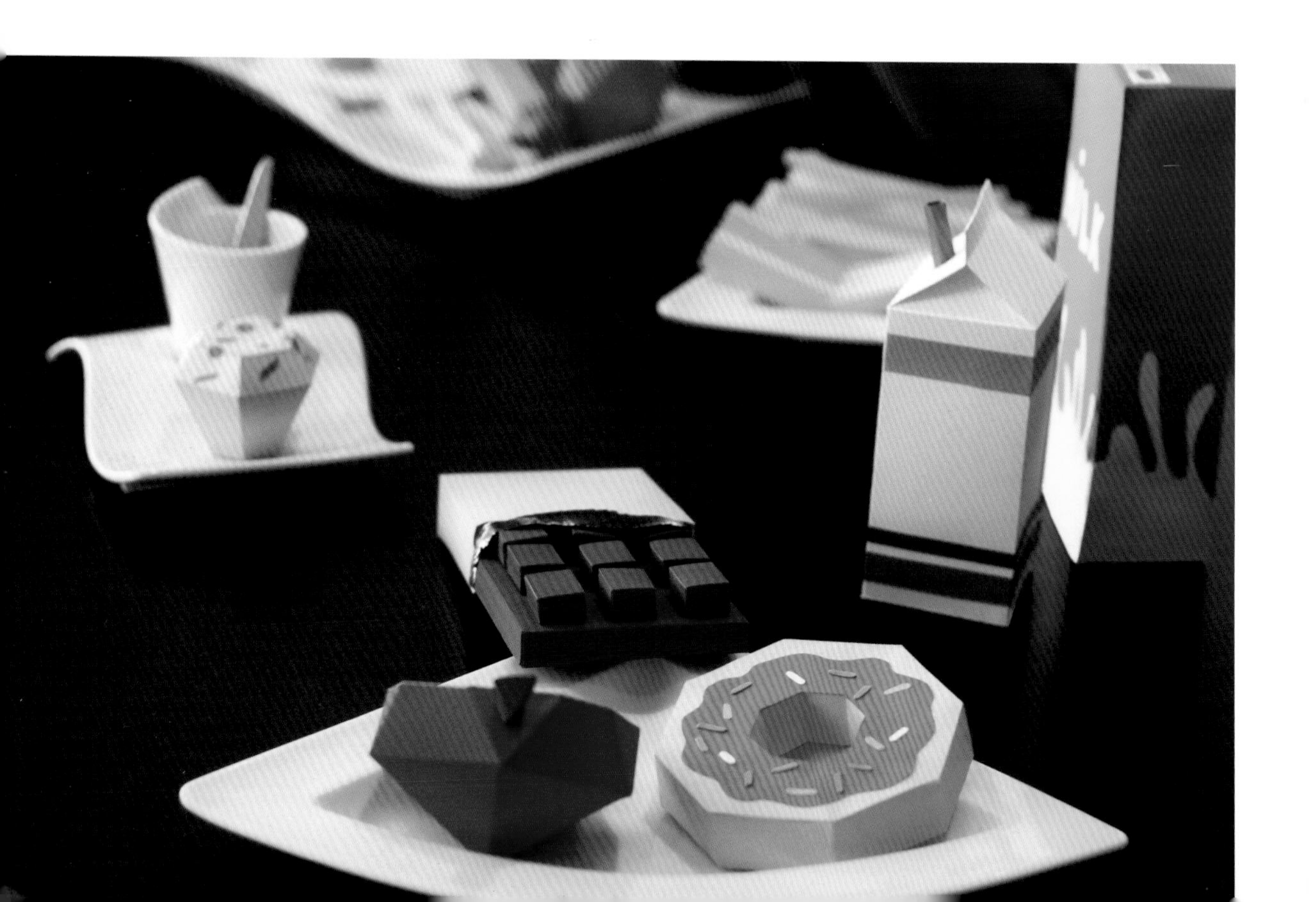

Work Type Fine arts Technique Die-cut

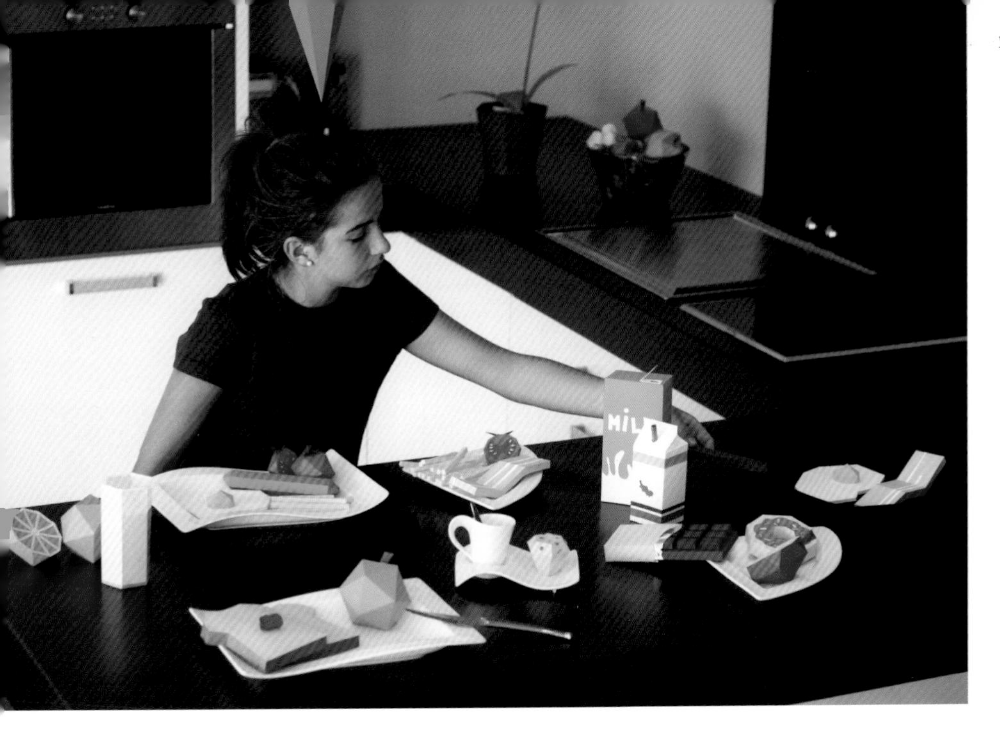

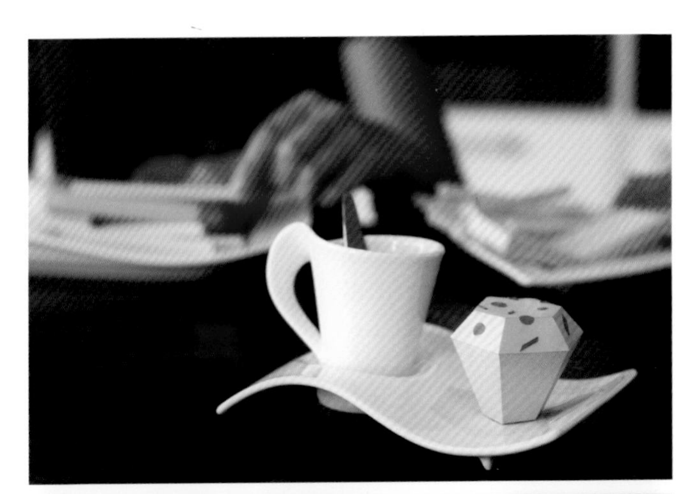

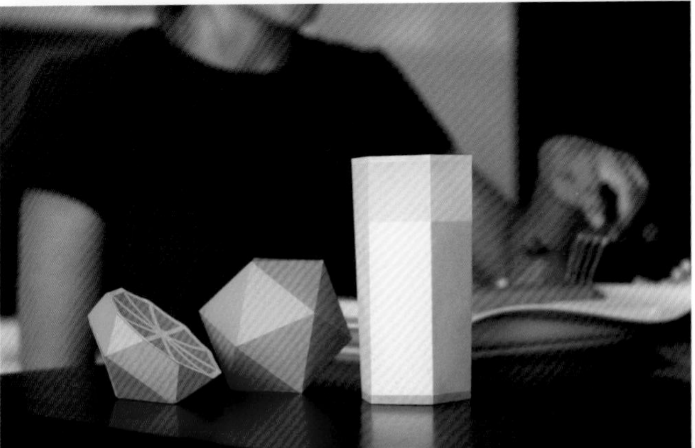

Design Agency Blast Client Arjowiggins Creative Papers Illustration Ian Wright

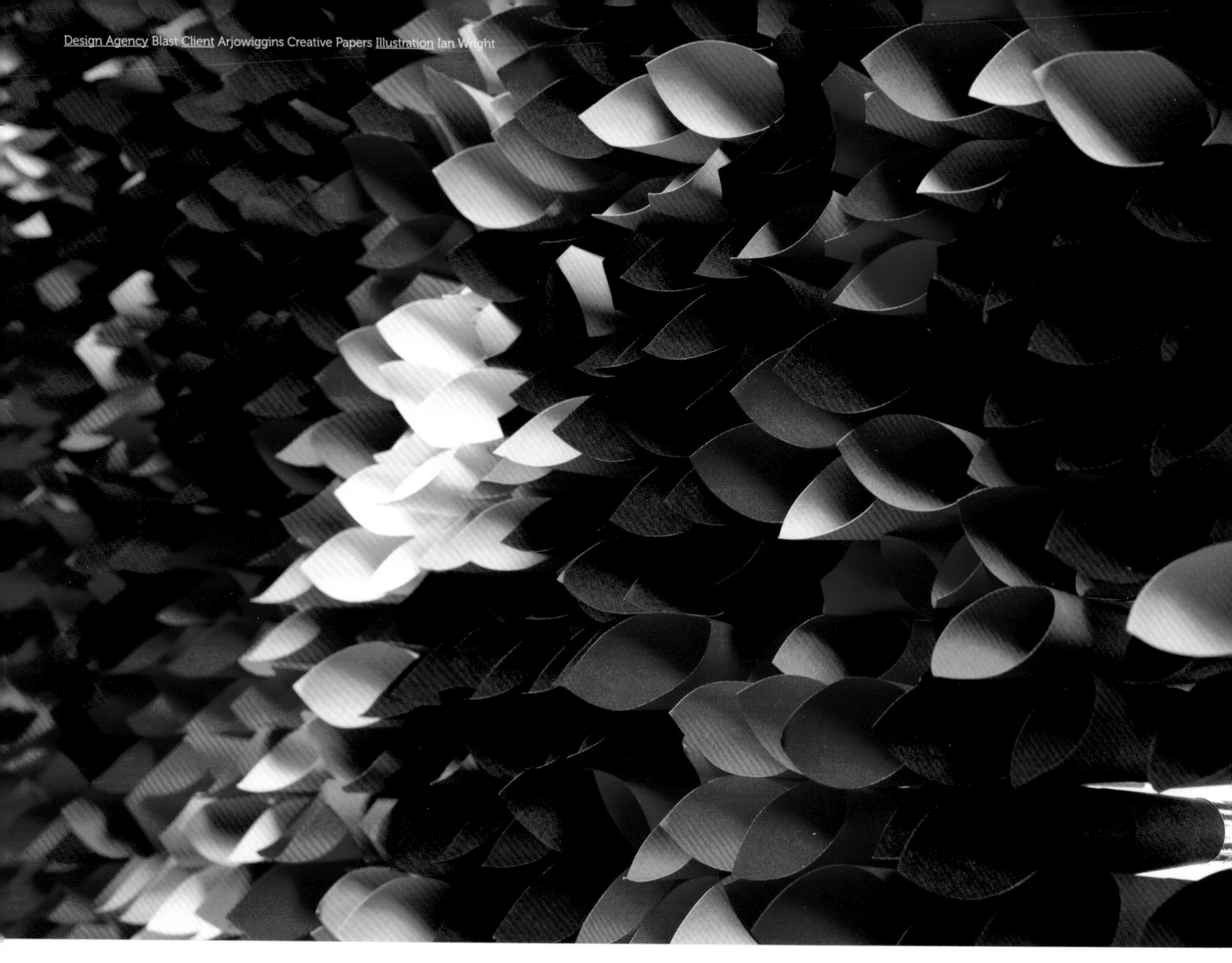

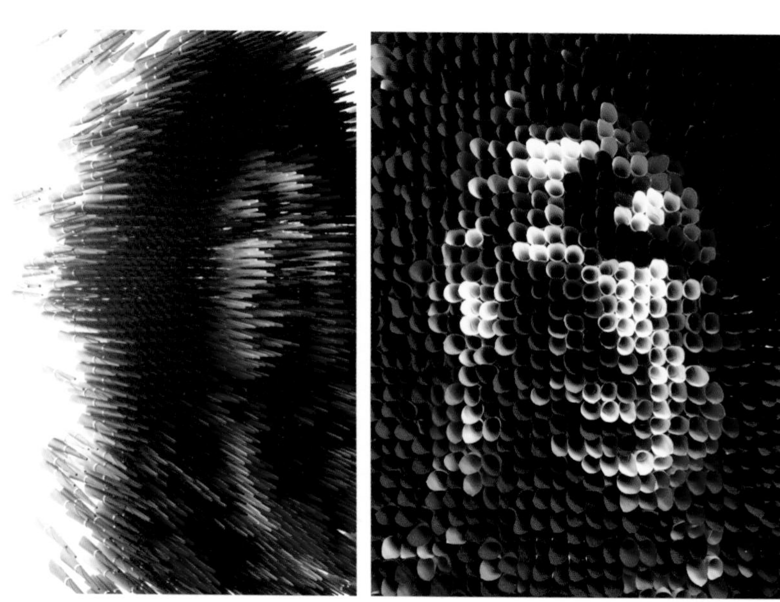

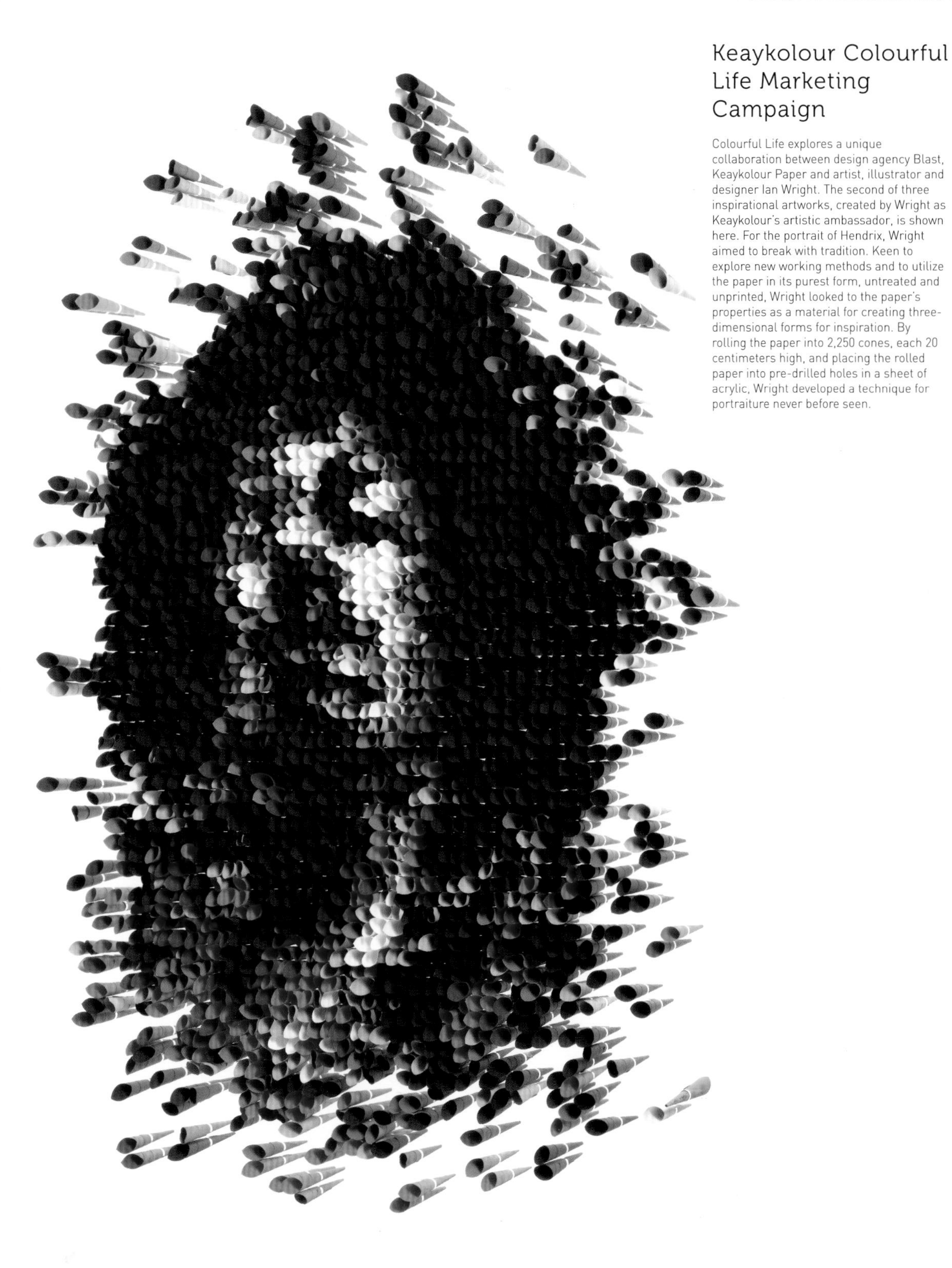

Keaykolour Colourful Life Marketing Campaign

Colourful Life explores a unique collaboration between design agency Blast, Keaykolour Paper and artist, illustrator and designer Ian Wright. The second of three inspirational artworks, created by Wright as Keaykolour's artistic ambassador, is shown here. For the portrait of Hendrix, Wright aimed to break with tradition. Keen to explore new working methods and to utilize the paper in its purest form, untreated and unprinted, Wright looked to the paper's properties as a material for creating three-dimensional forms for inspiration. By rolling the paper into 2,250 cones, each 20 centimeters high, and placing the rolled paper into pre-drilled holes in a sheet of acrylic, Wright developed a technique for portraiture never before seen.

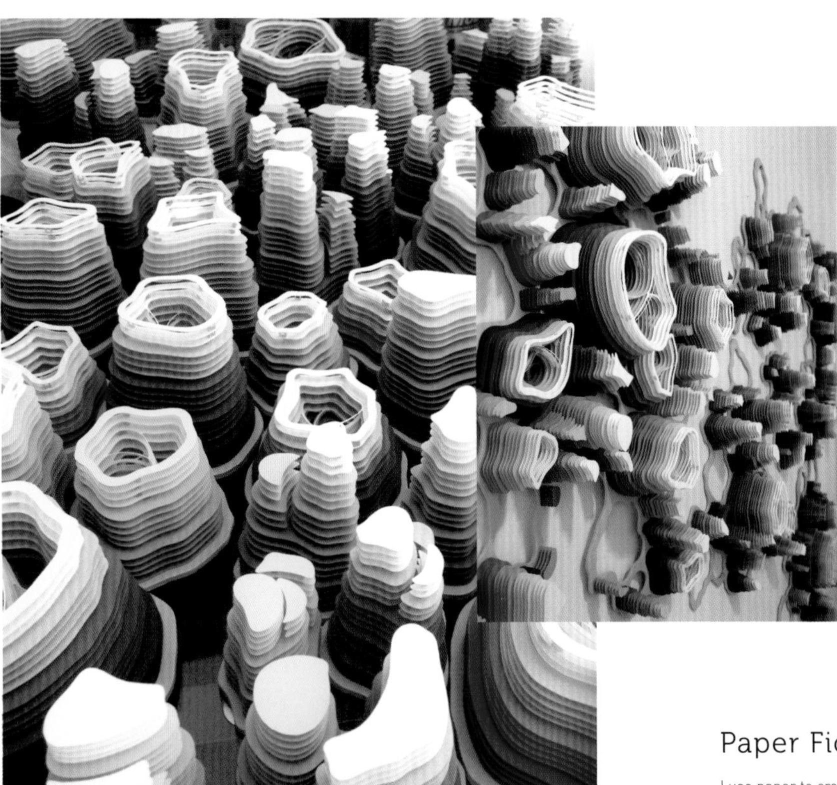

Paper Fiction

I use paper to create a world of fiction that challenges the viewer to suspend disbelief and venture into my fabricated reality. By layering paper I am able to build intriguing land formations that mimic viral colonies and concentric sound waves. These strange landmasses contaminate and infect the surfaces they inhabit, transforming the space into something suitable for their gestation. Towers of paper and color jut into the viewer's space inviting playful interactions between the viewer and this conceived world. These constructions question the notion of microbial outbreaks and their similarity to the visual representation of sound waves, transforming them into something more playful and inviting.

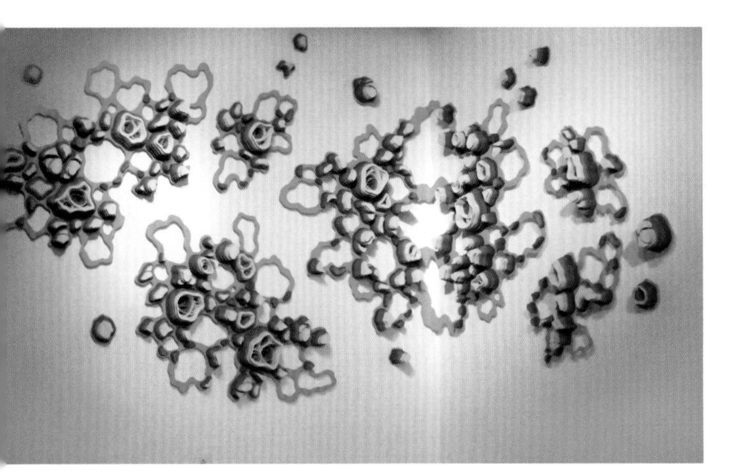

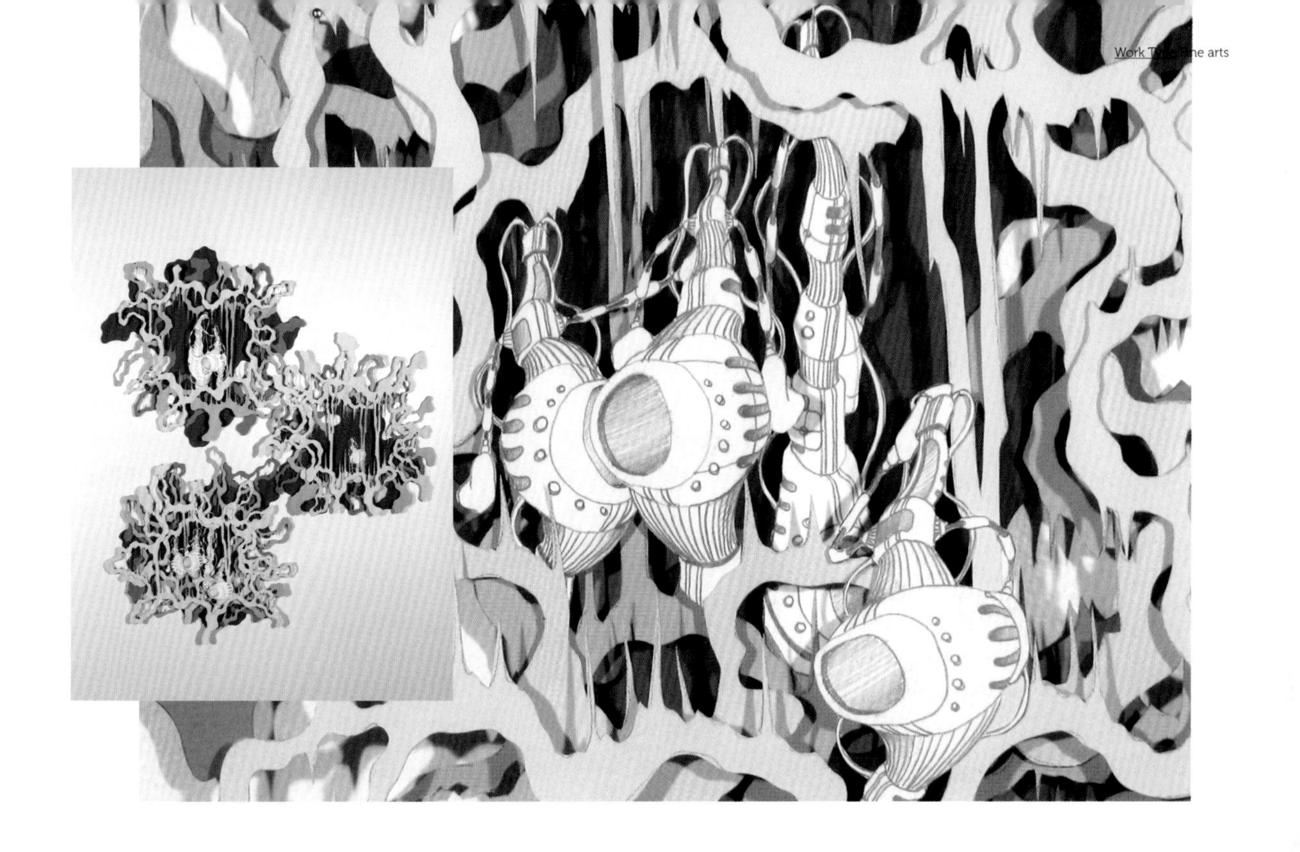

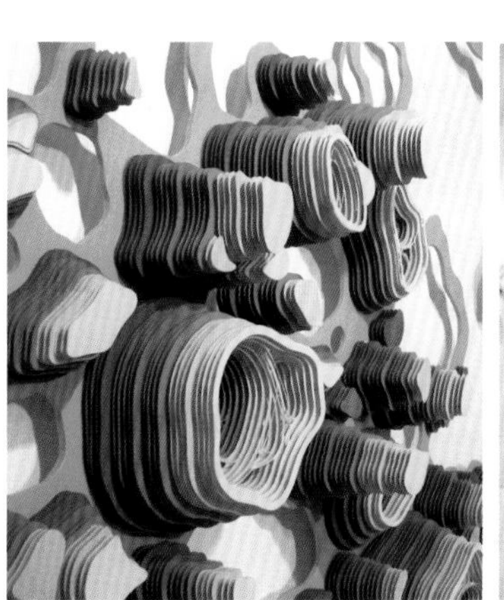

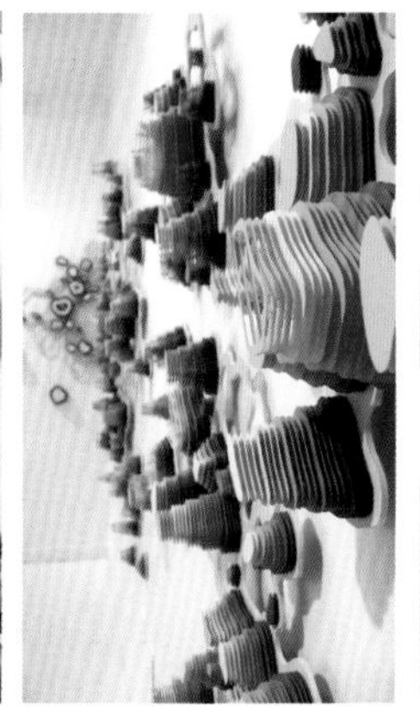

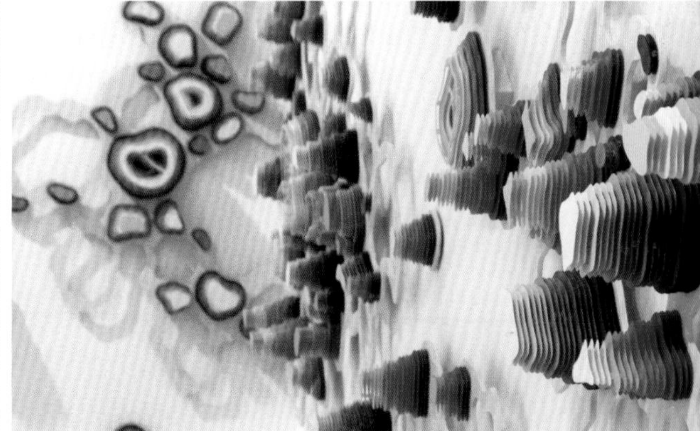

Artist Mikkel Wettre Photographer Mikkel Wettre

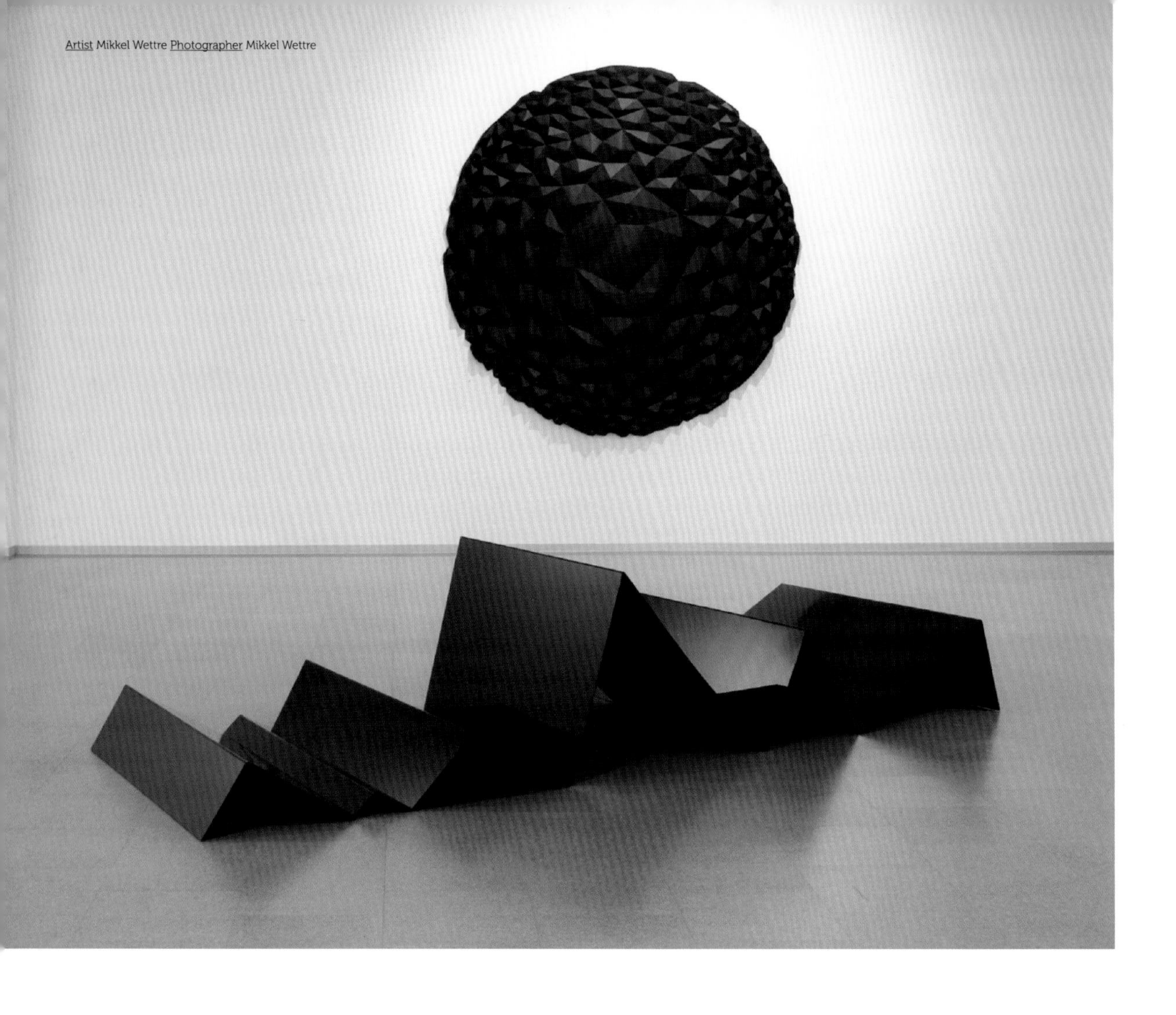

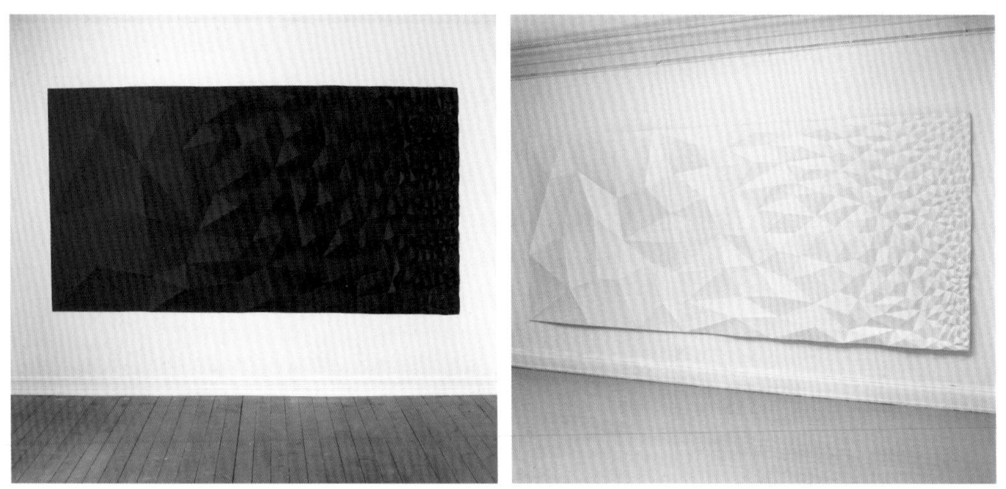

The End of Imagination & The Goblin's Raincoat

In The End of Imagination folded paper is used to create a continuum that explores spatial arrangement and subjective perception. The open-ended textures are tactile narrations that hold infinite potential and suggest the fold as a figure of human thought.

The Goblin's Raincoat takes a Japanese folktale as the starting point for explorations into abstraction and pictorial space. The story serves as an anecdotal reference and blends a mythological theme into the formal interplay of visible and invisible structures.

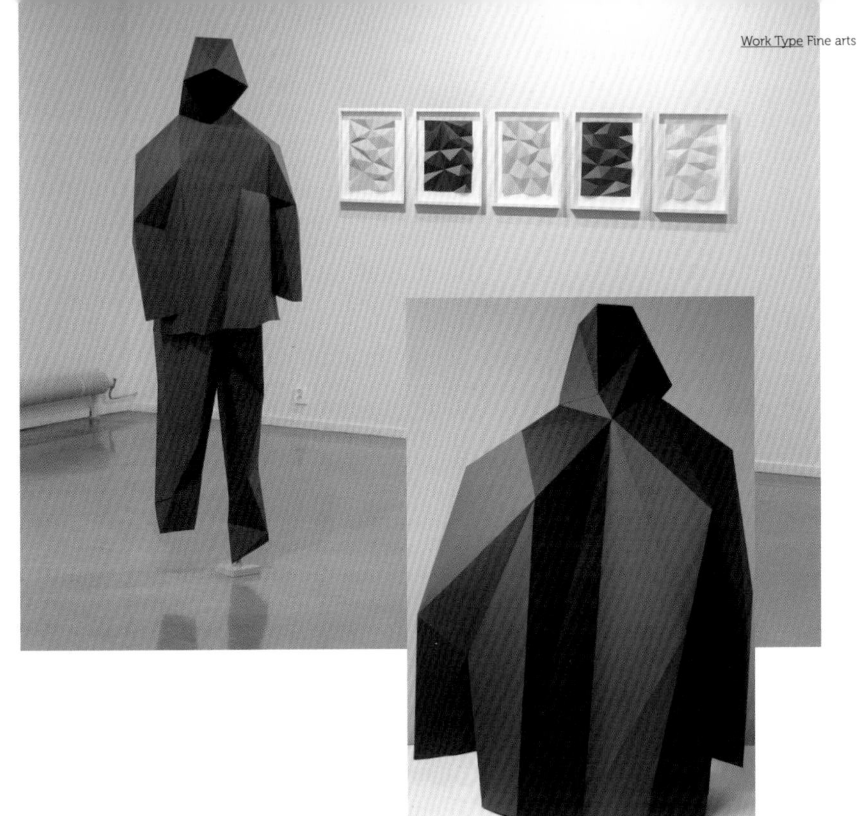

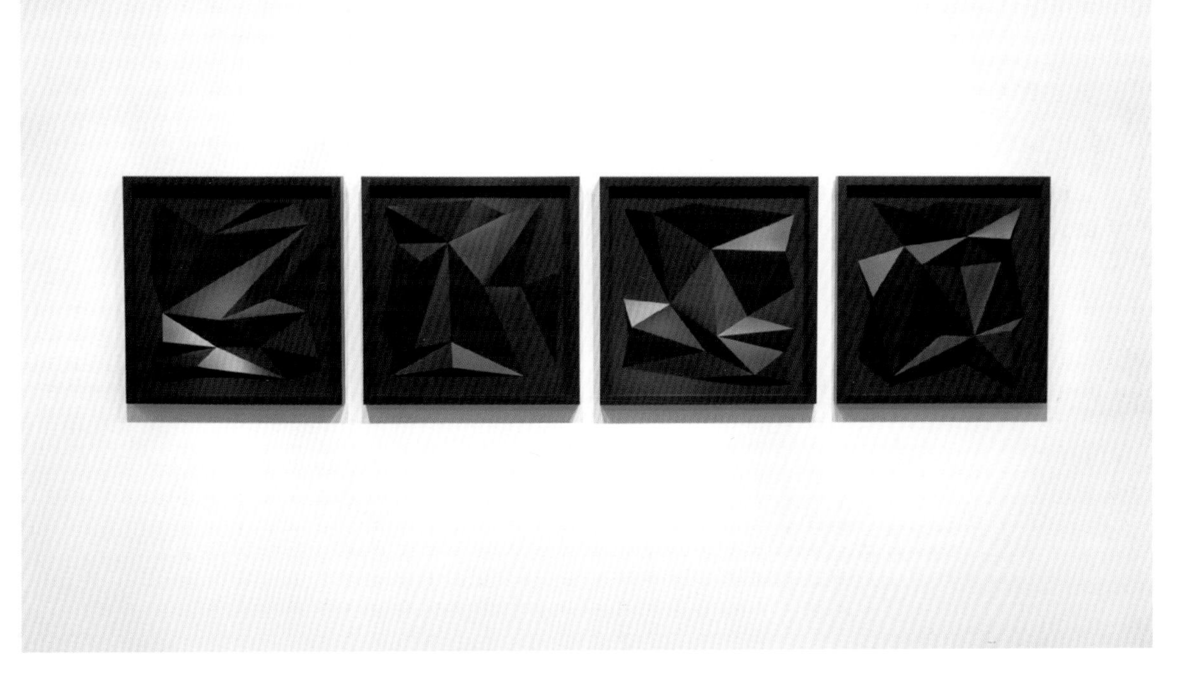

Artist Tommy Støckel Photographer Roland Schmidt, copyright Tommy Støckel & VG Bildkunst

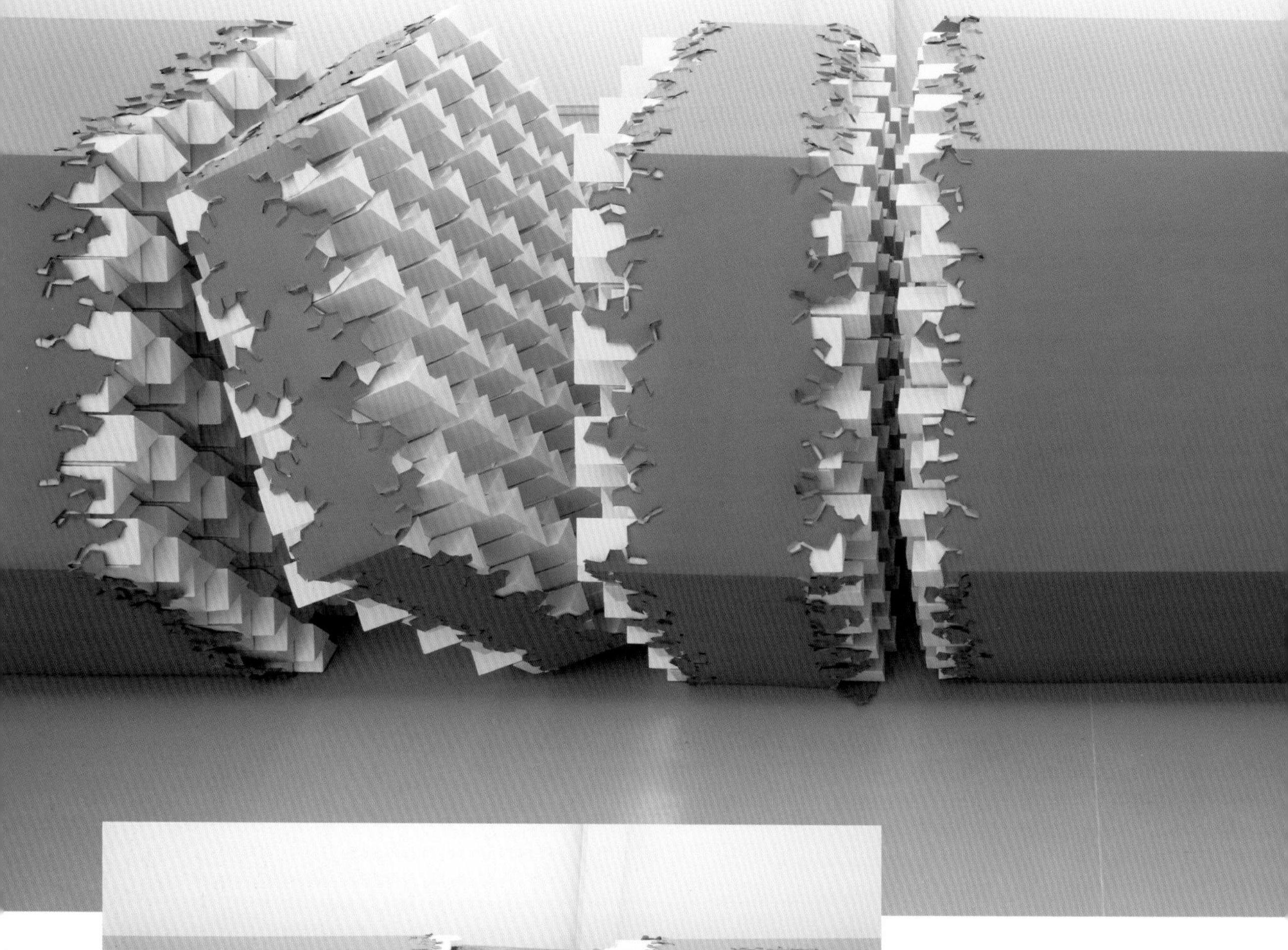

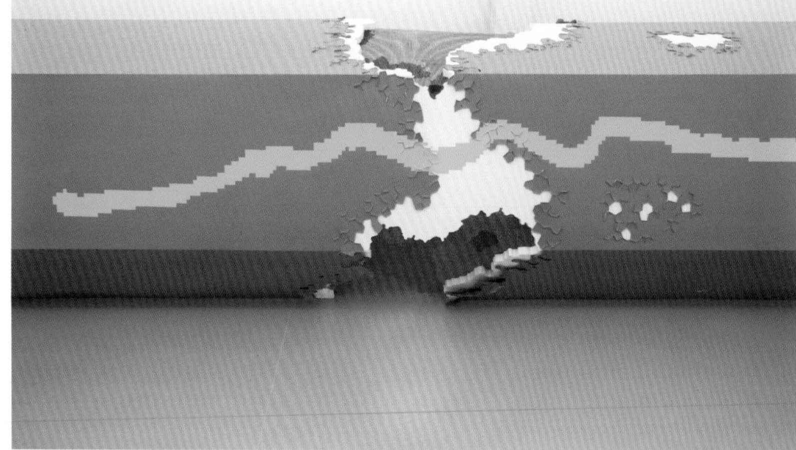

From Here to Then and Back Again

The 20 meter long sculpture was developed for a 24 meter long exhibition space. The artist thought that because of the length and shape of the space the sculpture is in, it has to be experienced in parts. Although it is constructed as one long uniform shape, the artist split it into many similar pieces; where the shape breaks, the interior of the structure is revealed. Each break of the sculpture contains a different interior, adding to the feeling of many sculptures in one.

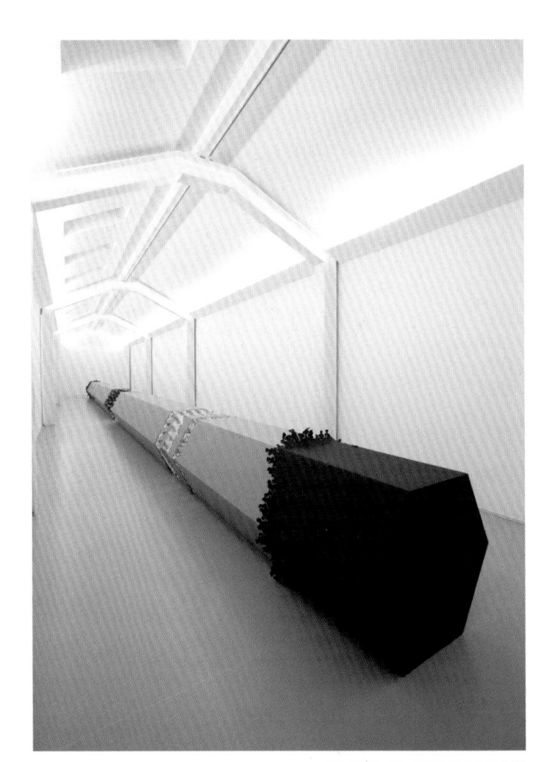

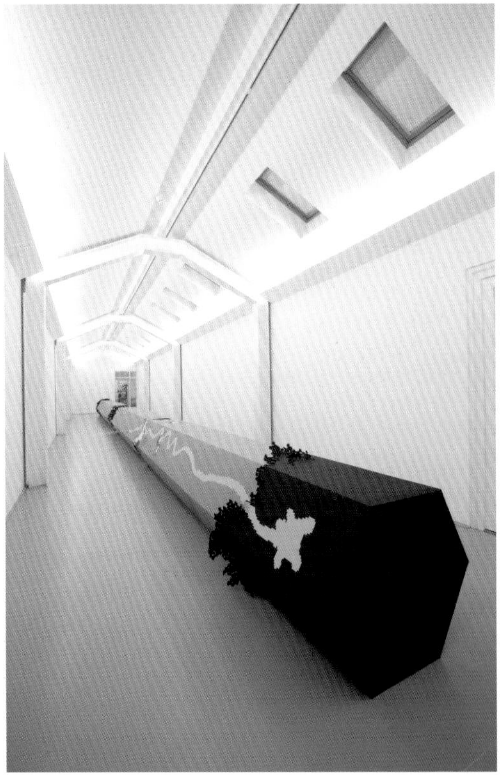

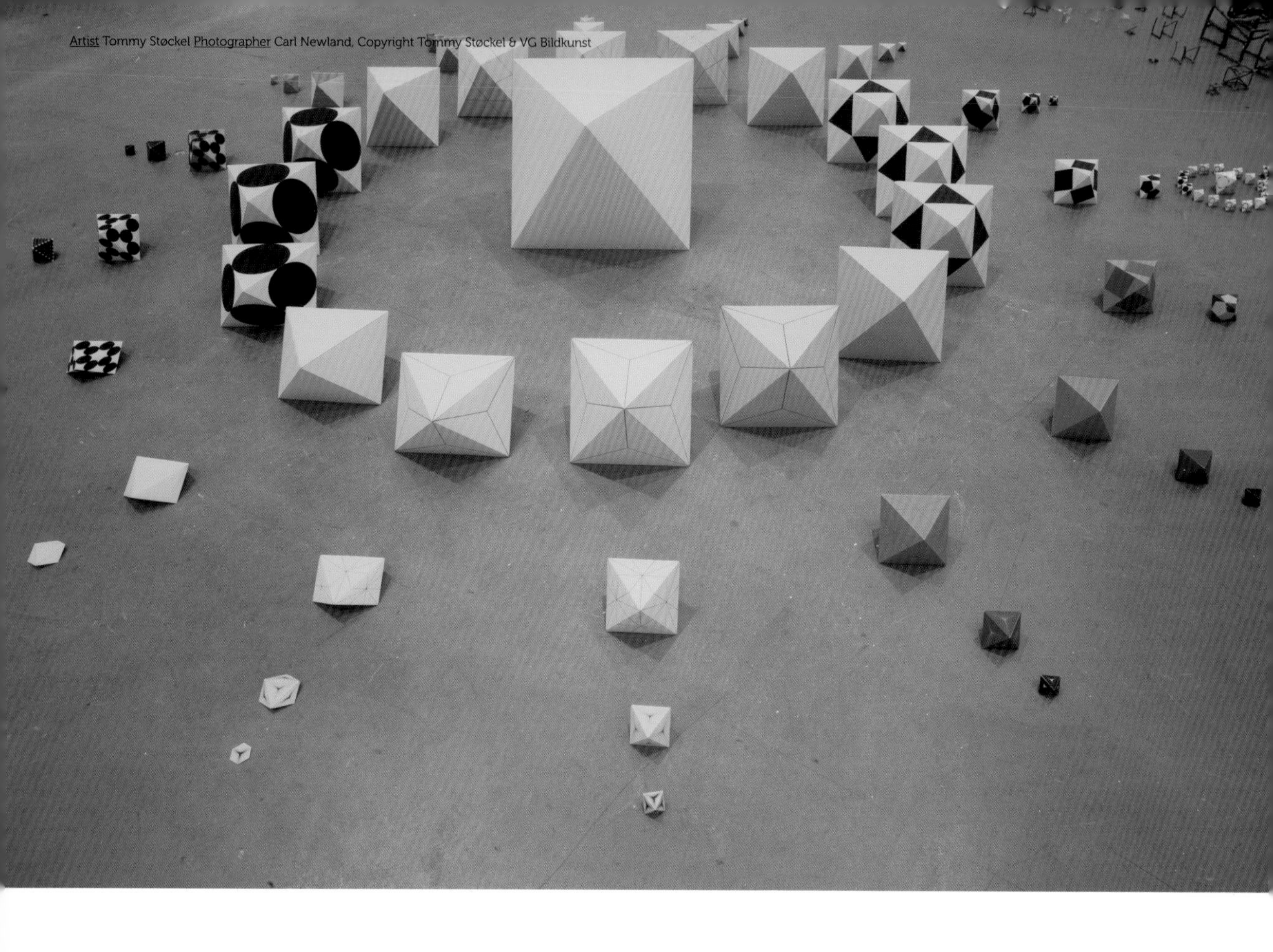

Artist Tommy Støckel Photographer Carl Newland, Copyright Tommy Støckel & VG Bildkunst

Tommy Støckel's Art of Tomorrow

This project was a sculptural diagram attempting to map out the possible developments in the works of Tommy Støckel. The 625 interconnected components were all examples of possible sculptures and derived from one single paper sculpture in the centre of the installation. Some of the possible developments were formal variations while others showed changes in materials or references. The predictions also saw the possibility of the artist moving away from fine arts and into such fields as architecture or furniture design.

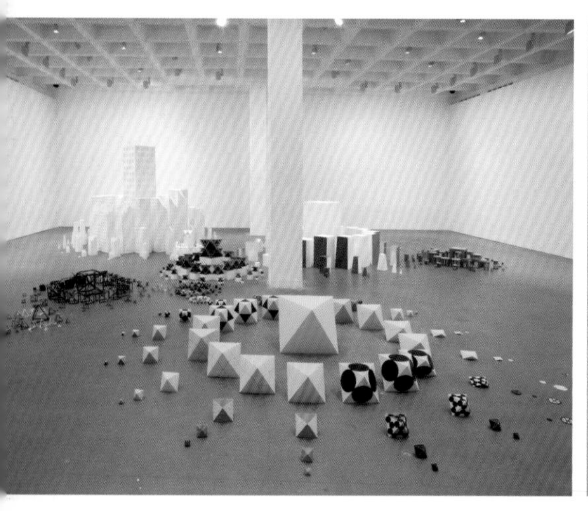

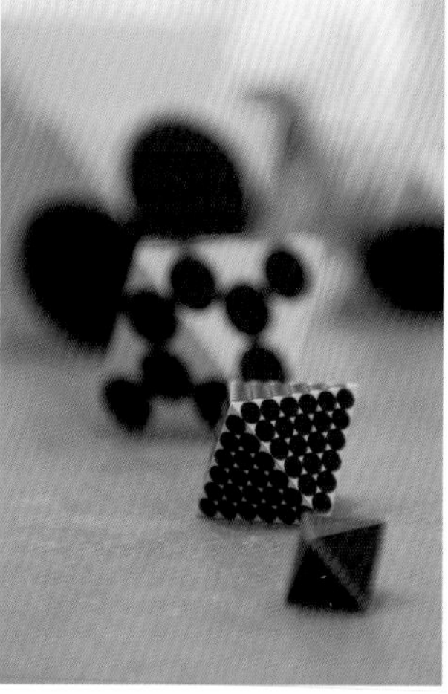

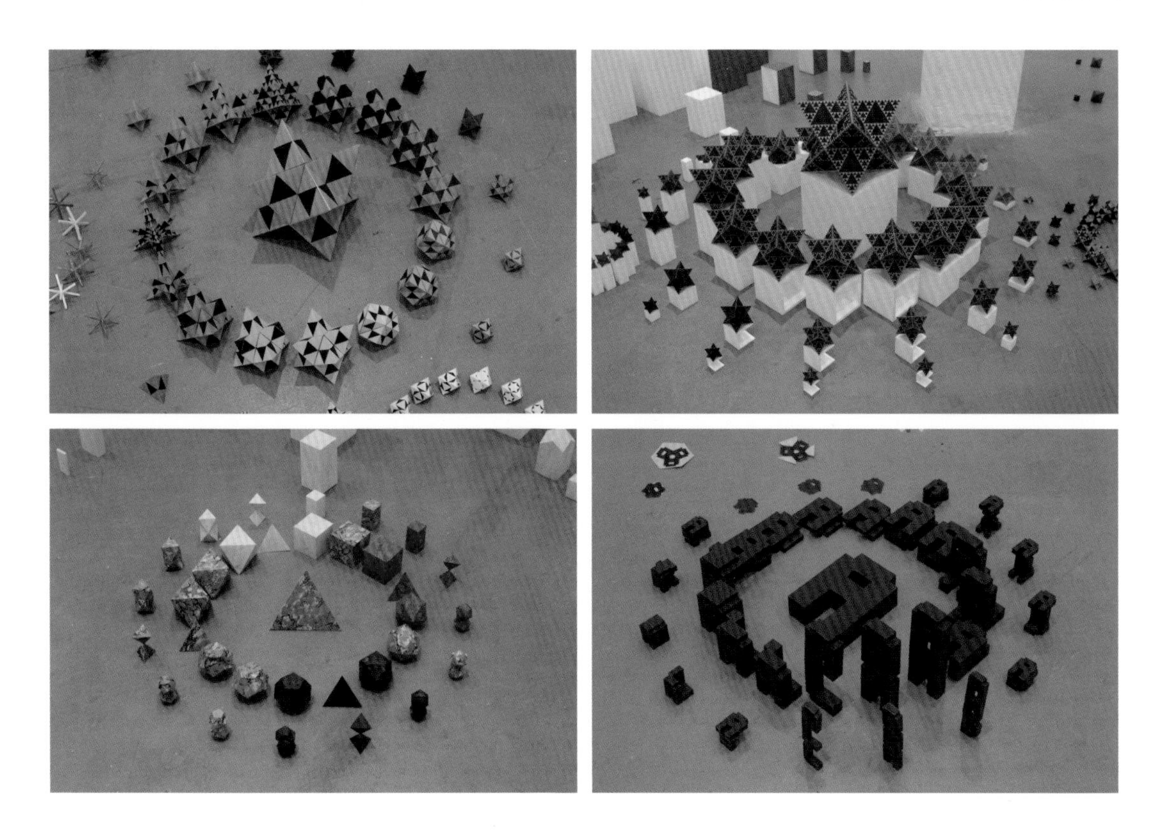

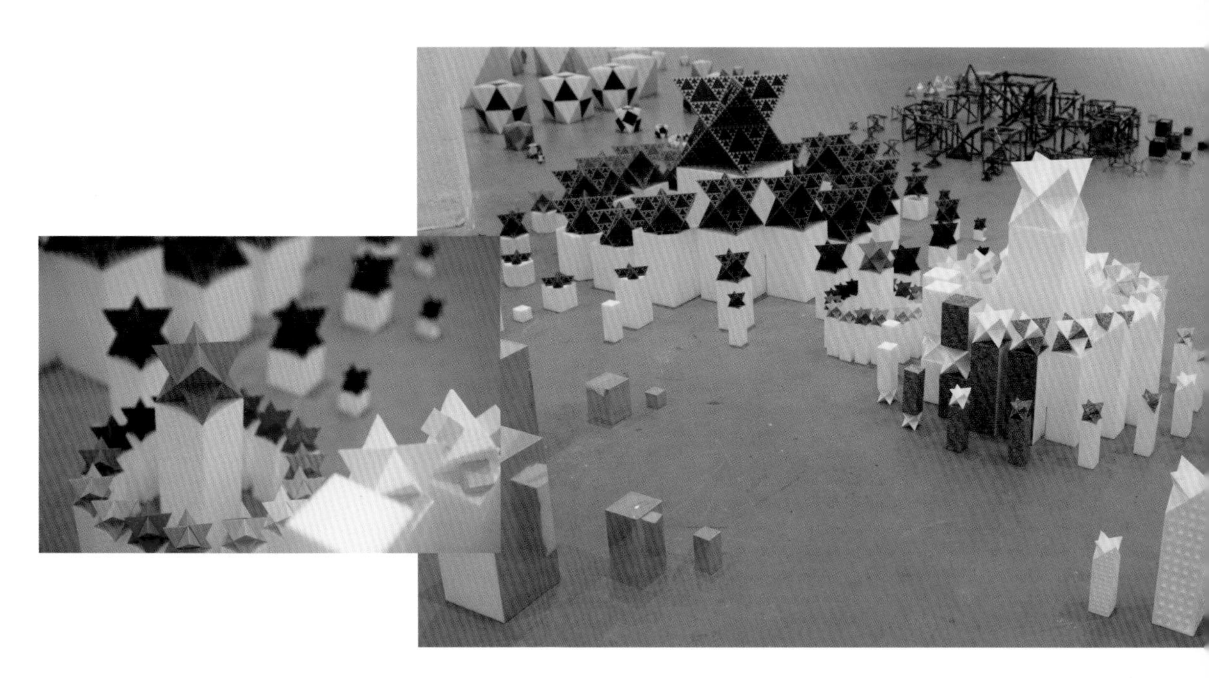

Design Agency Estudio Rosa Lázaro Designer Héctor Sos Photographer Xabier Mendiola Client Torras Papel

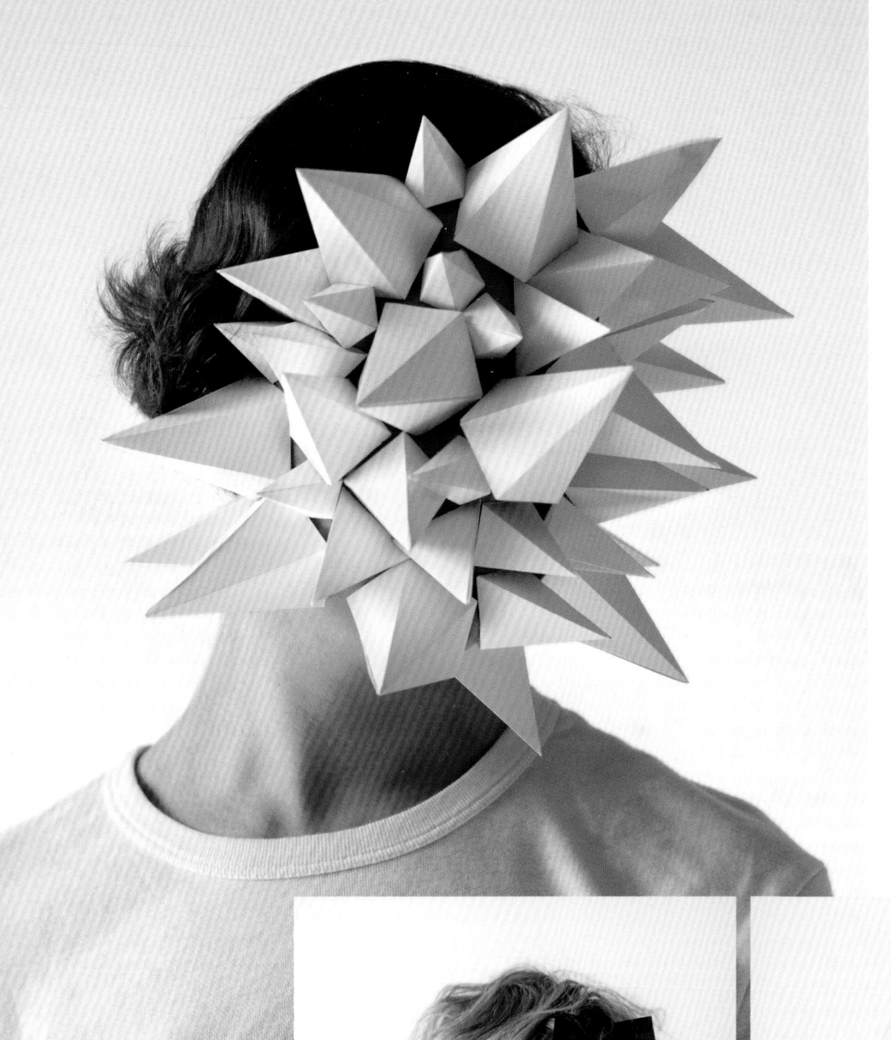

Paper Faces

The "Paper Faces" project was created with the intention of linking CreadorVol paper with the concept of the publishing industry as natural and alive — hence the visual metaphor between paper and face expressed by this design. This idea and the need to show the qualities of paper during the four-color printing process inspired a series of distinctive structures made out of paper; the models' faces were covered with the paper structures and then photographed. Paper and color are the elements that give strength to the project. The photo shoot intent was for the models to be captured in poses similar to those in a traditional portrait session: torso turned toward the camera, classic profile shot, or a three quarters view. These traditional poses were reinvented with an urban aesthetic to be both youthful and contemporary through the use of natural direct light. The light clarity unifies the images and gives the models a natural feeling of ease.

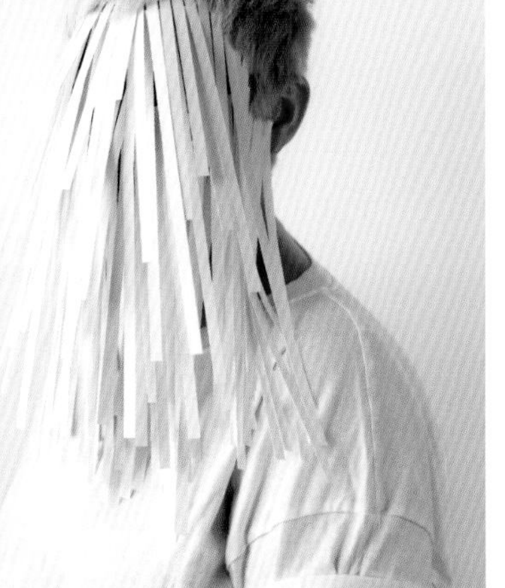

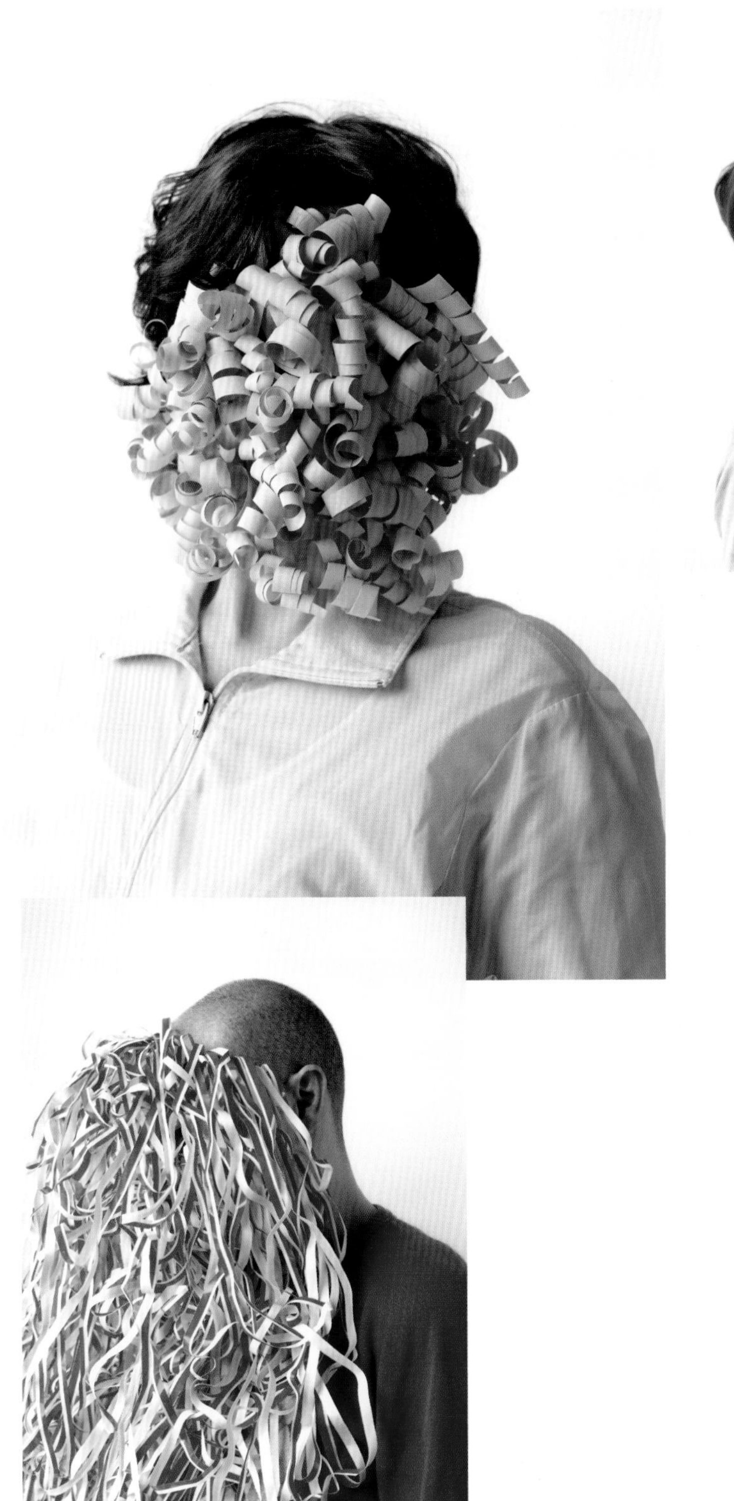

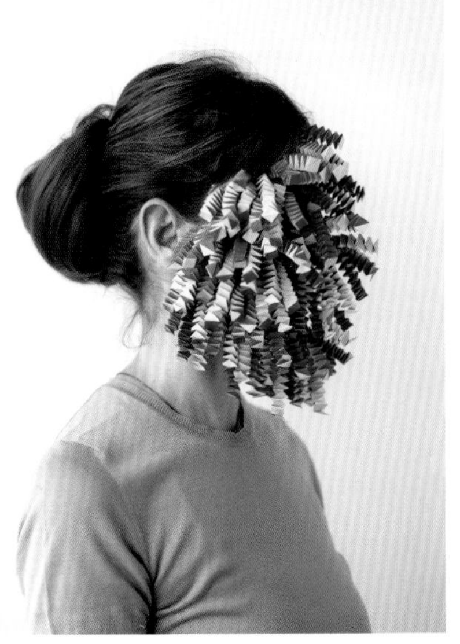

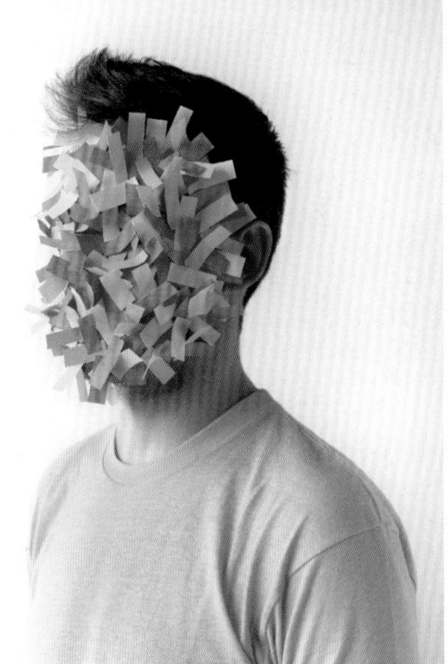

Architect Yo Shimada Photographer Yousuke Takeda Client Art Zone

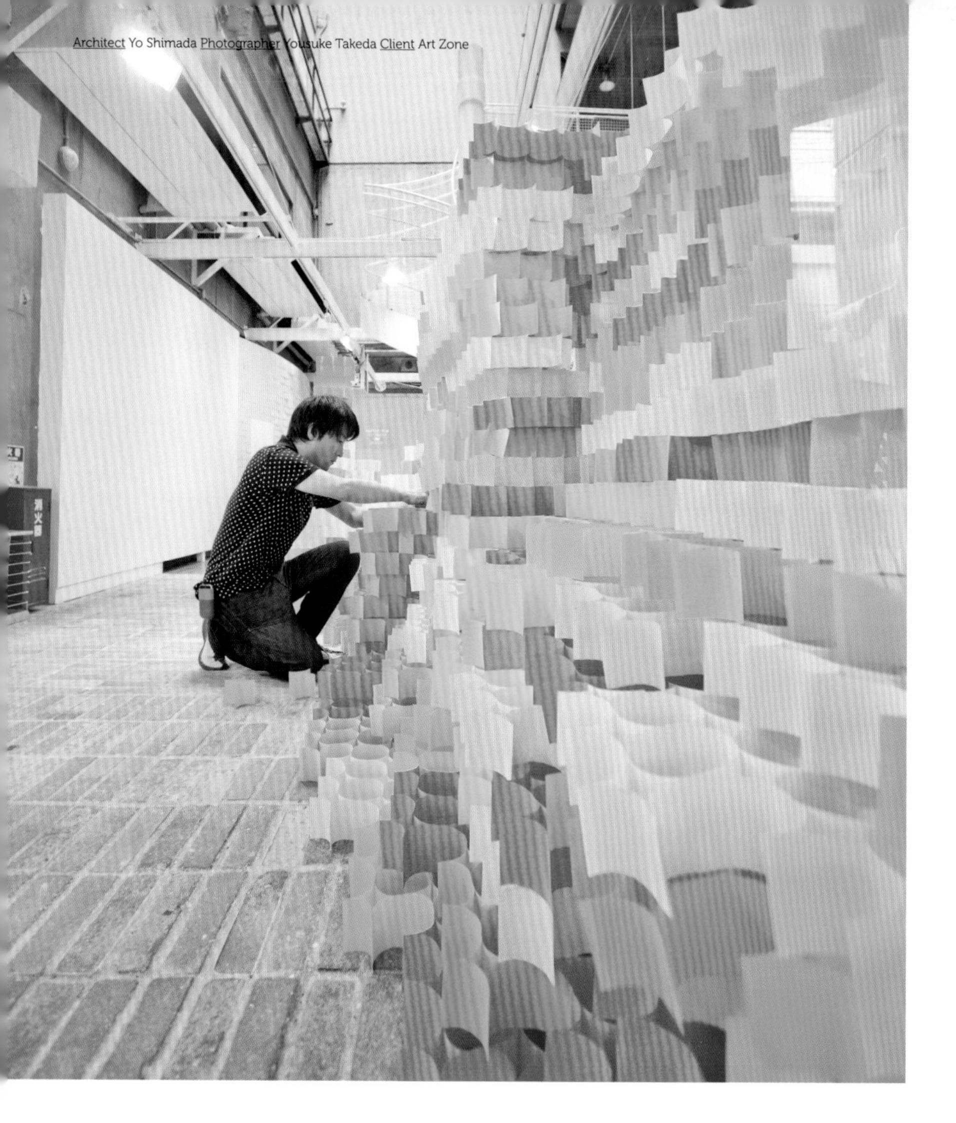

Post-it Structures

This is an art installation for an event of six dialogues held in Kyoto University of Art and Design. Yo Shimada from "tato architects" created the installation in three days in cooperation with the students. About 30 thousand post-its were used. The audience was instructed to jot down their impressions on a post-it and then add it to the front of the wall. Post-its were also used to create a structure for decorating the stage where architect Yo Shimada had an interview and discussion with Japanese calligrapher Miss Kasetsu. Prior to the discussion, Miss Kasetsu chose to remove a few post-its of a single shade, add her calligraphy to them, and then add them back into the installation.

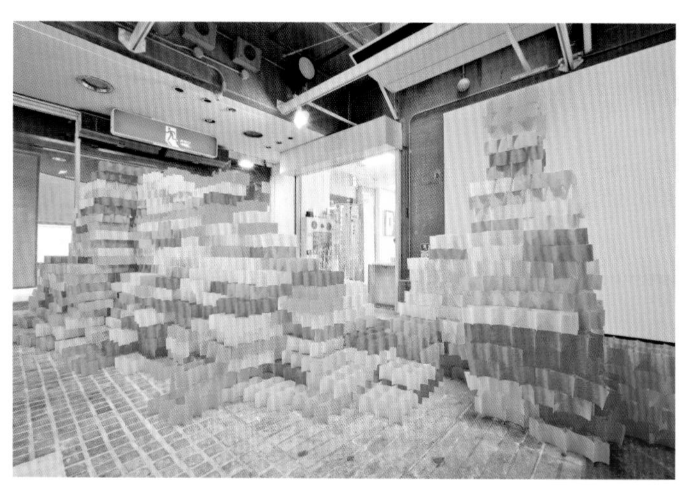

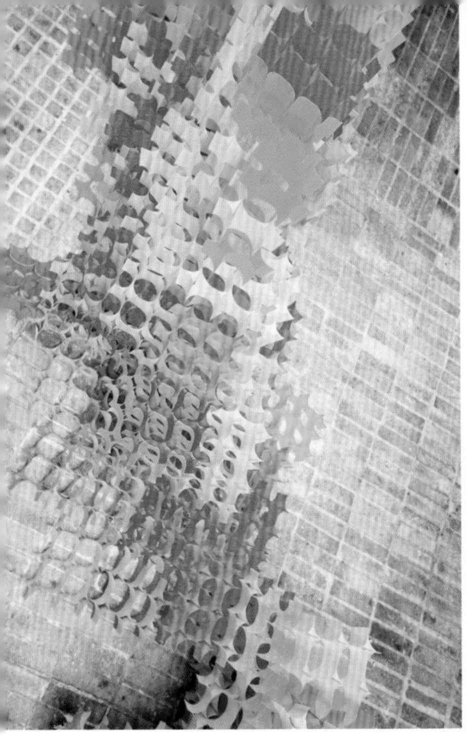

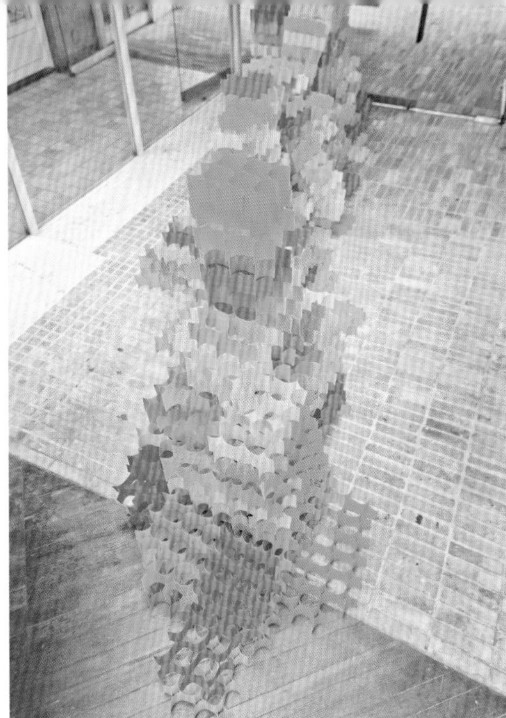

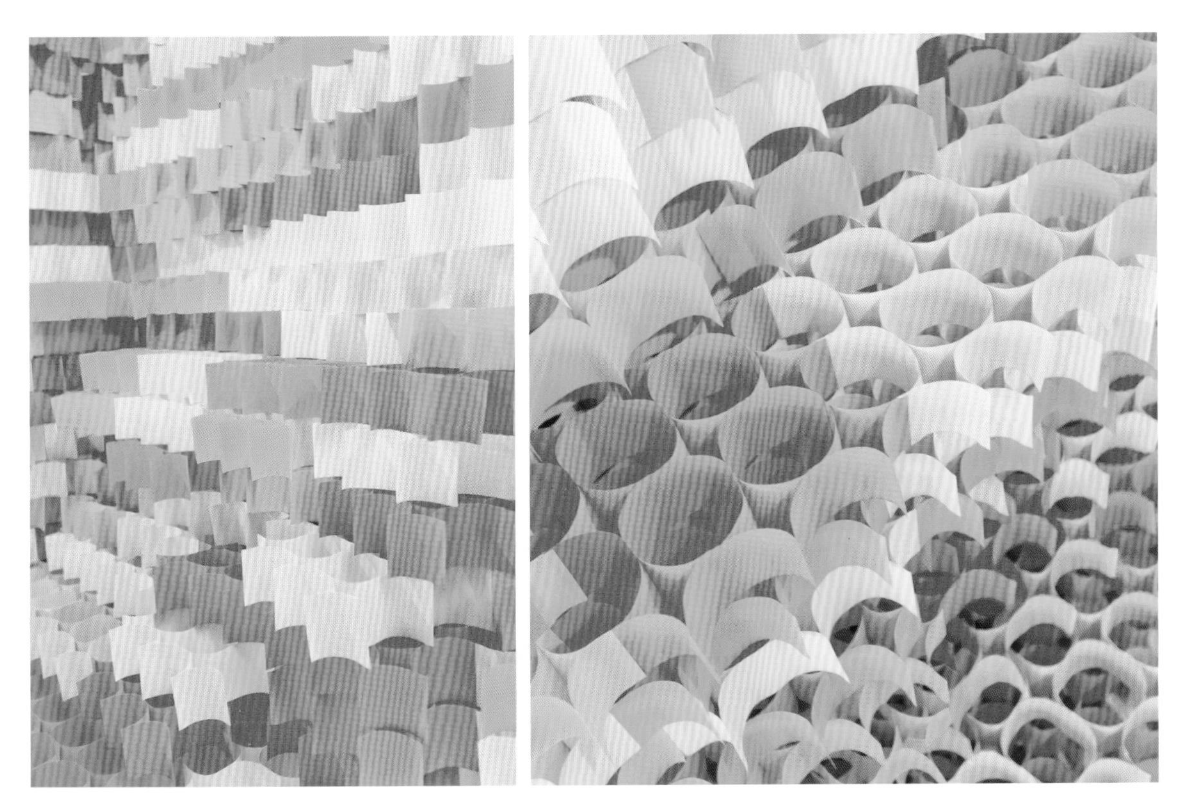

Body Anatomy

1 / Non-Prescription
2,3 / Parasite
4 / Extrasensory

Extrasensory elaborates on human anatomy to create a fictional new model based on physical ensation and imagination. Non-Prescription is based on the structure of children's pop-up books; this installation inside a medicine cabinet unfolds to reveal its contents as the door is opened to reveal an unexpected anatomy inside. Parasite is a sculptural drawing created for the Museum Bellerive in Zurich. This site-specific work incorporates vines, flowers, and other organic forms, with a very large bird embryo nestled inside.

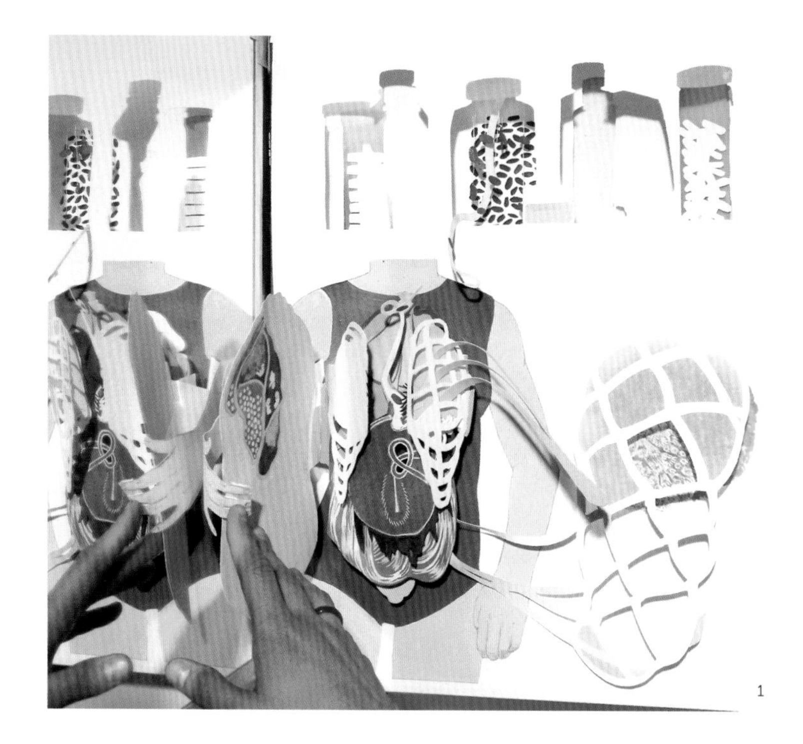

1

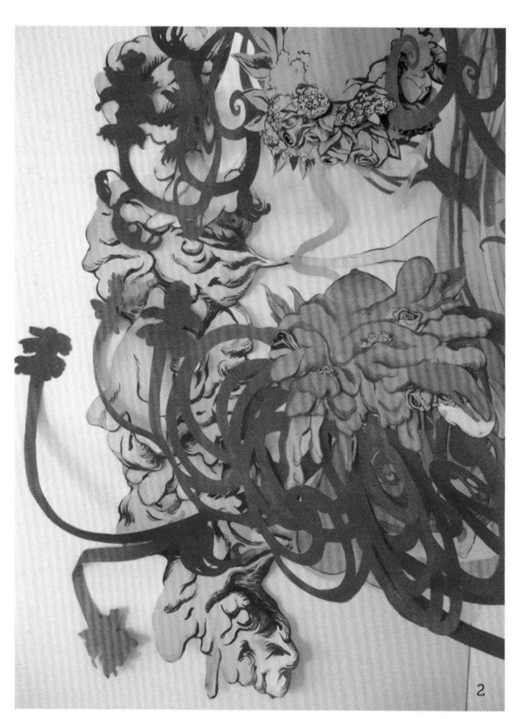

2

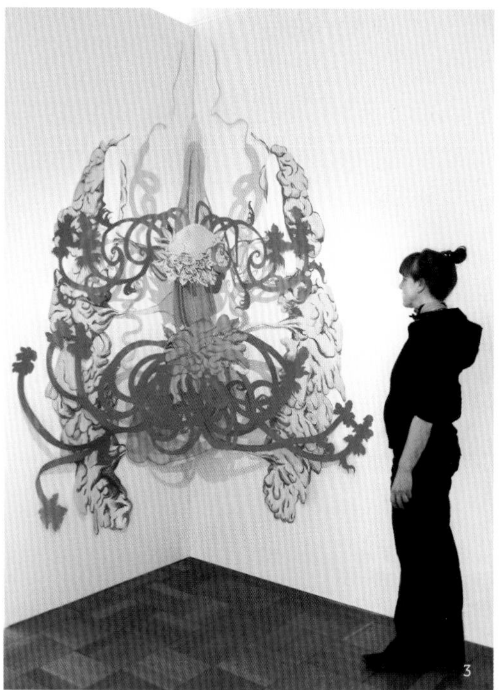

3

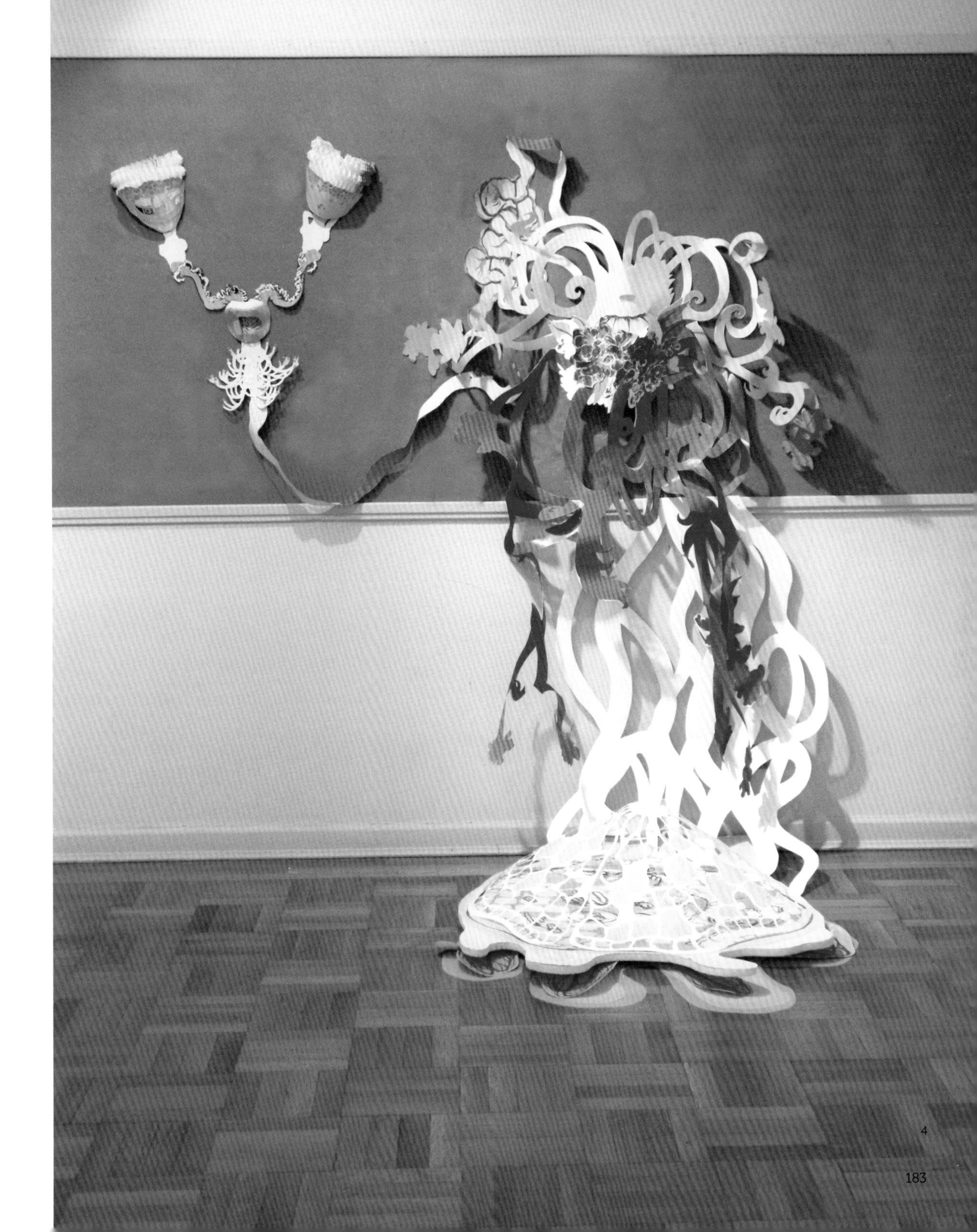

4

Design Agency SILNT Designer Ying Hui, Serene Wong, Jonathan Yuen, The Bureau, Hans Tan, Edwin Tan, Yanda Photographer Jae Hann Client Antalis Paper

Help Save Paper

1 / Untitled
2 / I dream of summer
3 / Wound
4 / Ultimate White
5 / Curious Translucent
6 / Sagittarius
7 / Dear Alice

This is a story about death. For sure, it begins with death, which gives birth to many things: fear, ingenuity and life. Once upon a time, paper was an important aspect of every part of our lives. It gave us privacy when it was a screen; it sheltered us from rain as an umbrella. It was an expression of artistry in the hands of skilled paper-makers. Due to the digital age, paper's numerous variants and breeds are dying out, leaving only the dull copier paper, most commonly found in offices. In such dire straits, we've called on twelve individuals from all artistic disciplines to create an object using only paper - to create things of beauty, things of usefulness or anything else they can imagine, as long as it elevates the status of paper from a printing surface to a versatile medium of brilliant creative potential.

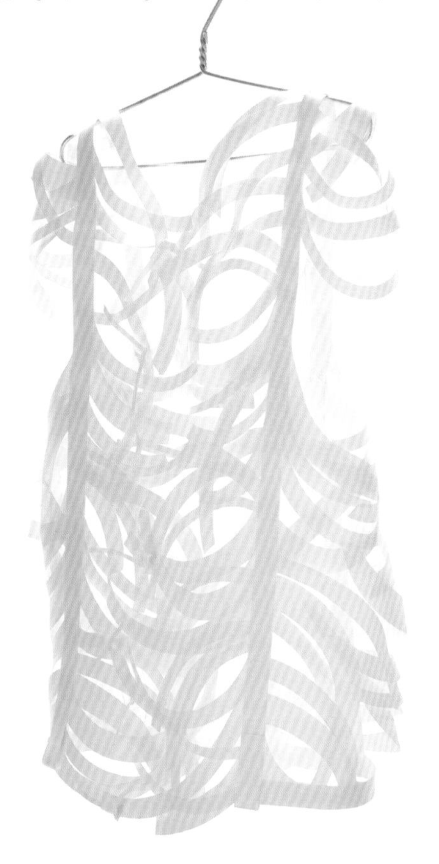

1

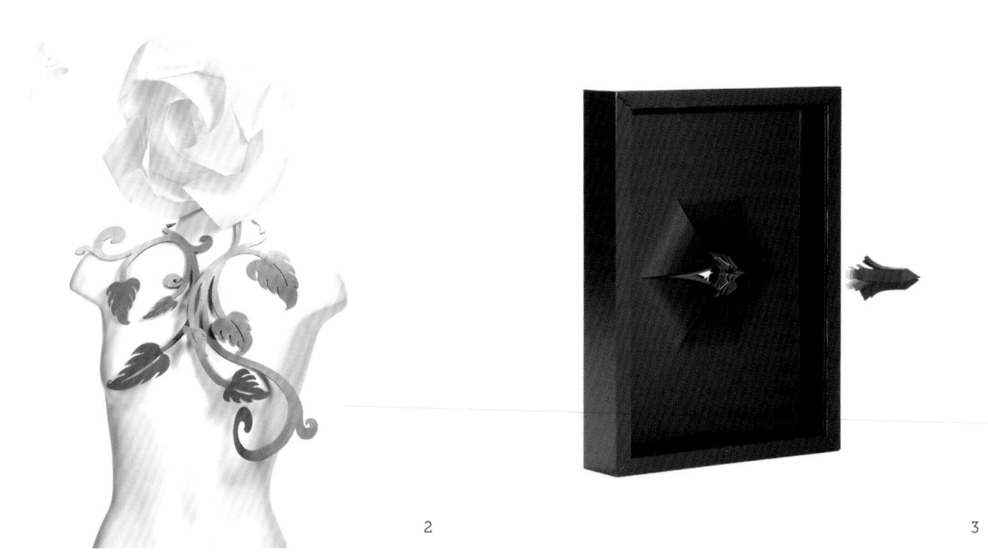

2

3

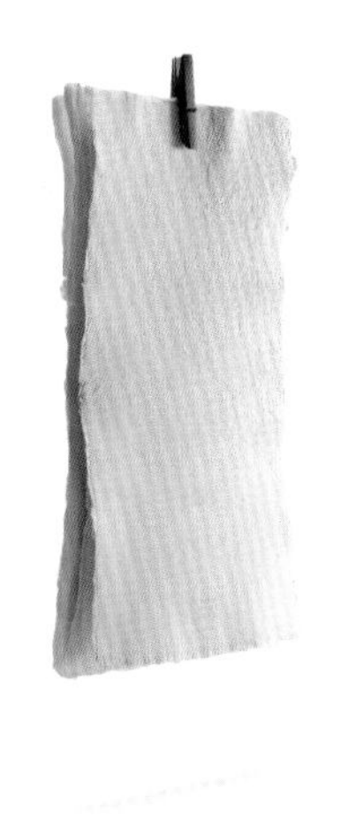

4

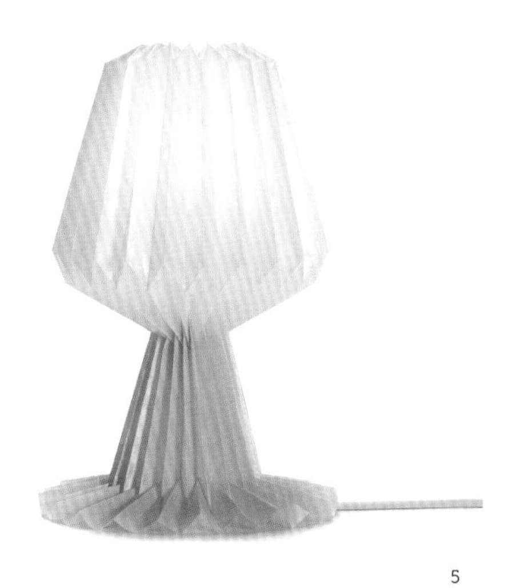

5

6

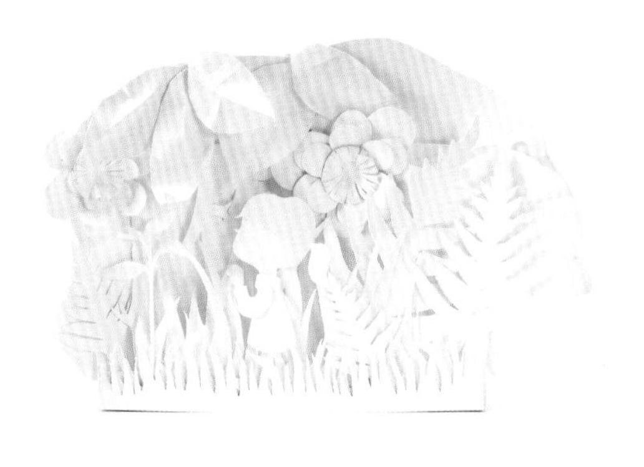

7

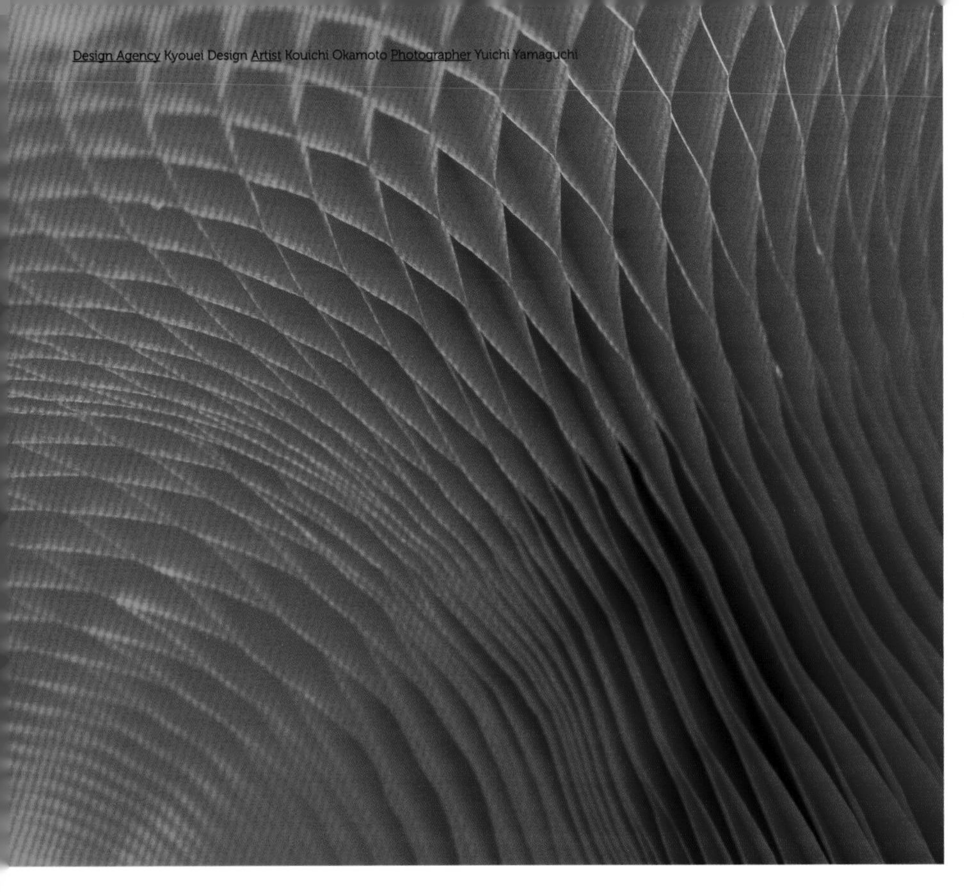

Design Agency Kyouei Design Artist Kouichi Okamoto Photographer Yuichi Yamaguchi

Honeycomb Lamp

We used "Denguri paper" for this Shade of a lamp. The "Denguri" paper is a local product of Shikoku region of Japan. When the paper construction is closed, it is only about 2 cms thick. When opened, the paper becomes a lamp shade held together at the edges by just a few pins. The project was created with delicate and time-consuming craftsmanship.

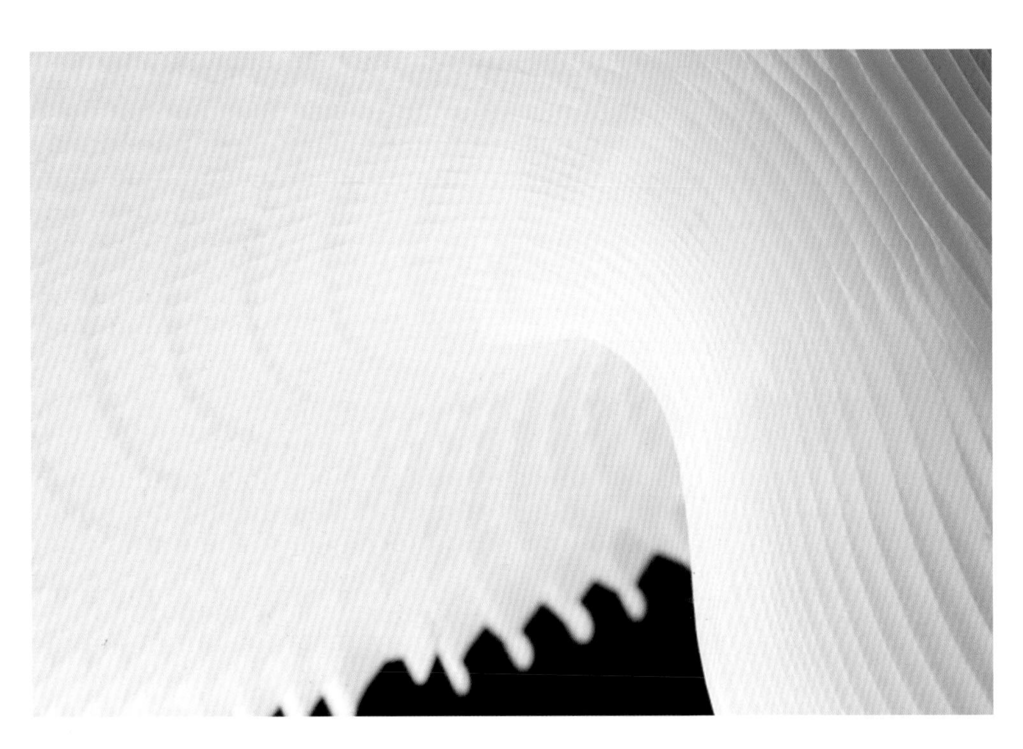

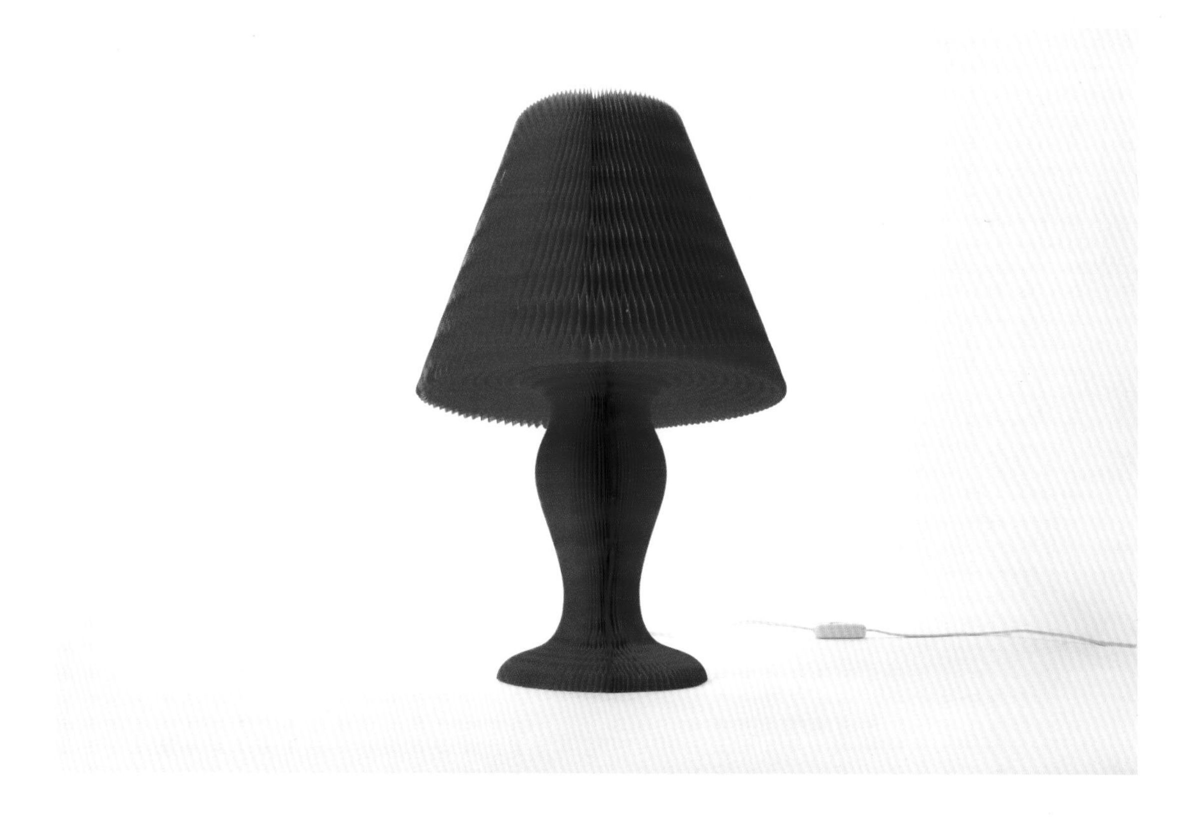

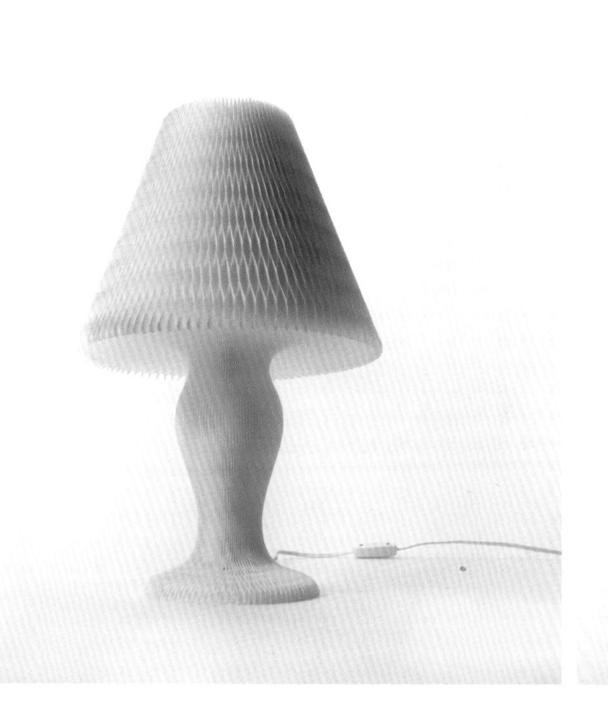

HONEYCOMBLAMP
made in Japan

Design Agency Kyouei Design Artist Kouichi Okamoto Photographer Yuichi Yamaguchi

Cube Letter Set

The cubic letter design was based on the traditional Japanese paper balloon. The writing paper, which is shaped like a cube, can be blown up like a balloon.

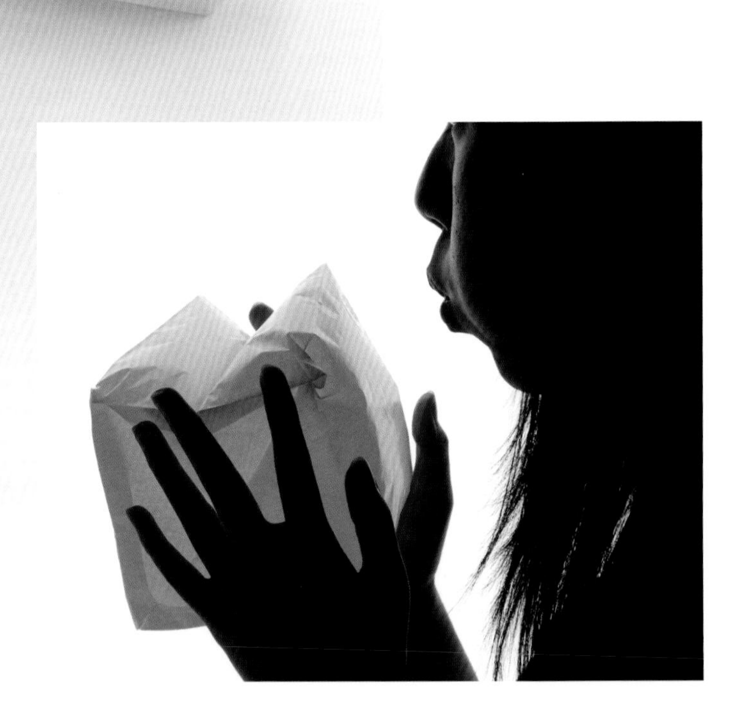

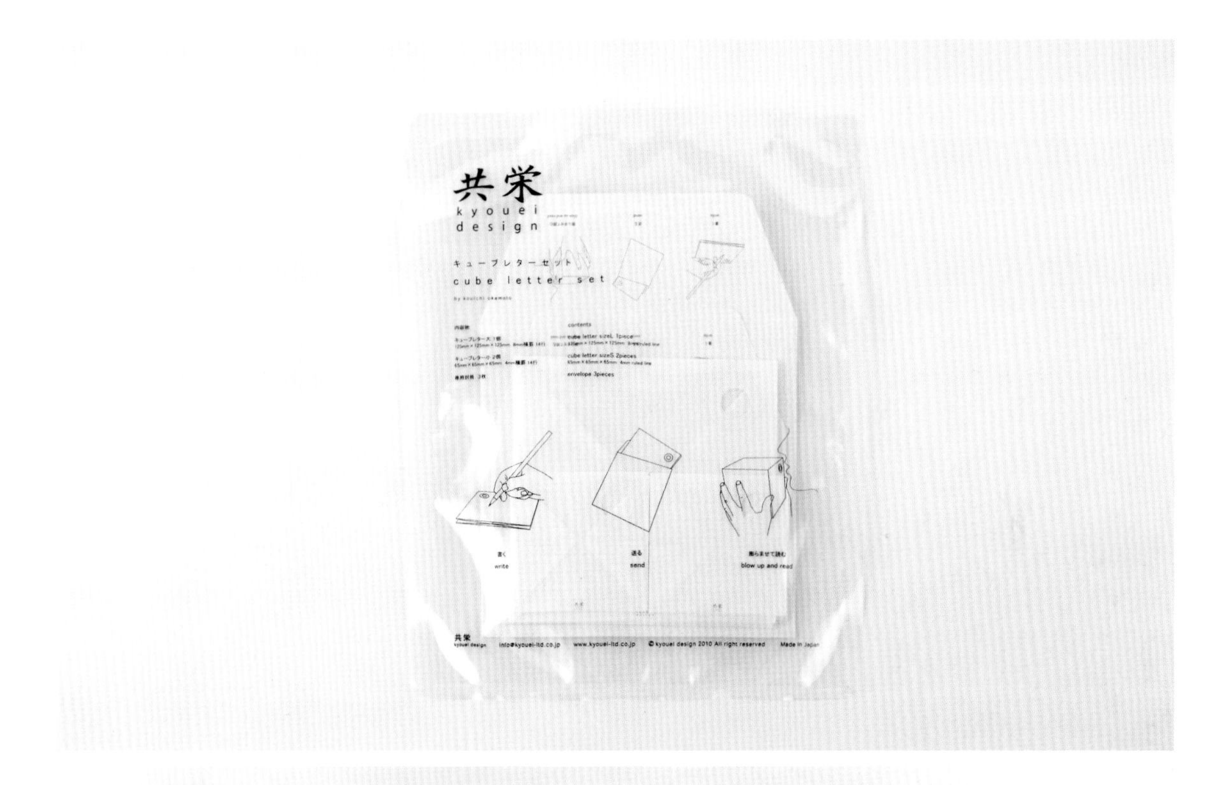
共栄
kyouei
design
キューブレターセット
cube letter set
contents
cube letter sizeS 2pieces
envelope 3pieces
書く
write
送る
send
blow up and read
共栄
kyouei design
info@kyouei-ltd.co.jp
www.kyouei-ltd.co.jp
© kyouei design 2010 All right reserved

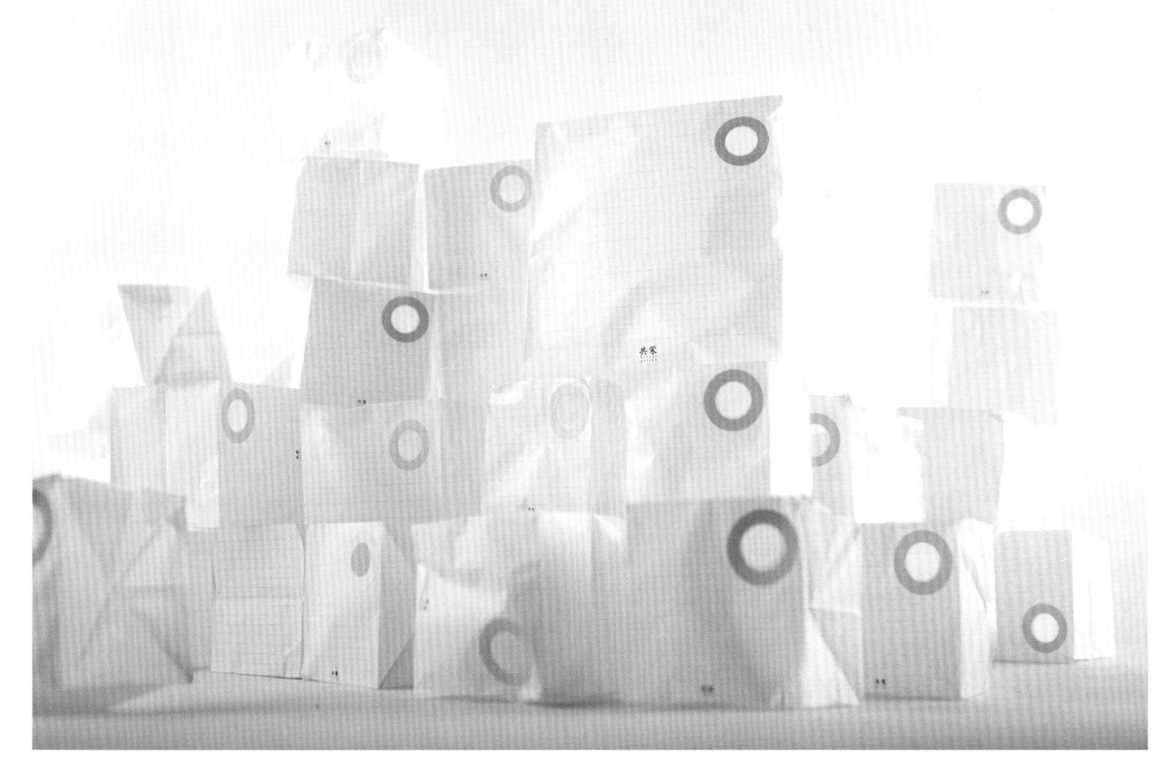

Designer Stephanie Chu

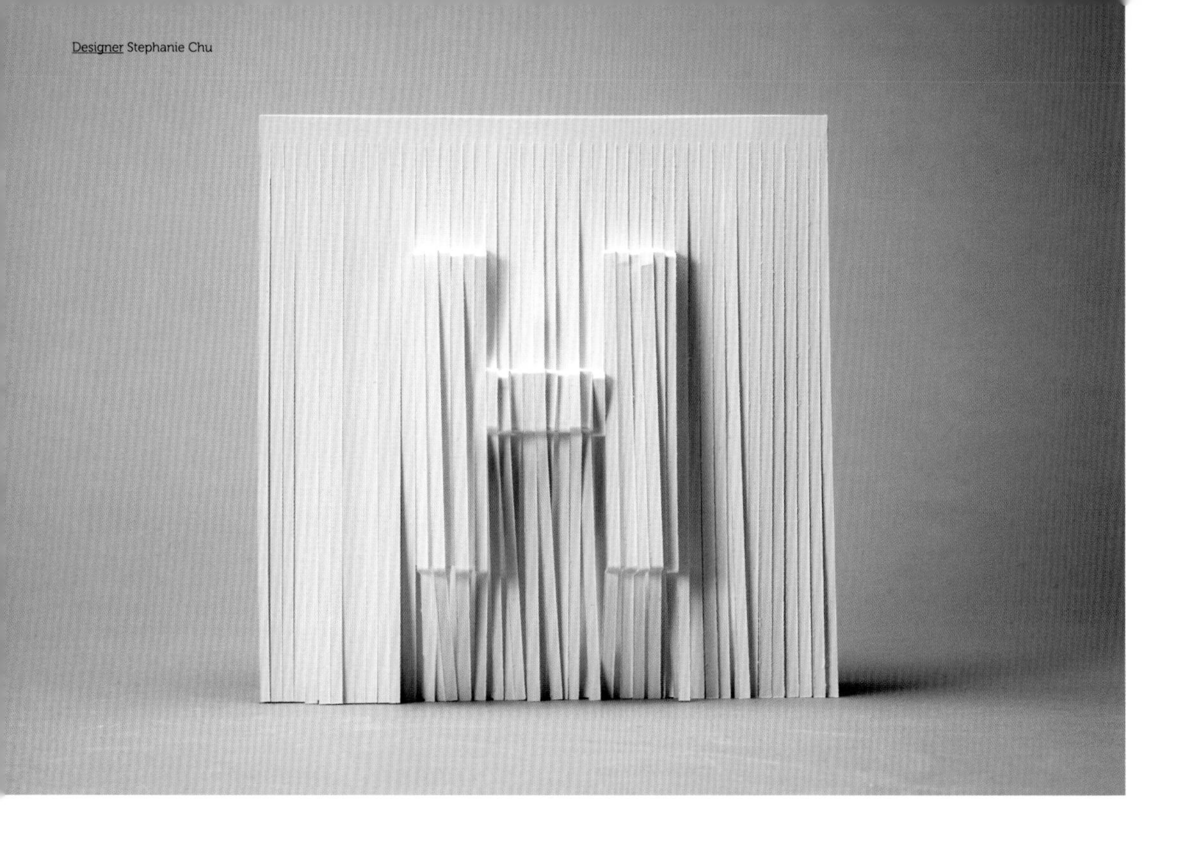

Paper ABC

When defining such a broad discipline as graphic design, it is not uncommon to find that many individuals will relate it to visual communication. Whether it is through the use of typography, symbols, or images, the final output is predominantly two dimensional. Magazines, posters, books, business cards, and letterheads are a few of the more common examples. With the advancement of technology and the rise in web design, user interface, and other digital media, graphic design is being used in two-dimensional planes more than ever before. As a result, "Paper ABC" became a personal exploration to discover if graphic design can lend itself to a three-dimensional space. Through the use of paper techniques and the Roman alphabet, each texture is appropriately applied based on the characteristics of each letterform. For example, a texture which lends itself to a curvilinear form is better suited for a letter with a rounded shape. In this way, a unique dialogue is created between what makes up the form and the form itself.

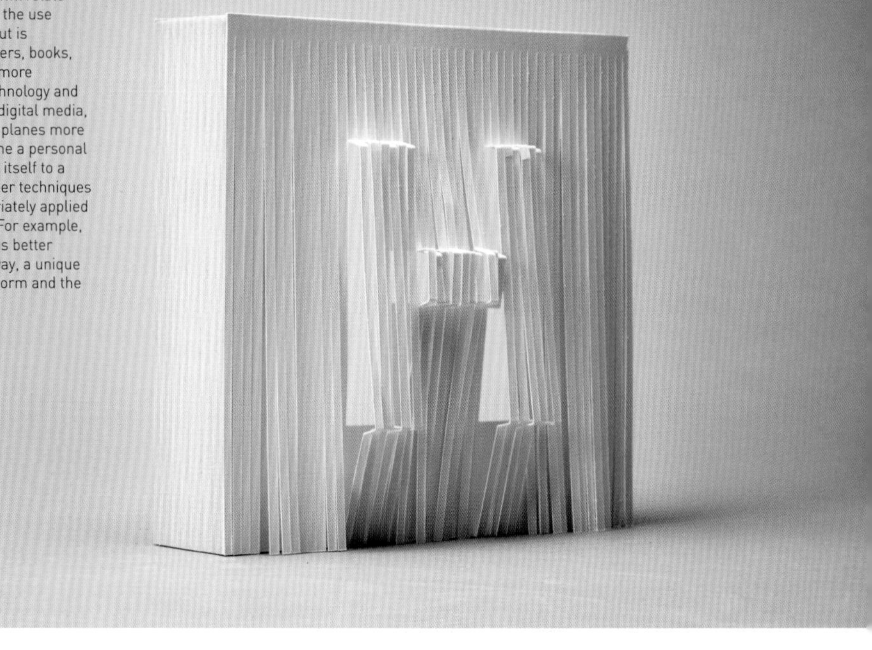

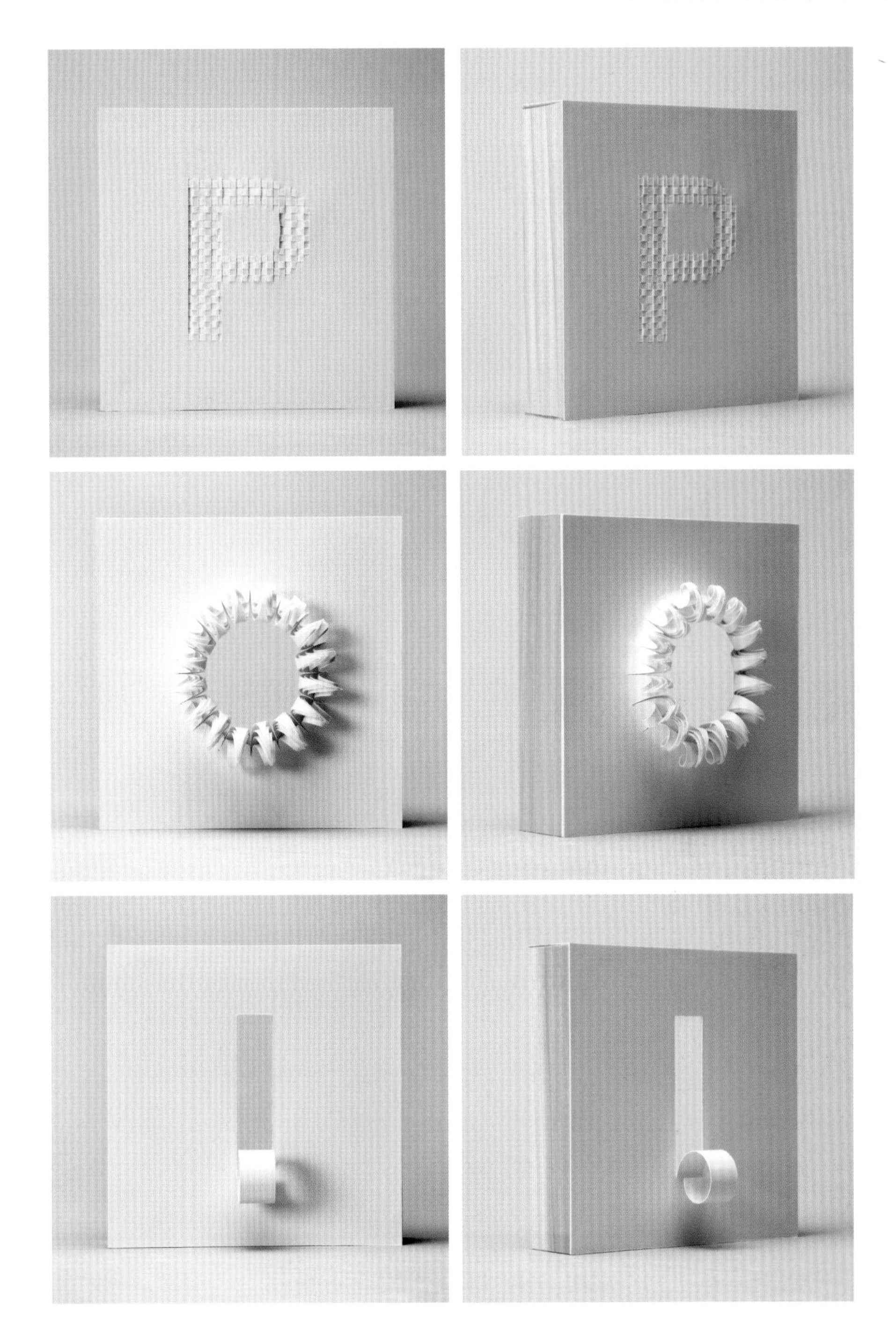

Designer Bianca Chang Photographer Jacob Ring

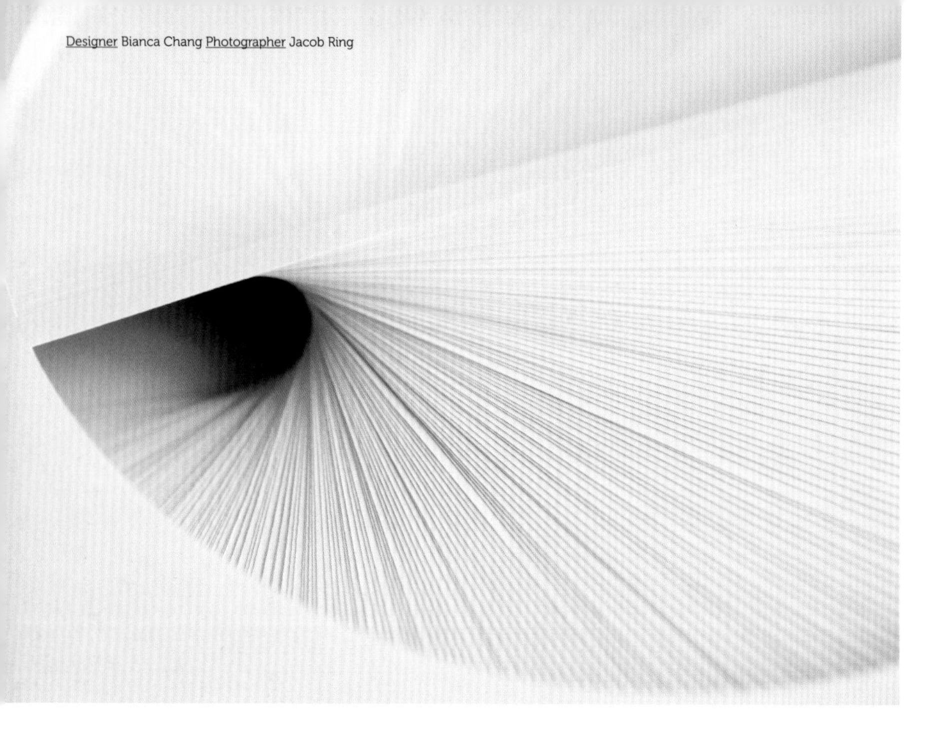

DOT & TWIN

Inspired by the subtlety of tone on signage and the shadow-play of three-dimensional letterforms, these sculptures were created by hand-plotting and cutting multiple sheets of 80gsm 100% recycled paper – minimizing the impact of paper consumption and consciously transforming a typically disposable medium into a long term piece of art.

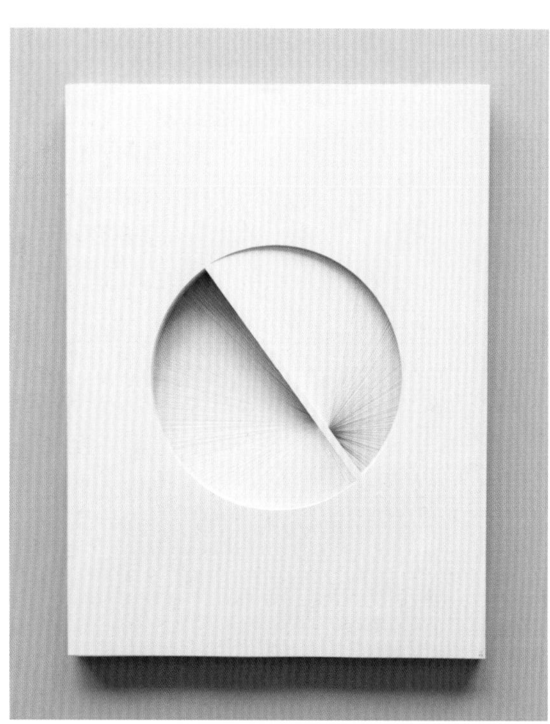

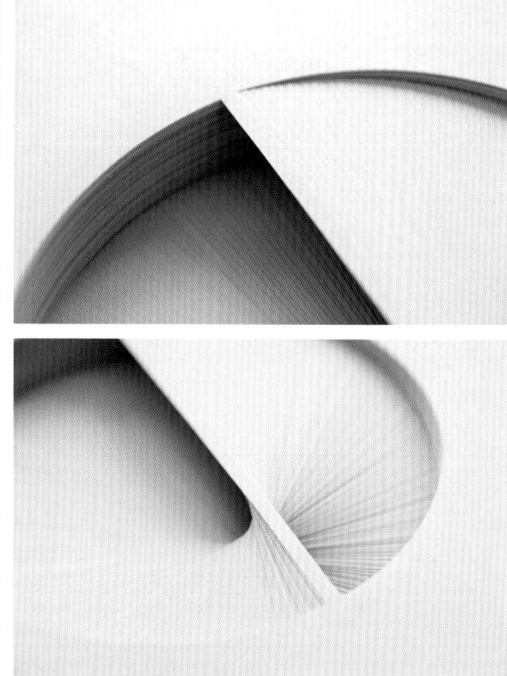

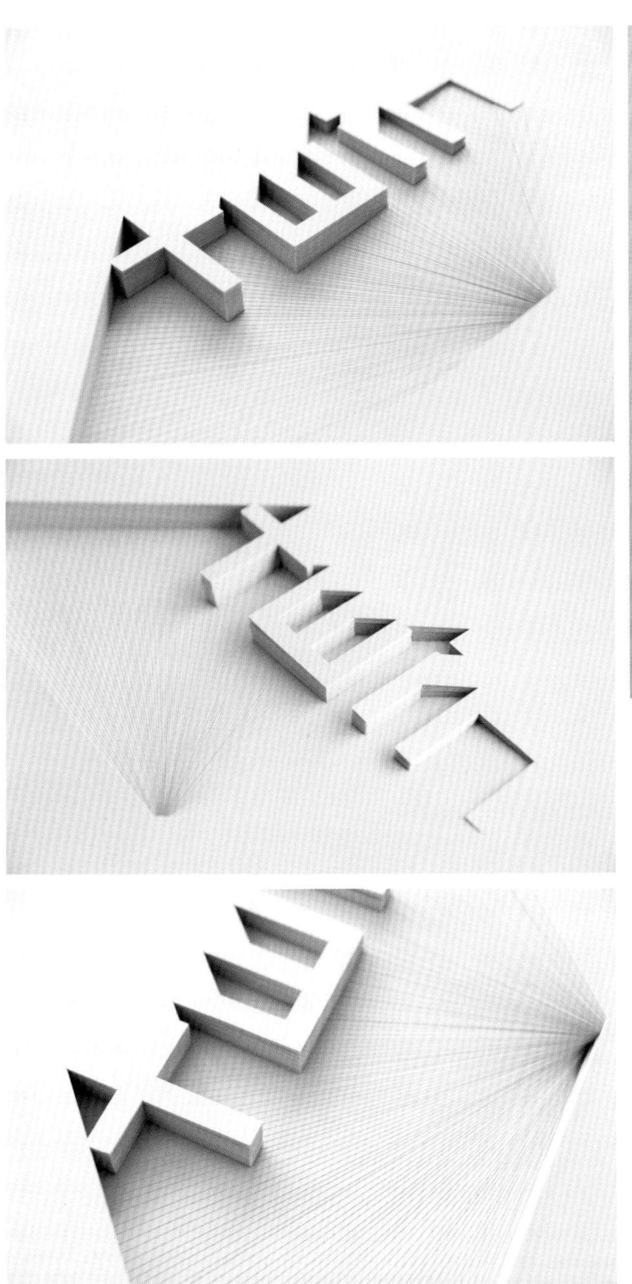
twin

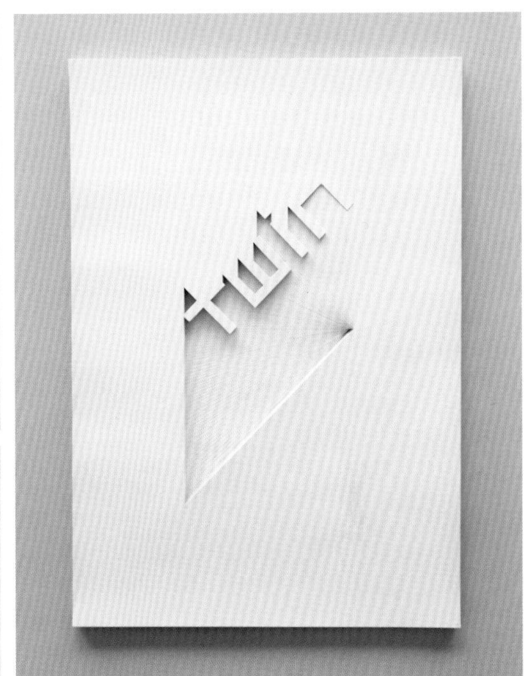
twin

Stripe Jewelry

As an artist I am mainly interested in the movement of lines and in my power to influence them. But I also need the resistance of the material. By experimentally exploring and developing ways to provoke the resistance of the fine drawing cardboard I use and push it to the limit. I put a hand in the material, grasp it, and elicit unimagined forces and tensions from it. These I use to steer the lines, create spatiality and new shapes.

My point of departure is a bundle of flat stripes. Once I have started to move the bundle and force different stripes on a single plane I can feel the resistance of the cardboard against my hands. This resistance releases the impulse to shape even further and the material responds to my hand and unfurls its curvature and shape – the concentrated process of artistic form finding is launched. I love my way of working mainly because of the openness required for this interaction with the material and the challenge to make the best decisions while creating each form.

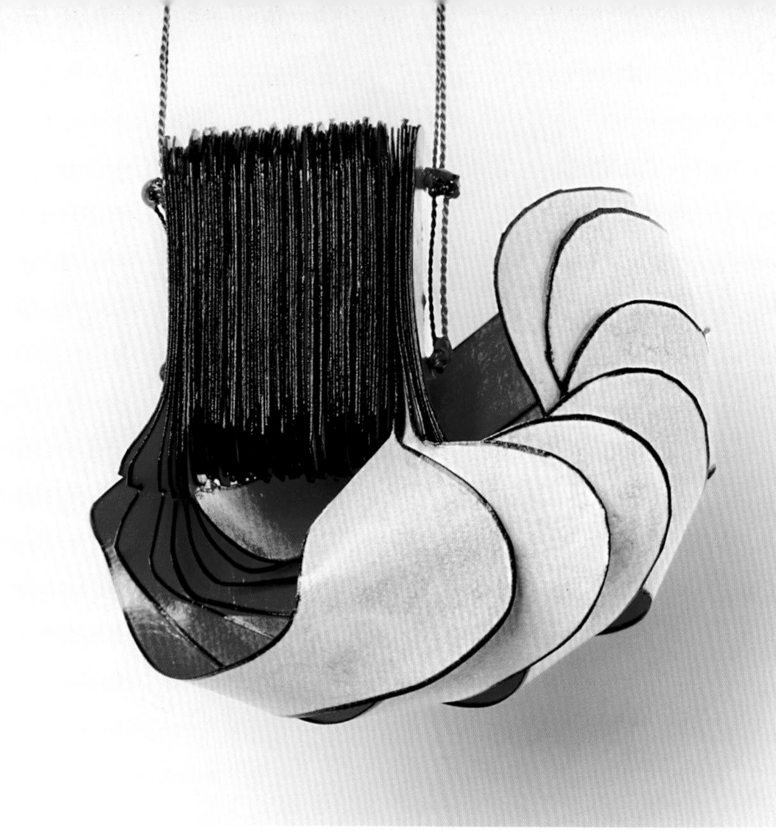

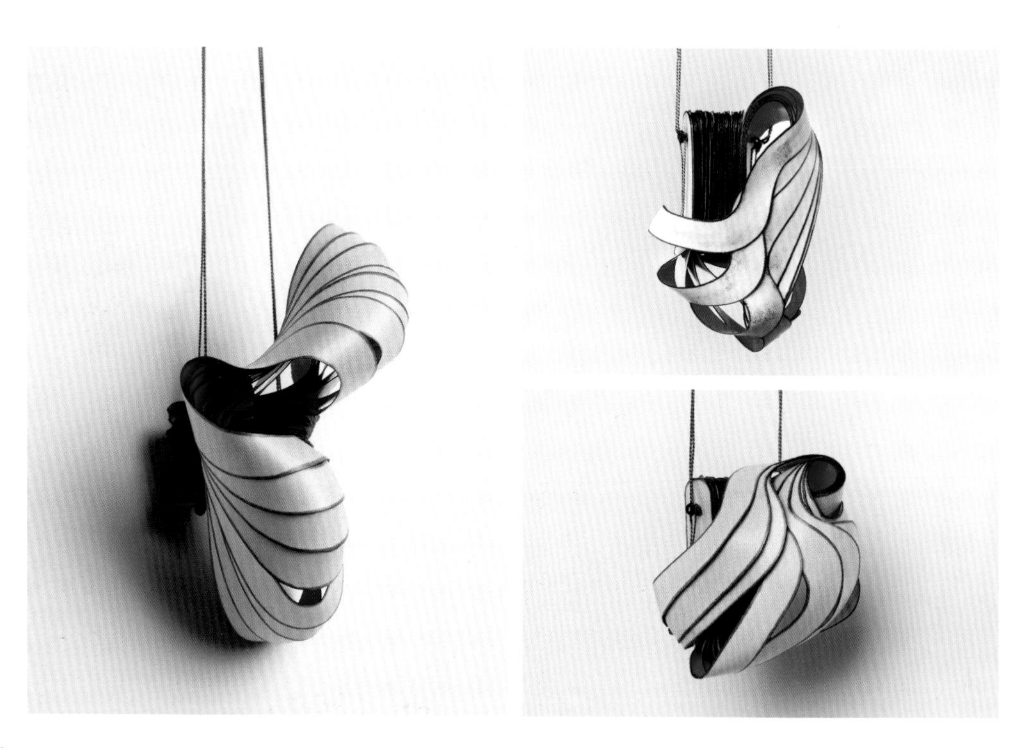

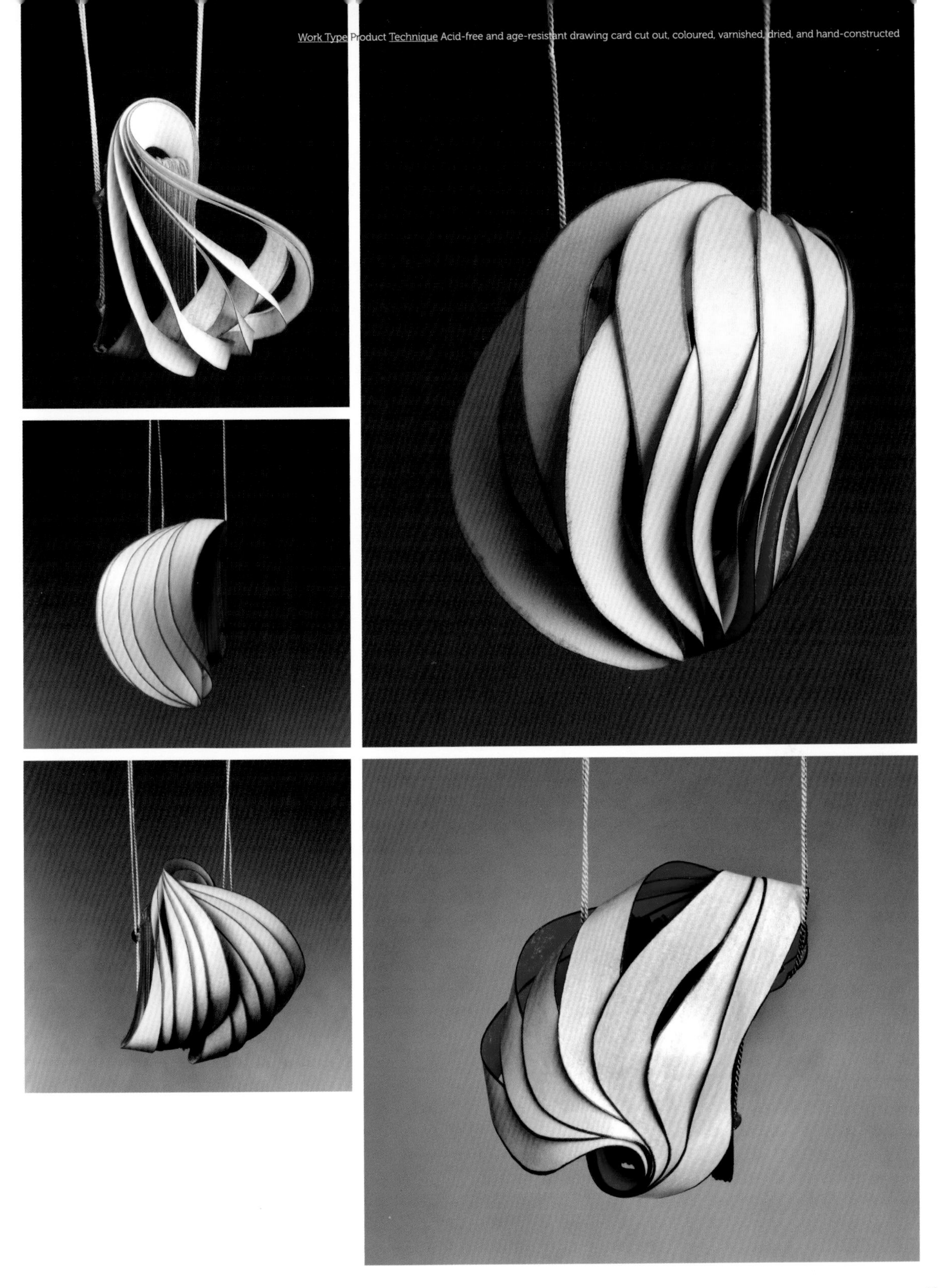

Work Type Product Technique Acid-free and age-resistant drawing card cut out, coloured, varnished, dried, and hand-constructed

Designer Sarah Kelly Photographer Gemma Dewson, Jennifer Peel & Lucas Brodowicz

To Cherish Collection

Influences for the Saloukee's "To Cherish" collection of jewelry include costume history and contemporary haute couture catwalk styles. By working primarily in the versatile medium of paper, Saloukee's pieces accomplish a simplicity and tactility that more durable materials would not achieve, while engaging with the fashion world and the ephemeral nature of its disposable trends. Saloukee's collection of paper jewelry innovates to combine traditional techniques and high tech advancements in laser cutting technologies. This unique use of materials justifies es wearable statement pieces, which confer preciousness on their wearers.

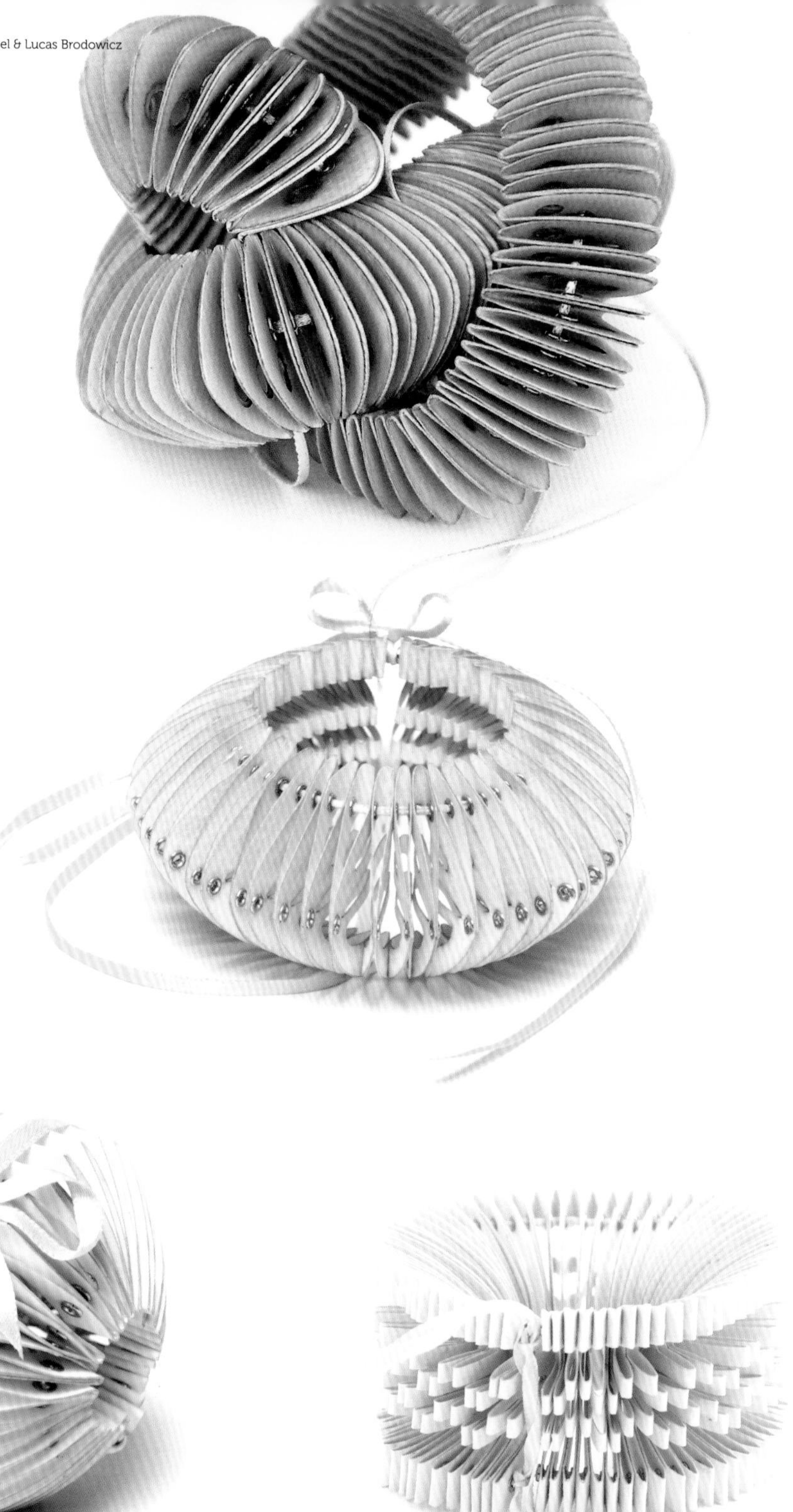

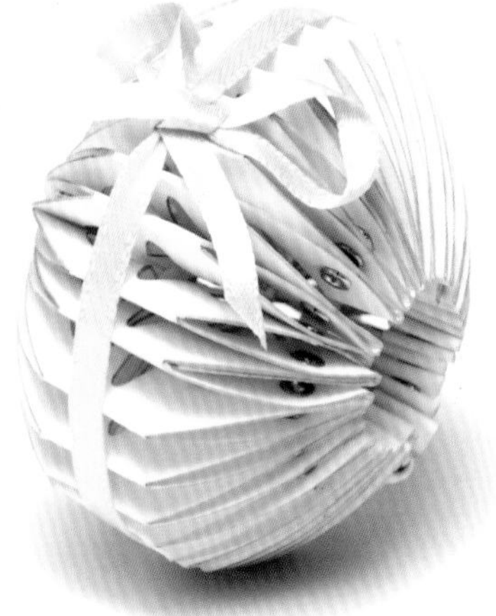

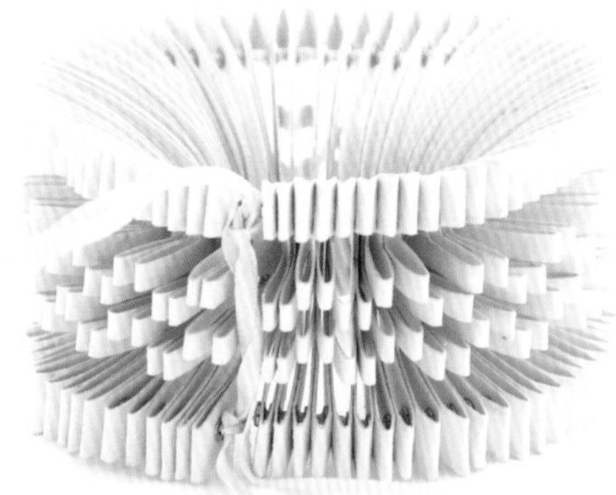

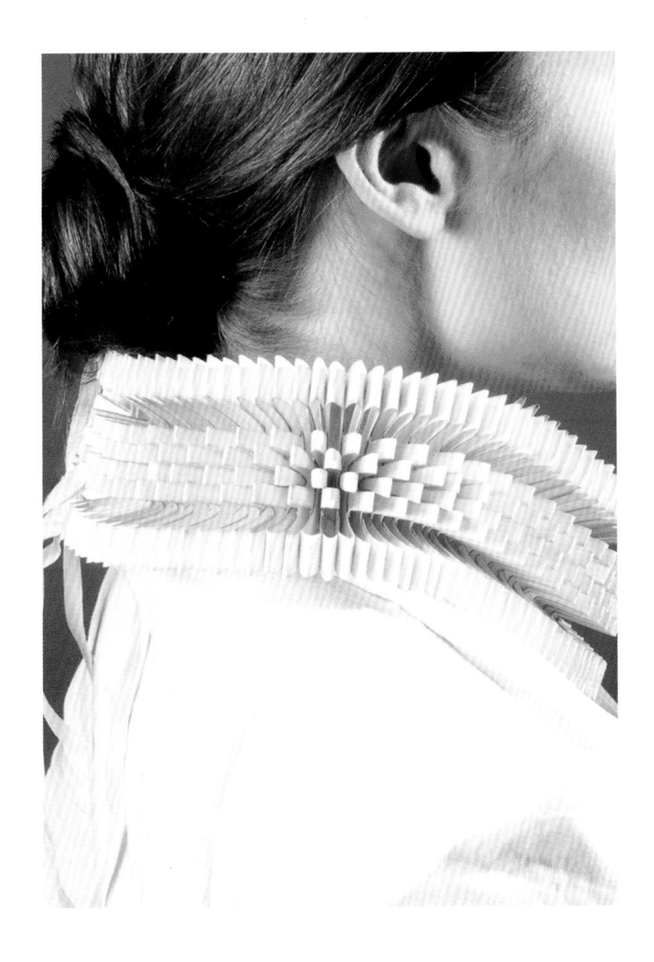

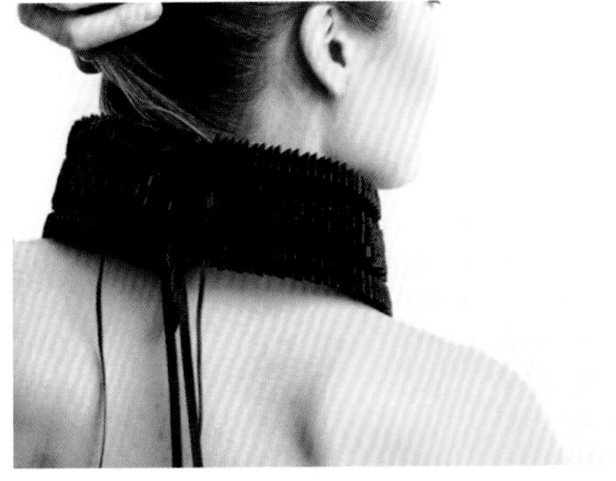

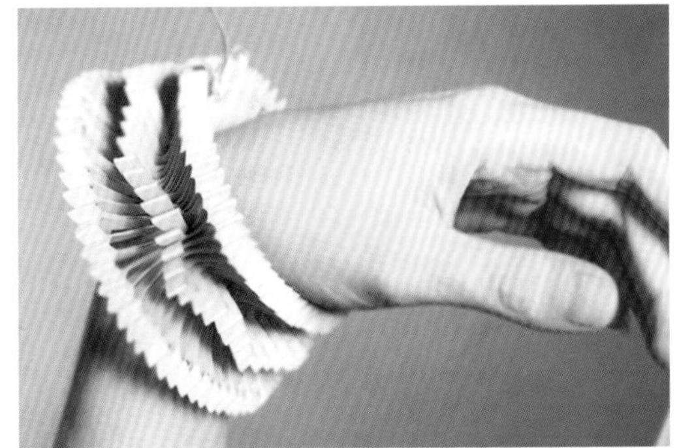

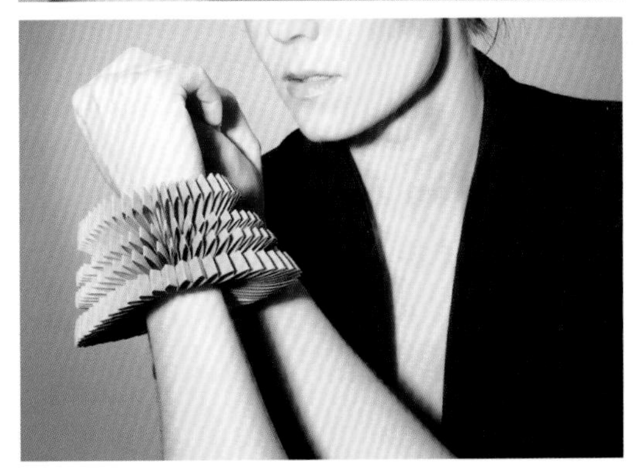

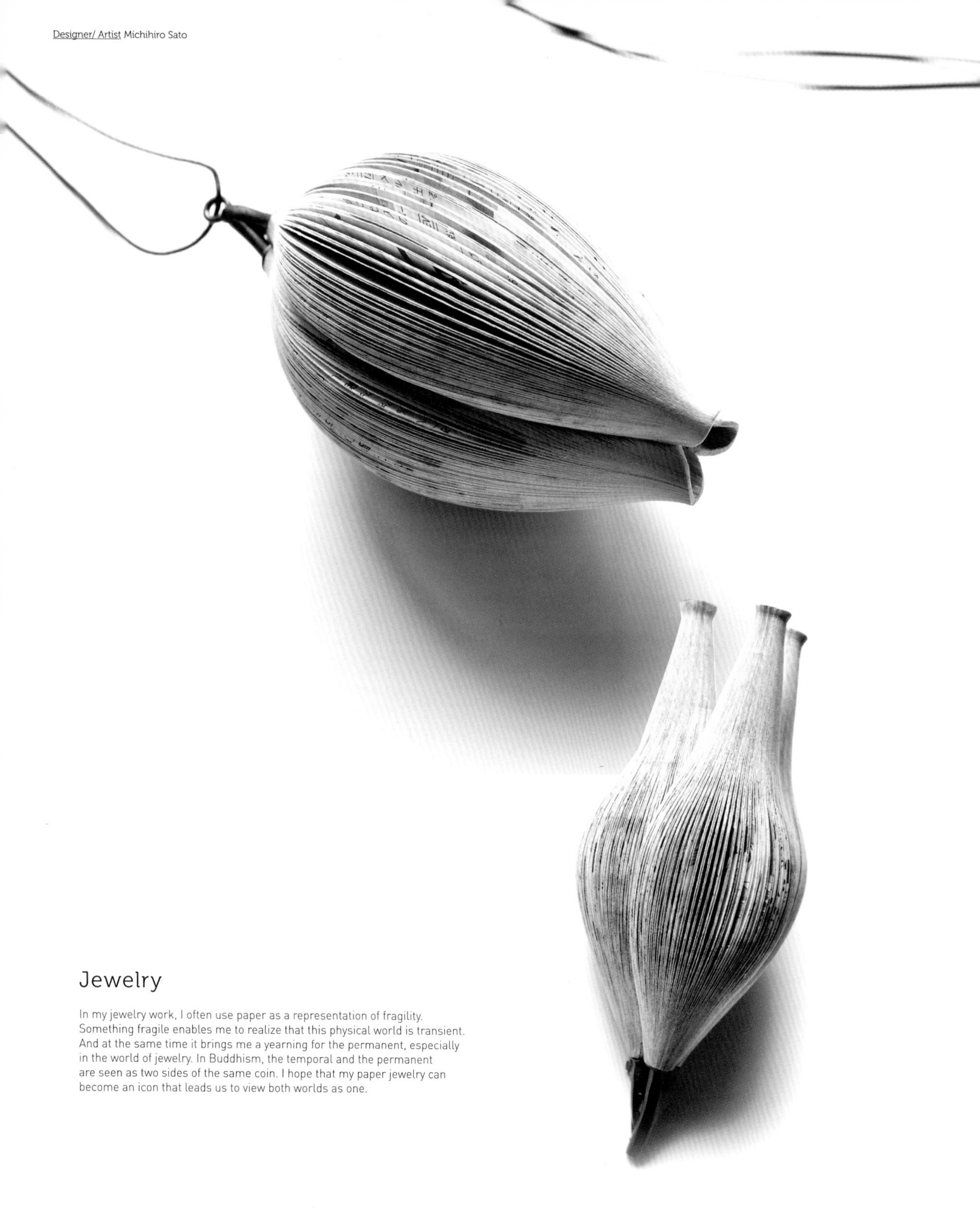

Jewelry

In my jewelry work, I often use paper as a representation of fragility. Something fragile enables me to realize that this physical world is transient. And at the same time it brings me a yearning for the permanent, especially in the world of jewelry. In Buddhism, the temporal and the permanent are seen as two sides of the same coin. I hope that my paper jewelry can become an icon that leads us to view both worlds as one.

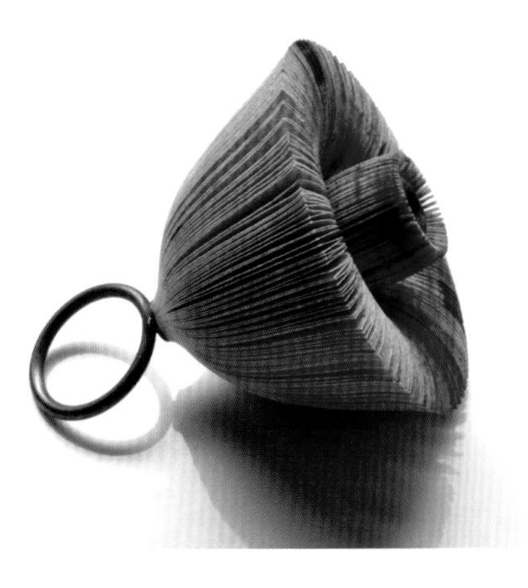

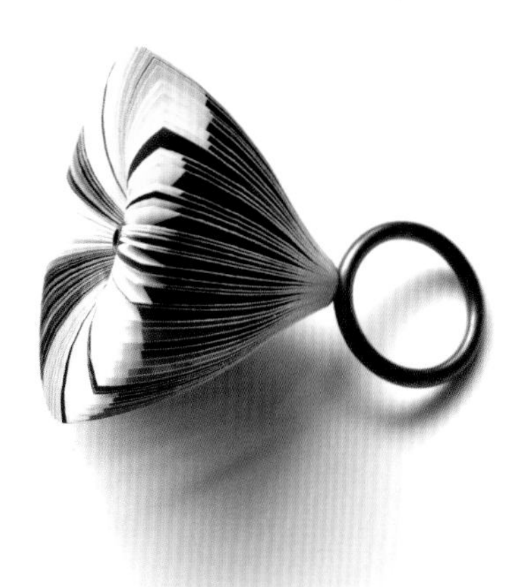

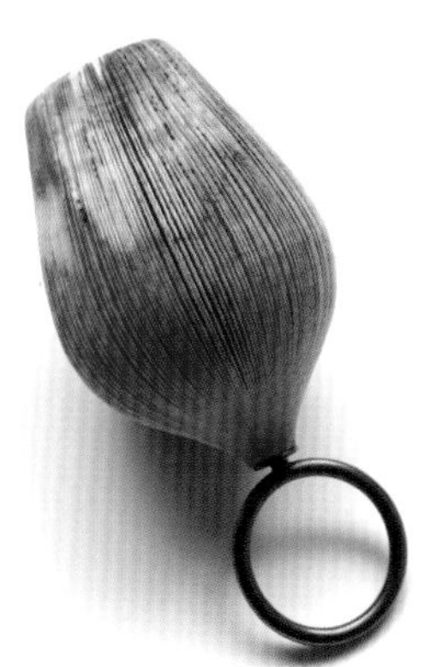

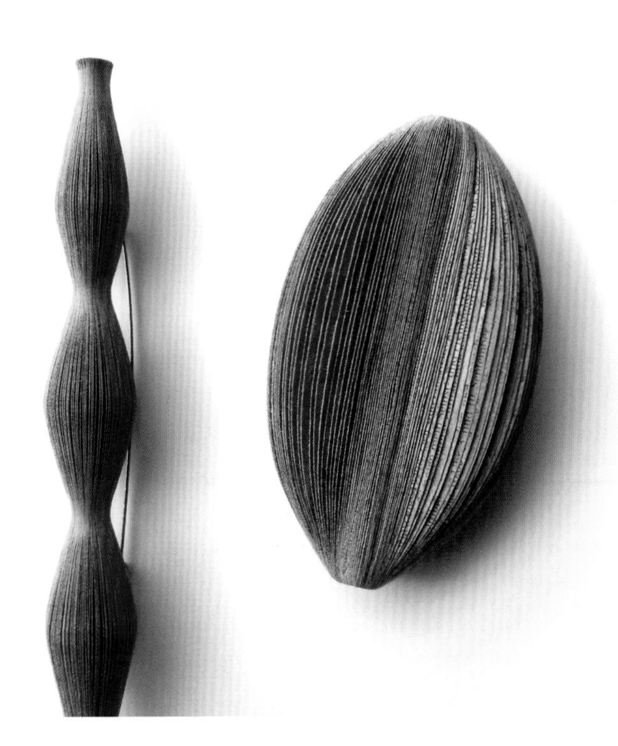

Kate Spade / July 2011

For two of their New York locations (Flatiron and Soho) this international brand commissioned a twenty-piece collection of black wigs inspired by famed American painter and photographer Lillian Bassman. The paper wigs were inspired by Kate Spade's capsule collection of accessories featuring "Touch of Dew," a 1961 photograph by Bassman.

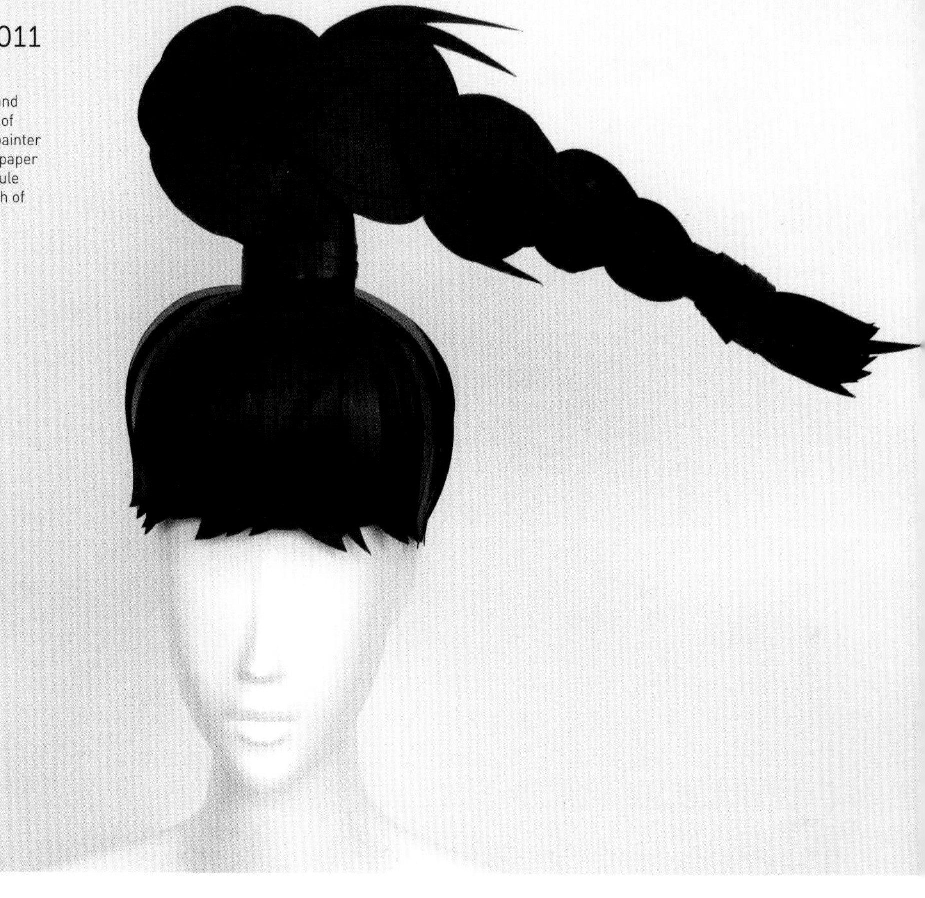

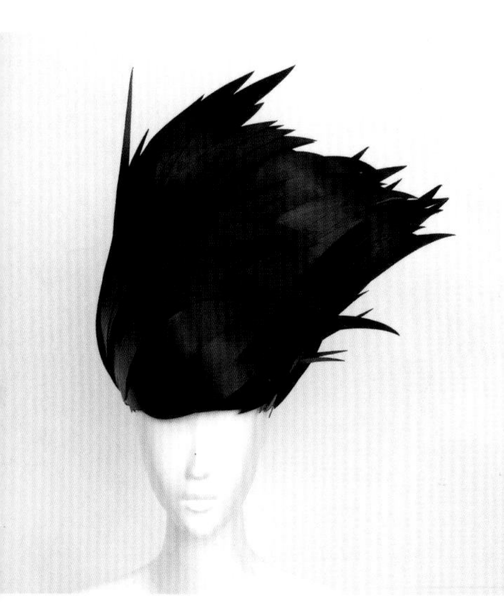

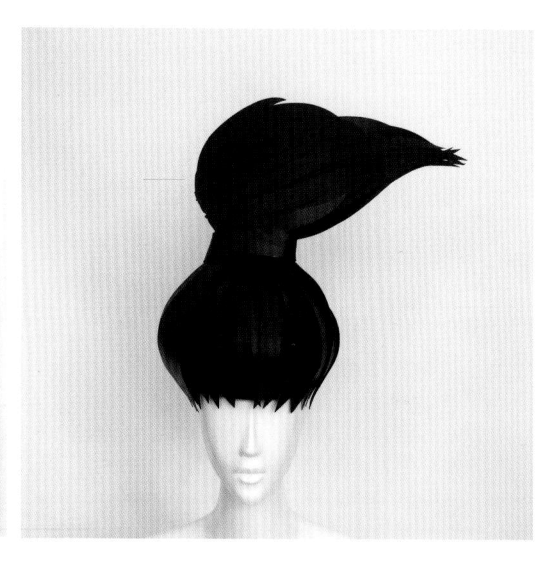

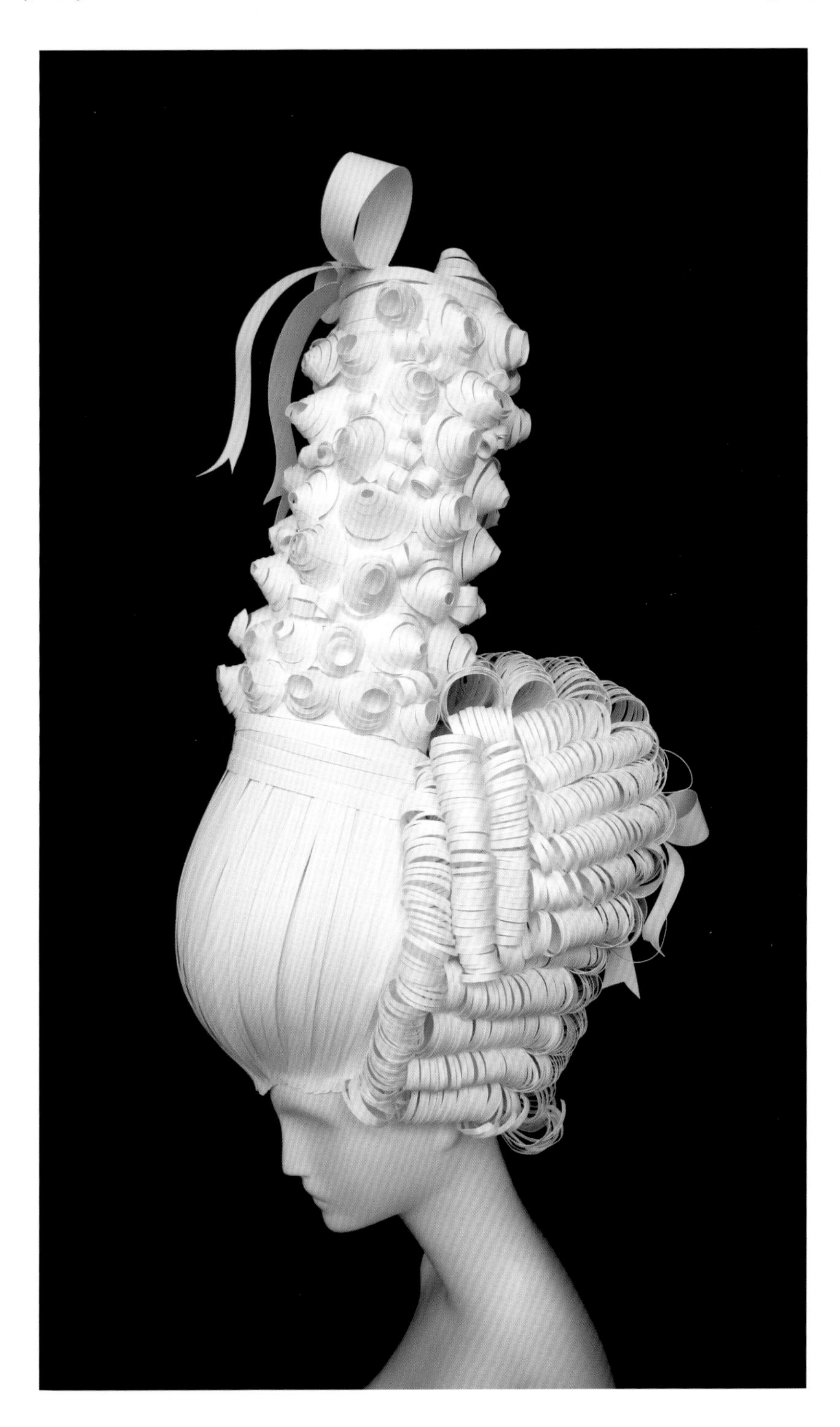

The Bay / December 2010

The Toronto-based luxury retailer commissioned a 15-piece collection of paper constructions inspired by 18th century wigs for their holiday windows at the company's downtown headquarters.

Design Agency Paper-Cut-Project Designer Amy Flurry, Nikki Nye

Jeffrey Paper Wigs/ January 2010

A collection of twenty wigs was installed storewide on mannequins at Jeffrey Atlanta and Jeffrey NY (simultaneously) for the month of January 2010.

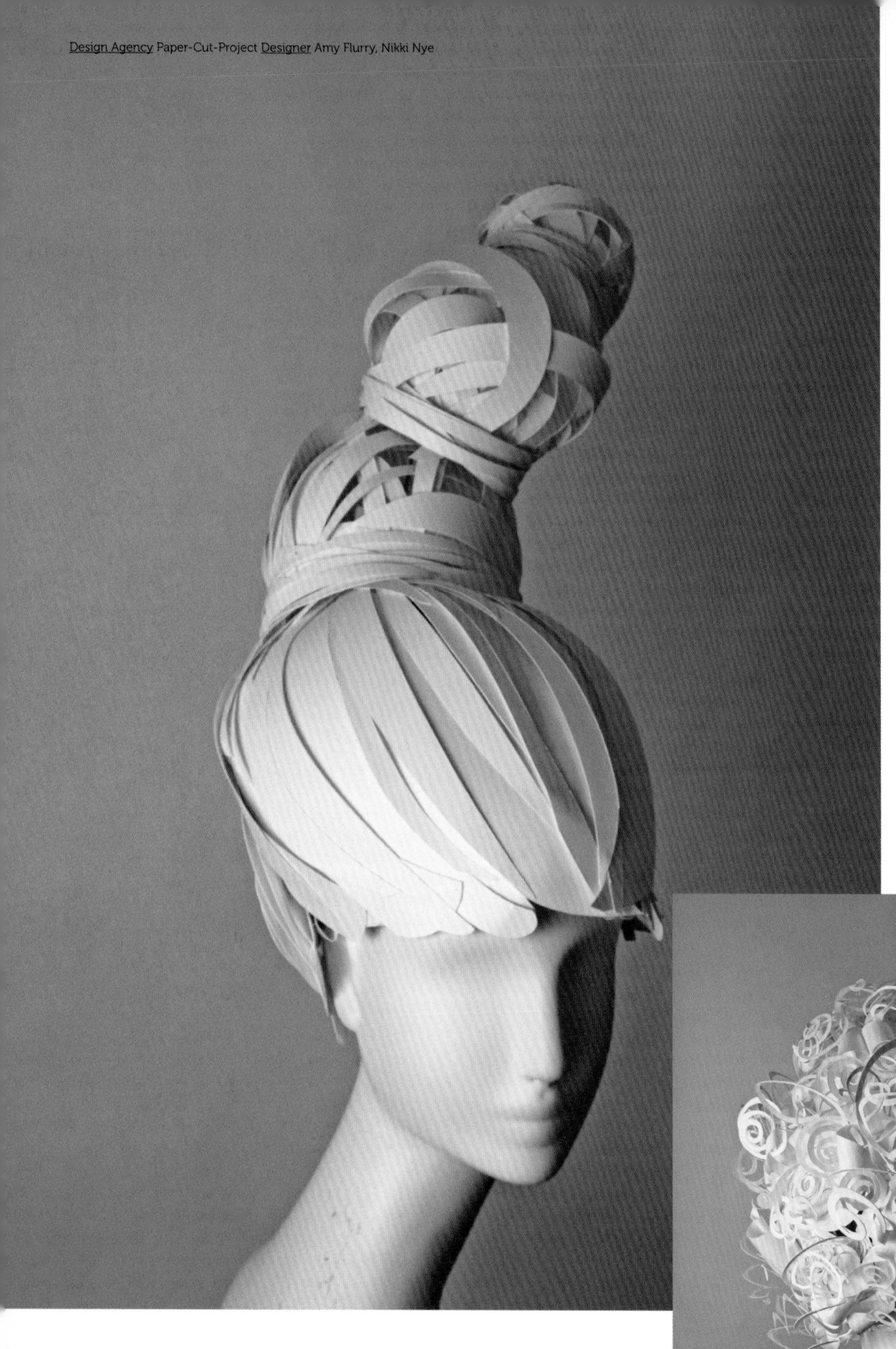

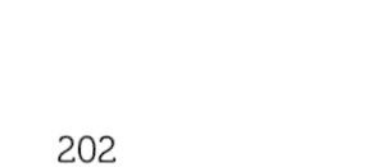

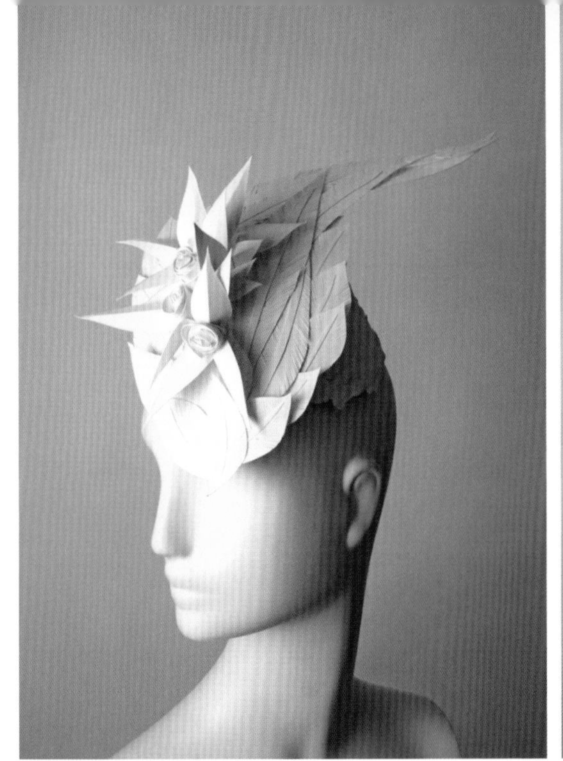

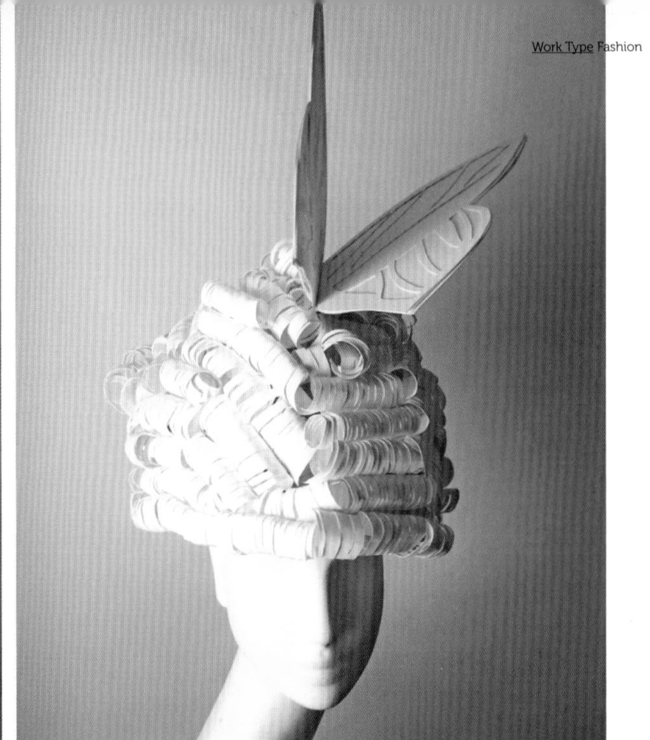

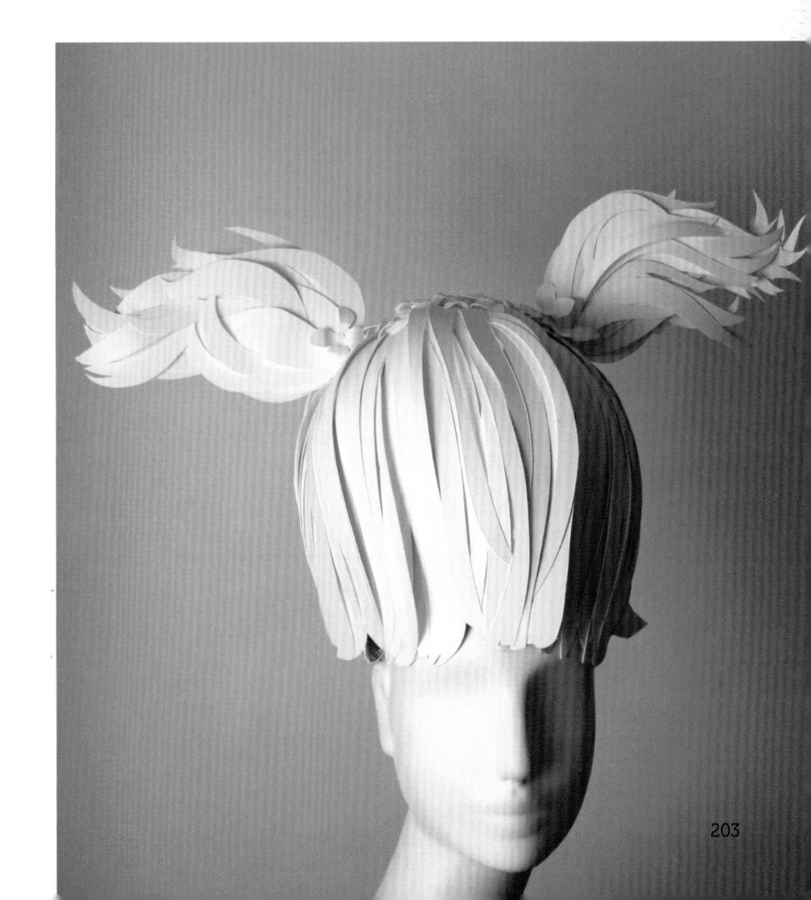

WASARA

With WASARA, we offer a new solution to disposable tableware. WASARA has been developed as beautifully designed and sustainable paper tableware, clearly distinct from anything else you have ever seen. The WASARA line of products is made from tree-free renewable materials, such as sugarcane waste, bamboo, and reed pulp, and is fully biodegradable and compostable. Featuring the aesthetic and sensitive design that invokes the feel of Japanese ceramics, WASARA fits comfortably in the hand, with an elegant form and sturdy support. Those details are backed by Japanese craftsmanship, excellent techniques of metallic molds, and the skills of trimming, which had never been used before in the paper tableware industry. We designed WASARA to accentuate the delicacy of cuisine and create a rich and warm atmosphere. While WASARA tableware is by design ephemeral, it represents the essence of Japanese tradition and spirit.

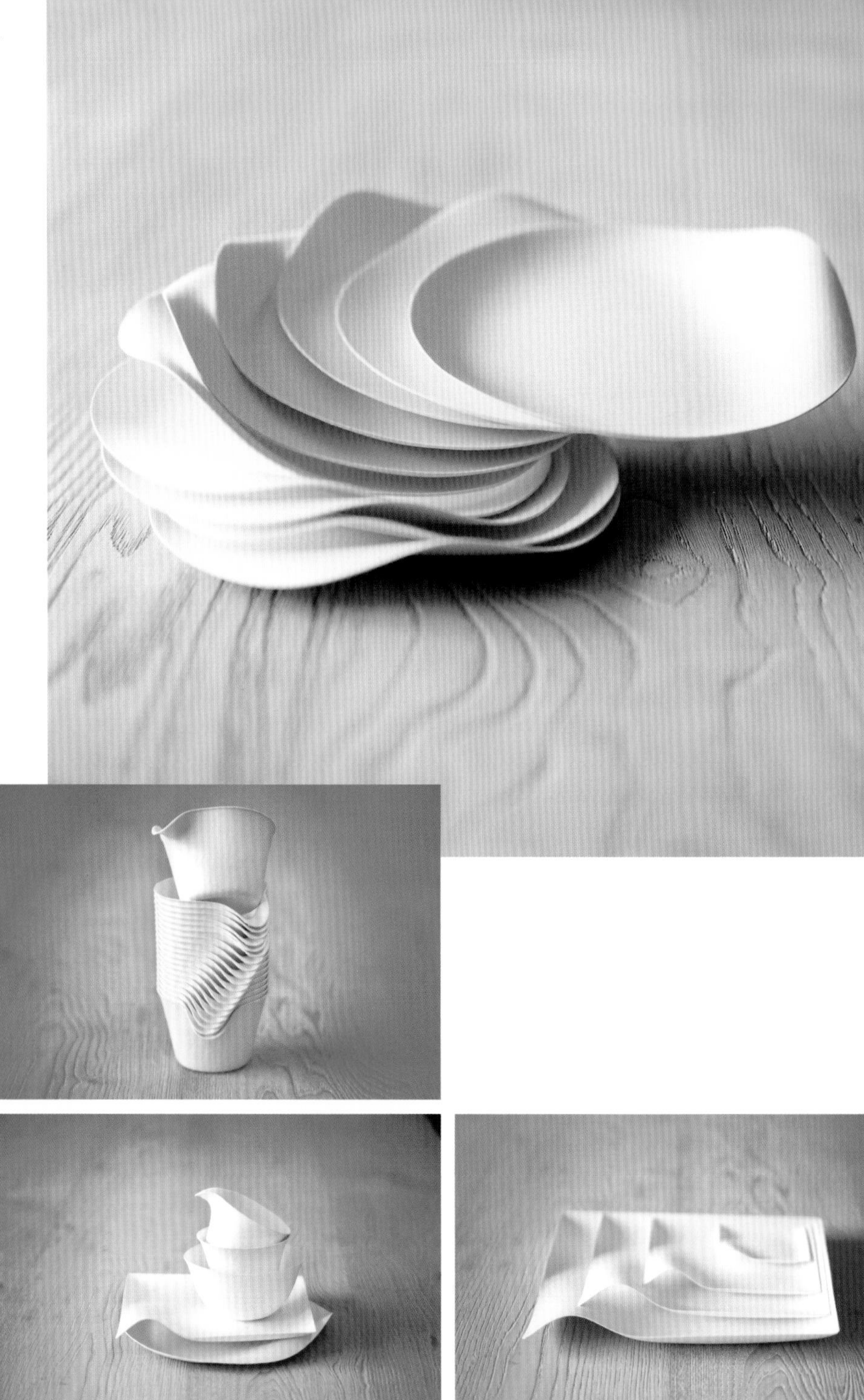

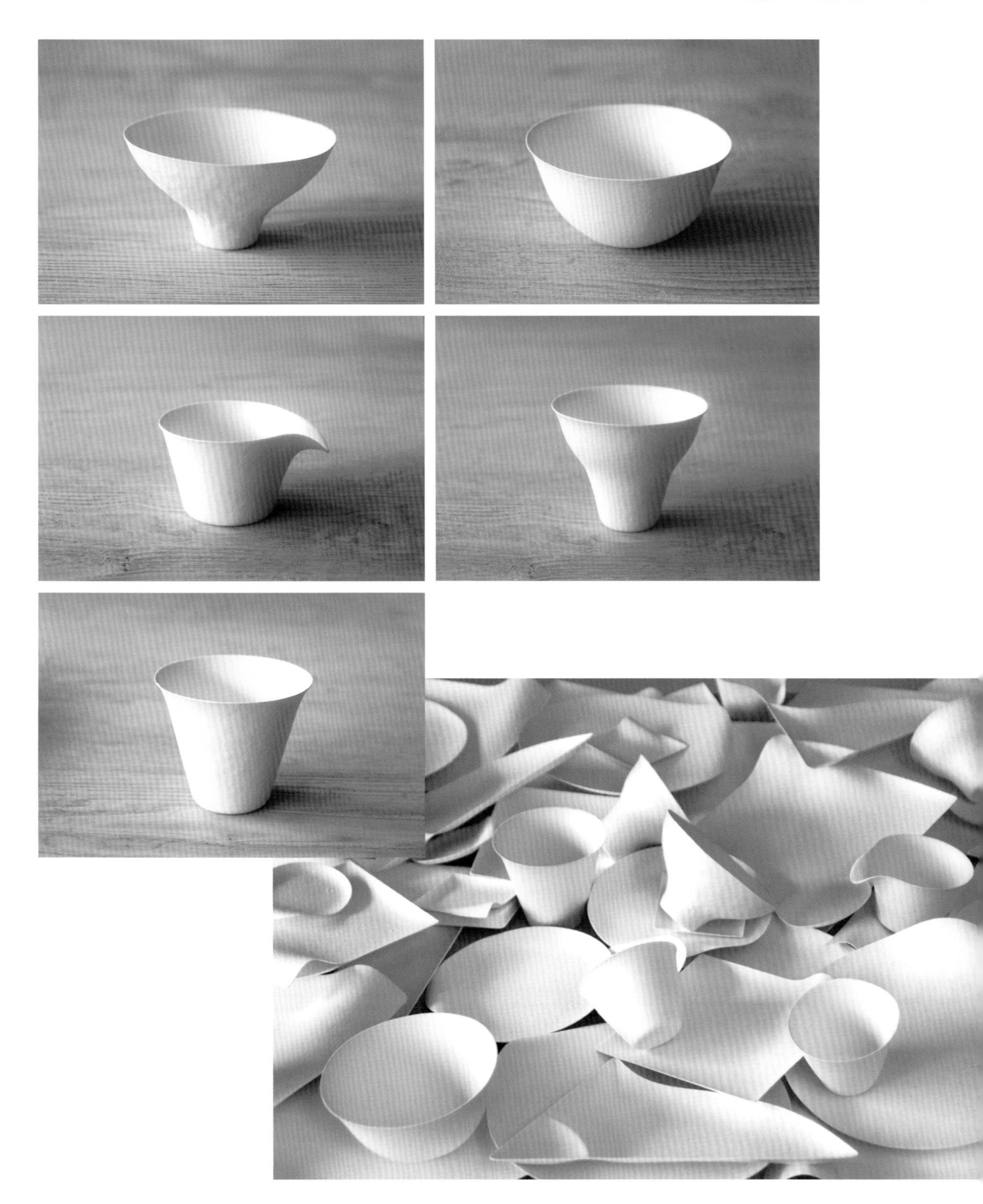

Artist Cecilia Levy Photographer Ann-Sofi Rosenkvist, Cecilia Levy

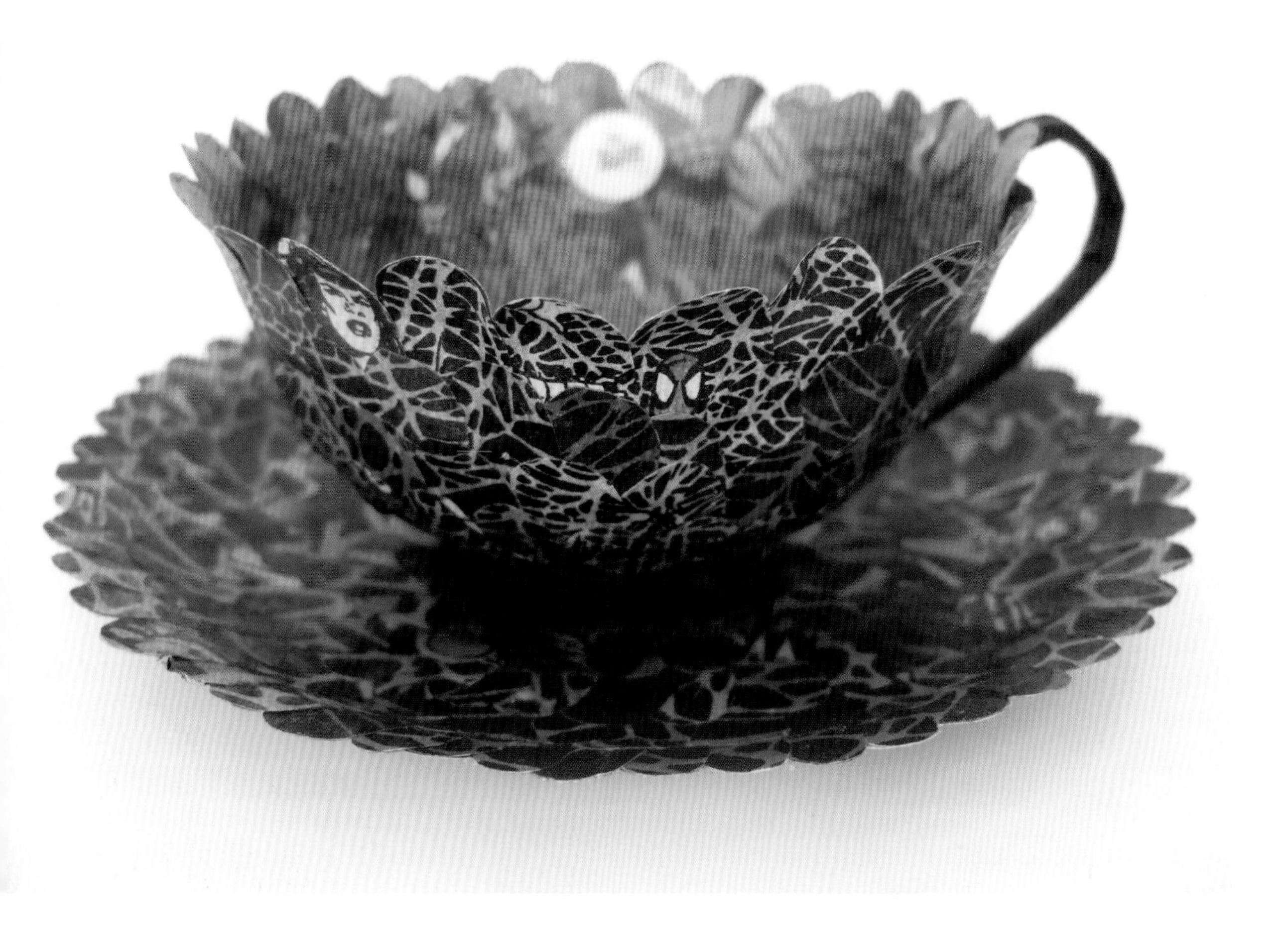

Petal Bowls & Paper Cups

Graphic design and papier mâché are combined in an entirely new way in these works by Cecilia Levy. Selected pages from old books are used, and new shapes – such as bowls, containers and cups – take form. The thin vessels Levy crafts are fragile yet remarkably steady. At first glance, it may be difficult to understand that they are made of paper. Levy has a passionate love of old paper. Her working material is found in old books from the beginning of the last century. She uses paper that has been around for a while, with wrinkles, discolorations and patina. It has character and personality; it carries a history. After cutting, tearing or shredding the paper, she pastes the pieces back together again. The new pieces take on a different physical form than the original – new life is breathed into these pages.

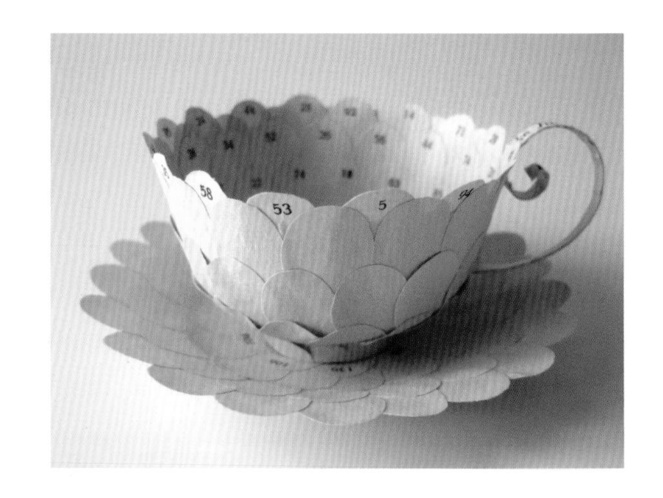

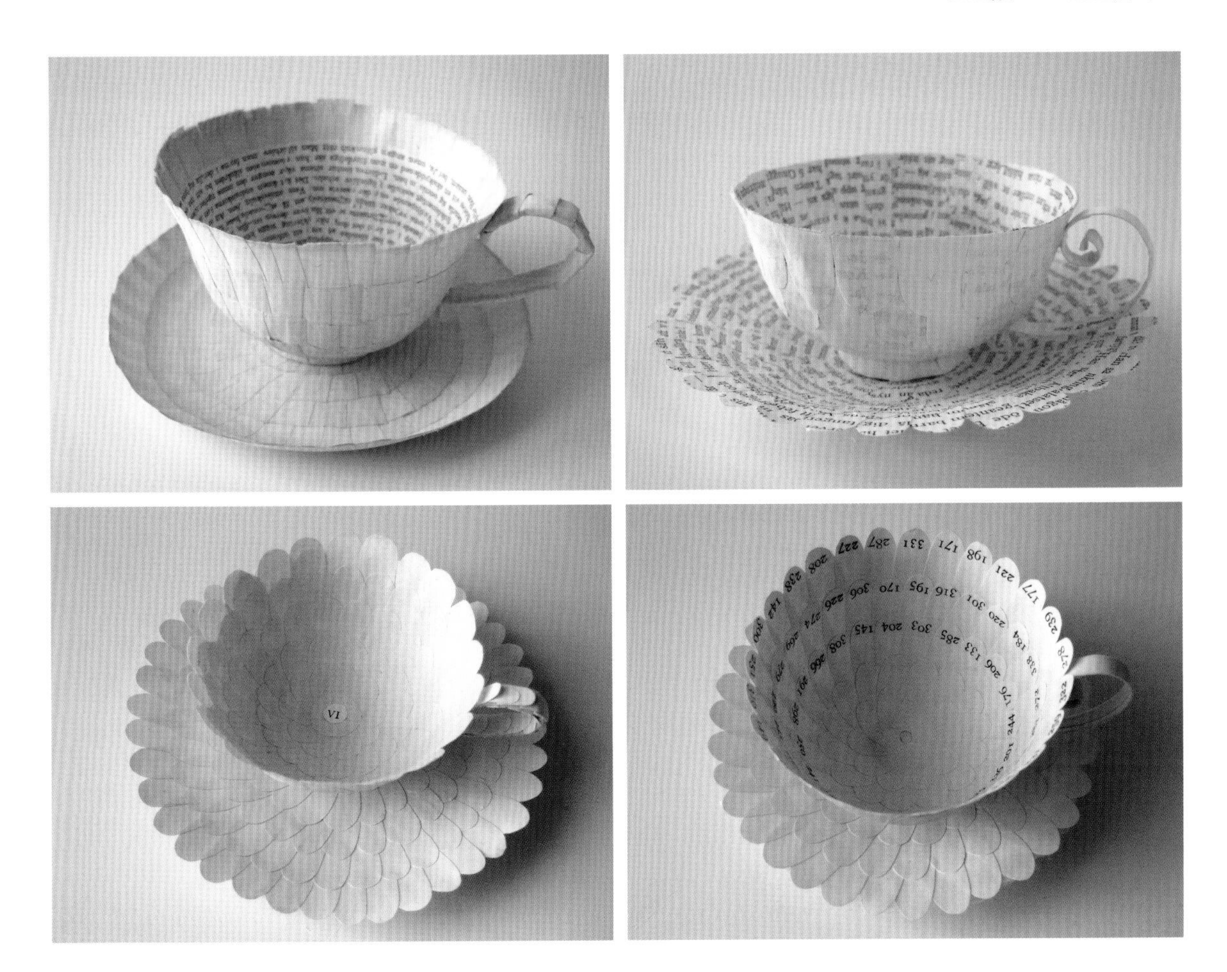

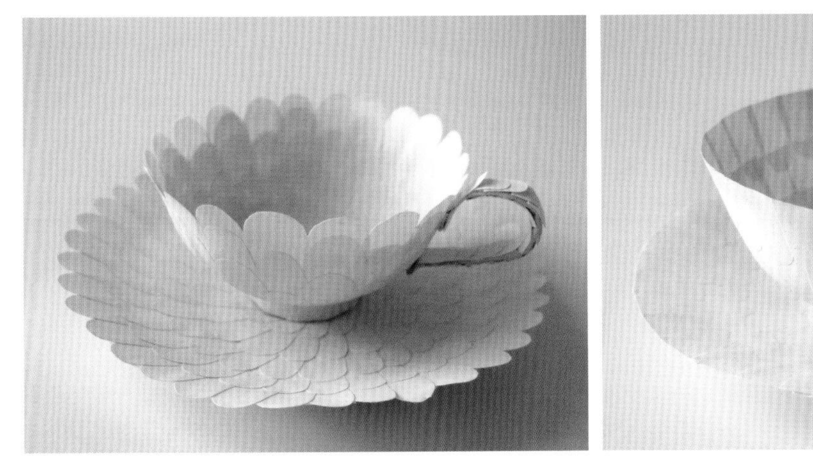

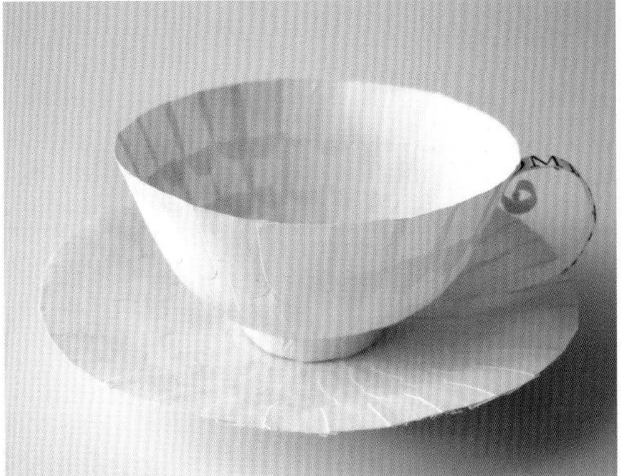

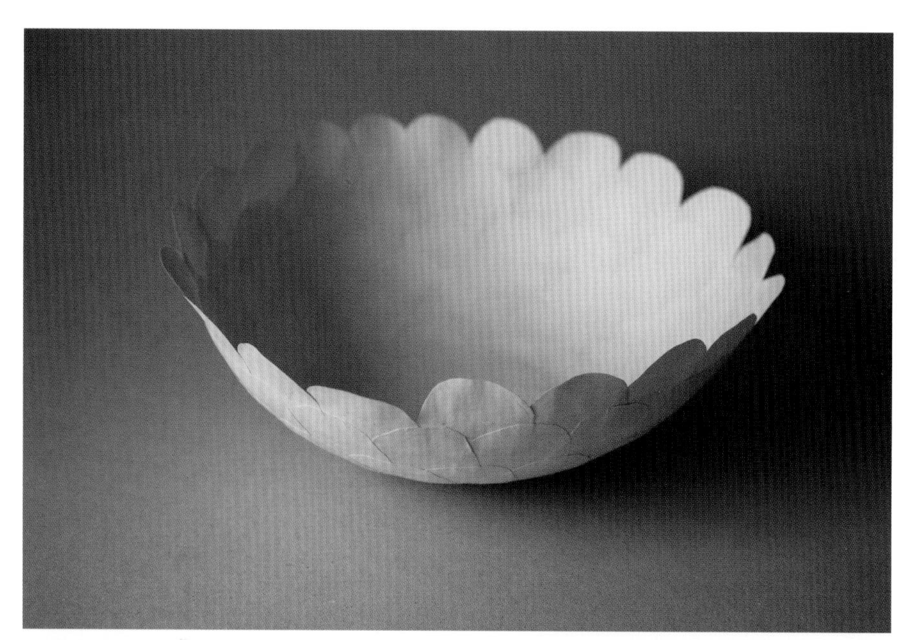

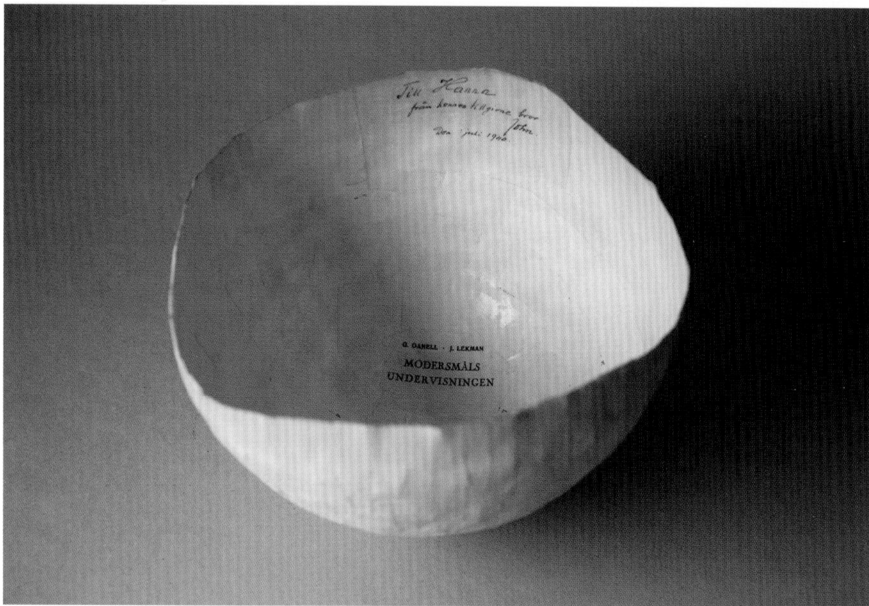
G. DANELL · J. LEKMAN
MODERSMÅLS
UNDERVISNINGEN

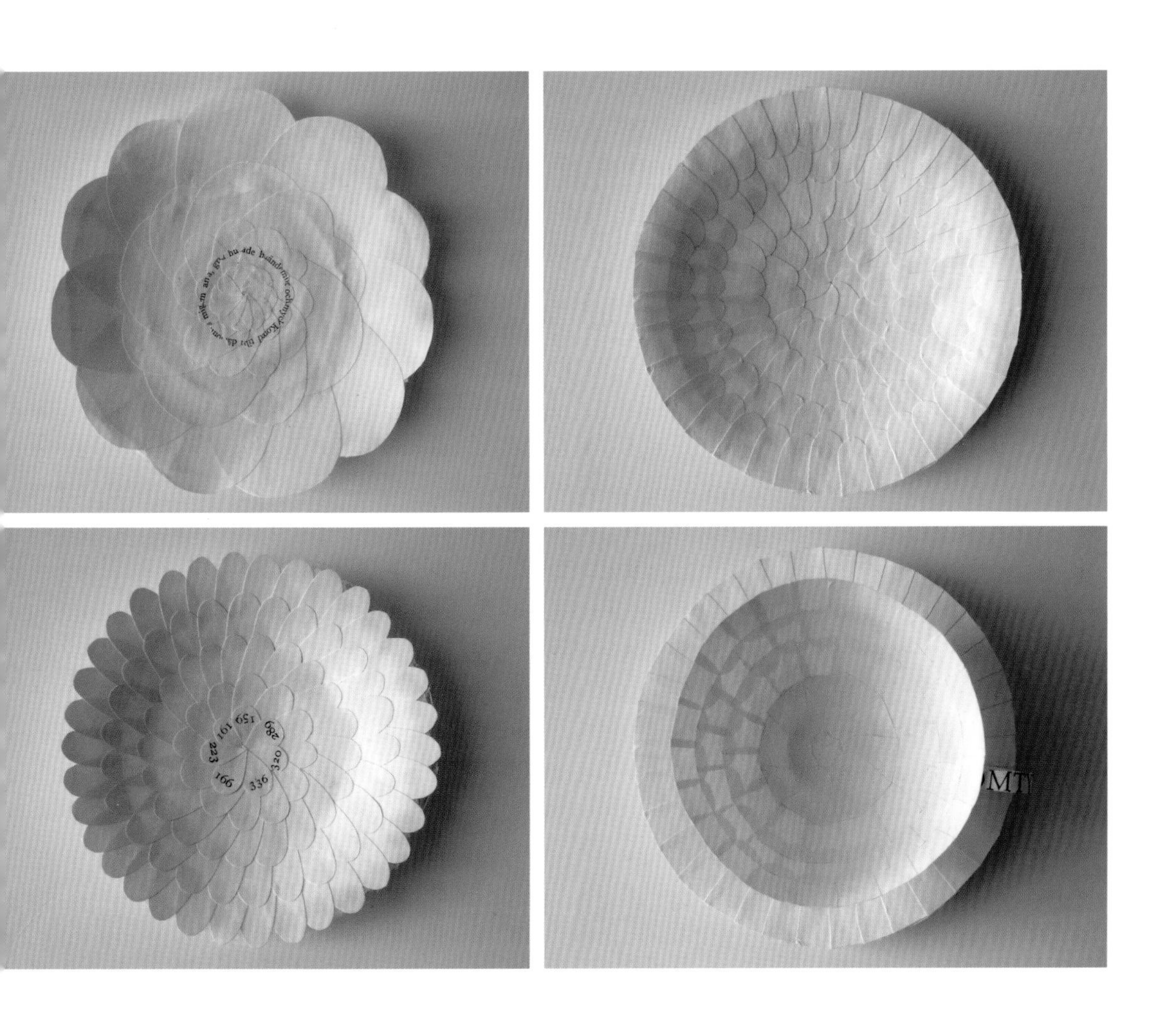

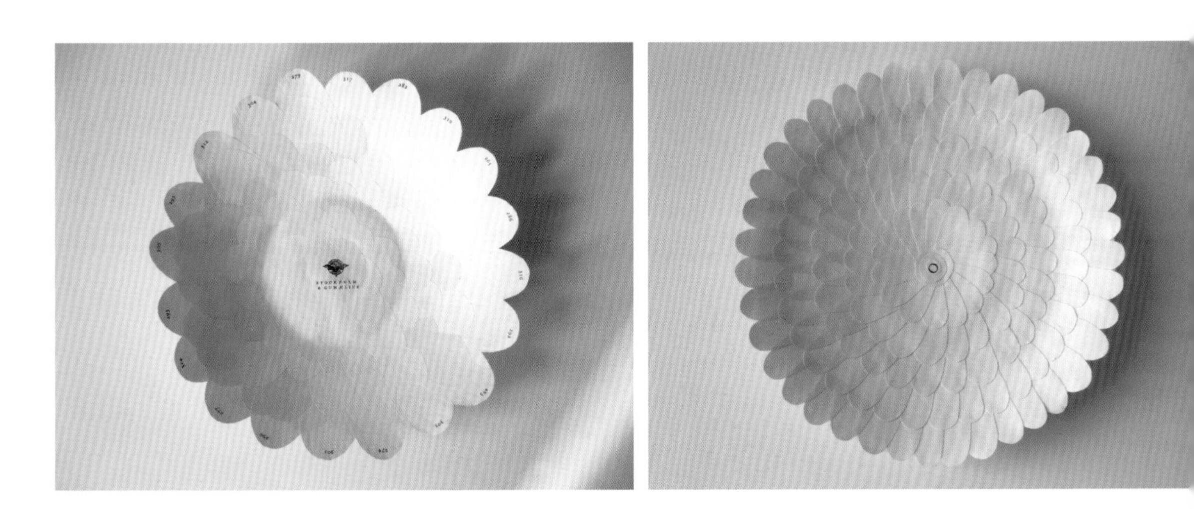

Artist Maryse Dugois Photographer Maryse Dugois

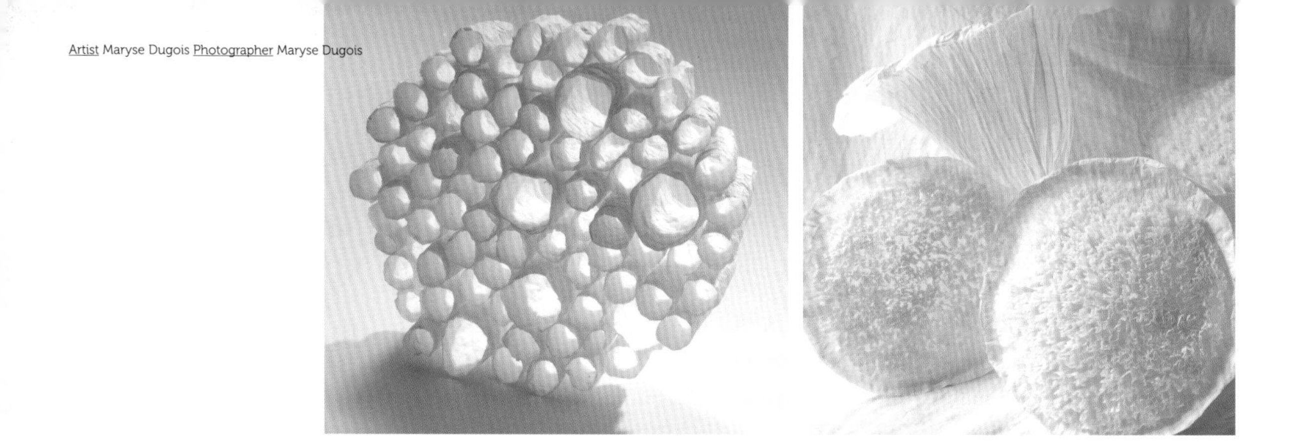

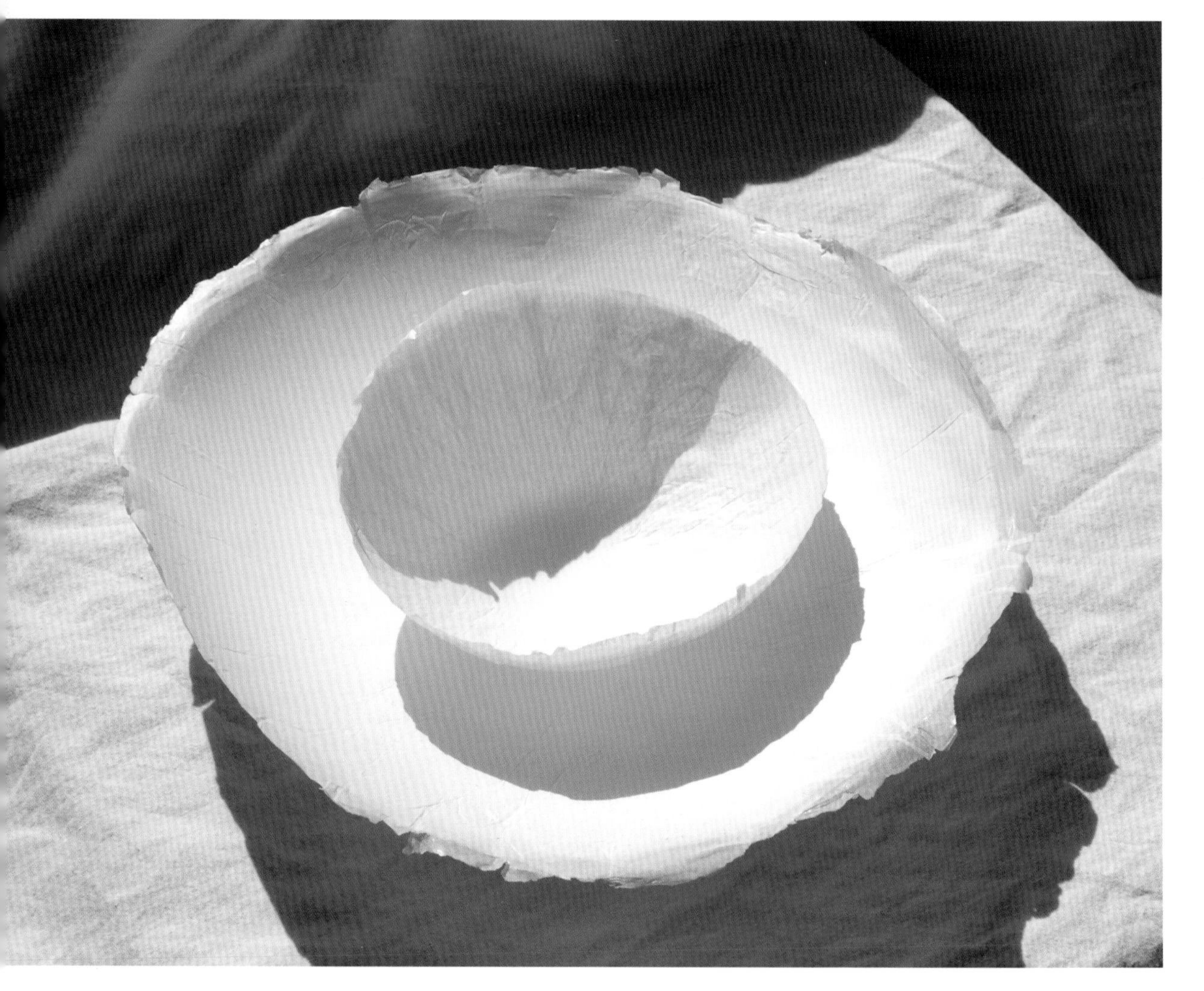

Creations in silk paper

Using the simplest, lightest materials available, I create pure forms, often inspired by nature, in order to produce sculptures and create atmospheres. The transparency of the silk paper allows light to be captured and the range of material used in my sculptures to be highlighted. All of them are adaptable in a poetic way for interior decorating, shop windows and events. I build on silk paper with the application of several layers of silk paper and glue. In order to bring transparency and lightness to my sculptures I use as little paper as possible and let the paper dry between each step.

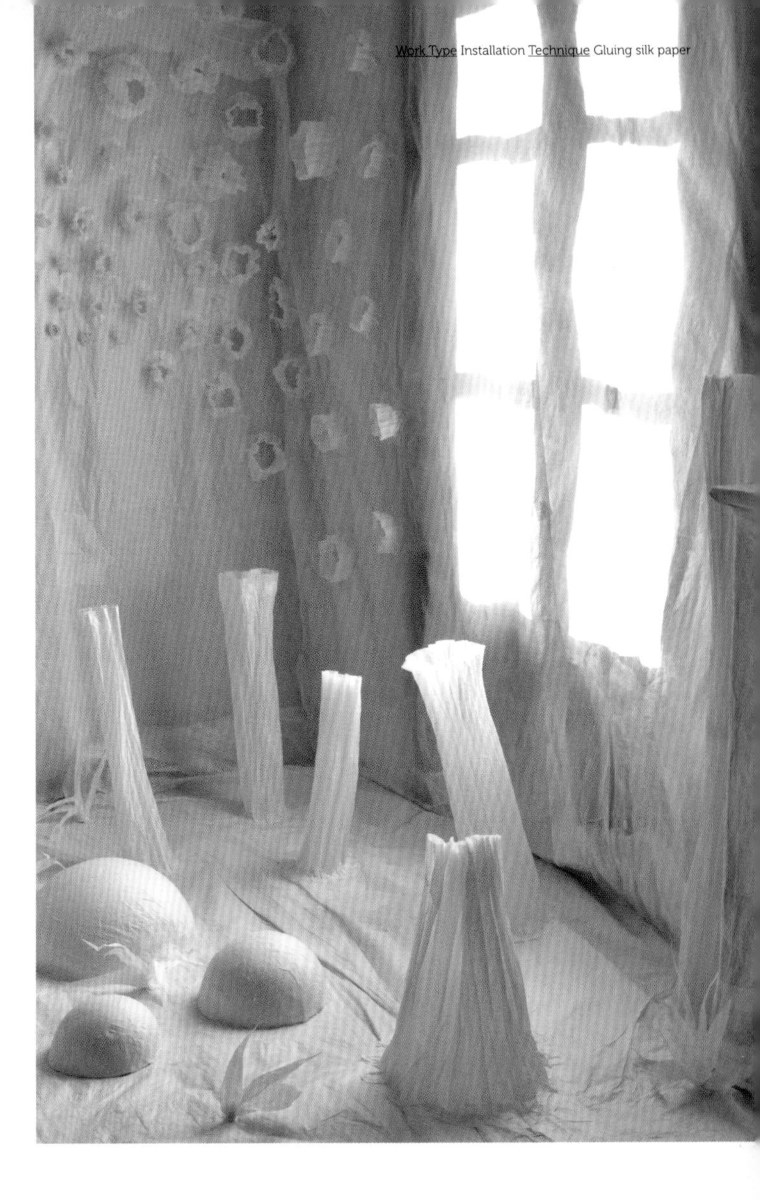

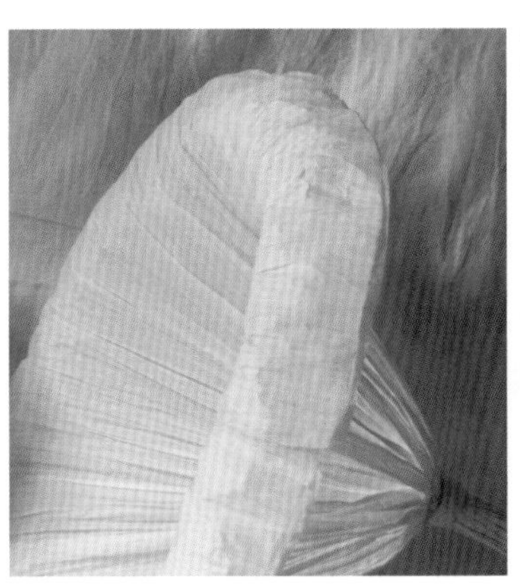

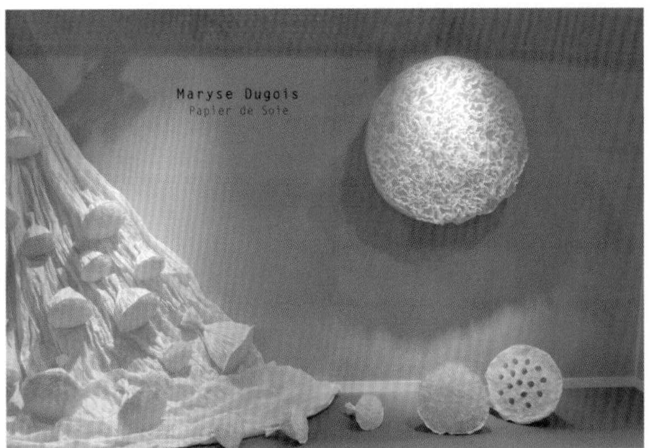

Artist duo The Makerie Studio Artist Julie Wilkinson, Joyanne Horscroft Photographer Nathan Gallagher

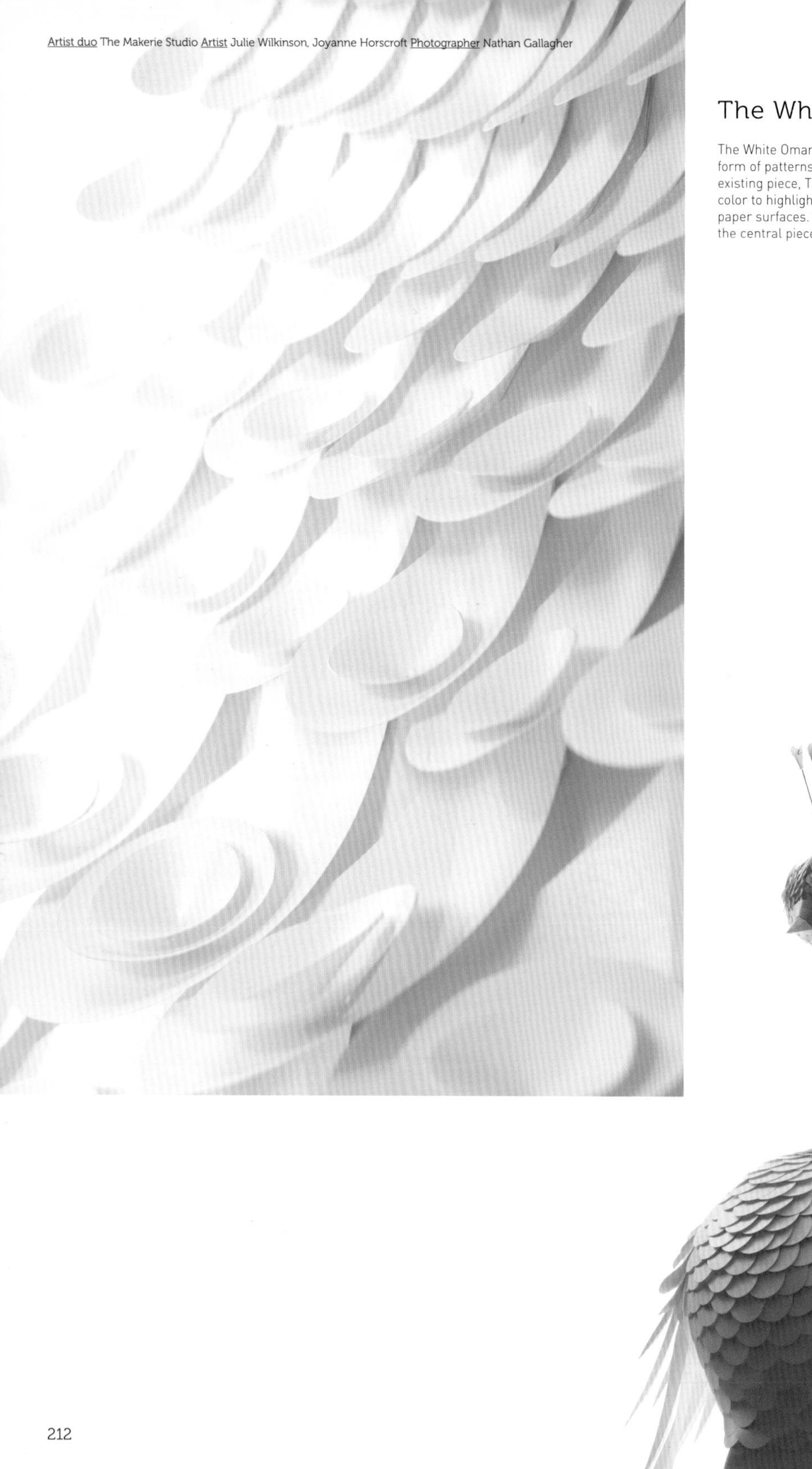

The White Omar

The White Omar is a piece that explores the structure and form of patterns and shapes previously developed for an existing piece, The Great Omar, as a way of stripping back color to highlight contours and the play of light across paper surfaces. The project is currently being developed as the central piece of a London boutique display.

Work Type Fine arts Technique Hand cutting paper feathers

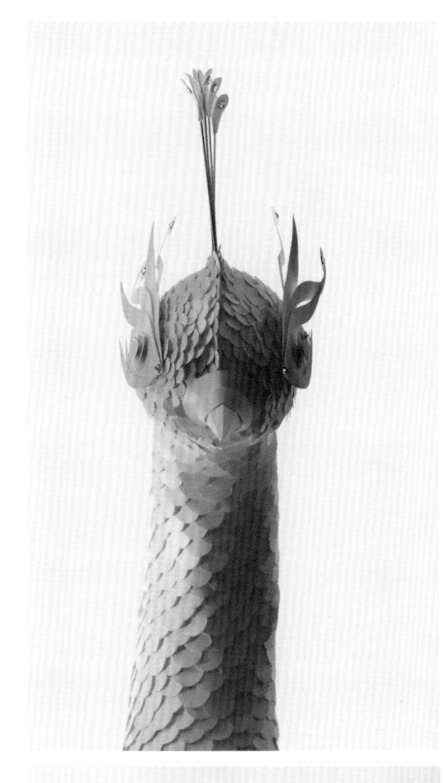

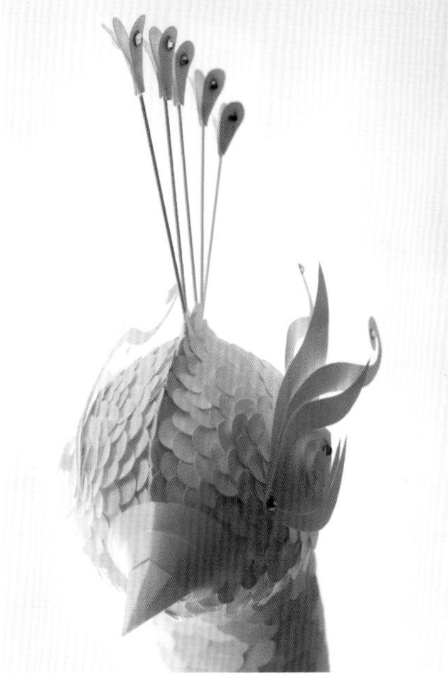

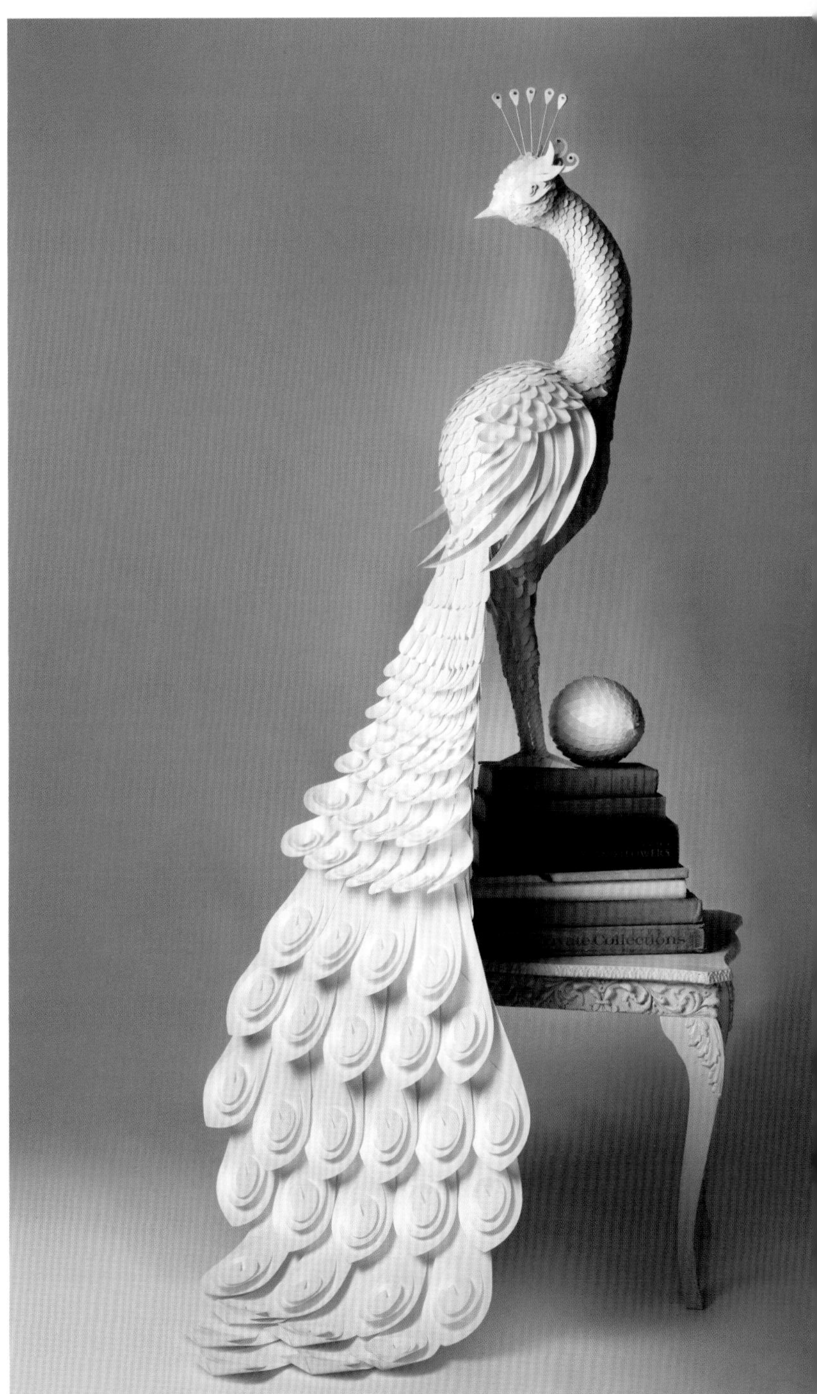

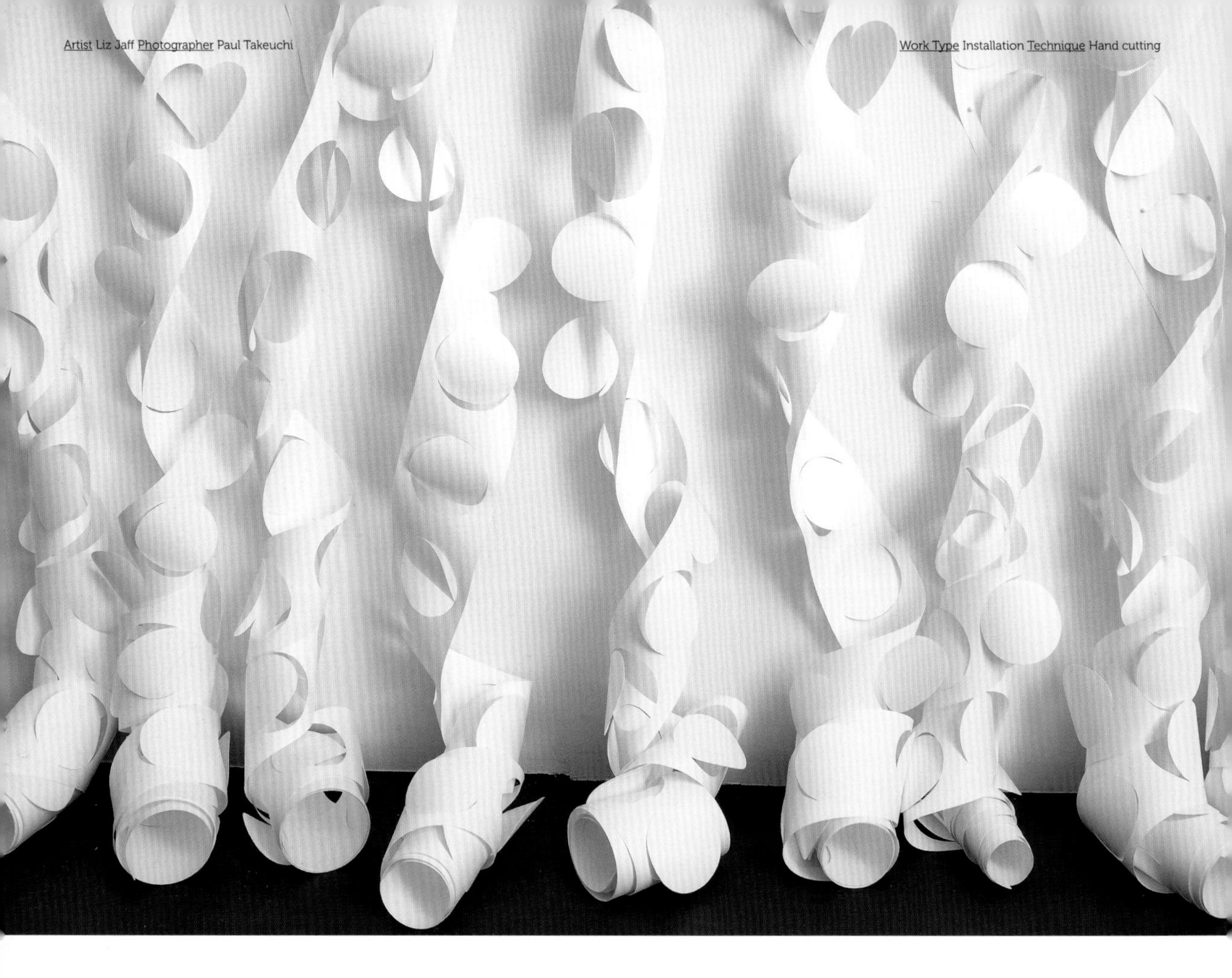

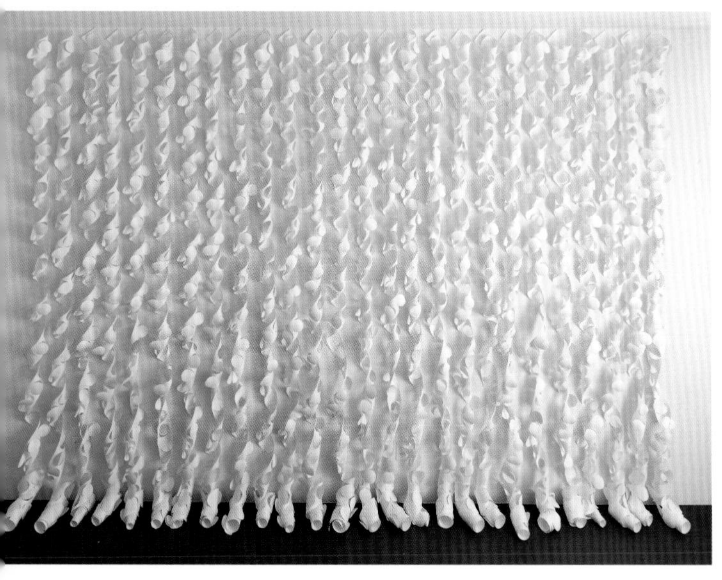

Plugs and Fuses

Plugs and Fuses is an installation that looks at the interplay of order and disorder. More than 20 strips of paper 12' long each are cut at regular intervals with uniform circular openings; the circles of paper are left partially attached. The resulting cascades of twisted strips reinterpret the traditional grid pattern, dissolving its order, and creating a new visual pattern.

Artist Liz Jaff Photographer Paul Takeuchi

Work Type Installation Technique Hand cutting, folding

Hedge

Hedge is a site-specific installation. The 2009 installation pictured here was constructed over a thirty-day period within the gallery, which was open to the public for the duration of its construction. Hedges are walls of foliage - organic barriers that surround, separate and protect. They create a dichotomy by defining public and private space. For this installation, the hedge is reinterpreted as an abstract wall relief composed of over 1, 714 parts. Each part begins as a circle that is hand cut with a scalpel and folded. It is an organic process, which allows me to maintain the feeling of my initial inspiration without creating a literal facsimile. Working in this manner I could reclaim and recreate a sense of the original place and experience and restructure it into a new one for the viewer.

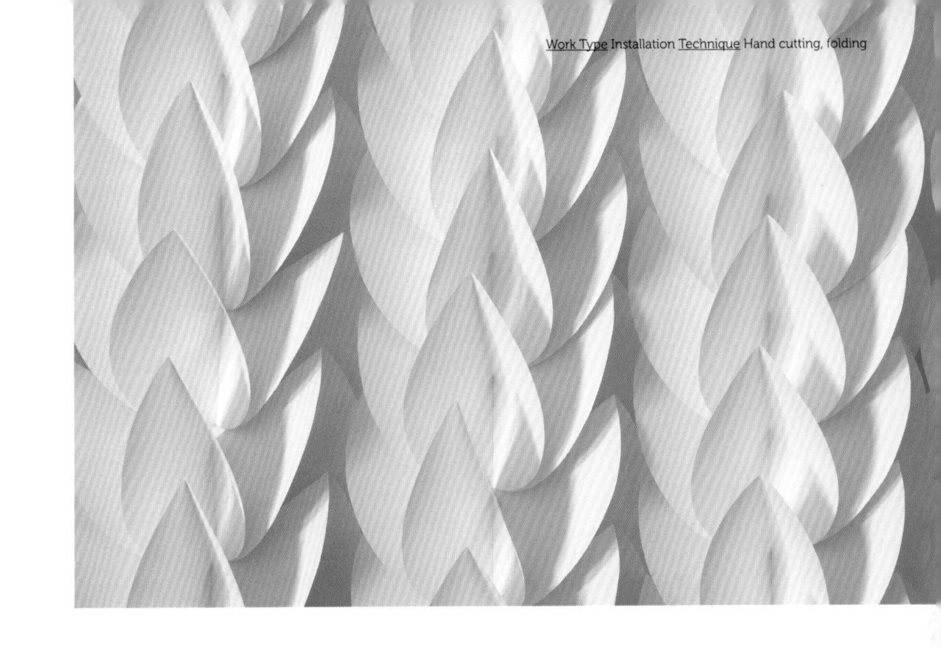

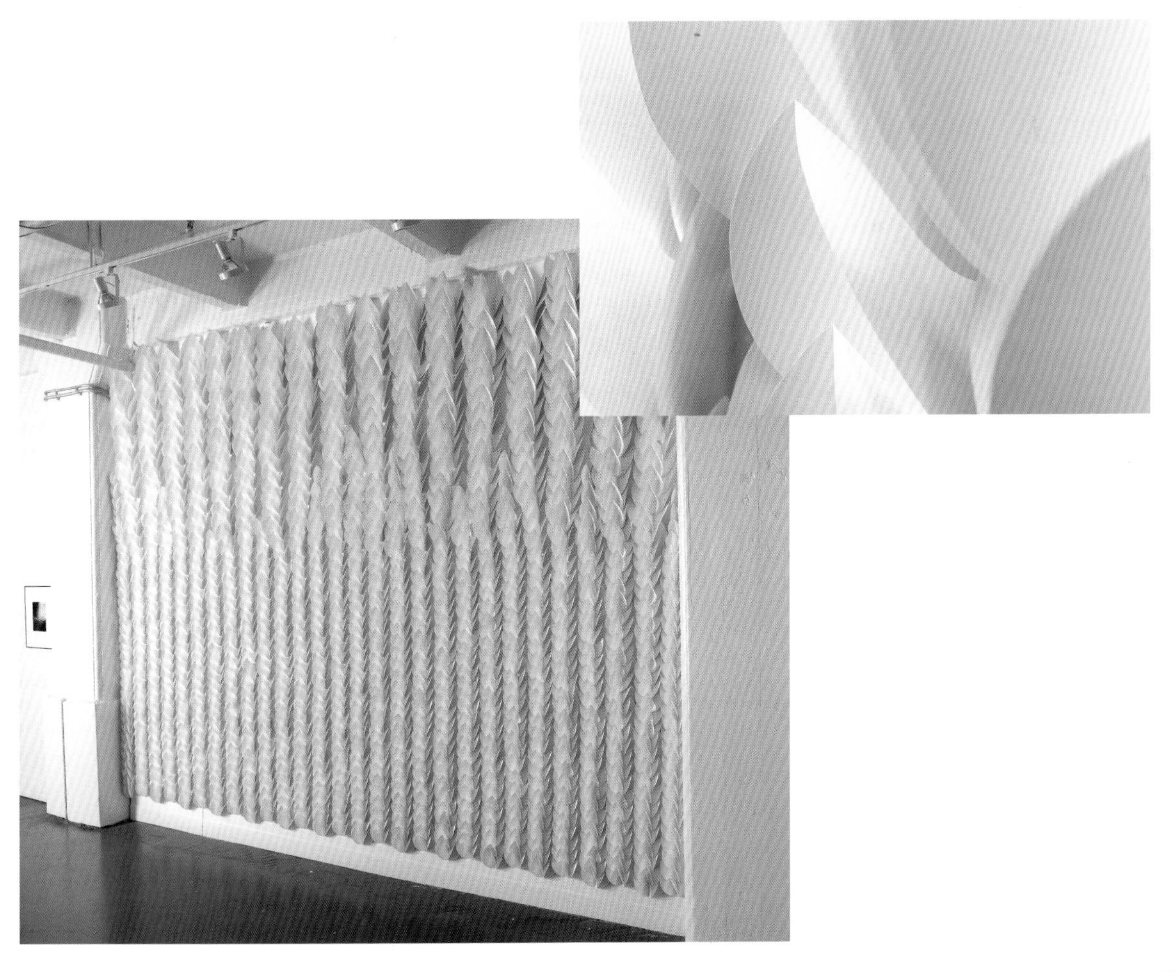

Design Agency Aichi Institute of Technology Designer Yoshinobu Miyamoto Client Research for Future Architecture Photographer Yoshinobu Miyamoto

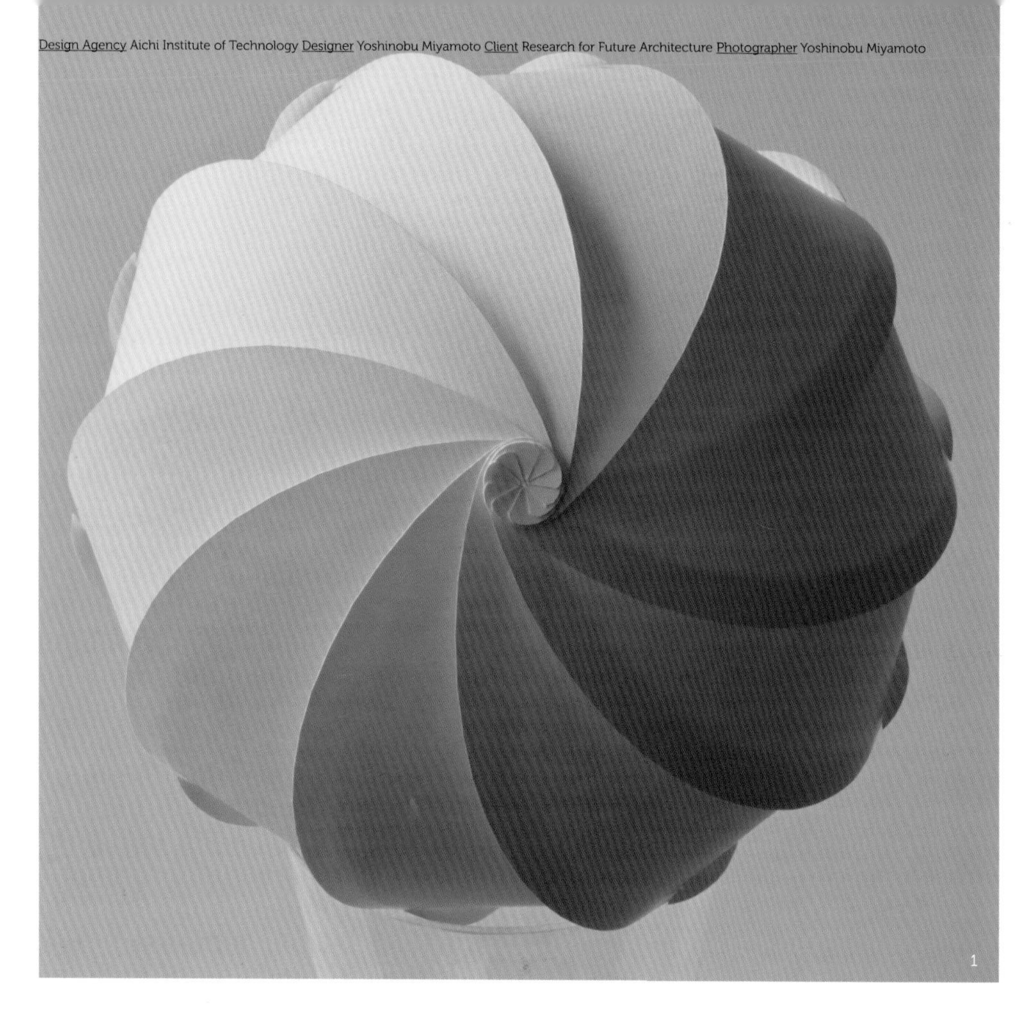

RES, SSS & ES

1 / ES-A (top view)
2 / ET
3 / ES-B
4 / ES-A, cut pattern & oval variation
5 / RES Variations

ES (Elastica Sphere) is made with full use of the elastic property of paper to form the shape with bent & twisted strips

ET (Elastica Torus) is made from a series of elastic bending curves.

RES (Rotational Erection System) is a novel method to make a 3D structure out of single 2D sheets only using cuts and folds.

I start with sketches on notebooks. Then I make 3D models with Google SketchUp. "Unfold plug-in" is useful to develop partial shapes. Cut and Crease patterns are generated from the 3D models and are edited with vector drawing software such as Adobe Illustrator. A small desktop cutting plotter is used to cut A4 or A5 size 0.2mm thick paper. Crease lines and curves are also done with the machine with blade pressure adjustment. Machine production takes several minutes and assembling and folding takes about ten minutes. Occasional mistakes in trials often bring new design ideas. Rapid prototyping with painless handiwork is a good drive for my creative motivation.

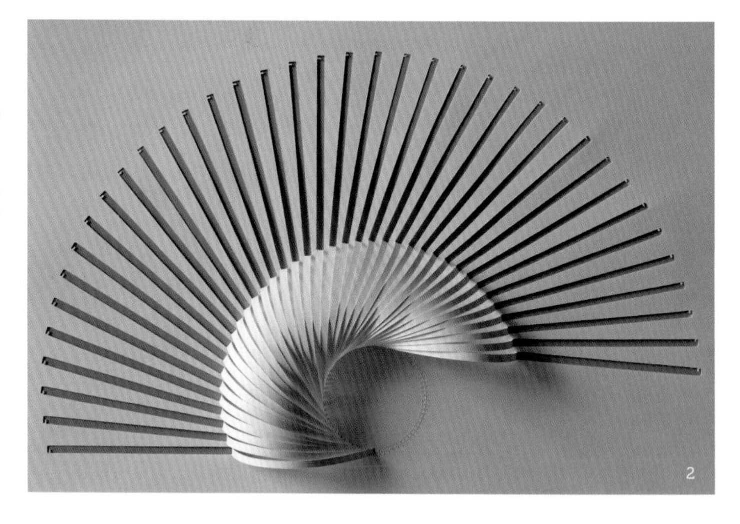

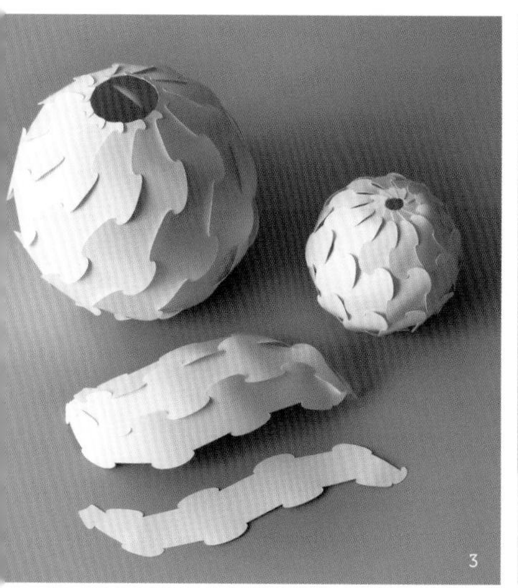
3

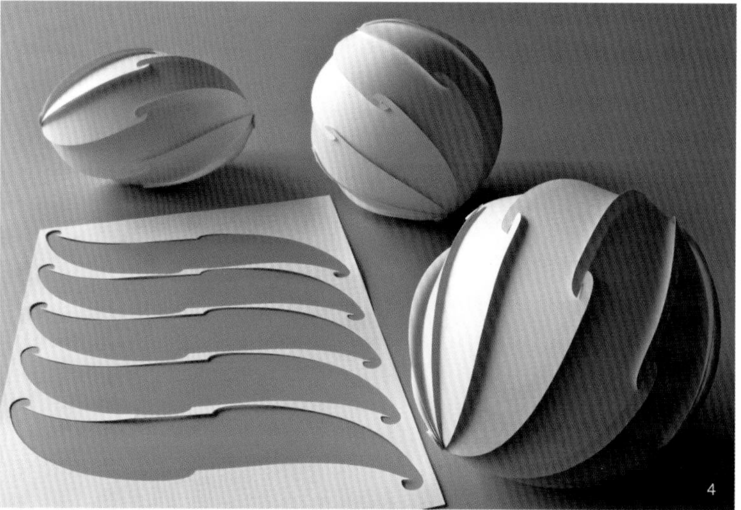
4

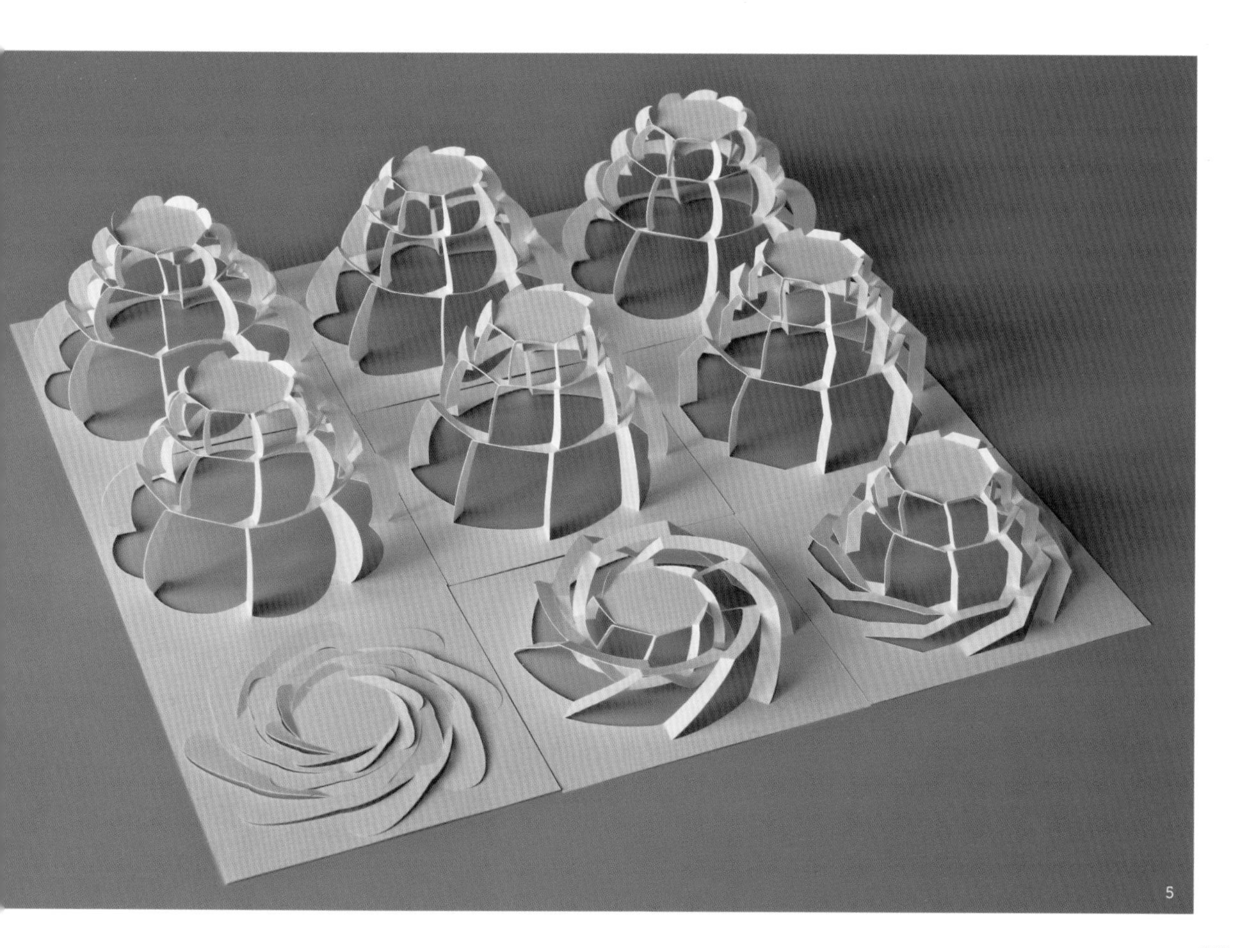
5

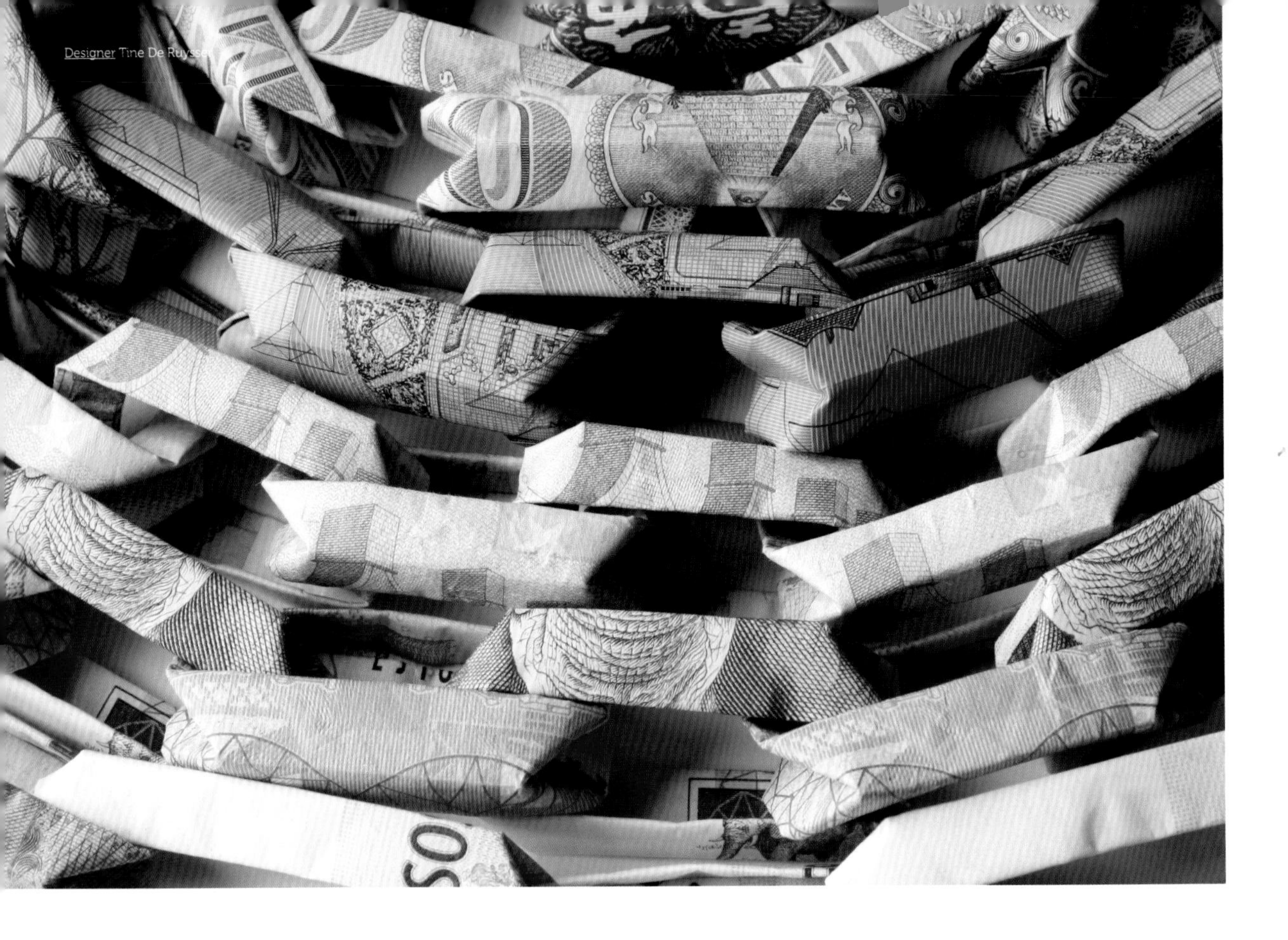

Money Jewelery

This jewelry collection is completely made from banknotes. All of the banknotes used were valid currency at the time the piece of jewelry was made. The banknotes are only folded and not damaged in any way: no cutting is used, nor is any glue applied. Each note can be unfolded and used as currency. The jewelry is surprisingly strong; it does not tear easily or fall apart quickly.

The collection is a comment on the perceived value of gold and money, and on the relationship between the two currencies. Can one replace the other? For this collection that is just what I have done: the precious necklaces and bracelets are made from banknotes instead of gold. They send out the same message (I'm rich!), and provide for financial back up in case of need.

At the same time the collection draws attention to the current worldwide economic crisis. What is money really? How much is it worth? What gives it value? How does one currency relate to the others? Why is one currency stronger than another, and for how long?

By replacing gold with money for these pieces of jewelry, I draw attention to Wealth. I hope to make people think about what money means to them and to society as a whole.

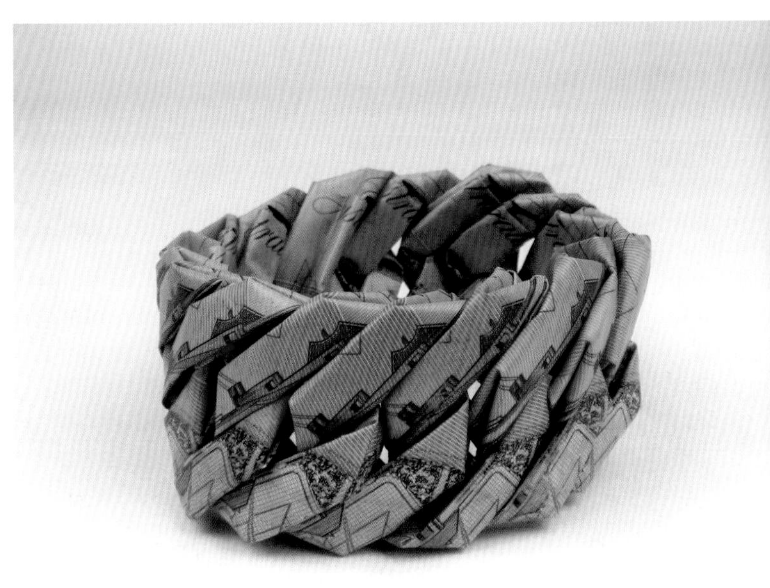

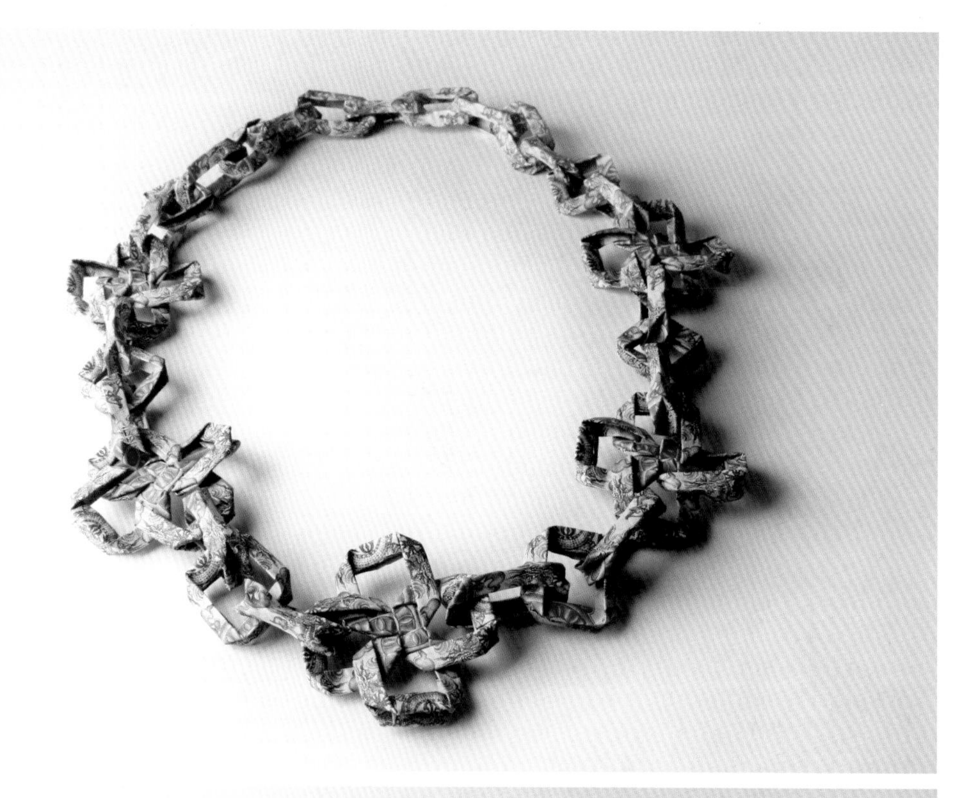

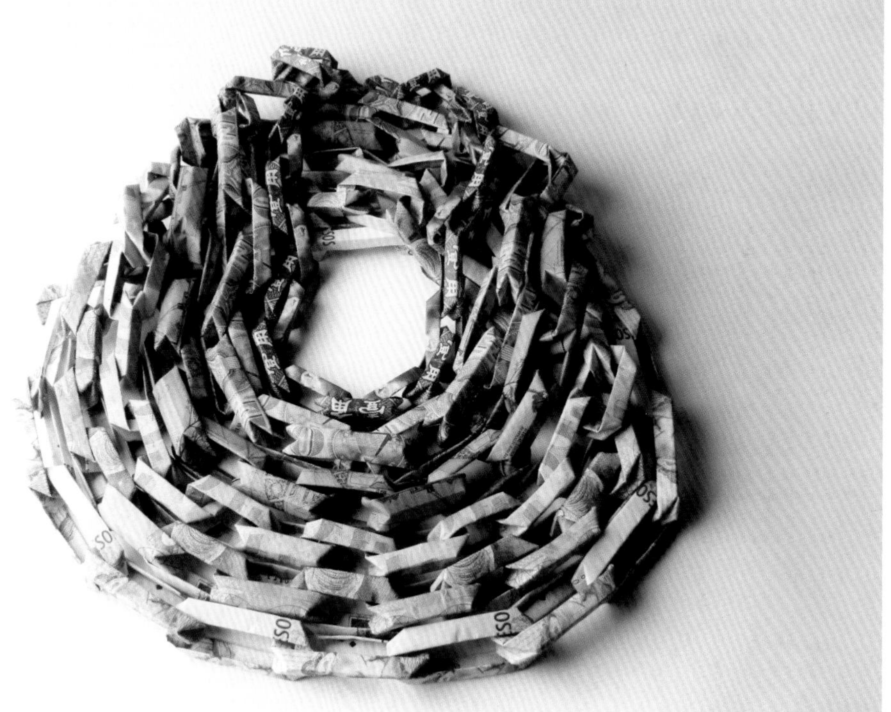

Book Pages Innovation

1 / Pink Curvy Roads Seanemone Brooch
2 / Deepblue Seanemone
3 / Here Black Brooch
4 / Orbit Neckpiece
5 / P. Red Brooch

My work concentrates on materials and experimenting with their qualities. The drive for these projects is a fascination with unexpected end results. I prefer organic materials as they all change with time, just like I make a change when starting to work with them. I am interested in the sculptural approach to these materials and also in finding unorthodox solutions to challenges. Although I use traditional goldsmith tools to create each piece, the basic materials and the techniques I use result in a very different type of jewelry than the classic gold pieces. I enjoy that each piece, even the similar ones look different and are unique, because every detail is handmade.

While the pieces each have a function, they also each have a unique identity. They become canvases on which a number of stories can play out. Jewelry can be nearly anything; this is the beauty of it. Given that the dimensions are more or less limited, each piece can be worn and therefore a mobile work of art.

1

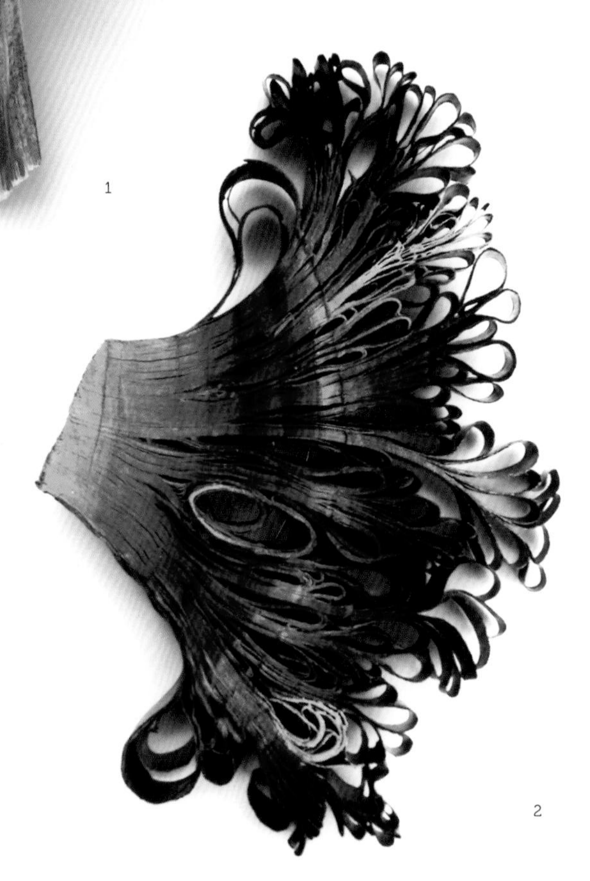

2

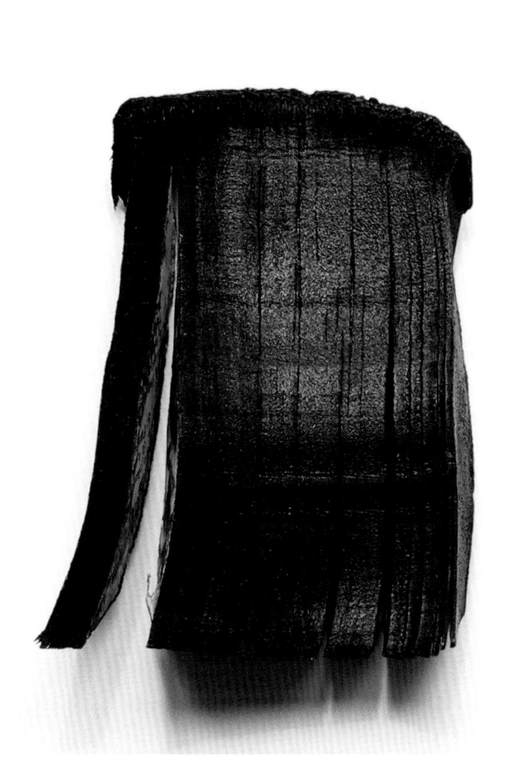

3

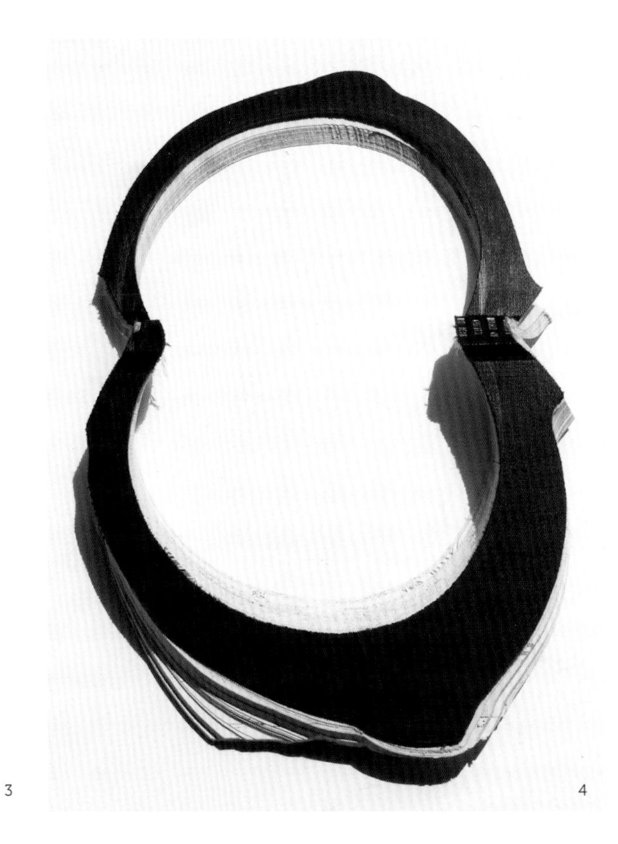

4

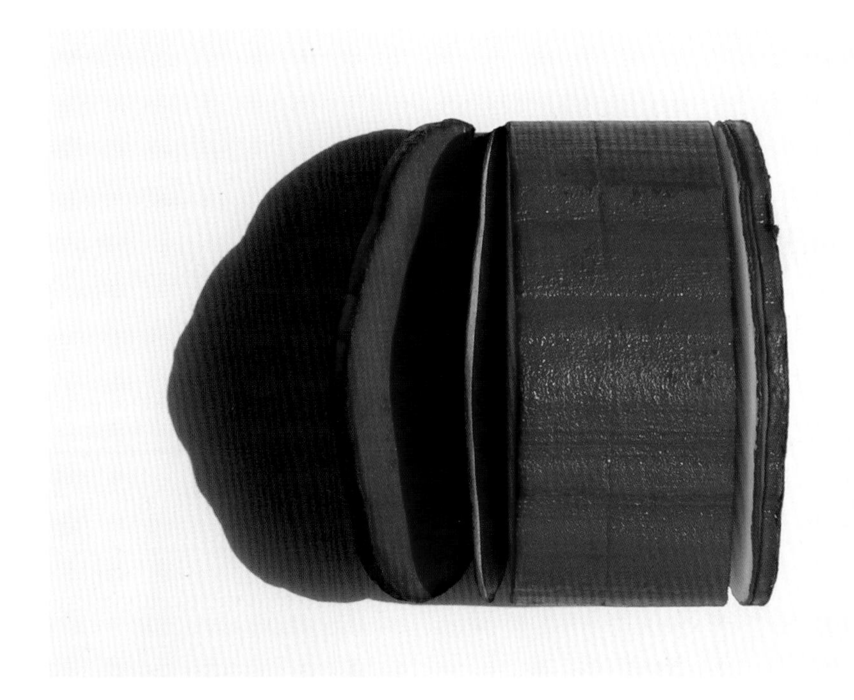

5

Design Agency THAT Designer Robert The

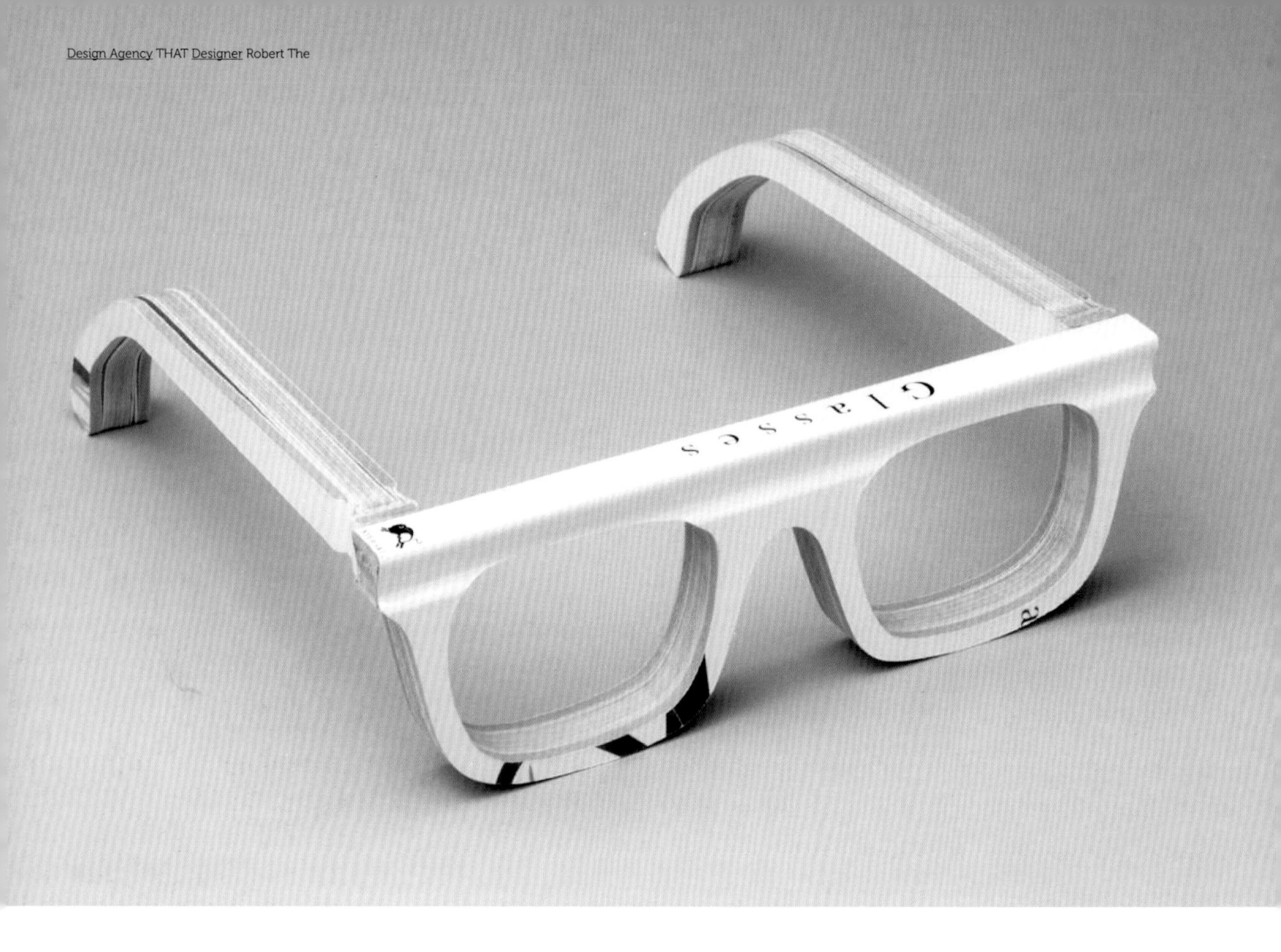

Book Works

Since the early 1990s, New York based artist Robert The has been precision altering books. His creations have been exhibited at Colette in Paris, MOMA New York, the Whitney Museum, the Guggenheim Berlin, and other international venues.

An obsession with the semiotic erosion of meaning and reality led him to alter texts so as to evangelize their own relevance by a direct fusion of word and form. Old editions of books (many culled from dumpsters and thrift store bins) are lovingly vandalized back to life so they can assert themselves against or reflect on the culture which turned them into debris.

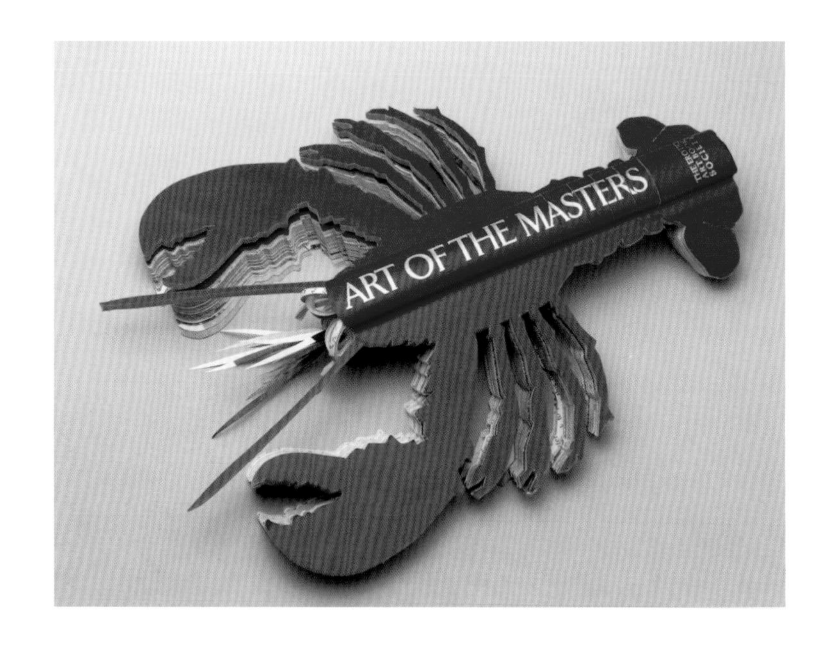

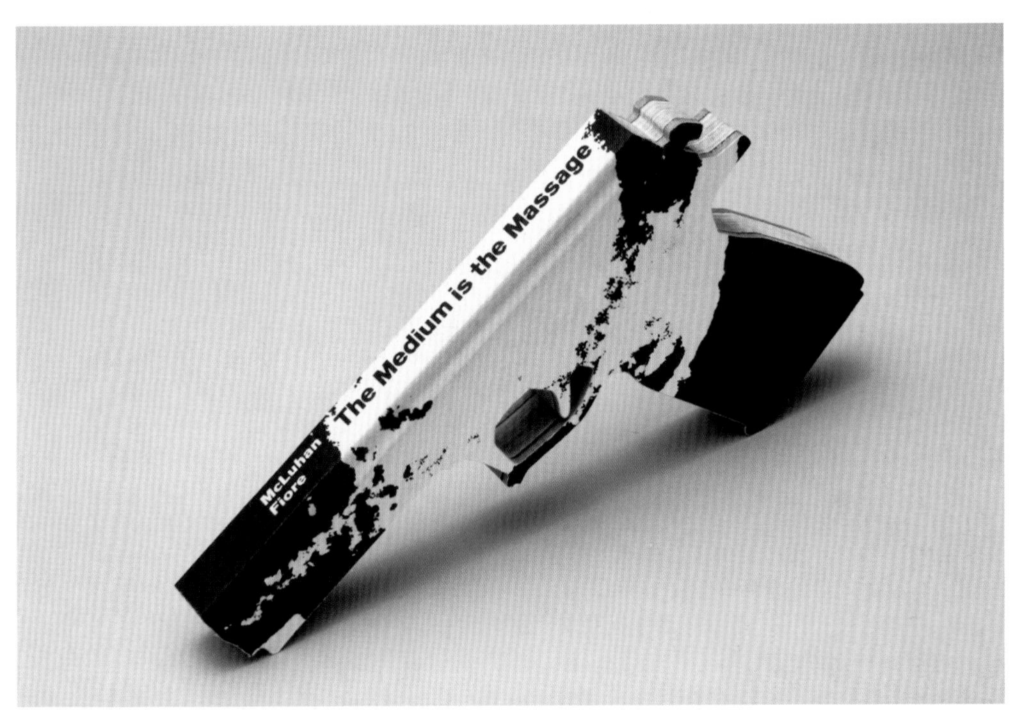
The Medium is the Massage
McLuhan
Fiore

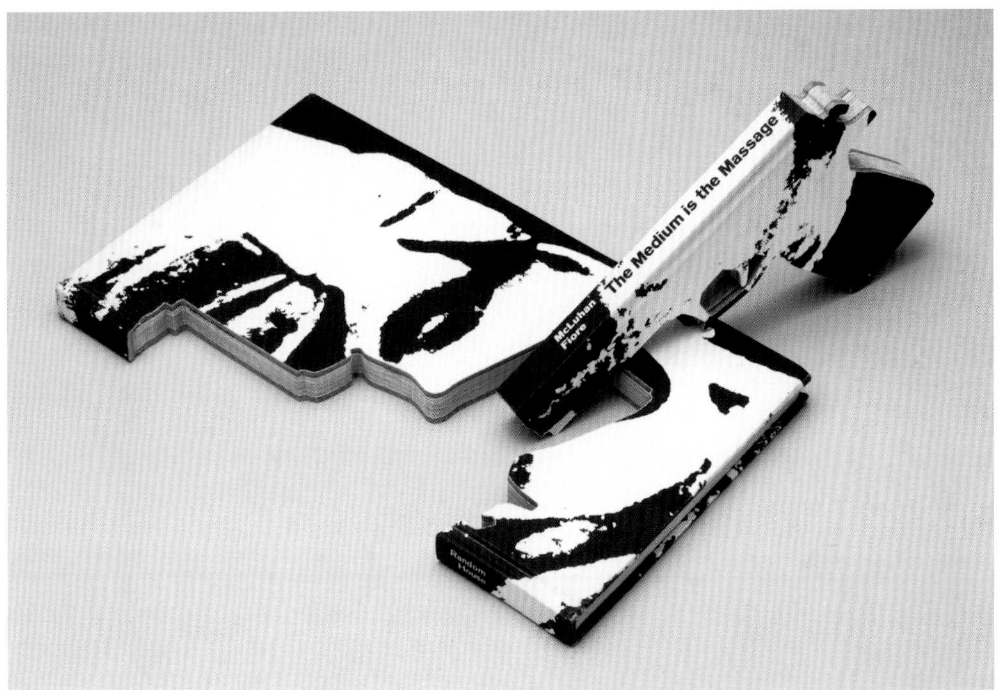
The Medium is the Massage
McLuhan
Fiore
Random
House

STARDREAM, MR PLIKE, IN/TO

These are three of a series of experimental sculptures that are part of a new collection produced to be used in an international magazine advertising campaign. The sculptures were made out of sheets of paper hand cut into strips and modules by the artist.

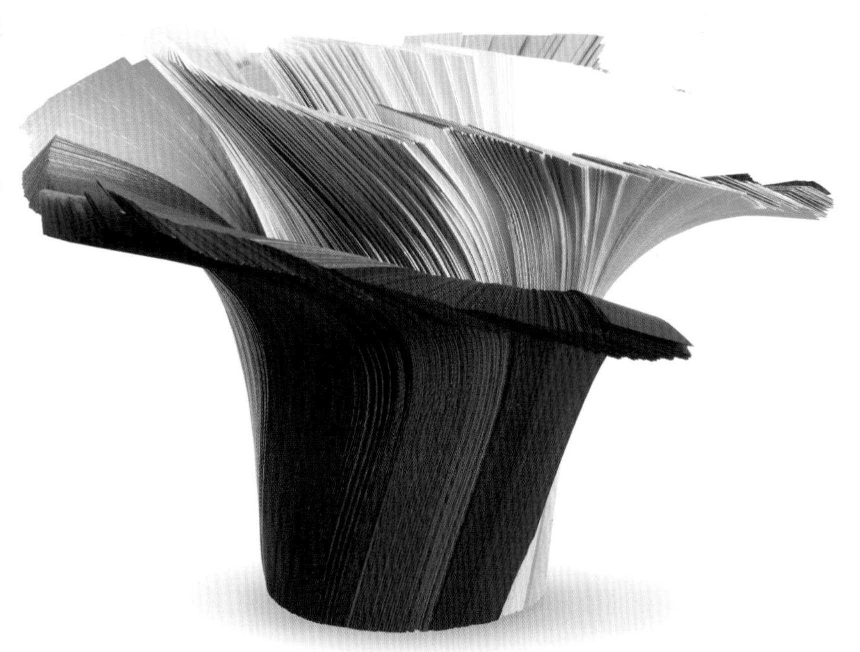

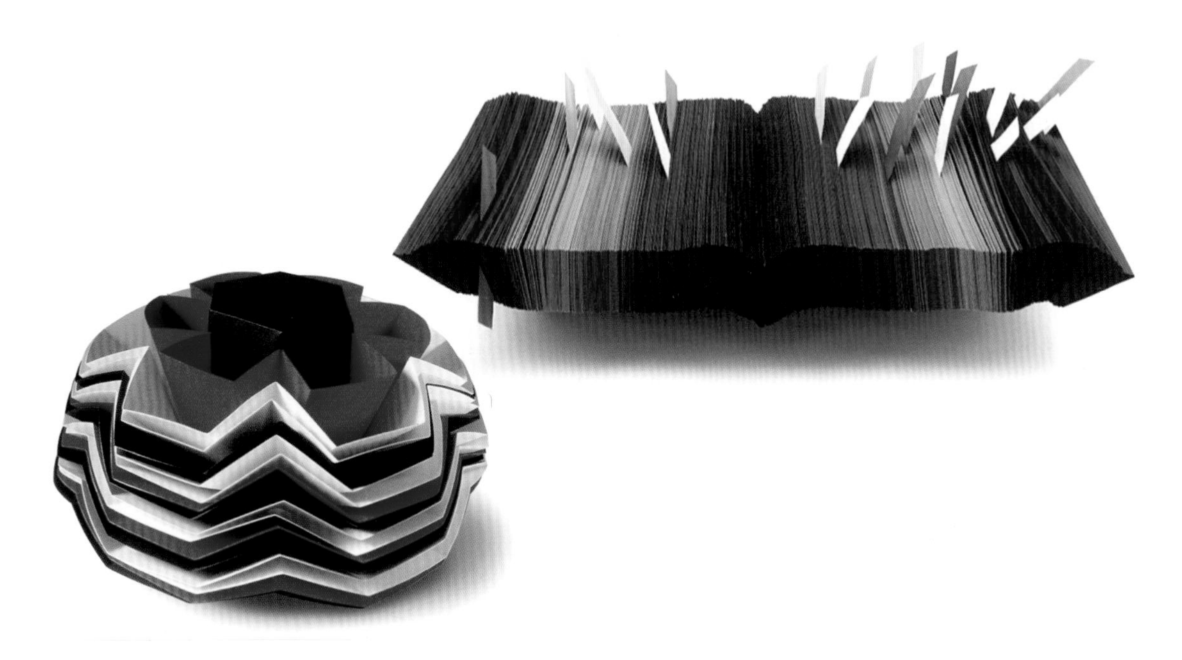

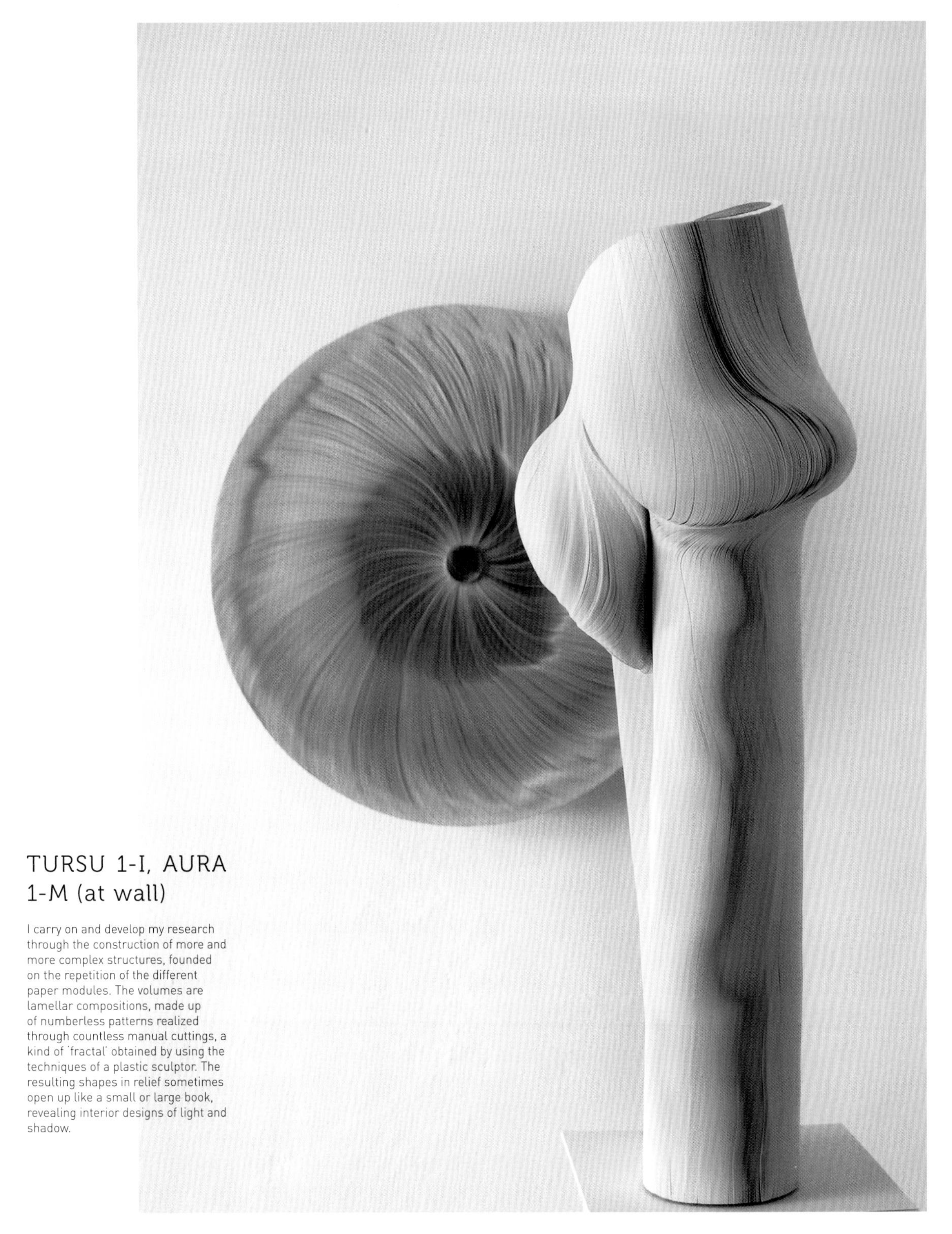

TURSU 1-I, AURA 1-M (at wall)

I carry on and develop my research through the construction of more and more complex structures, founded on the repetition of the different paper modules. The volumes are lamellar compositions, made up of numberless patterns realized through countless manual cuttings, a kind of 'fractal' obtained by using the techniques of a plastic sculptor. The resulting shapes in relief sometimes open up like a small or large book, revealing interior designs of light and shadow.

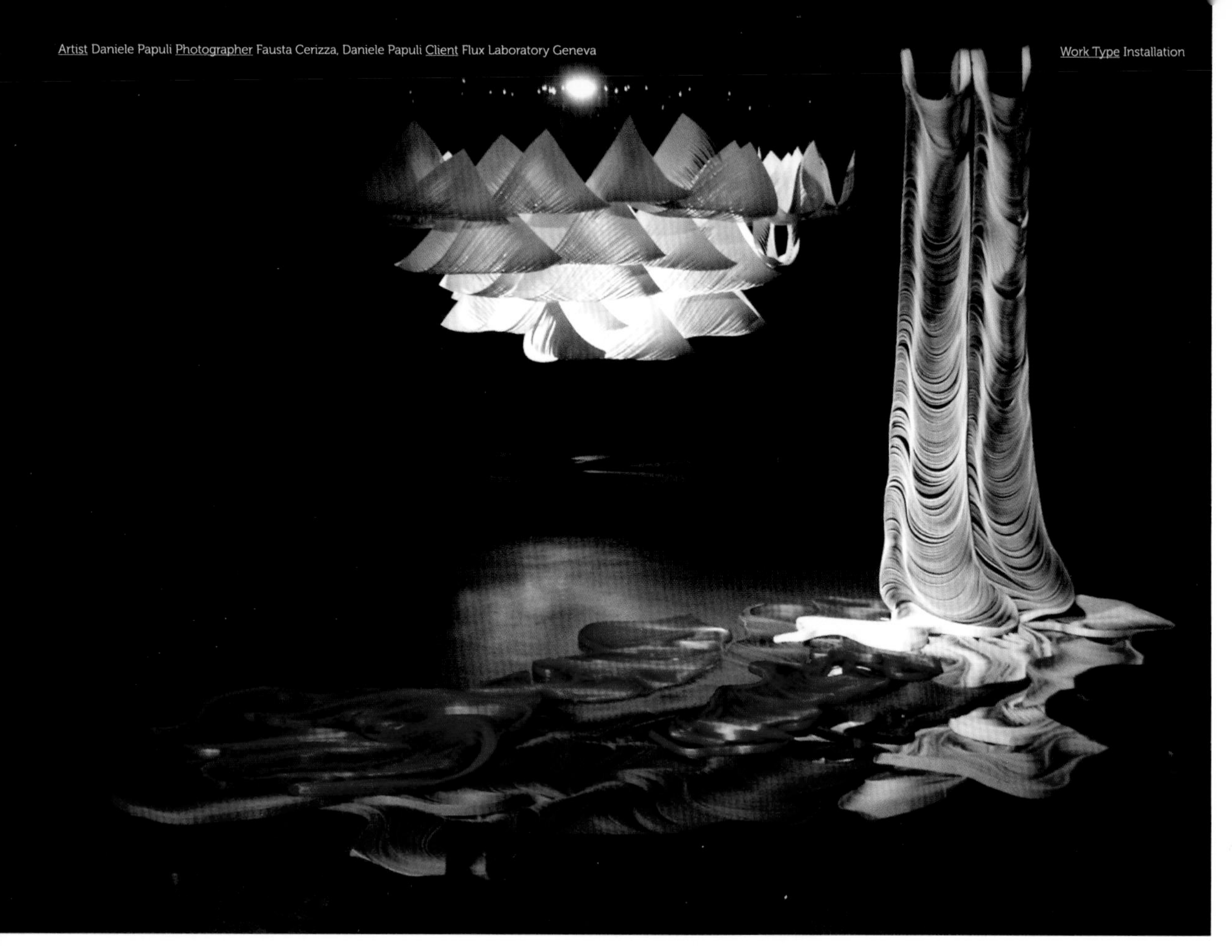

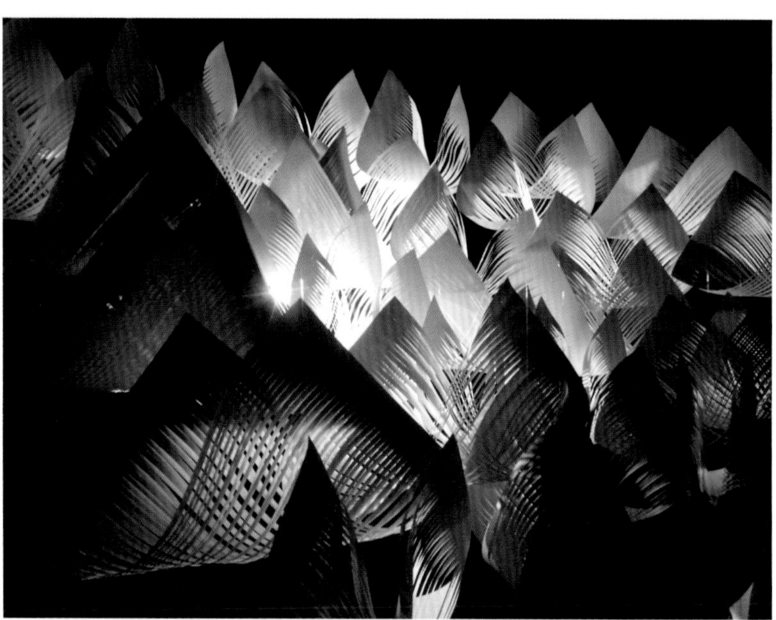

PANTA REI ET ULA

The project was four scenic structures that moved with the dancers through the space. Four dances were performed: attractions, projections, passages and crossings. All four dances interact with the sculptural paper within the space. The sculpture was conceived as a spatial construction and deconstruction of the original paper material. Panta rei consists of hundreds of strips of selected cards that make the paper appear to be a fluid material.

The project is composed of about 60 sheets of 50 x 70 white paper. The paper is shaped into geometric structures, such as kites, and these are then suspended in space to create patterns of light and shadow that correspond to the dance choreography.

Artist Daniele Papuli Photographer Salvatore Basile Client Aragonese Castle of Ischia - Italy

Work Type Installation

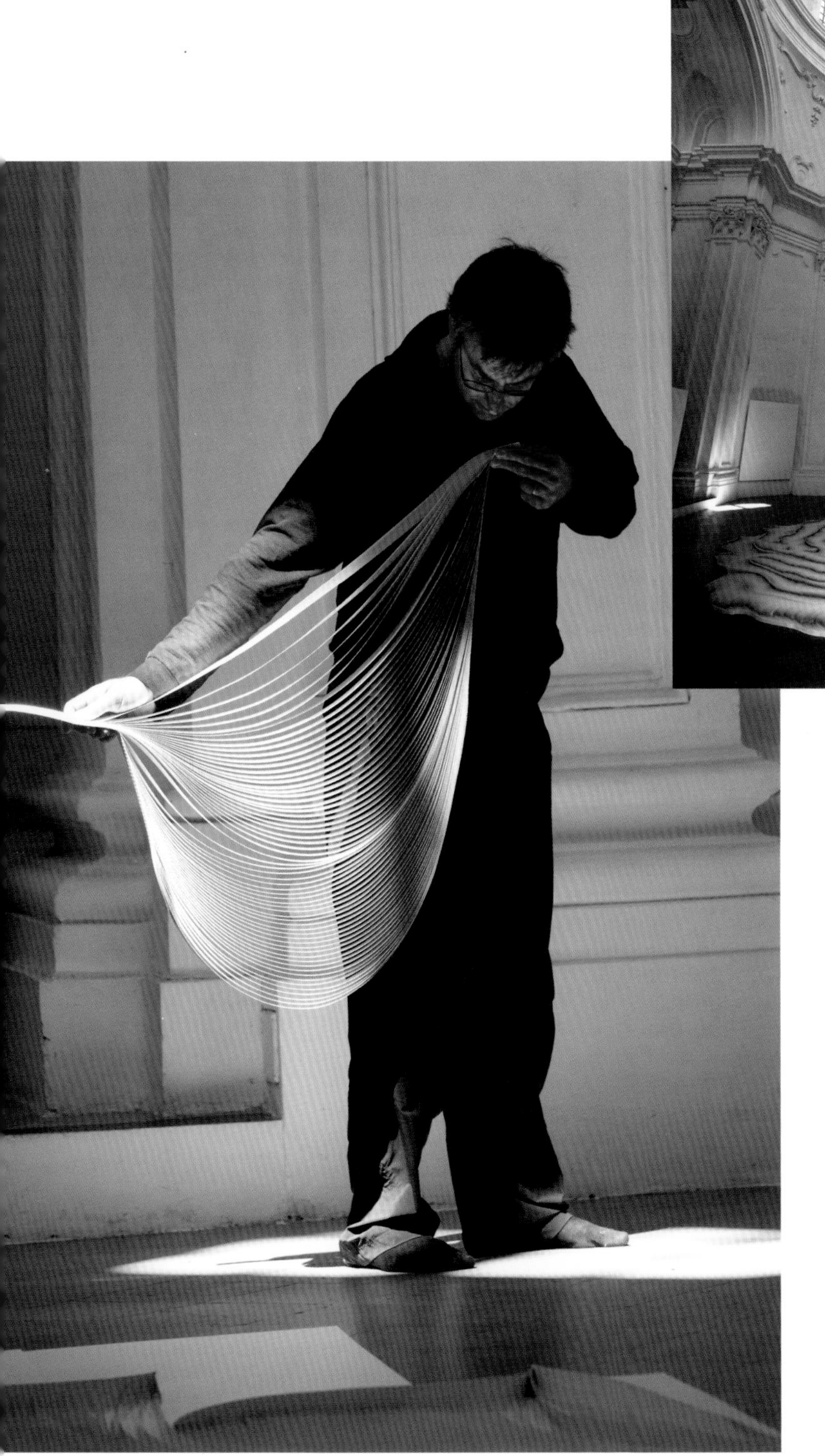

CARTOFRAMMA

This is a dialogue between the church space and the paper construction; the work is designed and built in response to the site. Cartoframma is a ground structure of 36 square metres made of modular paper reams. The island of paper in the center of the floor spreads out horizontally like a growing mass... generating reflections and refracting shadows and light.

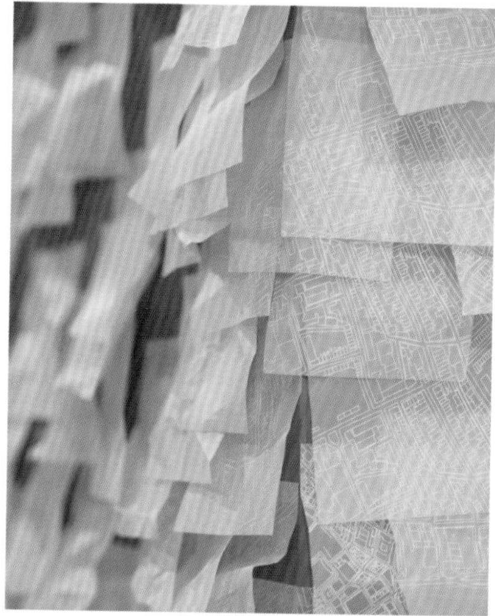

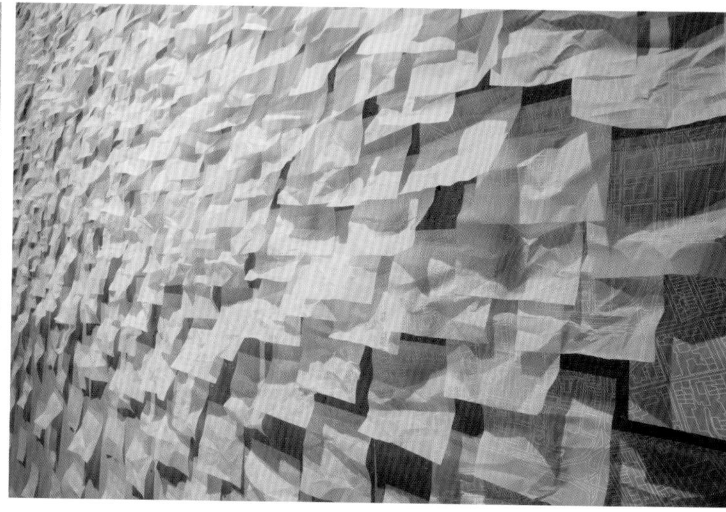

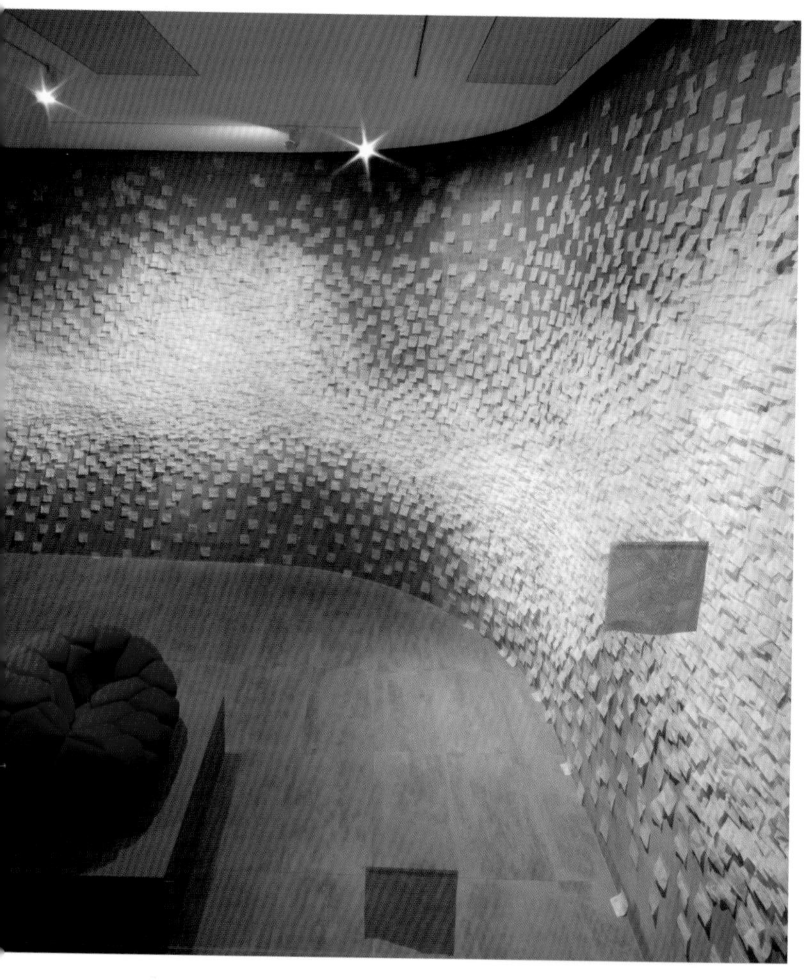

Established & Sons

The space design is for British design company Established & Sons' exhibition for the 2011 London Design Festival; it is presented in the company's showroom in east London. The collection's theme was "My London", so we pasted 25,000 maps of London neighbourhoods printed on tracing paper onto the walls, creating an installation that recollects that particular atmospheric phenomenon, the London fog. The installation, an accumulation of intimate individual feelings towards the city, becomes a physical, spatial expression of the dynamic, always ambiguous face of the city.

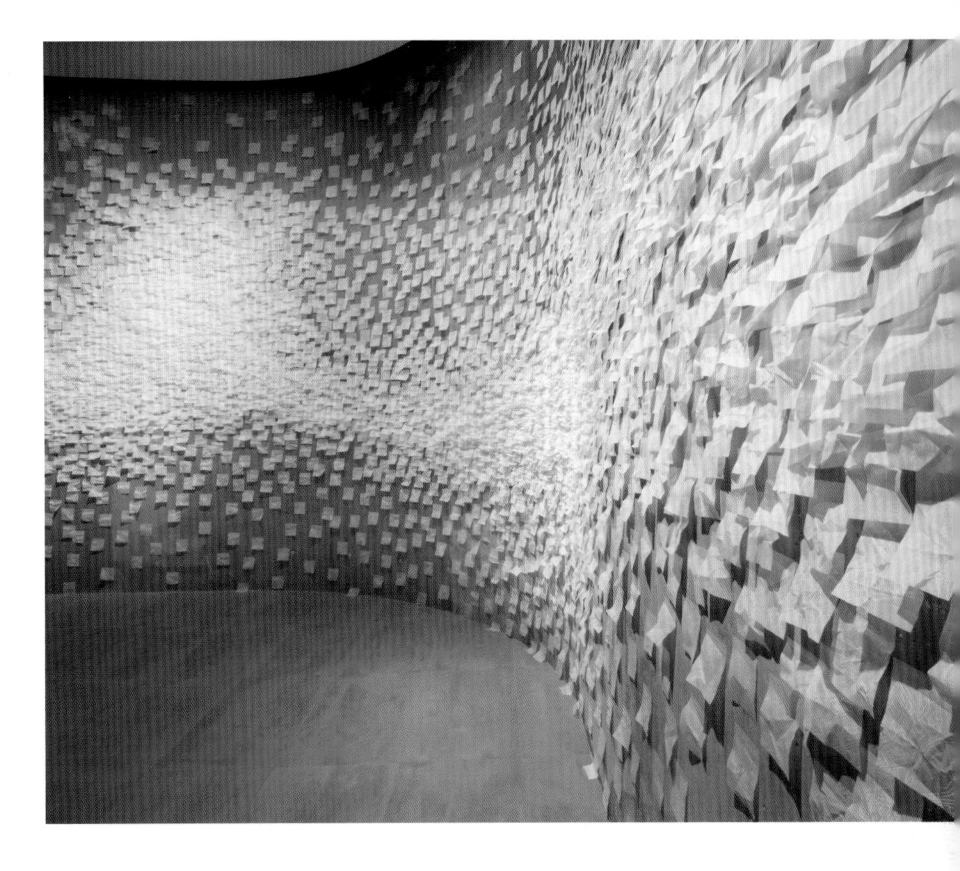

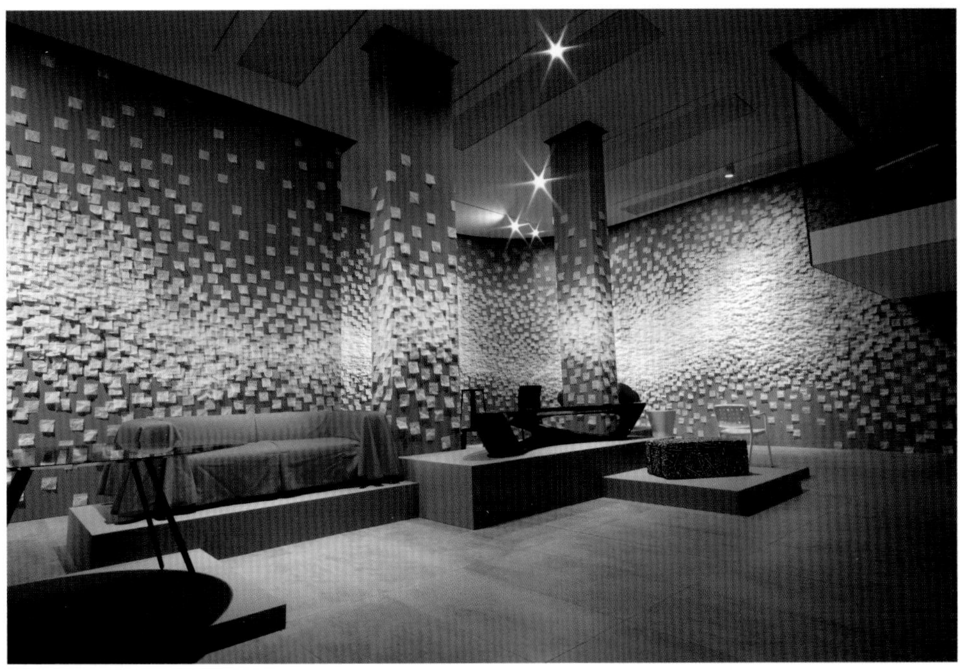

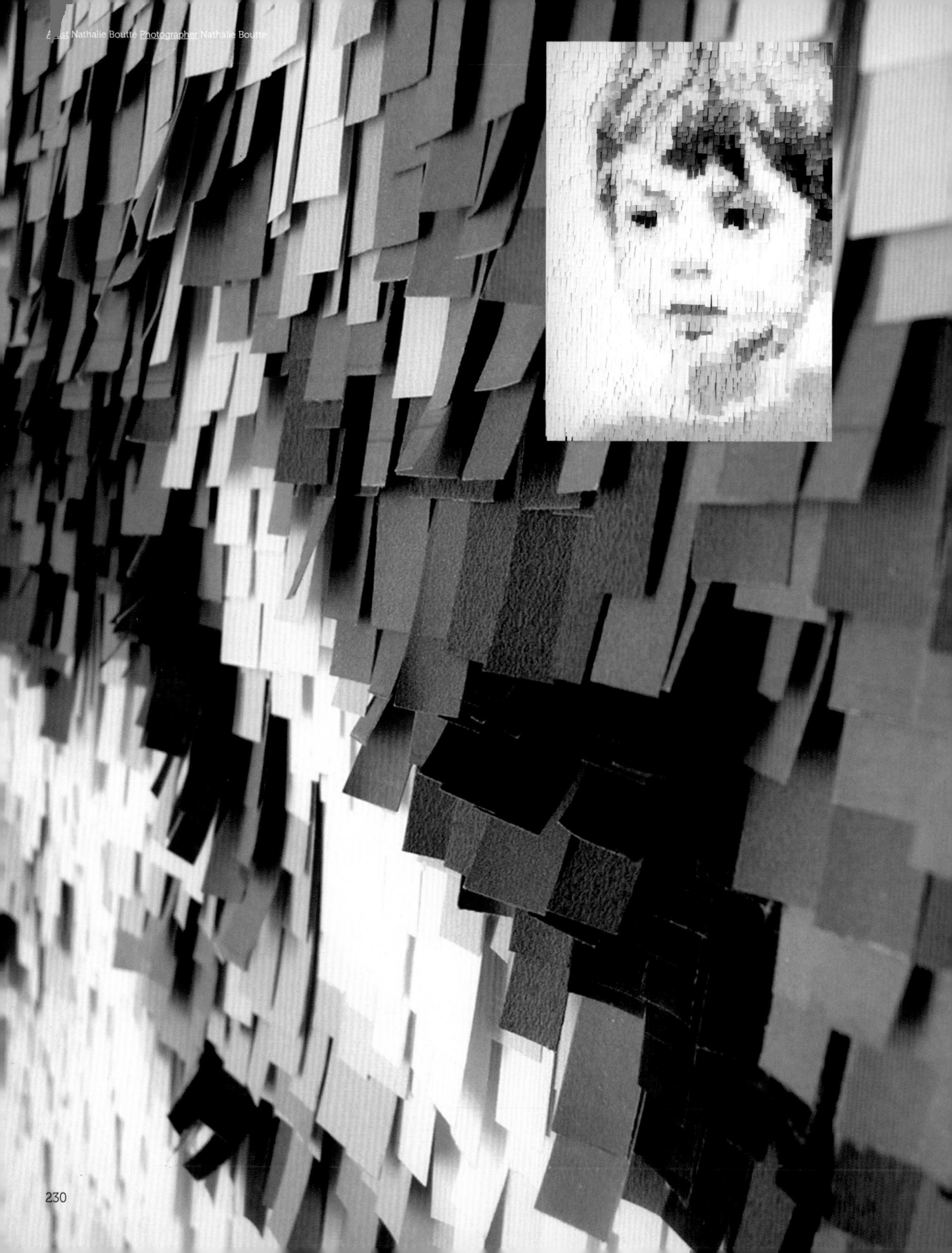

Artist Nathalie Boutté Photographer Nathalie Boutté

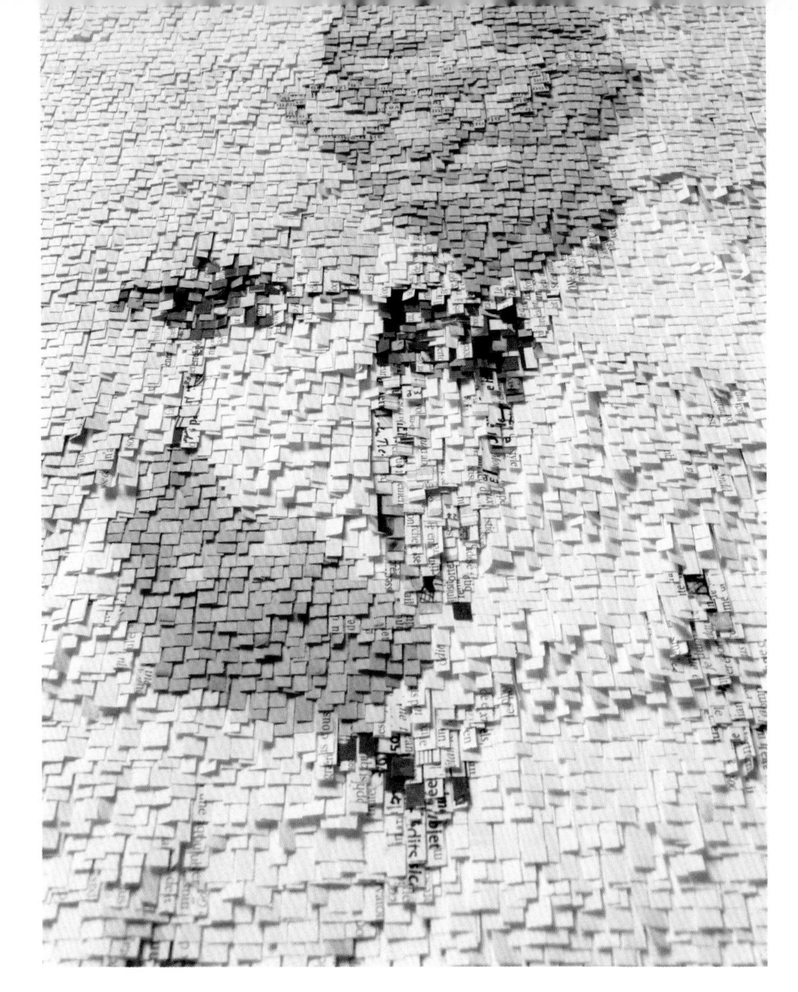

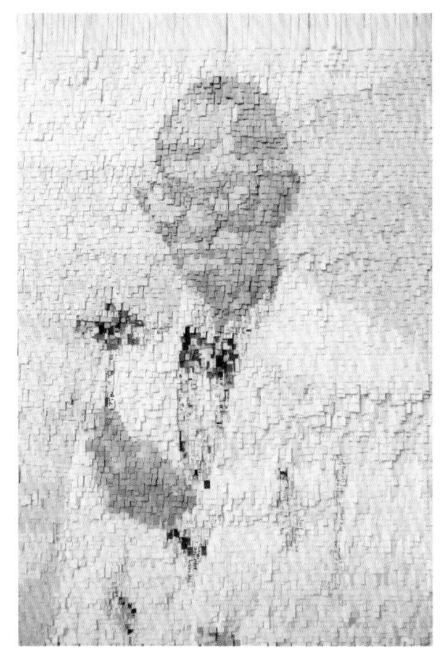

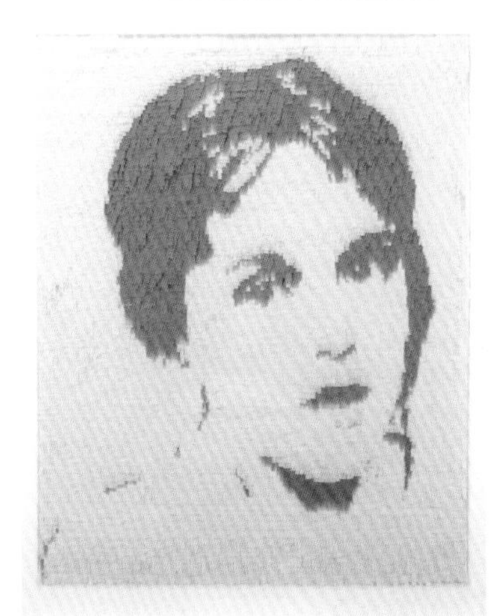

PAPER STRIPES

Nathalie Boutté constructs long narrow strips of paper that she patiently assembles from recycled tissue paper and discarded novels, creating a feather effect that is constantly evolving. She uses both grey and bright colors, sometimes mixing in Indian ink or gold sheets to create an even more varied effect. The strips are densely layered like thatch on a roof, exposing just the tips of each piece of paper, which creates an effect similar to pixels forming a larger image.

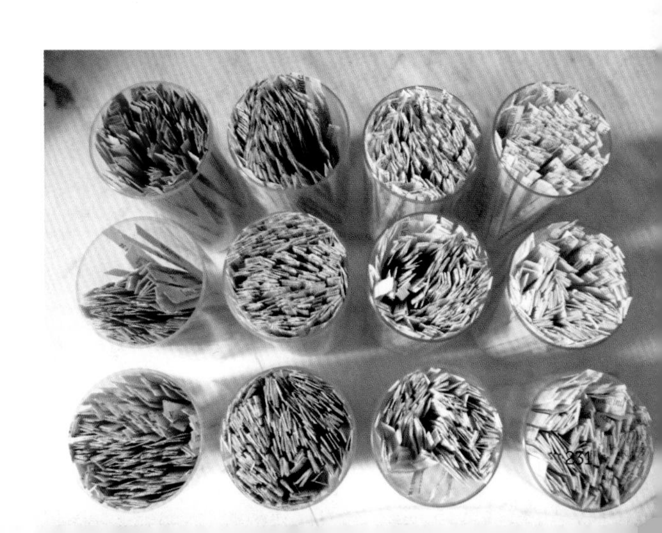

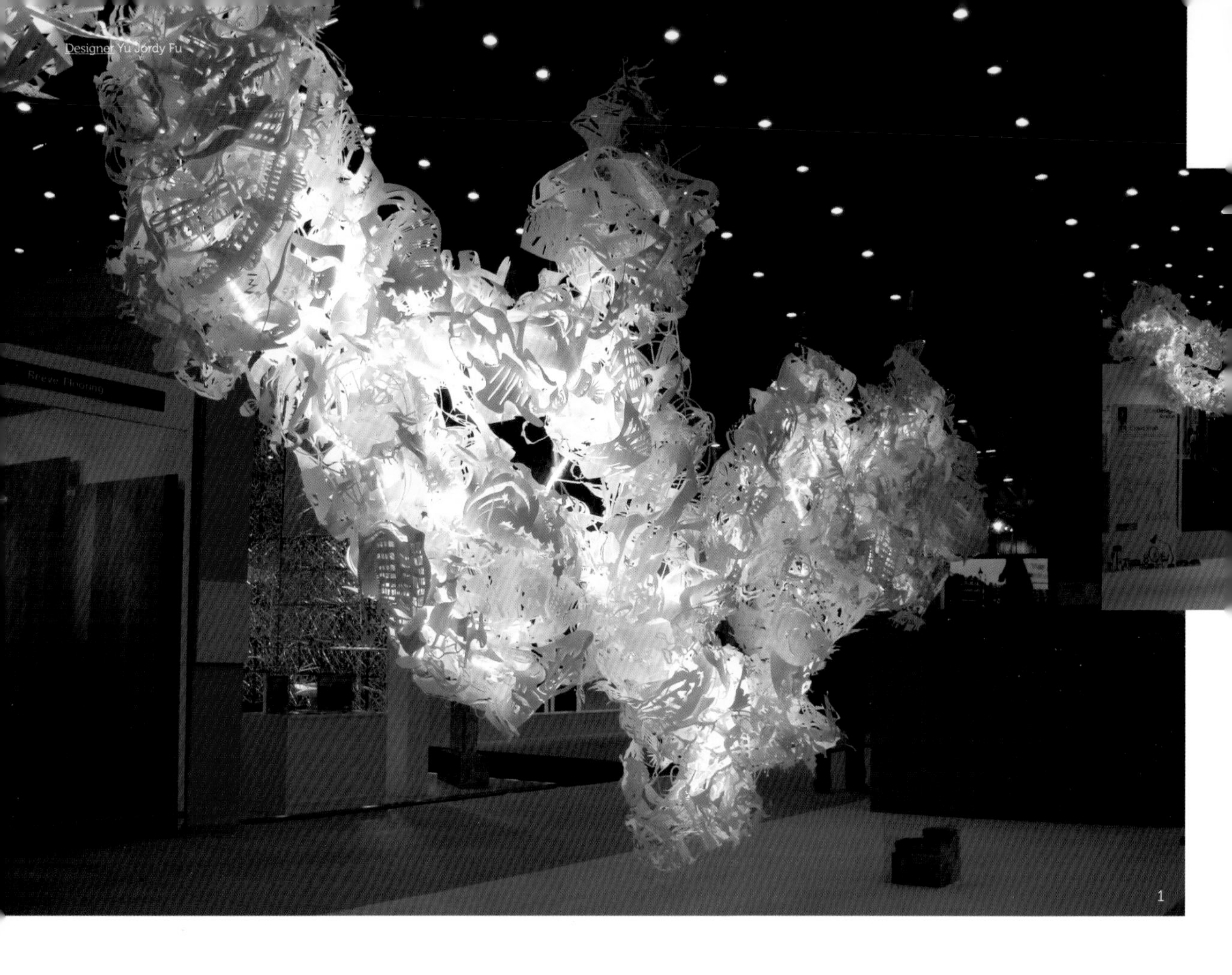

1

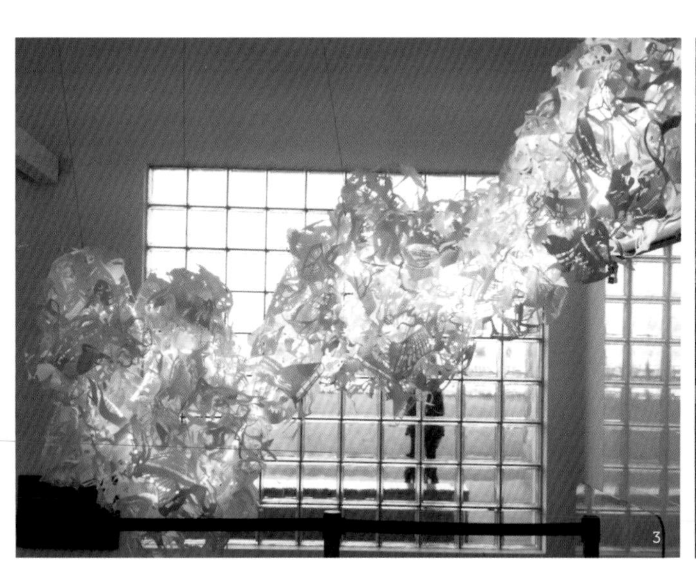

3

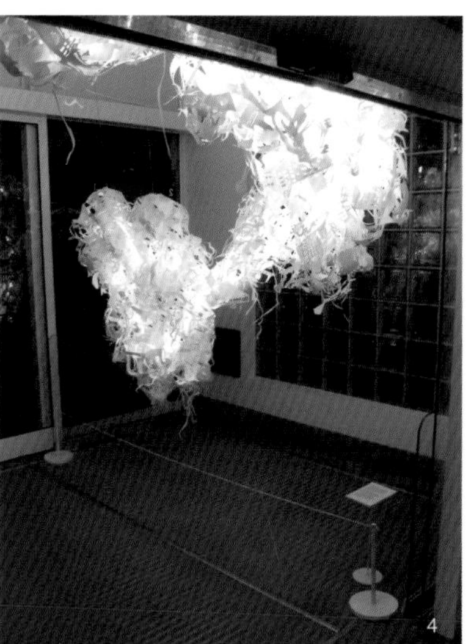

4

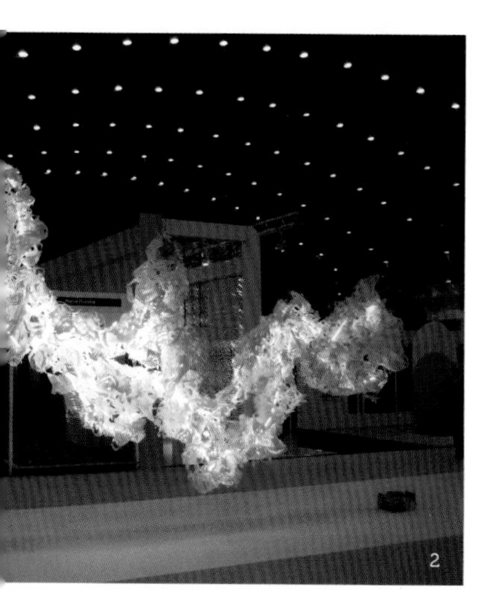

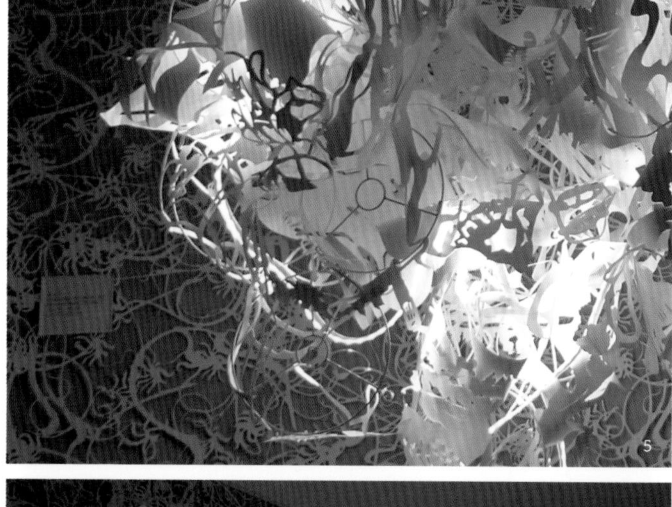

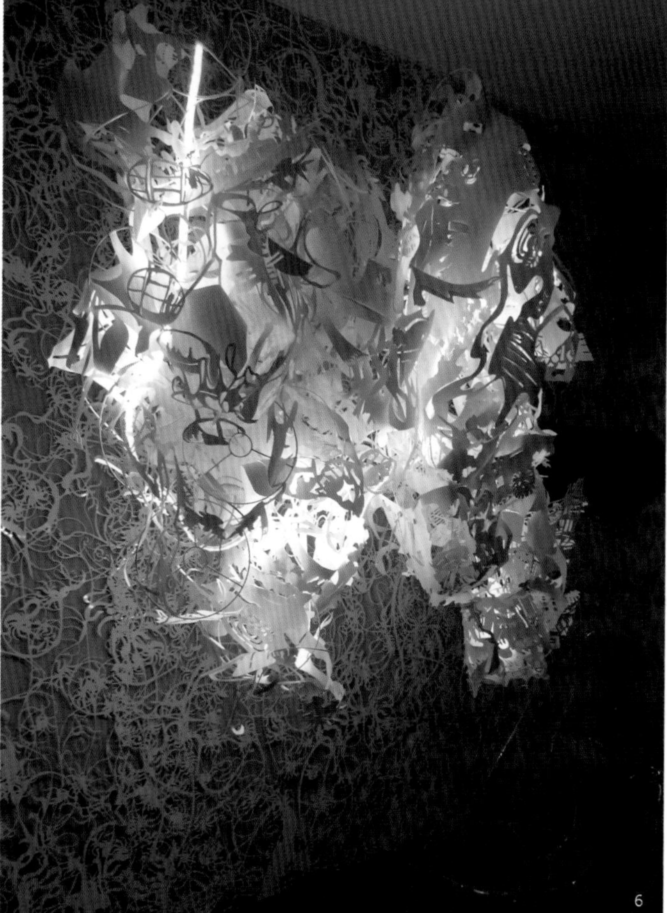

Handmade Recycled Paper with LED Lighting

1, 2 / Cloud Walk
3, 4 / Liquid Winter
5, 6 / Selfdiges Chandelier

Inspired by London, Cloud Walk celebrates the spatial relationship between people and the many facts of the city-the existing, proposed and imaginary London. Cloud Walk chandelier is modular; it can be installed and combined vertically or horizontally in a variety of shapes or sizes. For example, you may have one module (1200mm x 500mm x500mm) for your bedroom, two in a living room, nine in a hotel lobby, or thirteen in a bar. Selfridges Chandelier is a project commissioned by the Selfridges department store. A Cloud Chandelier was created for the rooftop restaurant run by renowned chef Pierre Koffmann. Liquid Winter draws from the interplay between the natural and man-made worlds. The installation is constructed of a series of lightweight modular "ripples" that were inspired by the views that can be seen inside or outside the Design Museum.

Designer Mia Pearlman Photographer 1, 2, 3 Jason Mandella 4, 6 Gene Bahng 5 Mia Pearlman

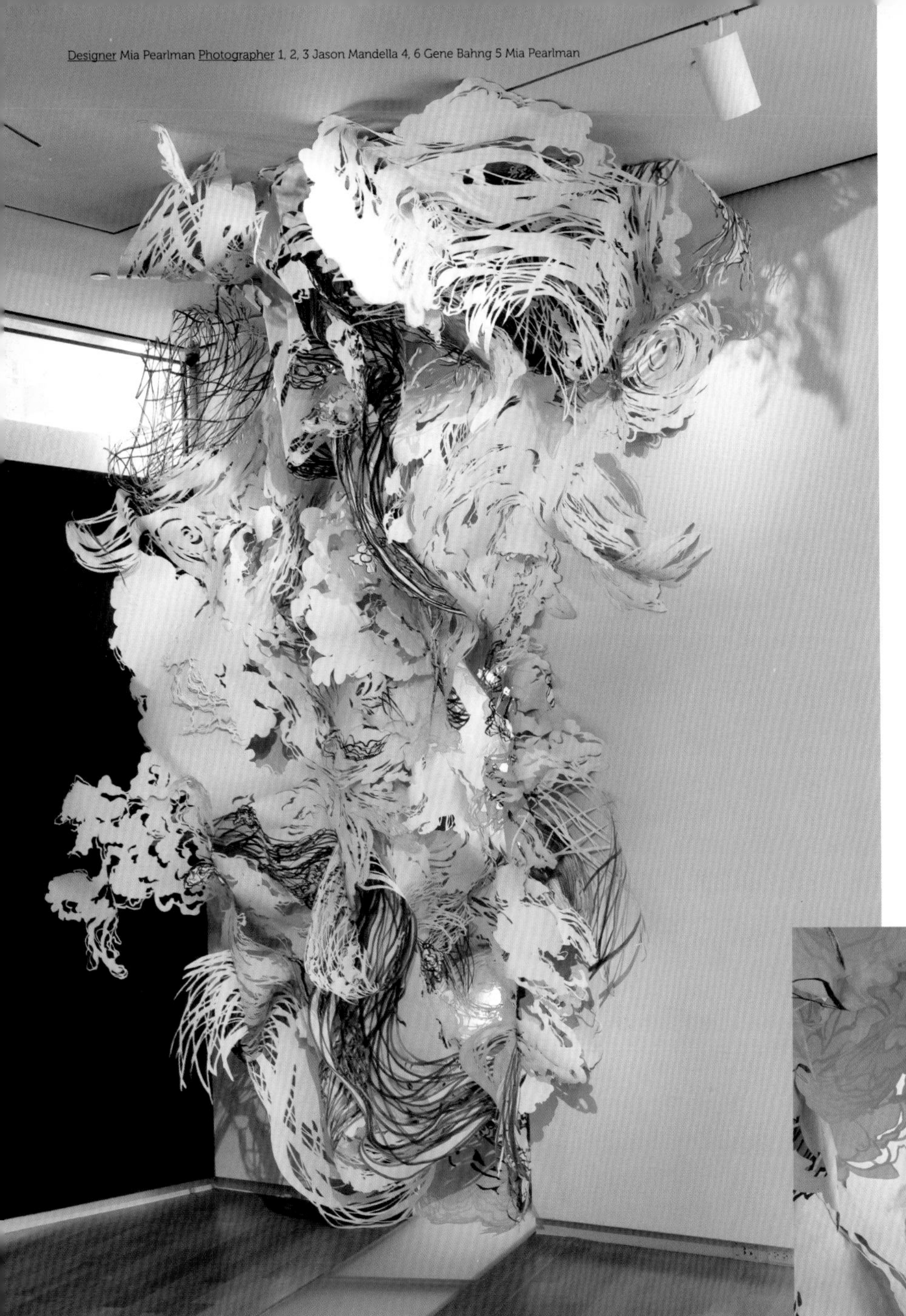

1

Imaginary Weather

1, 2 / INRUSH
3 / EDDY
4, 6 / GYRE
5 / EYE

I make site-specific cut paper installations-ephemeral drawings in both two and three dimensions that blur the lines between actual, illusionistic and imagined space. Sculptural, dynamic and often glowing with natural or artificial light, these imaginary weather systems appear frozen in an ambiguous moment, bursting through or hovering within a room.

My process is very intuitive, based on spontaneous decisions made in the moment. I begin by making loose line drawings in India ink on large rolls of paper. Then I cut out selected areas between the lines to make a new drawing in positive and negative space on the reverse. 30-80 of these cut paper pieces form the final installation, which I create on site by trial and error-a 2-3 day dance with chance and control. Existing only for the length of an exhibition, this weightless world totters on the brink of being and not being, continually in flux. It is my mediation on creation, destruction, and the transient nature of reality.

2

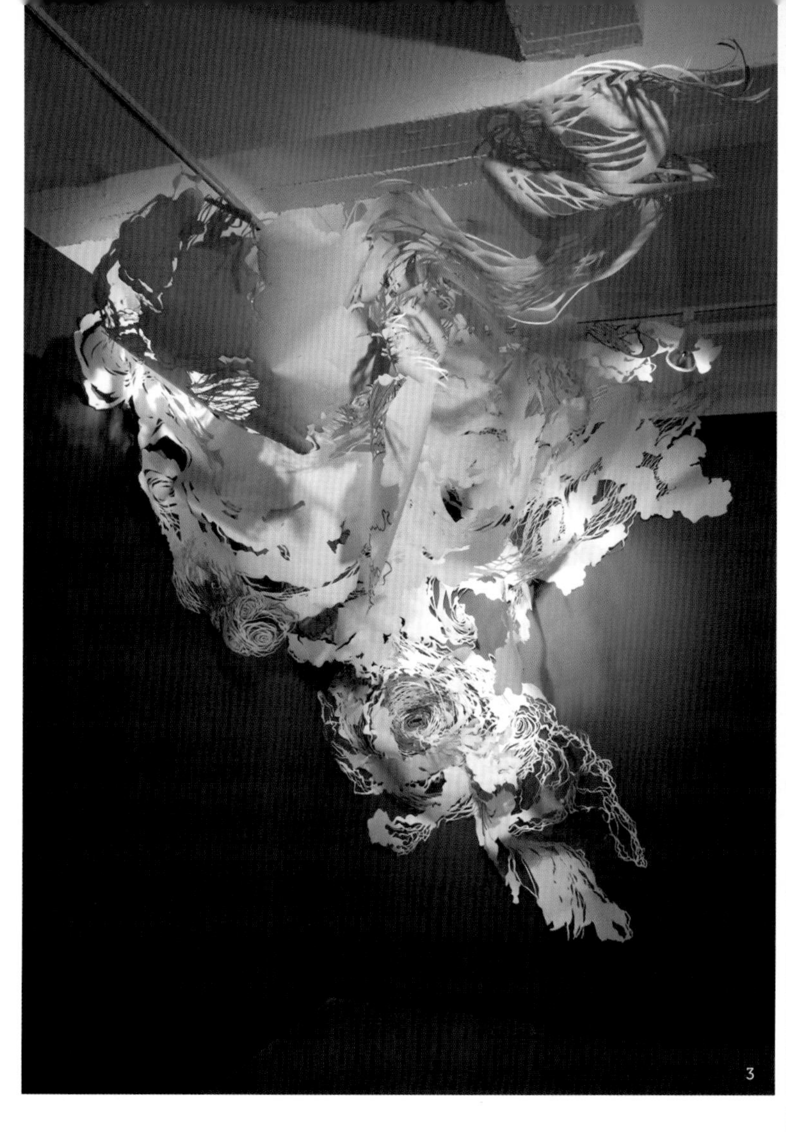
3

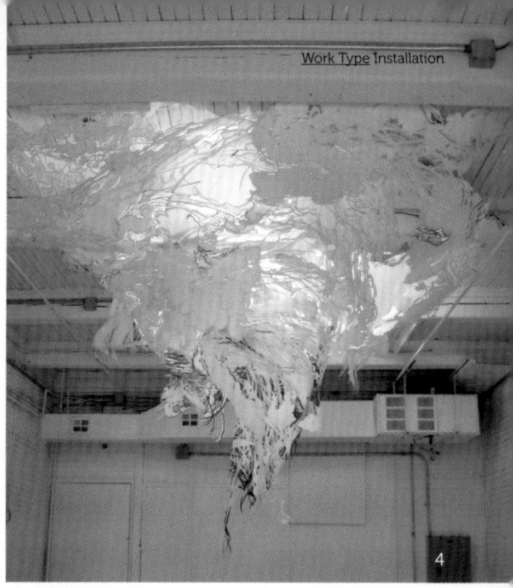
4

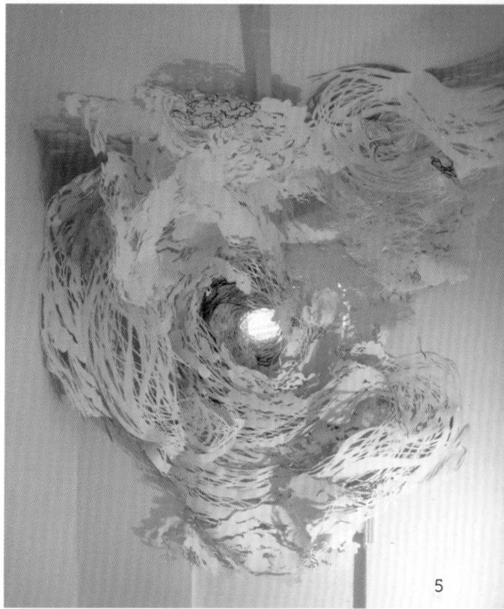
5

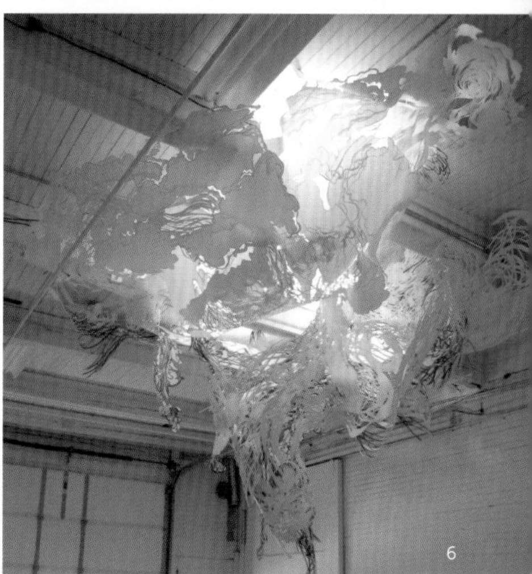
6

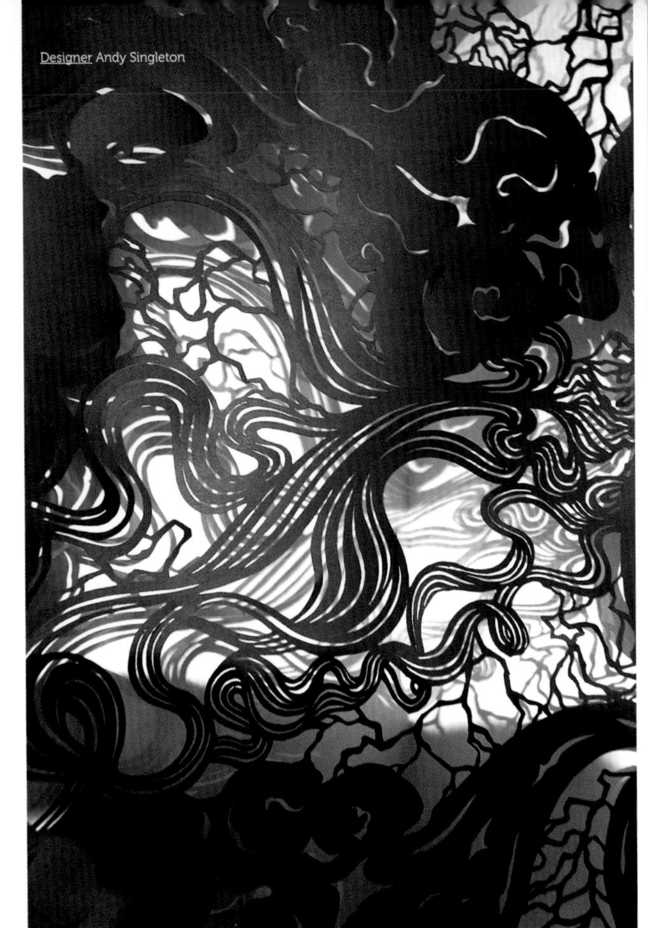

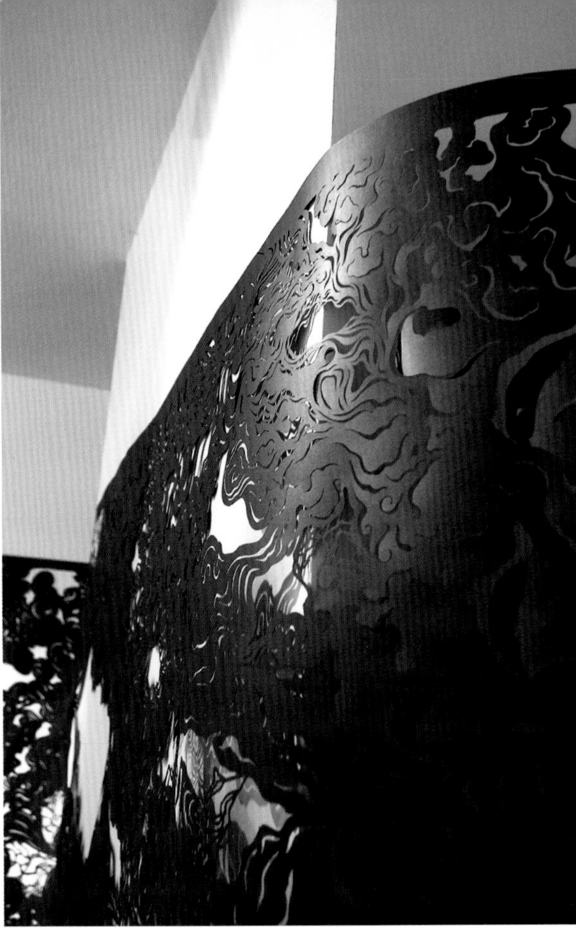

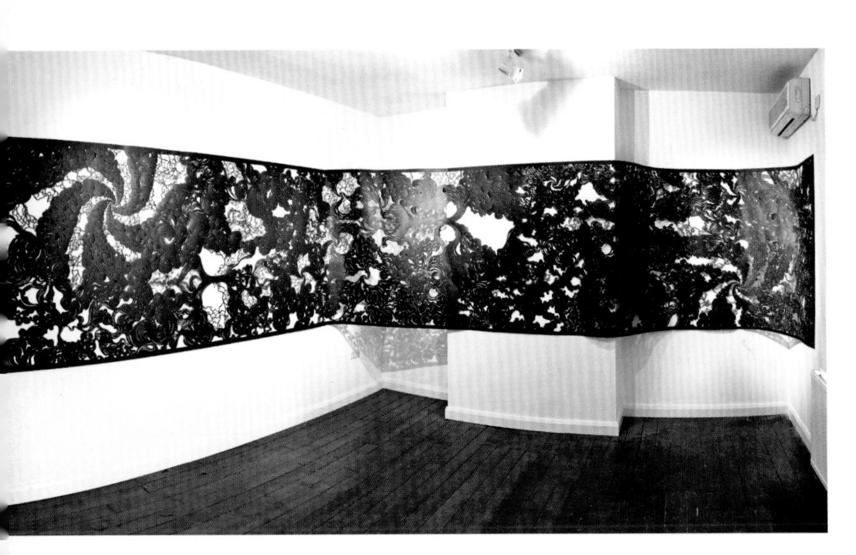

Dust Clouds in the Eagle Nebula

"Dust Clouds in the Eagle Nebula" is a hand cut paper installation created for the "Cutpaper" exhibition at the Bowery Gallery, Leeds. Inspired by photography from the Hubble space telescope, Andy Singleton attempts to explore the scale, intricacy and beauty of our universe. Choosing the medium of large scale paper cuttings, he hopes to inspire the same sense of awe that we feel when we look into the deepest regions of space. The work stretches 8 meters across and is 1.3m in width. The piece was entirely hand cut.

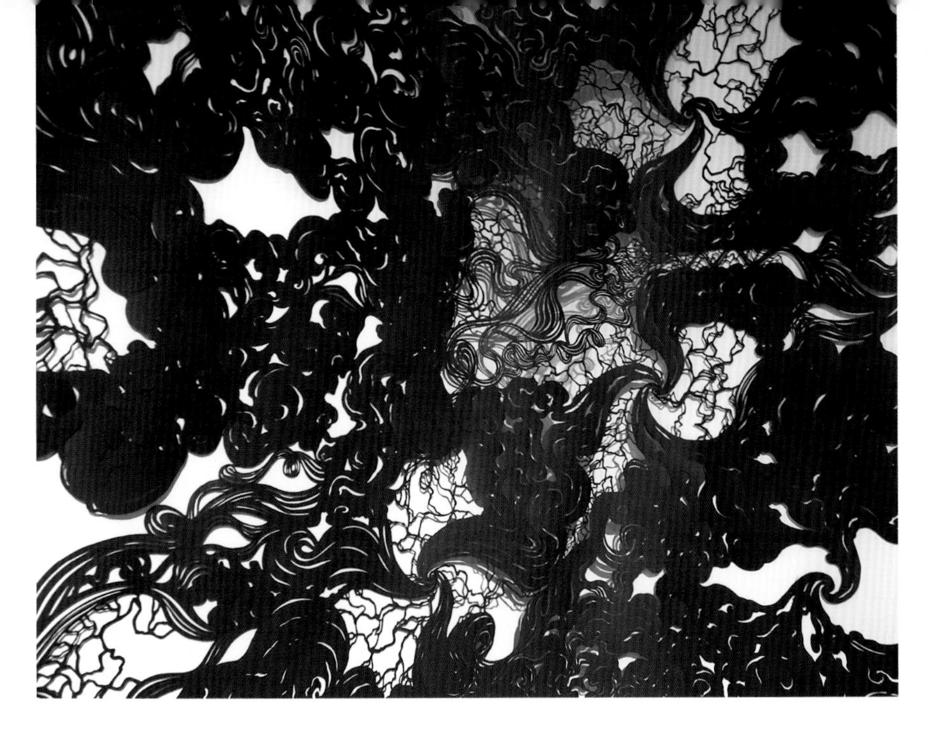

Work Type Installation Technique Hand cutting

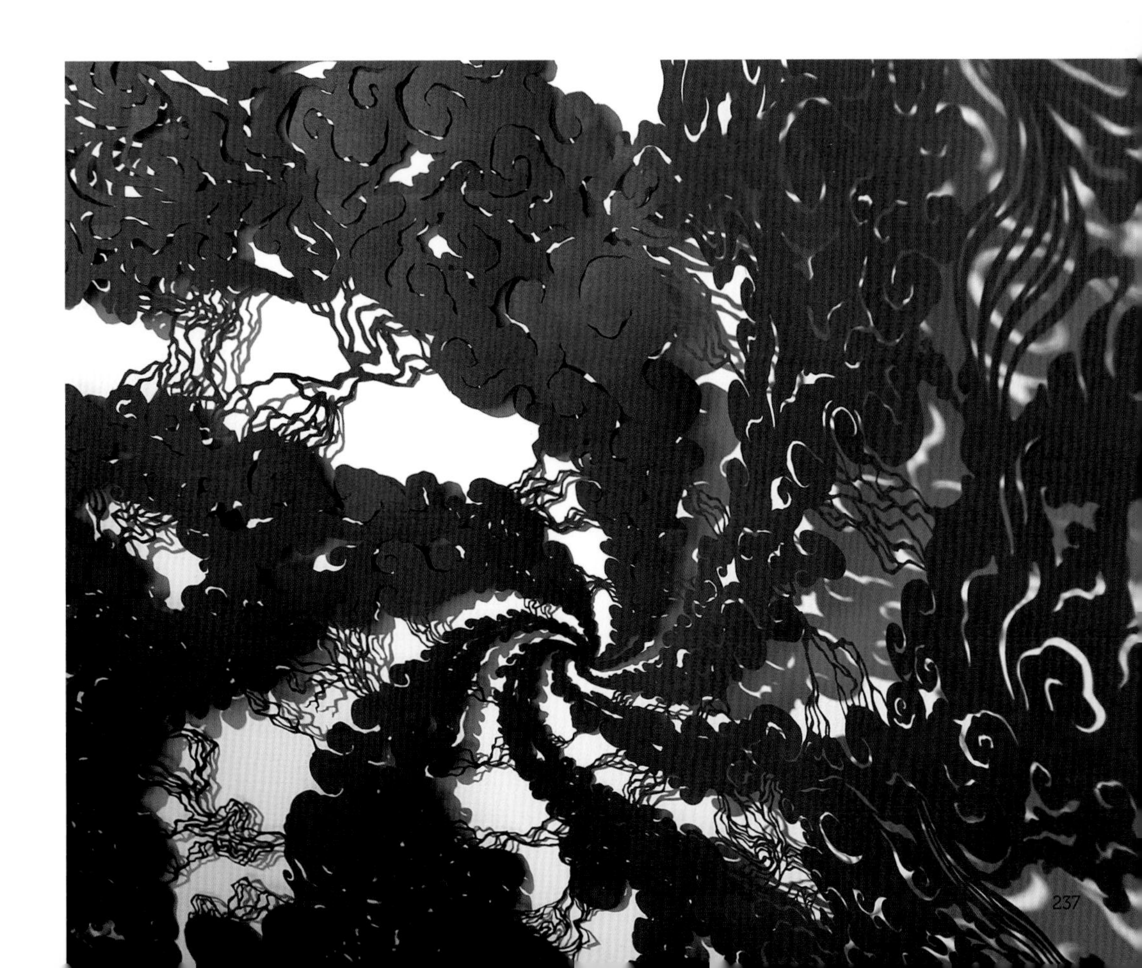

Designer Charlotte McGowan-Griffin Photographer 1, 2, 3 Kay Riechers / 6-11 Patricia Sevilla Ciordia

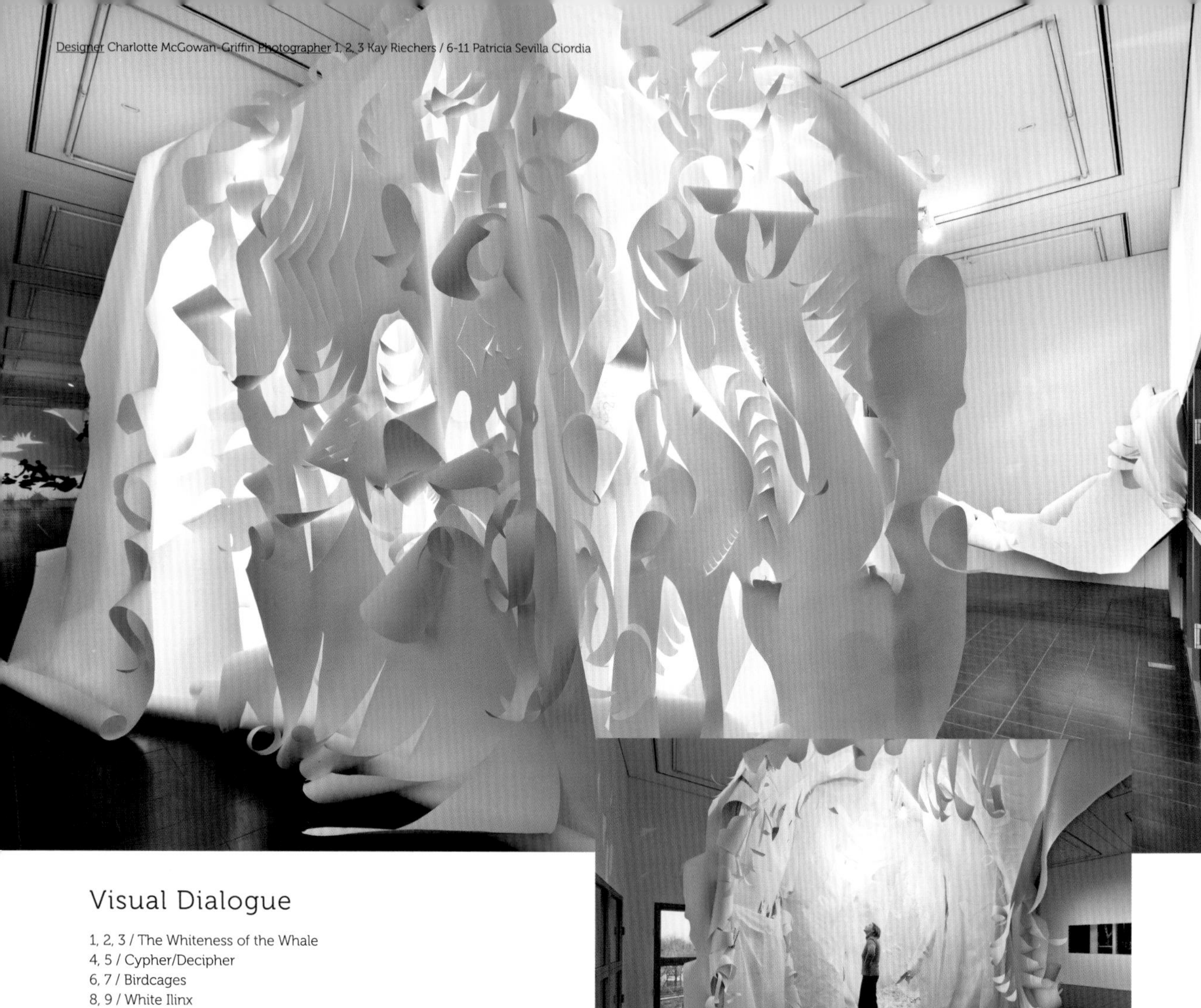

2

Visual Dialogue

1, 2, 3 / The Whiteness of the Whale
4, 5 / Cypher/Decipher
6, 7 / Birdcages
8, 9 / White Ilinx
10, 11 / Brainstorming

Charlotte McGowan-Griffin's cut paper work contains a complex visual language, juxtaposing symbols from the natural world with areas of ornamentation as well as looser, more gestural cuts. In her installation works, sculptural forms are silhouetted against a delicate sub-layer of illumination, projection and shadow, while her two-dimensional works, which feature landscapes populated by birds, birdcages, and mysterious areas of pattern, display the bolder aesthetic of traditional paper-cut silhouettes.

Since 2008 the artist complements her cutout works with a technique which she calls "cutting in", which not only contrasts with the standardised term "cutting out", but also references a chapter of Herman Melville's novel Moby-Dick, on which she based her installation project The Whiteness of the Whale (2009-10). Here the blank paper is hung before it is cut, and a long blade is used to slice into the paper. The cut pieces are left in the work, and in this way build up to form a textured, multi-layered sculptural relief.

During her numerous research visits to Japan, Charlotte has become increasingly interested in the specific associations and meanings that are transmitted through the visual and haptic qualities of different types of paper, and her most recent works are also explorations of these connotations.

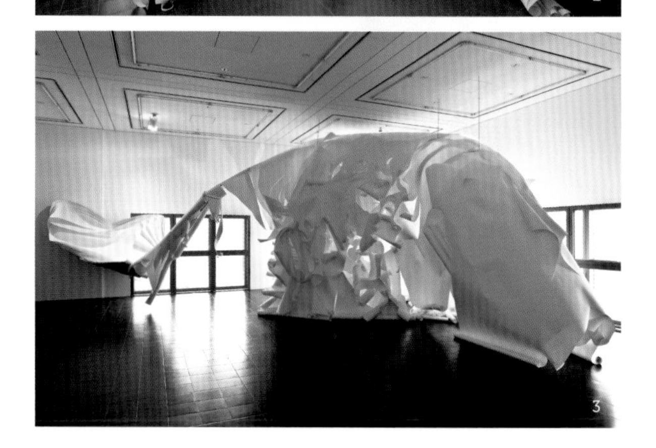

3

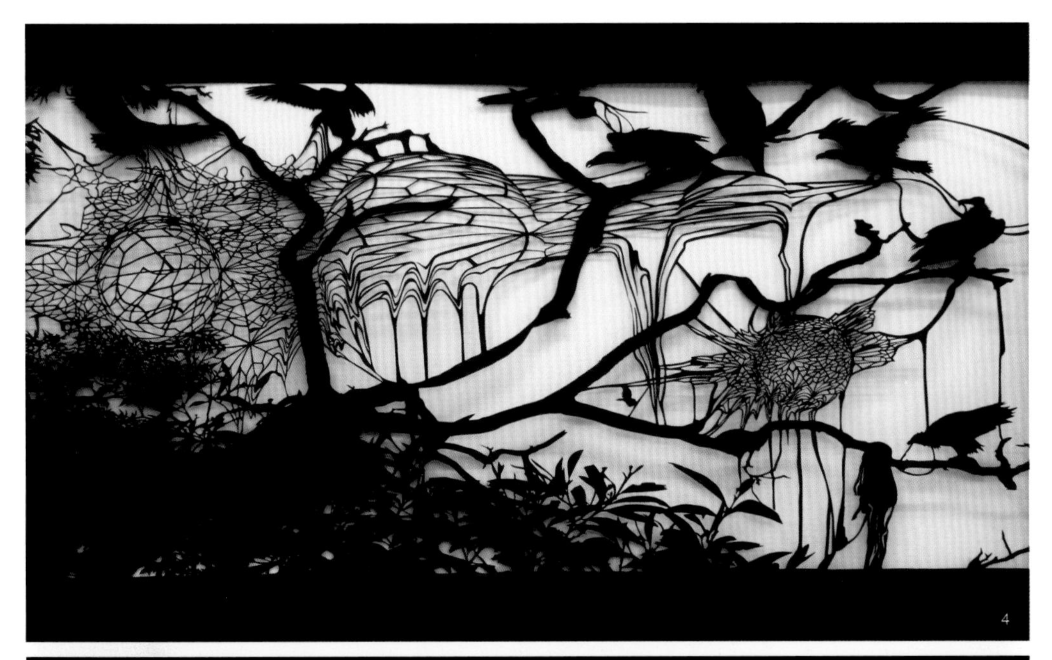

4

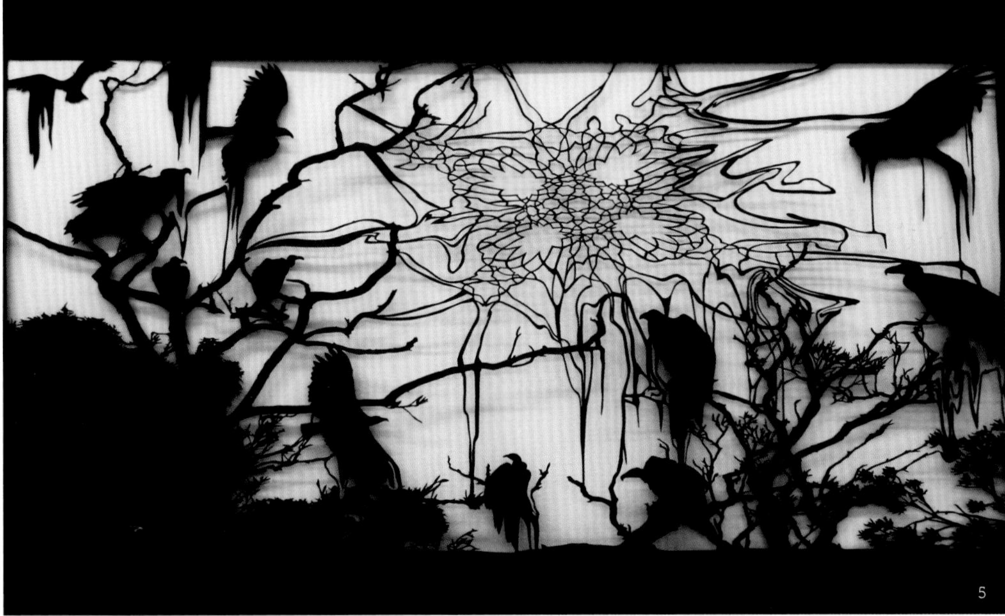

5

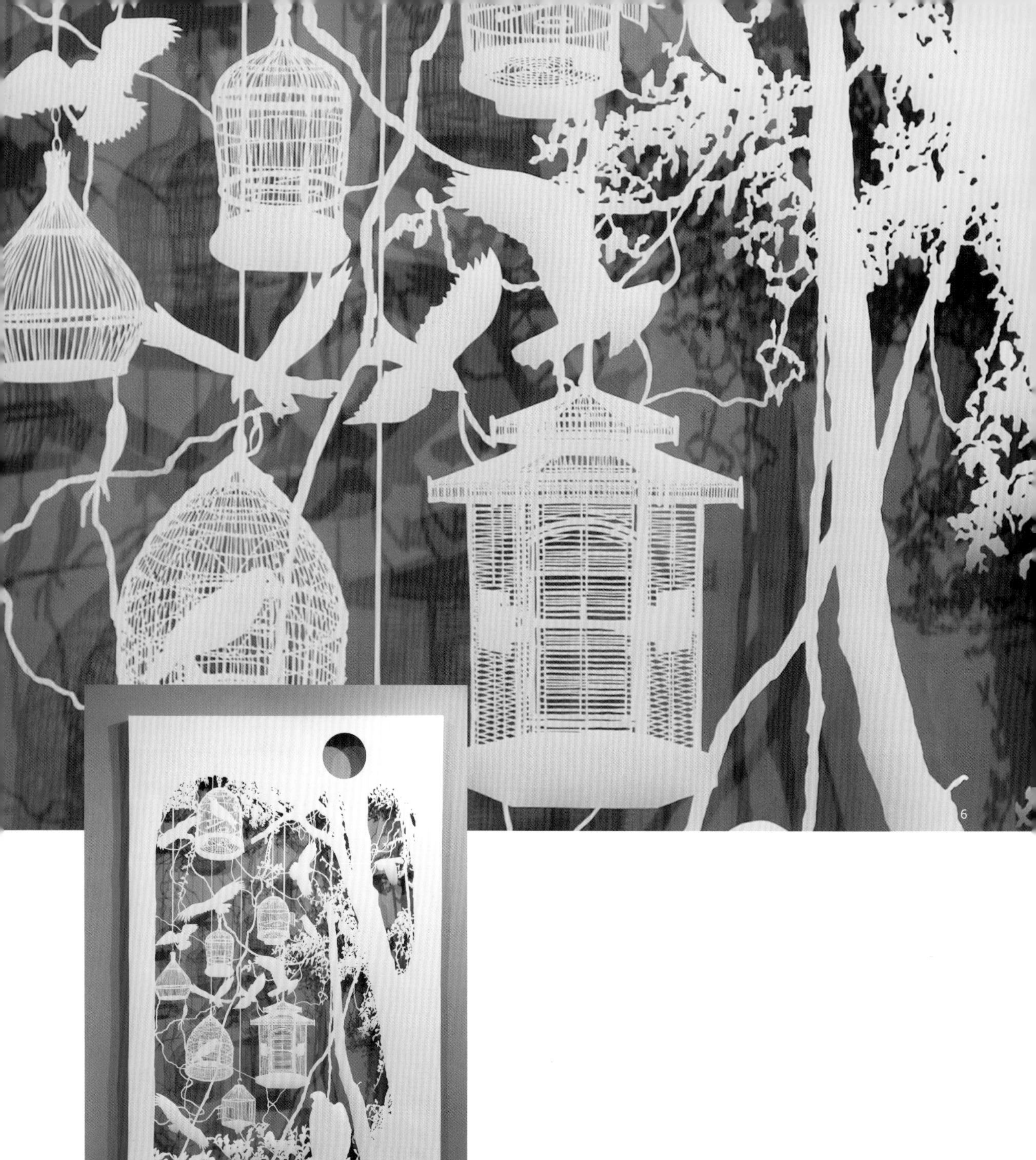
6
7

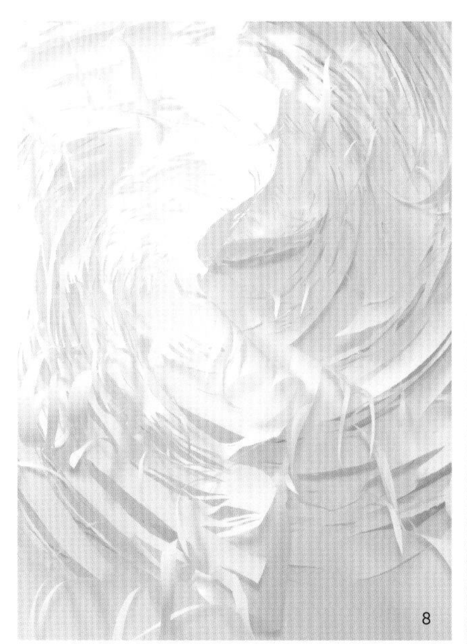
8

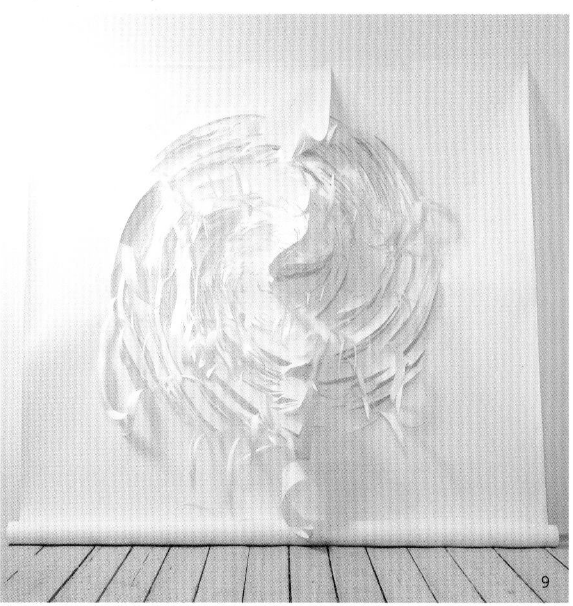
9

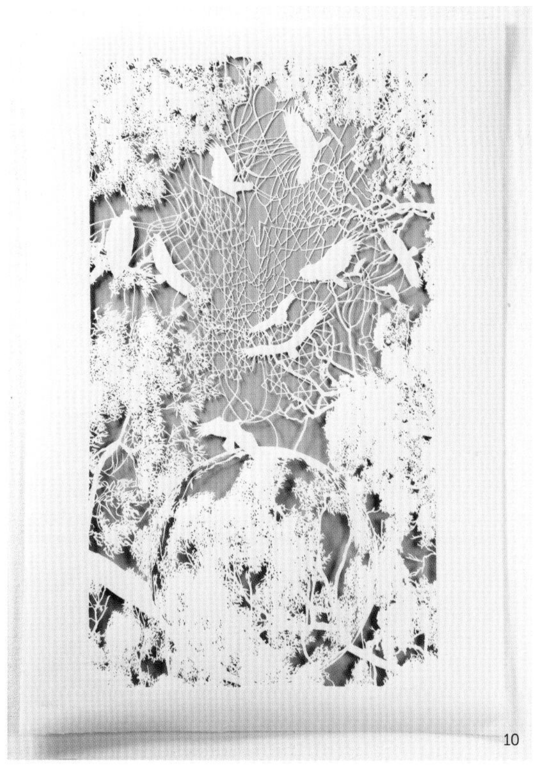
10

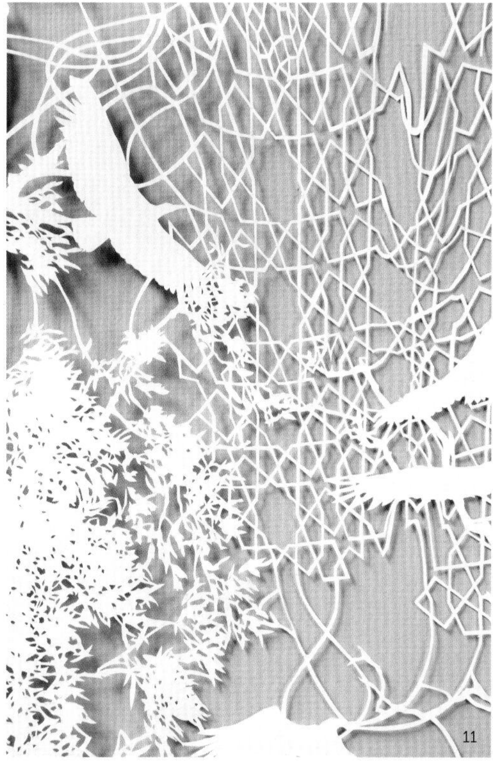
11

Designer Andy Singleton Photographer Andy Singleton, Nick Singleton Client Oriel Mostyn Gallery

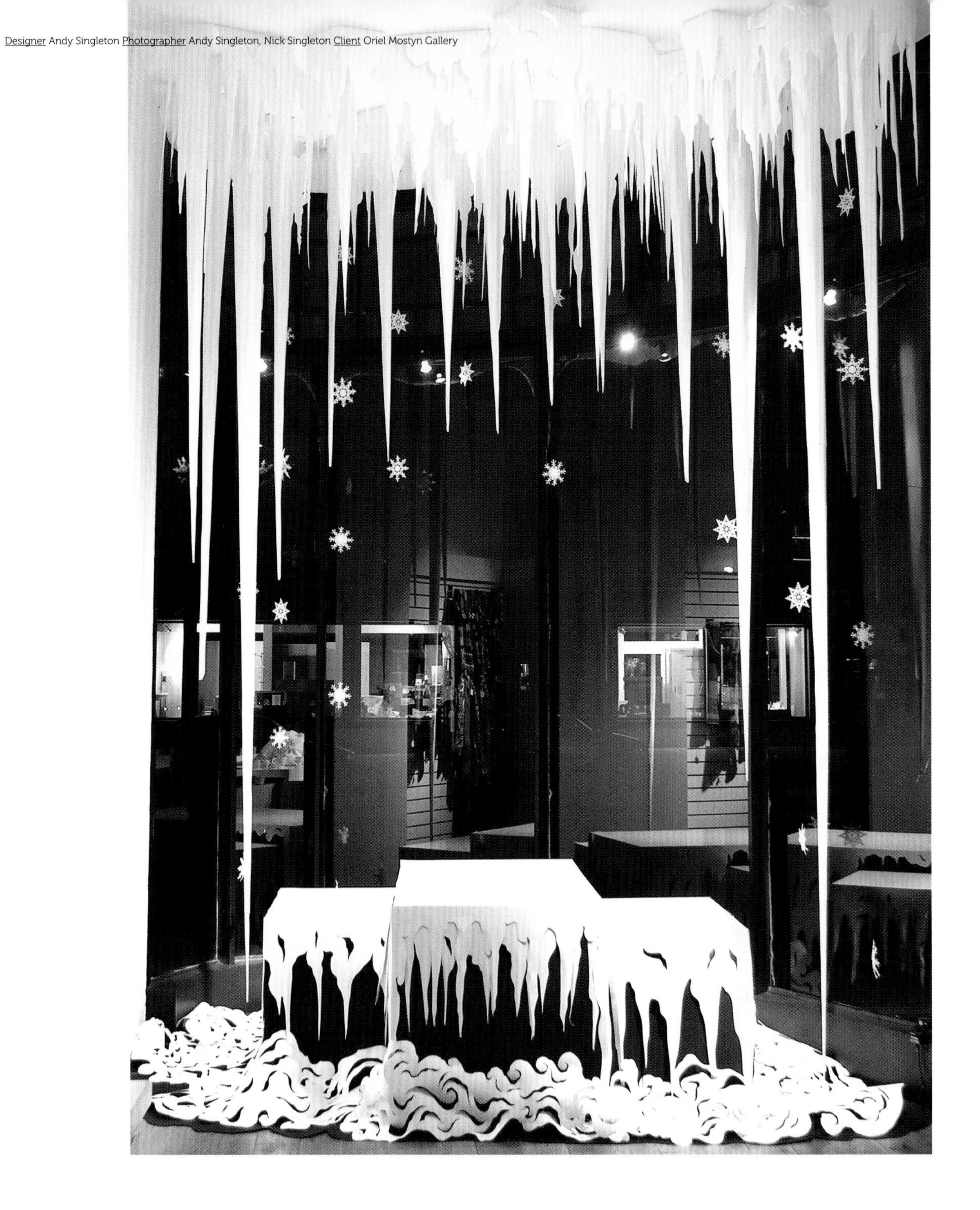

"Ice Caverns" Winter Window Installation

Andy Singleton was commissioned to create a winter window installation at the Oriel Mostyn Gallery in 2010. Singleton handmade 3D icicle sculptures and combined them with flowing 2D paper cut pieces to form the "ice caverns." The paper was finished with an iridescent glitter to add to the effect of sparkling ice formations.

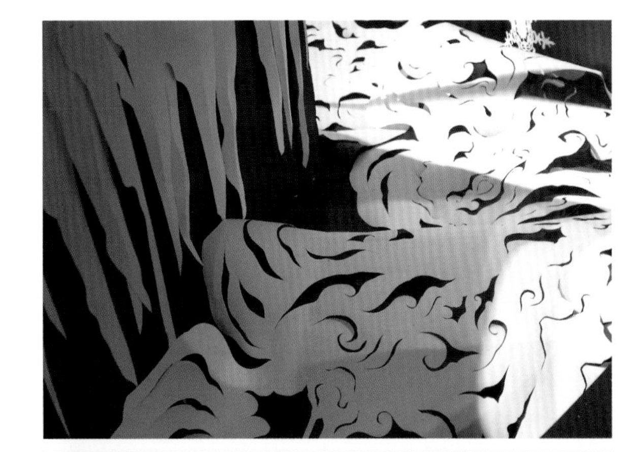

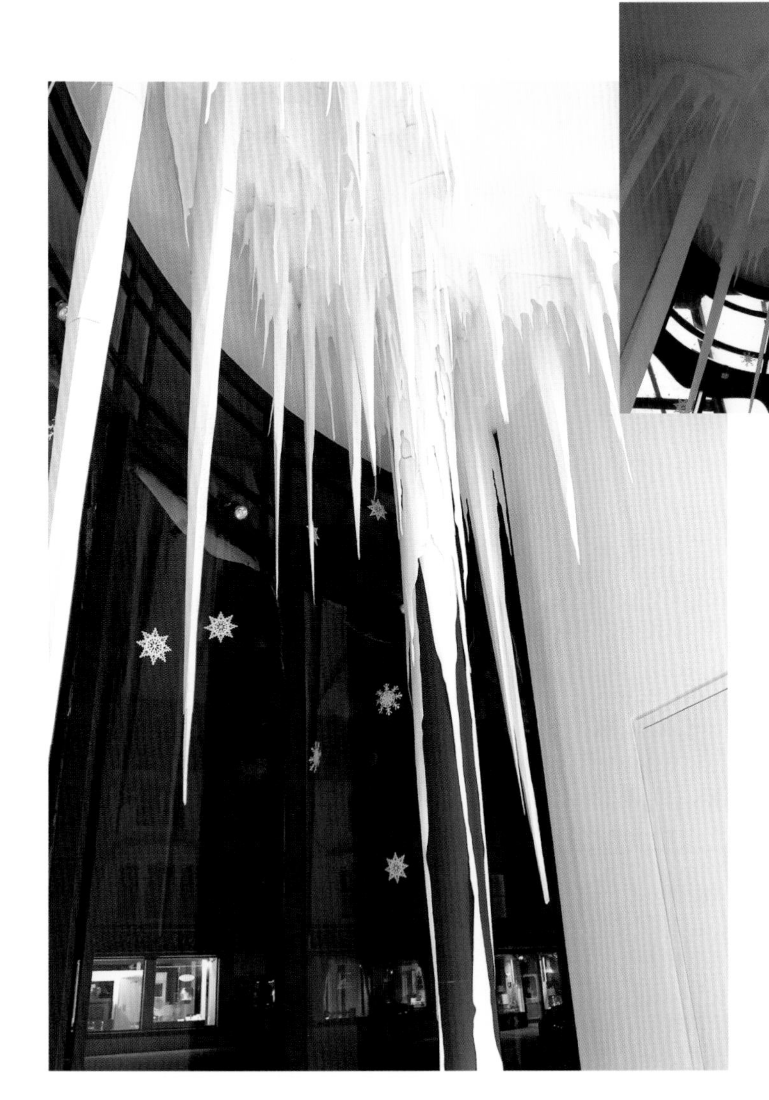

Finest Paperware

The Finest Paperware series is a response to modern throwaway culture. Our habits of consumption have changed and convenience and fashion take precedent. Consumption is increasingly more about having, using, and discarding objects, rather than about acquiring and cherishing them. The disposable paper cup is an icon of this trend in consumerism, and so here I have created a range of paperware that mimics traditional ceramic aesthetics, transposing the ceramic context onto the throwaway object.

To create "a symmetry of opposites" some of these cups are assembled from cast sheets of handmade paper; others are hand-built from sheets of a specially formulated porcelain and paper pulp mixture. The "Jasperware" set emulates Wedgewood's iconic range using stained paper and porcelain, and embossed relief details in white. The Dutch classic "Blue Delft" is alluded to in hand drawn details in blue biro, which have been scanned and digitally transformed into enamel decals for application to porcelain.

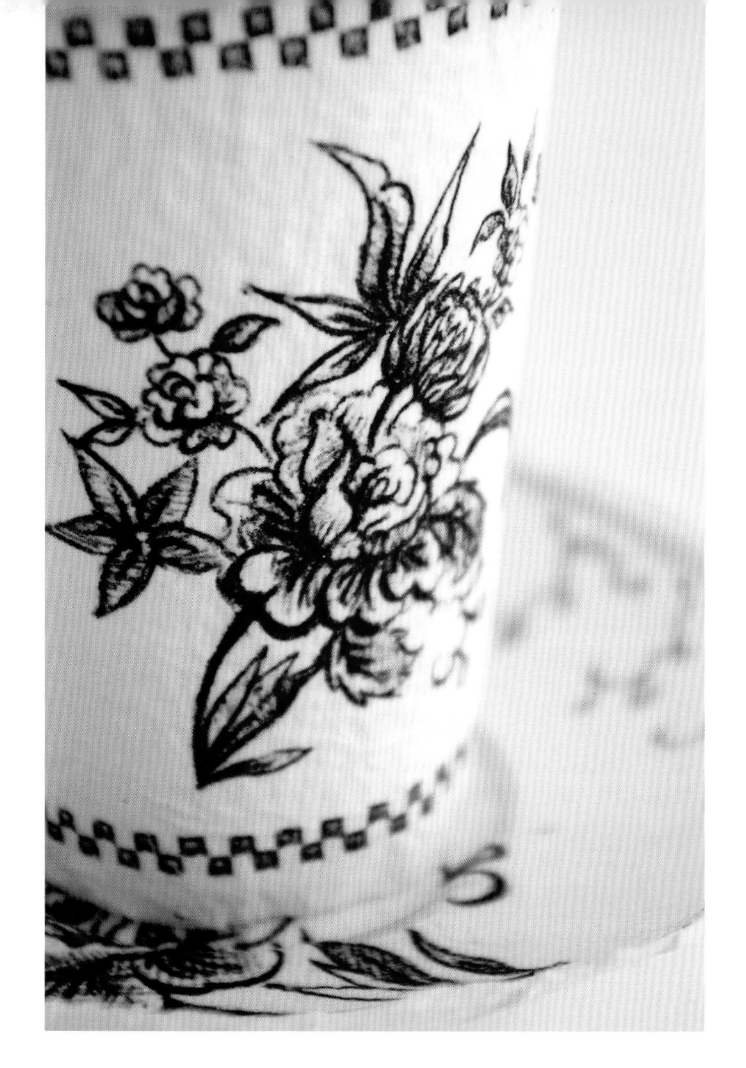

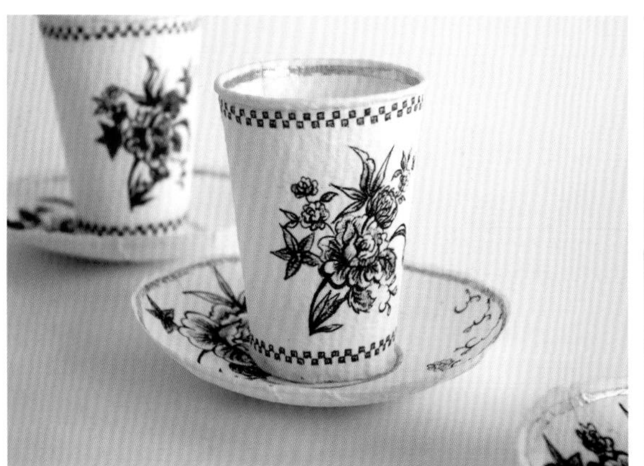

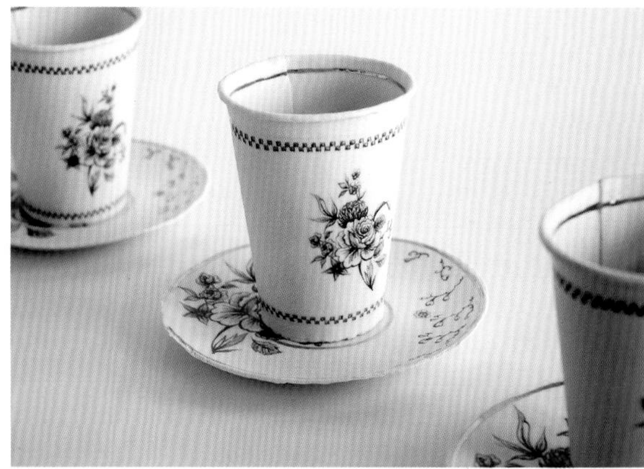

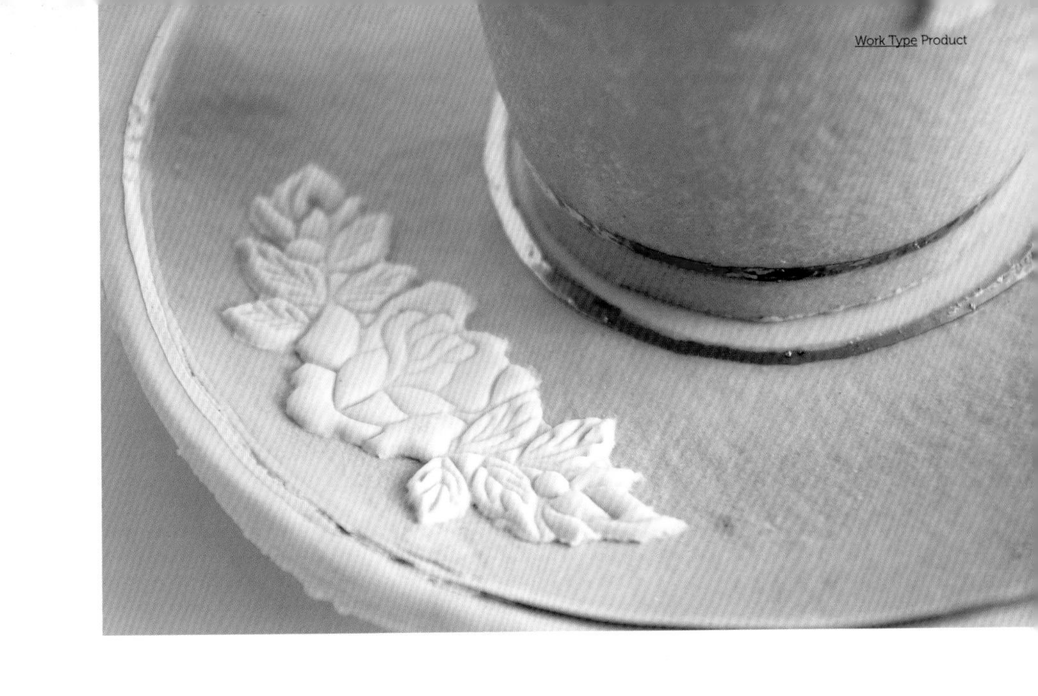

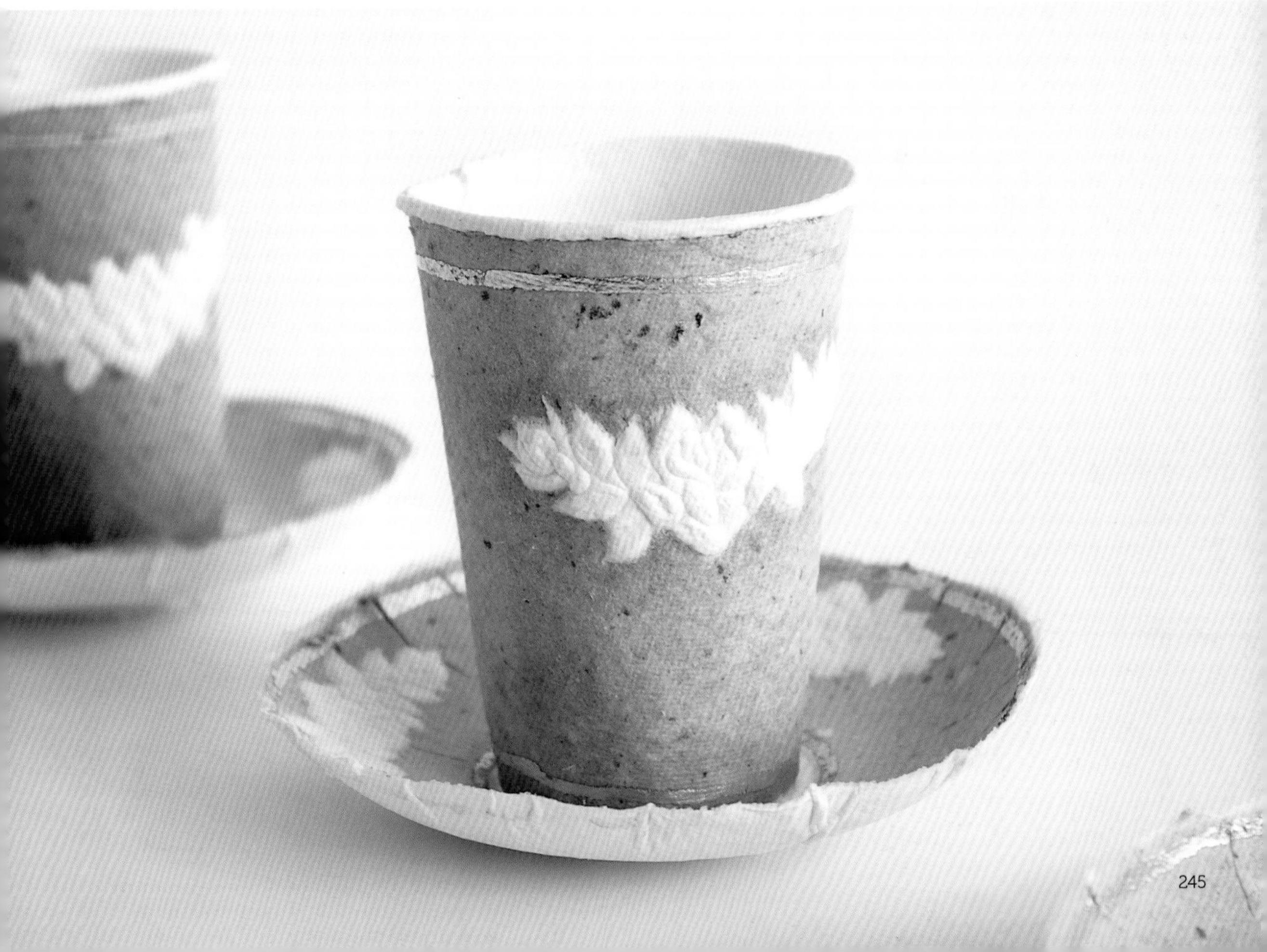

Vessel

1 / Blue Iris in Vessel
2 / Lavender in Vessel
3 / Singapore Orchid in Vessel
4 / Crucifix Orchid in Vessel
5 / Ginger Flower in Vessel
6-7 / Vessel Exhibition

My sculptural practice relies on a variety of images drawn from the natural world. Recently this has involved the hand-crafted removal of natural forms from domestic and commercial objects. Individual pages of books and paper stacks are carved with a scalpel to create a hollowed out space reserved for a variety of carefully-rendered bird and plant species. Thousands of holes were drilled into Venetian blinds to allow a new "view" of plant life to stream through a window. Large sections were cut out from a tower of plywood to reveal the elegant form of a potted plant. In each instance my work is presented with the intention of creating a multiplicity of readings both conceptual and personal. My pieces prompt the viewer to entertain the significance of the absent form and fill this space with ideas from the profound to the pragmatic.

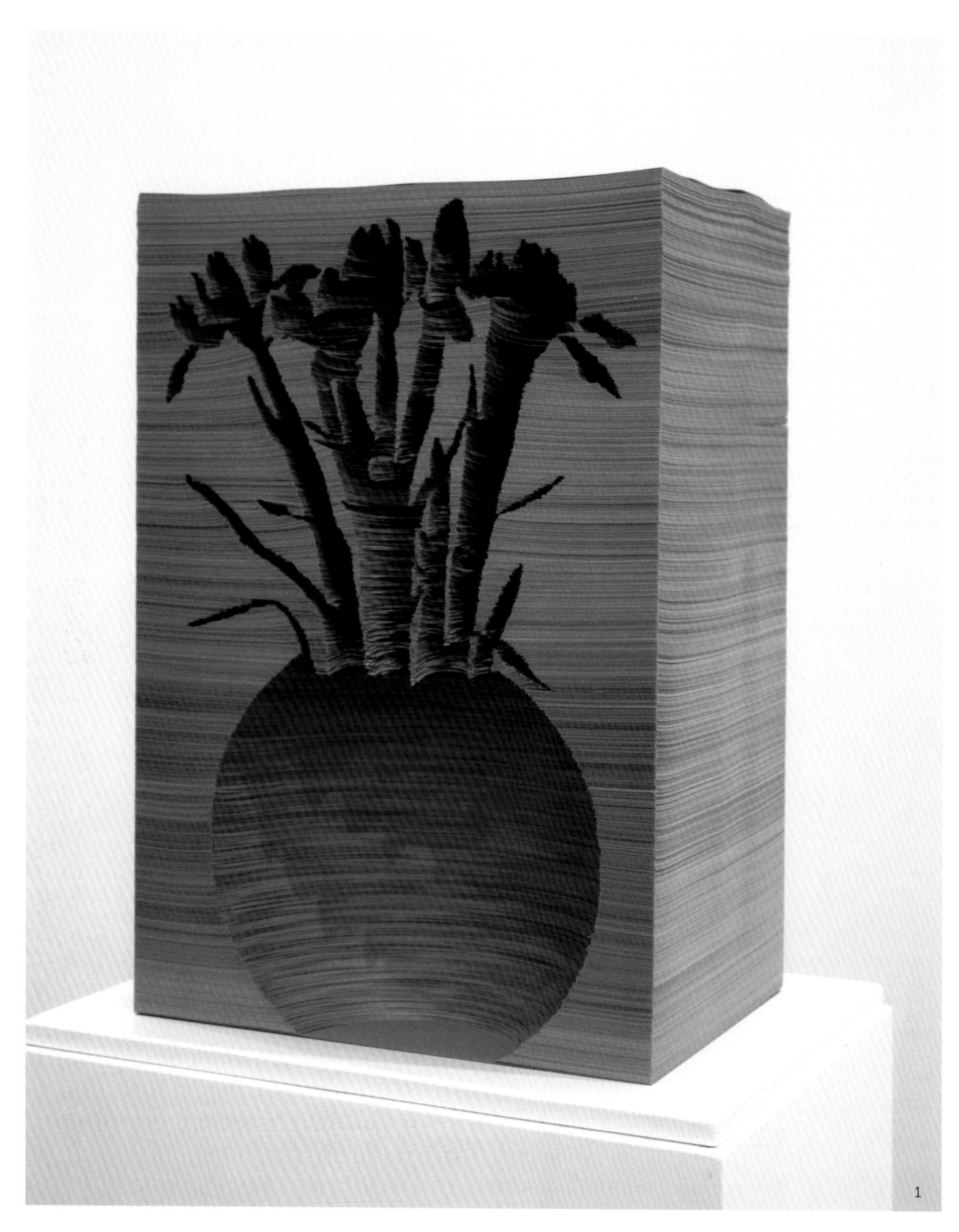

1

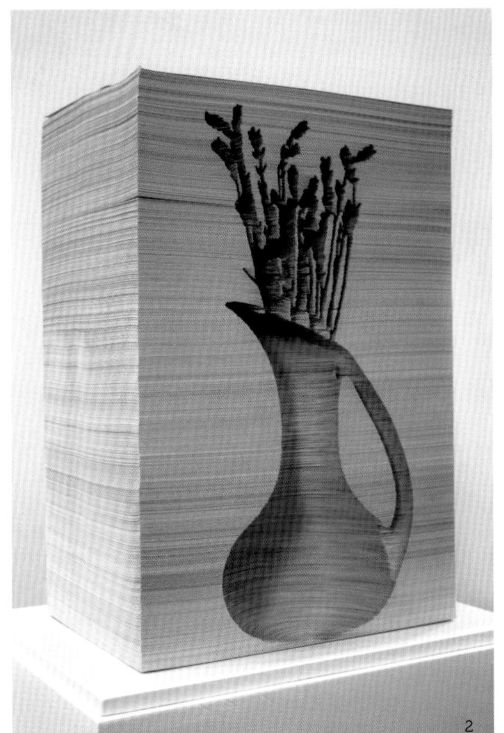
2

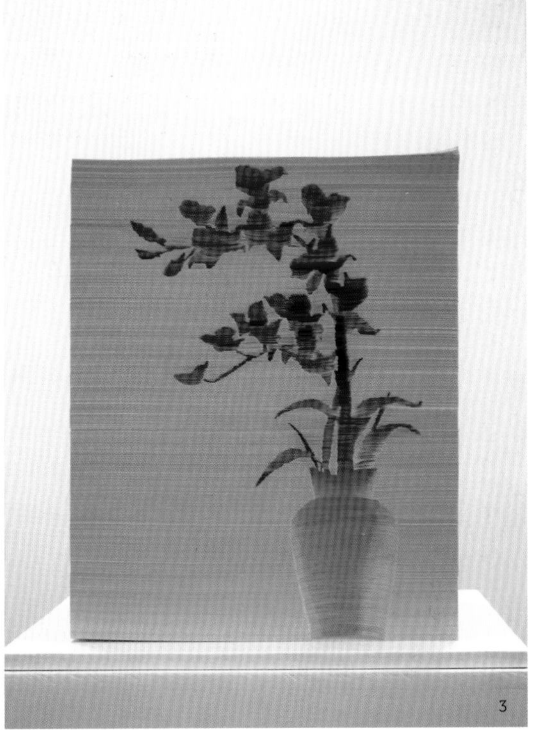
3

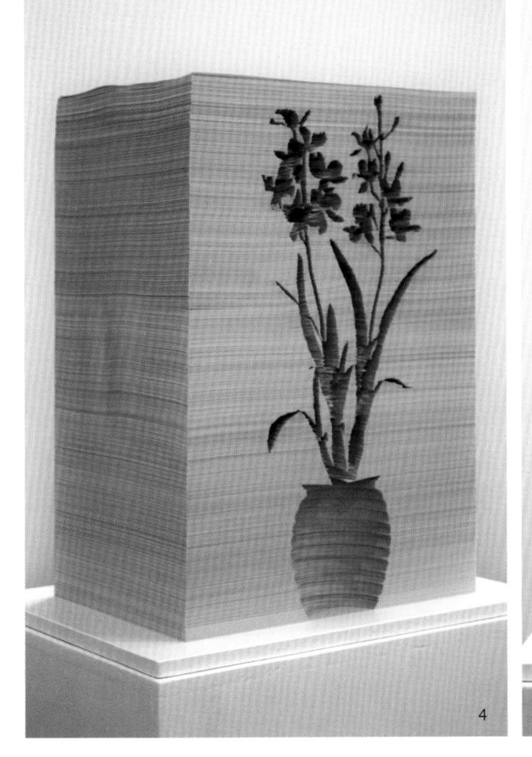
4

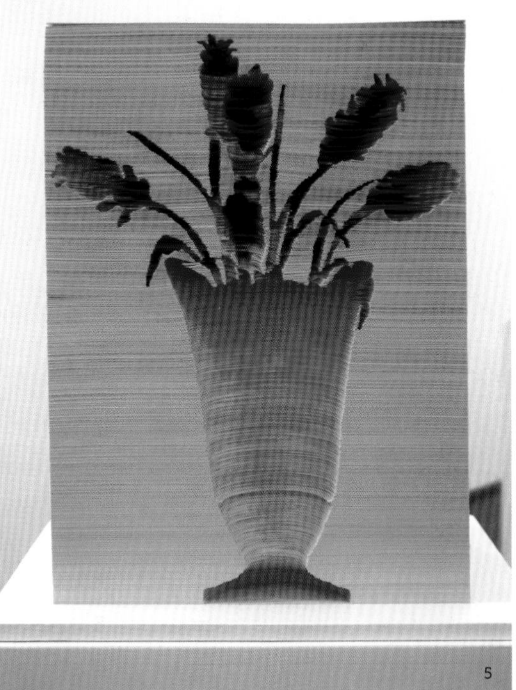
5

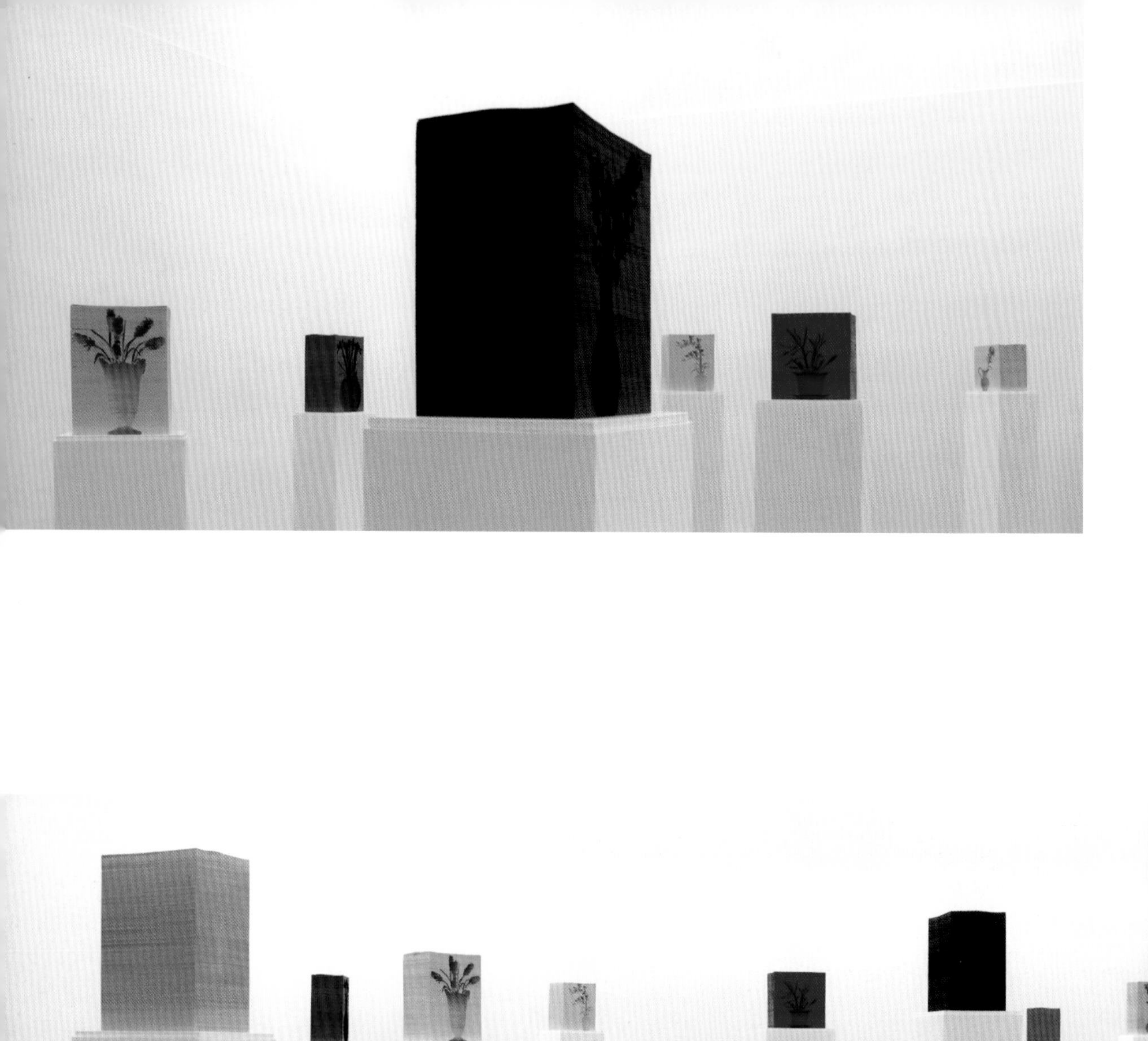

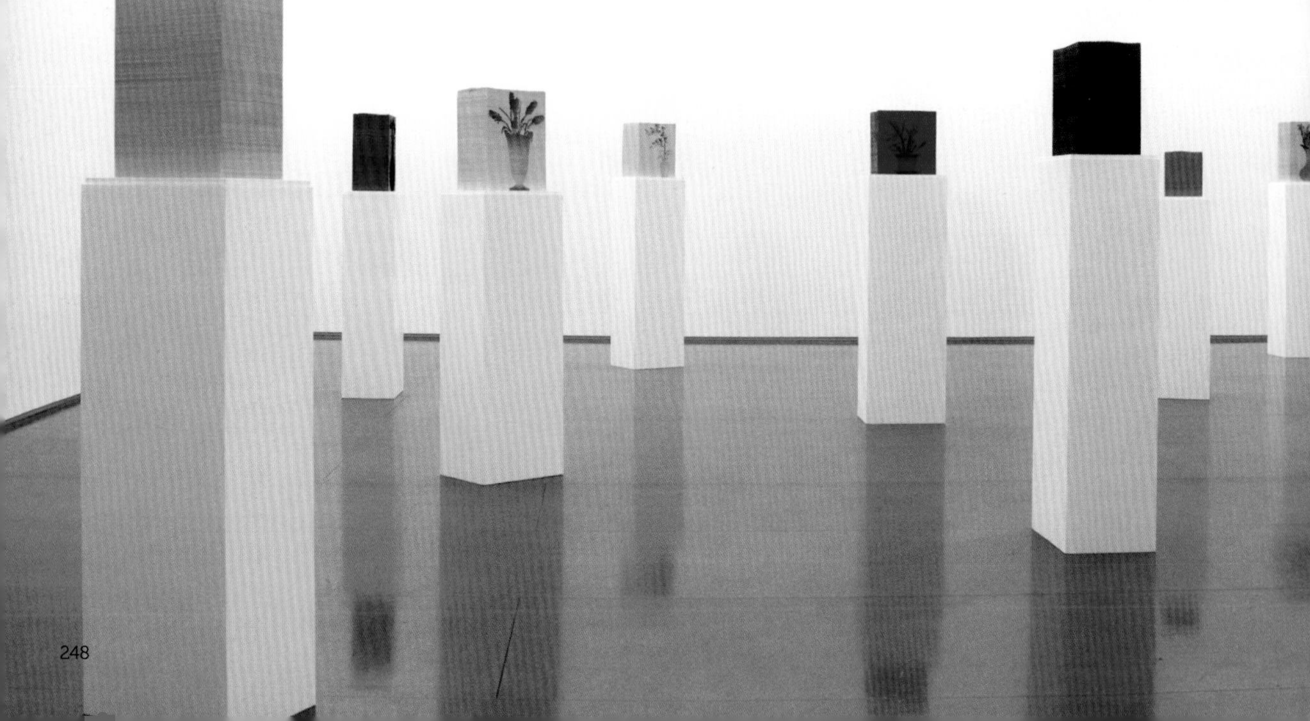

24°Studio

www.24d-studio.com
USA / Japan p.042-043

24° Studio is a multidisciplinary practice established by Fumio Hirakawa and Marina Topunova in 2008. We dedicate our investigation to working at the intersection of architecture, technology and environment. We collaborate with our vast network of experts to deliver new solutions to our clients and audiences in order to realize their goals. With ever changing global movements bringing us limitless inspirations, 24° Studio believes that the process of integrating multiple perspectives will lead to innovative results, thus redefining the connection between our body and our surroundings.

Adriane Colburn

www.adrianecolburn.com
USA p.128-129

Adriane Colburn is an artist based in San Francisco, CA and Athens, Georgia. She has exhibited her work throughout the US and internationally. She has been an artist in residence at the Headlands Center for the Arts, the Macdowell Colony, the Kala Institute and The Blue Mountain Center. Adriane's work consists of large-scale installations (comprised of layers of hand cut paper, digital prints and projected light) that investigate the complex relationships between human infrastructure, earth systems, technology and the natural world.

Amy Lau

www.amylaudesign.com
USA p.068-069

Amy Lau is a New York-based designer; she founded her interiors firm in 2001. From her headquarters in the West Chelsea arts district, she brings imagination and energy to furnishings, fabrics, and installations. Inspired by her passion for nature and abstract art, she combines expressive color with soft, organic shapes. Her love of form is reflected in the work, which balances scale, texture, and influences through the lens of modernism. Amy Lau Design creates refined, elegant, and optimistic spaces that are more curated than decorated.

Anastassia Elias

www.anastassia-elias.com
France p.076-077

Anastassia Elias was born in 1976. She completed philology and journalism studies. She lives in Paris, France now. As a full-time artist and illustrator, she mainly makes paper collages and paintings. She recently illustrated two children's books, both published in France.

Andy Singleton

www.andysingleton.co.uk
UK p.116 / p.147 / p.236-237 / p.242-243

Andy Singleton is a paper artist and illustrator based in Wakefield, England. He studied Animation with Illustration at Manchester Metropolitan University. His work is an exploration of the natural and manmade world through intricate paper cuttings, paper sculpture and hand drawn illustrations, working on both personal and commercial projects. Andy has produced work for a variety of clients, including the Crafts Council, Liberty, Hermés, The Hepworth and Lazerian. He has produced varied work for site specific installations, window displays, illustration, brand graphic, apparel and interiors.

Annie Vought

www.annievought.com
USA p.126-127

Annie Vought, born in 1977, is an artist based in Oakland, California. Her work explores people's emotional artifacts, specifically the handwritten letter. She has a far reaching presence on the web and has exhibited extensively. In 2009 Annie received her MFA from Mills College. Annie was raised in Santa Fe, New Mexico. Her growth is surrounded by the arts. Her father is a painter and her mother and stepfather are musicians. She now lives in Oakland with her husband and one large dog.

Ashburn Eng

www.testshootgallery.com
Singapore p.040-041

Having gained much success and recognition as a fashion stylist and creative director of Test Shoot Gallery, Ashburn Eng was the recipient of 2 top prizes (overall winner as well as best stylist) in the 2009 Iconique Societas Awards. Ashburn never fails to impart advice to the countless designers that he has worked with. Throughout the many years of his styling career, these designers have greatly benefited from his words-of-wisdom on clothing presentation and corrections.

Béatrice Coron

www.beatricecoron.com
USA p.052-053

Béatrice Coron tells stories inspired by life. Her own life colors her work: after briefly studying art at the Ecole des Beaux-Arts of Lyon, and Mandarin Chinese at the Université of Lyon III, Coron experienced life with a series of odd jobs. She has been, among others, a shepherdess, truck driver, factory worker, cleaning lady and New York City tour guide. She lived in France (her native country), Egypt and Mexico for one year each, and China for two years. She moved to New York in 1985, where she reinvented herself as an artist. Coron's oeuvre includes illustration, book arts, fine art and public art. She cuts her characteristic silhouette designs in paper and Tyvek. She also creates works in stone, glass, metal, rubber, stained glass and digital media. Her work has been purchased by major museum collections, such as the Metropolitan Museum, the Walker Art Center and The Getty. Her public art can be seen in subways, airports, and sports facilities among others.

Bianca Chang

www.biancachang.com
Australia p.192-193

Bianca Chang is a young designer, paper artist and image maker based in Sydney. After studying at the Queensland College of Art, she started her career working as an editorial designer in Singapore before relocating to Sydney. Armed with a love of type and wanting to explore it in three dimensions, she started working on a series of hand-cut graphic paper sculptures which she has since exhibited and continues to develop through gallery showings and private commissions. Bianca now works as a designer at Mark Gowing Design.

Blast

www.blast.co.uk
UK p.168-169

Established in 1996, Blast is a leading London based brand identity and communications design consultancy. They work across a variety of sectors, producing creative, effective brand strategies, identities, campaigns, publications and online communications.

Bovey Lee Studio

www.boveylee.com
China / Hong Kong p.114-115

Bovey Lee is a cut paper artist known for her highly intricate works hand cut on Chinese rice (xuan) paper. She was born in Hong Kong and is based in Pittsburgh, Pennsylvania, USA. Since 2005, Bovey has been creating cut paper works that combine her disparate expertise in both traditional and digital media. Her works have been exhibited at museums, galleries, and art fairs around the world. Her works are represented in the permanent collection of the Ashmolean Museum of Art at Oxford University, Fidelity Investments, and the Hong Kong Museum of Art, among others. Bovey's international commission projects include Hugo Boss, F.P Journe, Pacific Place, Annabelle magazine, and others. In addition to having received numerous grants and awards, Bovey's works have also been published in several books on paper art. Grotto Fine Art in Hong Kong and Rena Bransten Gallery in San Francisco, CA represent her works.

Brian Dettmer

www.briandettmer.com
USA p.072-075

Brian Dettmer is known for his detailed and innovative sculptures with books and other forms of tangible media. He is represented by Kinz + Tillou (New York), Packer Schopf (Chicago), MiTO (Barcelona), Toomey Tourell (San Francisco) and Saltworks (Atlanta). Dettmer's work has been exhibited internationally in several galleries, museums and art centers including the Museum of Arts and Design (NY), Museum of Contemporary Art (GA), the International Museum of Surgical Science (IL), and Museum Rijswijh (Netherlands). His work can be found in several public and private collections throughout the U.S, Latin America and Europe.

Cecilia Levy

www.cecilialevy.com
Sweden p.206-209

Swedish designer/artist Cecilia Levy combines the professions of graphic design, bookbinding and illustration; she does commission work and is a member of the arts and crafts cooperative Kaleido in Uppsala, north of Stockholm, where her handmade paper products are sold. As an artist she works with paper, creating 3-dimensional objects or drawings in pencil or ink. Her art is exhibited in solo and group shows in Sweden and abroad.

Charles Clary

percusiveart.blogspot.com
USA p.170-171

Charles Clary was born in 1980 in Morristown, Tennessee. He received his BFA in painting with honors from Middle Tennessee State University and his MFA in painting from the Savannah College of Art and Design. As an artist, Charles has exhibited regionally, nationally, and internationally in numerous solo and group shows. In 2011, Charles was featured in numerous print and Internet interviews. He is also represented by The Diana Lowenstein Gallery in Miami Fl, and currently living and working in Murfreesboro,TN.

Charlotte McGowan-Griffin

www.mcgowan-griffin.net
UK p.238-241

Charlotte McGowan-Griffin was born in London, and graduated from the Fine Art course at London's

Goldsmiths College in 1997. Since then, paper cutting has been her primary medium. During a residency in Japan in 2004 she began to combine the technique with light, shadow and projection to create large-scale installations. Whereas her two-dimensional cut-paper works might borrow from traditional paper-cutting practices, her installation projects tend to be site-specific and are increasingly oriented towards experimental modes of working.

Christa Donner

www.christadonner.com
USA p.182-183

Chicago-based artist Christa Donner uses paper and ink to examine the human body and our relationships to it through sensation and imagination. Her most recent work investigates questions about the role of biology in culture, building from the social structures of wasps, bacteria, and other organisms to imagine new anatomies driving symbiotic human societies. Donner's drawings, installations and zines are widely exhibited internationally.

Claire Brewster

clairebrewster.co.uk
UK p.058-059

I have been living and working in London for over 20 years, but started life in the semi-rural county of Lincolnshire. Using old maps, atlases and other found paper, I create beautiful, delicate and intricate paper cuts of flowers, birds and insects. My inspiration comes from nature and the urban environment in which I live and a desire to re-use the discarded, unwanted and obsolete. I exhibit my work nationally and internationally, showing regularly in London, other parts of the UK, USA, France, Germany and Italy. My work has been published in many magazines including: Vogue (UK and Greece), World of Interiors, Inside Out (Australia) and was featured in the book" Paper: Tear, Fold, Rip, Crease, Cut" (Blackdog Publishing 2009). I was commissioned to make a large scale work for the Corinthia hotel in London in 2011 and I have upcoming shows in the London Transport Museum (part of Cultural Olympiad 2012 and Manchester City Art Gallery, UK.

Clare Pentlow

www.cjpdesigns.co.uk
UK p.056-057

While studying Surface Pattern Design at University I became suddenly fascinated by paper and I started upon an exploration of the material working with the transformation of paper from a flat, basic material to a folded, cut and sculpted piece of art. This exploration is still continuing and I'm finding many new and exciting ways of changing the surface dynamics of an ordinary material and challenging people's perceptions of such an everyday material.

Daniele Papuli

www.danielepapuli.net
Italy p.224-227

Daniele Papuli was born in 1971 at Maglie, Puglia. His first approach to sculpture dates back to 1991 with his earliest stone, wood and plaster artefacts. In 1993, on the occasion of an international workshop in Berlin, he learned methods for manufacturing sheet paper. It was a crucial experience that brought him in 1995 to choose paper as the most suitable material for his research and his own language. He then experimented with the production of handmade paper and in 1997 made his first sculptures with different types of paper material. He proceeds more like an explorer than like a designer, transferring and amplifying images and suggestions of a design path undertaken on paper.

Elisabeth Lecourt

www.elisabethlecourt.com
France p.080-081

Elisabeth Lecourt was born in Oloron Saint Marie, France then moved to London to gain her MA at The Royal College of Art. She now exhibits in Europe, Asia and the USA. Lecourt's art is one of disclosure, using life events in works ranging from story telling, drawing, installation, painting, embroidered handkerchiefs and sculpture. Within "Les Robes Géographiques" Lecourt uses maps forming clothes and garments as a "rubbing" of the body and soul. It's a continuation of personal thoughts found throughout her work, which she creates using a range of materials to provoke and extract emotions.

Estudio Rosa Lázaro

www.rlazaro.com
Spain p.178-179

Since 1990, we have taken on every aspect of each project: conceptualization, art direction, design and production for both private sector and institutions, nationally and internationally. We do product development, packaging, naming, branding, editing, press, content management, identity, applied graphics, exhibitions and institutional communication. Our method is to work as a team with professionals and specialists: industrial designers, copywriters, journalists, curators, architects, interior designers, photographers, illustrators, programmers, motion graphics specialists...

Flóra Vági

www.floravagi.com
Hungary p.220-221

There are things we can think of, things we can name. Like 'bread', 'pane', 'kenyer', 'chlieb' and so on. But there are also lots of things we have no words for. Search, discover, transform.... surprise, all parts of the process I apply to the pieces. The materials get a 'return ticket' from me, and with their 'newly dressed souls' I send them back to the world, where they came from.

I make objects that are intimate and meaningful to their owners who carry them: jewelry, which not only adorns, but 'talks' or sometimes 'whispers'. I work in a language that is understood without words and the verbal explanation becomes secondary really, so...

Grégoire Alexandre

www.gregoirealexandre.com
France p.152-153

Normandy-born Grégoire Alexandre is now stationed in Paris. Because photography is his great interest, which gives him a greater sense of control and allows him to take something out of reality without having to set it up first, Alexandre takes photography as his career. Now he is a young talented photographer, and had quite an impressive and unique portfolio, ranging from advertising to high end editorial. He would like to create some amazing sets and props to help him capture the most beautiful images.

GAIAdesign

www.veasyble.com
Italy p.024-027

Four People + talking + occasional silence x time spent eating together = Problem Solution. Gloria, Arianna, Ilaria and Adele met at ISIA Firenze and reached immediate understanding and collaboration on projects of Product & Communication Design. They all reflect and work with inspiration and creativity on the issues of living, the spatial and conceptual barriers/boundaries, and the expression of the self in the domestic and urban environment.

Gonçalo Campos

www.goncalocampos.com
Portugal p.018-019

Gonçalo Campos (born 1986) is a Portuguese product designer. Graduating in product design in 2008, he soon after joined Fabrica, Benetton's communications research centre, in the design studio. This gave him the chance to work with brands such as SecondoMe, Seletti or Zanotta. In 2009, he worked in Sam Baron's studio. He is currently developing a series of objects, continuing to explore the possibilities of design through function and material. Campos prides himself on finding simple solutions, through the sound use of materials and production methods, in a process that starts from within the object and travels towards the outside. This results in recognizable "smart" objects, often with a certain humor; a relaxed way of thinking, and a curious attitude.

Hattie Newman

www.hattienewman.co.uk
UK p.146

Originally from the quiet countryside of Devon UK, Hattie studied Illustration in Bristol, graduating with a First Class BA (Hons) before moving to London to work as a Freelance Illustrator and Set Designer. Her colorful and optimistic style, alongside a passion for paper has led her to work on a breadth of projects including children's books, animation, set design, and window displays.

Hina Aoyama

hinaaoyama.com
France p.054-055

Hina Aoyama was born in Yokohama, Japan in 1970. She is a super fine lacy-paper-cutting artist. She started super fine Lacy-paper-cuttings in 2000. She currently lives and works in Ferney Volaire, France.

Hiroko Matsushita

www.hirokomatsushita.com
UK p.066-067

Hiroko's practice is placed within a realm of visual art, illustration and design using paper. She has been inspired by paper-engineering skills such as folding, cutting-out and layering that are primitive but creative techniques. A flat sheet of paper can be transformed in an instant into figures that expand into space, thus paper is a very malleable and imaginative material for her.

Her work explores a correlation between people and narrative as a cultural mirror. She often leads the audience to an open narrative aiming to stimulate their imagination and fantasy deriving from reminiscences in childhood. Folded or layered paper creates a sense of depth with shade and tone that makes theatrical ambience and the notion of front and back indicates there is a hidden story to be revealed behind a story we have been told.

Ingrid Siliakus

ingrid-siliakus.exto.org
the Netherlands p.140-143

Ingrid Siliakus first discovered paper architecture by seeing work by the originator of this art form Prof. Masahiro Chatani (an architect and professor in Japan), who developed this art form in the early 1980s. Ingrid was instantly fascinated by the ingenious manner in which these pieces were designed and by the beauty they radiated. Ingrid studied the originator's work for some years and then started to design herself. Ingrid states that working with this art form has given her personal means of expressing herself. Her design skills have grown over the years. Her specialties are buildings of master architects and intricate abstract sculptures. Her source of inspiration for these abstract sculptures is the work of artists like M.C. Escher. With buildings she feels attracted to the work of Berlage and Gaudi.

Jacob Dahlstrup Jensen

www.jacobdahlstrup.com
Denmark p.100-103

Jacob Dahlstrup Jensen was born in 1985 in Denmark. He gained a Bachelor of Fine Arts from The Glasgow School of Art, Scotland. He is currently living and working in Copenhagen, Denmark. The key to his practice is a process of calculated spontaneity and pre-planned coincidence through which he works primarily in a combination of drawing and installation. Through a merging of material and context he explores the visual language of nautical folklore, which tells the story of faith, hope, love, and the struggle to get to the non-existing point in the horizon.

Jeff Nishinaka

www.jeffnishinaka.com
USA p.106-107

Los Angeles native Jeff Nishinaka is the world's premier paper sculptor with a prolific career that spans 28 years. Nishinaka attended UCLA and graduated from the prestigious Art Center College of Design, where he first experimented with paper art and sculpture. Nishinaka began working in paper quite by accident. Nishinaka wanted to manipulate paper in the least invasive way, to keep the integrity and feel of it. Paper to him is a living, breathing thing that has a life of its own. He just tries to redirect that energy into something that feels animated and alive.

JK Keller

jk-keller.com
USA p.078-079

Jonathan Keller Keller, born in 1976 in Hutchinson, MN, is an artist currently living and working in Baltimore, MD. He received a Bachelors of Fine Arts in Interactive Multimedia from the Minneapolis College of Art + Design in 1999 and a Masters of Fine Arts from the Cranbrook Academy of Art in 2007. Working at the intersection of craft, collection, and computation, Keller seeks to transcend and transform everyday digital elements through obsessive, iterative, and generative processes. His online presence is felt widely throughout the internet, with video views in the millions, features on thousands of websites including NYTimes.com, BoingBoing, and the front page of Yahoo!. JK's work has been exhibited at Walker Art Center, Minneapolis, MN; Vögele Kultur Zentrum, Pfäffikon, Switzerland; I space Gallery, Chicago, IL; and the Australian Centre for Photography, Paddington, Australia; among other international galleries.

Johnny Kelly

www.nexusproductions.com
UK p.160-161

Johnny Kelly was born in Ireland. He was trained in graphic design at Dublin Institute of Technology before moving to animation. Johnny studied at The Royal College of Art where he completed an MA in Animation and was awarded the Conran Foundation Award by the Provost, Sir Terence Conran. His graduation short film, Procrastination, received global attention and won him the Jerwood Moving Image Prize 08 and the Best Animation, NYC Shorts 08 award. He was selected to be part of the Saatchi & Saatchi New Director Showcase and was also awarded Best New Director at the 2007 Shark Awards in Kinsale. Most recently he was the winner of a First Boards Award. He joined Nexus Productions in 2007 and has directed both music videos and commercials including spots for Adobe, UN, BMW, Bacardi and Google.

Jolynn Krystosek

www.jolynnkrystosek.com
USA p.044-045

Jolynn Krystosek was born in Fortuna, California in 1982. Jolynn's family moved extensively throughout the western United States, exposing her to a variety of landscapes and environments, which encouraged her interest in nature. She received her BFA from San Francisco State University in San Francisco, California and her MFA from Hunter College in New York, NY. She has exhibited throughout the United States including solo exhibitions at Lux Art Institute, Philadelphia Art Alliance, Lucas Schoormans Gallery, and The Horticultural Society of New York. Jolynn currently lives and works in Brooklyn, NY.

Julien Vallée

www.jvallee.com
Canada p.156-157

Julien Vallée is a graphic designer and art director from Montréal, Canada, who creates tangible images for clients from The New York Times Magazine to Swatch and MTV-One. Julien's work was granted recognitions such as the ADC Young Guns 6 Award and Creative Review Award 2010. It was featured in numerous publications and appeared on various book and magazine covers such as Computer Arts, IdN and Gestalten's book Tangible. It was also exhibited around the world in Berlin, Zurich, Montréal, London, Shangai and Seoul, just to name a few.

Jum Nakao

www.jumnakao.com.br
Brazil p.036-039

Jum Nakao is a fashion designer and a creative director. He lives in the city of São Paulo where his atelier is located. His work is part of the most important fashion shows of the century in the Fashion Museum of Paris. In 2008 The Enchanted World of Jum Nakao was presented at The New Dowse Museum. Japanese curator Yuko Hasegawa from MOT - Contemporary Art Museum from Japan selected his work luxdelix to be part of the international exhibition held in 2008 at São Paulo and Tokyo. His work is part of many fashion, design, and art publications around the world. Jum presents several lectures and workshops throughout the world about the creative process.

Kapsule Kollektive

www.dorakelemen.com
Hungary p.022-023

Kapsule Kollektive, a building couture and photography project, was established by young Hungarian fashion designer Dóra Kelemen and photographer Tamás Réthey-Prikkel. Kapsule Kollektive uses a collaborative approach exploring the theme of structure, a visual remix of the creation of three different art forms – fashion design, architecture and photography - and also a fantasyland where the features of a building magically are reflected in the characteristics of the attires. Kapsule Kollektive's unique viewpoint is bound to revolutionize building photography and promotion as we know it, as involving couture is adding a new, astoundingly forceful element to the conventional two-agent mix of architecture and photography.

Katsumi Hayakawa

www.katsumihayakawa.com
Japan p.132-133

Born in Tochigi Prefecture, Japan, and educated in Tokyo and New York City, Katsumi Hayakawa has held many solo and group exhibitions. Katsumi has also won many awards.

Kris Trappeniers

www.flickr.com/photos/kristrappeniers
Belgium p.118-119

Kris Trappeniers is a Belgium based graphic artist creating in a variety of mediums including spray paint, acrylics, ballpoint, paint markers, collages, hand-cut paper and stencils.

His stencil and paper cut designs are based on small intricate ink drawings. Often the stencil is used just once (as opposed to serigraphy). Afterwards, the pochoir is colored with acrylics and turns into a decorative artwork itself. This cycle forces the artist to continuously come up with new designs and run through the cycle again.

KRONA & LION

www.kronalion.com
Canada p.048

KRONA & LION consists of Kristen Lim Tung, Fiona Lim Tung, Lisa Keophila, and Jonathan Margono. They are a multi-disciplinary design collective with experience in architecture, graphic design, ceramics, and textiles. KRONA & LION are fully skilled in both low and high-tech contemporary craft techniques. They share a common goal of creating beautiful and cutting-edge pieces, with a strong conceptual base. KRONA & LION's work imparts beauty into often unexpected spaces with unexpected materials, lending a sense of fun, exuberance, and cheekiness. KRONA & LION have created installations and sets for private collections and editorial shoots, and have exhibited extensively. In addition, they have developed their signature flower design for retail mass production. KRONA & LION have worked with an extensive list of clients, artists, and designers and welcome future collaborations.

Kylie Stillman

www.kyliestillman.com
Australia p.246-248

After studying Painting at the Royal Melbourne Institute of Technology, Australian artist Kylie Stillman began working with found objects and domestic materials like books, Venetian blinds, paper stacks and plywood to create a set of unusual sculptures. Kylie Stillman has held numerous solo exhibitions. Additionally, she has participated in numerous curated group exhibitions. Kylie Stillman has also been the recipient of the following grants: Australia Council New York Residency in 2009; an Arts Victoria Presentation Grant and Arts House Studio Residency in 2007; an Australia Council Milan Residency in 2006; and an Australia Council Grant for New Work in 2004.

Kyouei Design

www.kyouei-ltd.co.jp
Japan p.186-189

Kyouei Design was founded by Kouichi Okamoto. He is a sound producer and product designer. He has been releasing his sounds on the Dutch techno label "X-Trax" since 1997. He founded Kyouei Design in 2006. Since then he has worked as a designer whose practice integrates his other activities as an artist and musician. He is elected as an artist of the project called "100 artists of contemporary culture NOVA" held in Brazil 2010-2011.

Laura Cooperman

lauracooperman.com
USA p.088-091

Laura Cooperman received her BFA from the Maryland Institute College of Art in 2006. While at MICA she was accepted into the New York Studio Program in New York City, where she worked as an assistant for Nancy Spero and Alan Sonfist as well as studied under the direction of many professional artists. Following her graduation, Laura was awarded the Grainger Marburg Travel Grant, which allowed her to live and work in Beijing, China and led to a yearlong period of extensive travel. In each new place, she created a collection of cut paper drawings and installations depicting the specific architectural landscape she found there. Through the amalgamation of these specific sites, Cooperman references the loss of localized meaning in our contemporary world. Traditional textile designs, architectural elements, wild vegetation and commercial products from different cultures find themselves pieced together in a new environment with new meaning and purpose attached.

Lauren Clay

www.laurenclay.com
USA p.012-013

Lauren Clay received an MFA in Painting and Printmaking from Virginia Commonwealth University, and BFA in Painting from Savannah College of Art and Design. She has had solo exhibitions at Larissa Goldston Gallery, New York; Tilt Gallery and Project Space in Portland, Oregon; and Whitespace Gallery in Atlanta, Georgia. In 2007 Lauren was the recipient of the Virginia Museum of Fine Art Fellowship. She has participated in artist residencies at Henry Street Settlement in New York City, and was a participant of the AIM program at the Bronx Museum of the Arts. Lauren grew up in Atlanta, Georgia, and currently lives and works in Brooklyn, New York. She is represented by Larissa Goldston Gallery in New York.

Lee Huey Ming

www.mingsrealm.com
Malaysia p.046-047 / p.117

Lee Huey Ming is a paper artist and graphic designer based in Auckland, New Zealand. She has a Master of Art and Design from Auckland University of Technology. Her works have been exhibited at various galleries in Auckland. Ming loves spending her time observing the intricacies of nature. Her love for the tactile and curiosity to explore handmade craftsmanship and actual, physically built objects is expressed in her intricate paper cuttings and paper sculptures. Her works investigate structures of nature and she is inspired by Ernst Haeckel.

Linus Hui

cargocollective.com/feelgoodfactory
China / Hong Kong p.158-159

My name is Linus Hui, and I am a paper artist working under the code name: Linus & The Feel Good Factory. I am based in Hong Kong, where I grew up. I studied Product Design at Hong Kong Polytechnic University. Since 2009, I have been working on some paper-crafted costumes for self-portraits. In June 2011, I designed some paper sculptures for Lane Crawford, a leading retailer with specialty stores selling designer label luxury goods in Hong Kong and China.

Liz Jaff

www.lizjaff.com
USA p.214-215

Paper's versatility is what attracted me to it as my primary medium. Its structural and aesthetic possibilities reveal themselves through my continuous experimentation. I have been folding paper for 12 years. I like repetition and rhythm. My first paper piece was conceived during a stay in Las Vegas and made with hotel stationery: the project was folded up and stowed away in the bottom of my suitcase. At that time I began working more abstractly as a way of representing my impressions of places and recollections. Paper became the perfect material to convey ephemeral experiences and the ultimate intangibility of memory. Transforming a two-dimensional surface into a three dimensional shape offers a variety of arrangements for the play of light and shadow on different flat planes. I use folding to investigate these opportunities, and the circle acts as a character to reveal and conceal form. When repeated, these forms are my substitute for the geometric grid.

Lizzie Thomas

www.lizziethomas.co.uk
UK p.062-063

Lizzie Thomas is an artist and maker based in Brighton, UK. She graduated from the University of Brighton with a degree in Wood, Metal, Ceramics and Plastics. She also studied at Nagoya University of Arts, Japan for a 4 month exchange. She mostly works with hand cut paper and wood and creates narrative pieces.

Lydia Hirte

www.lydiahirte.de
Germany p.194-195

Lydia Hirte studied Jewelry Design at the University of Jewelry design at the University of Applied Sciences Schwäbisch-Gmünd and the University of Applied Sciences (FHG) Pforzheim by Jens-Rüdiger Lorenzen and Johanna Dahm from 1986 to 1992. She lived in Ingolstadt in Germany in the next four years. After that she adopted two children and had a working break until 2004. Since 2004, she picked up the profession as an artist again. Her paper sculpture jewelry is really impressive. Through the nature of paper and creative ideas, Lydia always creates a unique element.

Maryse Dugois

www.marysedugois.fr
France p.210-211

After attending Boulle School in Paris, I became a teacher and later I created packaging and I was also an illustrator. At that time I refined my orientations and my choices, and working on paper became my main medium. Now I create paper sculptures and atmospheres for luxury brands.

Mia Pearlman

miapearlman.com
USA p.234-235

Since receiving a Bachelor of Fine Arts from Cornell University in 1996, Mia Pearlman has exhibited internationally in numerous galleries, non-profit spaces and museums, including the Museum of Arts and Design (NYC), Plaatsmaken (Netherlands), Roebling Hall Gallery (NYC). Her work has been featured in over a dozen books on contemporary art, and in both international and domestic press. Pearlman has also participated in many residency programs, such as Proyecto'Ace (Buenos Aires) and the Vermont Studio Center. In 2012 she will be a Fellow at the Liguria Study Center in Bogliasco, Italy. Currently, Pearlman lives and works in Brooklyn, NY.

Michael Kukla

mkukla.com
USA p.134-135

Michael Kukla is a sculptor and visual artist who works with organic forms: in stone, plywood, paper and panel. He received a BFA in painting from Castleton State College, VT. There he was smitten by the large amount of marble and slate quarries located in the area. This logically led to his pursuit of sculpture in stone. He studied at the Hochschule der Kunste (MFA) in Berlin, Germany under sculptor Joshimi Hashimoto where he learned to push the materiality of marble, granite and limestone. He lives and works in New York City and also works as a graphic designer.

Michihiro Sato

www.michihiro-sato.info
Japan p.198-199

Michihiro Sato was born in Takasaki, Gunma prefecture, Japan. He is currently living and working as a jewelry artist in Itami, Hyogo, Japan. He is also a teacher at Osaka University of Arts and Itami Jewellery College. Michihiro Sato has held many solo and group exhibitions around the world, such as COLLECT in the Saatchi Gallery in London, UK in 2011. He has also won many awards, both domestically and internationally.

Mikito Ozeki

www.mikito.jp
Japan p.120-121

Mikito Ozeki was born in Nagoya city in Japan. He began working with paper in 1997. He entirely improvises his paper cuttings and believes in experimentation.

Mikkel Wettre

www.mikkelwettre.com
Norway p.172-173

Mikkel Wettre, born in 1974, is a Norwegian artist. He works with a wide range of media, using sculptures, drawing and computer graphics to investigate questions of formal structure and organization, blending personal mythos with the iconography of modernism. His sculptures tend to be matter-of-fact, material statements that narrate concrete insights and observations as well as alluding to less rational sensations. Mikkel Wettre has worked extensively with paper, using complex folding as a basis for the tangible manipulation of space. The paper sculptures explore the limitless configurations of modular formation and geometry. Referring to both subjective perception and sophisticated craft, the sculptures are a physical analogy to human consciousness and the texture of thought.

Miriam Londoño

www.miriamlondono.com
The Netherlands p.124-125

Miriam Londoño studied Fine Arts in Medellin, Colombia and in Florence, Italy. In recent years she has experimented a great deal with paper fibbers, developing a personal technique to write and draw with paper as if it were ink.

Textiles and writing have been Miriam's sources of inspiration: textile as the underlying structure of things, and writing as a textile created by the continuous interlacing of words.

Her work has been exhibited in many countries around the world. Currently Miriam Londoño lives and works in The Hague, The Netherlands.

Molly Bosley

www.mollybosley.com
USA p.064-065

Molly Bosley currently lives in the Northeastern U.S. She explores many mediums involving textiles and alternative materials to create nostalgic and captivating artworks. Her fascination with found photographs, old books and history has led to a vast collection of resources for new creations. Molly's need to create is sustained by her hunger to learn and to experience both familiar histories and new adventures—desires which have bounced her around Europe and the Americas so far; and which will undoubtedly lead her further.

molo design

molodesign.com
Canada p.028-031 / p.049

molo was formed in 2003, when Stephanie Forsythe and Todd MacAllen partnered with long time friend Robert Pasut. Pasut brings an understanding of international business and a rigorous analytical perspective to the design of molo as a business. Forsythe + MacAllen began working together in 1994 at Architecture school. Constructing a number of houses and smaller scale objects, Forsythe + MacAllen won several international competitions for design projects and conceptual ideas which have become the foundation for the molo studio (www.forsythe-macallen.com). molo is now a collaborative design and production studio of 18 people working in a variety of roles in architecture, design, materials research, product development, production, graphics, business administration and sales. In addition, molo has an extended family of specialized manufacturers that they continuously work with in a beautiful endeavor to bring imagination to fruition.

Nathalie Boutté

www.nathalieboutte.com
France p.230-231

Nathalie Boutté was born in 1967; she lives and works in Montreuil, near Paris, France. For over 20 years she has worked at the various stages of production in traditional paper-based publishing and in doing so acquired an in-depth knowledge of paper-based production work. Nathalie is self-taught; she has no specialized degrees or training. She is not opposed to formal training, but she believes that the key to knowledge has always resided in the practical side of experimenting with materials. Her creations are always a beginning of something new, her technique is forever being enriched and improved. There is no certainty with her, no one truth, but there is always another experience, another achievement.

nendo

nendo.jp
Japan p.228-229

nendo is a design firm founded in 2002 by Oki Sato. Currently based in Tokyo and Milan, nendo's practice spans architecture, interiors, product and graphic design. Since achieving international recognition for bloomroom, an installation for Milan Design Week 2006, the firm has launched new products annually with manufacturers including Cappellini, De Padova, Guzzini, Oluce and Swedese.

Nikki Rosato

www.nikkirosato.com
USA p.122-123

Nikki Rosato is currently a MFA candidate at the School of the Museum of Fine Arts, Boston. Prior to studying at SMFA, Rosato received a Bachelor of Arts degree in Studio Art and Art History from the University of Pittsburgh. Rosato's work has received multiple awards, including a 2008 A.J. Schneider Award, and she has exhibited both nationally and internationally.

Packaging UQAM

www.packaginguqam.blogspot.com
Canada p.150-151

The packaging course given by professor Sylvain Allard at the University of Quebec in Montreal is part of the graphic design program. Sylvain Allard is also the director of the program. The course has become well known internationally because of the blog published by Professor Allard: http:// www.packaginguqam.blogspot.com.

Paper Donut

www.paperdonut.com
France p.166-167

Paper Donut is the work of Alexis Facca, a French freelance artist specialized in paper art and space scenography. I evolve in a geometric and colorful world which is very evocative, exciting and totally fun. As a freelance artist, I've been working for clients coming from various spheres and for different kind of projects: illustration, motion, scenography, and graffiti. My mission is to solve creatively all your challenges, whether it has to be seen, heard, touched or tasted. If you're interested in working with Paper Donut, want more information about my works, or just want to say hello, feel free to get in touch!

Paper-Cut-Project

www.paper-cut-project.com
USA p.034-035 / p.108-109 / p.200-203

Founded in October of 2009, Paper-Cut-Project is an installation design element using expressive paper sculpture. A collaboration between Amy Flurry and Nikki Nye, the Atlanta-based studio makes delicate paper cuts as an antidote to the ubiquity of mass-production, a return to something hands-on. Nye has long nurtured affection for the material through her own paper art. Flurry is a veteran writer and stylist. Together, they plotted a new way to channel their love of fantasy in storytelling as it plays out in campaigns, runway productions and fashion spreads.

PAPERSELF

www.paperself.com
UK p.020-021

Launched in 2009 by London based designer Chunwei Liao, Paperself unites artists, designers and manufacturers from East to West. Challenging conventions of product design, Paperself offers a stylish alternative in furniture, homeware and accessories for eco-conscious living. Paperself is fast gaining recognition for its inventive adaptations, having exhibited at numerous trade fairs and design forums across the globe, as well as being featured in some of the top international publications and online media venues. Continuing to expand and evolve, Paperself looks to the future, seeking out new talent, transcending traditions and promoting the perception of paper through new eyes. Paperself is a platform for the innovative exploration of paper for contemporary product design.

Pat Shannon

www.pat-shannon.com
USA p.130-131

Since receiving her diploma in studio art from the School of the Museum of Fine Arts Boston, Pat Shannon has exhibited regionally in numerous galleries, non-profit spaces and academic venues. Her work has also been included in selected group exhibitions and is held in private collections. She is the recipient of a 1999 and 2009 Massachusetts Cultural Council Fellowship Grant in Sculpture/Installation. Shannon lives and works in Boston, Massachusetts.

Peter Callesen

www.petercallesen.com
Denmark p.094-099

Peter Callesen was born in Herning, Denmark in 1967. He studied architecture, but then switched to studying art at the Jutland Art Academy and later at Goldsmiths College in the UK. Peter started his artistic career with paintings, video and performances, but has since then started working with cardboard and paper. He now mainly works with A4 paper. He cuts out a silhouette from which he makes a 3D figure, and he focuses on playing with the contrast between the positive and the negative. Peter currently lives and works in Copenhagen.

Petra Storrs

www.petrastorrs.com
UK p.070-071

Petra Storrs is a surrealistic multi-disciplinary, London-based artist whose acclaimed art direction explores elaborate set, fashion and costume design with a penchant for an otherworldly, wonderland aesthetic through photography. Her work for the likes of Lady Gaga, Paloma Faith and Dazed & Confused magazine evokes the essence of craft with an escapist romanticism. Storrs was recently commissioned to create an augmented reality animation "SkyRise" for the Becks Green Box projects, fusing cheer-leading, architecture and synchronised swimming into a smart phone viewable art exhibition, along with the V&A Museum, and has just been recognized by the Independent Newspaper as one of 15 artists that will define the future of British art.

Postlerferguson

www.postlerferguson.com
UK p.144-145

Postlerferguson is a London-based design agency specializing in product design, branding & research. Founded in 1977 in Germany and the USA, PostlerFerguson has operated from London since 2007. Educated at the Royal College of Art, Massachusetts Institute of Technology, and the Muthesius University of Architecture, Fine Art & Design, and having worked in the USA, Germany, UK, Japan, China and Hong Kong, the designers now work and reside in London. Recent clients include Selfridges, BBC, Goods of Desire, Walking With Robots, Puzhen and Levis, and the Victoria & Albert Museum.

Currently they are designers in residence at the Victoria & Albert Museum; their sister company, Papafoxtrot, produces wooden toys based on modern infrastructure.

Rebecca Wilson

www.rebeccawilsonceramics.com
UK p.244-245

Rebecca Wilson's ceramics turn everyday items into a collage of pleasurable extravagance. Rebecca uses luxurious porcelain and bone china but removes the formality of the materials so they simply drip with the desire of momentary self-indulgence. Using slip-casting techniques Rebecca produces high-quality items that defy the throwaway nature of their subject matter.

Robert The

www.bookdust.com
USA p.222-223

Born in Carmel, California in 1961, Robert The studied philosophy and mathematics at the University of Wisconsin, Madison from 1979 to 1984. He attended the Institute of Lettering Design in Chicago from 1986 to 1988 and currently lives in Kingston, New York.

Sangeeta Sandrasegar

sangeetasandrasegar.blogspot.com
Australia p.092-093

Sandrasegar works within a research-based practice, building narratives in which every new work connects to previous projects. Her practice is centered round postcolonial and hybridity theory and draws strongly from her mixed heritage. Sandrasegar is interested in the many ways the structures of culture, sexuality and identity have become intertwined in contemporary culture and the interpretation and representation of these shifts. These themes are explored through research and the development of a visual language concerned with shadows. Through installations of paper cut-outs and soft sculptures, the constructed shadow becomes a motif for themes of selfhood, otherness and in-between spaces. Simultaneously engaged with the history of the shadow in Art, in extending the scope of the art-object the cast shadows hint at cognitive alternatives, and sites of transformation. Sandrasegar has exhibited widely both locally and internationally, and is the recipient of several fellowships and prizes. She holds a Doctorate of Philosophy in Visual Arts from The University of Melbourne.

Sarah Kelly

www.saloukee.com
UK p.196-197

Sarah Kelly creates innovative, sculptured art jewelry made in paper under her company name "Saloukee." She began working with paper when creating mock ups for traditional silver jewelry and fashion accessories. It was at this point that she realized that she loved working with the malleable, ephemeral nature of paper, much more than the metals which she had been traditionally trained in.

Sarah Morpeth

www.sarahmorpeth.com
UK p.060-061

After an Art Foundation course, Sarah did a degree in Embroidery; this was a wide-ranging degree with a very broad approach to stitch. She came out of that degree making books and works in cut paper - applying Embroidery techniques but to paper rather than fabric. The rich history of Embroidery inspired her; techniques such as cut work and layering as well as stitch itself when transferred to paper can produce beautiful and sometimes unexpected results. All her work is underpinned by drawing from the landscape around her in the north of England; she draws with pencils and scalpels, finding paper the perfect medium, being robust enough to create three-dimensional structures as well as work in two dimensions. Sarah makes books and other work in cut paper, in the fields of fine art and illustration and works to commission as well as for exhibition.

Scholten & Baijings

www.scholtenbaijings.com
The Netherlands p.164-165

Stefan Scholten (1972) and Carole Baijings (1973) combine minimal forms and a balanced use of colour with traditional craft techniques and industrial production in a distinctive, almost un-Dutch design style. Scholten & Baijings have bridged the roles of designer, artisan and manufacturer. Their close involvement in the production process results in design with both a perfect finish and a personal signature. This perfection is the result of their comprehensive vision of the genesis of the product, executed in close collaboration with skilled craftspeople and leading producers. Widely differing ways of working are translated by Scholten & Baijings into products that are at once functional and individual. The finesse, entrancing colours and subtle use of materials in their work have earned considerable admiration in the international design world.

Shinichiro Ogata

www.wasara.jp
Japan p.204-205

With his beginnings in the interior design field, Ogata started his own design firm and laboratory, SIMPLICITY, in 1998 with the goal of creating a new contemporary Japanese culture. The proprietor and the genius behind HIGASHI-YAMA Tokyo, a new style of Japanese dining, and HIGASHIYA, a tea and confections brand, his creativity is behind everything from the menu to the interior design, the furniture to the tableware, and of course the food. These establishments are recognized as highly successful and redefine the Japanese experience in Tokyo today. Since then, he has opened several restaurants including the private salon YAKUMO-SARYO, and has been active in various interior design projects, for the hospitality and restaurant industries, including several projects with the world renowned chef and entrepreneur, Alain Ducasse. He has been the Creative Director of WASARA since its inception.

SILNT

www.silnt.com
Singapore p.184-185

Established in March 2005, the studio is made up of just two partners, Felix Ng and Germaine Chong. We work on a diverse range of projects from art direction and design, brand development and campaign services for esoteric luxury and lifestyle brands to curatorial direction and bespoke graphic art for independent stores and cultural institutions. Based in the cosmopolitan city of Singapore, we gather a bespoke team for each project and have presented over 50 projects in six cities - made possible through a growing network of individuals worldwide that consists of designers, artists, writers, architects, fashion designers, developers and musicians.

Simon Schubert

www.simonschubert.de
Germany p.104-105

Simon Schubert, born in 1976, is an artist based in Cologne, Germany, his birthplace. From 1997 to 2004 he trained at the Kunstakademie Düsseldorf in the sculpture class of Irmin Kamp. Inspired by Surrealism as well as by Samuel Beckett, Schubert's works imagine architectonical settings, common situations and objects, whereas the materials he uses are either simple or sophisticated - white paper folded or mixed media arrangements.

Sloppy James

www.sloppyjames.com
USA p.148-149

Sloppy James is an emerging American artist and freelance designer, a poet and a writer. He lived in 18 places growing up (so he calls the world his home), and he's still on the go. He makes art to be happy. He lives to create engaging works that have never been attempted before. Tucked away in his slightly cramped studio in Montreal, he knows that there is not enough time for all the ideas.

Stephanie Beck

www.stephaniebeck.org
USA p.136-139

Stephanie Beck creates drawings, prints, and cut-paper sculpture and stages public art interactions. Her work explores ideas of architecture, urban spaces, classification and mapping. She has a Master of Fine Arts from the Pennsylvania Academy of the Fine Arts, a Post-Baccalaureate Certificate from the School of the Museum of Fine Arts, Boston, and a Bachelor of Arts with Highest Distinction in Art History from the University of Virginia. Stephanie received a Joan Mitchell Foundation MFA Grant in 2007 and was nominated to apply for the Louis Comfort Tiffany Foundation Grant in 2009. Stephanie lives and works in Brooklyn, NY.

Stephanie Chu

www.cargocollective.com/schu
USA p.190-191

Born and raised in Pennsylvania, Stephanie Chu is a graphic designer who graduated with a BFA in Graphic Design from Rhode Island School of Design in 2010. She is interested in working in various mediums, particularly paper and ceramic, and is in love with beautiful and creative packaging. Through her experiences at design agencies such as Tank Design and Duarte Design, Stephanie has had the wonderful opportunity to work with various global brands and thought leaders.

Aside from design, Stephanie is passionate about the culinary arts as well. You can find her most weekends at the local Farmers Market, in her kitchen cooking, or dining out at a newly discovered restaurant or food festival. With food and culture linked closely together, it is no surprise that Stephanie is also interested in learning foreign languages, and has taken classes in Spanish, Chinese, Japanese, and Korean.

Stuart McLachlan

www.stuart-mclachlan.com
Australia p.014-017

Stuart McLachlan began his career as an illustrator in Adelaide after completing a degree in Illustration and Graphic Design. Since then his illustration has allowed him to live and work in Melbourne, Amsterdam, Montreal, Toronto, Vancouver and now Sydney. His illustrations have been published worldwide in such magazines as The Economist, The New Yorker and Newsweek.

Recently, Stuart developed a new technique of paper styling using cut paper to create images and art objects for the fashion, art editorial and advertising areas. These hand made pieces have been used extensively on the fashion runway and have been published in Vogue, Karen magazine, on book covers, posters, editorial and commissioned art. He hopes to progress his paper styling to complex and varied uses and is always open to new increasingly challenges in the art, fashion and illustration fields.

The Makerie Studio

www.themakeriestudio.com
UK / Italy p.212-213

The Makerie Studio consists of Julie Wilkinson and Joyanne Horscroft, friends from a Graphic Design degree at Bath Spa University who eventually decided that there is more to life than computers - namely ventures that seemed entirely plausible when we were five. At 25, after glitzy advertising jobs, design internships, photography courses, teaching expeditions and working away in other people's studios, we came back to our original childhood plans and joined forces to make lovely things. We now design and create bespoke paper sculptures using gorgeous papers, and love every minute of it.

Thomas Hillier

www.thomashillier.co.uk
UK p.082-087

Thomas Hillier was born and brought up in the always-sunny County of Dorset. Thomas's architectural interests go beyond the built environment to include art, design, story telling and installations with a particular interest in how literature can be directly translated into urban and architectural space. He attempts to look at architecture from a different perspective, using unorthodox narratives and programmes to create original and often surreal observations. These observations use innovative and poetic materials coupled with a technological and environmental understanding to enhance and blur the thresholds of spatial design. He is driven by a precise and meticulously crafted working method that is illustrated through drawings, models and assemblages. Most importantly he tries not to take architecture too seriously and aims for his work to be as humorous as it is serious.

Tine De Ruysser

www.tinederuysser.com
UK p.218-219

Dr Tine De Ruysser was trained as a jeweller at the Royal Academy of Fine Arts in Antwerp and the Royal College of Art in London, where she finished her PhD in 2010. Her work crosses the boundaries between art, jewellery, textiles and product design. She takes part in exhibitions worldwide, and has won several awards. She also travels to teach and lecture, specialising in the use of folding to create 3D shapes from sheet material.

Toby Edwards

www.tobyedwards.co.uk
UK p.162-163

Having graduated from Nottingham Trent University in 2010 after three years studying graphic design, I have since gained experience at a number of well established design companies in the UK. Currently, I'm employed at Mark Studio in Manchester, working on a range of creative briefs within brand identity, advertising and print design.

Tokujin Yoshioka

www.tokujin.com
Japan p.032-033

Tokujin Yoshioka was born in Saga, Japan in 1967. He established his own studio, Tokujin Yoshioka Design in 2000. He has done many projects with Issey Miyake in the past 20 years such as shop design and installation for A-POC and ISSEY MIYAKE. Also, he has collaborated with various companies in and outside Japan such as HERMES, TOYOTA, BMW, KDDI, SWAROVSKI, and other notables. Some of his most important works are displayed as a part of permanent collections in well-known museums.

Tommy Støckel

www.tommystockel.net
Germany p.174-177

Tommy Støckel was born in Copenhagen in 1972. He is presently living in Berlin. He concentrated on working with sculpture in the last decade and has been experimenting with its possibilities as a medium.

Through his work he has explored ideas such as reality and artificiality; fiction and history; handmade vs digital; the minimal and the baroque; systems and coincidences; futures and pasts as well as permanence and temporality. His solo exhibitions include "What Already Was and What Could Have Been", Helene Nyborg Contemporary, Copenhagen; "3 Sculptures", SMART Project Space, Amsterdam; "Tommy Støckel's Art of Tomorrow", Amolfini, Bristol; "From Here to Then and Back Again", Kunstverein Langenhagen, Langenhagen and "Ist das Leben nicht schon?" Frankfurter Kunstverein, Frankfurt am Main.

TORAFU ARCHITECTS

www.torafu.com
Japan p.009-011

Founded in 2004 by Koichi Suzuno and Shinya Kamuro, TORAFU ARCHITECTS employs a working approach based on architectural thinking. Works by the duo include a diverse range of products, from architectural design to interior design for shops, exhibition space design, product design, spatial installations and film making. They have received many prizes including the Design for Asia (DFA) Grand Award for the "TEMPLATE IN CLASKA" in 2005, and the Grand Prize of the Elita Design Awards 2011 with "Light Loom (Milano Salone 2011)". The airvase book and TORAFU ARCHITECTS Ideas + Process 2004-2011 were published in 2011.

Ufocinque

www.flickr.com/people/ufocinque/
Italy p.112-113

Matteo Capobianco, aka Ufocinque, was born in Novara in 1981. Originally an active member of the Italian writing scene, he gradually began to embrace a more extensive definition of street art while completing his Design studies at the Politecnico of Milan. As a firm believer in the endless possibilities of art as a communication tool, he began to experiment with different techniques beyond the restrictions of street art. Form is never without function and each element is sustaining each other to create an effortlessly beautiful world.

Yo Shimada

www.tat-o.com
Japan p.180-181

Yo Shimada was born in Kobe, Japan and graduated from Kyoto City University of the Arts in 1997. In the same year, Yo Shimada established Tato Architects in Kobe. He is convinced that architecture is a means to love the environment and is on a quest to create architecture to make the environment be more attractive. Yo Shimada's wonderful works have won him several awards, such as superior prize in the Kanden House Design competition in 2011.

Yoshinobu Miyamoto

www.flickr.com/photos/yoshinobu_miyamoto/sets/
Japan p.216-217

Yoshinobu Miyamoto designed the Bank of China Tower, Shanghai, the Aviation Museum Tokorozawa and the Chemical Institute of Japan when he was at Nikken Sekkei, Tokyo. He pursues novel architectural designs with paper as a form-finding tool as opposed to making miniatures of existing building designs. His works on Flickr inspire a wide range of designers in architecture, interiors, jewelry, graphics and origami.

Yu Jordy Fu

www.jordyfu.com
UK p.110-111 / p.232-233

Yu Jordy Fu is an artist, who had her first solo exhibition at Beijing Capital Museum at the age of six.

Jordy graduated from Central Saint Martins College of Art and Design London, with a first-class degree in Spatial Design, and then received a Master of Arts in Architecture and Interiors from the prestige Royal College of Art, London, UK. Currently she is the Creative Director at dwp (Design Worldwide Partnership www.dwp.com), leading large architecture and interior design projects in Asia, and she is also the Creative Director at Marques & Jordy - a London based studio specializing in sustainable objects and environments that engage emotions.

Yuko Takada Keller

www.yukotakada.com
Denmark p.154-155

Yuko Takada Keller was born in Japan and then moved to Denmark. She has been living in Helsinge, Denmark since 1997. She is a Japanese Paper Artist and shows her work not only in Denmark but also in some other European countries as well as Japan. She also curates some exhibitions to introduce Japanese artists in Denmark. Tracing paper is the main material of her works. Through this special paper, she conveys her philosophy towards life with the delicate works.

Yuriko Kaneko

cucumtea.exblog.jp
Japan p.050-051

Yuriko Kaneko was born in Toyko, Japan. She graduated from the Department of Oil Painting at Tama Art University in Tokyo in 2008.

ACKNOWLEDGEMENTS

We would like to thank all the artists and designers for their kind permission to publish their works, as well as all the photographers who have generously granted us the rights to use their images. We are also very grateful to many other people whose names do not appear in the credits but who made specific contributions and provided support. Without them, we would not be able to share these beautiful artistic projects with readers around the world.